REPORTS OF INTERNATIONAL ARBITRAL AWARDS

RECUEIL DES SENTENCES ARBITRALES

VOLUME XXXI

ST/LEG/RIAA/31

(The first twenty-two volumes in this series were issued without a document symbol.)

UNITED NATIONS PUBLICATION

Sales No. B.18.V.1

ISBN 978-92-1-033108-1

eISBN: 978-92-1-362892-8

Manufactured in the United States of America

REPORTS OF INTERNATIONAL ARBITRAL AWARDS

RECUEIL DES SENTENCES ARBITRALES

VOLUME XXXI

UNITED NATIONS — NATIONS UNIES

TABLE OF CONTENTS*

TABLE DES MATIÈRES**

PART I — PARTIE I

PART II — PARTIE II

* Information on the location of maps and diagrams attached to each Award is found in the Table of Contents accompanying each part of each Award.

** Pour savoir où trouver les cartes et diagrammes annexés à chaque sentence, veuillez vous reporter à la table des matières accompagnant chaque partie de sentence.

FOREWORD

The present volume reproduces the awards in two arbitration cases, namely, the case between Pakistan and India concerning the intended construction of a dam on their shared watercourse, and the case between Mauritius and the United Kingdom of Great Britain and Northern Ireland regarding the dispute over the Chagos Marine Protected Area.

This publication was originally conceived in 1948 as a collection of international awards or decisions rendered between States, including cases involving espousing or respondent Governments on behalf of individual claimants. In principle, awards between a private individual or body and a State or international organization were excluded. However, some awards between a State and other entities, or between non-State entities, have exceptionally been included, given the significance of the issues of general international law addressed.

In accordance with the practice followed in this series, the awards are presented in chronological order. Awards in English or French are published in the original language, as long as the original language text was available. Those in both languages are published in one of the original languages. Awards in other languages are published in English. A footnote indicates when the text reproduced is a translation made by the Secretariat. In order to facilitate consultation of the awards, headnotes are provided in both English and French. In line with previous volumes, only typographical errors made in the original awards have been edited by the Secretariat, with the remainder of the Award reproduced as in its original form of publication.

This volume, like volumes IV to XXX, was prepared by the Codification Division of the Office of Legal Affairs. Further information and electronic copies of each volume can be found at http://legal.un.org/riaa/.

AVANT-PROPOS

Le présent volume reproduit les sentences rendues dans deux affaires d'arbitrage, à savoir celle opposant le Pakistan à l'Inde concernant le projet de construction d'un barrage sur le cours d'eau que partagent les deux pays et le différend entre Maurice et le Royaume-Uni de Grande-Bretagne et d'Irlande du Nord concernant l'aire marine protégée des Chagos.

La présente publication a été conçue en 1948 en tant que Recueil de sentences et de décisions internationales rendues dans des affaires opposant des États, y compris celles dans lesquelles des gouvernements prenaient fait et cause pour des particuliers ou se portaient défendeurs à leur place. En étaient en principe exclues les sentences rendues dans les affaires opposant une personne de droit privé à un État ou à une organisation internationale. Certaines sentences rendues dans des affaires opposant un État à d'autres entités ou des entités non étatiques entre elles y ont toutefois été exceptionnellement incluses, compte tenu de l'importance des questions de droit international général qu'elles soulevaient.

Conformément à la pratique suivie dans le présent Recueil, les sentences sont reproduites ci-après par ordre chronologique. Les sentences rendues en anglais ou en français sont publiées dans la langue originale, dès lors que cette version originale était disponible. Celles qui ont été rendues en anglais et en français ont été reproduites dans une des deux langues originales. Le Recueil fournit une version anglaise des sentences rendues dans d'autres langues en spécifiant, dans une note de bas de page, si la traduction émane du Secrétariat de l'Organisation des Nations Unies. Pour faciliter autant que possible la consultation des sentences, celles-ci sont précédées d'un sommaire publié à la fois en anglais et en français. Comme dans les volumes précédents, seules les erreurs typographiques relevées dans les versions originales ont été corrigées par le Secrétariat, les sentences étant pour le reste reproduites telles quelles.

À l'instar des volumes IV à XXX, le présent volume a été compilé par la Division de la codification du Bureau des affaires juridiques. Des informations complémentaires et la version électronique de chaque volume sont disponibles à l'adresse http://legal.un.org/riaa/.

PART I

Award in the Arbitration regarding the Indus Waters Kishenganga between Pakistan and India

Order on Interim Measures of 23 September 2011

Partial Award of 18 February 2013

Decision on India's Request for Clarification or Interpretation of 20 December 2013

Final Award of 20 December 2013

PARTIE I

Sentence arbitrale relative à l'affaire « Eaux de l'Indus – barrage de Kishenganga » opposant le Pakistan et l'Inde

Ordonnance sur la demande de mesures provisoires du 23 septembre 2011

Sentence partielle du 18 février 2013

Décision sur la demande en précision ou en interprétation présentée par l'Inde en date du 20 décembre 2013

Sentence finale du 20 décembre 2013

Award in the Arbitration regarding the Indus Waters Kishenganga between Pakistan and India

Sentence arbitrale relative à l'affaire « Eaux de l'Indus – barrage de Kishenganga » opposant le Pakistan et l'Inde

1. Interim measures

Request for interim measures—"proceed at own risk" principle—test of "necessary" under Indus Waters Treaty 1960 ("Treaty") does not require "urgency" and "irreparable injury" as terms developed for provisional measures by International Court of Justice—"necessary" for interim measures equals preservation *pendent lite* of ability to render a warranted award in legal principles and in remedies.

Order—temporary halt to India's construction of certain elements of the dam.

2. Partial award

Bearing on right or claims to sovereignty over territory of Jammu and Kashmir—Treaty extends to use of waters of Indus system exclusively—award to have no bearing on territorial claims.

Intended diversion of water from Kish/Neelum River—Treaty restricts use of waters, not products generated by use—Kishenganga Hydro-Electric Project (KHEP) type of scheme envisaged under the Treaty—negotiating history shows purpose of delivery of water determines if action is a necessity—necessity defined in normal usage as "required, needed or essential"—delivery of water is required for designated purpose.

Intended diversion of water from Kish/Neelum River—interpretation of "then existing agricultural use or hydro-electric use by Pakistan" as limitation to construction under Treaty—context of such limitation combined with object and purpose of Treaty indicates "critical period" approach, intent coupled with action, followed by examination of "then existing uses"—totality of record supports India's stronger claim—right to divert water subject to Treaty constraints and relevant customary international law principles to ensure minimum flow of water—obligation to manage natural resources in line with principle of sustainable development—obligation for large-scale construction to undertake environmental impact assessment (EIA) and duty to prevent or mitigate against significant harm environment—request from Court for further data to determine sufficient minimum flow required.

Permissibility of reservoir depletion for "run-of-river plant" under Treaty—challenge to admissibility—no request for "neutral experts" by either Party—not mandatory for technical question to be sent to "neutral experts"—sediment accumulation not unforeseen emergency permitting reservoir depletion below designated level—method proposed by India specifically prohibited by Treaty to extent depletes water below designated level.

3. Request for clarification or interpretation

Request for interpretation of partial award by India—Court's finding on reservoir depletion applies to KHEP and to future construction on relevant rivers—consideration of alternative methods a component of interpretation of Treaty, not a site-specific application of facts—prohibition declared by Court is general, not site-specific.

4. Final award

Determination of minimum flow to be discharged downstream of KHEP—determination to balance mitigation of adverse effects against presumed right to operate the plant—in-depth EIA appropriate for project of such magnitude—customary international law principles cannot circumscribe nor negate express rights in Treaty—inappropriate to adopt "precautionary approach" or to permit environmental factors to override all other rights and obligations—Court sets designated minimum flow of water—life of Final Award not to be extended into circumstances in which reasoning no longer accords with reality by operation of *res judicata*—mechanism for review after seven-year period and monitoring to be conducted by standing Permanent Indus Commission and Treaty mechanisms.

1. Mesures provisoires

Demande de mesures provisoires – principe de l'action « à ses risques et périls » – le critère de nécessité prévu dans le Traité de 1960 sur les eaux de l'Indus (le « Traité ») n'implique pas les notions d'« urgence » et de « préjudice irréparable » définies par la Cour internationale de Justice en matière de mesures conservatoires – appliqué aux mesures provisoires, le critère vise à préserver pendente lite la faculté de rendre une sentence justifiée sur le plan des principes de droit et celui des mesures de réparation.

Ordonnance : suspension temporaire de la construction de certains éléments du barrage par l'Inde

2. Sentence partielle

Incidence sur le droit ou les revendications de souveraineté visant le territoire du Jammu-et-Cachemire – le Traité se rapporte exclusivement à l'utilisation des eaux du réseau de l'Indus – la sentence ne doit avoir aucune incidence sur les revendications territoriales.

Intention de détourner les eaux de la rivière Kish/Neelum – le Traité limite l'utilisation des eaux, mais pas celle des produits résultant de cette utilisation – le Projet hydroélectrique de Kishenganga relève des catégories visées par le Traité – d'après l'historique des négociations, le but de l'approvisionnement en eau détermine si la mesure est nécessaire – dans son sens courant, le mot « nécessaire » se dit d'une chose dont on a besoin, qui est requise ou indispensable – l'approvisionnement en eau est requis dans un but précis.

Intention de détourner les eaux de la rivière Kish/Neelum – l'utilisation existante par le Pakistan à des fins agricoles ou pour la production d'énergie hydroélectrique est interprétée comme une limitation à la construction imposée par le Traité – le contexte entourant cette limitation, combiné aux objet et but du Traité, tend à favoriser la théorie de la « période critique », la mise à exécution de l'intention, puis l'examen des « utilisations existantes » – l'ensemble du dossier étaye la position plus solide de l'Inde – le droit de détourner les eaux est assujetti aux contraintes définies dans le Traité et aux principes du droit international coutumier visant à assurer un débit d'eau minimal – obligation de gérer les ressources naturelles conformément au principe du développement durable – obligation, dans le cadre des grands projets de construction, de procéder à une étude d'impact sur l'environnement (EIE) et de prévenir ou d'atténuer les dommages importants causés à l'environnement – demande émise par le Tribunal pour obtenir des informations supplémentaires en vue de déterminer le débit minimal suffisant.

Licéité, au regard du Traité, de l'épuisement des réservoirs pour les besoins d'une centrale au fil de l'eau – contestation de la recevabilité : ni l'une ni l'autre des parties n'a demandé l'intervention d'« experts impartiaux » – il n'est pas obligatoire de renvoyer les questions techniques à des « experts impartiaux » – l'accumulation de sédiments n'est pas une situation d'urgence imprévue justifiant que les réservoirs soient vidés en deçà de la limite fixée – la méthode proposée par l'Inde est spécifiquement interdite par le Traité car elle entraîne l'épuisement des réservoirs en deçà de la limite fixée.

3. Demande en précision ou en interprétation

Demande en interprétation de la sentence partielle présentée par l'Inde – la conclusion du Tribunal sur l'épuisement des réservoirs s'applique au Projet hydroélectrique de Kishenganga et aux projets de construction à venir sur les rivières concernées – la recherche d'autres méthodes relève de l'interprétation du Traité et non de l'application des faits à tel ou tel lieu – l'interdiction prononcée par le Tribunal est de portée générale et non liée à un lieu en particulier.

4. Sentence finale

Détermination du débit minimal en aval du Projet hydroélectrique de Kishenganga – le niveau fixé doit permettre d'atténuer les effets dommageables tout en préservant le droit présumé d'exploiter l'usine – il convient d'effectuer une EIE approfondie pour les projets d'une telle ampleur – les principes du droit international coutumier ne sauraient limiter les droits expressément énoncés dans le Traité ou en empêcher l'exercice – il n'est pas acceptable de recourir au principe de précaution ou de permettre que les facteurs environnementaux fassent obstacle à tous les autres droits et obligations – le Tribunal fixe le débit d'eau minimal – l'application de la sentence finale ne doit pas, au nom du principe de l'autorité de la chose jugée, être étendue à des faits devenus incompatibles avec le raisonnement – la Commission permanente de l'Indus et les mécanismes conventionnels pourront procéder à un réexamen après sept ans et assurer le suivi nécessaire.

* * * * *

In the matter of the Indus Waters Kishenganga arbitration

-before-

The Court of Arbitration constituted
in accordance with the Indus Waters Treaty 1960
between the Government of India
and the Government of Pakistan
Signed on September 19, 1960

-between-

The Islamic Republic of Pakistan

-and-

The Republic of India

Order on the Interim Measures Application of Pakistan dated June 6, 2011

Court of Arbitration:

Judge Stephen M. Schwebel (Chairman)
Sir Franklin Berman KCMG QC
Professor Howard S. Wheater FREng
Professor Lucius Caflisch
Professor Jan Paulsson
H.E. Judge Bruno Simma
H.E. Judge Peter Tomka

Secretariat:

The Permanent Court of Arbitration

September 23, 2011

Agents, Counsel, and other Representatives of the Parties

Agent for Pakistan:

— Mr. Kamal Majidulla, Special Assistant to the Prime Minister on Water Resources and Agriculture

Agent for India:

— Mr. Dhruv Vijay Singh, Secretary to the Government, Ministry of Water Resources

Co-Agents for Pakistan:

— Mr. Khalil Ahmad, Ambassador at Large
— Mr. Mohammad Karim Khan Agha, Additional Attorney General for Pakistan
— Mr. Sheraz Jamil Memon, Pakistan Commissioner for Indus Waters

Co-Agents for India:

— Mr. Y.K. Sinha, Joint Secretary (PAI), Ministry of External Affairs
— Mr. Narinder Singh, Joint Secretary & The Legal Adviser, Ministry of External Affairs
— Mr. G. Aranganathan, Commissioner (Indus), Ministry of Water Resources

Counsel for Pakistan:

— Professor James Crawford, Whewell Professor of International Law, University of Cambridge
— Professor Vaughan Lowe, Chichele Professor of Public International Law, Oxford University
— Barrister Samuel Wordsworth, Essex Court Chambers
— Ms. Shamila Mahmood, Senior Legal Consultant, Government of Pakistan

Counsel for India:

— Mr. Fali S. Nariman, Senior Advocate, Supreme Court of India
— Mr. R.K.P. Shankardass, Senior Advocate, Supreme Court of India
— Professor Stephen C. McCaffrey, Professor of International Law, University of the Pacific, McGeorge School of Law

— Professor Daniel Barstow Magraw, Professor of International Law, Johns Hopkins University
— Mr. Rodman Bundy, Partner, Eversheds LLP
— Mr. S.C. Sharma, Advocate, Supreme Court of India

Advisors for India:

— H.E. Ms. Bhaswati Mukherjee, Ambassador of India, The Hague
— Mr. A.K. Bajaj, Chairman, Central Water Commission
— Dr. Pankaj Sharma. Minister, Indian Embassy, The Hague
— Mr. K.S. Nagaraja, Executive Director, NHPC Ltd.
— Mr. Darpan Talwar, Senior Joint Commissioner (Indus), Ministry of Water Resources

TABLE OF CONTENTS

I. Procedural History

A. The Indus Waters Treaty and the Initiation of Arbitration

1. On September 19, 1960, the Government of India and the Government of Pakistan signed the Indus Waters Treaty 1960 (the "Treaty"). Instruments of ratification were exchanged between the Parties on January 12, 1961; upon ratification, the Treaty entered into force retroactively as of April 1, 1960.[1]

2. Article IX of the Treaty provides for a system for the settlement of differences and disputes that may arise in relation to the Treaty. In its relevant part, Article IX states:

> **Article IX**
>
> **Settlement of Differences and Disputes**
>
> [...]
>
> (4) Either Government may, following receipt of the report referred to in Paragraph (3), or if it comes to the conclusion that this report is being unduly delayed in the Commission, invite the other Government to resolve the dispute by agreement. [...]
>
> (5) A Court of Arbitration shall be established to resolve the dispute in the manner provided by Annexure G
>
> (*a*) upon agreement between the Parties to do so; or
>
> (*b*) at the request of either Party, if, after negotiations have begun pursuant to Paragraph (4), in its opinion the dispute is not likely to be resolved by negotiation or mediation; or
>
> (*c*) at the request of either Party, if, after the expiry of one month following receipt by the other Government of the invitation referred to in Paragraph (4), that Party comes to the conclusion that the other Government is unduly delaying the negotiations.
>
> [...]

3. In turn, Paragraph 2 of Annexure G of the Treaty provides as follows:

> 2. The arbitration proceeding may be instituted
>
> [...]
>
> (*b*) at the request of either Party to the other in accordance with the provisions of Article IX (5) (*b*) or (*c*). Such request shall contain a statement setting forth the nature of the dispute or claim to be submitted to arbitration, the nature of the relief sought and the names of the arbitrators appointed under Paragraph 6 by the Party instituting the proceeding.

[1] *See* Article XII, Indus Waters Treaty 1960.

4. Through a "Request for Arbitration" dated May 17, 2010, the Islamic Republic of Pakistan initiated arbitration proceedings pursuant to Article IX and Annexure G to the Treaty against the Republic of India.

5. In its Request for Arbitration, Pakistan stated that the Parties had failed to resolve the "Dispute" concerning the Kishenganga Hydro-Electric Project ("KHEP") by agreement pursuant to the terms of Article IX(4) of the Treaty.

6. Pakistan identified "two questions that are at the centre" of the dispute in the following way:

> *a.* Whether India's proposed diversion of the river Kishenganga (*Neelum*) into another Tributary, i.e. the Bonar Madmati Nallah, being one central element of the Kishenganga Project, breaches India's legal obligations owed to Pakistan under the Treaty, as interpreted and applied in accordance with international law, including India's obligations under Article III(2) (let flow all the waters of the Western rivers and not permit any interference with those waters) and Article IV(6) (maintenance of natural channels)?
>
> *b.* Whether under the Treaty, India may deplete or bring the reservoir level of a run-of-river Plant below Dead Storage Level (*DSL*) in any circumstances except in the case of an unforeseen emergency?[2]

B. The Constitution of the Court of Arbitration

7. Pursuant to Article IX(5) of the Treaty, a Court of Arbitration has been established. Seven arbitrators were appointed in accordance with Paragraph 4 of Annexure G to the Treaty.

8. On May 17, 2010, Pakistan appointed His Excellency Judge Bruno Simma and Professor Jan Paulsson as arbitrators in accordance with Paragraphs 4 and 6 of Annexure G.

9. On June 16, 2010, India appointed His Excellency Judge Peter Tomka and Professor Lucius Caflisch as arbitrators in accordance with paragraphs 4 and 6 of Annexure G.

10. Having failed to maintain a Standing Panel of umpires as provided under Paragraph 5 of Annexure G or to reach an agreement on the remaining umpires as specified in Paragraph 7(*b*)(i), the Parties proceeded to select umpires in accordance with the procedure set out in Paragraph 7(*b*)(ii) of Annexure G, which provides:

> 7. The umpires shall be appointed as follows:
>
> (*a*) […];
>
> (*b*) If a Panel has not been nominated in accordance with Paragraph 5, or if there should be less than three names on the Panel in any category

[2] Pakistan's Request for Arbitration, para. 4.

or if no person in a category accepts the invitation referred to in Paragraph 7(*a*), the umpires, or the remaining umpires or umpire, as the case may be, shall be appointed as follows: –

(i) By agreement between the Parties.

(ii) Should the Parties be unable to agree on the selection of any or all of the three umpires, they shall agree on one or more persons to help them in making the necessary selection by agreement; but if one or more umpires remain to be appointed 60 days after the date on which the proceeding is instituted, or 30 days after the completion of the process described in sub-paragraph (*a*) above, as the case may be, then the Parties shall determine by lot for each umpire remaining to be appointed, a person from the appropriate list set out in the Appendix to this Annexure, who shall then be requested to make the necessary selection.

11. The Parties not having been able to agree on the persons to be appointed as umpires, in accordance with Paragraph 7(*b*)(ii) of Annexure G, three of the persons provided in the Appendix to Annexure G—the Secretary-General of the United Nations (for selection of the Chairman), the Rector of the Imperial College of Science and Technology, London, England (for selection of the Engineer Member), and the Lord Chief Justice of England (for selection of the Legal Member)—were called upon to appoint the umpires.

12. On October 12, 2010, the Secretary-General of the United Nations appointed Judge Stephen M. Schwebel as umpire and Chairman of the Court in accordance with Paragraphs 4(*b*)(i), 7, and 8 of Annexure G.

13. On December 12, 2010, the Lord Chief Justice of England and Wales appointed Sir Franklin Berman KCMG QC as umpire, in accordance with Paragraphs 4(*b*)(iii) and 7 of Annexure G.

14. On December 17, 2010, the Rector of Imperial College, London, appointed Professor Howard S. Wheater FREng as umpire, in accordance with Paragraphs 4(*b*)(ii) and 7 of Annexure G.

15. At the First Meeting of the Court on January 14, 2011, the Court made the following appointments with the consent of the Parties pursuant to Paragraph 15(*a*) of Annexure G: (i) the Permanent Court of Arbitration (the "PCA") as Secretariat; (ii) Mr. Aloysius P. Llamzon, Legal Counsel of the PCA, as Registrar; and (iii) Mr. Brooks W. Daly, Deputy Secretary-General and Principal Legal Counsel of the PCA, as Treasurer.

16. Following the First Meeting, draft Terms of Appointment were sent to the Parties for comment and approval, resulting in the signing of the Terms of Appointment by the Parties, the Chairman, and the Secretary-General of the PCA, with effect from March 8, 2011. In Paragraph 2.11 and 2.12 of the Terms of Appointment, the Parties confirmed that (*a*) "the members of the Court have been validly appointed in accordance with the Treaty," and (*b*) they "have no objection to the appointment of any member of the Court on the

grounds of conflict of interest and/or lack of independence or impartiality in respect of matters known to them at the date of the signature of these Terms of Appointment."

C. The First Meeting of the Court of Arbitration

17. By e-mail communication dated December 17, 2010, the Chairman invited the Parties, pursuant to Paragraph 14 of Annexure G, to meet with the members of the Court at the premises of the PCA in The Hague on January 14, 2011. Paragraph 14 of Annexure G provides as follows:

> 14. The Court of Arbitration shall convene, for its First Meeting, on such date and at such place as shall be fixed by the Chairman.

18. By e-mail communications dated December 26 and 27, 2010, the Parties accepted the Chairman's invitation to the First Meeting of the Court. Thereafter, the Chairman transmitted for the Parties' comment a draft agenda for the meeting drafted pursuant to Paragraph 15 of Annexure G. The Parties' comments thereon were incorporated as annotations to the agenda.

19. On January 14, 2011, the Court of Arbitration's First Meeting was held at the Peace Palace, The Hague, the Netherlands. Immediately following the First Meeting, the PCA transmitted to the Parties a verbatim transcript of the day's discussions, which was signed by the Chairman and constituted minutes for the purposes of Paragraph 19 of Annexure G. The Court also issued Procedural Order No. 1 dated January 21, 2011, memorializing many of the matters agreed to by the Parties during the First Meeting.

20. During the First Meeting, one of the items discussed amongst the Court and the Parties pursuant to Paragraph 16 of Annexure G was the determination of what supplemental procedural rules might be employed for the conduct of this arbitration. After hearing the Parties' views during the First Meeting and further exchanges made pursuant to paragraph 2 of Procedural Order No. 1, the Court issued Procedural Order No. 2 dated March 16, 2011, in which *inter alia* it adopted a set of "Supplemental Rules of Procedure" which apply in these proceedings subject to the Treaty, procedural orders of the Court, and the Terms of Appointment (signed by the Parties, the Chairman, and the PCA Secretary-General, and dated as of March 8, 2011).[3]

D. Confidentiality

21. During the First Meeting, the Parties agreed that all written pleadings and any other documents or evidence relating to these proceedings are to remain confidential until otherwise agreed. The Court noted this agreement in paragraph 7 of Procedural Order No. 1, while also establishing a timeline for further consultation between the Parties concerning the possible opening

[3] Procedural Order No. 2, para. 1.1.

of the hearing on the merits to the public, and the publication of the written pleadings, supporting documents, and the Award to be rendered by the Court.

E. The Site Visit

22. In the course of discussions during the First Meeting of the Court, the Parties agreed that it would be desirable for the Court of Arbitration to conduct a site visit to the pertinent facilities and locations of the KHEP and to those of the Neelum Valley.

23. Pursuant to Procedural Order No. 1, the Court invited the Parties to confer and agree upon a joint itinerary and other arrangements for the site visit by March 18, 2011.

24. After further communication between the Parties, on March 21, 2011, the PCA transmitted to the Parties the Court's decision concerning the site visit, providing that the dates of June 15–21, 2011 would be set aside for the conduct of the site visit and requesting that the Parties propose an itinerary—including the related logistical arrangements—by no later than April 29, 2011.

25. On May 10, 2011, having considered the Parties' respective communications concerning the site visit itinerary, the Court issued Procedural Order No. 3, deciding, *inter alia*, the itinerary of the proposed visit, the size of the delegations, matters concerning the confidentiality of the site visit and the manner in which the costs were to be apportioned between the Parties.

26. From June 15, 2011 to June 21, 2011, a site visit to the Neelum-Jhelum and Kishenganga hydro-electric projects and surrounding areas located on the river Kishenganga/Neelum was conducted. The Court arrived in Islamabad on June 15, 2011, visited the Neelum Valley by helicopter, and inspected components of the Neelum-Jhelum Hydro-Electric Project. The Court then crossed the line of control on June 17, 2011 and proceeded to Srinagar. On June 18 and 19, 2011, it inspected components of the KHEP located in the Gurez valley and the area near Bandipura north of Wular Lake. The Court then departed from India by way of New Delhi on 20–21 June 2011.

27. Pursuant to paragraph 6 of Procedural Order No. 3, on August 2, 2011, the PCA transmitted to the Parties and the members of the Court a set of four DVD-format discs containing videos of the various presentations made during the site visit, and numerous photographs of the site visit.

F. Provisional Measures

28. Paragraph 28 of Annexure G of the Indus Waters Treaty provides:

> 28. Either Party may request the Court at its first meeting to lay down, pending its Award, such interim measures as, in the opinion of that Party, are necessary to safeguard its interests under the Treaty with respect to the matter in dispute, or to avoid prejudice to the final solution or

aggravation or extension of the dispute. The Court shall, thereupon, after having afforded an adequate hearing to each Party, decide by a majority consisting of at least four members of the Court, whether any interim measures are necessary for the reasons hereinbefore stated and, if so, shall specify such measures: Provided that

a) the Court shall lay down such interim measures only for such specified period as, in its opinion, will be necessary to render the Award: this period may, if necessary, be extended unless the delay in rendering the Award is due to any delay on the part of the Party which requested the interim measures in supplying such information as may be required by the other Party or by the Court in connection with the dispute; and

b) the specification of such interim measures shall not be construed as an indication of any view of the Court on the merits of the dispute.

29. In Paragraph 10 of its Request for Arbitration, Pakistan stated:

Accordingly, pursuant to Annexure G, paragraph 28 of the Treaty, Pakistan will request the Court at its first meeting to lay down, pending its Award, interim measures both to safeguard Pakistan's interests under the Treaty with respect to the matters in dispute, and to avoid prejudice to the final solution and aggravation or extension of dispute.

30. Pakistan sought, *inter alia*, the following relief in its Request for Arbitration:

An interim order restraining India from proceeding further with the planned diversion of the river Kishenganga/Neelum until such time as the legality of the diversion is finally determined by a Court of Arbitration.[4]

31. On January 14, 2011, during the Court's First Meeting, Pakistan made the following statement in respect of provisional measures:

Our assessment of the present situation in Kishenganga is that while the plan certainly envisages works on the Indus that would breach the Indus Waters Treaty and cause great harm to Pakistan, the project is not yet so far advanced that such harm is imminent.

We are aware of the principle of international law, applied for example by the International Court in paragraphs 30–33 of its Order on provisional measures in the Great Belt case, that in cases such as the present a State engaged in works that may violate the rights of another State can proceed only at its own risk. The court may, in its decision on the merits, order that the works must not be continued or must be modified or dismantled.

We are content at this stage to rely upon that principle.

Major construction projects are, however, not easily reversible processes. The excavation of construction sites and the filling of dams cannot easily be undone. Equally importantly, costs are not incurred in a regular and

[4] Pakistan's Request for Arbitration, para. 54(*a*).

> uniform fashion. There are points at which major investments of capital and resources have to be made. Beyond those points a State might find it more difficult to abandon the project and restore the *status quo ante*.
>
> We therefore invited India to give an undertaking to inform the Court, and at the same time the Government of Pakistan, of any actual or imminent developments or steps in relation to the Kishenganga project that it considers would have a significant adverse effect upon the practicality of abandoning the project and restoring the *status quo ante*, or would in any other way seriously jeopardize Pakistan's interests.
>
> On that basis, and on the understanding that we may apply to the Court for provisional measures at any point in the future should it become apparent (whether as a result of a communication from India or otherwise) that the ordering of such measures is an urgent necessity, we have decided to make no application for provisional measures at this meeting.

32. By e-mail communication dated March 6, 2011, counsel for Pakistan requested that counsel for India provide, by March 17, 2011, its comments on, *inter alia*: (1) India's understanding of the "proceed at your own risk" principle first outlined in the *Great Belt* case[5] before the International Court of Justice, providing that in respect of provisional measures a "State engaged in works that may violate the rights of another State can proceed only at its own risk;" (2) the status of the undertaking to inform Pakistan and the Court of "any actual imminent steps in relation to the KHEP that it considers would have a significant adverse effect upon the practicability of abandoning the project and restoring the *status quo ante* or would in any other way seriously jeopardize Pakistan's interests;" (3) information on the current state of works at the site; and (4) the planned date for diversion of the river.

33. By e-mail communication dated March 17, 2011, counsel for India replied to counsel for Pakistan to the effect that: (1) India considered that in its understanding the "proceed at your own risk" principle was "covered by the existing International Law"; (2) as a consequence of Pakistan's decision, expressed at the January 14, 2011 meeting, to forego lodging an application for provisional measures, India considered it inappropriate for Pakistan to be "seeking any unilateral undertakings on the part of India"; (3) India would address the status of current construction in "substantive pleadings on the merits according to the schedule laid down by the Court"; and (4) the "planned date of diversion is not before 2015".

34. On June 6, 2011, Pakistan submitted an Application for Provisional Measures (the "Application") by e-mail.

35. By e-mail communication dated June 7, 2011, India wrote to the PCA, requesting "adequate time to respond to Pakistan's [A]pplication." India submitted that in its view Pakistan's application should have been filed earli-

---

[5] *Passage through the Great Belt* (Finland *v.* Denmark), Provisional Measures, Order of 29 July 1991, *I.C.J. Reports 1991*, p. 12.

er, especially because "India's last letter to Pakistan was on 17 March 2011." India also recalled that at the Court's First Meeting, Pakistan had stated that it would not pursue an application for provisional measures.

36. After considering the comments of the Parties on the manner and timing on which the Court should consider Pakistan's "Application for Provisional Measures," the Court issued Procedural Order No. 4 on June 12, 2011 deciding, *inter alia*, on a schedule for written submissions and hearing.

37. By e-mail communication dated June 30, 2011, Pakistan recalled to the Court, *inter alia*, the statement made by India during the course of the site visit according to which "the temporary tunnel at the Kishenganga dam site is 100% complete" and the "river would be dammed at the site in November 2011." Pakistan submitted that a

> section of the Kishenganga/Neelum would be diverted as a result, however, the interference in the flow of the river at this section is intended to be permanent—the former riverbed would be lost, and would become a construction site for the permanent 37m high dam structure … Pakistan considers that the imminence of these works adds a further element of urgency to its Application.

By e-mail communication dated July 1, 2011, the PCA, on behalf of the Chairman of the Court, invited India to comment on Pakistan's communication of June 30, 2011 as part of its Response to Pakistan's Application, due on July 22, 2011.

38. On July 22 2011, India submitted its Response to Pakistan's Application for Provisional Measures.

39. After consulting with the Parties, on July 26, 2011, the Court issued Procedural Order No. 5, deciding, *inter alia*, the time, place and conduct of the hearing on interim measures. The Court determined that the hearing would be organized in two rounds of oral argument: starting with statements by Pakistan on the first day, India on the second, and reply and closing statements by both Parties on the final day of the hearing.

40. On August 3, 2011, Pakistan submitted its Reply to India's Response on Pakistan's Application for Provisional Measures.

41. On August 15, 2011, India submitted its Rejoinder to Pakistan's Reply.

42. On August 25–27, 2011 an interim measures hearing was held at the Great Hall of Justice, the Peace Palace, The Hague. Present at the hearing were the following persons:

The Court of Arbitration

Judge Stephen M. Schwebel (Chairman)
Sir Franklin Berman KCMG QC
Professor Howard S. Wheater FREng
Professor Lucius Caflisch
Professor Jan Paulsson

H.E. Judge Bruno Simma

H.E. Judge Peter Tomka

Pakistan

Mr. Kamal Majidulla, Agent for Pakistan

H.E. Khalil Ahmed, Ambassador at Large, Co-agent

Mr. Mohammad Karim Khan Agha, Additional Attorney General for Pakistan, Co-agent

Mr. Aijaz Ahmed Pitafi, Joint Commissioner for Indus Waters

Professor James Crawford (*by telephone conference*)

Professor Vaughan Lowe, Legal Counsel

Barrister Samuel Wordsworth, Legal Counsel

Ms. Shamila Mahmood, Legal Counsel

H.E. Ambassador Aizaz Chaudhry, Ambassador for Pakistan to the Netherlands

Mr. Asif Baig, Technical Expert

Mr. Mehr Ali Shah, Technical Expert

India

Mr. Dhruv Vijai Singh, Agent for India

H.E. Bhaswati Mukherjee, Ambassador of India, The Hague

Mr. A.K. Bajaj, Chairman, Central Water Commission, Technical Advisor

Dr. Pankaj Sharma, Minister, Indian Embassy, The Hague

Mr. Fali S. Nariman, Counsel for India

Mr. R.K.P. Shankardass, Counsel for India

Professor Stephen C. McCaffrey, Counsel for India

Mr. Rodman Bundy, Counsel for India

Prof. Daniel Magraw, Counsel for India

Mr. S.C. Sharma, Counsel for India

Mr. Y.K. Sinha, Co-Agent for India

Mr. Narinder Singh, Co-Agent for India

Mr. K.S. Nagaraja, Executive Director NHPC

Mr. G. Aranganathan, Co-Agent for India

Mr. Darpan Talwar, SJC (Indus), Technical Advisor

Registry

Mr. Aloysius Llamzon, Registrar and Legal Counsel

Mr. Dirk Pulkowski, Legal Counsel

Mr. Garth Schofield, Legal Counsel

Ms. Anna Vinnik, Assistant Legal Counsel

Ms. Willemijn van Banning, Legal Secretary

Court Reporters

Mr. David Kasdan

Mr. Randy Salzman

43. At the hearing, the following persons presented oral arguments before the Court on behalf of Pakistan:

Mr. Kamal Majidulla, Agent for Pakistan

Barrister Samuel Wordsworth, Legal Counsel

Professor Vaughan Lowe, Legal Counsel

44. The following persons presented oral arguments before the Court on behalf of India:

Mr. Dhruv Vijai Singh, Agent for India

Mr. Fali S. Nariman, Counsel for India

Mr. R.K.P. Shankardass, Counsel for India

Mr. Rodman Bundy, Counsel for India

Professor Stephen C. McCaffrey, Counsel for India

Professor Daniel Magraw, Counsel for India

45 In the morning of August 27, 2011, the third day of the hearing, a member of the Court, Professor Wheater, requested that India provide information on the following points with respect to the technical aspects of the proposed Kishenganga Dam:

(1) One or more cross-sections of the dam.

(2) A drawing of the dam elevation showing the location of the proposed spillways and any other discharge outlets with respect to design levels of water elevation, such as the drawing provided for the Baglihar dam in Volume 7 of Pakistan's Memorial at Figure 5.2.1. on Page 141.

(3) Specification of the hydraulic design of the proposed spillways and any other downstream outlet works; the capacity of the dam to transmit flows downstream as a function of the ponded water level.

(4) The intended mode of operation of India, including the transmission of flows downstream to meet the needs of existing uses as specified in the Treaty, including any environmental flows and for sediment flushing.

(5) A diagram showing the upstream extent of inundation at the Full Pondage Level and under surcharge storage; that is, during the passage of the design flood, including the location of any nearby upstream ripar-

ian settlements, and such a document could be a plan view of the inundated areas.

(6) India's Environmental Impact Assessment for the dam.

(7) An outline schedule of the proposed construction works; that is including the currently proposed timing of key phases of the dam.[6]

46. During the afternoon of the third hearing day, the Chairman of the Court requested that India provide the technical data and construction schedules requested by Professor Wheater by no later than September 2, 2011, and that Pakistan submit its comments on that data, should it wish to make any comments, by no later than September 7, 2011.[7]

47. In response, the Agent for India pointed out that some of the information requested by the Court "is very much part of" India's Counter-Memorial[8] and needed to be placed within proper context, as it would be in the Counter-Memorial. The Agent for India requested that the Court allow India to submit only such information as is "absolutely necessary and which does not pre-empt our filing of the Counter-Memorial."[9]

48. The Chairman replied that the Court recognized that "the time offered is short" but requested that India nonetheless submit "such papers as it quickly can put in" and assured the Agent for India that the Court did not "expect a comprehensive revelation of all the data that it [India] will bring into play in its Counter-Memorial ... Clearly, what is left for the merits should be left for the merits, and we don't anticipate that our order will go into the merits."[10]

49. By letter dated August 29, 2011, the PCA sent the Parties copies of documents provided by India to the Court and Pakistan during the hearing, including a set containing several of the documents requested by Professor Wheater.

50. On September 2, 2011, India wrote the Court in relation to the question posed by Professor Wheater during the interim measures hearing. India's Agent confirmed that most of the documents requested had been provided earlier to Pakistan, and identified those that were included as documentary exhibits in Pakistan's Memorial. It was also confirmed that apart from those documents already provided by India during the interim measures hearing on August 27, 2011, further documentation (including those concerning India's environmental impact assessment for the dam) would be provided in India's Counter-Memorial.

---

[6] Interim Measures Hearing Transcript, 201:6–202:25.

[7] Interim Measures Hearing Transcript, 294:10–17.

[8] Interim Measures Hearing Transcript, 294:21–23.

[9] Interim Measures Hearing Transcript, 295:4–5.

[10] Interim Measures Hearing Transcript, 296:3–10.

51. On September 7, 2011, Pakistan commented on India's September 2, 2011 communication and provided the Court with two additional documents previously referred to by Pakistan during the interim measures hearing.

II. The requested interim measures

52. As specified in Paragraph 15 of its Application, Pakistan requests that the Court "issue an order for provisional measures in the following terms":

(i) India shall cease work on the KHEP until such time as the Court renders its award on the merits in these proceedings;

(ii) India shall inform the Court and Pakistan of any actual or imminent developments or steps in relation to the Kishenganga project that may have a significant adverse effect upon restoring the *status quo ante* or that may in any other way seriously jeopardise Pakistan's rights and interests under the Treaty;

(iii) Any steps that India has taken or may take in respect of the KHEP are taken at its own risk and without prejudice to the possibility that the Court may in its decision on the merits order that the works must not be continued or must be modified or dismantled; and

(iv) Such further relief as the Court considers to be necessary.

53. In its response, India requests the Court "to reject Pakistan's Application for Provisional Measures, and to decide that the circumstances of the case are not such to justify the ordering of interim measures under the 1960 Treaty."

III. Summary of the Parties' arguments

54. The arguments raised by the Parties may be summarized as follows.

A. Pakistan's Decision not to Seek Interim Measures at the First Meeting

55. Paragraph 28 of Annexure G of the Indus Waters Treaty provides that "[e]ither Party may request the Court at its first meeting to lay down, pending its Award, such interim measures as, in the opinion of that Party, are necessary to safeguard its interests under the Treaty ..."

56. During the First Meeting of January 14, 2011, Pakistan informed the Court that it had chosen to forego the immediate pursuit of an order for interim measures, but that it would reserve the right to make such an application should it later determine that "the ordering of such measures is an urgent

necessity."[11] An exchange of correspondence between Pakistan's and India's counsel followed in March 2011.[12] On June 6, 2011, Pakistan submitted its Application for Provisional Measures.

Pakistan's Position

57. In its Application, Pakistan noted the following developments in relation to its pursuit of interim measures at that stage in the proceedings:

> Work on the KHEP continues. Pakistan is seriously concerned by India's unwillingness to commit itself to adherence to the 'proceed at own risk' principle, and to give an undertaking to inform the PCA and Pakistan of any actual or imminent developments or steps in relation to the Kishenganga project that would have a significant adverse effect upon the practicability of abandoning the project and restoring the *status quo ante* or would in any other way seriously jeopardise Pakistan's interests. Pakistan regards India's response as a reservation of its position that amounts to a refusal to accept those principles.[13]

58. At the January meeting, Pakistan argues, "India had not carefully and deliberately refused to confirm that it proceeded at its own risk and had not carefully and deliberately refused to give an undertaking as to informing the Court and Pakistan of any actual or imminent steps in relation to KHEP."[14] According to Pakistan, the communications made by India only after the January meeting "explain [ ] why the application was not made then,"[15] as do the "conflicting reports about the state of readiness of the [KHEP]"[16] that Pakistan had received. Additionally, Pakistan observes that practical considerations, including work on its Memorial in April and May 2011[17] and the need for the Application to be made prior to the site visit "and with sufficient notice for the matter to be dealt with in this hearing slot,"[18] influenced the precise timing of its request for interim measures. Overall, Pakistan submits that the reasons for the timing of its Application have been addressed, and that continued attention to the issue "is a distraction."[19]

59. Having advanced the foregoing explanation for its decision not to seek interim measures at the First Meeting of January 14, 2011, Pakistan rejects India's position that a later application carries an 'enhanced' burden of proof.[20] Falling in with such a suggestion, Pakistan submits, would "contradict the

[11] First Meeting Transcript, 21:6–12.

[12] *See supra*, paras. 32–33.

[13] Pakistan's Application for Provisional Measures, para. 9.

[14] Interim Measures Hearing Transcript, 203:25 to 204:4.

[15] Interim Measures Hearing Transcript, 15:11–13.

[16] Pakistan's Reply, para. 4.

[17] Interim Measures Hearing Transcript, 18:7–10.

[18] Interim Measures Hearing Transcript, 18:4–5.

[19] Interim Measures Hearing Transcript, 203:18–19.

[20] Pakistan's Reply, para. 3.

concept of provisional measures as a procedural mechanism necessary to preserve the efficacy and the fairness of judicial proceedings."[21]

India's Position

60. India agrees that Pakistan's decision not to pursue interim measures at the First Meeting does not mean that it is "precluded" from pursuing such measures at the present moment.[22] India accepts that "after the Court's first meeting, circumstances could arise of a compelling nature whereby a Request for Interim Measures would be justified."[23]

61. Nevertheless, India submits that if "circumstances genuinely dictated the appropriateness, at least in Pakistan's mind, of provisional measures at the time, that first meeting in January was the appropriate time and place to file a request."[24] In India's view, such timing would correspond to the Treaty drafters' expectation that the grounds for interim measures "would be apparent" at the time of the First Meeting, "given the history of a dispute."[25]

62. Pakistan's statements at the First Meeting also indicate, in India's view, that Pakistan had accepted that there was "no imminent harm to Pakistan in view of its assessment of the status of the Kishenganga Project."[26] Specifically, India relies upon the following observation of the Agent for Pakistan:

> Mr. President, members of the Court, our assessment for the present situation along the Kishenganga is that while the plan certainly envisages works that would breach the Indus Waters Treaty and cause great harm to Pakistan, the project is not yet so far advanced that such harm is imminent.[27]

63. Against this backdrop, India argues that Pakistan "bears a heavy burden to show that the situation has later changed justifying a subsequent request for such measures."[28] Far from meeting this burden, India submits that Pakistan has "made no attempt—no attempt—to explain why Pakistan suddenly considered interim measures to be warranted in June when it had taken the exact opposite position in January and again at the end of May,"[29] when it submitted its Memorial on the merits, which did not include the prayer for interim measures previously set out in its Request for Arbitration.[30] Moreover, India maintains that "assertions about conflicting reports and limited

---

[21] Pakistan's Reply, para. 3.

[22] Interim Measures Hearing Transcript, 249:23 to 250:3.

[23] Interim Measures Hearing Transcript, 250:4–6.

[24] Interim Measures Hearing Transcript, 249:15–18.

[25] India's Response, para. 47.

[26] India's Response, para. 3. *See also* Interim Measures Hearing Transcript, 128:6–15.

[27] First Meeting Transcript, 19:22 to 20:2.

[28] India's Response, para. 48.

[29] Interim Measures Hearing Transcript, 144:5–9.

[30] Interim Measures Hearing Transcript, 142:18–25.

information" as a reason for the submission of the Application only in June 2011 "are not backed up by a shred of evidence ... filed in these proceedings."[31]

64. India also considers that the June 6, 2011 Application was Pakistan's "second request" for interim measures, the same having been raised prior to the First Meeting in Pakistan's original Request for Arbitration.[32]

B. The "Proceed at Own Risk" Principle

65. During the January 14, 2011 First Meeting, Pakistan invoked the principle (considered by Pakistan to be one of international law) applied by the International Court of Justice ("ICJ") in the *Passage through the Great Belt* case[33] that "a state engaged in works that may violate the rights of another state can proceed only at its own risk. The court may in its decision on the merits order that the works must not be continued or must be modified or dismantled."[34] During that meeting, Pakistan stated that in reliance upon this principle, it would not seek interim measures at that time.[35]

66. Thereafter, on March 6, 2011, Pakistan's counsel wrote to India's counsel, requesting that India affirm its adherence to the principle articulated by the ICJ in the *Great Belt* case. Pakistan further reiterated its invitation, expressed during the First Meeting, that India provide an undertaking not to take steps that would have a "significant adverse effect" on its ability to abandon the project and return to the *status quo ante*.[36]

Pakistan's Position

67. According to Pakistan, the justification for its counsel's March 6, 2011 communication was India's silence on what Pakistan considered to be "an essential, if relatively uncontentious point."[37] Pakistan contends that India's letter of March 17, 2011 and subsequent submissions demonstrate that "India has ... in various notably elaborate ways and on three separate occasions refused to say that it proceeds at risk ..."[38] India's statement that the "proceed at own risk" principle is "covered by provisions of existing international law"[39] provides, in Pakistan's view, "no clue there as to what provisions India considers to apply, how India interprets those provisions, [or] how India considers that they

[31] Interim Measures Hearing Transcript, 130:9–11.

[32] India's Response, para. 2.

[33] *Passage Through the Great Belt* (Finland *v.* Denmark), Provisional Measures Order, ICJ Reports 1991, p. 12.

[34] First Meeting Transcript, 20:7–11.

[35] First Meeting Transcript, 20:12–13.

[36] Letter from Pakistan's Counsel, dated March 6, 2011.

[37] Interim Measures Hearing Transcript, 13:1–3.

[38] Interim Measures Hearing Transcript, 13:23–25.

[39] Letter from India's Counsel dated March 17, 2011.

apply to it in the current circumstances."[40] Moreover, Pakistan argues, India's understanding appears to contemplate at most a risk that it would be required to open the spillways of the KHEP and allow the Kishenganga to flow unhindered—but not the possibility that it might be required to dismantle the dam.[41]

68. In Pakistan's view, India's unwillingness to confirm "well-established principles of international law concerning the conduct of parties during the pendency of litigation ... can only be construed as a reservation of the right to violate [these principles]."[42] India's purportedly equivocal statements in this regard are said to stand in stark contrast to the assurances provided in the "clearest of terms" by India[43] in the *Baglihar* case[44] or the undertaking by Uruguay during the hearing on provisional measures in the *Pulp Mills on the River Uruguay* case[45] before the ICJ.[46]

69. In evaluating India's statements on this question, Pakistan rejects the argument that the March 2011 correspondence exchanged among counsel for the two Parties occurred outside the parameters of this arbitration or could be distinguished from the Parties' own positions.[47] In any event, Pakistan submits that even if some "relatively fine line could be drawn between inter-counsel correspondence sent pursuant to instructions of the Parties and correspondence between the Agents of the two states," the positions stated in those letters were later "adopted and reflected" in the Parties' official submissions.[48]

India's Position

70. At the close of the hearing, India stated that it "is committed to proceed on 'the own-risk principle' of international law ... [and] that any actual or imminent development or steps in relation to the Kishenganga Project during the progress of this arbitration that would have significant adverse effect on Pakistan's stated rights or interests will be promptly intimated to the Court and to Pakistan."[49]

71. Within the context of this assurance, India disputes that the response of its counsel to counsel for Pakistan's March 6, 2011 letter was insufficient, or that this exchange of correspondence can provide any basis for Pakistan's request for interim measures. As an initial matter, India submits

[40] Interim Measures Hearing Transcript, 14:13–16.

[41] Interim Measures Hearing Transcript, 16:20 to 17:9.

[42] Pakistan's Reply, paras. 5–6.

[43] Interim Measures Hearing Transcript, 20:7 to 21:11.

[44] R. Lafitte, "Determination of Neutral Expert on the Baglihar Project" of 12 February 2007 (Exhibit PK-230).

[45] *Pulp Mills on the River Uruguay* (Argentina *v.* Uruguay), Provisional Measures, Order of 13 July 2006, *I.C.J. Reports 2006*, p. 113.

[46] Interim Measures Hearing Transcript, 17:10–21.

[47] Interim Measures Hearing Transcript, 13:14–22.

[48] Interim Measures Hearing Transcript, 13:17–21.

[49] Interim Measures Hearing Transcript, 269:24 to 270:6.

that it was under no obligation to respond to the letter from Pakistan's counsel or to offer supplemental information on developments in the KHEP outside the Treaty provisions for the exchange of information. [50] The response from India's counsel was "as a matter of courtesy"[51] and "was taken outside of the arbitration proceedings on a counsel-to-counsel basis."[52] India further maintained that even if it had refused to answer the questions posed by Pakistan's counsel, Pakistan gave "no indication of being dis-satisfied with the response of India's counsel,"[53] and that, whatever its content, a "counsel-to-counsel letter cannot be a valid reason for the Court to grant interim measures under Paragraph 28."[54]

72. More importantly, in India's view, "international law contains no duty requiring one State to accede to a demand by another State that the first State recognize a principle of international law."[55] In any case, India asserts that there has been "no refusal—much less a continuing refusal—on the part of India to say that it accepts well-established legal principles."[56] India further notes that the principle of international law enunciated in the *Great Belt* case must be applied to both Parties in the dispute, and extend with equal force to Pakistan's Neelum-Jhelum project.[57]

73. Finally, as to the alleged unwillingness of India to acknowledge the possibility that the dam would be ordered to be dismantled, counsel for India expressed skepticism that the physical dismantling of the dam could ever be necessary. Nonetheless, counsel for India made the following statement: "Yes, I agree to a dismantling. I say that there is no occasion in this case. You could modify, you could do it, and the cases do say you can order a dismantling."[58] The Agent for India assured the Court that India has "no hesitation in committing that we will fully and wholly abide by any decision taken by the Court of Arbitration."[59]

C. Applicable Legal Standards

74. Paragraph 28 of Annexure G of the Indus Waters Treaty provides as follows:

> Either Party may request the Court at its first meeting to lay down, pending its Award, such interim measures as, in the opinion of that Par-

[50] India's Response, para. 25.

[51] India's Response, para. 25.

[52] India's Response, para. 24.

[53] India's Response, para. 28.

[54] Interim Measures Hearing Transcript, 95:4–5.

[55] India's Response, para. 66.

[56] India's Rejoinder, para. 28.

[57] India's Response, para. 57; Interim Measures Hearing Transcript, 159:3–11.

[58] Interim Measures Hearing Transcript, 281:6–8.

[59] Interim Measures Hearing Transcript, 289:5–6.

ty, are necessary to safeguard its interests under the Treaty with respect to the matter in dispute, or to avoid prejudice to the final solution or aggravation or extension of the dispute. The Court shall, thereupon, after having afforded an adequate hearing to each Party, decide, by a majority consisting of at least four members of the Court, whether any interim measures are necessary for the reasons hereinbefore stated and, if so, shall specify such measures: Provided that

a) the Court shall lay down such interim measures only for such specified period as, in its opinion, will be necessary to render the Award: this period may, if necessary, be extended unless the delay in rendering the Award is due to any delay on the part of the Party which requested the interim measures in supplying such information as may be required by the other Party or by the Court in connection with the dispute; and

b) the specification of such interim measures shall not be construed as an indication of any view of the Court on the merits of the dispute.

Pakistan's Position

75. Pakistan submits that its Application for Provisional Measures is based solely on Paragraph 28 of Annexure G to the Treaty, which provides a self-contained set of rules. In Pakistan's view, "[n]o other reasons or criteria are relevant; and no reference to other sources of law is necessary or permissible in order to interpret or apply paragraph 28 of Annexure G."[60] In particular, Pakistan objects to India's reliance on the decisions on provisional measures of the ICJ rendered under the terms of Article 41 of that Court's Statute. In particular, ICJ jurisprudence on "questions of urgency and necessity" is, in Pakistan's view, "not relevant."[61]

76. Pakistan accepts that "Paragraph 29 of Annexure G permits the Court to apply other treaties and customary international law,"[62] but emphasizes that this provision is a general applicable law clause not specifically tied to interim measures and restricts recourse to such supplementary sources to instances "necessary" for the interpretation and application of the Treaty.[63] This provision constitutes, in Pakistan's view, a "very deliberately formulated hurdle" to the application of law beyond the text of the Treaty,[64] and Pakistan maintains that "India has made out no case for recourse to Paragraph 29. It has offered no explanation as to why it is necessary to go beyond the perfectly clear text of Paragraph 28 and have recourse to these other sources."[65]

[60] Pakistan's Reply, para. 18.

[61] Pakistan's Reply, para. 17.

[62] Interim Measures Hearing Transcript, 54:13–14.

[63] Interim Measures Hearing Transcript, 54:15 to 55:2.

[64] Interim Measures Hearing Transcript, 47:4–5.

[65] Interim Measures Hearing Transcript, 55:3–6.

77. For Pakistan, "Paragraph 28 of Annexure G is perfectly clear in its own terms."[66] The Parties were free to "adopt the wording in the [ICJ] Statute or at least to use it as a model," yet elected not to do so.[67] Given this background, Pakistan argues, "other texts cannot be used as substitutes for reading what the Treaty that governs these proceedings actually says."[68]

78. Pakistan argues that, interpreted on its own terms, "the test established by Paragraph 28 of Annexure G is not the same as the test in Article 41 of the ICJ Statute."[69] In Pakistan's view, *urgency*, "which is an important consideration in the ICJ jurisprudence, is not an element in the test prescribed in ... paragraph 28."[70] Nor, Pakistan contends, is the Court sitting as a court in equity, bound to apply a balance-of-convenience test found nowhere in the Treaty.[71] Rather than imposing a formula from the ICJ or any other court, Pakistan submits that "the Court is simply to exercise its discretion under Paragraph 28 and ask: Is this order needed now?"[72]

India's Position

79. In contrast to the view that Paragraph 28 is self-contained, India maintains that "the terms of Paragraph 28 are quite spare. They don't provide the Court with much guidance as to the conditions under which interim measures should be granted, and those conditions are a matter of great moment..."[73] Paragraph 28 "does not purport to lay down a legal standard; rather it empowers the Court to order interim measures for certain stated reasons,"[74] and there is, India notes, no "code nor any experience accumulated or otherwise relating to the granting of interim measures under Paragraph 28."[75]

80. Against this background, India believes that recourse to the decisions of other international courts is appropriate insofar as those bodies were also faced with interpreting spare textual guidance; the ICJ in particular has interpreted its Statute in a manner that ensured "that provisional measures are granted only when absolutely necessary and clearly justified."[76] Recourse to such jurisprudence is permissible, India argues, because Paragraph 29 of Annexure G permits recourse to both "[i]nternational conventions establishing rules which are expressly recognized by the Parties [and] customary inter-

[66] Interim Measures Hearing Transcript, 53:22–23.

[67] Interim Measures Hearing Transcript, 46:18–21.

[68] Interim Measures Hearing Transcript, 55:16–18.

[69] Interim Measures Hearing Transcript, 46:16–18.

[70] Pakistan's Reply, para. 19.

[71] Interim Measures Hearing Transcript, 47:6–16.

[72] Interim Measures Hearing Transcript, 226:5–6.

[73] Interim Measures Hearing Transcript, 148:21–25.

[74] India's Rejoinder, para. 11.

[75] Interim Measures Hearing Transcript, 150:6–8.

[76] Interim Measures Hearing Transcript, 150:14–15.

national law."[77] The Court is entitled to have recourse to customary international law insofar as "any clarification is needed as to ... whether provisional measures are necessary within Paragraph 28."[78] Pakistan's objections to the use of ICJ precedents in this regard are belied, in India's view, by its willingness to invoke the *Great Belt* case in support of its own position.[79]

81. Turning to the experience of the ICJ, India submits that four criteria guide the indication of provisional measures: "first, plausibility of the alleged rights whose protection is being sought; second, a link between these rights and the Measures requested; third, risk of irreparable prejudice; and, fourth, urgency: a real and imminent risk that irreparable prejudice may be caused to the rights in dispute before the Court has given its final decision."[80] India notes in particular the need to show irreparable harm and urgency and emphasizes that "as a matter of customary international law, it can be safely said that urgency is a criterion for the ordering of provisional measures."[81]

82. Additionally, in India's view, a "balance of convenience test" is inherent in the nature of the Court as a court of justice—whether such a test is described in those terms or in the language of the "justice of the case."[82] Accordingly, in evaluating Pakistan's request, the Court must look also to the effect of the requested interim measures on India. Equal treatment of the Parties, India submits, is a fundamental principle of international law, and is incorporated in the Treaty through Paragraph 29 of Annexure G as well as under Article 7 of the Court's Supplemental Rules of Procedure.[83] In particular, India argues, in evaluating the plausibility of the rights to be protected by interim measures, the Court should bear in mind that "India's right to construct the Kishenganga Project is at the very least plausible"[84] and that the measures requested by Pakistan would in India's view inflict irreparable harm upon it.[85]

D. Urgency and Irreversibility

Pakistan's Position

83. Consistent with its view on the non-applicability of the requirements for the granting of provisional measures found in ICJ case-law, Pakistan submits that Paragraph 28 of Annexure G does not "refer to urgency as a

---

[77] India's Response, para. 36; Interim Measures Hearing Transcript, 154:6–22.

[78] Interim Measures Hearing Transcript, 254:15–20.

[79] India's Rejoinder, para. 19; Interim Measures Hearing Transcript, 129:1–25.

[80] Interim Measures Hearing Transcript, 153:9–14.

[81] Interim Measures Hearing Transcript, 254:21–23; *see also* India's Response, para. 38.

[82] Interim Measures Hearing Transcript, 84:2 to 85:1.

[83] Interim Measures Hearing Transcript, 156:14–18.

[84] Interim Measures Hearing Transcript, 161:18–20.

[85] India's Response, paras. 83–89.

condition for the ordering of provisional measures."[86] Nevertheless, Pakistan maintains that "there is in fact urgency in this case."[87] This urgency stems in the first instance from India's continued refusal to accept the obligation "not to prejudice the solution of the dispute, not to aggravate the dispute, and to avoid harm to Pakistan's interests under the [Treaty]."[88] A "further element" of urgency was said to have been added when Pakistan discovered during the site visit that the local diversion of the Kishenganga River through the by-pass tunnel is contemplated to take place in November 2011.[89]

84. For Pakistan, the possibility that the ultimate diversion of the Kishenganga would take place only in 2015 does not negate the urgency of its Application. The 2015 diversion, Pakistan contends, is "no more than one particularly serious act in a project that has been unlawful from its inception."[90]

85. In response to India's assertion that information regarding the by-pass tunnel had been available to Pakistan for some time, Pakistan submits that it is not arguing that it had only recently become aware of the by-pass tunnel's construction. Rather, it was only "during the site visit [that] it learned of the imminent local diversion of the Kishenganga."[91] This "imminent local diversion," Pakistan argues, reveals India's plans to make "significant modifications to the hydraulics of the Kishenganga"[92] and to accelerate work on the KHEP.[93] For Pakistan, the local diversion is itself a violation of the Treaty, and is submitted as reason enough for the Court to order interim measures.[94] In respect of future developments, however, Pakistan maintains that it is under no obligation to identify the precise point at which India's construction of the KHEP will be irreversible, such information being available only to India.[95] For this reason, Pakistan argues, the second element of its requested interim measures—an obligation for India to provide information—is necessary. [96]

86. Finally, with respect to urgency, Pakistan does not agree with the proposition that "all projects involving the building of dams are in a sense physically reversible."[97] First, Pakistan questions India's acceptance of the possibility that it could in fact be required to dismantle the KHEP.[98] Second,

[86] Pakistan's Application for Provisional Measures, para. 14; *see also* Pakistan's Reply, para. 19.

[87] Pakistan's Application for Provisional Measures, para. 14.

[88] Pakistan's Reply, para. 10.

[89] Pakistan's Reply, para. 14.

[90] Pakistan's Reply, para. 8.

[91] Interim Measures Hearing Transcript, 207:14–25.

[92] Pakistan's Reply, para. 14.

[93] Pakistan's Reply, para. 20.

[94] Pakistan's Reply, para. 23.

[95] Pakistan's Reply, para. 34.

[96] Interim Measures Hearing Transcript, 70:9–18.

[97] Interim Measures Hearing Transcript, 16:23–25; India's Response, para 36.

[98] Interim Measures Hearing Transcript, 17:4–9.

Pakistan argues that it "cannot realistically be denied that it is significantly less likely that the dam would be demolished than that India would refrain from building it in the first place, and that is what we mean by prejudice to Pakistan's interests."[99] In Pakistan's view, India's insistence that Pakistan's concerns can be addressed by India regulating the flow rather than dismantling the works ignores a "central purpose" of the Treaty, which is to "limit the extent to which India has a tap in its hands which it can turn on and off as it pleases."[100]

India's Position

87. Paragraph 28 of Annexure G speaks of the laying down of interim measures when "necessary" on the grounds provided therein. India submits that because the KHEP will not be operational until 2015, Pakistan cannot possibly show that it is "urgent" or "necessary" to grant interim measures.[101] At present, India argues, construction of the KHEP continues, without acceleration, in a manner which is not different from the situation that existed at the time of the First Meeting of the Court on January 14, 2011.[102]

88. With respect to assurances, India argues that it has not reserved the "right to take 'irreversible or pre-emptive action' at any moment."[103] Rather, India submits, it has repeatedly offered assurances that the diversion of the Kishenganga's waters will not take place before 2015. In India's view, the Court should consider its willingness to offer assurances sufficient and refuse to order interim measures, as was done by the ICJ in the *Great Belt* case.[104]

89. With respect to the temporary by-pass tunnel, the operation of which was allegedly discovered during the site visit, India submits that no urgency or necessity for the specification of interim measures arises from it. First, India argues that the by-pass tunnel is expressly permitted under the Treaty insofar as Article I(15) provides that a "temporary by-pass ... shall not be deemed to be an interference with the waters."[105] Second, India notes that the by-pass will have "no impact on the volume or timing of the flow of the water as it flows to the Line of Control ("LOC") because there will be no withdrawal of water."[106] Third, India maintains that Pakistan's communications in respect of interim measures have confounded the meaning of "diversion."[107] The "diversion" against which Pakistan sought relief in its Request for Arbitration is the diversion—or "delivery" in the terms of the Treaty—of waters from the Kishenganga into another tributary of the Jhelum, *not* a temporary local

[99] Interim Measures Hearing Transcript, 62:12–16.

[100] Interim Measures Hearing Transcript, 17:7–9.

[101] India's Response, para. 61.

[102] India's Response, para. 52.

[103] India's Response, para. 73.

[104] India's Response, para. 73.

[105] India's Rejoinder, para. 27; Interim Measures Hearing Transcript, 21–25; 132:21–25.

[106] India's Response, para. 15; *see also* India's Response, para. 77.

[107] India's Response, para. 15.

diversion of the river.[108] India notes that "there were no questions of by-pass tunnels" in Pakistan's Application for Provisional Measures.[109] Finally, India contests as a matter of fact any contention that Pakistan learned of the by-pass tunnel only during the site visit. In India's view, Pakistan was provided information on the progress of the by-pass at meetings of the Indus Commission in November 2004 and never objected to its construction.[110] In sum, India argues, Pakistan's attempt to justify interim measures on the basis of the by-pass tunnel is "no more than an *ex post facto* attempt to justify its application for provisional measures based on alleged urgency."[111]

90. From a broader perspective, India argues that a construction project such as the KHEP can never, in and of itself, justify interim measures because construction is reversible. According to India, "all projects involving the building of dams are, in a sense, physically reversible, particularly a Run-of-River project like Kishenganga, since mechanisms always exist in every dam which can regulate the flow of water."[112]

91. India rejects Pakistan's argument that interim measures could be justified merely by the difficulty of abandoning the project after a certain point or of restoring the *status quo ante*.[113] Nor does India agree that urgency exists because of the construction of "spillway gates" which, according to Pakistan, India might not be willing to undo at a later date.[114] The irreversibility complained of by Pakistan, India contends, concerns only the physical structure—but does not imply the irreversibility of the uninterrupted flow across the Line of Control.[115] In this respect, India cites the ICJ's *Gabčíkovo-Nagymaros Project*[116] decision as support for the proposition that it is the putting into operation of a project that gives rise to a wrongful act justifying the granting of provisional measures, not the preparation and construction of those works.[117] In any case, India maintains that the construction of the spillway is not a matter before the Court and should be decided by a Neutral Expert.[118] In India's view, Pakistan has otherwise failed to identify what the stage of construction making the project irreversible might be.[119]

---

[108] India's Response, paras. 12–13.

[109] Interim Measures Hearing Transcript, 256:25 to 257:1–2.

[110] Interim Measures Hearing Transcript, 106:5–107:16.

[111] India's Response, para. 76.

[112] India's Response, para. 63.

[113] India's Response, para. 62.

[114] India's Rejoinder, para. 30.

[115] India's Rejoinder, para. 30.

[116] *Case Concerning the Gabčíkovo-Nagymaros Project* (Hungary/Slovakia), *I.C.J. Reports 1997*, p. 7.

[117] India's Response, para. 60.

[118] India's Rejoinder, para. 30.

[119] India's Response, para. 63.

92. While the construction of the KHEP is said to be reversible, and therefore cannot give rise to an urgent need for provisional measures, India submits that the harm that those measures would inflict on India would indeed be irreparable, *inter alia*, because the State of Jammu and Kashmir is "seriously short of power."[120] According to India, any interim measure ordering India to cease work on the KHEP would add "enormous financial costs" to the project and impact the lives of India's citizens currently engaged in the project who would lose their "jobs and their livelihood."[121]

93. In response to Pakistan's fear that India will "turn off the tap, "[122] India argues that the Treaty "provides ample safeguards"[123] against this, which include: (1) Paragraph 18 of Annexure E, which stipulates that there must be prior agreement between the Parties before the reservoirs are filled; (2) a limited period for filling the reservoirs in case no agreement is reached; and (3) the dispute resolution mechanism under the Treaty in case Pakistan comes to the conclusion that these provisions have not been complied with.[124] India also argues that "the whole point of run of river dams is that they allow water to pass through without storage."[125] India submits that it would be physically impossible to transform these plants into storage facilities in order to turn off the tap.[126]

94. Finally, concerning Pakistan's second requested interim measure—that of obliging India to provide information to the Court and Pakistan of actual or imminent developments or steps in relation to the KHEP that may have a significant adverse effect upon restoring the *status quo ante*—counsel for India made the following additional representation with respect to the provision of information:

> [t]hat any actual or imminent development or steps in relation to the Kishenganga Project during the progress of this arbitration that would have significant adverse effect on Pakistan's stated rights or interests will be promptly intimated to the Court and to Pakistan.[127]

[120] India's Response, para. 86.

[121] India's Response, para. 87–88.

[122] Interim Measures Hearing Transcript, 160:1.

[123] Interim Measures Hearing Transcript, 160:4.

[124] Interim Measures Hearing Transcript, 160:3–10.

[125] Interim Measures Hearing Transcript, 160:11–13.

[126] Interim Measures Hearing Transcript, 160:18–19.

[127] Interim Measures Hearing Transcript, 270:2–6.

E. The Issuance of Interim Measures on Grounds of "Safeguarding [the Applicant's] Interests under the Treaty with Respect to the Matter in Dispute"

95. In its Application for Provisional Measures, Pakistan submits that the specification of interim measures is necessary to "safeguard its interests under the Treaty with respect to the matter in dispute."[128]

Pakistan's Position

96. According to Pakistan, "it has rights to secure itself against violations of India's duty to let flow the Kishenganga waters and not to permit any interference with them."[129] It has "rights not to have the flow obstructed by the Kishenganga Dam or the waters diverted away from the river."[130] And it has a right not to have India "build a dam to meet the needs of a people in a different River Basin."[131]

97. While the Treaty "refers to the *interests* and not to the *rights*" of a Party[132] (in contrast to the language used in the ICJ Statute, which refers to the "rights of the parties"),[133] this difference does not, in Pakistan's view, permit the protection of any rights whatsoever, with no relation to the Treaty, as India is said to suggest.[134] Rather, the use of the term "interests" indicates that it is "not necessary at this stage for Pakistan to prove that it has a right under the Indus Waters Treaty that would, itself, be violated by continued construction of the Kishenganga plant."[135] In Pakistan's view, "it is enough that Pakistan has an interest in not having these claimed rights prejudiced pending the decision of this Court."[136]

98. As set forth by Pakistan, its interests under the Treaty include preventing the deprivation of the aforementioned substantive rights,[137] as well as "interests in ensuring that the Indus Waters Treaty system for … the safeguarding of those rights works."[138] In Pakistan's view, India understates Pakistan's essential interests under the Treaty by suggesting that Pakistan's interests extend only to the delivery of a quantity of water over the Line of

---

[128] Pakistan's Application for Provisional Measures, paras. 11–13.

[129] Interim Measures Hearing Transcript, 59:22–24.

[130] Interim Measures Hearing Transcript, 59:25 to 60:1.

[131] Interim Measures Hearing Transcript, 60:2–3.

[132] Interim Measures Hearing Transcript, 59:9–10. (italics supplied)

[133] Pakistan's Reply, para. 27.

[134] Interim Measures Hearing Transcript, 59:12–17.

[135] Interim Measures Hearing Transcript, 59:18–21.

[136] Interim Measures Hearing Transcript, 60:6–8.

[137] Interim Measures Hearing Transcript, 61:8–10; *see supra*, para. 96.

[138] Interim Measures Hearing Transcript, 61:11–14.

Control—rather than to the unrestricted usage of the Western Rivers, subject only to limited, enumerated rights granted to India.[139]

99. In respect of its substantive interests, Pakistan maintains that interim measures are necessary to prevent the creation of a *fait accompli* and harm to the likelihood of any remedy that the Court may order being effective in the "real world."[140] Pakistan submits that "[i]f the work on the dam goes ahead now, it significantly reduces the practical possibility of the Court effectively upholding Pakistan's rights if it upholds Pakistan's claim."[141] In respect of Pakistan's interest in the Indus Waters Treaty system, Pakistan submits that interim measures are necessary to preserve the Court's freedom of action and to protect the principle that "neither State can press ahead with projects … in the face of an ongoing Court proceeding concerning the legality of that very question."[142]

India's Position

100. India emphasizes that Pakistan "prayed in its Memorial only to restrain India from diverting the waters of the Kishenganga to a Tributary."[143] There can be no ground for the specification of interim measures, India submits, given the categorical assertion—made by India in its counsel's March 17, 2011 correspondence—that there will be no such diversion until 2015.[144] In India's view, "the un-interrupted flow, the only thing that is of material consequence to Pakistan … will remain the same …"[145]

101. India rejects Pakistan's invocation of wider interests, as well as its distinction of "interests" under the Treaty from "rights."[146] In India's view, this would permit Pakistan to advance "any 'interest' that suited its particular agenda," however far removed from "legally protected interests, i.e. rights recognized by the Treaty."[147] Specifically, India submits that Pakistan is asserting rights in excess of those it actually possesses and without reference to India's corresponding rights. According to India, "[t]here is no question of the Treaty giving Pakistan a right of veto of, or prior consent to, India's construction and operation of" projects such as the KHEP.[148] For India, "the Treaty, while granting Pakistan's right to waters of the Western Rivers in Article III(1), clearly protects India's rights under Article III(2) … an aspect Pakistan rarely

[139] Pakistan's Reply, paras. 9, 29; Interim Measures Hearing Transcript, 229:1–21.

[140] Interim Measures Hearing Transcript, 61:20 to 62:20.

[141] Interim Measures Hearing Transcript, 62:16–19.

[142] Interim Measures Hearing Transcript, 65:7–10.

[143] Interim Measures Hearing Transcript, 112:16–17.

[144] India's Response, para. 8; Interim Measures Hearing Transcript, 124:7–9, 132:24 to 133:8, 182:17–20.

[145] India's Rejoinder, para. 30.

[146] India's Rejoinder, para. 35.

[147] India's Rejoinder, para. 35.

[148] India's Rejoinder, para. 38.

mentions or simply ignores."[149] Denying India's rights in this context is "tantamount" to denying the treaty.[150]

102. Finally, India maintains that "there is no link between the rights under the Treaty whose protection Pakistan seeks and the Measures she requests."[151] Insofar as, in India's view, "Pakistan's Neelum-Jhelum Project is not within her territory," the specification of interim measures relating to the project is unrelated to the rights Pakistan "undoubtedly" possesses to construct dams "within her own territory on the Western Rivers."[152]

F. The Issuance of Interim Measures on Grounds of Avoidance of "Prejudice to the Final Solution … of the Dispute"

103. Under Paragraph 28 of Annexure G, a Party may request that the Court lay down interim measures when necessary, *inter alia*, "to avoid prejudice to the final solution … of the dispute." Pakistan accordingly submits that interim measures are necessary in this case to avoid prejudice to the final solution of the dispute.[153]

Pakistan's Position

104. Pakistan considers that India's "[p]roceeding with the Kishenganga Project now while this case is in progress, self-evidently increases the difficulty and costs of reversing the process, and the obvious fear is that India will plead the difficulty and cost of reversing the project as a reason constraining the Court's exercise of discretion …"[154] Interim measures, Pakistan notes, are necessary when needed to "avert the possibility of the taking of a step by which one or the other Party could, in effect, box the Court in and limit the Court's practical ability to resolve the case in accordance with the law."[155]

105. Pakistan is particularly concerned that the ongoing work on the KHEP will render certain remedies technically unfeasible or will supply India with additional arguments to the effect that it would be "inequitable" to halt the project in light of sunk costs.[156] The costs of reversing the project, Pakistan notes, and the remedies available to the Court, do not necessarily progress gradually, but may pass through "step changes" that substantially increase the difficulty of certain solutions to the dispute. In particular, Pakistan points to

[149] Interim Measures Hearing Transcript, 116:5–11.

[150] India's Rejoinder, para. 37.

[151] Interim Measures Hearing Transcript, 162:9–11.

[152] Interim Measures Hearing Transcript, 162:8–16.

[153] Pakistan's Reply, para. 30.

[154] Interim Measures Hearing Transcript, 68:3–8.

[155] Interim Measures Hearing Transcript, 67:25 to 68:3.

[156] Pakistan's Reply, para. 32.

the commencement of construction on the lower phases of the Kishenganga dam and the inclusion of large low-level outlets—to which Pakistan objects—in the dam design.[157]

106. The potential physical reversibility of the KHEP, Pakistan submits, does not lessen this concern.[158] According to Pakistan, while it may be physically possible to remove the dam and other works, India may create a situation in which work on the project is so far along that the Court will be forced to consider alternatives to abandoning the KHEP.[159] While the Court may order the complete demolition of the dam, Pakistan submits that this is "not the question."[160] Rather, according to Pakistan, the question is "whether the possibility of restoring the *status quo ante* is prejudiced by India's continued work on the Kishenganga Project, and in particular by the opening of the by-pass, the draining of the river and the construction of a dam on the riverbed."[161] For Pakistan, "once that work is started, the chances of removing this obstruction to the flow of the waters of the Kishenganga will be reduced, and that is why we need this order, and that is why we need it now: to keep alive the possibility of the maintenance of the *status quo*."[162] Is it "really credible," Pakistan asks, "to say that it is as easy for this Court to say demolish as it is for this Court to say pause?"[163]

India's Position

107. India disputes the idea that the Court would feel constrained in the remedies it could adopt in this case, and rejects the idea that the possibility of such a feeling can justify the imposition of interim measures.[164] In particular, India points to the way this issue was forthrightly handled by the ICJ in the *Great Belt* case, noting Pakistan's own invocation of that precedent. Faced with the assertion by Denmark that an order to dismantle its project would be out of the question, India points out that the ICJ explicitly noted the possibility of an order "that such works must not be continued or must be modified or dismantled."[165] Observing that the ICJ did not "feel that it was in a box or in any other way constrained," India questions why the present Court "would feel any more boxed in."[166]

108. While maintaining that, "as a matter of principle," the Court is unlikely to feel constrained, India further submits that the question of dis-

[157] Pakistan's Reply, paras. 32, 35.

[158] Pakistan's Reply, para. 36.

[159] Pakistan's Reply, para. 36.

[160] Interim Measures Hearing Transcript, 231:14.

[161] Interim Measures Hearing Transcript, 231:15–19.

[162] Interim Measures Hearing Transcript, 233:4–8.

[163] Interim Measures Hearing Transcript, 232:5–7.

[164] Interim Measures Hearing Transcript, 159:3–23; 184:6–25.

[165] Interim Measures Hearing Transcript, 159:18–19.

[166] Interim Measures Hearing Transcript, 159:20–22.

mantling is "unlikely to arise."[167] This is not, India hastens to add, due to what it considers its likely success on the merits. Rather, India is of the view that even if all of Pakistan's claims were granted, it would still be permissible under the Treaty for India to operate the KHEP during at least a portion of the year. Accordingly, while the Court might need to regulate the flows that India would be obligated to provide,[168] it is unlikely to confront any issue of dismantling, "simply because on [Pakistan's] own admission it is only for six months of the year during the lean season that the flow to Pakistan ... would be affected."[169]

G. The Issuance of Interim Measures on Grounds of "Aggravation or Extension of the Dispute"

109. Under Paragraph 28 of Annexure G, a Party may request that the Court lay down interim measures when necessary, *inter alia*, to avoid "aggravation or extension of the dispute."

Pakistan's Position

110. Pakistan submits that "India's accelerating work on the KHEP, and its continuing refusal to say that it accepts well-established legal principles, is itself aggravating the dispute," thereby justifying the specification of interim measures.[170]

111. Moreover, in Pakistan's view, the introduction of claims relating to sovereignty or territorial control over the area in which Pakistan's Neelum-Jhelum Project is being prepared "threatens to extend the dispute in a very regrettable manner."[171]

India's Position

112. India rejects the proposition that any of its actions or arguments have had the effect of aggravating or extending the dispute, such that interim measures might be contemplated.[172] As India puts it, "[t]he third possible ground is aggravation or extension of the dispute, and Pakistan has failed to demonstrate in any way that the interim measures are necessary in order to do that."[173]

113. First, in India's view, continuing "work on the KHEP does not aggravate or extend the dispute" as Pakistan's own exposition of the issues in dispute is said to be limited to "(*a*) whether India may deliver water from the

---

[167] Interim Measures Hearing Transcript, 263:5–11.

[168] Interim Measures Hearing Transcript, 263:22–264:9.

[169] Interim Measures Hearing Transcript, 279:22–280:1.

[170] Pakistan's Reply, para. 42.

[171] Interim Measures Hearing Transcript, 9:6–8; see also Pakistan's Reply, paras. 43–44.

[172] India's Rejoinder, paras. 46–47.

[173] Interim Measures Hearing Transcript, 186:10–13.

KHEP to another tributary of the Jhelum, and (*b*) the permissibility of the lowering of the water level below the Dead Storage Level."[174] Second, India denies that it has accelerated the pace of construction: "there has in fact been a slight slippage in the progress of works as against the targeted dates ..."[175] Third, in respect of any "refusal to say that it accepts well-established legal principles" (which it also contests as a matter of fact), India submits that Pakistan has not established "how such a 'refusal' (assuming quod non there was one) could aggravate or extend the dispute."[176] Finally, India argues that its use of terms such as "Pakistan-occupied Kashmir ... is a reflection of a fact ... [that] should be carefully kept in mind while considering whether provisional measures should be imposed,"[177] but "is not what we call an 'aggravation of the dispute.'"[178] On the contrary, India observes that "a real danger of aggravation of the dispute" exists "if India is restrained from further works ... while Pakistan continues work on a project that is not even situated in its territory."[179]

H. The Parties' Characterization of the Historical Record

114. In the course of their arguments on interim measures, the Parties introduced and commented on various historical events that are alleged to have a bearing on these proceedings.

Pakistan's Position

115. In Pakistan's view, its Application for Provisional Measures must be approached by the Court in light of the "stark deficit in trust between the parties"[180] and the historical experience of 1948 "when the East Punjab Government cut off all the canals supplying West Punjab."[181] Pakistan observes that these experiences formed the background for the negotiation of the Indus Waters Treaty and

> led to around a decade of hard-fought negotiations, leading ultimately to the carefully constructed and as a matter of engineering quite remarkable solution of the 1960 Treaty. The essence of that solution is that there is no equitable apportionment of uses, but rather a literal and permanent division of the Indus System of rivers; the Eastern Rivers go to India, the Western Rivers go to Pakistan, and that is as established by Articles 2 and 3 of the Treaty. That solution is a radical one, but it is readily understandable given the background of the Treaty. And it is Pakistan's inter-

[174] India's Rejoinder, para. 46.

[175] India's Rejoinder, para. 28.

[176] India's Rejoinder, para. 47.

[177] Interim measures Hearing Transcript, 82:6–11.

[178] Interim Measures Hearing Transcript, 82:3–5.

[179] Interim Measures Hearing Transcript, 82:11–14.

[180] Pakistan's Reply, para. 39.

[181] Interim Measures Hearing Transcript, 24:3–4.

ests in the finally agreed treaty regime that Pakistan seeks to protect by its current Application.[182]

116. Equally, this history makes clear the extent to which the Indus Rivers system is "fundamental to [Pakistan's] existence and the health and livelihood of its people."[183] "India's dam construction program," Pakistan believes, "is an existential issue."[184]

117. These concerns, Pakistan observes, are far from "anachronistic."[185] As it was developed, the bargain agreed upon depends upon "limitations on India's capacity to manipulate the timing of flows," a matter that "was hard-wired into the Treaty. This was done by limiting the amount of live storage ... for changing the timing of flows on each and every hydropower dam that India could construct on the two rivers."[186] With the recent *Baglihar* case, however, Pakistan has, in its view, been left without physical protection against the manipulation of flow on the Indus system.[187]

India's Position

118. India denies the relevance of events that occurred in the immediate aftermath of partition, prior to the Indus Waters Treaty, for the present issue of interim measures.[188] In India's view, the 1948 incident took place "during a period of some confusion between two new States ... that were sorting out their respective rights."[189] Moreover, "it was done by East Punjab without any consultation with India's central government. It was opposed by India's central government as soon as India's central government learned about it, and in fact it was terminated almost immediately after the central government learned of it."[190] Finally, "[n]othing remotely like that has occurred in the ensuing 63 years."[191]

119. In India's view, references to 1948 represent an attempt on the part of Pakistan to portray itself as the victim.[192] The same, India submits, is true with respect to the finding of the neutral expert in the *Baglihar* case and with India's other pending hydro-electric projects on the Western Rivers—which do not "have anything to do with Pakistan's Application for Provisional Measures."[193]

182 Interim Measures Hearing Transcript, 28:17–25, 29:3.
183 Interim Measures Hearing Transcript, 23:20–21.
184 Interim Measures Hearing Transcript, 23:24–25.
185 Interim Measures Hearing Transcript, 25:8.
186 Interim Measures Hearing Transcript, 25:24 to 26:3.
187 Interim Measures Hearing Transcript, 26:23 to 27:1.
188 India's Rejoinder, para. 43.
189 India's Rejoinder, para. 43.
190 Interim Measures Hearing Transcript, 171:19–23.
191 Interim Measures Hearing Transcript, 171:25 to 172:1.
192 India's Rejoinder, para. 44.
193 India's Rejoinder, para. 44.

120. In fact, India argues, the implementation of the Treaty has been "relatively smooth" over more than fifty years,[194] and the assertion that the Baglihar Dam was filled in such a way as to harm Pakistan is factually incorrect.[195] In India's view, the evidence introduced on this matter should be disregarded as "inaccurate, emotion-laden and inflammatory."[196]

IV. Analysis of the Court

A. India's Assurances and Representations

121. This case marks the first instance in the fifty-year history of the Indus Waters Treaty that a court of arbitration has been constituted to resolve a Treaty dispute between the Parties. Vital interests are at stake for both Pakistan and India. The importance of launching arbitral proceedings under the Treaty for the first time, and on issues so profoundly affecting those vital interests, coupled with Pakistan's having applied for the laying down of interim measures, may give the impression that little common ground exists between the Parties. But the far-reaching and intricate terms of the Indus Waters Treaty, and the fact that it has endured and has been applied by the Parties for more than fifty years despite difficulties in their relations, attest to the essential mutuality of their interests, and to the skill of the World Bank in melding those mutual interests in the terms of the Treaty. It is accordingly important at the outset for the Court to record that key matters of agreement have emerged in the course of this arbitration concerning how India will conduct itself in its construction of the KHEP. Those elements of agreement bode well for the continuing vitality of the Treaty.

122. The first and apparently most contentious of the assurances sought by Pakistan was for India to recognize explicitly the "proceed at own risk" principle. The content of that principle is expressed by Pakistan, on the basis of the ICJ's *Passage Through the Great Belt* provisional measures order, to be as follows: "a State engaged in works that may violate the rights of another State can proceed only at its own risk."[197] The extent to which India did or did not agree with this principle was the subject of sustained debate through the written submissions and the hearing on interim measures. But any doubt about India's acceptance of this principle was put to rest during the last day of

---

[194] Interim Measures Hearing Transcript, 80:6–13.

[195] Interim Measures Hearing Transcript, 175:5–6.

[196] Interim Measures Hearing Transcript, 179:21–24 to 180:6.

[197] Pakistan's Application for Provisional Measures, para. 6, *citing* Letter of Counsel for Pakistan to Counsel for India dated March 6, 2011. That letter quoted directly from the *Great Belt* case as follows: "... it is for Denmark, which is informed of the nature of Finland's claim, to consider the impact which a judgment upholding it could have upon the implementation of the Great Belt project, and to decide whether or to what extent it should accordingly delay or modify that project" (*Passage through the Great Belt* (Finland *v.* Denmark), Provisional Measures, Order of 29 July 1991, *I.C.J. Reports 1991*, p. 18, para. 33).

the hearing on interim measures, when counsel for India stated, "in unequivocal terms," that "in this case, India is committed to proceed on the 'own-risk principle' of international law."[198]

123. Second, Pakistan sought in its Application that the Court issue an order providing that India "inform the Court and Pakistan of any actual or imminent developments or steps in relation to the Kishenganga project that may have a significant adverse effect upon restoring the *status quo ante* or that may in any other way seriously jeopardise Pakistan's rights and interests under the Treaty."[199] India has, in response, accepted in almost *verbatim* terms Pakistan's request that it provide such information.[200]

124. Third, in response to Pakistan's request for information concerning the "planned date for diverting the river and putting the KHEP into operation,"[201] India has assured both Pakistan and the Court that "the planned date of diversion is not before 2015."[202]

125. A fourth, much lesser point of seeming contention was the extent to which Paragraph 28 of Annexure G ("[e]ither Party may request the Court *at its first meeting* to lay down, pending its Award, such interim measures …") imposes a temporal limitation on the ability of a State to apply for interim measures. Pakistan argued that it did not, and in response to a query from the Court, India confirmed that it "does not take the position—that Pakistan or any Party is precluded from requesting provisional measures at a later time."[203]

126. Finally, India has given an unequivocal assurance that, regardless of the outcome, it will comply with the Court's Award. The Agent of India's statement in this regard merits quotation:

> I had said in my Opening Statement that India wants peace and friendship with its neighbors, and we have striven very hard to build friendship, build confidence and trust, and this even now guides us in our approach. India believes in the sanctity of [the] Indus Waters Treaty, not only the Indus Waters Treaty, all our international legal commitments, and I have no hesitation in committing that we will fully and wholly abide by any decision taken by the Court of Arbitration.[204]

---

[198] Interim Measures Hearing Transcript, 269:23 to 270:1.

[199] Pakistan's Application for Provisional Measures, para. 15.

[200] During the hearing on interim measures, counsel for India said: "But let me state here, in unequivocal terms, … that any actual or imminent development of steps in relation to the Kishenganga Project during the progress of the arbitration that would have 'significant adverse effect' … on Pakistan's stated rights or interests will be promptly intimated to the Court and to Pakistan." Interim Measures Hearing Transcript, 269:5–10.

[201] E-mail Letter of March 6, 2011 from counsel for Pakistan, Appendix A, Application for Provisional Measures dated June 6, 2011.

[202] E-mail Letter of March 17, 2011 from counsel for India, Appendix B, Application for Provisional Measures dated June 6, 2011. *See also* Interim Measures Hearing Transcript 258:22–25, 278:12–14.

[203] Interim Measures Hearing Transcript, 250:1–3.

[204] Interim Measures Hearing Transcript, 288:25 to 289:7.

127. The assurances sought from India by Pakistan have thus to a great extent been met. These assurances have reduced the need for the Court to pass upon some of Pakistan's claims. Moreover, these assurances have helped foster a spirit of cooperation that conduces to the efficient conduct of these proceedings and, more than that, to the continued effectiveness of the Treaty.

B. The Court's Power to Specify Interim Measures: Paragraph 28 of Annexure G to the Treaty

128. Paragraph 28, Annexure G to the Treaty governs the issuance of interim measures. It provides:

> Either Party may request the Court at its first meeting to lay down, pending its Award, such interim measures as, in the opinion of that Party, are necessary to safeguard its interests under the Treaty with respect to the matter in dispute, or to avoid prejudice to the final solution or aggravation or extension of the dispute. The Court shall, thereupon, after having afforded an adequate hearing to each Party, decide, by a majority consisting of at least four members of the Court, whether any interim measures are necessary for the reasons hereinbefore stated, and, if so, shall specify such measures: Provided that
>
> (*a*) the Court shall lay down such interim measures only for such specified period as, in its opinion, will be necessary to render the Award: this period may, if necessary, be extended unless the delay in rendering the Award is due to any delay on the part of the Party which requested the interim measures in supplying such information as may be required by the other Party or by the Court in connection with the dispute; and
>
> (*b*) the specification of such interim measures shall not be construed as an indication of any view of the Court on the merits of the dispute.

129. As set out above,[205] the Parties, having been afforded an adequate hearing, differ over the interpretation of Paragraph 28. The essence of their difference is whether, to be "necessary," interim measures must be required urgently and so as to avoid irreparable injury to the interests of the Party seeking those measures.

130. In the view of the Court, an interpretation of the term "necessary" in Paragraph 28 that engrafts the requirements of "urgency" and "irreparable injury," as those concepts have been developed by the International Court of Justice in its case-law on provisional measures,[206] is not required. One evident

[205] *See supra* paragraphs 83–94.

[206] *See, e.g., Passage through the Great Belt* (Finland *v.* Denmark), Order of 29 July 1991, *I.C.J. Reports 1991*, p. 17, para. 23. ("Whereas provisional measures under Article 41 of the Statute are indicated 'pending the final decision' of the Court on the merits of the case, and are therefore only justified if there is urgency in the sense that action prejudicial to the rights of either party is likely to be taken before such final decision is given;"); *Frontier Dispute* (Burkina Faso/Republic of Mali), Order of 10 January 1986, *I.C.J. Reports 1986*, p. 10, para. 21 ("Whereas the facts that have given rise to the requests of both Parties for the indication of provisional measures expose

reason not wholly to import the ICJ's provisional measures requirements is, of course, the difference in the respective wording of Article 41 of the ICJ Statute[207] and Paragraph 28 of Annexure G. Paragraph 28 sets out three distinct, specific grounds on the basis of which the meaning of "necessary" can be ascertained. It thus functions as a kind of *lex specialis* prescribed by the framers of that provision that makes unnecessary the imposition of further requirements.

131. Under Paragraph 28, the Court is empowered—and indeed appears to be obliged—in three instances to specify interim measures if it concludes that those measures are necessary:

(i) to safeguard the interests of the requesting Party with respect to the matter in dispute; or
(ii) to avoid prejudice to the final solution of the dispute; or
(iii) to avoid aggravation or extension of the dispute.

132. In specifying the three grounds on which interim measures may be granted, the framers of the Treaty chose to use a disjunctive "or" rather than the conjunctive "and," thus indicating that the measures required need only meet one of these criteria in order that interim measures may be ordered.[208]

133. Each of the three grounds for interim measures enunciated in Annexure G has a different focus: the first places the Parties' "interests" as the central consideration, while the third requires the demonstration of the likelihood of aggravation or extension of the dispute.

134. The second ground is conceived in even broader terms; as worded, interim measures may be required in order to avoid potential prejudice

the persons and property in the disputed area, as well as the interests of both States within that area, to serious risk of irreparable damage; and whereas the circumstances consequently demand that the Chamber should indicate ... ").

[207] Article 41 of the ICJ Statute provides:

"1. The Court shall have the power to indicate, if it considers that circumstances so require, any provisional measures which ought to be taken to preserve the respective rights of either party.

2. Pending the final decision, notice of the measures suggested shall forthwith be given to the parties and to the Security Council."

[208] The use of the disjunctive word "or" has a logical meaning, creating alternative elements which can each satisfy a given condition. In *Plama* v. *Bulgaria*, the question before the tribunal was whether the Claimant was a legal entity owned or controlled by citizens or nationals of a third state under Article 17(1) of the Energy Charter Treaty. The Tribunal determined that the word "or" in that provision must signify that "ownership and control are alternatives: in other words, only one need be met for the first limb to be satisfied ..." *Plama Consortium Ltd. (Cyprus) v. Bulgaria*, Decision on Jurisdiction, ICSID ARB/03/24, para. 170, February 8, 2005. In the *Anglo-Iranian Oil Co.* case, ICJ Judge John Read observed that a plain reading of the disjunctive word "or" in the clause "with regard to situations or facts relating directly or indirectly to the application of treaties or conventions accepted by Persia" had an "unequivocal meaning." He reasoned that the use of that word had been "deliberate" and had the effect of broadening the scope of the declaration in question beyond those instruments which were "directly" accepted by Persia, to those having an indirect relationship to the treaties or conventions in question. *Anglo-Iranian Oil. Co. Case* (United Kingdom *v.* Iran), *I.C.J. Reports 1952*, p. 142 at p. 146 (dissenting opinion of Judge Read).

to the final outcome of the arbitration. This ground for the specification of interim measures appears to be primarily intended to safeguard the Court of Arbitration's own freedom to prescribe what it in due course considers to be the correct outcome on the substance of a given dispute. Other international courts and tribunals, including the ICJ, have acknowledged the cogency of this concern even in the face of less specific guidance.[209] The terms of Paragraph 28 of Annexure G make it plain that the need not to constrain the Court in its findings or choice of remedies by "facts on the ground" constitutes a legitimate and independent basis for an order of interim measures.

135. Yet, as broad as the scope of Paragraph 28 may be, the Court nonetheless recognizes that interim measures under the Treaty remain an extraordinary recourse. Consistent with the general practice of international and national courts and tribunals, the Court must be satisfied that, without prejudice to its decision on the merits, the claims set forth by the Party seeking interim measures appear to be at least "plausible."[210] Regardless of the conditions under which a court is authorized under its rules to indicate interim relief, such relief cannot be said to be "necessary" under any of those conditions if it is apparent to that court at an early stage that it is unlikely to have jurisdiction or that the applicant has failed to present a plausible case on the merits.

C. The Necessity "to avoid prejudice to the final solution ... of the dispute" under Paragraph 28 of Annexure G to the Treaty

136. Having found that any one of the three grounds provided under Paragraph 28 would be sufficient for the Court to specify interim measures, the Court now addresses the ground that, in its view, bears the most relevance to these proceedings—that of ordering provisional measures when "necessary ... to avoid prejudice to the final solution." In the circumstances of the present case, the Court finds merit in the argument that direction from the Court in

---

[209] Article 41 of the ICJ Statute, for example, does not expressly mention prejudice to the proceedings before the Court as a criterion of which account is to be had in considering provisional measures applications. Yet then ICJ President Jiménez de Aréchaga, in reflecting on the essential function of provisional measures pursuant to the ICJ Statute, noted that "[t]he essential object of provisional measures is to ensure that the execution of a future judgment on the merits shall not be frustrated by the actions of one party *pendente lite*." *Aegean Sea Continental Shelf* (Greece *v.* Turkey), Order on Interim Protection, *I.C.J. Reports 1976*, p. 3, at p. 16 (separate opinion of President Jiménez de Aréchaga.).

[210] In the terminology used by the ICJ: *see, e.g., Request for Interpretation of the Judgment of* 15 *June 1962 in the Case Concerning the Temple of Preah Vihear* (Cambodia *v.* Thailand), Order on Provisional Measures of 18 July 2011, para. 33. Indeed, some jurisdictions would require the demonstration of something more than a plausible case, such as a *prima facie* determination that the case is meritorious. Under the UNCITRAL Model Law (2006 Revisions), the party requesting interim measures must satisfy the arbitral tribunal that, *inter alia,* "[t]here is a reasonable possibility that the requesting party will succeed on the merits of the claim." Article 17A(1)(*b*).

the form of interim measures—albeit not in as far-reaching a form as requested by Pakistan—is necessary to "avoid prejudice to the final solution" of the present dispute as it may be prescribed in the Court's eventual Award.

137. The circumstances in which it will be appropriate for the Court of Arbitration to exercise its powers under Paragraph 28 in the interest of avoiding "prejudice to the final solution" of the dispute will necessarily vary depending on the alleged violation of the Treaty and the facts of the dispute insofar as they may by then appear to have been established. In the present proceedings, the Parties principally look to this Court of Arbitration to assist them in the authoritative interpretation of certain provisions of the Treaty that raise questions, none of which have been decided before by a court of arbitration under the Treaty. The specific remedies regarding the construction of the KHEP requested by Pakistan are contingent on the interpretation of the Treaty that the Court will adopt. Accordingly, what must be preserved *pendente lite* is the Court's ability eventually to render an award with the content that it considers is warranted both in terms of legal principle and in terms of the remedies that it may order, once it has had the benefit of a complete exposition of fact and law by both Parties.

138. In addition, the Court must be satisfied that an order of interim measures at the present stage is "necessary" in the circumstances of this case. As noted earlier, the urgency and irreparable injury criteria developed in the ICJ's case-law on provisional measures are not dispositive under Paragraph 28 of Annexure G. At the same time, the Court cannot rule out the possibility that its interpretation of the first ground for interim measures—"to safeguard its interests under the Treaty" —might be usefully informed by the ICJ's case-law on the phrase "to preserve the respective rights of either party" in the ICJ Statute, not so much by virtue of any particular relevance of the ICJ Statute for the interpretation of the Indus Waters Treaty, but by virtue of the comparable position in which the applicant finds itself in both situations. The Court however fails to see how either criterion—that of urgency or that of irreparable harm to a party—would affect the interpretation of the phrase "necessary ... to avoid prejudice to the final solution ... of the dispute," as this second ground, on which the present order relies, is essentially intended to protect the *Court's* position rather than the rights or interests of a party.

139. The Court sees no reason to read the term "necessary" in Paragraph 28 as embodying any special meaning beyond the normal use of the term, expressing simply the idea that an action is required, needed or essential for a particular purpose.[211] Thus, under the second head of Paragraph 28, interim measures are necessary to avoid prejudice to the final solution of a dispute when, in the absence of their issuance, there would be the risk of a *fait accompli*

[211] The Oxford English Dictionary (Concise 11th ed. 2008) defines "necessary" as a synonym of "required to be done, achieved, or present; needed." (at p. 956). Similarly, the New Oxford American Dictionary (3d ed., 2010) provides the following synonyms for "necessary": "required to be done, achieved, or present; needed; essential."

that compromises the liberty of the Court of Arbitration to render its Award in the manner it considers to be legally warranted, or the Parties' ability to implement such award without prohibitive delays or costs.

D. Conclusions

1. Pakistan's Claims Satisfy the Test of Plausibility

140. Pakistan's claims of Treaty violation challenge the permissibility of the construction and operation of the KHEP on the river Kishenganga/Neelum. At this stage in the proceedings, the Court has not and cannot form any views as to the merits of Pakistan's claims.[212] That said, the Court is satisfied that Pakistan has presented a plausible, provisionally tenable argument under the Treaty in support of its case. Having reviewed Pakistan's arguments as they are stated in its Memorial, the Court cannot exclude the possibility that India's planned installations, or elements of those installations, on the Kishenganga/Neelum would not be in conformity with the Treaty.[213]

2. Temporarily enjoining India's construction of many components of the KHEP (including the headrace tunnel and powerhouse facility) is not necessary to avoid prejudice to the Award.

141. In considering which aspects of the KHEP present a real risk of "prejudice to the final solution" of the dispute, the construction schedule of the KHEP as compared to the procedural timetable of the present arbitration is of critical importance.[214] Under the current timetable, the Court intends

---

[212] In this context, the Court stresses the provision of Paragraph 28(*b*) of Annexure G, pursuant to which "the specification of such interim measures shall not be construed as an indication of any view of the Court on the merits of the dispute."

[213] Article III of the Treaty, "Provisions regarding Western Rivers," provides:

(1) Pakistan shall receive for unrestricted use all those waters of the Western Rivers which India is under obligation to let flow under the provisions of Paragraph (2).

(2) India shall be under an obligation to let flow all the waters of the Western Rivers, and shall not permit any interference with these waters, except for the following uses, restricted ... in the case of each of the rivers, The Indus, The Jhelum and The Chenab, to the drainage basin thereof:

[...]

(*d*) Generation of hydro-electric power, as set out in Annexure D.

Whether or not construction and operation of the KHEP on the Kishenganga River is or would be an "interference" with the flow of the waters of the Indus River system into and through Pakistan or is or would be an authorized exception to such interference is a question—indeed, the question—for the merits of the dispute before the Court. It cannot and will not be addressed in this Order.

[214] An updated construction schedule was handed by the Government of India to the Court of Arbitration and the Government of Pakistan on the last day of the hearing on interim measures. It forms part of the case file as Exhibit IN-21.

to communicate its final Award to the Parties late in 2012 or early in 2013.[215] It follows that it cannot be "necessary" to order a halt of any construction activity on the KHEP that will take place after the issuance of the Court's final Award.[216] On the other hand, specific works put at issue in the dispute that are scheduled to commence soon, and are likely to have reached a certain degree of permanence by the time the Award will be rendered, create by that token a risk of "prejudice to the final solution ... of the dispute," thereby rendering an interim measures order "necessary."

142. In the Court's view, the suspension of many of the key components of construction activity of the KHEP, such as the boring of tunnels and the construction of the power house, does not appear to be "necessary" to safeguard its ability to render an effective Award. As seen during the Court's site visit, the construction and completion of these elements of the KHEP occur at some distance from the Kishenganga/Neelum riverbed, and would thus not in and of themselves affect the flow of the river. Thus, even under the hypothesis that the Court finds at the merits stage that Pakistan's claims, or elements of those claims, are meritorious and the KHEP cannot be completed and put into operation as planned, no violations of Pakistan's rights would have been caused by the tunneling and power house construction aspects of the KHEP, and no particular remedies seem to be available from the Court in this regard (at least as far as the Court can see at this early phase in the proceedings).

143. In the Court's view, the continuation of such activity is appropriately governed by the "proceed at own risk" principle of international law, as specifically recognized by India during the hearing. The situation would merely be one in which India would have invested considerable sums of money without reaping the benefit of the operation of the KHEP as currently envisaged. This, however, is precisely the risk that India has declared it is willing to assume, and there seems to be no further risk of "prejudice to the final solution," in terms of the Court's Award, in allowing these aspects of the KHEP's construction works to proceed.

---

[215] The Court notes, in this regard, that the hearing on the merits in this case is currently scheduled for August 20 to 31, 2012 (Procedural Order No. 1, para. 5.2.2(*a*)), and that the Court "shall endeavour to render its Award within 6 months of the close of the hearings." (Supplemental Rules of Procedure, Art. 16).

[216] In this connection, the Court refers to India's assurances that the delivery of the waters from the Kishenganga into the Bonar-Madmati Nallah will not occur before 2015 (E-mail Communication of March 17, 2011 from counsel for India, Application for Provisional Measures dated June 6, 2011, Appendix B), and that India will inform the Court and Pakistan of any significant developments concerning the construction schedule of the KHEP (Interim Measures Hearing Transcript, 270:2–6).

3. Temporarily enjoining the operation of the bypass tunnel is not necessary to avoid prejudice to the Award

144. In its pleadings[217] and during the hearing on interim measures,[218] India maintains that the construction and operation of the KHEP's by-pass tunnel[219] at the Gurez site does not violate the Treaty, as that tunnel is a permitted "temporary by-pass" under Article I(15)(*b*) of the Treaty, and is therefore not an "interference with the waters" of the Kishenganga/Neelum. Pakistan disagrees with this interpretation.[220]

145. At this stage in the proceedings, the Court finds that this issue has not been fully briefed. Nonetheless, consistent with the nature of interim measures, the Court, on a provisional basis, cannot exclude that the by-pass tunnel of the KHEP at the Gurez site is a "temporary by-pass" within the meaning of Article I(15)(*b*), as that provision relates to Article III(2) of the Treaty. The Court also notes that, as described by India, the KHEP by-pass tunnel is, by its very nature, intended to be essentially of temporary use and would thus not by itself be capable of rendering more or less likely the implementation of any remedies that the Court may decide upon in its Award. The same can be said for the temporary cofferdams.

4. Temporarily enjoining India's construction of certain elements of the dam at the Kishenganga/Neelum riverbed is necessary to avoid prejudice to the Award

146. Conversely, the Court considers that the construction of the permanent dam which India proposes to emplace in and on the Kishenganga/Neelum riverbed falls squarely within the category of works that create a significant risk of "prejudice to the final solution." Although the dam component of the KHEP presumably accounts for only a fraction of the overall construction costs, Pakistan's legal arguments are, in essence, conditional upon its completion. It is the dam that would eventually enable India to exercise a certain degree of control over the volume of water that will reach Pakistan; the temporary obstruction of the river and its channeling through a by-pass tunnel does not have any such effect. Moreover, it is the dam that would eventually place India in a position to divert parts or all of the waters of the Kishenganga/Neelum river into the Bonar-Madmati Nallah, thus potentially affecting water supplies in downstream areas of the Neelum valley.

147. Accordingly, while the dam is of course intended to function as only one (albeit integral) part of a complex hydro-electric installation, it is clear that it is a key component of Pakistan's complaints of breaches of the

---

[217] India's Response, paras. 78–79.

[218] Interim Measures Hearing Transcript, 182:23 to 183:8.

[219] Also called the "diversion tunnel" in India's Exhibit IN-21.

[220] Interim Measures Hearing Transcript, 63:1–18.

Treaty. A temporary halt to the construction of the dam would, in the Court's view, go a long way toward avoiding any situation of potential inconsistency with the Treaty while these proceedings are ongoing. It is the Court's conclusion that so holding is in accordance with the purport of the Indus Waters Treaty system, which the arbitration mechanism in Article IX and Annexure G is intended to serve.

148. Moreover, even if the Court were ultimately to reject Pakistan's arguments regarding the alleged illegality of the KHEP in all its elements, as it fully retains the option of doing, the Court at this stage cannot rule out that adjustments to the design of the KHEP dam or related works at the Gurez site may be required. The entirely unconstrained construction of the KHEP *pendente lite* thus presents a risk of constricting the legal principles to which the Court may have recourse in its Award. Continued construction may also have the effect of foreclosing, delaying the implementation of, or rendering disproportionately large the cost of particular remedies that the Court may choose to order.[221] It is not difficult to envisage a situation where the construction of permanent works leading to the erection of a dam on the riverbed runs the risk of a prejudicial *fait accompli*, as the existence of such works would inevitably need to be taken into account in any consideration of remedies should a breach of the Treaty be determined to have occurred.

149. The Court understands that activities to prepare the construction of the dam in the riverbed at the Gurez site are set to commence in November 2011, some two-odd months away; such activity is thus imminent. Even under the assumption that any construction activity will slow down significantly over the winter months, the work on the dam could progress at least during the late spring, summer, and early fall of 2012. Based upon the Parties' submissions and the construction schedule, and bearing in mind the Court's inspection of the dam site during the site visit, the Court is persuaded that, while the present proceedings are underway, works on the dam are likely to advance to a point where the possible restoration of the flow of the Kishenganga/Neelum to its natural channel will be rendered significantly more difficult and costly to the potential prejudice of any prescriptions that may be made by the Court in its Award.

---

[221] The Court recalls the argument made by India that the ICJ, acting under Article 41 of its Statute, has never found it appropriate to order the suspension of construction activity for the duration of the proceedings of installations that were potentially in violation of international law (*See, e.g.*, Interim Measures Hearing Transcript, 255:5 to 256:7; at 256:2–6: "In these kinds of cases dealing with construction activities which may or may not be legitimate under a convention or a treaty, all you have to do is look at *Great Belt* and *Pulp Mills* to see that provisional measures were not so ordered.").

In the Court's view of Paragraph 28 of Annexure G within the context of the Indus Waters Treaty—which deals with legitimate uses of the Indus waters system, including precisely the kind of large-scale construction projects as the KHEP—it is reasonable to conclude that the drafters of the Treaty had contemplated the possibility that an interim order to suspend construction works can be issued under appropriate circumstances.

150. In the circumstances, the Court concludes that the construction of this portion of the KHEP is capable of leading to "prejudice to the final solution … of the dispute," and that it is necessary to enjoin India from proceeding with the construction of permanent works on or above the Kishenganga/Neelum riverbed that may inhibit the full flow of that river to its natural channel until the Court renders its Award.

151. The Court considers that while this arbitration is pending, and subject to any agreement between the Parties as to the implementation of the present Order, India may: (i) erect temporary cofferdams and operate the by-pass tunnel it has said to have completed; (ii) temporarily dry out the riverbed of the Kishenganga/Neelum at the Gurez valley; (iii) excavate the riverbed; and (iv) proceed with the construction of the sub-surface foundations of the dam. However, as specified above, until the Court renders its Award, India may not construct any other permanent works on or above the riverbed that may inhibit the restoration of the full flow of that river to its natural channel.

V. Order

152. Having found that it is necessary to lay down certain interim measures in order to "avoid prejudice to the final solution … of the dispute" as provided under Paragraph 28 of Annexure G to the Indus Waters Treaty, the Court unanimously rules that:

(1) For the duration of these proceedings up until the rendering of the Award,

(*a*) It is open to India to continue with all works relating to the Kishenganga Hydro-Electric Project, except for the works specified in (*c*) below;

(*b*) India may utilize the temporary diversion tunnel it is said to have completed at the Gurez site, and may construct and complete temporary cofferdams to permit the operation of the temporary diversion tunnel, such tunnel being provisionally determined to constitute a "temporary by-pass" within the meaning of Article I(15) *b*) as it relates to Article III(2) of the Treaty;

(*c*) Except for the sub-surface foundations of the dam stated in paragraph 151(iv) above, India shall not proceed with the construction of any permanent works on or above the Kishenganga/Neelum riverbed at the Gurez site that may inhibit the restoration of the full flow of that river to its natural channel; and

(2) Pakistan and India shall arrange for periodic joint inspections of the dam site at Gurez in order to monitor the implementation of sub-paragraph 1(*c*) above. The Parties shall also submit, by no later than December 19, 2011, a joint report setting forth the areas of agreement and any points of disagreement that may arise between the Parties concerning the implementation of this Order.

153. The Court shall remain actively seized of this matter, and may revise this Order or issue further orders at any time in light of the circumstances then obtaining.

Done at the Peace Palace, The Hague

Dated: 23 September 2011

[*Signed*]
PROFESSOR LUCIUS CAFLICH

[*Signed*]
PROFESSOR JAN PAULSSON

[*Signed*]
H.E. JUDGE BRUNO SIMMA

[*Signed*]
H.E. JUDGE PETER TOMKA

[*Signed*]
PROFESSOR HOWARD S. WHEATER FREng

[*Signed*]
SIR FRANKLIN BERMAN KCMG QC

[*Signed*]
JUDGE STEPHEN M. SCHWEBEL, CHAIRMAN

[*Signed*]
MR. ALOYSIUS LLAMZON, REGISTRAR

In the matter of
the Indus Waters Kishenganga arbitration

-before-

The Court of Arbitration constituted
in accordance with the Indus Waters Treaty 1960
between the Government of India
and the Government of Pakistan
Signed on 19 September, 1960

-between-

The Islamic Republic of Pakistan

-and-

The Republic of India

Partial Award

Court of Arbitration:

Judge Stephen M. Schwebel (Chairman)
Sir Franklin Berman KCMG QC
Professor Howard S. Wheater FREng
Professor Lucius Caflisch
Professor Jan Paulsson
Judge Bruno Simma
H.E. Judge Peter Tomka

Secretariat:

The Permanent Court of Arbitration

18 February 2013

Agents, Counsel, and Other Representatives of the Parties

Agent for Pakistan:

— Mr. Kamal Majidulla, Special Assistant to the Prime Minister on Water Resources and Agriculture

Agent for India:

— Mr. Dhruv Vijay Singh, Secretary to the Government of India, Ministry of Water Resources

Co-Agents for Pakistan:

— Mr. Khalil Ahmad, Ambassador at Large

— Mr. Mohammad Karim Khan Agha, Prosecutor General, National Accountability Bureau

— Mr. Mirza Asif Baig Mirza, Pakistan Commissioner for Indus Waters

Co-Agents for India:

— Mr. Y.K. Sinha, Additional Secretary (PAI), Ministry of External Affairs

— Dr. Neeru Chadha, Joint Secretary & The Legal Adviser, Ministry of External Affairs

— Mr. G. Aranganathan, Indian Commissioner for Indus Waters

Counsel for Pakistan:

— Professor James Crawford SC, University of Cambridge, Matrix Chambers

— Professor Vaughan Lowe QC, University of Oxford, Essex Court Chambers

— Mr. Samuel Wordsworth, Essex Court Chambers

— Ms. Shamila Mahmood, Senior Legal Consultant, Government of Pakistan

Counsel for India:

— Mr. Fali S. Nariman, Senior Advocate, Supreme Court of India

— Mr. R.K.P. Shankardass, Senior Advocate, Supreme Court of India

— Mr. Rodman Bundy, Eversheds LLP, Paris

— Professor Stephen C. McCaffrey, McGeorge School of Law, University of the Pacific

— Professor Daniel Barstow Magraw, Johns Hopkins University

— Mr. S.C. Sharma, Advocate, Supreme Court of India

Representatives for Pakistan

— Mr. Aamir Shoukat, Chargé d'affaires, Embassy of Pakistan
— Mr. Faris Qazi, Deputy Commissioner for Indus Waters

Representatives for India

— H.E. Bhaswati Mukherjee, Ambassador of India to the Netherlands
— Mr. Darpan Talwar, Senior Joint Commissioner (Indus), Ministry of Water Resources, Technical Adviser
— Mr. P.K. Saxena, Director, Central Water Commission, Technical Adviser
— Mr. Balraj Joshi, General Manager, NHPC Ltd., Project representative

Representative for the Government of Azad Jammu and Kashmir:

— Mr. Sardar Raheem, Secretary of Irrigation and Agriculture

Expert Witnesses for Pakistan:

— Mr. Vaqar Zakaria, Managing Director, Hagler Bailly Pakistan
— Mr. Syed Muhammad Mehr Ali Shah, Principal Engineer, NESPAK
— Dr. Gregory L. Morris, GLM Engineering COOP
— Dr. Jackie King, River Ecology and Environmental Flow Specialist, Southern Waters

Expert Witnesses for India:

— Dr. K.G. Rangaraju, Hydraulic Engineering Consultant & Former Head of Civil Engineering, IIT, Roorkee
— Dr. S. Sathyakumar, Scientist, Wildlife Institute of India, Dehra Dun
— Mr. Jesper Goodley Dannisøe, Senior Project Manager, DHI (Water & Environment), Denmark
— Dr. Niels Th. Jepsen, Senior Scientist, Section for Freshwater Fisheries Ecology, Technical University of Denmark

Technical Experts for Pakistan:

— Mr. Manzar Naeem Qureshi, Power Economics Expert, Hagler Bailly Pakistan

— Mr. .Saleem Warsi, Flow Measurement Expert, Water Resources and Power Development Authority
— Dr. Jens Christian Refsgaard, Geological Survey of Denmark and Greenland (GEUS)
— Mr. Hans Beuster, Hydrologist, Beuster, Clarke and Associates
— Dr. Cate Brown, River Ecology and Environmental Flow Specialist, Southern Waters

TABLE OF CONTENTS

FIGURES AND MAPS

* Secretariat note: these maps and diagrams are located in the front pocket of this volume.

Glossary of Defined Terms

1898 Gleichen Handbook	"Handbook of the Sudan" compiled in the Intelligence Division, War Office by Captain Count Gleichen (1898)
1954 Proposal	Proposal by the World Bank for a "Plan for the Development and Use of the Indus Basin Waters" dated 5 February 1954 (Annex PK-2)
***Baglihar* (or *Baglihar* Determination)**	Raymond Lafitte, Determination of Neutral Expert on the Baglihar Project dated 12 February 2007 (Annex PK-230)
Commission	The Permanent Indus Commission established by Article VIII of the Treaty
Commissioners	The Pakistani Commissioner and the Indian Commissioner
Counter-Memorial	India's Counter-Memorial dated 23 November 2011
Court	The Court of Arbitration in these proceedings as constituted pursuant to Article IX(5) and Annexure G of the Treaty
CWPC	India's Central Water and Power Commission
CWPC Letter	Letter from the Chairman of the CWPC to India's Ministry for Irrigation and Power dated 16 May 1960 (Annex IN-54)
Dead Storage	As defined at Paragraph 2(*a*) of Annexure D to the Treaty, "that portion of storage which is not used for operational purposes."
Dead Storage Level	As defined at Paragraph 2(*a*) of Annexure D to the Treaty, "the level corresponding to Dead Storage"
EIA	Environmental impact assessment
First Dispute	As stated in Pakistan's Request for Arbitration, the dispute between the Parties as to: Whether India's proposed diversion of the river Kishenganga (Neelum) into another Tributary, i.e. the Bonar-Madmati Nallah, being one central

	element of the Kishenganga Project, breaches India's legal obligations owed to Pakistan under the Treaty, as interpreted and applied in accordance with international law, including India's obligations under Article III(2) (let flow all the waters of the Western rivers and not permit any interference with those waters) and Article IV(6) (maintenance of natural channels)
First Meeting	Meeting convened by the Court with the Parties on 14 January 2010 pursuant to Paragraph 14 of Annexure G to the Treaty
ICOLD	International Commission on Large Dams
Indian Commissioner	Commissioner for Indus Waters appointed by India pursuant to Article VIII(1) of the Treaty
Kishenganga/Neelum River (or Kishenganga/Neelum or River)	The river called the "Kishenganga" by India and the "Neelum" by Pakistan
KHEP	Kishenganga Hydro-Electric Project
11 **March 2009 Letter**	Pakistani Commissioner's letter to the Indian Commissioner dated 11 March 2009 (Annex PK-194)
MCM	Million cubic metres
Memorial	Pakistan's Memorial dated 27 May 2011
Morris Report	Expert report by Dr. Gregory L. Morris submitted by Pakistan with its Reply; "Response to Items A, B and C in Chapter 7, Counter-Memorial of the Government of India"
Neutral Expert	The neutral expert appointed pursuant to Annexure F to the Treaty who rendered the Baglihar Determination
NJHEP	Neelum-Jhelum Hydro-Electric Project
Order on Interim Measures	Order on the Interim Measures Application of Pakistan dated June 6, 2011
Pakistani Commissioner	Commissioner for Indus Waters appointed by Pakistan pursuant to Article VIII(1) of the Treaty
Parties	The Islamic Republic of Pakistan and the Republic of India
PCA	Permanent Court of Arbitration

Rejoinder	India's Rejoinder dated 21 May 2012
Reply	Pakistan's Reply dated 21 February 2012
Request for Arbitration	Pakistan's Request for Arbitration dated 17 May 2010
Run-of-River Plant	As defined at Paragraph 2(*g*) of Annexure D to the Treaty, "a hydro-electric plant that develops without Live Storage as an integral part of the plant, except for Pondage and Surcharge Storage."
Schleiss Report	"Note on Second Dispute regarding Drawdown Flushing," expert report by Prof. Dr. Anton J. Schleiss submitted by India with its Rejoinder
Second Dispute	As stated in Pakistan's Request for Arbitration, the dispute between the Parties as to: Whether under the Treaty, India may deplete or bring the reservoir level of a run-of-river Plant below Dead Storage Level (DSL) in any circumstances except in the case of an unforeseen emergency
Storage Work	As defined in Paragraph 2(*a*) of Annexure E to the Treaty, "a work constructed for the purpose of impounding the waters of a stream; but excludes (i) a Small Tank, (ii) the works specified in Paragraph 3 and 4 of Annexure D, and (iii) a new work constructed in accordance with the provisions of Annexure D"
Treaty	Indus Waters Treaty 1960 Between the Government of India, the Government of Pakistan and the International Bank for Reconstruction and Development signed at Karachi on 19 September 1960, 419 U.N.T.S. 126
VCLT	Vienna Convention on the Law of Treaties, 1969, 1155 U.N.T.S. 331
World Bank	International Bank for Reconstruction and Development

I. Procedural History

A. The Indus Waters Treaty and the Initiation of this Arbitration

1. On 19 September 1960, the Government of the Republic of India and the Government of the Islamic Republic of Pakistan (the "Parties") signed the Indus Waters Treaty 1960 (the "Treaty").[1] The Treaty was also signed by the International Bank for Reconstruction and Development (the "World Bank") in respect of the World Bank's role under certain provisions of the Treaty. Instruments of ratification were exchanged between the Parties on 12 January 1961; the Treaty entered into force on that date with retroactive effect as of 1 April 1960 as stated in Article XII(2).

2. Article IX of the Treaty provides for a system for the settlement of differences and disputes that may arise under the Treaty. Article IX states in part:

> **Article IX**
>
> **Settlement of differences and disputes**
>
> (1) Any question which arises between the Parties concerning the interpretation or application of this Treaty or the existence of any fact which, if established, might constitute a breach of this Treaty shall first be examined by the Commission, which will endeavour to resolve the question by agreement.
>
> (2) If the Commission does not reach agreement on any of the questions mentioned in Paragraph (1), then a difference will be deemed to have arisen, which shall be dealt with as follows:
>
> (*a*) Any difference which, in the opinion of either Commissioner, falls within the provisions of Part 1 of Annexure F shall, at the request of either Commissioner, be dealt with by a Neutral Expert in accordance with the provisions of Part 2 of Annexure F;
>
> (*b*) If the difference does not come within the provisions of Paragraph (2)(*a*), or if a Neutral Expert, in accordance with the provisions of Paragraph 7 of Annexure F, has informed the Commission that, in his opinion, the difference, or a part thereof, should be treated as a dispute, then a dispute will be deemed to have arisen which shall be settled in accordance with the provisions of Paragraphs (3), (4) and (5);
>
> Provided that, at the discretion of the Commission, any difference may either be dealt with by a Neutral Expert in accordance with the provisions of Part 2 of Annexure F or be deemed to be a dispute to be settled

[1] *Indus Waters Treaty 1960 Between the Government of India, the Government of Pakistan and the International Bank for Reconstruction and Development*, 19 September 1960, 419 U.N.T.S. 126 ("Treaty").

> in accordance with the provisions of Paragraphs (3), (4) and (5), or may be settled in any other way agreed upon by the Commission.
>
> [...]
>
> (4) Either Government may, following receipt of the report referred to in Paragraph (3), or if it comes to the conclusion that this report is being unduly delayed in the Commission, invite the other Government to resolve the dispute by agreement. [...]
>
> (5) A court of Arbitration shall be established to resolve the dispute in the manner provided by Annexure G
>
> (*a*) upon agreement between the Parties to do so; or
>
> (*b*) at the request of either Party, if, after negotiations have begun pursuant to Paragraph (4), in its opinion the dispute is not likely to be resolved by negotiation or mediation; or
>
> (*c*) at the request of either Party, if, after the expiry of one month following receipt by the other Government of the invitation referred to in Paragraph (4), that Party comes to the conclusion that the other Government is unduly delaying the negotiations.
>
> [...]

3. In turn, Paragraph 2 of Annexure G to the Treaty provides in relevant part as follows:

> 2. The arbitration proceeding may be instituted
>
> [...]
>
> (*b*) at the request of either Party to the other in accordance with the provisions of Article IX (5)(*b*) or (*c*). Such request shall contain a statement setting forth the nature of the dispute or claim to be submitted to arbitration, the nature of the relief sought and the names of the arbitrators appointed under Paragraph 6 by the Party instituting the proceeding.

4. Through a Request for Arbitration dated 17 May 2010, Pakistan initiated proceedings against India pursuant to Article IX and Annexure G of the Treaty.

5. In its Request for Arbitration, Pakistan stated that the Parties had failed to resolve the "Dispute" concerning the Kishenganga Hydro-Electric Project (the "KHEP") by agreement pursuant to Article IX(4) of the Treaty. Pakistan identified "two questions that are at the centre" of the dispute in the following manner:

> *a*. Whether India's proposed diversion of the river Kishenganga (*Neelum*) into another Tributary, i.e. the Bonar-Madmati Nallah, being one central element of the Kishenganga Project, breaches India's legal obligations owed to Pakistan under the Treaty, as interpreted and applied in accordance with international law, including India's obligations under Article III(2) (let flow all the waters of the Western rivers and not permit any interference with those waters) and Article IV(6) (maintenance of natural channels)?

b. Whether under the Treaty, India may deplete or bring the reservoir level of a run-of-river Plant below Dead Storage Level (*DSL*) in any circumstances except in the case of an unforeseen emergency?[2]

6. These disputes will be referred to, as in the Request for Arbitration, as the "First Dispute" and the "Second Dispute," respectively.

B. The Constitution of the Court of Arbitration

7. The Court of Arbitration (the "Court") was established pursuant to Article IX(5) and Annexure G of the Treaty. Paragraph 4 of Annexure G calls for the appointment of seven Members of the Court.

8. On 17 May 2010, Pakistan appointed His Excellency Judge Bruno Simma and Professor Jan Paulsson as arbitrators in accordance with Paragraphs 4 and 6 of Annexure G.

9. On 16 June 2010, India appointed His Excellency Judge Peter Tomka and Professor Lucius Caflisch as arbitrators in accordance with Paragraphs 4 and 6 of Annexure G.

10. In the absence of a standing panel of umpires as provided under Paragraph 5 of Annexure G or an agreement on the remaining umpires as specified in Paragraph 7(*b*)(i) of that Annexure, the Parties proceeded to select umpires in accordance with the procedure set out in Paragraph 7(*b*)(ii), which provides:

> (ii) Should the Parties be unable to agree on the selection of any or all of the three umpires, they shall agree on one or more persons to help them in making the necessary selection by agreement; but if one or more umpires remain to be appointed 60 days after the date on which the proceeding is instituted, or 30 days after the completion of the process described in sub-paragraph (*a*) above, as the case may be, then the Parties shall determine by lot for each umpire remaining to be appointed, a person from the appropriate list set out in the Appendix to this Annexure, who shall then be requested to make the necessary selection.

11. The Parties called upon three of the persons provided in the Appendix to Annexure G—the Secretary-General of the United Nations (for selection of the Chairman), the Rector of the Imperial College of Science and Technology, London, England (for selection of the Engineer Member), and the Lord Chief Justice of England (for selection of the Legal Member)—to appoint the umpires.

12. On 12 October 2010, the Secretary-General of the United Nations appointed Judge Stephen M. Schwebel as umpire and Chairman of the Court in accordance with Paragraphs 4(*b*)(i), 7 and 8 of Annexure G.

[2] Pakistan's Request for Arbitration, para. 4.

13. On 12 December 2010, the Lord Chief Justice of England and Wales appointed Sir Franklin Berman KCMG QC as umpire, in accordance with Paragraphs 4(*b*)(iii) and 7 of Annexure G.

14. On 17 December 2010, the Rector of Imperial College London appointed Professor Howard S. Wheater FREng as umpire, in accordance with Paragraphs 4(*b*)(ii) and 7 of Annexure G.

15. The Members of the Court signed and delivered declarations of independence and impartiality, which the Chairman communicated to the Parties on 27 December 2010.

C. The First Meeting of the Court and the Adoption of Procedural Rules

16. Paragraph 14 of Annexure G to the Treaty provides:

> 14. The Court of Arbitration shall convene, for its first meeting, on such date and at such place as shall be fixed by the Chairman.

17. By e-mail communication dated 17 December 2010, the Chairman of the Court invited the Parties, pursuant to Paragraph 14 of Annexure G, to meet with the Members of the Court at the premises of the Permanent Court of Arbitration (the "PCA") in The Hague on 14 January 2011.

18. The Parties accepted the Chairman's invitation in e-mail communications dated 26 and 27 December 2010. Thereafter, the Chairman transmitted for the Parties' comments a draft agenda for the meeting, prepared in accordance with Paragraph 15 of Annexure G, which provides:

> 15. At its first meeting the Court shall:
>
> (*a*) establish its secretariat and appoint a Treasurer;
>
> (*b*) make an estimate of the likely expenses of the Court and call upon each Party to pay to the Treasurer half of the expenses so estimated: Provided that, if either Party should fail to make such payment, the other Party may initially pay the whole of the estimated expenses;
>
> (*c*) specify the issues in dispute;
>
> (*d*) lay down a programme for submission by each side of legal pleadings and rejoinders; and
>
> (*e*) determine the time and place of reconvening the Court.

19. The Parties' comments thereon were incorporated as annotations to the agenda.

20. The Court of Arbitration held its first meeting on 14 January 2010 (the "First Meeting"). Immediately following the First Meeting, the PCA transmitted to the Parties a verbatim transcript of the day's discussions which was signed by the Chairman and constituted minutes for the purpose of Paragraph 19 of Annexure G.

21. Following the First Meeting, draft Terms of Appointment were sent to the Parties for comment and approval, resulting in the signing of the Terms of Appointment by the Parties, the Chairman and the Secretary-General of the PCA, with effect from 8 March 2011. In paragraphs 2.11 and 2.12 of the Terms of Appointment, the Parties confirmed that: (1) the Members of the Court had been "validly appointed in accordance with the Treaty"; and that (2) they had "no objection to the appointment of any member of the Court on the grounds of conflict of interest and/or lack of independence or impartiality in respect of matters known to them at the date of the signature of these Terms of Appointment."

22. At the First Meeting, having paid regard to Paragraph 24 of Annexure G, the Parties and the Court agreed, in keeping with prevailing practice, that all Members of the Court (whether arbitrators or umpires) would receive the same fees, and that all such fees would be paid by the Treasurer without any direct Party payments to the arbitrators.

23. On 21 January 2011, the Court issued Procedural Order No. 1, incorporating the matters agreed to by the Parties during the First Meeting:

> 1. Seat of Arbitration
>
> 1.1 Taking note of the agreement expressed by the Parties during the First Meeting, the Court determines that the seat of arbitration for these proceedings shall be The Hague, The Netherlands.
>
> 2. Supplemental Rules of Procedure
>
> 2.1 Pursuant to Paragraph 16 of Annexure G, the Court will determine, after receiving the Parties' views, supplemental Rules of Procedure for the conduct of these proceedings.
>
> 2.2 Based on the Parties' comments prior to and during the First Meeting, the Court notes that two options for supplementing Annexure G are under consideration:
>
> *a.* the PCA Optional Rules for Arbitrating Disputes Between Two States; or
>
> *b.* rules of procedure similar to those used by arbitral tribunals constituted under the United Nations Convention on the Law of the Sea in proceedings administered by the PCA.
>
> 2.3 In either case, the rules would be subject to amendment by the Court, in consultation with the Parties, to account for the particularities of these proceedings.
>
> 2.4 The Parties are invited to confer and agree upon one of the foregoing options or, in the absence of agreement, to provide the Court with their respective comments on this matter. The Parties shall appraise the Court of their agreement or provide their respective comments by no later than February 3, 2011.
>
> 2.5 After having considered the Parties' views, the Court shall adopt supplemental rules of procedure in due course.

3. Programme for Submission of Written Pleadings

3.1 Pursuant to Paragraph 15(*d*) of Annexure G, and taking note of the views of the Parties expressed during the First Meeting, the Court lays down the following programme for the submission of written pleadings:

3.1.1 The written pleadings in these proceedings shall include:

(*a*) A Memorial by Pakistan.

(*b*) A Counter-Memorial by India.

(*c*) A Reply by Pakistan, which shall be restricted to matters raised in rebuttal to India's Counter-Memorial.

(*d*) A Rejoinder by India, which shall be restricted to matters raised in rebuttal to Pakistan's Reply.

3.1.2 Pakistan shall submit its Memorial no later than 180 days from the date of the First Meeting, i.e., no later than July 13, 2011. The Court acknowledges that Pakistan has the prerogative to accelerate the proceedings by submitting its Memorial before this deadline.

3.1.3 India shall submit its Counter-Memorial no later than 180 days from receipt of the Memorial of Pakistan.

3.1.4 Pakistan shall submit its Reply no later than 90 days from receipt of the Counter-Memorial of India.

3.1.5 India shall submit its Rejoinder no later than 90 days from receipt of the Reply of Pakistan.

4. Preliminary Objections of India

4.1 In its comments of January 11, 2011 on the draft agenda for the First Meeting, India gave notice that it "will urge preliminary objections which go to the maintainability of Pakistan's Request for Arbitration, including the competence of the Court of Arbitration to deal with the differences mentioned in the Request for Arbitration." After having discussed the matter with the Parties during the First Meeting, the Court determines that the preliminary objections of India shall be considered in the following manner:

4.1.1 India shall lodge its preliminary objections no later than 30 days from the submission of the Memorial of Pakistan.

4.1.2 Pakistan shall submit its Reply to India's preliminary objections no later than 30 days from receipt of India's submission.

4.1.3 The Court shall thereafter determine a time and place for the conduct of a hearing on preliminary objections in accordance with paragraphs 5.2.1 and 5.3 herein.

4.1.4 Following the hearing on preliminary objections, the Court shall endeavour to render its Decision on Preliminary Objections expeditiously, and if possible before the deadline for submission of India's Counter-Memorial.

4.2 The proceedings on preliminary objections shall not affect the schedule for the submission of written pleadings provided under paragraph 3 herein.

5. Time and Place of Reconvening the Court

5.1 Taking note of the views of the Parties expressed during the First Meeting and the schedule established under paragraphs 3 and 4 herein, the Court will notify the Parties in due course of the time and place of its reconvening.

5.2 Without prejudice to any further developments that may arise in these proceedings, the Court hereby informs the Parties of its availability to reconvene for hearings on the following dates:

5.2.1. For the hearing on preliminary objections:

(*a*) In the event that Pakistan submits its Memorial between April 15, 2011 and the end of May 2011, the Tribunal has provisionally set aside August 29 and 30, 2011 as possible hearing dates, in The Hague.

(*b*) In the event that Pakistan submits its Memorial on or after June 1, 2011, the Tribunal has provisionally set aside November 17 and 18, 2011 as possible hearing dates, in The Hague.

5.2.2 For the hearing on the merits:

(*a*) In the event that Pakistan submits its Memorial between April 15, 2011 and the end of May 2011, the Tribunal has provisionally set aside August 20 to 31, 2012 as possible hearing dates.

(*b*) In the event that Pakistan submits its Memorial on or after June 1, 2011, the Tribunal has provisionally set aside December 3 to December 14, 2012 as possible hearing dates.

5.3 Should Pakistan submit its Memorial substantially earlier than April 15, 2011, the Court may, to the extent practicable, propose earlier dates for the conduct of hearings.

6. Specification of the Issues in Dispute

6.1 Pursuant to Paragraph 15(*c*) of Annexure G and with regard to the Parties' opening statements during the course of the First Meeting, the Court takes note of the issues in dispute as found in Pakistan's Request for Arbitration of May 17, 2010, without prejudice to further development of the issues by the Parties in their respective pleadings.

7. Confidentiality

7.1 Taking note of the Parties' agreement, all written pleadings and any other documents or evidence relating to these proceedings are to remain confidential at this time.

7.2 In due course, and in any event no later than 30 days before the opening of the hearing on the merits (*should such be necessary*), the Parties shall inform the Court as to:

7.2.1 whether they agree to open to the public any hearings on the merits that may be conducted in these proceedings and, if so, whether they agree that the hearings may be broadcast;

7.2.2 whether they agree to make public the written pleadings, supporting documents, Rules of Procedure, and procedural orders utilized in these proceedings; and

7.2.3 whether they agree to make public the award rendered by the Court.

8. Site Visit

8.1 Taking note of the Parties' agreement during the First Meeting that the Court should conduct a site visit to the pertinent facilities and locations of the Kishenganga hydro-electric facility and to those of the Neelum Valley, the Court invites the Parties to confer and agree on a joint itinerary for the visit. The Parties are particularly encouraged to agree upon the optimum dates for conducting the site visit and on attendant security arrangements, as well as air transport between their respective sites if feasible.

8.2 Unless the Parties jointly apply for more time to discuss the matter, the Parties' respective views on the time, place, and other arrangements relating to the proposed site visit (*including any points that may have been agreed to between them*) shall be communicated to the Court no later than March 18, 2011.

8.3 The Court shall thereafter issue an order deciding upon the further steps to be taken in regard to the site visit.

8.4 The Court takes note of the views expressed by the Parties during the First Meeting regarding the possible conduct of the site visit within the months of February 2011 or March 2011. Regrettably, upon review of the calendars of its members, the Court has decided that it would not be possible to conduct the visit within the first quarter of 2011.

9. Appointment of Secretariat, Registrar, and Treasurer

9.1 Pursuant to Paragraph 15(*a*) of Annexure G and with the Parties' approval, the Court made the following appointments during the First Meeting:

9.1.1 The Permanent Court of Arbitration as Secretariat,

9.1.2 Mr. Aloysius P. Llamzon, Legal Counsel of the PCA, as Registrar, and

9.1.3 Mr. Brooks W. Daly, Deputy Secretary-General and Principal Legal Counsel of the PCA, as Treasurer.

10. Transcription of Hearings and Meetings

10.1 The Court takes note of the Parties' agreement that verbatim transcripts of hearings and meetings be taken in these proceedings.

10.2 In accordance with Paragraph 19 of Annexure G, the Secretariat shall arrange for the verbatim transcription of hearings and meetings.

Such transcripts, when signed by the Chairman, shall constitute minutes for the purposes of Paragraph 19 of Annexure G.

24. After hearing the Parties' views during the First Meeting and receiving further communications from the Parties pursuant to paragraph 2 of Procedural Order No. 1, the Court issued Procedural Order No. 2 dated 16 March 2011, in which it adopted a set of "Supplemental Rules of Procedure" to apply in these proceedings subject to the Treaty, the procedural orders of the Court, and the Terms of Appointment.[3]

25. As recorded in paragraph 4.1 of Procedural Order No. 1, India gave notice, prior to the Court's First Meeting, that it would "urge preliminary objections which go to the maintainability of Pakistan's Request for Arbitration, including the competence of the Court of Arbitration to deal with the differences mentioned in the Request for Arbitration." Procedural Order No. 1 set out a schedule for the consideration of any preliminary objections.

26. However, by e-mail communication dated 7 July 2011, India informed the Court that it no longer intended to "lodge preliminary objections to jurisdiction," and that "[o]bjections to admissibility, pursuant to Article 12(2) of the Supplemental Rules of Procedure, would be addressed at the appropriate stage of the proceedings."

D. Confidentiality

27. With respect to confidentiality, Paragraph 19 of Annexure G provides:

> The Chairman of the Court shall control the discussions. The discussions shall not be open to the public unless it is so decided by the Court with the consent of the Parties. The discussions shall be recorded in minutes drawn up by the Secretaries appointed by the Chairman. These minutes shall be signed by the Chairman and shall alone have an authentic character.

28. During the First Meeting, the Parties agreed that all written pleadings and any other documents or evidence relating to these proceedings were to remain confidential unless otherwise agreed. The Court noted this agreement in paragraph 7 of Procedural Order No. 1, while also establishing a timeline for further consultation between the Parties concerning the possible opening of the hearing on the merits to the public, and the publication of the written pleadings, supporting documents, rules of procedure, procedural orders and the Award to be rendered by the Court.

29. On 10 July 2012, the Court invited the Parties to submit to the Court their agreed views on the matters set out in paragraph 7 of Procedural Order No. 1.

30. By e-mail communication dated 20 July 2012, India stated its view that the pleadings and case documents should be made available to the public

[3] Procedural Order No. 2, para. 1.1.

at the start of the oral hearing. It also suggested that the hearing be broadcast and open to the public. Finally, India supported making the Award available to the public.

31. By e-mail communication dated 7 August 2012, Pakistan stated its wish to keep the proceedings confidential. Pakistan was willing however to support the issuance of a press release at the conclusion of the hearing and the publication of the Court's Award.

32. After further discussion between the Parties and with the Chairman at the hearing on the merits, the PCA issued, on 20 August and 1 September 2012, two press releases concerning the opening and closing of the hearing respectively.[4]

E. The Court's First Site Visit

33. During the First Meeting of the Court, the Parties had agreed that it would be desirable for the Court to conduct a site visit to the pertinent facilities and locations of the KHEP as well as to the Neelum Valley and Pakistan's Neelum-Jhelum Hydro-Electric Project (the "NJHEP").

34. Pursuant to Procedural Order No. 1, the Court invited the Parties to confer and agree upon a joint itinerary and other arrangements for the site visit. The Parties exchanged views on 18 March 2011.

35. By e-mail communication dated 21 March 2011, the PCA transmitted to the Parties the Court's instructions concerning the site visit, providing that: (1) the dates of 15–21 June 2011 would be set aside as the optimum dates for the conduct of the site visit; (2) the Court would be prepared to conduct the site visit in accordance with a "jointly agreed itinerary proposed by the Parties," which the Parties were requested to propose by no later than 29 April 2011; and (3) the Court had provisionally reserved 12–18 February 2012 for the possible conduct of a second site visit should such a visit be deemed necessary or appropriate.

36. Having considered further communications from the Parties regarding the site visit, the Court issued Procedural Order No. 3 on 10 May 2011, deciding the itinerary of the proposed visit, the size of the delegations, matters concerning the confidentiality of the site visit and the manner in which the costs were to be apportioned between the Parties. The operative parts of Procedural Order No. 3 are as follows:

> 1. The Site Visit Program
>
> 1.1 The Court takes note of the Parties' agreement on the "broad outline of the itinerary", as follows:

[4] *See* http://www.pca-cpa.org/showpage.asp?pag_id=1392.

Day	*Details of visit*	*Proposed day and date*	*Start time*
Day 1	Arrival of members of [the Court] and Indian Delegation at Islamabad	Wednesday/Thursday, June 15/16, 2011	
Day 2	Visit to the Neelum Valley	Thursday, June 16, 2011	0800 hours
	Return to Hotel	29°00’00” E	1500 hours
Day 3	Visit to NJ Power House Sites	Friday, June 17, 2011	0800 hours
	Proceed to Chakothi Border on Muzaffarabad Srinagar Road, Crossing the [Line of Control] and immigration process		1300 hours
	Departure to Srinagar for night stay		1800 hours
Day 4	Visit to Dam Site of Kishenganga	Saturday, June 18, 2011	0800 hours
	Departure to Srinagar for night stay		1500 hours
Day 5	Visit to Kishenganga Power House Site	Sunday, June 19, 2011	0800 hours
	Departure to Srinagar for night stay		1530 hours
Day 6	Srinagar to Delhi, stay in New Delhi	Monday, June 20, 2011	1100–1400 hours
	Departure of members of [the Court] and Pakistan Delegation to their respective destinations		

1.2 Having found the foregoing acceptable, the Court hereby adopts the outline of the itinerary proposed by the Parties on April 29, 2011.

2. Size of Delegations

2.1 The Court takes note of the Parties' agreement that their respective delegations (*including the Agent, Co-Agents, counsel, and experts*) each be limited to not more than 10 persons for logistical reasons.

2.2 The Court's delegation shall similarly be comprised of not more than 10 persons, including all the Members of the Court, the Registrar, and the members of the Secretariat involved in documentation and logistical support to the Court.

3. Confidentiality; Press Release

3.1 While both Parties have affirmed the importance of the rules on confidentiality in relation to the site visit, the Court takes note of the Parties' lack of agreement on whether a press release should be issued by the Court upon the conclusion of the visit. India has proposed that a press release whose text has been agreed between the Parties be issued by the Court at the end of the visit, while Pakistan maintains that confidentiality is necessary under the circumstances and does not wish the Court to issue such a press release.

3.2 Recalling the principles on confidentiality that govern this arbitration (*including Paragraph 7 of Procedural Order No. 1*) and taking into account the lack of agreement between the Parties, the Court considers that no public disclosure of the site visit, including any statement to the press emanating from the Court, can be made.

3.3 The Court hereby orders that:

(*a*) There shall be no advance public announcements of the fact that a site visit shall be conducted, nor of the dates and itineraries thereof. The Parties are enjoined to ensure the absolute confidentiality of all information relating to the site visit until the visit has been concluded.

(*b*) If both Parties agree at any point before or during the site visit, the Court may issue a press release in consultation with the Parties, to be issued only after the conclusion of the visit on June 21, 2011. However, if both Parties do not so agree, then no press release nor other public statement shall be issued by the Court.

4. Hospitality/Social Events

4.1 The Court takes note of the Parties' agreement that the site visit "be as discreet as possible without any social events", of India's suggestion that "this should not exclude any reasonable hospitality by Government authorities", and of Pakistan's request that India clarify the meaning of "reasonable hospitality".

4.2 Without limiting the Parties' freedom to reach agreement on this matter, the Court expresses its availability to attend any simple dinner event that a Party may wish to prepare, if that dinner includes and is restricted to the members of both delegations participating in the site visit.

5. Presentations During the Site Visit

5.1 The Court takes note of the Parties' agreement that any presentations made during the site visit be limited to objective, technical presentations made by experts (*whether members of the official delegations or other experts*), and that legal issues or arguments should not be discussed at any point during such presentations. The Court agrees with this approach and wishes to emphasize that presentations should be succinct and remain neutral in tone.

5.2 The Members of the Court shall be free to put questions at any time during a presentation. No member of any delegation shall be permitted to ask questions during or after a presentation. With the Chairman of the Court's leave, the non-presenting delegation may respond to a point made in a presentation, such response shall be limited strictly to technical or factual matters.

5.3 Any materials meant to be distributed during such presentations (*including maps, plans, technical illustrations, and similar documents*), shall be provided to the Court and the other Party no later than May 31, 2011.

5.4 For the avoidance of doubt, the site visit (*including the presentations made therein*) shall not be considered "oral hearings" or "oral submissions" within the meaning of Article 14 of the Supplemental Rules of Procedure.

6. Record of the Site Visit

6.1 The Court takes note of Pakistan's statement that "on the matter of record of the site visit, no doubt that members of the delegation would be taking notes; however, we are of the view that it would be useful to have a permanent record" of the presentations made during the site visit, and of its proposal that the PCA "make necessary arrangements for a video recording of the entire visit." For its part, India has suggested that "[e]ither side will arrange videography/photography on its side" while expressing that it is "open to any directions from the Court" on this point.

6.2 Within their respective delegations, the Parties are free to take their own notes. These need not be shared with the Court or the other Party.

6.3 The Members of the Court and its Secretariat shall be free to take notes and photographs for exclusive use in internal deliberations. The Secretariat shall also take charge of producing a video recording of all presentations made, and shall make a copy thereof for each Party.

7. Costs of the Site Visit

7.1 The Court takes note of the Parties' agreement that each Party shall bear all costs of the site visit within their respective territories, including hotel accommodations and internal transportation.

7.2 Pursuant to Article 21 of the Supplemental Rules of Procedure, all other expenses relating to the site visit shall be borne equally by the Parties.

8. Further Arrangements

8.1 The Court takes note of India's statement that "[i]f the proposed outline programme of the visit to India and Pakistan is generally acceptable to the Court, then we can mutually discuss the further details, including the logistics", and Pakistan's observation that the Parties have yet to "reach agreement on some of the modalities" of the site visit.

8.2 Within the framework of this Order, the Court invites the Parties to continue conferring on the remaining logistical issues, and to report back to the Court with further points of agreement no later than May 23, 2011. The logistical issues to be agreed upon should include but not necessarily be limited to the following: (*a*) arrangements to ensure the security of each member of the Court at all times; (*b*) a detailed (by-the-hour) itinerary, to the extent possible; (*c*) provisions for medical support; (*d*) lists of the Parties' delegations and experts that will address the Court during the site visit, (*e*) hotel arrangements, and (*f*) modes of internal transportation.

37. By e-mail communications dated 12 June 2011, India and Pakistan submitted slides and visual aids to be used during the site visit. By e-mail communication of 13 June 2011, India objected to Pakistan's submitted presentations and on 14 June 2011, the Court informed India that it would be afforded the opportunity to raise its objections to any particular presentation of Pakistan after that presentation was made during the site visit. India's objections were subsequently expressed during Pakistan's presentations and were noted by the Court.

38. From 15 to 21 June 2011, a site visit to the KHEP, the NJHEP and surrounding areas located on the Kishenganga/Neelum River was conducted. Thirty persons, ten representatives from each Party[5] plus a ten-member delegation from the Court of Arbitration,[6] participated in it. The Court arrived in Islamabad on 15 June 2011, visited the Neelum Valley by helicopter, and inspected components of the NJHEP. The Court then crossed the Line of Control on 17 June 2011 and proceeded to Srinagar. On 18 and 19 June 2011, travelling by helicopter and ground transport, the Court inspected components of the KHEP located in the Gurez Valley and the area near Bandipura north

[5] Pakistan's delegation was comprised of: Mr. Kamal Majidulla, Agent for Pakistan and Special Assistant to the Prime Minister on Water Resources and Agriculture; Mr. Khalil Ahmad, Ambassador at Large, Co-agent; Mr. Mohammed Karim Khan Agha, Additional Attorney General for Pakistan, Co-agent; Mr. Sheraz Jamil Memon, Pakistan's Commissioner for Indus Waters, Co-agent; Prof. James Crawford, Counsel; Mr. Samuel Wordsworth, Counsel; Ms. Shamila Mahmood, Counsel; Mr. Farhat Mir, Secretary of Planning and Development, Government of Azad Jammu and Kashmir; Mr. Mirza Asif Baig, Expert; and Mr. Mehr Ali Shah, Expert.

India's delegation was comprised of: Mr. Dhruv Vijai Singh, Agent for India and Secretary, Ministry of Water Resources; Mr. Narinder Singh, Co-agent; Mr. G. Aranganathan, Co-agent; Mr. A. K. Bajaj, Chairman, Central Water Commission; Mr. R.K.P. Shankardass, Counsel; Prof. Stephen C. McCaffrey, Counsel; Prof. Daniel Magraw, Counsel; Mr. Darpan Talwar, Senior Joint Commissioner (Indus), Ministry of Water Resources; Mr. Balraj Joshi, Expert; and Dr. S. Sathyakumar, Expert.

[6] The Court's delegation included all the Members of the Court as well as three members of the Secretariat: Mr. Aloysius Llamzon, Registrar and Legal Counsel; Mr. Dirk Pulkowski, Legal Counsel; and Mr. Garth Schofield, Legal Counsel.

of Wular Lake. It then departed from India by way of New Delhi on 20 and 21 June 2011.

39. On 22 June 2011, the PCA published a press release approved by both Parties concerning the site visit as well as a photograph of the Court taken during the site visit.

40. Pursuant to paragraph 6 of Procedural Order No. 3, on 2 August 2011, the PCA transmitted to the Parties and the Members of the Court a set of four DVD-format discs containing videos of the various presentations made during the site visit, and photographs of the site visit.

F. Pakistan's Application for Interim Measures

41. Paragraph 28 of Annexure G to the Treaty provides:

> 28. Either Party may request the Court at its first meeting to lay down, pending its Award, such interim measures as, in the opinion of that Party, are necessary to safeguard its interests under the Treaty with respect to the matter in dispute, or to avoid prejudice to the final solution or aggravation or extension of the dispute. The Court shall, thereupon, after having afforded an adequate hearing to each Party, decide, by a majority, consisting of at least four members of the Court, whether any interim measures are necessary for the reasons hereinbefore stated and, if so, shall specify such measures: Provided that
>
> *a*) the Court shall lay down such interim measures only for such specified period as, in its opinion, will be necessary to render the Award: this period may, if necessary, be extended unless the delay in rendering the Award is due to any delay on the part of the Party which requested the interim measures in supplying such information as may be required by the other Party or by the Court in connection with the dispute; and
>
> *b*) the specification of such interim measures shall not be construed as an indication of any view of the Court on the merits of the dispute.

42. In paragraph 10 of its Request for Arbitration, Pakistan stated:

> Accordingly, pursuant to Annexure G, paragraph 28 of the Treaty, Pakistan will request the Court at its first meeting to lay down, pending its Award, interim measures both to safeguard Pakistan's interests under the Treaty with respect to the matters in dispute and to avoid prejudice to the final solution and aggravation or extension of the dispute.

43. Pakistan sought:

> An interim order restraining India from proceeding further with the planned diversion of the river Kishenganga/Neelum until such time as the legality of the diversion is finally determined by a Court of Arbitration.[7]

[7] Pakistan's Request for Arbitration, para. 54(*a*).

44. During the Court's First Meeting, Pakistan made the following statement in respect of provisional measures:

> Our assessment of the present situation along the Kishenganga is that while the plan certainly envisages works on the Indus that would breach the Indus Waters Treaty and cause great harm to Pakistan, the project is not yet so far advanced that such harm is imminent.
>
> We are aware of the principle of international law, applied for example by the International Court [of Justice] in paragraphs 30–33 of its Order on provisional measures in the Great Belt case, that in cases such as the present a State engaged in works that may violate the rights of another State can proceed only at its own risk. The court may, in its decision on the merits, order that the works must not be continued or must be modified or dismantled.
>
> We are content at this stage to rely upon that principle.
>
> Major construction projects are, however, not easily reversible processes. The excavation of construction sites and the filling of dams cannot easily be undone. Equally importantly, costs are not incurred in a regular and uniform fashion. There are points at which major investments of capital and resources have to be made. Beyond those points a State might find it more difficult to abandon the project and restore the *status quo ante.*
>
> We therefore invite India to give an undertaking to inform the Court, and at the same time the Government of Pakistan, of any actual or imminent developments or steps in relation to the Kishenganga project that it considers would have a significant adverse effect upon the practicality of abandoning the project and restoring the *status quo ante*, or would in any other way seriously jeopardize Pakistan's interests.
>
> On that basis, and on the understanding that we may apply to the Court for provisional measures at any point in the future should it become apparent (whether as a result of a communication from India or otherwise) that the ordering of such measures is an urgent necessity, we have decided to make no application for provisional measures at this meeting.[8]

45. By e-mail communication dated 6 March 2011, Pakistan requested that India provide, by 17 March 2011, its comments on: (1) India's understanding of the "proceed at your own risk" principle outlined by the International Court of Justice in the *Great Belt* case;[9] (2) the status of the undertaking to inform Pakistan and the Court of "any actual imminent steps in relation to the KHEP that it considers would have a significant adverse effect upon the practicability of abandoning the project and restoring the *status quo ante* or would in any other way seriously jeopardize Pakistan's interests"; (3) the current state of works at the site; and (4) the planned date for diversion of the river.

---

[8] First Meeting Tr., 14 January 2010, at 19:22 to 21:12.

[9] *Passage through the Great Belt (Finland* v. *Denmark)*, Provisional Measures, Order of 29 July 1991, *I.C.J. Reports 1991*, p. 12.

46. By e-mail communication dated 17 March 2011, India replied that: (1) in its understanding the "proceed at your own risk" principle was "covered by the existing International Law"; (2) as a consequence of Pakistan's decision, expressed at the First Meeting of the Court, to forego lodging an application for provisional measures, it would be inappropriate for Pakistan to be "seeking any unilateral undertakings on the part of India"; (3) India would address the question of the status of current construction in "substantive pleadings on the merits according to the schedule laid down by the Court"; and (4) the "planned date of diversion is not before 2015."

47. By e-mail communication dated 6 June 2011, Pakistan submitted an application for provisional measures.

48. On 7 June 2011, India requested "adequate time to respond to Pakistan's application" and submitted that Pakistan's application should have been filed earlier, especially because "India's last letter to Pakistan was on 17 March 2011." India also recalled that at the Court's First Meeting, Pakistan had stated that it would not make an application for provisional measures.

49. Through the Registrar, the Court communicated a proposed procedural schedule for considering Pakistan's application for provisional measures. After considering the comments of the Parties, the Court issued Procedural Order No. 4 on 12 June 2011 deciding on a schedule for written submissions and on a hearing to be held at the Peace Palace in The Hague, from 25 to 27 August 2011.

50. By e-mail communication dated 30 June 2011, Pakistan recalled to the Court the statement made by India during the course of the site visit according to which "the temporary tunnel at the Kishenganga dam site is 100% complete" and the "river would be dammed at the site in November 2011." Pakistan submitted that a

> section of the Kishenganga/Neelum River would be diverted as a result, however, the interference in the flow of the river at this section is intended to be permanent—the former riverbed would be lost, and would become a construction site for the permanent 37m high dam structure ... Pakistan considers that the imminence of these works adds a further element of urgency to its Application.

51. On 22 July 2011, India submitted a response to Pakistan's application for provisional measures.

52. After consulting the Parties, on 26 July 2011, the Court issued Procedural Order No. 5, determining that the hearing on interim measures would be organized in two rounds of oral argument, starting with statements by Pakistan on the first day, by India on the second, and reply and closing statements by both Parties on the final day of the hearing.

53. On 3 August 2011, Pakistan submitted a reply to India's response to Pakistan's application for provisional measures. On 15 August 2011, India submitted a rejoinder to Pakistan's reply.

54. The Court held a hearing on interim measures at the Peace Palace in The Hague, from 25 to 27 August 2011. The following persons participated:

The Court of Arbitration

Judge Stephen M. Schwebel (Chairman)
Sir Franklin Berman KCMG QC
Professor Howard S. Wheater FREng
Professor Lucius Caflisch
Professor Jan Paulsson
H.E. Judge Bruno Simma
H.E. Judge Peter Tomka

Pakistan

Mr. Kamal Majidulla, Agent
H.E. Khalil Ahmed, Ambassador at Large, Co-agent
Mr. Mohammad Karim Khan Agha, Additional Attorney General for Pakistan, Co-agent
Mr. Aijaz Ahmed Pitafi, Joint Commissioner for Indus Waters
Professor James Crawford (*by telephone conference*)
Professor Vaughan Lowe, Legal Counsel
Mr. Samuel Wordsworth, Legal Counsel
Ms. Shamila Mahmood, Legal Counsel
H.E. Ambassador Aizaz Chaudhry, Ambassador for Pakistan to the Netherlands
Mr. Asif Baig, Technical Expert
Mr. Mehr Ali Shah, Technical Expert

India

Mr. Dhruv Vijai Singh, Agent
H.E. Bhaswati Mukherjee, Ambassador of India, The Hague
Mr. A.K. Bajaj, Chairman, Central Water Commission, Technical Advisor
Dr. Pankaj Sharma, Minister, Indian Embassy, The Hague
Mr. Fali S. Nariman, Counsel
Mr. R.K.P. Shankardass, Counsel
Professor Stephen C. McCaffrey, Counsel
Mr. Rodman Bundy, Counsel
Professor Daniel Magraw, Counsel
Mr. S.C. Sharma, Counsel

Mr. Y.K. Sinha, Co-Agent
Mr. Narinder Singh, Co-Agent
Mr. K.S. Nagaraja, Executive Director NHPC
Mr. G. Aranganathan, Co-Agent
Mr. Darpan Talwar, SJC (Indus), Technical Advisor

The Secretariat

Mr. Aloysius Llamzon, Registrar and Legal Counsel
Mr. Dirk Pulkowski, Legal Counsel
Mr. Garth Schofield, Legal Counsel
Ms. Anna Vinnik, Assistant Legal Counsel
Ms. Willemijn van Banning, Legal Secretary

Court Reporters

Mr. David Kasdan
Mr. Randy Salzman

55. The following persons presented oral arguments before the Court on behalf of Pakistan:

Mr. Kamal Majidulla, Agent for Pakistan
Prof. Vaughan Lowe, Legal Counsel
Mr. Samuel Wordsworth, Legal Counsel

56. The following persons presented oral arguments before the Court on behalf of India:

Mr. Dhruv Vijai Singh, Agent for India
Mr. Fali S. Nariman, Counsel
Mr. R.K.P. Shankardass, Counsel
Mr. Rodman Bundy, Counsel
Prof. Stephen C. McCaffrey, Counsel
Prof. Daniel Magraw, Counsel

57. On 27 August 2011, Professor Wheater requested India to provide information on the following points with respect to the technical aspects of the proposed KHEP dam:

(1) One or more cross-sections of the dam.

(2) A drawing of the dam elevation showing the location of the proposed spillways and any other discharge outlets with respect to design levels of water elevation, such as the drawing provided for the Baglihar dam in Volume 7 of Pakistan's Memorial at Figure 5.2.1. on Page 141.

> (3) Specification of the hydraulic design of the proposed spillways and any other downstream outlet works; that is, the capacity of the dam to transmit flows downstream as a function of the ponded water level.
>
> (4) The intended mode of operation of India, including the transmission of flows downstream to meet the needs of existing uses as specified in the Treaty, any environmental flows and for sediment flushing.
>
> (5) A diagram showing the upstream extent of inundation at the Full Pondage Level and under surcharge storage; that is, during the passage of the design flood, including the location of any nearby upstream riparian settlements, and such a document could be a plan view of the inundated areas.
>
> (6) India's Environmental Impact Assessment for the dam.
>
> (7) An outline schedule of the proposed construction works; that is including the currently proposed timing of the key phases of the construction of the dam.[10]

58. The Chairman of the Court asked India to provide the technical data and construction schedules requested by Professor Wheater at the latest by 2 September 2011, and Pakistan to submit its comments on those data, should it wish to do so, no later than on 7 September 2011.[11]

59. On 2 September 2011, India wrote to the Court in relation to the data requested by Professor Wheater. India's Agent confirmed that most of the documents requested had been provided earlier to Pakistan, and identified those that were included as documentary exhibits in Pakistan's Memorial. He also confirmed that apart from the documents already provided by India during the hearing on interim measures, further documentation (including that concerning India's environmental impact assessment for the dam) would be produced in India's Counter-Memorial.

60. On 7 September 2011, Pakistan commented on India's communication of 2 September 2011 and provided the Court with two additional documents previously referred to by Pakistan during the hearing.

61. The Court issued its Order on the Interim Measures Application of Pakistan dated June 6, 2011 ("Order on Interim Measures") on 23 September 2011. The operative provisions of the Order read:

> 152. Having found that it is necessary to lay down certain interim measures in order to "avoid prejudice to the final solution … of the dispute" as provided under Paragraph 28 of Annexure G to the Indus Waters Treaty, the Court unanimously rules that:
>
> (1) For the duration of these proceedings up until the rendering of the Award,

---

[10] Interim Measures Hearing Tr., (Day 3), 27 August 2011, at 201:6 to 202:25.

[11] Interim Measures Hearing Tr., (Day 3), 27 August 2011, at 294:10–16.

(*a*) It is open to India to continue with all works relating to the Kishenganga Hydro-Electric Project, except for the works specified in (*c*) below;

(*b*) India may utilize the temporary diversion tunnel it is said to have completed at the Gurez site, and may construct and complete temporary cofferdams to permit the operation of the temporary diversion tunnel, such tunnel being provisionally determined to constitute a "temporary by-pass" within the meaning of Article I(15)(*b*) as it relates to Article III(2) of the Treaty;

(*c*) Except for the sub-surface foundations of the dam stated in paragraph 151(iv) above, India shall not proceed with the construction of any permanent works on or above the Kishenganga/Neelum River riverbed at the Gurez site that may inhibit the restoration of the full flow of that river to its natural channel; and

(2) Pakistan and India shall arrange for periodic joint inspections of the dam site at Gurez in order to monitor the implementation of sub-paragraph 1(*c*) above. The Parties shall also submit, by no later than December 19, 2011, a joint report setting forth the areas of agreement and any points of disagreement that may arise between the Parties concerning the implementation of this Order.

153. The Court shall remain actively seized of this matter, and may revise this Order or issue further orders at any time in light of the circumstances then obtaining.

62. On 26 September 2011, as directed by the Court, the PCA made the Order on Interim Measures available to the public through the PCA's website, where it remains.[12]

G. The Implementation of the Order on Interim Measures

63. Pursuant to paragraph 152(2) of the Order on Interim Measures, providing that "Pakistan and India shall arrange for periodic joint inspections of the dam site at Gurez in order to monitor the implementation of sub-paragraph 1(*c*) above," the Parties exchanged communications in October and early November 2011 discussing the timing and other aspects of the joint inspections.

64. As the Parties were unable to agree on dates for the joint inspections, on 8 November 2011, India sent the Court a letter enclosing the communications exchanged by the Parties and requested that the Court give the Parties "suitable directions."

65. On 24 November 2011, after receiving the Parties' respective views on India's request for directions, the Court indicated that the joint report required by paragraph 152(2) of the Order on Interim Measures "is meant to provide an opportunity for the Parties to raise any issues they may have

---

[12] *See* http://www.pca-cpa.org/showpage.asp?pag_id=1392.

concerning the interpretation and implementation of the Order, including the timing and frequency of periodic joint inspections of the dam site at Gurez.... If the parties are unable to agree on such a schedule, that disagreement should be articulated in the Report."

66. After further correspondence discussing areas of agreement and disagreement, the Parties jointly submitted a report on 19 December 2011 pursuant to paragraph 152 of the Order on Interim Measures. In that report, the Parties stated that they disagreed about: (1) the scope of the Order; (2) the timing and frequency of the joint inspections; (3) the size of the delegations for the first joint inspection; and (4) the duration of that inspection. The Parties agreed that the expenses for any joint inspection would be borne equally by the Parties.

67. On 30 December 2011, the Court issued Procedural Order No. 6 (*Concerning the Joint Report dated December 19, 2011 Submitted Pursuant to Paragraph 152(2) of the Order on Interim Measures*), in which it decided that: (1) two joint inspections, one to be conducted at the earliest practicable time in spring 2012 and the other at the latest practicable time in fall 2012, would be sufficient to monitor the implementation of the Order on Interim Measures; (2) the delegation of each Party for the joint inspections would comprise up to three members; and (3) in good weather, the joint inspections would last two days if the delegations were to travel by helicopter and three to four days if they were to travel by road.

68. After a series of e-mail communications in April 2012, the Parties agreed to hold a joint inspection of the Gurez dam construction site during the week of 7 May 2012.

69. On 8 May 2012, a three-member delegation from each Party[13] travelled to Srinagar and proceeded by helicopter to the Gurez dam site.

70. Pursuant to paragraph 152(2) of the Order on Interim Measures, the Parties notified the Court of their attempts to agree on a joint report on the joint inspection of 8 May 2012. In the absence of agreement on the content of a joint report, the Parties agreed to submit separate reports regarding the joint inspection. These were received by the Court on 31 May 2012.

71. In its report, Pakistan quoted paragraph 152 of the Order on Interim Measures and further stated:

> Thus, the purpose of the inspection was to determine: (1) the status of the temporary diversion tunnel and cofferdam, (2) the status of sub-surface foundations, and (3) the status of any permanent works on or above the Kishenganga/Neelum River riverbed that may inhibit restoration of the full flow of that river to its natural channel.
>
> Itinerary:

[13] Pakistan's delegation was comprised of Mr. Asif Baig, Dr. Gregory Morris and Ms. Shamila Mahmood. India's delegation was comprised of Mr. G. Aranganathan, Mr. Darpan Talwar and Prof. K.G. Rangaraju.

The site inspection was initiated by a thirty minute military helicopter flight which departed the Srinagar airport at approximately 8:30 AM. After landing, approximately thirty additional minutes were required for transport by automobile to the dam site.

Shortly after arrival at the dam site the Pakistan delegation walked the length of the works in the company of the Indian representatives, including representatives of the construction contractor. The works in progress were observed and queries were raised which were answered by the contractor's representatives. However, photography of the works, the surrounding area or the river was not allowed during the inspection. As such, there is no photographic documentation.

The site visit was concluded with refreshments and snacks. We began the road journey back to the helicopter at noon for the return flight.

Observations:

The following observations were made during the site visit.

1. Status of the temporary diversion tunnel and cofferdam. Excavation of the diversion tunnel was reportedly completed, but we did not enter the tunnel to confirm. The vertical sluice gate at the tunnel entrance was not yet installed, as concrete work was still in progress and neither the gate guides or other operating mechanisms had been installed or were visible on site. Work had not been initiated on the cofferdam.

2. Status of sub-surface foundations. There was no evidence that any foundation work for the dam had been initiated, and not having diverted the river such work would be essentially impossible to undertake in any event.

3. Status of any permanent works on or above the Kishenganga/Neelum River riverbed that may inhibit restoration of the full flow of that river to its natural channel. The only "permanent" work that was visible during the visit was rock excavation on the left abutment, in the general area where the spillway and related works will be located. There was a large mass of rock spoil on the left overbank of the river but there was no evidence that concrete work has been initiated in this area, other than the portals for the river diversion tunnel. Although the river channel was somewhat restricted by placement of the construction road, the rusted condition of the gabions running along the left riverbank gave evidence that this condition has been present for some time.

72. In its report, India also quoted from paragraph 152 of the Order on Interim Measures and further summarized as follows:

B. The areas of agreement between the Parties:

4. India has not proceeded with the construction of any permanent works on or above the Kishenganga/Neelum River riverbed at the Gurez site that may inhibit the restoration of the full flow of that river to its natural channel.

C. The areas of disagreement between the Parties:

5. Pakistan takes a broader view of the scope of inspection than is specified by the Court Order.

73. On 5 October 2012, after further correspondence between the Parties, the Court issued Procedural Order No. 11 (*Concerning the Second Joint Inspection conducted pursuant to Paragraph 152(2) of the Order on Interim Measures and Paragraph 2.2 of Procedural Order No. 6*):

1. Scope of the Joint Inspection

1.1 The Court understands the disagreement between the Parties on the scope of the joint inspection to center on the parts of the dam site at Gurez that should be made available to Pakistan for inspection. India maintains that "*as per the Court's Order [on Interim Measures] dated 23 September 2011 the visit would be limited to inspecting the status of construction of permanent works, if any, on or above the Kishenganga/Neelum riverbed that may inhibit the restoration of the full flow of that river to its natural channel. Temporary diversion tunnels and cofferdams are not permanent works and, in our view, do not fall within the ambit of the joint inspection.*" By contrast, Pakistan "*is of the considered view that the Order requires the Parties to conduct joint inspections of the dam site at Gurez and does not limit the extent of the inspection or exclude any works from inspection. An inspection of all works and the entire site is considered necessary to determine the permanence and capability of the works constructed and whether these works will or will not inhibit the restoration of the full flow of the river to its natural channel.*"

1.2 Having considered the Parties' positions, the Court determines that the monitoring of compliance with the Interim Measures Order necessitates the inspection of all works at the dam site at Gurez that are constructed on or above the Kishenganga/Neelum's natural riverbed.

1.3 Accordingly, in carrying out the joint inspection of the dam site at Gurez pursuant to paragraph 152(*2*) of the Order on Interim Measures, the Parties may undertake the following:

(*a*) view and inspect the reach of the Kishenganga/Neelum River from the upstream cofferdam through to the downstream cofferdam; and

(*b*) view and inspect any works, existing or under construction, that are physically located on or above the Kishenganga/Neelum's natural riverbed in the area between the upstream cofferdam and the downstream cofferdam.

1.4 For the avoidance of doubt, the Court emphasizes that although the Parties may see during the inspection the cofferdams and any excavation works or subsurface foundations of the dam located on the riverbed, such works are expressly permitted by the Court's Order on Interim Measures and shall not be construed as a breach of the Order so long as they comply with paragraph 152(*1*)(*c*) of the Order.

2. Joint Inspection Report

> 2.1 In preparing any report to the Court on the conduct of the joint inspection, the Parties are not restricted to identifying the existence or otherwise of "permanent works on or above the Kishenganga/Neelum riverbed at the Gurez site that may inhibit the restoration of the full flow of that river to its natural channel." The Parties may, to the extent necessary to give context to the joint report, briefly describe the condition of the river and its bed in the area between the cofferdams, along with the status of any works (*existing or under construction*) or features viewed over the course of the inspection that bear direct relevance to the monitoring of compliance with the Interim Measures Order.
>
> 2.2 In the event that the Parties are unable to reach agreement on the content of a joint report, they may submit a joint report setting forth the remaining areas of disagreement or, if necessary, submit separate reports.

74. On 14 October 2012, a second joint inspection was conducted, during which three-member[14] delegations of the Parties visited the KHEP site at Gurez.

75. Having been unable to reach agreement on the content of a joint report on the second joint inspection, the Parties submitted separate reports to the Court on 26 and 30 November 2012. In its report, Pakistan quoted paragraph 159 of the Order on Interim Measures and from Procedural Order No. 11, and further stated:

> Thus, the purpose of the inspection was to determine: (1) the status of the river diversion works, (2) the status of sub-surface foundations, and (3) the status of any permanent works on or above the Kishenganga/Neelum riverbed that may inhibit restoration of the full flow of that river to its natural channel.
>
> A. Itinerary:
>
> [...]
>
> B. Observations:
>
> The following observations were made during the site visit.
>
> 1. Status of the temporary diversion tunnel and cofferdam. The upstream cofferdam had been constructed of rock and earth, and contained a clay core. It was in operation and river flow was being diverted into the diversion tunnel. Based on the evidence of sediment deposits along the river banks, the backwater area created by the diversion tunnel extends approximately one kilometre upstream of the cofferdam.
>
> The downstream cofferdam extended almost the full width of the river, but was stopped about two meters from the opposite bank so that water can still pass this cofferdam.
>
> There was no evidence of disturbance to the riverbed upstream or downstream of the two cofferdams, except that a gravel crushing plant and

[14] Pakistan's delegation was comprised of Mr. Asif Baig, Dr. Gregory Morris and Ms. Shamila Mahmood. India's delegation was comprised of Mr. G. Aranganathan, Dr. Neeru Chadha and Prof. K.G. Rangaraju.

stockpiles are located on the wide left-hand gravel bar a little more than a kilometre upstream of the dam, where the river starts to open into the Gurez Valley. This plant was also present during the May 2012 site visit.

2. Status of sub-surface foundations. There was no evidence that any foundation work for the dam had been initiated. Waste material from rock excavation on either abutment (*including stones as large as 1.5 m diameter*) had either fallen or been placed into the riverbed, and the riverbed extending approximately 100 meters downstream from the cofferdam had been filled with stone 2 to 3 meters deep. However, at the dam axis the original river bed was visible in places, and there was no evidence of any foundation work or other permanent structures. A concrete foundation approximately ½ meter thick had been placed along the axis of the cut-off wall, upstream of the dam axis. Upon enquiring, it was explained that this foundation was to support the drilling equipment that was going to determine the depth to bedrock, to create the template for cut-off wall construction. Although some drilling pipe was on the site, no drilling had been initiated and the drilling foundation was not yet completed.

3. Status of any permanent works on or above the Kishenganga/Neelum riverbed that may inhibit restoration of the full flow of that river to its natural channel. The only "permanent" work that was visible during the visit was rock excavation on both abutments, plus the diversion tunnel. A large mass of rock spoil had been placed along the left side of the river from the dam axis upstream for a distance of nearly one kilometre, but there is still ample width for the river to flow freely with inconsequential flow obstruction.

All of the stone that has been placed in the riverbed is loose material that can be removed by heavy equipment to restore the river to its pre-construction geometry. There is no evidence of any concrete or other permanent works in the riverbed.

76. In its report, India also quoted from paragraph 152 of the Order on Interim Measures and Procedural Order No. 11 and further stated:

4. The Parties inspected the following works:

   i. Upstream Cofferdam

   ii. The reach of the river and river flow to the extent visible from its top.

   iii. Inlet of the temporary diversion or by-pass tunnel with the river flow entering into it

   iv. Reach between upstream cofferdam through to the downstream cofferdam

      1. Preparation for sub-surface excavation

      2. Hill slope on either side of the reach.

   v. Downstream cofferdam

vi. The reach of the river and river flow to the extent visible from its top.

vii. Outlet of the temporary diversion or by-pass tunnel with the river flow being discharged from the diversion or by-pass tunnel into the natural course of the river downstream

5. There was no permanent work *on or above the Kishenganga/Neelum riverbed* that may inhibit the restoration of the full flow of that river to its natural channel at the dam site.

6. The Parties have no disagreement concerning the implementation of the "Court Order" as per the scope defined therein.[15]

H. The Court's Second Site Visit

77. In an e-mail communication dated 6 December 2011, Pakistan requested the Court to conduct a second site visit in February 2012 as had been canvassed in the Court's letter to the Parties dated 21 March 2011 concerning the June 2011 site visit (see paragraph 35 above). The Court invited India to comment on Pakistan's request.

78. On 21 December 2011, India offered comments in an e-mail communication in which it stated that it would "leave the decision to the Court" about whether to conduct a second site visit.

79. On 30 December 2011, the Court transmitted to the Parties a draft of Procedural Order No. 7 (*Concerning the Second Site Visit*) for their comments, noting that it determined a second site visit to be appropriate.

80. The Parties provided their comments on the draft order on 9 January 2012. On 14 January 2012, Pakistan also provided the Court with a suggested itinerary for the second site visit.

81. The Court issued Procedural Order No. 7 on 16 January 2012, providing that: (1) the second site visit would take place from 3 to 6 February 2012; (2) the Court's delegation would be comprised of three persons: two Members of the Court, Sir Franklin Berman and Professor Howard Wheater, and one member of the Secretariat;[16] (3) those Members of the Court not present would view the photos and video of the visit taken by the Secretariat; (4) experts who were not members of the official delegations would be allowed to brief and assist the delegations when *in situ*; and (5) there would be no advance public announcements of the visit, but a press release containing a text and photo-

---

[15] Emphasis in the original.

[16] With respect to the size of the Court's delegation, the Court stated as follows:

The Court takes note of both Parties' willingness to accommodate a second site visit involving fewer than all Members of the Court if necessary, though the Court acknowledges that both Parties expressed their preference that the full Court or as many of its Members as possible attend. Regrettably, upon review of the calendar of its Members and other limiting factors, the Court has determined it would not be possible for all the Members of the Court to physically participate in the second site visit.

graph to be approved by the Parties and the Court would be prepared by the Secretariat for publication on the PCA website following the conclusion of the visit. In other respects, Procedural Order No. 7 provided that the arrangements for the second site visit would follow the practice established during the first site visit.

82. With the transmission of Procedural Order No. 7 and in response to India's comments of 9 January 2012 concerning potential factual presentations by Pakistan during the site visit and India's ability to reply, the Court indicated:

> The purpose of the second site visit is to give the Members of the Court a background impression of the relevant projects and areas surrounding the Kishenganga/Neelum River. As the Secretariat will be providing both Parties with copies of the photographs and video recordings taken, the Parties are free to submit any evidence they deem relevant in their future submissions in accordance with the Supplemental Rules.
>
> [...]
>
> The Court is of the view that the second site visit does not constitute a "transaction of business" within the meaning of Paragraph 11 of Annexure G. The site visit is not an "oral hearing" in which "oral submissions" are made by the Parties, and those Members of the Court not present during the second visit will have an opportunity to review the video and photographic materials from the site visit (including videos of any presentations made) individually, just as they each review any submission or communication of the Parties. The Court also assures the Parties that its two physically participating Members shall not by themselves "transact business" at any point during the visit.

83. By e-mail communication dated 25 January 2012, India requested that the Court "direct Pakistan to make available to India by 27 January 2012 all presentations and all technical and factual matters proposed to be presented or briefed orally by Pakistan during the second site visit." India further commented that such a direction was necessary to "maintain the equality of the Parties" so that India would not "be expected to respond spontaneously to the points to be made in Pakistan's presentations and oral briefings."

84. By e-mail communication dated 25 January 2012, Pakistan commented on India's e-mail communication of the same date, arguing that India's request was "superfluous" in light of the Parties' prior opportunity to comment on the draft order.

85. On 27 January 2012, the Registrar conveyed to the Parties the following statement from the Chairman of the Court:

> I acknowledge the Parties' respective e-mail communications of January 25, 2012, regarding the conduct of the second site visit. I take particular note of the Agent of Pakistan's assurance (i) that no formal presentations of the type made during the first site visit are anticipated, and (ii) that the experts would only conduct "an informal briefing at the site with

the intention of describing what the Members of the Court happened to be looking at."

On the basis of these representations from Pakistan, and noting that Pakistan's experts will not discuss legal issues or arguments, and that the experts' statements must be succinct and neutral in tone (para. 5.1, Procedural Order No. 7), I am of the view that:

(1) the procedure to be followed with respect to any presentations or statements made during the second site visit—including the need for formal presentation materials (if any) to be provided in advance of the visit—has been addressed in Procedural Order No. 7, and no further directives from the Court are necessary in this regard; and

(2) these proceedings afford the Parties no shortage of opportunity to address or comment on any matter arising from the second site visit; however, should any circumstance arise during the second site visit that one Party considers to be of grave prejudice that cannot be addressed over the ordinary course of the proceedings, immediate recourse to the Members of the Court present (and the Court itself, if necessary) is always available.

Finally, I trust that all representatives of the Parties understand the basic rule prohibiting *ex parte* discussions with Members of the Court during the course of these proceedings. In the case of the second site visit, I trust that any potentially contentious matter, whether of substance or procedure, will not be raised *ex parte* by any Party representative to any member of the Court or Secretariat.

86. From 3 to 6 February 2012, a site visit to the Neelum Valley was conducted. Arriving in Islamabad on 3 February 2012, the Court's delegation, together with representatives from India and Pakistan,[17] travelled to Muzaffarabad. On 4 February, the delegation proceeded by road into the Neelum Valley and visited the gauge-discharge observation site at Dudhnial. The delegation also visited a water-pumping installation in the vicinity of Athmuqam and was briefed on lift irrigation practices in the Neelum Valley. The delegation returned to Islamabad on 5 February, and left Pakistan on 6 February 2012.

87. On 15 February 2012, the PCA published a press release approved by both Parties concerning the second site visit as well as three photographs taken during the visit.

88. Pursuant to Procedural Order No. 7, on 28 March 2012, the PCA transmitted to the Parties and the Members of the Court a set of two DVD-format disks containing videos of the presentations made during the second site visit, along with photographs.

[17] Pakistan's delegation for the second site visit comprised Mr. Kamal Majidulla, Ms. Shamila Mahmood and Mr. Mirza Asif Baig. India's delegation consisted of Mr. Dhruv Vijai Singh, Mr. Ram Chandra Jha and Mr. Darpan Talwar. The Court's delegation consisted of Sir Franklin Berman and Prof. Howard Wheater, assisted by Mr. Garth Schofield of the Secretariat.

I. The Parties' Written Submissions on the Merits; Requests for Documents and Further Information

89. On 27 May 2011, Pakistan submitted its Memorial, accompanied by witness statements and expert reports. On 4 July 2011, Pakistan submitted a Volume 3 *bis* and a correction sheet addressing certain errata in the Memorial.

90. On 23 November 2011, India submitted its Counter-Memorial, accompanied by expert reports, technical documents, legal authorities and a list of errata.

91. By e-mail communication dated 22 December 2011, the Agent for Pakistan requested that the Agent for India provide copies of three documents referred to in India's Counter-Memorial: (1) a unredacted version of a letter dated 16 May 1960 from the Chairman of India's Central Water and Power Commission (the "CWPC") to India's Ministry for Irrigation and Power (known to the Parties as "Document IN-54" or "Annex IN-54" and hereinafter referred to as the "CWPC Letter"); (2) a letter dated 13 January 1958 referred to in the CWPC Letter; (3) the preliminary hydro-electric survey for the Indus basin which accompanied the letter of 13 January 1958; and (4) the revised or additional environmental impact assessments ("EIAs") and other surveys and reports prepared in respect of the reconfiguration of the KHEP in 2006.

92. By e-mail communication dated 5 January 2012, Pakistan also requested from India "further information as to the purpose for the construction of Adit 1 and the range of uses to which it could be put in the operation of the KHEP (including any use in diverting water from the valley in which its entrance is located into the KHEP plant)."

93. By e-mail communication dated 13 January 2012, India responded to Pakistan's request for documents. India further requested Pakistan to provide: (1) a copy of the EIA, environmental management plan, and socio-economic impact assessment studies for the NJHEP; and (2) the technical details and EIAs of the four projects being planned upstream of the NJHEP.

94. On 21 January 2012, Pakistan submitted to the Court an application for production of a full copy of the CWPC Letter, arguing that an unredacted copy was essential for the presentation of its case.

95. Also on 21 January 2012, Pakistan responded to India's e-mail communication of 13 January 2012. Pakistan requested further information "as to where the [CWPC Letter] was located by India" as well as confirmation as to whether India's response regarding Pakistan's request for certain environmental reports "is that (i) the documents sought are not in existence or (ii) the documents are not being supplied for some other reason." Pakistan asked India for more specific information regarding its first request and referred India to paragraph 3.35 of Pakistan's Memorial for the identification of the four projects noted by India.

96. By e-mail communication dated 30 January 2012, India commented on Pakistan's application for production of a full copy of the CWPC Letter. Pakistan responded by e-mail communication dated 31 January 2012.

97. On 1 February 2012, the Court notified the Parties of the following procedure for consideration of Pakistan's application for production of the CWPC Letter:

> India is requested to provide to all Members of the Court (through the Registrar) a full copy of [the CWPC Letter] at India's earliest convenience, but in no case later than Tuesday, February 7, 2012.
>
> By no later than Tuesday, February 7, 2012, India is invited to provide its views on any applicable principle of State secrecy or privilege that the Court should take into account in deciding Pakistan's disclosure application.
>
> Pakistan is invited to comment on India's submission by no later than Friday, February 10, 2012.

98. By letter dated 4 February 2012, India provided to the Court a full copy of the CWPC Letter, a copy of the Official Secrets Act 1923 (India), and a copy of the Official Secrets Act 1923 (Pakistan). India and Pakistan then re-stated their respective positions on 7 and 9 February 2012.

99. To resolve this impasse, on 14 February 2012 the Court issued Procedural Order No. 8 which provided:

> 1. Procedural History
>
> [...]
>
> 2. Summary of the Parties' Positions
>
> 2.1 Pakistan contends that India ought to produce an unredacted copy of Annex IN-54 because Annex IN-54 is "of central importance" to India's argument. It maintains that India refers to the document "on multiple occasions in support of the contention that: 'The planning, development, and construction of the [Kishenganga Hydro-Electric Plant ('*KHEP*')] dates back to a period when the Treaty was being negotiated, and was a key reason why specific provisions were included in Annexure D of the Treaty allowing India to engage in inter-tributary transfers for Run-of-River projects on tributaries of the Jhelum.'"
>
> 2.2 Pakistan argues that the Court is empowered to order the production of documents it considers "appropriate and necessary" pursuant to Paragraph 20 of Annexure G of the Treaty. Pakistan acknowledges that "redactions may be justified in appropriate cases, e.g. where dictated by issues of confidentiality or security" but argues that, based on India's prior communications, such factors "do not apply in the current case." On these grounds, Pakistan concludes that Annex IN-54 is likely to be relevant to the disputes before the Court, and that it is both appropriate and necessary for the Court to see the document in its entirety. Pakistan further asserts that it requires Annex IN-54 in its entirety to respond to India's argument as articulated in the Counter-Memorial.

2.3 India makes three principal arguments. First, India maintains that the deleted passages of Annex IN-54 are not relevant to matters before the Court, noting that the redacted passages pertain to the Indus and the Chenab Rivers, not involved in the present dispute. Second, India argues the redacted passages need not be disclosed because India does not rely on them "in terms of Rule 11(i)(*a*) of the Supplemental Procedural Rules." Third, India indicates that the disclosure of an unredacted copy of Annex IN-54 risks "prejudice to India." India also makes reference to the Official Secrets Act, 1923 in force in both India and Pakistan. Referring to Paragraph 20 of Annexure G, India requests the Court not to disclose these redacted sections of Annex IN-54.

2.4 With respect to India's arguments, Pakistan comments that India does not explain why the Official Secrets Act, 1923 is applicable in the instant case nor articulate what prejudice it might suffer.

3. Decision of the Court

3.1 As noted by the Parties, Paragraph 20 of Annexure G of the Treaty provides that the Court may "require from the Agents of the Parties the production of all papers and other evidence it considers necessary."

3.2 The Court acknowledges Pakistan's position concerning the potential relevance of the redacted passages of Annex IN-54 and the adverse impact redaction may have on Pakistan's ability to respond to India's arguments, as well as India's position that the redacted passages contain "internal opinions with respect to matters that are not before this Court," the disclosure of which may result in "prejudice to India." The Court understands that India's objection to Pakistan's Application is based principally on the lack of relevance of the redacted portions of the document to this proceeding, and not on the Official Secrets Act, 1923.

3.3 As a general rule, the Court believes that any Party offering a document in evidence should provide the full document. The practice of redacting portions of exhibits has the understandable tendency to raise concerns on the part of the other Party, even where the material in question may be irrelevant. To address this concern, Paragraph 20 of Annexure G and Article 13(*2*) of the Supplemental Rules of Procedure empower the Court to request, either *motu propio* or upon application of a Party, the production of the full, unredacted document.

3.4 In the exercise of this power the Court would, in appropriate circumstances, seek an examination of the redacted material. Accordingly, India's offer to provide the Court with a copy of the unredacted Annex IN-54 *in camera* is a welcome development, as it allows the Court to determine for itself the degree of relevance of those redacted portions.

3.5 The Court has carefully reviewed the unredacted copy of Annex IN-54 in light of the Parties' concerns regarding prejudice to the interests of either Party that may result from the disclosure or non-disclosure of the redacted passages. In the Court's view, the unredacted passages of Annex IN-54 are not directly relevant to the issues in dispute as currently defined in the pleadings of the Parties, and the non-disclosure of the redacted passages will not hamper Pakistan's ability to respond to the arguments made in India's Counter-Memorial that refer to Annex IN-54.

3.6 The Court therefore concludes that at this stage in the proceedings, it is not necessary to order that India supply Pakistan a complete and unredacted copy of the communication affixed to India's Counter-Memorial as Annex IN-54.

3.7 The Court shall remain seized of the matter. Should further submissions by the Parties or other developments in the proceedings lead the Court to consider revisiting this determination, the Parties will be invited to provide further comments at that time. Pakistan may also renew its application for production of a full copy of Annex IN-54 should new matters arise in the course of proceedings that it believes justifies such disclosure.

100. By e-mail communication dated 15 February 2012, India asked Pakistan to be more specific regarding its request of 21 January 2012 for environmental reports. India further commented on the relevance of the environmental impact report requested by India in relation to the NJHEP and the discussion of that report during the first site visit. India also noted that, insofar as detailed project reports and environmental impact assessments did not exist for Pakistan's four potential projects, India considered any effect of the KHEP to be "speculative" and that such sites were not "existing" hydro-electric uses.

101. By e-mail communication dated 20 July 2012, Pakistan asked India for further technical information regarding the construction and use of Adit 1 of the KHEP construction.

102. At the hearing on the merits, in response to further queries made by Pakistan, India stated that Adit 1 is intended to be used for construction and maintenance, not for diversion of waters.[18]

103. On 21 February 2012, Pakistan submitted its Reply, accompanied by an annexure.

104. On 21 May 2012, India submitted its Rejoinder.

J. Expert Witnesses and Testimony by Video Link

105. Pursuant to paragraph 3.2 of Procedural Order No. 9, on 15 June 2012, the Parties conveyed to each other and to the Court the names of witnesses and experts they intended to cross-examine at the hearing on the merits.

106. On 16 July 2012, Pakistan notified India that one witness India intended to cross-examine, Professor Michael Acreman, could not be present at the hearing in The Hague. Pakistan suggested the possibility of making Professor Acreman available by telephone or video-conference.

[18] Hearing Tr., (Day 5), 24 August 2012, at 145:15 to 146:8.

107. On 23 July 2012, India replied to Pakistan's message of 16 July, urging Pakistan to take steps to present Professor Acreman in person for cross-examination, noting that cross-examination "via a video link would obviously be less effective than an in person examination, and would thus result in prejudicing India."

108. By e-mail communication dated 9 August 2012, Pakistan asked the Registrar to place the matter of Professor Acreman's testifying by videoconference before the Court as India had not agreed to permit Professor Acreman's videoconference testimony. Pakistan confirmed that Professor Acreman was not available to come to The Hague.

109. India reiterated its objection to Pakistan's request by e-mail communication dated 13 August 2012, stating that Pakistan had known as far back as January 2011, when the dates of the hearing were finalized, that Professor Acreman could possibly be required to come to The Hague at that time. Referring to paragraph 3.3 of Procedural Order No. 9, which states that "(t)he Parties shall ensure that experts are present and available sufficiently in advance of the time they are anticipated to be called," India maintained that cross-examination by telephone or video link was not as effective as in-person examination and that it contravened the Court's Orders.

110. In an e-mail communication dated 13 August 2012, Pakistan pointed out that it accepted that prejudice may be caused to India by Professor Acreman's availability only by telephone, but that on balance, Pakistan would suffer more prejudice from Professor Acreman's unavailability to participate in person.

111. On 15 August 2012, the Court issued Procedural Order No. 10 (*Concerning Pakistan's Request for Permission to Present Dr. Acreman for Cross-Examination by Telephone Link*), in which it directed:

> 1. Articles 10 and 14 of the Supplemental Rules establish the procedure for the submission of expert evidence in support of the Parties' factual and legal arguments. A Party wishing to submit such evidence must append to its written pleadings the expert's witness report, which will stand as evidence in chief, while the other Party may request to cross-examine the expert. In accordance with Section 3.3 of Procedural Order No. 9, each Party is responsible for summoning to the hearing those of its experts that the other Party wishes to cross-examine. Consistent with these provisions and with general practice in international arbitration, the expert is expected to appear for cross-examination in person during the scheduled hearing. These provisions provide no guidance for a situation such as this one, where the expert is not presented in person due to a professed prior commitment.
>
> 2. At the outset, the Court notes that in international arbitration there are serious consequences to a party's failure to present an expert witness for cross-examination without cogent reasons: in general, that expert's

report would be stricken from the record, and would form no part of the evidence on which an award can be based.

3. The Court considers that it is the norm for cross-examination of a witness or expert to be conducted in the physical presence of counsel for the other party and the tribunal. Where, as here, alternative means of cross-examination are proposed, to protect against a violation of the procedural due process rights of the other party, the Court would ordinarily need to be satisfied that: (1) at the time the expert report was presented, the Party did not know that the expert would not be available for cross-examination in person due to a prior commitment; (2) there is good reason, by virtue of the nature of the expert's duties at the time of examination, for excusing the expert's physical presence during the hearing; and (3) the alternative means of cross-examination satisfactorily approximates in-person cross-examination.

4. For reasons of liberality and because of the imminence of the hearing, the Court is willing to forego further analysis of requirements (1) and (2) on a *pro hac vice* basis.

5. As to (3), Pakistan offers to present Dr. Acreman for cross-examination by telephone link. In the Court's view, cross-examination by telephone link does not satisfactorily approximate in-person cross-examination, as visual contact with the expert, possible in person but not by telephone, is essential for an effective cross-examination.

6. By contrast, the Court is of the view that video-conferencing is, under certain circumstances, an acceptable substitute for in-person cross-examination. By providing a synchronous audio and visual connection between the witness or expert, the cross-examining counsel, and the arbitral tribunal, video-conferencing can potentially approximate the conditions of in-person cross-examination. The Court notes in this regard that cross-examination of expert and fact witnesses by video-conferencing has been allowed in a number of international arbitral hearings.[fn1] That said, based on the actual conduct of cross-examination by video-conferencing, the weight to be given to testimony made through that medium rests with the Court.[fn2]

7. Pakistan contends that Dr. Acreman is unable to make himself available for video-conferencing because his assignment involves fieldwork (which presumably requires frequent changes of location), the detailed schedule of which will not be known until some time during the week of August 13, 2012. In this context, it appears that video-conferencing could be arranged once Dr. Acreman's schedule and itinerary become known. The hearing is scheduled to take place from August 20 to August 31, 2012, and the Court would be prepared to allow Dr. Acreman's cross-examination to take place on any weekday from August 20 to 28, provided that advanced notice of at least three working days is given.

8. The Court therefore *denies* Pakistan's Request and urges Pakistan to present Dr. Acreman for cross-examination in person or, if not possible, by video-conferencing.

9. Should cross-examination of Dr. Acreman occur not in person but through video-conference, the Court reserves the possibility, in the light of the quality of the video link achieved, of deciding to reconvene at a later stage in order to hear Dr. Acreman in person. If so reconvened, the attendant cost consequences will follow.

---

fn1 *See e.g. Murphy Exploration and Production Company International* v. *Republic of Ecuador*, ICSID Case No. ARB/08/4, Award on Jurisdiction of December 15, 2010, para. 16; *S.D. Myers, Inc.* v. *Government of Canada*, UNCITRAL, Second Partial Award, 21 October 2002, para. 76; *Sergei Paushok, CJSC Golden East Company and CJSC Vostokneftegaz Company* v. *Government of Mongolia*, UNCITRAL, Award on Jurisdiction and Liability of 28 April 2011, para. 61; *Fraport AG Frankfurt Airport Services Worldwide* v. *Republic of the Philippines*, ICSID Case No. ARB/03/25, Award of 16 August 2007, para. 43; *EDF (Services) Limited* v. *Romania*, ICSID Case No. ARB/05/13, Award of 8 October 2009, para. 38; *SGS Société Générale de Surveillance S.A.* v. *Republic of Paraguay*, ICSID Case No. ARB/07/29, Award of 10 February 2012, para. 23.

fn2 Art. 13(1) of the Supplemental Rules provides that "[t]he Court shall determine the admissibility, relevance, materiality, and weight of the evidence adduced." [19]

112. In the course of the hearing on the merits, the Chairman announced that he was informed by Pakistan that it "proved impossible to link up with Dr. Acreman in the remote reaches of Australia … and therefore his testimony has been withdrawn."[20]

113. By e-mail communication dated 9 August 2012, Pakistan stated that it intended to "call Professor Jens Christian Refsgaard as an expert witness in the forthcoming hearing." It indicated that Professor Refsgaard was willing to "provide a brief note on his comments [that he wishes to make in light of the reports submitted by India with its Rejoinder]" for the Court's reference during his examination, should the Court wish to have such a written note.

114. By e-mail communication dated 13 August 2012, India objected to Pakistan's notification of 9 August concerning Professor Refsgaard, arguing that "any notification by a Party that it intends to call a particular expert-witness to be heard was required to be filed by 21 July 2012 at the latest" according to the Supplemental Rules of Procedure (Article 14, paragraph 3). India recalled its e-mail communication dated 17 July 2012 in which it notified the Court and Pakistan that it did not seek to cross-examine Professor Refsgaard. Thereafter Pakistan had given no indication that it wished to call Professor Refsgaard. India argued, thus, that calling Professor Refsgaard "at this late stage would also be fundamentally prejudicial to India."

115. Pakistan responded to India's objection by e-mail communication dated 14 August 2012, in which it acknowledged its "inadvertent and minor

---

[19] Emphasis in the original.

[20] Hearing Tr., (Day 2), 21 August 2012, at 1:3–7.

failure to comply with Article 14.3" of the Supplemental Rules of Procedure but submitted that it was not appropriate to prevent Professor Refsgaard from testifying at the hearing, given that Article 14.3, unlike some other articles of the Rules, did not stipulate a strict consequence for a failure to comply. Further, Pakistan contended that India would not be prejudiced by Pakistan's failure to make an Article 14.3 communication as India had planned to cross-examine Professor Refsgaard until "late July." To the contrary, to prevent Professor Refsgaard from testifying at the hearing would not be consistent with the requirements of equality and the need to give each Party a full opportunity to be heard because India would have had the opportunity to criticize Professor Refsgaard without giving him a chance to respond.

116. India reiterated its objection to Professor Refsgaard's participation by e-mail communication dated 15 August 2012, arguing that granting Pakistan the opportunity to present a written submission by Professor Refsgaard would severely prejudice India, as would giving him the opportunity to testify.

117. In a letter to the Parties dated 17 August 2012, the Court denied Pakistan's request for direct oral examination of Professor Refsgaard during the hearing on the merits, stating that permitting such testimony would raise serious issues of procedural fairness. The Court's full communication of 17 August 2012 reads as follows:

> 1. The Court acknowledges receipt of the Parties' respective communications of August 9, 13, and 14, 2012 concerning the proposed direct testimony of the expert witness put forth by Pakistan, Professor Jens Christian Refsgaard, at the Hearing on the Merits.
>
> 2. Pakistan has indicated its intention to directly examine Professor Refsgaard during the Hearing and has sought guidance as to whether a written note outlining Professor Refsgaard's additional comments would be preferred. India has objected to the Court hearing further testimony from Professor Refsgaard. The Court recalls that India originally indicated, on June 15, 2012, its intention to cross-examine Professor Refsgaard. However, on July 17, 2012 India informed the Court that it no longer considered Professor Refsgaard's presence to be necessary.
>
> 3. As a general matter, Articles 10 and 14 of the Supplemental Rules of Procedure establish the procedure for the submission of expert evidence in support of the Parties' factual and legal arguments. A Party wishing to submit such evidence must append to its written pleadings the expert's witness report, which will stand as evidence in chief, while the other Party may request to cross-examine the expert. Article 14(5) establishes that, "subject to the control of the Court", the examination of expert witnesses during the Hearing "will be limited to cross-examination and re-direct, and to questions that may be put by the Court." This procedure was established to minimize the possibility of surprise to either Party during the Hearing—cross-examination would be based on expert reports provided to the other Party well before the Hearing is to take place. It follows from this that an expert witness would not testify

on direct examination in the ordinary course of events, absent a request for cross-examination from the other Party *or* an application for leave to conduct direct examination by the Party which is granted by the Court. Although not expressed in these terms, the Court will interpret Pakistan's August 9 and 14, 2012 communications as such an application.

4. India has also raised the failure of Pakistan to indicate its intention to conduct direct examination of Mr. Refsgaard at least 30 days prior to the Hearing, in violation of Article 14(3) of the Supplemental Rules. Pakistan has admitted that it had inadvertently failed to comply with this rule, but maintains that such a failure is minor and that the appropriate remedy "could not conceivably be the draconian measure that India calls for". The Court agrees that if a Party can demonstrate the necessity of allowing one of its witnesses or experts to be directly examined during a hearing, a violation of the 30 day rule embodied in Article 14(3) would alone not be fatal to that application.

5. There is a more fundamental point on procedural fairness raised by India, however, that merits serious consideration from the Court. In approaching Pakistan's application, the Court considers that its paramount duty is to maintain *both* Parties' due process rights, in particular the right to be heard on the matters on which the Court will render its decision, and the equally important right of the other Party to have adequate opportunity to contradict all those matters. Procedures and time limits for the identification of witnesses and experts in advance of a hearing are intended to insure that neither party is surprised by the issues to be raised and that counsel are able to adequately prepare.

6. In this instance, Professor Refsgaard's reports consist of expert commentary on the methodologies employed in the hydrology reports prepared respectively by National Engineering Services Pakistan (Pvt) Limited ("NESPAK") and by the Indian Central Waters Commission ("CWC"). To the extent that the CWC report or the report of Dr. George Annandale (which touches on the same subject)—both appended to India's Rejoinder—raise issues not adequately addressed by Professor Refsgaard's earlier testimony, the Court considers that the appropriate procedure would have been for Pakistan to call Dr. Annandale and a representative of the CWC for cross-examination, and if necessary, to also apply for leave to either submit a further expert report or, if not possible, for direct testimony from Professor Refsgaard. Pakistan did not call for the cross-examination of the CWC Report or of Dr. Annandale.

7. Under these circumstances, the Court is of the view that permitting additional direct testimony from Professor Refsgaard would raise serious issues of procedural fairness, as it would introduce additional evidence in a manner that would not allow India an adequate opportunity for contradiction. Professor Refsgaard would be given the opportunity to criticize the testimony of Dr. Annandale and the CWC experts and lay out new testimonial evidence in support of his view; and crucially,

neither the CWC experts nor Dr. Annandale would be able to respond, not being in attendance at the Hearing as far as the Court can tell.

8. In view of these considerations, the Court *denies* Pakistan's request for direct oral examination of Professor Refsgaard during the Hearing. The Court notes that it is open to Pakistan to raise any issues it may have concerning India's Rejoinder in its oral pleadings, including any concerns it may have on the expert reports contained in the Rejoinder.

9. Nonetheless, in order to ensure every orderly opportunity for each Party to present its case, *if*, within five days after the conclusion of the Hearing (i.e., by September 5, 2012), Pakistan believes that there are critical matters Dr. Refsgaard would have raised that could not be dealt with through agent/counsel argument at the Hearing, Pakistan may submit a further expert report from Professor Refsgaard, which shall be limited to matters raised in India's Rejoinder. India would then be given a period of three weeks (i.e., until September 26, 2012) to submit any additional expert reports it wishes to in response.

10. Finally, the Court wishes to emphasize that at any time during or after the Hearing, if the Court considers that it would benefit from further expert assistance from either or both Parties, then the Court will require a supplementary procedure at that time.[21]

118. On the first day of the hearing, Pakistan reiterated a request for the direct examination of Professor Refsgaard, to which India objected.[22] The Court reaffirmed its ruling of 17 August 2012 denying Pakistan's request while noting that Pakistan would have the option of applying to the Court for leave to submit a further expert report by Professor Refsgaard if it "believes there are critical matters to Professor Refsgaard's testimony that cannot be adequately dealt with through counsel argument during this hearing."[23]

K. The Hearing on the Merits

119. Pursuant to paragraph 5.2.2 of Procedural Order No. 1, a two-week hearing was scheduled to be held from 20 to 31 August 2012.

120. On 4 June 2012, after receiving the views of the Parties, the Court issued Procedural Order No. 9, which provided for the conduct of the hearing.

121. The hearing on the merits took place at The Hague as scheduled. The following persons were present:

The Court of Arbitration

Judge Stephen M. Schwebel (Chairman)

Sir Franklin Berman KCMG QC

[21] Emphasis in the original.

[22] Hearing Tr., (Day 1), 20 August 2012, at 57:17–20.

[23] Hearing Tr., (Day 1), 20 August 2012, at 57:20 to 28:5.

Professor Howard S. Wheater FREng

Professor Lucius Caflisch

Professor Jan Paulsson

Judge Bruno Simma

H.E. Judge Peter Tomka

Pakistan

Mr. Kamal Majidulla, Agent, Special Assistant to the Prime Minister for Water Resources and Agriculture

Mr. Khalil Ahmad, Co-agent, Ambassador at Large

Mr. Karim Khan Agha, Co-agent, Prosecutor General, National Accountability Bureau

Mr. Asif Baig, Co-Agent, Pakistan Commissioner for Indus Waters

Mr. Vaqar Zakaria, Technical Expert, Managing Director, Hagler Bailly Pakistan

Dr. Muhammad Rafiq, Technical Expert, Hagler Bailly Pakistan

Mr. Manzar Naeem Qureshi, Power Economics Expert

Mr. Syed Muhammad Mehr Ali Shah, Technical Expert, Principal Engineer, NESPAK

Mr. Faris Qazi, Technical Expert, Deputy Commissioner for Indus Waters

Mr. Saleem Warsi, Flow Measurement Expert, Water Resources and Power Development Authority

Mr. Sardar Raheem, Representative of the Government of Azad Jammu and Kashmir, Secretary of Irrigation and Agriculture

Dr. Gregory Morris, Technical Expert

Dr. Jens Christian Refsgaard, Technical Expert

Dr. Jackie King, Technical Expert

Mr. Hans Beuster, Technical Expert

Dr. Cate Brown, Technical Expert

Prof. James Crawford, Counsel

Prof. Alan Vaughan Lowe, Counsel

Ms. Shamila Mahmood, Counsel

Mr. Samuel Wordsworth, Counsel

Mr. Aamir Shouket, Counsellor, Embassy of Pakistan

India

Mr. Dhruv Vijai Singh, Agent, Secretary to the Government of India, Ministry of Water Resources

Dr. Neeru Chadha, Co-agent, Joint Secretary and Legal Adviser, Ministry of External Affairs

Mr. G. Aranganathan, Co-agent, Indian Commissioner for Indus Waters

H.E. Bhaswati Mukherjee, Ambassador of India to the Netherlands

Mr. Raj Kumar Singh, Deputy Chief of Mission, Embassy of India, The Hague

Dr. A. Sudhakara Reddy, First Secretary (Legal), Embassy of India, The Hague

Mr. Fali S. Nariman, Counsel

Mr. R.K.P. Shankardass, Counsel

Prof. Stephen C. McCaffrey, Counsel

Mr. Rodman Bundy, Counsel

Prof. Daniel Magraw, Counsel

Mr. S.C. Sharma, Counsel

Mr. Jesper Goodley Dannisøe, Expert Witness

Dr. Niels Jepsen, Expert Witness

Dr. S. Sathyakumar, Expert Witness and Advisor

Dr. K.G. Rangaraju, Expert Witness and Advisor

Dr. Alka Upadhyay, Advisor

Mr. Darpan Talwar, Advisor, Senior Joint Commissioner, Ministry of Water Resources

Mr. P.K. Saxena, Advisor, Director, Central Water Commission

Mr. Balraj Joshi, Advisor

Dr. Shahid Ali Khan, Advisor

Mr. Rajeev Baboota, Advisor

Ms. Swarupa Reddy, Research Assistant

Mr. S.P. Bhatt, Attaché (Legal)

The Secretariat

Mr. Aloysius P. Llamzon, Registrar and Legal Counsel

Mr. Garth Schofield, Legal Counsel

Ms. Kathleen Claussen, Assistant Legal Counsel

Ms. Evgeniya Goriatcheva, Assistant Legal Counsel

Ms. Willemijn van Banning, Case Manager

Court Reporter

Mr. Trevor McGowan

122. The following persons presented oral arguments before the Court on behalf of Pakistan:

Mr. Kamal Majidulla, Agent

Prof. James Crawford, Counsel

Prof. Alan Vaughan Lowe, Counsel

Ms. Shamila Mahmood, Counsel

Mr. Samuel Wordsworth, Counsel

123. The following persons presented oral arguments before the Court on behalf of India:

Mr. Dhruv Vijai Singh, Agent

Dr. Neeru Chadha, Co-agent

Mr. Fali S. Nariman, Counsel

Mr. R.K.P. Shankardass, Counsel

Mr. Rodman Bundy, Counsel

Prof. Stephen C. McCaffrey, Counsel

Prof. Daniel Magraw, Counsel

124. Pursuant to the Parties' notifications of 15 June 2012, Pakistan presented the following experts for cross-examination:[24]

Mr. Mehr Ali Shah

Dr. Jackie King

Mr. Vaqar Zakaria, and

Dr. Gregory Morris

India presented the following experts for cross-examination:

Dr. K.G. Rangaraju

Dr. S.K. Sathyakumar

Mr. Jesper Goodley Dannisøe, and

Dr. Niels Jepsen

125. By letter dated 12 September 2012, the Court distributed the certified transcript for the hearing on the merits, which constituted minutes for the purpose of Paragraph 19 of Annexure G and "pronounced the discussions closed" in accordance with Paragraph 22 of Annexure G.[25]

---

[24] *See also* paras. 106–110 of this Partial Award concerning the presentation of Dr. Acreman.

[25] Paragraph 22 of Annexure G provides:

When the Agents and Counsel of the Parties have, within the time allotted by the Court, submitted all explanations and evidence in support of their case, the Court shall pronounce the discussions closed. The Court may, however, at its discretion re-open the dis-

II. BACKGROUND

126. This arbitration marks the first instance that a court of arbitration has been constituted since the Indus Waters Treaty was concluded over half a century ago. The proceedings have arisen out of a dispute between Pakistan and India concerning the interpretation and implementation of the Treaty in relation to the construction and operation of the Kishenganga Hydro-Electric Project. The Treaty sets forth the rights and obligations of the Parties on the use of the waters of the Indus system of rivers. The KHEP is an Indian hydro-electric project located on one such river—known as the "Kishenganga" in India-administered Jammu and Kashmir and as the "Neelum" in Pakistan-administered Jammu and Kashmir (the "Kishenganga/Neelum River," "Kishenganga/Neelum," or "River").[26]

127. The KHEP is designed to generate power by diverting water from a dam site on the Kishenganga/Neelum River (within the Gurez valley, an area of higher elevation) to another river of the Indus system (lower in elevation and located near Wular Lake) through a system of tunnels, with the water powering turbines having a capacity of up to 330 megawatts. In essence, the Parties disagree as to whether the planned diversion of water and other technical design features of the KHEP are in conformity with the provisions of the Treaty. The Parties also disagree over the permissibility under the Treaty of the use of the technique of drawdown flushing for sediment control in Run-of-River Plants.

A. The Geography

128. The Indus system of rivers is composed of six main rivers: the Indus, the Jhelum and the Chenab (together with their tributaries, the "Western Rivers"), and the Sutlej, the Beas and the Ravi (together with their tributaries, the "Eastern Rivers").[27] These rivers and their tributaries rise primarily in the Himalayas and course through Afghanistan, China, India and Pakistan before merging into the Indus river and draining into the Arabian Sea southeast of the port of Karachi in Pakistan.[28] The Indus system of rivers and its catchment area are depicted on the following map provided by Pakistan.[*]

129. The Kishenganga/Neelum River, on which the KHEP is located, is a tributary of the Jhelum. The River originates in India-administered Jam-

cussions at any time before making its Award. The deliberations of the Court shall be in private and shall remain secret.

[26] The terminology used in this Partial Award to denote geographic locations is intended to be neutral and should not be construed as the adoption by the Court of any position with regard to any matters of territorial sovereignty. *See* the discussion of the territorial scope of the Treaty at paras. 359–363 of this Partial Award. Pakistan-administered Jammu and Kashmir is sometimes referred to by the Parties as "Azad Jammu and Kashmir" or "Pakistan Occupied Kashmir." India-administered Jammu and Kashmir is sometimes referred to by the Parties as "India," "Indian-occupied Kashmir" or "Indian-held Kashmir."

[27] Treaty, Arts. 1(5)–(6); India's Counter-Memorial, para. 2.2.

[28] Pakistan's Memorial, para. 1.14; India's Counter-Memorial, para. 2.2.

[*] Secretariat note: See map located in the front pocket of this volume (Map 1).

mu and Kashmir at latitude 34°33'N and longitude 75°20'E at an elevation of 4400 metres.[29] It flows through India-administered Jammu and Kashmir, crosses the Line of Control separating India-administered Jammu and Kashmir from Pakistan-administered Jammu and Kashmir, and joins the Jhelum River at Muzaffarabad in Pakistan-administered Jammu and Kashmir. The flow in the Kishenganga/Neelum River is strongly seasonal. The highest flows occur from May to August, associated with seasonal snowmelt in the upper catchment, and monsoon rain in the lower reaches. In contrast, there is a long low flow season from early October to the middle of March.[30]

B. The Indus Waters Treaty

130. The need for a treaty regulating the use of the waters of the Indus river system arose in 1947 with the independence of India from British rule and its partition into the Dominion of Pakistan (now the Islamic Republic of Pakistan and the People's Republic of Bangladesh) and the Union of India (now the Republic of India).[31]

131. Before partition, use of the waters was negotiated between the relevant provinces and states of British India, and any disputes were resolved by the British Secretary of State for India, and later by the Government of India.[32] After partition, parts or all of the upper reaches of the six main rivers of the Indus system were located in India, with their downstream stretches flowing through Pakistan.[33] A temporary agreement for the allocation of the use of these waters between East Punjab (an Indian state from 1947 to 1956) and West Punjab (a province of Pakistan from 1947 to 1955) expired on 31 March 1948.[34]

132. In April 1948, an incident occurred during which East Punjab discontinued the flow of water in the canals leading to West Punjab.[35] An agreement was reached by the two states and the flow of water in the canals concerned was restored within one month, but this incident exposed the two states' differing views on their respective rights and obligations regarding the waters of the Indus river system.[36]

133. In August 1951, Mr. David E. Lilienthal, the former head of the Tennessee Valley Authority in the United States, visited the region at the invitation

[29] India's Counter-Memorial, para. 2.8.

[30] *See* Pakistan's Memorial, para. 3.21; India's Counter-Memorial, para. 2.11.

[31] Pakistan's Memorial, paras. 1.26–1.27; India's Counter-Memorial, paras. 2.22, 2.24.

[32] Pakistan's Memorial, para. 1.28; India's Counter-Memorial, para. 2.23.

[33] Pakistan's Memorial, para. 1.26; India's Counter-Memorial, para. 2.24.

[34] Pakistan's Memorial, paras. 1.27, 1.33, referring to Marjorie M. Whiteman, *Digest of International Law*, vol. 3, 1963, pp. 1022–1023, (Annex PK-LX-18).

[35] Pakistan's Memorial, para. 1.33, referring to Marjorie M. Whiteman, *Digest of International Law*, vol. 3, 1963, pp. 1022–1023, (Annex PK-LX-18); India's Counter-Memorial, paras. 2.25–2.28.

[36] Pakistan's Memorial, para. 1.34, referring to Inter-Dominion Agreement, Between the Government of India and the Government of Pakistan, on the Canal Water Dispute Between East and West Punjab, 4 May 1948, 54 U.N.T.S. 45, included in Annexure A to the Treaty; India's Counter-Memorial, para. 2.28.

of the Prime Minister of India Mr. Jawaharlal Nehru and after his visit published an article recommending that the World Bank facilitate the negotiation of the joint development of the Indus waters basin by India and Pakistan.[37]

134. In pursuance of Mr. Lilienthal's proposal, on 6 September 1951, the World Bank offered to assist India and Pakistan in elaborating a cooperative regional approach to the development of the Indus river system's water resources.[38] Both States accepted this offer.[39]

135. The first two years of negotiations were not successful. The two States were unable to prepare jointly a comprehensive plan and, when invited to each prepare their own comprehensive plan, made proposals that "differed widely in concept and in substance."[40] From the World Bank's perspective, the difficulties resulted not from technological complexity, but from: (1) the inadequacy of the resources of the Indus system of rivers to satisfy all the needs of the area; (2) the involvement of two sovereign States in the development of the Indus basin as an economic unit; and (3) the fact that while Pakistan considered that existing uses of the waters should be continued from existing sources, India believed that, although existing uses should be continued, they did not need to be continued from existing sources (i.e., that some waters of the Eastern Rivers used by Pakistan could be released for use by India and replaced by waters from the Western Rivers).[41]

136. To end the impasse, on 24 February 1954, the World Bank put forward a substantive proposal (the "1954 Proposal"), suggesting a division of the waters of the Indus river system between the two States. The 1954 Proposal allocated to Pakistan the "exclusive use and benefit" of the "entire flow of the Western Rivers (Indus, Jhelum and Chenab)," and to India the "exclusive use and benefit" of the "entire flow of the Eastern Rivers (Ravi, Beas and Sutlej)." It also provided for a transitional period during which India would continue to supply Pakistan with its "historic withdrawals" from the Eastern Rivers, while Pakistan constructed link canals that would allow it to replace water it had previously secured from the Eastern Rivers by water from the Western Rivers.[42]

137. Four years of intensive negotiation and discussion followed, at the conclusion of which agreement was reached on the Treaty's general principles, largely in keeping with the 1954 Proposal. Beginning in August 1959, the World Bank proposed and the Parties exchanged views on increasingly detailed

[37] Letter from Eugene R. Black, President of the World Bank, to Pakistan's Prime Minister Liaquat Ali Khan, 6 September 1951, (Annex IN-31), (an identical letter was sent to India's Prime Minister Jawaharlal Nehru).

[38] *Ibid.*

[39] India's Counter-Memorial, para. 2.46.

[40] Proposal by the International Bank Representative for a Plan for the Development and Use of the Indus Basin Waters, 5 February 1954, (Annex PK-2), paras. 1–2 ("1954 Proposal").

[41] 1954 Proposal, (Annex PK-2), paras. 5–16.

[42] 1954 Proposal, (Annex PK-2), para. 24.

drafts.[43] Among other matters, agreement was reached on the restricted uses India would be permitted to make of the waters of the Western Rivers.[44]

138. The Parties, as well as the World Bank, finally signed the Treaty on 19 September 1960. The Treaty entered into force on 12 January 1961, upon the exchange of documents of ratification, with retroactive effect from 1 April 1960.[45]

139. In addition to regulating the allocation of the use of the waters of the Indus system of rivers, the Treaty created the Permanent Indus Commission (the "Commission") to establish and maintain cooperative arrangements for the implementation of the Treaty. The Commission is formed of a Commissioner for Indus Waters appointed by India (the "Indian Commissioner") and a Commissioner for Indus Waters appointed by Pakistan (the "Pakistani Commissioner") (together, the "Commissioners"), each acting as a representative of his Government and as the regular channel of communications for all matters related to the Treaty. The full range of the Commission's duties is set out in Article VIII of the Treaty. Sub-paragraph 4 of this provision specifies that these functions include:

> (*a*) to study and report to the two Governments on any problem relating to the development of the waters of the Rivers which may be jointly referred to the Commission by the two Governments: [...]
>
> (*b*) to make every effort to settle promptly, in accordance with the provisions of Article IX(1), any question arising thereunder;
>
> (*c*) to undertake, once in every five years, a general tour of inspection of the Rivers for ascertaining the facts connected with various developments and works on the Rivers;
>
> (*d*) to undertake promptly, at the request of either Commissioner, a tour of inspection of such works or sites on the Rivers as may be considered necessary by him for ascertaining the fact connected with those works or sites;
>
> [...]

C. The History of the Disputes

140. The documentary history of the present disputes within the Commission dates back to 1988. At that time, it came to the Pakistani Commissioner's notice that "work on a scheme envisaging diversion of the waters of the Kishenganga River into Wullar Lake had been taken in hand."[46] By telegram dated 14 December 1988, the Pakistani Commissioner requested that India interrupt its work and provide Pakistan with information on the project. In the

[43] Pakistan's Memorial, paras. 1.50–1.69; India's Counter-Memorial, paras. 2.60–2.61.

[44] Pakistan's Memorial, paras. 1.54–1.63.

[45] *See* Treaty, Art. XII(2).

[46] Pakistani Commissioner's telegram to the Indian Commissioner, 14 December 1988, (Annex PK-38).

same telegram, the Pakistani Commissioner stated his view that "the scheme if implemented would adversely affect Pakistan's hydro-electric projects and other uses on the [Kishenganga/Neelum River]."[47]

141. By telegram dated 16 December 1988, the Indian Commissioner explained that geological investigations regarding the proposed project on the Kishenganga/Neelum River had only just begun and that India "would communicate to Pakistan information specified in the Treaty at least six months in advance of beginning of work on the project."[48]

142. By letter dated 22 April 1989, the Pakistani Commissioner, recalling a meeting of the Commission on 17–20 December 1988, informed India "again" of the construction by Pakistan of the NJHEP on the Kishenganga/ Neelum River in Pakistan-administered Jammu and Kashmir.[49]

143. By letter dated 12 May 1989, the Indian Commissioner recalled that, in accordance with Paragraph 10 of Annexure E to the Treaty, which regulates Indian Storage Works on the Western Rivers, any Indian Storage Work located on a tributary of the Jhelum must be "so designed and operated as not to adversely affect the then existing Agricultural Use or hydro-electric uses on that Tributary." The Indian Commissioner therefore requested the Pakistani Commissioner to provide information regarding Pakistan's agricultural and hydro-electric uses on the Kishenganga/Neelum River and, in particular, the NJHEP.[50] By letter dated 15 March 1990, the Pakistani Commissioner provided the requested information.[51]

144. By letter dated 2 June 1994, the Indian Commissioner furnished the Pakistani Commissioner with the details of the KHEP "in accordance with Paragraph '12' of Annexure 'E'" to the Treaty.[52]

145 From that time, the Commissioners exchanged voluminous correspondence setting forth their respective positions with regard to the KHEP. The Pakistani Commissioner objected to the KHEP on the grounds that: (1) the planned diversion was not permitted by Annexure E to the Treaty; (2) the KHEP would have a significant adverse impact on Pakistan's agricultural and hydro-electric uses on the Kishenganga/Neelum River, and in particular on the NJHEP, thus contravening Paragraph 10 of Annexure E to the Treaty; and (3) the KHEP's design did not conform to the design criteria of

[47] *Ibid.*

[48] Indian Commissioner's telegram to the Pakistani Commissioner, 16 December 1988, (Annex PK-39).

[49] Pakistani Commissioner's letter to the Indian Commissioner, 22 April 1989, (Annex PK-40).

[50] Indian Commissioner's letter to the Pakistani Commissioner, 12 May 1989, (Annex PK-41).

[51] Pakistani Commissioner's letter to the Indian Commissioner, 15 March 1990, (Annex PK-53).

[52] Indian Commissioner's letter to the Pakistani Commissioner, 2 June 1994, (Annex PK-63).

Paragraph 11 of Annexure E to the Treaty.[53] The Pakistani Commissioner also stated that India had provided insufficient information with respect to the KHEP.[54] The Indian Commissioner, by contrast, was of the view that the KHEP was permitted by Annexure E to the Treaty, so long as the KHEP did not affect Pakistan's pre-existing agricultural and hydro-electric uses. The Indian Commissioner further argued that Pakistan had continuously failed to substantiate its agricultural and hydro-electric uses on the Kishenganga/Neelum River.[55] On the basis of the information provided by Pakistan and of the 1991 and 1996 tours of inspection to the Neelum Valley, the Indian Commissioner contended that the NJHEP did not constitute a "then existing" hydro-electric use on the Kishenganga/Neelum River, as it was no more than a "proposed" project, and that little, if any, agricultural use of the River's water was being made in the Neelum Valley.[56]

146. Pakistan's objections to the KHEP were discussed at meetings of the Commission held in 2004 and 2005 without leading to any settlement of the Parties' disagreement.[57]

147. By letter dated 7 February 2006, the Pakistani Commissioner informed the Indian Commissioner that, in his view, a dispute had arisen with respect to the KHEP.[58] On 26 March 2006, in accordance with Article IX(3) of the Treaty, he provided a draft report to be submitted to the Governments of India and Pakistan.[59]

148. By letter dated 20 April 2006, the Indian Commissioner informed the Pakistani Commissioner that, due to local concerns over the submer-

[53] Pakistani Commissioner's letter to the Indian Commissioner, 8 September 1994, (Annex PK-64); Pakistani Commissioner's letter to the Indian Commissioner, 11 October 1997, (Annex PK-77).

[54] Indian Commissioner's letter to the Pakistani Commissioner, 21 February 1991, (Annex PK-56); *see also* Pakistani Commissioner's letter to the Indian Commissioner, 8 September 1994, (Annex PK-64), para. 4; Pakistani Commissioner's letter to the Indian Commissioner, 11 October 1997, (Annex PK-77), para. 7.

[55] India's Counter-Memorial, paras. 3.11, 3.98–3.104, 3.114–3.122, referring to Pakistani Commissioner's letter to the Indian Commissioner, 9 September 1991, (Annex IN-88); Pakistani Commissioner's letter to the Indian Commissioner, 7 November 1991, (Annex PK-59); Pakistani Commissioner's letter to the Indian Commissioner, 11 May 1992, (Annex PK-62); Record of the 92nd Meeting of the Commission, Lahore, 27-29 November 2004, (Annex PK-28), para. 5; Record of the 97th Meeting of the Commission, New Delhi, 30 May to 4 June 2007, (Annex PK-33), pp. 11–12, 17–18; Indian Commissioner's letter to the Pakistani Commissioner, 26 May 2007, (Annex PK-174), pp. 3–4.

[56] Indian Commissioner's letter to Pakistani Commissioner, 21 February 1991, (Annex PK-56); Indian Commissioner's letter to the Pakistani Commissioner, 7 February 1992, (Annex PK-61); Indian Commissioner's letter to the Pakistani Commissioner, 29 January 1997, (Annex PK-76).

[57] Pakistan's Memorial, para. 2.18, referring to Record of the 92nd Meeting of the Commission, Lahore, 27–29 November 2004, (Annex PK-28).

[58] Pakistani Commissioner's letter to the Indian Commissioner, 7 February 2006, (Annex PK-157).

[59] Pakistani Commissioner's letter to the Indian Commissioner, 26 March 2006, (Annex PK-159).

gence of villages, the KHEP had been re-configured to a Run-of-River Plant falling under Article III(2)(*d*) and Annexure D of the Treaty.[60] Accordingly, "any proposal for reference of any dispute ... would no longer be relevant or necessary."[61] On 19 June 2006, the Indian Commissioner provided information concerning the re-configured KHEP "as specified in Appendix II to Annexure D" to the Treaty.[62]

149. By letters dated 21 July and 24 August 2006, the Pakistani Commissioner observed that the KHEP was a new Run-of-River Plant, and that India was accordingly required to submit information under the relevant provisions of Annexure D. He raised specific objections to the re-configured KHEP on the basis that: (1) the proposed diversion of the Kishenganga/Neelum River would violate India's obligation under the Treaty to "let flow" the waters of the Western Rivers; and (2) the new design of the KHEP contravened the design criteria of Paragraph 8 of Annexure D to the Treaty.[63] By letter dated 25 May 2007, the Indian Commissioner rejected all of Pakistan's objections.[64] The Indian Commissioner nevertheless communicated some updated details and plans to Pakistan in May 2007 and in May and June 2008.[65]

150. Pakistan's objections to the re-configured KHEP were discussed at the 99th, 100th and 101st meetings of the Commission held respectively from 30 May to 4 June 2007, 31 May to 4 June 2008 and 25 to 28 July 2008. However, no agreement was reached.[66]

151. By letter dated 11 March 2009, the Pakistani Commissioner informed his Indian counterpart of his view that the First Dispute and the Second Dispute had arisen between the Parties in relation to the KHEP (the "11 March 2009 Letter"). The Letter enclosed a draft report for submission to the Governments of India and Pakistan in accordance with Article IX(3) of the Treaty.[67] Upon request by the Government of India, Pakistan agreed, without prejudice to its position that disputes had arisen under Article IX of the Treaty, that the KHEP be discussed again at the 103rd meeting of the Commission that was to be held from 31 May to 5 June 2009. [68] Yet again, the Parties did not reach agreement during that meeting. Moreover, India maintained its position that no dispute had arisen.[69]

[60] Indian Commissioner's letter to the Pakistani Commissioner, 20 April 2006, (Annex PK-161).

[61] Indian Commissioner's letter to the Pakistani Commissioner, 20 April 2006, (Annex PK-161).

[62] Indian Commissioner's letter to the Pakistani Commissioner, 19 June 2006, (Annex PK-163).

[63] Pakistani Commissioner's letter to the Indian Commissioner, 24 August 2006, (Annex PK-166).

[64] Indian Commissioner's letter to the Pakistani Commissioner, 25 May 2007, (Annex PK-174/IN-98).

[65] *Ibid.*; Indian Commissioner's letter to the Pakistani Commissioner, 1 June 2009, (Annex IN-101).

[66] Pakistan's Memorial, paras. 2.27–2.32.

[67] Pakistani Commissioner's letter to the Indian Commissioner, 11 March 2009, (Annex PK-194).

[68] India's Note Verbale, 19 May 2006, (Annex PK-206); Pakistan's Note Verbale, 30 May 2009, (Annex PK-210).

[69] Record of the 103rd Meeting of the Commission, New Delhi, 31 May to 5 June 2009, (Annex PK-36), item (xi).

152. By Note Verbale dated 10 July 2009, in accordance with Article IX(4) of the Treaty, Pakistan invited India to resolve the disputes by agreement and nominated two negotiators for this purpose.[70] By Note Verbale dated 20 August 2009, India indicated that in its view appointment of negotiators was "not warranted at present."[71]

153. By a Request for Arbitration dated 17 May 2010, Pakistan commenced the present arbitration.

D. The KHEP and the NJHEP—Technical Characteristics

154. The Parties agree that the KHEP was first conceived as a Storage Work within the meaning of Annexure E to the Treaty. According to its original design, the KHEP was intended to store water during the high flow season in a reservoir with a gross storage capacity of 220.00 million cubic metres ("MCM") behind a 77-metre high dam. The stored water was intended to be used for enhanced power generation during the winter months when the natural flow of the river was at its lowest.[72]

155. The KHEP was re-designed in 2006.[73] As described in India's letter of 19 June 2006[74] and in Annex I and Appendix 2 to India's Counter-Memorial, the new design comprises: (1) a 35.48 metre high dam over the Kishenganga/Neelum River located in the Gurez valley in India-administered Jammu and Kashmir, at latitude 34°39'00"N and longitude 75°45'08"E, approximately 12.07 kilometres upstream of the Line of Control; (2) a reservoir with a gross storage capacity of 18.35 MCM, located behind the dam; (3) a 23.5 kilometre head-race tunnel through which up to 58.4 m3/s of water can be diverted from the Kishenganga/Neelum River at the dam site to the powerhouse; (4) a powerhouse at the downstream end of the tunnel at latitude 34°28'18"N and longitude 75°38'28"N; and (5) a tail-race channel which, after power generation, will deliver water diverted from the Kishenganga/Neelum River into the Bonar Nallah, another tributary of the Jhelum. The diverted water will then rejoin the Jhelum River through Wular Lake, at a point upstream of the Jhelum River's juncture with the Kishenganga/Neelum River. The design of the KHEP thus makes use of the natural 666-metre denivelation between the dam and the powerhouse for the generation of power.[75]

---

[70] Pakistan's Note Verbale, 10 July 2009, (Annex PK-212).

[71] India's Note Verbale, 20 August 2009, (Annex PK-214).

[72] India's Counter-Memorial, Appendix 2, paras. 5–7; *see also* India's Counter-Memorial, Annex 1.

[73] The re-designed KHEP is a Run-of-River Plant within the meaning of Annexure D to the Treaty. *See* para. 383 of this Partial Award.

[74] Indian Commissioner's letter to the Pakistani Commissioner, 19 June 2006, (Annex PK-163).

[75] India's Counter-Memorial, Appendix 2, para. 2.

156. Pakistan renders the KHEP schematically as follows:

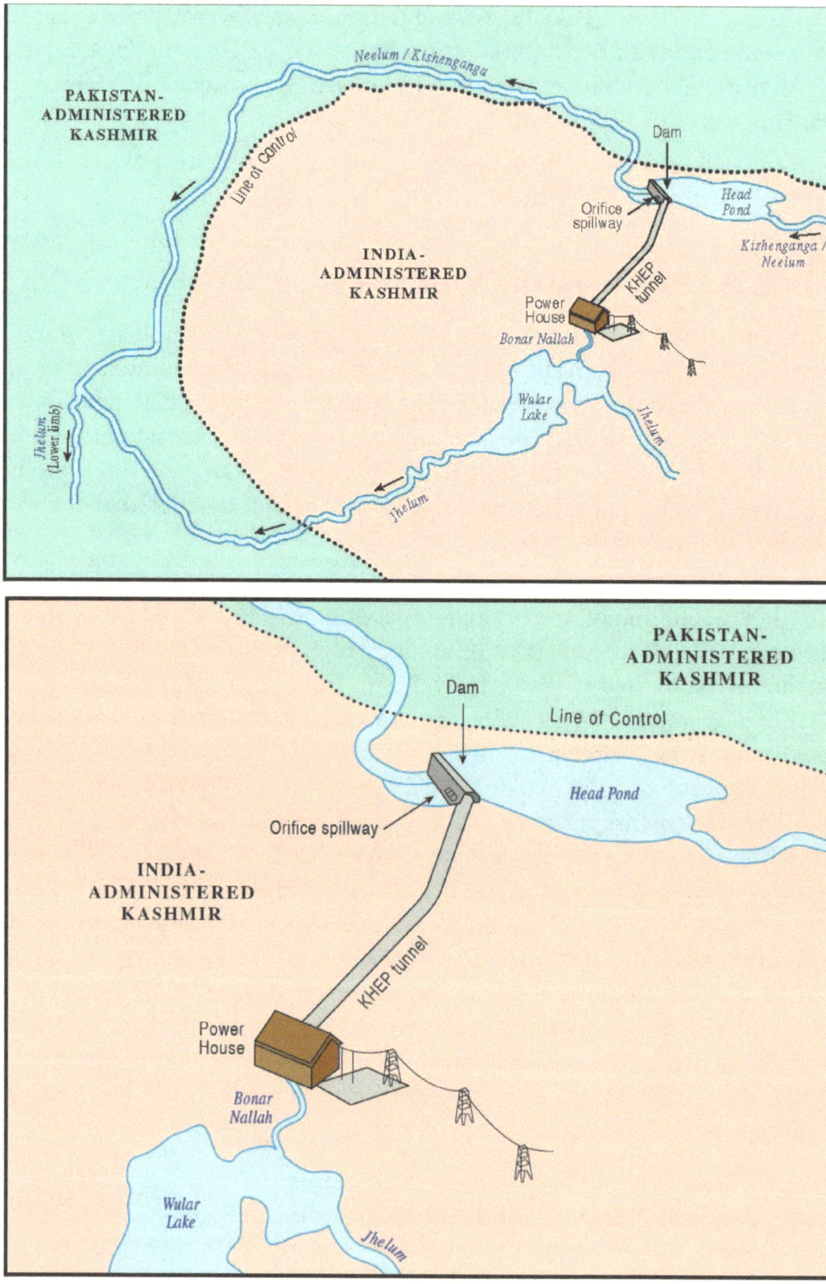

Source: Pakistan's Memorial, volume 2, Figure 9.

157. As stated by India, the KHEP is designed to have an installed capacity of 330 megawatts and is intended to generate 1350 gigawatt hours in a 90 percent dependable year for India's northern regional grid, comprising the states of Himachal Pradesh, Punjab, Haryana, Uttar Pradesh, Uttaranchal, Rajasthan, Union Territory of Chandigarh & Delhi and India-administered Jammu and Kashmir.[76]

158. As described in Pakistan's Memorial, the NJHEP's design includes: (1) a 41.5-metre dam to be constructed on the Kishenganga/Neelum River at Nauseri, in Pakistan-administered Jammu and Kashmir, 158 kilometres downstream of the KHEP and a short distance upstream of Muzaffarabad; and (2) a tunnel of approximately 30 kilometres through which water will be diverted from the Kishenganga/Neelum River to an underground powerhouse at Chatter Kalas. After power generation, the water will be returned to the Jhelum River near Zaminabad. The NJHEP has a design capacity of 969 megawatts and is intended to provide peaking power from 18:00 to 22:00 hours throughout the year and full-time operation during the high flow season. [77]

159. The respective locations of the KHEP and the NJHEP can be seen on the following map.*

E. The Impact of the KHEP on the NJHEP

160. It is undisputed between the Parties that the operation of the KHEP would to some extent affect the power-generating capacity of the NJHEP, although the precise numbers cited by the Parties differ somewhat.[78] The Parties' contentions as to the potential effect of the KHEP on the volume of water in the Kishenganga/Neelum River available for power generation at Nauseri (from where water is diverted to the NJHEP's power station) and on potential energy production by the NJHEP may be summarized as follows:[79]

[76] India's Counter-Memorial, Appendix 2, para. 3.

[77] Pakistan's Memorial, paras. 3.19–3.20; Pakistan's Memorial, vol. 3, Tab B, National Engineering Services Pakistan Limited, "Kishenganga/Neelum River: Hydrology and Impact of Kishenganga Hydroeletric Plant on Energy Generation in Pakistan," April 2011, p. ES-1.

* Secretariat note: See map located in the front pocket of this volume (Map 2).

[78] *See* paras. 247 and 252 of this Partial Award for a discussion of the reasons for this discrepancy.

[79] Pakistan's Memorial, paras. 3.29–3.33, referring to Pakistan's Memorial, vol. 3, Tab B, National Engineering Services Pakistan Limited, "Kishenganga/Neelum River: Hydrology and Impact of Kishenganga Hydroeletric Plant on Energy Generation in Pakistan, April 2011, p. 86, table 14, p. 89, table 16; Pakistan's Memorial, Tab A, Jens Christian Refsgaard, "Review of NESPAK Report: Hydrology and Impact of Kishenganga Hydroeletric Plant on Energy Generation in Pakistan," 12 May 2011, para. 2.5; India's Counter-Memorial, paras. 5.13, 5.16, table 5.2, referring to India's Counter-Memorial, Tab A, Central Water Commission, Government of India, "Hydrology Report on Kishenganga Hydro-Electric Project," October 2011, p. 48.

	Average Flow Reduction at Nauseri (in percent)		**Average Energy Production Reduction at NJHEP (in percent)**	
	In Pakistan's submission	*In India's submission*	*In Pakistan's submission*	*In India's submission*
October to March	33	29.88	35	29.9
April to September	11	4.59	6	4.6
Annually	14	11.2	13	11.2

III. ARGUMENTS OF THE PARTIES

161. This Chapter first summarizes the Parties' arguments on the First Dispute (Part A) and then those on the Second Dispute (Part B).

A. The Diversion of the Kishenganga/Neelum River under the Terms of the Treaty

162. As stated in Pakistan's Request for Arbitration and at the outset of its Memorial, the First Dispute concerns the following:

> Whether India's proposed diversion of the river Kishenganga (Neelum) into another Tributary, i.e. the Bonar-Madmati Nallah, being one central element of the Kishenganga Project, breaches India's legal obligations owed to Pakistan under the Treaty, as interpreted and applied in accordance with international law, including India's obligations under Article III(2) (let flow all the waters of the Western rivers and not permit any interference with those waters) and Article IV(6) (maintenance of natural channels).[80]

163. The First Dispute thus centers on whether the intended diversion of water from the Kishenganga/Neelum River as part of the KHEP is prohibited under the Treaty. Pakistan alleges three principal Treaty violations: (1) breach of the general obligation to "let flow" the waters of the Western Rivers; (2) breach of requirements pertaining to the permissible use of the waters for the generation of hydro-electric power; and (3) breach of the obligation to use best endeavours to maintain the natural channels of the Western Rivers.

[80] Pakistan's Request for Arbitration, para. 4(*a*); Pakistan's Memorial, para. 1.12.

1. The Parties' arguments on the governing principles of the Treaty for use of the waters of the Western Rivers

164. Underlying the Parties' disagreement on hydro-electric projects such as the KHEP is a more fundamental divergence about the principles established by the Treaty for the use of the waters of the Western Rivers. Before turning to the Treaty's specific treatment of hydro-electric power generation, this section outlines the Parties' contrasting views on the governing principles through which the Treaty regulates the use of the Western Rivers.

165. Article III of the Treaty provides that:

> (1) Pakistan shall receive for unrestricted use all those waters of the Western Rivers which India is under obligation to let flow under the provisions of Paragraph (2).
>
> (2) India shall be under an obligation to let flow all the waters of the Western Rivers, and shall not permit any interference with these waters, except for the following uses, restricted (except as provided in item (*c*) (ii) of Paragraph 5 of Annexure C) in the case of each of the rivers, The Indus, The Jhelum and The Chenab, to the drainage basin thereof:
>
> (*a*) Domestic Use;
>
> (*b*) Non-Consumptive Use;
>
> (*c*) Agricultural Use, as set out in Annexure C; and
>
> (*d*) Generation of hydro-electric power, as set out in Annexure D.

166. Pakistan contends that the KHEP's proposed diversion of water from the Kishenganga/Neelum River into the Bonar Nallah tributary violates India's obligation under Article III(1) to "let flow" the waters of the Western Rivers (including those of the Jhelum and its tributaries) and constitutes an "interference" with those waters prohibited by Article III(2).[81] Pakistan stresses that India's obligations to "let flow" and "not permit any interference with" the waters of the Western Rivers limit the scope of the exceptions to these obligations listed in Article III(2).[82]

167. In India's view, Pakistan's interpretation of Article III nullifies the four Article III(2) exceptions to the "let flow" obligation,[83] the fourth of which permits the construction of the KHEP. According to India, Pakistan's reading of the Article would destroy India's right to build and operate any hydro-electric project on the Western Rivers.[84] India contends that the Treaty intends to create a distribution that achieves the "most complete and satisfactory utilisation of the waters" rather than to mandate any guiding principle with respect to the appropriate flow of the waters.[85]

---

[81] Pakistan's Memorial, para. 5.6; Hearing Tr., (Day 4), 23 August 2012, at 11:5–8.

[82] Pakistan's Memorial, para. 5.8.

[83] India's Counter-Memorial, paras. 1.5, 1.7, 1.24, 4.16.

[84] India's Rejoinder, paras. 1.4, 2.15.

[85] India's Counter-Memorial, paras. 1.4, 4.61, 4.62, quoting Treaty, Preamble.

(a) The meaning of the Treaty text

Pakistan's arguments

168. Pakistan argues that Article III imposes two general obligations on India. The first and most important, which Pakistan refers to as the "let flow" obligation, is a positive obligation according to which "all the waters of each River must be permitted to flow, i.e., to flow in accordance with their natural patterns."[86] In Pakistan's view, India's obligation to "let flow all the waters" constitutes a right for Pakistan to the unrestricted flow of the water "at the time when, and in the location where, it would naturally flow."[87] The obligation refers not only to the volume of water but also to the maintenance and timing of the flow.[88]

169. The second general obligation that Pakistan identifies is the prohibition in Article III(2) of "any interference with the waters" of the Western Rivers (including the waters of the Jhelum and its tributaries). As an initial matter, Pakistan notes that "interference with the waters" is a term of art in the Treaty, defined in Article I(15) as "[a]ny act of withdrawal [from the waters]" or "[a]ny man-made obstruction to their flow which causes a change in the volume ... of the daily flow of the waters." Pakistan submits that "the diversion of waters to an entirely different location would be inimical to this prohibition."[89]

170. Although Pakistan recognizes certain exceptions to the "let flow" and non-interference obligations, which are stated in Article III(2), it emphasizes that the foregoing obligations, as made clear by both Articles II and III, are the "fundamental principle underlying the Treaty." [90] The flow of the waters of the Western Rivers is, to Pakistan, a matter of "existential importance."[91] Thus, Pakistan contends that the exceptions in Article III(2) should be interpreted in light of India's central obligations under the Treaty to "let flow" and "not permit any interference with" those waters.[92] Moreover, it is an elementary concept of legal drafting, Pakistan maintains, that "exceptions should not be given a wide interpretation."[93] Pakistan's position is that the burden of

---

[86] Pakistan's Memorial, para. 5.6a.

[87] Pakistan's Memorial, para. 5.6a.

[88] Pakistan's Memorial, paras. 1.7, 1.94.

[89] Pakistan's Memorial, para. 5.6b.

[90] Pakistan's Memorial, para. 1.97. Article II of the Treaty provides, in relevant part:

(1) All the waters of the Eastern Rivers shall be available for the unrestricted use of India, except as otherwise expressly provided in this Article.

(2) Except for Domestic Use and Non-Consumptive Use, Pakistan shall be under an obligation to let flow, and shall not permit any interference with, the waters of the Sutlej Main and the Ravi Main in the reaches where these rivers flow in Pakistan and have not yet finally crossed into Pakistan.

[91] Pakistan's Memorial, para. 5.7.

[92] Pakistan's Reply, para. 2.45.

[93] Pakistan's Memorial, para. 1.97.

demonstrating that its project falls within the "very limited exceptions" available under the Treaty rests with India.[94]

171. While the language of the Preamble acknowledges the importance of attaining the "most complete and satisfactory" utilization of the waters of the Indus river system, for Pakistan, the phrase does not carry as much significance as India attributes to it.[95] In Pakistan's view, it is the Treaty's "precise stipulation of rights and obligations" that "give[s] definition to what is complete and satisfactory."[96] At the same time, Pakistan maintains, other restrictions specified in the Treaty "cannot be interpreted away on the basis of the Preamble's reference to complete and satisfactory utilisation."[97]

India's arguments

172. India disagrees with Pakistan's interpretation of the "let flow" and non-interference obligations. India's position is that Pakistan has a right under Article III(1) to receive for its unrestricted use in Pakistan "all those waters of the Western Rivers which India is under an obligation to let flow … but only those waters, and Pakistan has a right to their unrestricted use *only* after she has actually received them."[98]

173. Contrary to Pakistan's position, India insists that there is no absolute principle in the Treaty of non-interference and of letting flow all the waters. Rather, the obligation to "let flow" the waters is subject to specific exceptions within which the KHEP squarely falls.[99] Likewise, the prohibition in Article III(2) of "any interference with" is followed by the phrase "except for the following uses," the effect of which is, India submits, to reverse the obligations preceding it so that India may "interfere" to carry out any of the uses enumerated thereafter.[100]

174. India considers that the words of the Treaty "must be presumed to be the authentic expression of the intentions of the parties"[101] and be interpreted in accordance with their ordinary meaning as prescribed by the customary international law of treaty interpretation.[102] Thus, the text of Arti-

[94] Pakistan's Memorial, para. 2.33.

[95] Pakistan's Reply, para. 2.30.

[96] Pakistan's Reply, para. 2.30.

[97] Pakistan's Reply, para. 2.30.

[98] India's Counter-Memorial, para. 4.26. Emphasis in the original. *See also* India's Rejoinder, para. 2.30.

[99] India's Counter-Memorial, para. 2.71.

[100] India's Counter-Memorial, paras. 4.28, 4.30.

[101] India's Counter-Memorial, para. 4.50, quoting *Commentary of the International Law Commission on what became art. 31 of the Vienna Convention,* Y.B. Int'l L. Comm'n, vol. II, 1966, (Annex IN-LX-8), p. 220. As a general proposition, India acknowledges that while neither Party is a party to the Vienna Convention on the Law of Treaties, 23 May 1969, 1155 U.N.T.S. 331 ("VCLT"), the principles of that Convention are part of customary international law. India's Counter-Memorial, para. 4.48.

[102] India's Counter-Memorial, para. 4.47.

cle III(2) should be taken on its face, as a whole; and at most, the Preamble should be taken into account to provide context.[103] According to India, the Preamble guides the Court to the goals pursued by the Parties at the time of signature, namely, to achieve the "most complete and satisfactory utilisation of the waters."[104]

(b) The Treaty's drafting history

Pakistan's arguments

175. Pakistan maintains that draft texts and communications exchanged during the negotiation of the Treaty support its reading. Relying on these documents, Pakistan asserts that the Treaty is premised on the idea that "the flow of the waters that make up the Indus Basin system should be definitively and permanently divided between the two States." Each State was to receive control of three rivers and their tributaries and to be bound by certain obligations regarding the flow in its territory of the rivers allocated to the other State.[105] Pakistan argues that this approach constitutes the "control/let flow" principle—a "primary point of reference in the Treaty"[106] that was carefully crafted to safeguard the water supply on which the people of Pakistan depend.[107]

176. Highlighting the unique features of the Indus river system, Pakistan emphasizes that the Treaty drafters never considered an equal division of the waters between the two States and that India never suggested such a division during the negotiations. Pakistan notes that India, unlike Pakistan, does not depend on the rivers of the Indus system for its principal water supplies.[108] Moreover, Pakistan's position as a downstream State puts it in a permanent position of vulnerability. Pakistan submits that this position explains its willingness to agree to the division set out in the Treaty.[109] In particular, the restrictions imposed by Annexure D on the design, construction and operation of new hydro-electric plants were important to Pakistan at the time of signing because without them, India could have controlled the flow of the waters at will; that is, India would have been able to "turn off the tap" of Pakistan's water supply.[110]

177. Pakistan puts emphasis on the World Bank's 1954 Proposal, which, in its view, introduced the "control/let flow" principle; it suggests that this proposal gave rise to the Treaty's overall approach that control of the rivers

[103] India's Counter-Memorial, para. 4.57; India's Rejoinder, para. 2.8.

[104] Hearing Tr., (Day 5), 24 August 2012, at 17:2–25.

[105] Pakistan's Memorial, paras. 1.88–1.89.

[106] Pakistan's Memorial, para. 1.92.

[107] Pakistan's Memorial, paras. 1.90–1.91.

[108] Pakistan's Reply, para. 2.41.

[109] Pakistan's Reply, para. 2.5.

[110] Pakistan's Memorial, para. 6.3.

would be divided.[111] According to Pakistan, the two central principles of the 1954 Proposal were that: (1) historical withdrawals must be continued but not necessarily from existing sources; and (2) control over the rivers would be divided.[112] Pakistan also relies on the 1957 "Head of Agreement" prepared by the World Bank, which states that "the entire flow of the three Western Rivers ... shall be available for the exclusive use and benefit of Pakistan";[113] in Pakistan's view, this indicates the Treaty's concern with ensuring that India would not diminish the flow of water to Pakistan.[114]

178. Pakistan further argues that India's reliance on the 8 November 1951 letter from the World Bank to argue that the object and purpose of the Treaty is one of cooperative development ("in such a manner as most effectively to promote the development of the Indus basin viewed as a unit") is misplaced and neglects the tenor of subsequent negotiations and the Treaty that was actually concluded.[115]

179. To the extent that maximization of development was an objective of the Treaty, Pakistan maintains that it led "to an obligation of cooperation, not unilateral rights of use or development."[116] This is apparent from the only specific Treaty provision dedicated to the subject—Article VII(1), which states:

> The two Parties recognize that they have a common interest in the optimum development of the Rivers, and, to that end, they declare their intention to co-operate, by mutual agreement, to the fullest possible extent. [...]

Thus, it is not for India to impose on Pakistan what it considers to be optimal for development.[117]

180. Pakistan argues that its interpretation of the Treaty is supported by the World Bank's communications with the Parties. Pakistan points to a letter dated 6 February 1960 from the President of the World Bank to the Pakistani Finance Minister in which the former stated that he was "satisfied that there is no doubt and no reservation in the mind of any one, either in the Indian delegation, or the Bank, that the present language of Article III(1) and (2) imposes the treaty obligation on India to allow to flow down *all* waters of the Western Rivers... ."[118]

[111] Pakistan's Reply, paras. 2.33–2.34.

[112] Pakistan's Reply, para. 2.34; *see also* Pakistan's Memorial, paras. 1.37–1.54.

[113] Pakistan's Memorial, para. 1.51, quoting Letter of the World Bank, 13 May 1957, Annex Setting Out Some Suggestions for "Head of Agreement," (Annex PK-5), Art. 1.

[114] Pakistan's Reply, paras. 2.36–2.38. Pakistan argues that the World Bank's press release on the conclusion of the Treaty contains a "clear statement of the control/let flow principle," contrary to India's argument. Pakistan's Reply, para. 2.38, referring to World Bank's press release, 19 September 1960, (Annex IN-51), p. 6.

[115] Pakistan's Reply, para. 2.33.

[116] Pakistan's Reply, para. 2.31.

[117] Pakistan's Reply, para. 2.32.

[118] Pakistan's Memorial, para. 5.6, fn. 175, quoting President of the World Bank's letter to the Pakistani Finance Minister, 6 February 1960, (Annex PK-16). Emphasis in the original.

181. Pakistan disputes that the 1957 *Lake Lanoux* arbitral award (delivered while the Treaty was being negotiated), to which India refers, bears any relevance to the determination of the permissibility under the Treaty of the planned diversion of the Kishenganga/Neelum waters.[119] In that case, France had developed a plan to divert water for the generation of hydro-electricity from Lake Lanoux, which is situated in the French Pyrenees near the border with Spain, and to return an equivalent amount of water to the Carol River before it flows into Spain.[120] Spain objected, claiming that the French project breached the treaty governing the parties' use of the waters by removing water from its natural flow into Spain.[121] The *Lake Lanoux* Tribunal ruled that France's diversion was compliant with its treaty obligations toward Spain. In Pakistan's view, even assuming its relevance, *Lake Lanoux* can be distinguished from the present situation as the waters in that case were to be pumped back into the Carol River before they reached Spain.[122] In contrast, the KHEP contemplates a diversion of the waters that does not allow those waters to rejoin the Kishenganga/Neelum River.

182. In sum, for Pakistan, concern over India's control of the waters was a constant element of the Treaty-drafting process. The balance achieved was the result of many years of negotiations aimed at bridging the Parties' conflicting interests; the result of that process should be maintained.[123]

India's arguments

183. In India's view, Pakistan misconstrues the *travaux préparatoires* of the Treaty. India maintains that evidence from the Treaty's negotiating history suggests that Pakistan wanted "control/let flow" to be a purpose of the Treaty, but India "would never have agreed to that, and even the Bank firmly rejected it."[124] Not once, India argues, does the drafting history state or imply that the Treaty drafters had the objective of ensuring that India not diminish the flow of water to Pakistan.[125] The word "control" does not appear in the relevant articles.[126]

184. According to India, Pakistan agreed to proceed on the basis of the principles set out in the World Bank's letter of 8 November 1951 which stated that "[t]he water resources of the Indus basin should be co-operatively developed and used in such a manner as most effectively to promote the economic

[119] Pakistan's Reply, paras. 2.6–2.7, referring to *Affaire du Lac Lanoux (France* v. *Spain)*, Award of 16 November 1957, 12 R.I.A.A. 281 (French original), 1974 Y.B. Int'l L. Comm'n, vol. 2, part 2, p. 194 (1976) (English translation) (Annex IN-LX-2) ("*Lake Lanoux*").

[120] *Ibid.*

[121] *Ibid*, p. 196.

[122] Pakistan's Reply, para. 2.7, fn. 5.

[123] Pakistan's Memorial, paras. 1.47, 1.55.

[124] India's Counter-Memorial, para. 2.77.

[125] India's Counter-Memorial, para. 2.75.

[126] Hearing Tr., (Day 5), 24 August 2012, at 36:1–2.

development of the Indus Basin as a unit."[127] The World Bank rejected Pakistan's proposal to structure the Treaty around a concept of "protecting existing uses from existing sources" and instead proposed that the waters be divided; both Parties agreed to this approach which formed the basis for the further conclusion of the Treaty.[128] India considers that the Treaty was purposefully designed around a "principle of freedom of action," while also giving the Parties different rights, as appropriate to their differing interests and geographies.[129]

185. India additionally maintains that a key principle to the Treaty was that "there should be nothing in the [T]reaty which would stand in the way of optimum utilisation of the water resources allocated to either party."[130] This fundamental principle was affirmed, in India's view, in the determination made in 2007 by a neutral expert regarding a difference arising under the Treaty in relation to India's Baglihar hydro-electric project located on the Chenab river ("*Baglihar*").[131] The Neutral Expert determined that both States' "rights and obligations ... should be read in the light of new technical norms and new standards as provided for by the Treaty."[132]

186. India contends that the production of hydro-electric power has "always been contemplated as an integral part, and indeed objective," of the approach to the development of the Indus basin taken by the Treaty.[133] India relies on a 1951 letter from the President of the World Bank, referring to power generation, and to similar exchanges during the course of the nine-year negotiation period.[134] It also refers to a statement by India's principal representative to the negotiations that to deny India the right to develop hydro-electric power would be "contrary to the purposes and the spirit of the Bank Proposal."[135] India asserts that by 1959 Pakistan had accepted India's right to generate hydro-electric power on the Western Rivers, as reflected in the Heads of Agreement of 15 September 1959.[136] India also cites the press release issued on

[127] India's Counter-Memorial, para. 2.47, quoting Letter from Eugene R. Black, President of the World Bank to Pakistan's Prime Minister Khawaja Nazimuddin, 8 November 1951, (Annex IN-33), (an identical letter was sent to India's Prime Minister Jawaharlal Nehru).

[128] India's Counter-Memorial, paras. 2.55, 2.57.

[129] India's Counter-Memorial, paras. 2.75–2.76, 2.81–2.85.

[130] India's Counter-Memorial, para. 4.14, quoting Niranjan Das Gulhati, *Indus Waters Treaty: an exercise in international mediation* (Allied Publishers, 1973), p. 266.

[131] India's Counter-Memorial, para. 4.15, referring to Raymond Lafitte, *Determination of Neutral Expert on the Baglihar Project*, 12 February 2007, (Annex PK-230), ("*Baglihar* Determination").

[132] India's Counter-Memorial, para. 4.15, quoting *Baglihar* Determination, executive summary p. 5.

[133] India's Counter-Memorial, para. 4.4.

[134] India's Counter-Memorial, paras. 4.4, referring to Letter from Eugene R. Black, President of the World Bank to Pakistan's Prime Minister Khawaja Nazimuddin, 8 November 1951, (Annex IN-33), (an identical letter was sent to India's Prime Minister Jawaharlal Nehru).

[135] India's Counter-Memorial, para. 4.9, quoting Niranjan Das Gulhati's letter to W.A.B. Iliff, Vice President of the World Bank, 24 December 1957, (Annex IN-47).

[136] India's Counter-Memorial, para. 4.12, referring to Heads of Agreement, 15 September 1959, (Annex PK-10).

the signing of the Treaty which specifically mentions that the Treaty permits India's use of the upstream water for the generation of hydro-electric power, as well as for irrigation.[137]

187. India compares this case to the 1957 *Lake Lanoux* arbitration between France and Spain. In India's view, *Lake Lanoux* is similar insofar as Spain argued there that the French project was "calculated to enable it ... to bring pressure to bear on the other signatory" and sought to prevent it.[138] In that case, the Tribunal stated that it was not for it

> to judge the reasons or experiences which might lead the Spanish Government to give expression to a certain anxiety.... Moreover, the French Government's proposals ... include 'the assurance that it will not in any case, interfere with the regime thus established.' ... The Tribunal must, therefore, answer the question submitted by the *compromis* on the basis of this assurance.[139]

Like Spain, Pakistan cannot insist on a further guarantee that India does not intend to harm Pakistan: bad faith cannot be presumed.[140] India believes that "fifty years of interference-free practice" under the Treaty "should be assurance enough for Pakistan"[141] and that Pakistan's "tap" concern is an unjustified preoccupation with the 1948 East Punjab/West Punjab incident.[142] Since that initial, isolated incident, India emphasizes, no further interference with deliveries to Pakistan has occurred.[143]

188. India also refers to the *Lake Lanoux* Tribunal's concluding observation that there is not, "in the generally accepted principles of international law, a rule which forbids a State, acting to protect its legitimate interests, from placing itself in a situation which enables it in fact, in violation of its international obligations, to do even serious injury to a neighbouring State."[144] Although India emphasizes that it has no intention to harm Pakistan in this way, international law does not prohibit activities merely on the basis of a potential to harm. "If it did, no State could situate a chemical plant, a nuclear power plant, or any other kind of potentially hazardous activity in a border region."[145]

189. Finally, India contends that Pakistan has not identified any support for its claim that India has no right permanently to divert the entirety of the waters of the Kishenganga/Neelum.[146] Subject to the express conditions for

---

[137] India's Counter-Memorial, para. 2.20, referring to World Bank's press release, 19 September 1960, (Annex IN-51).

[138] India's Counter-Memorial, para. 4.19, quoting *Lake Lanoux*, p. 196.

[139] *Lake Lanoux*, p. 196.

[140] India's Counter-Memorial, para. 4.21, referring to *Lake Lanoux*, p. 196.

[141] India's Counter-Memorial, para. 4.21.

[142] India's Counter-Memorial, para. 4.51; *see also* para. 132 of this Partial Award.

[143] India's Counter-Memorial, paras. 2.34–2.41.

[144] India's Counter-Memorial, para. 4.22, quoting *Lake Lanoux*, p. 196.

[145] India's Counter-Memorial, para. 4.22.

[146] India's Counter-Memorial, paras. 4.80–4.81.

diversion, India maintains that the Treaty gives it an "unrestricted" right in this regard,[147] as discussed further in the next section.

2. The Parties' arguments on the Treaty provisions governing hydro-electric projects

190. Consistently with the Parties' disagreement on the governing principles of the Treaty (outlined in the previous section), the Parties also disagree on the Treaty's regulatory framework for hydro-electric projects on the Western Rivers. Both Parties accept that the construction of the KHEP is permitted by the Treaty only if it falls under Article III(2)(*d*) which allows for "[g]eneration of hydro-electric power, as set out in Annexure D." Annexure D elaborates specifically on the "Generation of Hydro-electric Power by India on the Western Rivers." The Parties accept that the KHEP would be permitted if it met the requirements of Annexure D, but differ as to the nature of those requirements.[148]

191. The Parties' arguments focus, first, on analyzing the language of Article III(2) concerning the permitted uses of the waters within the drainage basin of the river in question.[149] Next, they turn to the purpose and meaning of the relevant paragraphs of Annexure D, particularly Paragraph 15, which dictates the scope of permissible diversion of waters for purposes of a hydro-electric power plant.[150] Finally, the Parties disagree about the conditions governing

[147] India's Counter-Memorial, para. 4.81.

[148] Pakistan's Memorial, paras. 5.10–5.17; India's Counter-Memorial, para. 4.79; Pakistan's Reply, para. 2.50.

[149] Article III(2) provides:

> India shall be under an obligation to let flow all the waters of the Western Rivers, and shall not permit any interference with these waters, except for the following uses, restricted (except as provided in item (*c*)(ii) of Paragraph 5 of Annexure C) in the case of each of the rivers, The Indus, The Jhelum and The Chenab, to the drainage basin thereof:
>
> (*a*) Domestic Use;
>
> (*b*) Non-Consumptive Use;
>
> (*c*) Agricultural Use, as set out in Annexure C; and
>
> (*d*) Generation of hydro-electric power, as set out in Annexure D.

[150] Paragraph 15 of Annexure D provides:

> ... [T]he works connected with a Plant shall be so operated that (*a*) the volume of water received in the river upstream of the Plant, during any period of seven consecutive days, shall be delivered into the river below the Plant during the same seven-day period, and (*b*) in any one period of 24 hours within that seven-day period, the volume delivered into the river below the Plant shall be not less than 30%, and not more than 130%, of the volume received in the river above the Plant during the same 24-hour period: Provided however that:
>
> [...]
>
> (iii) Where a Plant is located on a Tributary of the Jhelum on which Pakistan has any Agricultural use or hydro-electric use, the water released below the Plant may be delivered, if necessary, into another Tributary but only to the extent that the then existing Agricultural

whether the water released below a hydro-electric plant may be delivered into another tributary.

192. Pakistan's view is that the KHEP's planned diversion of the Kishenganga/Neelum River is incompatible with the meaning of the term "Run-of-River Plant" under the Treaty. Pakistan argues that the provision of Annexure D permitting delivery of water released below a hydro-electric plant into another tributary does not establish a right to divert permanently the entirety of the waters. Even if the KHEP is permitted under this provision, Pakistan contends that the use of the electricity generated must be restricted to the Jhelum River's drainage basin. India contests each of Pakistan's assertions.

(a) *"Restricted ... to the drainage basin thereof"*

193. The Parties first disagree on the scope of the language in Article III(2) that restricts permissible Indian uses of the waters of the Western Rivers to the drainage basin of the appropriate river—here, the Jhelum.

Pakistan's arguments

194. Pakistan submits that Article III(2) prohibits India from utilizing the waters of any tributary of the Jhelum River (including the Kishenganga/Neelum) for the generation of power for general use outside the drainage basin of the Jhelum, as is envisaged with respect to the power to be generated by the KHEP. Put differently, any electricity generated under the exception to the "let flow" obligation of Article III(2) must be used within the drainage basin of the Jhelum.[151] Pakistan maintains that under India's alternative interpretation, the drainage basin restriction would "add nothing so far as the generation of hydro-electric power is concerned."[152] Pakistan is particularly concerned that were the Treaty to be interpreted otherwise, India's potential uses on the Western Rivers would be limitless, depleting a resource that is critical for Pakistan.[153]

195. Pakistan refers to the 15 September 1959 Head of Agreement draft of what became Article III, which treated hydro-electric uses separately from the other three exceptions.[154] According to a table of amendments pre-

Use or hydro-electric use by Pakistan on the former Tributary would not be adversely affected.

[151] Pakistan's Memorial, para. 5.26.

[152] Pakistan's Reply, paras. 2.46–2.47.

[153] Pakistan's Memorial, para. 5.25.

[154] Pakistan's Memorial, referring to Article IV of the Heads of Agreement, 15 September 1959, (Annex PK-10), provides as follows:

Arrangements Concerning Western Rivers

(1) India shall let flow the waters of the Western Rivers free from any interference except for the following uses restricted in the case of each river to the drainage basin of that river.

(i) Domestic uses;

pared by Pakistan, the language appearing in the final version of the Treaty reflects a purposeful change, describing the generation of hydro-electric power "more mildly as a use and not as something to which India is 'entitled'" and restricting this use "in the case of each of the Western Rivers to the drainage basin thereof."[155]

196. By way of comparison, Pakistan discusses how Annexure C to the Treaty contains an express exception to Article III(2)'s drainage basin restriction with respect to India's agricultural use of the Western Rivers. According to Pakistan, Annexure C permits India to withdraw specified maximum quantities of water for a small area outside the drainage basin of the Chenab. This exception is, in Pakistan's view, the only deviation from the foundational principle prohibiting use outside the drainage basin.[156]

India's arguments

197. India argues that Pakistan misinterprets the word "use" in the phrase "except for the following uses." For India, the "use" in question under Art. III(2)(*d*) is the use *of the waters* for the generation of hydro-electric power, not the use *of the electricity* generated. Power generation must take place in the drainage basin, but the power can be transported elsewhere.[157] India maintains that there is no textual support for Pakistan's argument. Rather, Treaty provisions allowing the return of water to another tributary confirm the framers' intent to control the water rather than the electricity produced by the water.[158] Referring to Article XI(1)(*a*) of the Treaty, which provides: "(1) It is expressly understood that (*a*) this Treaty governs the rights and obligations of each Party *with respect only to the use of the waters of the Rivers* and matters incidental thereto," India argues that it is clear that how India makes use of the electricity generated from the KHEP is not governed by the Treaty.[159]

(ii) Non-consumptive uses; and

(iii) Consumptive uses as set out below

The question of consumptive uses is being approached on the basis of fixing a quantum of use to be specified in the treaty.

(2) India shall be entitled to generate hydro-electric power on the Western Rivers in accordance with the provisions of Annex. "B".

(3) Pakistan shall be entitled to the unrestricted use of the waters of the Western Rivers, except to the extent specified in Paragraphs (1) and (2) of this Article.

This text was modified in the final text of the Treaty to include hydro-electric use alongside other uses restricted to the drainage basin of a particular river.

[155] Pakistan's Memorial, paras. 5.29–5.32, quoting Comparative Table of Provision of the Heads of Agreement of 15 September 1959 and the Draft Indus Waters Treaty, (Annex PK-14), (originally appended to Mueeneddin's letter to W. Shaikh, 15 December 1959, (Annex PK-13).

[156] Pakistan's Memorial, para. 5.28.

[157] India's Counter-Memorial, para. 4.39.

[158] India's Counter-Memorial, para. 4.76.

[159] India's Rejoinder, para. 1.37, quoting Treaty, Art. XI(1)(*a*), emphasis added by India.

198. India further observes that Pakistan has not previously raised this objection in relation to at least four projects in other locations which contribute their generated power to locations outside their respective drainage basins.[160]

(b) *Run-of-River Plants*

199. In light of India's present design of the KHEP as a Run-of-River Plant, both Parties look to the Treaty provisions regulating this type of hydro-electric project as the criteria for assessing the legality of the design and operation of the KHEP. Part 3 of Annexure D sets out considerations for the design and operation of new Run-of-River Plants such as the KHEP. Paragraph 15, on which the Parties focus their attention, provides:

> Subject to the provisions of Paragraph 17, the works connected with a Plant shall be so operated that (*a*) the volume of water received in the river upstream of the Plant, during any period of seven consecutive days, shall be delivered into the river below the Plant during the same seven-day period, and (*b*) in any one period of 24 hours within that seven-day period, the volume delivered into the river below the Plant shall be not less than 30%, and not more than 130%, of the volume received in the river above the Plant during the same 24-hour period: Provided however that:
>
> [...]
>
> (iii) where a Plant is located on a Tributary of The Jhelum on which Pakistan has any Agricultural Use or hydro-electric use, the water released below the Plant may be delivered, if necessary, into another Tributary but only to the extent that the then existing Agricultural Use or hydro-electric use by Pakistan on the former Tributary would not be adversely affected.

200. Pakistan argues that the KHEP does not meet the criteria of Part 3 of Annexure D and therefore falls outside the realm of permissible projects. India asserts the contrary, maintaining that the KHEP meets the relevant provisions of Annexure D and that Pakistan's present position contradicts its earlier representation—upon which India appropriately relied—that the diversion of waters into another tributary is permitted under Annexure D.

Pakistan's arguments

201. According to Pakistan, Part 3 of Annexure D contains two sets of provisions: one addressing the design of a Run-of-River Plant and a second concerning the operation of such a Plant. In this respect, Pakistan submits that Paragraphs 8 to 13 of Part 3 of Annexure D relate to design, while Paragraphs 14 to 17 deal with the operation of the Plant.[161] In particular, Paragraph 15 "presumes and provides for the operation of a plant."[162]

[160] India's Counter-Memorial, paras. 4.40–4.41.

[161] Pakistan's Memorial, para. 5.14; Hearing Tr., (Day 4), 23 August 2012, at 15:10 to 16:4, 16:15 to 18:1.

[162] Pakistan's Memorial, para. 5.17; Hearing Tr., (Day 4), 23 August 2012, at 18:1–3.

202. Pakistan argues that the KHEP is not designed to operate within the bounds of Paragraph 15, particularly the criteria on the delivery of water into another tributary. In Pakistan's view, this provision allows the occasional delivery of waters to another tributary but does not provide for a project based on a large-scale and permanent diversion to a "quite different location."[163] Pakistan considers that Paragraph 15(iii) "does not seek to establish the basis for a right to design a wholly new type of plant, i.e. a plant that does not allow the river to flow, but instead dams that river [and] permanently channels the entirety of its waters."[164] The KHEP does not even meet India's own definition of a Run-of-River Plant, Pakistan notes; the Bureau of Indian Standards states that "[i]n such stations, the normal course of the river is not materially altered."[165]

203. In further support of the incompatibility of the KHEP with the provisions for Run-of-River Plants, Pakistan points out that Appendix II to Annexure D sets out particular information regarding new projects that India is obliged to submit to Pakistan and that—although such information includes statistics related to the design of the head-race and tail-race of the new Plant—there is "no equivalent category to allow for details of a power tunnel such as India seeks to construct."[166] For this reason, Pakistan asserts that such an arrangement was not contemplated and is therefore not permitted by the Treaty.

204. Turning to the Treaty's drafting history, Pakistan rejects India's premise that Paragraph 15(iii) was introduced into the Treaty with the Kishenganga project in mind. Pakistan insists that the CWPC Letter on which India relies reveals nothing about the meaning of Annexure D and the subject of this dispute. Pakistan points out that the part of the CWPC Letter on which India places emphasis discusses "Storage Works," which are regulated by Annexure E, and offers no insight into the drafters' intentions regarding Annexure D. A draft of Paragraph 15(iii), Pakistan observes, had already been introduced into Annexure D on 23 April 1960; thus, "[i]f a comment with respect to a Kishenganga project had been intended to influence the wording of Annexure D, it is evident that a comment would have been made by reference to the draft of Annexure D that the Chairman [of the CWPC] had before him."[167] Accordingly, Pakistan concludes, the CWPC Letter cannot shed light on the meaning of Paragraph 15(iii) of Annexure D.[168]

205. As to India's assertion that no prohibition of inter-tributary transfers was incorporated into Annexure E in anticipation of a project like the

[163] Pakistan's Memorial, para. 5.17. *See also* para. 220 of this Partial Award concerning Pakistan's argument that Paragraph 15 permits diversion in case of an emergency.

[164] Pakistan's Memorial, para. 5.20; Pakistan's Reply, para. 2.55. In speaking of the diversion of the "entirety" of the waters, Pakistan refers to the 58.4 m3/s that will be diverted at the KHEP dam.

[165] Pakistan's Reply, para. 1.35, referring to India's Counter-Memorial, para. 7.30.

[166] Pakistan's Memorial, para. 5.20, fn. 185.

[167] Pakistan's Reply, para. 1.12, referring to Draft of Treaty, Annexure D, 23 April 1960, (Annex PK-20).

[168] Pakistan's Reply, para. 2.62.

KHEP, Pakistan submits that if India had genuinely intended in 1960 to realize such a project, India would have sought its express inclusion.[169] India identified no record of such an attempt. Pakistan also contests India's submission that Paragraph 10 of Annexure E was included in the Treaty to make the implementation of the KHEP possible. Paragraph 10 of Annexure E provides that "any Storage Work to be constructed on a Tributary of The Jhelum on which Pakistan has any Agricultural Use or hydro-electric use shall be so designed and operated as not to adversely affect the then existing Agricultural Use or hydro-electric use on that Tributary." Nothing in Paragraph 10, Pakistan emphasizes, suggests permission for an inter-tributary transfer.[170]

India's arguments

206. India maintains that the KHEP conforms to the specifications of Annexure D and submits that there is no basis for Pakistan's argument that Paragraph 15(iii) does not establish a right to divert permanently the entirety of the waters of the Kishenganga/Neelum into another tributary. First, India disputes Pakistan's contention that the latter portion of the Annexure, including Paragraph 15, pertains to the Plant's operation rather than to considerations of design. India argues that the design and operation of a Plant are inextricably linked;[171] to disregard Paragraph 15 because it supposedly addresses operation rather than design would, in India's view, be senseless, as India must necessarily refer to provisions regarding operation in the course of arriving at the design of the project. Furthermore, India considers Pakistan's interpretation of Paragraph 15(iii) to be incompatible with the "unrestricted" nature of India's right to use the waters of the Western Rivers. Provided that India complies with the express restrictions of Annexure D, the latter makes clear that its ability to generate hydro-electric power is to be unrestricted.[172] India also notes that Pakistan's complaint that the KHEP will divert the entirety of the waters is in conflict with the river flow data and fails to take into account the waters contributed to the Kishenganga/Neelum from tributaries below the Gurez site.[173] It would be impossible for India to divert the "entirety" of the waters.[174]

207. According to India, inter-tributary transfer was envisaged at the time of the Treaty's drafting.[175] India contends that it "knew in the mid-1950s"

---

169 Pakistan's Reply, para. 1.15.

170 Pakistan's Reply, para. 1.16.

171 India's Rejoinder, para. 1.52.

172 India's Counter-Memorial, para. 4.31.

173 India's Counter-Memorial, paras. 4.82–4.85. According to India, the data, and the geography, make clear that additional waters not accounted for in Pakistan's data will contribute to the flow below Gurez. Even without accounting for these, Pakistan's own studies show that the KHEP will not divert the entirety of the waters (showing an average 3.1 m3/s of water would be available from the catchment downstream of the KHEP up to the Line of Control even in January, the month of lowest flow). India maintains that even with the KHEP, 89 percent of the flows would still be available for power generation at NJHEP.

174 India's Counter-Memorial, para. 4.83.

175 India's Counter-Memorial, para. 4.77.

that a diversion project on the Kishenganga/Neelum was possible and that it ensured that the Treaty contained a provision designed to permit the implementation of such a project.[176] India argues that the CWPC Letter shows that India was contemplating hydro-electric projects on the Kishenganga/Neelum "that would involve inter-tributary deliveries of water, and that the Treaty framers were aware that such a project was envisaged in the Jhelum Basin."[177]

208. In India's view, Pakistan also recognized the possibility of inter-tributary transfers in 1960. The Pakistani Cabinet decisions of 15 February 1960 recommended that a protection against prejudice to downstream use of the waters be reflected in Annexure D, "so that the uses in the Azad Kashmir [are] not affected adversely by inter-tributary diversions."[178] Thus, Pakistan "may be said to have implicitly accepted the fact that the KHEP could be constructed on the basis of ... Pakistan's acceptance of that provision [Paragraph 15(iii)]."[179]

209. Since 1960, India observes, Pakistan has repeatedly accepted that inter-tributary transfer is permitted by Annexure D.[180] In one instance, in 2005, the Pakistani Commissioner stated Pakistan's belief that inter-tributary transfers were not permitted under Annexure E for Storage Works, but were permitted under Annexure D for Run-of-River Plants.[181] After having agreed that inter-tributary transfer was permitted for Run-of-River Plants, however, Pakistan changed its position (upon learning of India's change in design) to argue that diversion is not permitted under the Treaty.[182]

(c) "Where a Plant is located on a Tributary of the Jhelum ... water released below the Plant may be delivered ... into another Tributary"

210. Pakistan argues that the planned KHEP diversion delivers the water from upstream of the Plant into another tributary despite the Treaty's

---

[176] India's Counter-Memorial, para. 4.23. According to India, Paragraph 15(iii) was intentionally inserted in the Treaty on the basis of a 1954 hydro-electric survey of the Indus basin carried out by India's CWPC, which identified the possibility of building a hydro-electric scheme on the Kishenganga. *See* India's Counter-Memorial, para. 4.70.

[177] India's Counter-Memorial, para. 3.19–3.20. India also considers that the CWPC Letter makes clear that "'there is only one tributary of the Jhelum' where a scheme such as the KHEP is possible." India's Counter-Memorial, para. 4.92. A proposal by the Jammu and Kashmir State Government in 1981 stated that "a project delivering waters from the Kishenganga through a[n] underground tunnel to a point just above Lake Wullar was the only suitable location based on engineering and geological considerations." India's Counter-Memorial, para. 3.23, referring to Outline Proposal on KHEP, December 1981, (Annex IN-57).

[178] India's Rejoinder, para. 2.76, quoting Decisions of the Cabinet Committee on the Draft of the Treaty, Meeting, 15 February 1960, (Annex PK-17).

[179] India's Counter-Memorial, para. 4.70.

[180] India's Rejoinder, para. 2.44.

[181] India's Counter-Memorial, para. 4.78, referring to Record of the 93rd Meeting of the Commission, New Delhi, 9–13 February 2005, (Annex PK-29), para. 38.

[182] India's Rejoinder, para. 2.44.

requirement that only "the water released below the Plant" be diverted. Pakistan also contests India's reading of the words "another tributary."

Pakistan's arguments

211. In Pakistan's view, the KHEP does not fall within the scheme laid out by Paragraph 15(iii) because the KHEP is not a "Plant located on a Tributary of The Jhelum" as required by that Paragraph. Only the KHEP's dam is located on a tributary of the Jhelum (the Kishenganga/Neelum), as the "power plant" is 23 kilometres away in a separate catchment area.[183] Pakistan maintains that with this design the KHEP "cannot correctly be characterized as a 'Plant located on a Tributary of The Jhelum.'"[184]

212. Pakistan also refers to the requirement in Appendix II to Annexure D that India provide a map "showing the location of the site" and "the catchment area of the Tributary above the site."[185] As both provisions refer to "the site" of the Plant, Pakistan argues that the Treaty drafters and Parties accepted that the powerhouse and the "Tributary above the site" are to be located in the same catchment area. The KHEP powerhouse, however, is located in the Bonar Nallah catchment area rather than that of the "Tributary above the site" of the dam, the Kishenganga.[186]

213. Even if the KHEP were to be characterized as a Plant on the Kishenganga, Pakistan maintains that it falls outside the scheme of Paragraph 15(iii) because it is not designed in compliance with the Paragraph's requirement that "water released below the Plant may be delivered, if necessary, into another Tributary"; rather, in the case of the KHEP, the water only reaches the Plant *after* it has been delivered elsewhere.[187] According to Pakistan, India plans to deliver the water to another tributary upstream of the Plant, rather than below it. Pakistan considers that such delivery is only permitted after the water has passed through the turbines of the Plant.[188]

214. Furthermore, Pakistan contends that the Bonar Nallah is not "another Tributary," as intended by the Treaty, as it is not within the watershed of the Kishenganga. According to Pakistan, the "basic rule" of Paragraph 15 is that "water in a given river above/below a given Plant should equal out over a seven day period." To be consistent with this principle, the tributary into which the water is released below the Plant must be located within the same watershed as the tributary where the Plant is located.[189] Here, unless the waters flow into a tributary of the Kishenganga, these flow provisions will be ineffectual.

[183] Pakistan's Reply, paras. 1.32–1.33.

[184] Pakistan's Reply, para. 1.32.

[185] Pakistan's Reply, para. 1.33, quoting Treaty, Annexure D, Appendix II, Paras. 1 and 2(*a*).

[186] Pakistan's Reply, para. 1.33.

[187] Pakistan's Reply, para. 1.30.

[188] Hearing Tr., (Day 4), 23 August 2012, at 35:8–25.

[189] Pakistan's Reply, para. 1.34.

In other words, Pakistan contends that waters that pass through the KHEP should go back into the same river, "hence balancing out the overall impacts of operation of the Plant."[190]

215. Finally, Pakistan submits that the design of the KHEP also violates the Treaty by creating storage in the Wular Lake, after the water flows from the KHEP into the Bonar Nallah. Storage on the Jhelum Main (which includes the Wular Lake as a "connecting lake") is not permitted to India at all, and neither Paragraph 15(iii) nor Annexure D generally create an exception to this rule.[191]

India's arguments

216. India asserts that the KHEP falls within the express terms of Paragraph 15(iii) of Annexure D because the Plant is located on the Kishenganga—a "Tributary" within the meaning of Paragraph 15(iii). In India's view, Pakistan misinterprets the term "Plant," which properly refers to the entire complex from the dam, through the tunnel and powerhouse, and to the tailrace.[192] Therefore, the water released below "the Plant" will indeed be delivered into another tributary as required by the Treaty: "it will be released from the tailrace of the Plant into the Bonar Nallah."[193]

217. India also interprets "another Tributary" differently. India maintains that the construction of Paragraph 15(iii) makes it clear that "another Tributary" means any other tributary of the Jhelum and is not limited to a tributary within the watershed of the river on which the Plant is located. In India's view, Pakistan's argument contradicts the terms of Paragraph 15(iii), which first refers to "a Tributary of the Jhelum" and then refers to "another Tributary," implying a further reference to tributaries of the Jhelum.[194]

218. To make use of the difference in elevation to generate power, it is inevitable, India claims, that the release of the waters below the Plant into another tributary will involve delivery into a different catchment area.[195] Annexure D is not an obstacle. India's obligation to provide a map of the "catchment area of the Tributary above site" pursuant to Appendix II to Annexure D is unrelated to the location of the powerhouse.[196] When Paragraph 15(iii) refers to the location of a "Plant" on a tributary, it is referring to the dam. When it refers to the water released below the "Plant," it is referring

[190] Pakistan's Reply, para. 1.34. Hearing Tr., (Day 4), 23 August 2012, at 19:4–19.

[191] Hearing Tr., (Day 3), 22 August 2012, at 178:11–18, 191:9 to 192:24; (Day 4), 23 August 2012, at 68:15–17.

[192] India's Rejoinder, paras. 2.60–2.70, referring to a 1959 draft of the Article that uses "powerhouse" rather than "Plant" before the drafters concluded that "Plant" was more appropriate. Heads of Agreement, 15 September 1959, (Annex PK-10); Hearing Tr., (Day 9), 30 August 2012, at 28:15–32:23.

[193] India's Rejoinder, para. 1.46(ii); *see also* Hearing Tr., (Day 5), 24 August 2012, at 159:1–2.

[194] India's Rejoinder, para. 2.73.

[195] India's Rejoinder, paras. 1.34–1.35.

[196] India's Rejoinder, para. 2.74.

to the powerhouse.[197] Accordingly, Pakistan's argument that the powerhouse and the "Tributary above the site" are to be located in the same catchment area is unfounded. Moreover, to interpret this provision as Pakistan suggests would defy gravity, requiring the powerhouse to be located upstream of the dam.[198]

(d) "If necessary"

219. The Parties also diverge as to the meaning of the phrase "if necessary" under Paragraph 15(iii), which limits circumstances under which diversion of water is permitted.

Pakistan's arguments

220. The ordinary meaning of "necessary," Pakistan argues, is "indispensable, requisite, needful; that cannot be done without."[199] Pakistan contends that India has not shown that the KHEP diversion is "necessary" pursuant to Paragraph 15(iii), in accordance with this ordinary meaning; rather, Pakistan maintains, India has given a misguided interpretation to the term "necessary." Pakistan notes that the Indian Commissioner's letter dated 25 May 2007 defines "necessity" in terms of maximizing the utility of the natural head difference for hydro-electric power.[200] From this, Pakistan concludes that India (wrongly) seeks to define "necessary" as "desirable." According to Pakistan, India's proposed low-threshold meaning would make any hydro-electric project possible under the Treaty by reference to its engineering or economic feasibility.[201] In Pakistan's view, by interpreting "necessary" as meaning only what is necessary for the generation of hydro-electric power, India arrives at too narrow a restriction that is without basis in the Treaty or elsewhere.[202] Rather than focusing on India's energy needs, Pakistan submits that the scope of "necessity" must be reasoned and based on evidence, which leads to the conclusion that diversion is to be used only in case of emergency.[203]

221. Pakistan turns to a variety of sources to elaborate the scope of necessity. It first refers to the meaning of "necessary" in the context of treaties of "Friendship, Commerce, and Navigation." The necessity-based exceptions of several of these treaties were discussed in the *Nicaragua*[204] and *Oil Platforms*[205]

---

[197] India's Rejoinder, para. 2.70.

[198] India's Rejoinder, para. 2.74.

[199] Pakistan's Memorial, para. 5.39, quoting the Shorter Oxford Dictionary.

[200] Pakistan's Memorial, para. 5.36, referring to the Indian Commissioner's letter to the Pakistani Commissioner, 25 May 2007, (Annex PK-174), at pp. 2–3.

[201] Pakistan's Memorial, para. 5.37.

[202] Pakistan's Reply, para. 2.65.

[203] Hearing Tr., (Day 4), 23 August 2012, at 27:23 to 28:20.

[204] *Case Concerning the Military and Paramilitary Activities in and Against Nicaragua (Nicaragua* v. *United States of America)*, Merits, Judgment, *I.C.J. Reports 1986*, p. 14, pp. 141–142.

[205] *Oil Platforms (Islamic Republic of Iran* v. *United States of America)*, Judgment, *I.C.J. Reports 2003*, p. 161, p. 183.

cases by the International Court of Justice, where that Court emphasized that conduct alleged to fall within such a provision must be necessary—in the sense of "essential"—to the purpose of the provision.[206] Looking also to the interpretation of necessity in arbitrations under bilateral investment treaties and in the context of the World Trade Organisation, Pakistan submits that the term carries a "continuum" of meanings.[207] Within such a continuum, however, the diversion could only be necessary in the very broadest sense, insofar as India (like any other State) needs electricity.[208] In Pakistan's view, however, the Treaty contemplates far more urgent necessity.[209]

222. Pakistan further posits that an element of proportionality is inherent in the term "necessary," as developed in international law jurisprudence.[210] The effect of the KHEP on Pakistan's rights under international law, in particular international environmental law, is relevant, in Pakistan's view, to whether the KHEP is proportionate, and therefore necessary.[211] Pakistan notes "the general obligation of States to ensure that activities within their jurisdiction and control respect the environment of other States or of areas beyond national control," as stated by the Tribunal in the *Iron Rhine* arbitration and by the International Court of Justice in the *Gabčíkovo-Nagymaros* judgment.[212] According to Pakistan, that principle is relevant in the present case and requires "a strict approach to the question of what is necessary and/or proportionate," insofar as any adverse impact on the environment resulting from India's acts would be contrary to customary international law.[213]

223. To make any proportionality analysis possible, Pakistan submits that India should have taken a number of steps. First, Pakistan contends that to establish what is "proportionate and/or necessary," India would have had to conduct an environmental impact assessment (or work with Pakistan to carry out one) to evaluate downstream effects.[214] In Pakistan's view, India has not made the compulsory assessment because the EIA that took place does not address the area below the dam site.[215] Second, Pakistan argues that India

[206] Pakistan's Memorial, para. 5.40.

[207] Pakistan's Memorial, para. 5.41.

[208] Pakistan's Memorial, para. 5.42.

[209] Pakistan's Memorial, para. 5.42. Pakistan posits the example of a drought in the basin of one tributary, giving rise to a need for inter-tributary transfer.

[210] Pakistan's Memorial, para. 5.43. Hearing Tr., (Day 4), 23 August 2012, at 114:8–11; 117:7–9.

[211] Pakistan's Memorial, para. 5.44; Hearing Tr., (Day 4), 23 August 2012, at 115: 14–15.

[212] Pakistan's Memorial, para. 5.44; Pakistan asserts that the principle articulated by the International Court of Justice in the *Pulp Mills* judgment that States must exercise due diligence with respect to activities bearing an impact on the environment of other States is also relevant to the interpretation of "necessary." Pakistan's Memorial, para. 5.44, referencing *Pulp Mills on the River Uruguay (Argentina* v. *Uruguay)*, Judgment, *I.C.J. Reports 2010*, p. 14.

[213] Pakistan's Memorial, para. 5.45.

[214] Pakistan's Memorial, paras. 5.44–5.49.

[215] Pakistan's Reply, para. 4.41. Pakistan refers to its expert assessment of India's EIA which "highlights a long series of shortcomings" in the EIA, but in particular, Pakistan notes

should have applied a precautionary approach to its activities, in line with the Rio Declaration on Environment and Development of 1992, particularly in light of the pristine environment below the dam site.[216]

224. Finally, Pakistan submits that "necessary" cannot be understood to be self-judging or subjective. Where other provisions of the Treaty were intended to be self-judging this was expressly indicated; with no such qualification in Annexure D, "necessary" must be understood as an objective test.[217]

India's arguments

225. Based on the Treaty Preamble's attention to "complete and satisfactory utilisation of the waters" and the negotiating record of the Treaty, India argues that "necessary" was intended to refer to that which was "optimal for power generation."[218] The "most complete and satisfactory utilisation" of the waters, India argues, cannot be attained without taking advantage of the difference in elevation between the Kishenganga/Neelum and the Bonar Nallah.[219] Moreover, India notes, the term "necessary" was introduced only late in the negotiations, at the time when Paragraph 15(iii) was modified from a prohibitory to an enabling provision; before that change, necessity was not an element in determining whether diversion was permissible. This was, indeed, a change proposed by India, and India submits that it did not intend for the term to be used in the strict sense of "cannot be done without."[220] On the contrary, India submits that it had in mind during the negotiation of Paragraph 15(iii) the possibility of a transfer from the Kishenganga/Neelum to Wular Lake.[221]

226. India refers to the Court's 23 September 2011 Order on Interim Measures, noting that therein the Court defined "necessary" as meaning that an action is "required, needed, or essential for a particular purpose"[222] and that this is consistent with India's textual reading that diversion is required for "much needed" power generation.[223] In India's view, Pakistan has failed to consider the area's topography, which makes it necessary to have the water delivered into a second tributary of the Jhelum; production of significant

that the most important area was not part of the Assessment at all. Pakistan's Reply, para. 4.42.

[216] Pakistan's Memorial, para. 5.48.

[217] Pakistan's Memorial, para. 5.39. Hearing Tr., (Day 4), 23 August 2012, at 31:7–16.

[218] India's Counter-Memorial, paras. 4.91–4.108, 4.116. India considers Pakistan's recourse to other treaties and case law to interpret "necessary" to be inapposite and is of the view that the meaning of the term can be ascertained within the terms of the Treaty and its negotiating record. In India's view, the other cases and treaties mentioned by Pakistan provide no guidance to the present arbitration as they involved neither the Parties nor the subject-matter of the case at hand. *See* India's Counter-Memorial, para. 4.86 and accompanying footnotes.

[219] India's Counter-Memorial, para. 4.91.

[220] India's Counter-Memorial, paras. 4.100, 4.102.

[221] India's Counter-Memorial, para. 4.103.

[222] Order on Interim Measures, para. 139.

[223] India's Rejoinder, paras. 1.46, 2.80.

hydro-electric power would not be feasible otherwise.[224] Further, India argues that "necessary" should be seen together with the fact that India's use of the waters "shall be unrestricted"; as India's use is unrestricted, it follows that it is for India to decide whether delivery into another tributary is necessary.[225]

227. India rejects Pakistan's importation of environmental harm principles into the meaning of "necessary" as, in its view, "necessary" concerns the generation of hydro-electric power—not the protection of the environment.[226] Pakistan is wrong, according to India, to say that any harm caused to it by the KHEP is a violation of the Treaty. At the outset, India contends that it conducted an appropriate EIA with respect to all areas for which it was able to obtain information.[227] Next, India submits that, contrary to Pakistan's assertion, no obligation is set forth in the *Pulp Mills* judgment or elsewhere that requires it to seek the assistance of another State to arrange a joint EIA.[228] Moreover, even if the contrary were true, India could only decide what is "necessary" with full details from Pakistan—which Pakistan refused to provide.[229] Finally, India disputes Pakistan's position that a precautionary approach is mandated by the applicable customary law. According to India, "some major countries take the strongly held view that precaution is not customary international law."[230] Moreover, India argues that the concept of precaution could not be applied in a principled manner here due to its many possible meanings.[231]

(e) Interpretation of the phrase "then existing Agricultural Use or hydro-electric use"

228. The Parties dispute the nature of the requirement that delivery into another tributary not cause adverse impact on the "then existing Agricultural Use or hydro-electric use by Pakistan." In particular, the Parties disagree on the meaning of the terms "then existing."

Pakistan's arguments

229. With respect to the timing indicated by the word "then," Pakistan submits that a "then existing use" is—in the ordinary meaning of the words—the use existing at the time of the water's release into the other tributary. Paki-

---

[224] India's Rejoinder, para. 2.84.

[225] India's Rejoinder, para. 2.81.

[226] India's Counter-Memorial, para. 4.116.

[227] India's Counter-Memorial, para. 6.47.

[228] India's Counter-Memorial, para. 6.48. Moreover, in India's view, the *dicta* from the *Pulp Mills* case on which Pakistan relies could not apply to the present dispute because the region affected here is part of India's territory under India's Constitution. India's Counter-Memorial, para. 6.49.

[229] India's Rejoinder, para. 2.104.

[230] India's Counter-Memorial, para. 6.102.

[231] India's Counter-Memorial, para. 6.102.

stan maintains that this reading of the phrase is consistent with the nature of an operational provision; that is, the question of adverse impact is to be tested "at the time of operation."[232] Pakistan contends that this point in time is further evidenced by the use of the present tense in the qualifier "where a Plant is located," which indicates that the Plant is already built and in operation.[233]

230. Pakistan notes that the phrase "then existing" appears in Annexures C, D and E, but submits that there is no common meaning across the different provisions; rather, each contemplates the "moment of action relevant to the particular provision."[234] In Annexure C, which governs agricultural use, "then existing use" refers to the time at which India makes a new agricultural use.[235] The phrase also appears in Annexure E, regarding Storage Works in the following terms:

> Notwithstanding the provisions of Paragraph 7 [which concerns the aggregate storage capacity of all Reservoirs], any Storage Work to be constructed on a Tributary of The Jhelum on which Pakistan has any Agricultural Use or hydro-electric use shall be so designed and operated as not to adversely affect the then existing Agricultural Use or hydro-electric use on that Tributary.[236]

231. The use of the phrase in Annexure E, Pakistan emphasizes, is different from that in Annexure D. Annexure E requires a cut-off date because it addresses a Storage Work "to be constructed" and expressly applies to the design of the Storage Work. In contrast, Paragraph 15(iii) of Annexure D addresses a Run-of-River Plant that "is located" and operating on a given tributary and refers to the time at which water is released from the Plant. Accordingly, Pakistan rejects India's contention of any "common thread" across the meaning of "then existing use" in the different Annexures.[237]

India's arguments

232. India interprets the phrase "then existing use" to mean that any new development by India should not disturb downstream activity by Pakistan as of the date when India communicates to Pakistan its "firm intention" to proceed with a project.[238] To interpret the Treaty as Pakistan suggests, as referring to the time the water is released or "whenever Pakistan might undertake

---

[232] Pakistan's Memorial, para. 5.52.

[233] Pakistan's Reply, paras. 2.74, 2.75.

[234] Hearing Tr., (Day 3), 22 August 2012, at 186 *et seq.*

[235] Paragraph 9 of Annexure C provides in full: "On those Tributaries of The Jhelum on which there is any Agricultural Use or hydro-electric use by Pakistan, any new Agricultural Use by India shall be so made as not to affect adversely the then existing Agriculture Use or hydro-electric use by Pakistan on those Tributaries."

[236] Treaty, Annexure E, Para. 10.

[237] Pakistan's Reply, paras. 2.77–2.83.

[238] India's Counter-Memorial, para. 4.139.

[its use]," would have a chilling effect on any new construction and supplant construction already underway, leading to substantial economic waste.[239]

233. India maintains that Pakistan's position regarding the operational focus of the provision in interpreting "then existing use" is untenable. In Pakistan's operational perspective, "existing use" would have to be read as "intended use"—contrary to the plain meaning of the phrase.[240] India further contends that Pakistan's interpretation would deprive India of its legitimate expectation to be entitled to the most complete and satisfactory utilization of the waters as guaranteed by the Treaty.[241]

234. According to India, the *travaux préparatoires* indicate that a cut-off date was intended by the Treaty drafters.[242] India relies on a letter from the President of the World Bank to the Prime Ministers of India and Pakistan dated 8 November 1951 identifying as an "essential principle" that the "Indus basin water resources are sufficient to continue all existing uses and to meet the further needs of both countries."[243] In India's view, this demonstrates that "existing" refers to "historic" uses and is distinct from those which might be developed to meet future—or "further"—needs. In its 1954 Proposal, the Bank outlined the Parties' views on the approach to "existing uses" and, according to India, "rejected Pakistan's concept of 'protecting existing uses from existing sources' because this would render a 'fair and adequate comprehensive plan' impossible of achievement and unduly limit the flexibility need[ed] for the efficient use of the waters."[244]

235. To identify the appropriate cut-off date, India notes that the provisions of Annexure D require India to provide Pakistan with complete information about its intended design six months before beginning construction. In synchrony with that point in time, India maintains that "uses by Pakistan have to be frozen at the stage when the design is being finalized."[245] In the case of the KHEP, India submits that the cut-off date was—at the latest—June 1994 when the finalized KHEP design (as a Storage Work) was provided to Pakistan.[246]

236. While India did not announce to Pakistan that the KHEP would be a Run-of-River Plant until 2005–2006, India maintains that the change should not affect the cut-off date for ascertaining downstream uses.[247] In any case, the

[239] India's Counter-Memorial, paras. 4.127, 4.128–4.134.

[240] India's Rejoinder, paras. 2.51, 2.53, 2.55, 2.105.

[241] India's Rejoinder, para. 1.18.

[242] India's Counter-Memorial, para. 4.139.

[243] India's Counter-Memorial, para. 4.128, referring to Letter from Eugene R. Black, President of the World Bank to India's Prime Minister Jawaharlal Nehru, 8 November 1951, (Annex IN-33).

[244] India's Counter-Memorial, para. 4.133.

[245] India's Counter-Memorial, para. 4.123.

[246] India's Counter-Memorial, para. 4.124.

[247] India also argues, in the alternative, that even if the cut-off date were determined by reference to the change of the KHEP to a Run-of-River Plant, the NJHEP would still not have

revised Run-of-River design is largely the same as the earlier design: "neither the axis of the dam, the location and layout of the project, nor its installed capacity or diversion works have changed … [nor has the] delivery of water to Bonar-Madmati Nallah."[248] Moreover, India considers the revisions advantageous to Pakistan: the height of the dam and the pondage capacity upstream of the dam were reduced.[249]

237. In support of its interpretation, India emphasizes the context given to "then existing" by the word "located" in the opening phrase of Paragraph 15(iii), which begins with "where a Plant is located on a Tributary." Appendix II to Annexure D, India notes, requires India to provide to Pakistan—in advance of construction—information on the Plant's planned design, including a section of information relating to the "Location of Plant." In India's view, "[h]aving identified the location of the planned Plant and having provided that information to Pakistan …, India is deemed to have 'located' the Plant."[250] A Plant does not need to be in operation to be "located," and the time at which a Plant is located through the exchange of information with Pakistan provides the time by reference to which "then existing" uses are to be assessed.

238. As further support, India compares the meaning of "then existing use" in Paragraph 15 to the context of the phrase in other provisions of the Treaty. India argues that it is clear from the placement of the phrase in Annexures C and E that a common meaning was intended: any new development by India should avoid disturbing the activities by Pakistan downstream which are already using the water of the river.[251]

(f) Whether Pakistan has established an "existing … use"

239. Turning to the concept of "existing use," the Parties agree that where Pakistan has shown an agricultural or hydro-electric use to exist at the relevant time, India's Run-of-River Plant cannot have an adverse impact on that use. The Parties disagree, however, as to what constitutes an "existing … use" and as to whether Pakistan has demonstrated existing uses on the Kishenganga/Neelum that must be taken into account.

Pakistan's arguments

240. Pakistan argues that India's plans to build a hydro-electric project in accordance with the Treaty must take account of "specific plans for uses" of the waters at specific locations to which Pakistan is "firmly committed."[252]

---

been a "then existing use" as construction on the NJHEP was initiated only in 2008. India's Counter-Memorial, para. 4.124.

[248] India's Counter-Memorial, para. 3.50.

[249] India's Counter-Memorial, para. 3.16.

[250] India's Rejoinder, para. 2.57.

[251] India's Counter-Memorial, para. 4.136.

[252] Pakistan's Reply, para. 5.15.

Pakistan notes that India was aware that it was engaged in the planning of the NJHEP from December 1988.[253] Indeed, India had requested details about the NJHEP in 1989, "specifically in the context of the determination of 'existing ... uses.'" Pakistan then provided such details in March 1990.[254]

241. With respect to agricultural uses, Pakistan argues that "agriculture downstream" of the KHEP depends on the flow from India and that the KHEP would "disrupt current projects aimed at the improvement of irrigated agriculture in Pakistan."[255] Pakistan points to the aerial photography of the Neelum Valley included in its EIA as evidence of extensive agricultural activity. Although much of this activity is dependent upon tributaries, Pakistan submits that irrigation is also drawn from the Kishenganga/Neelum itself, and that "plans have been developed to expand the area under irrigation by pumping water" from the main river.[256]

India's arguments

242. India submits that Pakistan has not shown the existence of any agricultural use that would be relevant for Paragraph 15(iii).[257] India maintains that it requested information from Pakistan regarding any "then existing" agricultural or hydro-electric uses both when it contemplated a Storage Work (as early as 1994[258]) and again when the KHEP was changed to a Run-of-River Plant.[259] Pakistan's only response was to provide, in 1990, the figure of 133,000 hectares of irrigated land, but without specifying the location of irrigation works or the areas irrigated by them. Nor were such works observed during a tour of the area.[260] In fact, India argues that Pakistan's own evidence and its submission in this arbitration demonstrates that the "very limited" agriculture in the Neelum Valley is "observed to be based on rainfall" and on channels fed by side streams, rather than on the Kishenganga/Neelum itself.[261]

243. India recognizes the NJHEP as a potential hydro-electric use but argues that Pakistan only announced its commitment to build the NJHEP in 2008 (14 years after the finalization of the KHEP under its original design

[253] Pakistan's Memorial, para. 2.13; Pakistan's Memorial, para. 2.12, citing the Pakistani Commissioner's letter to the Indian Commissioner, 22 April 1989, informing him of the construction of the NJHEP: "the waters of the Neelum (Kishenganga) River [stand] committed to this project."

[254] Pakistan's Reply, para. 3.36.

[255] Pakistan's Memorial, para. 1.21.

[256] Pakistan's Memorial, para. 3.51; Pakistan's Memorial, Hagler Bailly Pakistan, Water Matters, Southern Waters & Beuster, Clarke and Associates, "Kishenganga/Neelum River Water Diversion: Environmental Assessment" at exhibits 1.4, 1.5, 6.10, 6.11 (May 2011).

[257] Hearing Tr., (Day 5), 24 August 2012, at 174 to 180.

[258] India's Rejoinder, para. 1.55–1.56; India's Rejoinder, para. 2.129 *et seq.*

[259] India's Counter-Memorial, para. 3.54.

[260] India's Counter-Memorial, para. 4.142, India's Rejoinder, paras. 2.115–2.117.

[261] India's Counter-Memorial, para. 4.143.

and two years after the revised design had been submitted to Pakistan).[262] India traces the timeline of the development of the plan for the KHEP, beginning in 1960 with the CWPC Letter. At that time, India notes, nothing in the record indicates a possible project at Nauseri.[263] By 1971, India had produced a document entitled "Kishenganga Hydroelectric Project" which, in its view, demonstrates that it had the project in mind.[264] During this period, there was no evidence of a Pakistani project on the river. Thereafter, and through the 1980s, India continued collecting data and carrying out exploratory work.[265] In comparison, it was not until 1989, when Pakistan wrote to India regarding the NJHEP, that the record indicates anything with respect to a Pakistani project.[266]

244. According to India, following India's communication to Pakistan of technical information concerning the KHEP in 1994, and as late as 2005, Pakistan only assured India that it would provide "relevant information" concerning the impact of the KHEP on the NJHEP.[267] Thus, India concludes that the NJHEP fails Pakistan's own definition of an "existing use" as Pakistan made no "firm commitment" or "active engagement" in the project until 2007–2008.[268] Even during an inspection in 2008, India submits, there was no evidence that preparatory construction work was under way.[269]

(g) Whether the diversion of the Kishenganga/Neelum River would cause an adverse effect

245. The Parties strongly disagree about the content and weight of evidence suggesting any potential adverse effect to Pakistani uses as a result of the KHEP. While they agree that the effect must be more than a minimal ("*de minimis*") effect, they again differ with respect to the meaning of "*de minimis*" in this context.

Pakistan's arguments

246. Pakistan considers it "self-evident that the planned diversion … would materially reduce the flows downstream" which would lead to a reduction in planned electricity generation at the NJHEP, as well as at other sites that have been considered for future hydro-electric development. Potential

---

[262] India's Counter-Memorial, para. 4.148.

[263] Hearing Tr., (Day 9), 30 August 2012, at 51:2–11.

[264] Hearing Tr., (Day 9), 30 August 2012, at 51:12–21, referencing Comments of the CWPC, 13 May 1971, (Annex IN-55) and Communication of the Government of Jammu and Kashmir to the Indian Ministry of Irrigation and Power, 3 April 1973, (Annex IN-56).

[265] Hearing Tr., (Day 9), 30 August 2012, at 51:25 to 53:13.

[266] Hearing Tr., (Day 5), 24 August 2012, at 148:15 *et seq.*

[267] Hearing Tr., (Day 5), 24 August 2012, at 150:3–5.

[268] India's Rejoinder, para. 1.59.

[269] India's Counter-Memorial, para. 4.147, noting that during two tours of inspection to the NJHEP site in 1991 and 1996, no construction was observed.

sites of future hydro-electric projects include Suti/Taobat, Followai, Kel and Dudhnial.[270] Overall, Pakistan predicts an annual loss in electricity generation of 13 percent at the NJHEP, equivalent to a loss of USD 141.3 million,[271] and a further annual loss of USD 74.1 million at its other planned sites.[272]

247. Insofar as the hydrological flow data presented by the Parties differs, Pakistan maintains that its daily data series of the flow at the NJHEP site is more accurate and gives a more representative understanding of the impact of the KHEP than does India's monthly series.[273] Pakistan rejects the suggestion that its statistical processing of observed data is somehow inappropriate. In Pakistan's view, raw data must be subjected to such analysis to produce useable results.[274] Pakistan also notes that in attempting to minimize the effect on power generation at the NJHEP, India misconstrues the planned mode of operation of the Plant, supposing that Pakistan seeks to generate only "peaking power" during a portion of the day, rather than full-time operation.[275] In addition, Pakistan observes that even India's own data show significant reduction in flows at the NJHEP due to the operation of the KHEP.[276]

248. Pakistan further rejects India's argument that the impact at the NJHEP would be mitigated by an overall increase in power generation in the region. Pakistan maintains that arguments concerning alleged beneficial impacts on other hydro-electric projects, such as the planned Kohala hydro-electric project, are irrelevant. Those projects are located on other tributaries and do not fall within the scope of this dispute.[277] Furthermore, India assumes wrongly that storage at the proposed Pakistani Dudhnial hydro-electric project would offset the impact of reduced flow at the NJHEP.

---

[270] Pakistan's Memorial, paras. 5.56, 5.58.

[271] Pakistan makes its calculation on the basis of an oil price of USD 115 per barrel. Pakistan's Memorial, para. 3.33.

[272] Pakistan's Memorial, paras. 5.57–5.58. Pakistan relies on the data presented in the National Engineering Services Pakistan Limited Report (NESPAK Report). This Report was then submitted for peer review to Prof. Jens Christian Refsgaard of the Geological Survey of Denmark and Greenland who provided a Review Report. In his Review Report, Prof. Refsgaard concludes:

> A diversion of 58.4 m3/s at Kishenganga will reduce the annual flow at the NJHEP site at Nauseri in Pakistan by 14%, while the winter and summer season flows will be reduced by 33% and 11%, respectively. The corresponding reduction figures at upstream sites closer to the [KHEP] will be much higher, e.g. 33% (annual), 74% (winter) and 26% (summer) at Suti/Taobat.

[273] Pakistan's Reply, paras. 4.16, 4.25–4.27.

[274] Pakistan's Reply, para. 4.12. For example, Pakistan argues that the seasonal regression equations in the NESPAK Report that India argued were unreliable, having been based on an assessment of the annual hydrological relationship, are in fact more reliable than India's figures, which are based on only six or seven data points. Pakistan's Reply, para. 4.9. Likewise, Pakistan objects to India's argument that the data from the Muzaffarabad gauge site are unreliable, contending that its streamflow measurement methodology is in accordance with good hydrological practice. Pakistan's Reply, para. 4.11.

[275] Pakistan's Reply, para. 4.24.

[276] Pakistan's Reply, para. 4.15.

[277] Pakistan's Reply, para. 4.29.

This is incorrect, Pakistan argues, first because it is unlikely that the Dudhnial project will be constructed as a storage scheme, as India assumes,[278] and second because India's calculation in this respect does not account for the fact that the Dudhnial project would itself suffer reduced water availability and an adverse impact from the KHEP.[279]

249. Additionally, Pakistan submits that the diversion will affect its agricultural use of the waters by "depriv[ing] the riverine communities of [the water that will be diverted]."[280] In particular, according to Pakistan, there will be no flow immediately below the dam site for six months of the year.[281] The impact on agricultural activities in the region will "depend on the precise location of given crop areas ... where irrigation is dependent on water taken from the Kishenganga/Neelum River," but an adverse impact would be expected to current and planned irrigation projects.[282]

250. In Pakistan's view, the evaluation of adverse effect under the Treaty "does not invite a general balancing act that seeks to bring into account alleged positive impacts to Agricultural Use or hydroelectric use on other Tributaries," as India implies through its analysis of "compensation" effects at other hydro-electric plants.[283] Pakistan urges the Court to bear in mind the scale of harm that would result from what may appear as an insignificant overall reduction in flow and argues that the data bear out that the overall adverse effect is significant.[284] As Pakistan stated at the hearing on the merits, "there is no particular size below which farmers or hydro-electric plants can simply be ignored by India."[285] In Pakistan's view, if there is an interference with the flow that is not insignificant and incidental, and that does have an adverse effect upon downstream uses, India is no longer permitted to divert the river pursuant to Paragraph 15(iii).[286]

India's arguments

251. India maintains that the KHEP will not have any significant adverse effect on the NJHEP.[287] To the contrary, India contends that the KHEP would have a net positive effect on the generation of hydro-electric power in the region: it will increase the flow of water going into Pakistan's planned Kohala hydro-electric project, thereby increasing its capacity to generate electricity during the winter months and substantially offsetting the loss of capacity at

---

[278] Pakistan's Reply, para. 4.31.

[279] Pakistan's Reply, para. 4.32.

[280] Pakistan's Memorial, para. 3.52.

[281] Pakistan's Memorial, para. 3.26.

[282] Pakistan's Memorial, para. 5.55.

[283] Pakistan's Reply, paras. 2.86, 4.29.

[284] Pakistan's Reply, para. 2.85.

[285] Hearing Tr., (Day 4), 23 August 2012, at 45:7–9.

[286] Hearing Tr., (Day 4), 23 August 2012, at 46:18–23.

[287] India's Counter-Memorial, para. 4.150.

the KHEP.[288] Such offset effects, along with a gain in energy at the NJHEP as a result of Pakistan's planned Dudhnial Storage Work, will increase total power output.[289] Accounting for these two projects in calculating the effect of the KHEP on Pakistan, as well as additional projects planned further downstream, it is India's view that "the impact of the KHEP will be largely moderated."[290] Even without such offsets, India submits that the relevant flow data from the area do not demonstrate any material adversity to Pakistan's hydro-electric use; rather, the water released at the KHEP would continue to suffice for the NJHEP to operate as a peaking plant, as intended by Pakistan.[291]

252. India disputes Pakistan's presentation of its flow data, criticizing its calculations for their inconsistencies and oversight,[292] the limits on the span of the data on which it relies,[293] and its transparency with respect to both data and calculation methodology.[294] In India's view, Pakistan's calculations depicting losses at the NJHEP during the high flow season, in particular, are based on an approach chosen to exaggerate its potential losses.[295] India contends that, "given the limitations of the various data sets, there can be no definite conclusion on the impact of [the] KHEP on power generation in [the] NJHEP."[296] Even if

---

[288] India's Counter-Memorial, paras. 5.31, 5.33.

[289] India's Counter-Memorial, para. 5.38. India notes that Pakistan informed India in 1990 that Dudhnial was intended to be developed as a storage project. India's Rejoinder, para. 3.57.

[290] India's Counter-Memorial, para. 5.39. "The entire system as a whole will benefit from the KHEP 4,703 MU [gigawatt hours]," whereas without the KHEP there will be a net loss to both Parties. India's Counter-Memorial, para. 5.41; India's Rejoinder, paras. 3.64–3.65.

[291] India's Counter-Memorial, paras. 5.12–5.13, 5.24.

[292] India finds the NESPAK Report's regression analysis to show concurrent flow between Gurez and Muzaffarabad to be inappropriate as it does not accommodate seasonal variability. "Pakistan's argument that one regression equation based on monthly flows be used does not take account of the natural processes in the development of hydrologic time series." India, by contrast, calculates each season's flows separately. India's Rejoinder, para. 3.16.

[293] India's Rejoinder, para. 3.22. India notes that Pakistan used an 18-month data set to develop a long-term series for flow at Nauseri and comments that a period of 18 months is too short for any reliable regression analysis. In addition, it observes that one of Pakistan's consultants discarded Nauseri data from 1991 to 1996 because these data were "said to be underestimated by about 8%," but that Pakistan did not take this into account and retained the data. India's Rejoinder, para. 3.23. India also rejects Pakistan's flow data from Muzaffarabad which it claims was measured only intermittently (two or three times per month). India's Rejoinder, para. 3.24.

[294] India argues, first, that Pakistan withheld gauge and discharge information observed at Nauseri and Dudhnial which prevented India from verifying it. India's Rejoinder, para. 3.21. Next, India rejects Pakistan's "modification" of the data from Muzaffarabad, that is, Pakistan's claim that earlier collected data was "raw" and needed to be further processed before being provided to India. India's Rejoinder, paras. 3.28–3.29. To India, the presence of three different sets of flow data from a single gauging station has not been sufficiently explained. India's Rejoinder, para. 3.26.

[295] India's Rejoinder, para. 3.45. In fact, India contends, any daily flow variations in the high flow season can be accommodated by Pakistan without a reduction in the power-generating capacity of the NJHEP; Pakistan has not taken into account that the NJHEP has live storage that can even out variations across a ten-day period. India's Rejoinder, para. 3.47.

[296] India's Rejoinder, para. 3.33. Further, in response to Pakistan's criticism about India's use of a ten-day time-step rather than daily flow, India argues that ten-day average flow calculations are an accepted norm and consistent with the Treaty, whereas Pakistan's daily flow analysis

the Court were to conclude that there is an adverse effect on hydro-electric power at the NJHEP, India argues, a minor adverse effect would not under the Treaty prevent delivery into the Bonar Nallah.[297] The Treaty requires an adverse effect "to a significant extent."[298]

253. Similarly, in India's view, Pakistan has not explained how the KHEP would have an impact on Pakistan's downstream agricultural use.[299] India states: "If Pakistan's concerns were that, in the reach of the Kishenganga (Neelum) Tributary below the KHEP, the timing of flow for irrigation essential to ensure food security would be significantly affected, its Memorial again does not throw any light in support of this statement. In fact, the irrigation water requirements for agricultural uses in the Neelum [V]alley are nominal and will not be affected by the reduction in volume of flow in this reach due to the KHEP."[300] Nor, India notes, did Pakistan provide any evidence to support its assertion that delivery of water to the Wular Lake would delay downstream flows and affect the early growing season.[301]

3. The Parties' arguments on Article IV(6) of the Treaty

255. In addition to its arguments regarding Article III and Annexure D, Pakistan claims that the construction of the KHEP breaches Article IV(6) of the Treaty, which provides:

> Each Party will use its best endeavours to maintain the natural channels of the Rivers, as on the Effective Date, in such condition as will avoid, as far as practicable, any obstruction to the flow in these channels likely to cause material damage to the other Party.

255. The Parties disagree as to the meaning of their obligation to "maintain the natural channels" and the scope of the obligation to "use their best endeavours" in doing so.

Pakistan's arguments

256. Pakistan accepts that Article IV(6) imposes a "best endeavours" obligation but submits that India has failed to live up to this standard.[302] As an initial matter, Pakistan claims that India is obliged, under Article IV(6), to avoid (as far as practicable) creating obstructions to the flow of the waters

is not reliable as it gives only a "single snapshot value at a particular time in the day." India's Rejoinder, paras. 3.41–3.43.

[297] India's Counter-Memorial, paras. 4.150; 5.25–5.33.

[298] India's Counter-Memorial, para. 4.150.

[299] India's Counter-Memorial, para. 4.36. With respect to the Muzaffarabad data, India contests Pakistan's data on the basis of the limited number of days included in Pakistan's study. India's Counter-Memorial, paras. 5.7, 5.8.

[300] India's Counter-Memorial, para. 4.36.

[301] India's Rejoinder, para. 2.122, referencing Pakistan's Reply, para. 4.50.

[302] Pakistan's Memorial, para. 5.59.

of the rivers that cause material damage to Pakistan. Because the KHEP will divert waters from their natural channels—"a *prima facie* breach of the requirement to maintain the natural channels"—and cause the deterioration of those channels,[303] it will, in Pakistan's view, obstruct the flow and result in material damage.[304]

257. In Pakistan's view, "material damage," as the term is used in Article IV(6), extends beyond the direct obstruction and degradation of the natural channel of the Kishenganga/Neelum, and encompasses harm to the ecology of the riverine environment in that channel.[305] As described by Pakistan, the KHEP will contribute to substantial material damage downstream.[306] Pakistan describes "a large loss of natural habitat, biota and ecosystem functions" immediately downstream of the Line of Control, as well as a decline in abundance of fish species and important changes to socio-economic conditions downstream.[307] Further, Pakistan contends that protecting the flow of the waters in their natural channels is "an essential element in ensuring food security."[308] The KHEP will interfere with Pakistan's capacity to manage the irrigation of its crops.

258. Relying on India's own data on the anticipated flow below the KHEP, Pakistan is unconvinced that any fixed minimum environmental flow would avoid significant harm to the environment in the affected areas.[309] At the least, Pakistan argues, for India to employ its best endeavours to avoid these harms would require it to assess the damage its diversion is likely to cause. Thus, in Pakistan's view, India failed to use its best endeavours when it neither carried out an adequate EIA,[310] nor shared with Pakistan information

---

[303] Pakistan's Memorial, para. 5.63. Pakistan states that immediately downstream of the Line of Control, the "hydrological dry season would become more than two months longer and start about six weeks earlier" with the operation of the KHEP. Further, the "flood season would start about a week later and would finish a month earlier, while its peak flows would be about 14% lower." Pakistan's Memorial, para. 3.45.

[304] Pakistan's Memorial, para. 5.63.

[305] Pakistan's Memorial, para. 3.52; Pakistan's Reply, para. 2.88.

[306] Pakistan's Memorial, paras. 3.45–3.50.

[307] Pakistan's Memorial, para. 5.46. Referring to an EIA carried out by a consortium of specialists, Pakistan describes how at Dudhnial four fish species are expected to show a decline in abundance of 30 to 40 percent. "[T]he reduction in fish population ... would reduce the revenues of local businesses and people associated with sport fishing." Pakistan's Memorial, para. 3.49. Further, reductions in the availability of water will affect its use for drinking and reduce "the navigational/transportation uses ... for around six months in an average year." Pakistan's Memorial, para. 3.50.

[308] Pakistan's Memorial, para. 1.7.

[309] Hearing Tr., (Day 10), 31 August 2012, at 34.

[310] In response to India's contention that it carried out an EIA in 2002, Pakistan maintains that this EIA is insufficient to ensure that its Treaty rights are upheld since only 12 pages are concerned with the impacts of the KHEP and the analysis undertaken is inadequate. Pakistan also observes that India requested information from Pakistan for it to carry out an EIA in 2008, but this request came two years after India had already finalized its plans for the KHEP. Pakistan's Reply, paras. 5.22, 5.23.

on the anticipated impact of its project, despite Pakistan's requests for such information.[311] Pakistan relies on the judgment of the International Court of Justice in the *Pulp Mills* case to support its position.[312] There, the Court stated: "it may now be considered a requirement under general international law to undertake an environmental impact assessment where there is a risk that the proposed industrial activity may have a significant adverse impact in a transboundary context, in particular, on a shared resource."[313] In Pakistan's view, this requirement applies to the KHEP, notwithstanding the unique status of the Line of Control; the *Pulp Mills* judgment refers to the obligation on States to ensure that activities "within their jurisdiction and control" respect the environment of other States or of areas "beyond their national control," a construction that applies equally to Indian activities having an effect on Pakistan-administered Jammu and Kashmir.[314]

India's arguments

259. According to India, the purpose of Article IV(6) is to maintain the "geometry of the channels" of the rivers.[315] The term "obstruction" cannot relate to projects permitted by other provisions of the Treaty; otherwise no development work would be possible.[316] India points to comments made by Pakistan's negotiator in 1959 indicating that Article IV(6) was intended to prevent India from placing "'temporary bunds,' or dikes, 'across the Eastern Rivers'"—and not to prevent inter-tributary transfers.[317] Moreover, India submits that Article IV(6) does not "provide a strong obligation [on the Parties], if in fact it provides an obligation at all." The word "will," rather than "shall," in the phrase "Each Party will use its best endeavours ..." is, for India, an indication of intent rather than of obligation.[318]

260. In India's view, its interpretation is confirmed by the surrounding paragraphs in Article IV (all of which relate to drainage), which confirm

---

[311] Pakistan's Memorial, para. 5.60.

[312] Pakistan's Memorial, paras. 5.61–5.62.

[313] Pakistan's Memorial, para. 5.61, citing *Pulp Mills on the River Uruguay (Argentina* v. *Uruguay)*, Judgment, *I.C.J. Reports 2010*, p. 14, p. 83. Pakistan locates additional support for its assertion that customary international law includes a prohibition on transboundary harm in Principle 21 of the Stockholm Declaration of the United Nations Conference on the Human Environment which, according to Pakistan, sets out a requirement that States not cause transboundary harm. Stockholm Declaration of the United Nations Conference on the Human Environment, (16 June 1972), UN Doc. A/CONF.48/14/Rev.1.

[314] Pakistan's Reply, para. 5.22. Pakistan also submits that India has admitted, in an environmental assessment and management plan upon which it relies, that the Line of Control is an international boundary, thereby rendering the decision in *Pulp Mills* directly relevant. *See* Pakistan's Reply, para. 5.21, referencing para. 6.55 of India's Counter-Memorial, and a report titled, *Comprehensive Management Action Plan for Wular Lake, Kashmir.*

[315] India's Counter-Memorial, paras. 4.155, 4.157.

[316] India's Counter-Memorial, paras. 4.152, 4.157.

[317] India's Rejoinder, para. 2.155.

[318] India's Rejoinder, para. 2.168.

that Paragraph 6 was intended to ensure effective drainage and smooth downstream flow—and not to maintain any particular volume of flow.[319] India submits that its interpretation is supported by the *travaux préparatoires*, insofar as an early draft of Article IV(6) used the phrase "natural flow in the Rivers," only to have this replaced by "flow in these channels." According to India, this change represents the drafters' recognition that "it would have been impossible to maintain the 'natural flow in the Rivers' as on the Effective Date in view of the uses India was permitted."[320]

261. India dismisses criticism of the scope of its EIA, noting that Pakistan refused to provide the information that would have permitted an environmental assessment covering the entire region.[321] India further defends the soundness of its EIA, arguing that this assessment considered impacts at the dam site and conformed to international best practices at the time.[322] Moreover, India observes, the EIA carried out by Pakistan contains flaws of its own, including a failure to consider the environmental effects of the NJHEP (and four other dams that Pakistan proposes to build) as well as the lack of consideration of environmental impacts in the area between Nauseri and Muzaffarabad.[323]

262. Finally, India rejects what it considers to be an attempt to import principles of international environmental law that are applicable neither to the interpretation of Article IV(6) nor to this dispute as a whole.[324] In India's view, environmental principles not found in the Treaty fall outside the jurisdiction of the Court.[325] Nevertheless, India emphasizes that it takes environmental considerations seriously. It notes, first, that the KHEP meets all requirements of Indian environmental law[326] and, second, that the evidence India collected in its EIA in 2000 establishes that the KHEP would not cause irreversible harm to the environment.[327] India also notes that the KHEP will not have a significant impact on any terrestrial species, nor lead to an increased risk of disease in the valley.[328] At the hearing on the merits, the Agent for India further

[319] India's Counter-Memorial, paras. 4.155, 4.157. For example, India refers to Paragraphs 4, 5, and 8 addressing maintenance of drainages, deepening or widening of drainages, and use of the natural channels for the discharge of excess waters, respectively.

[320] India's Counter-Memorial, para. 4.161.

[321] India's Counter-Memorial, para. 6.86.

[322] India's Rejoinder, paras. 3.75–3.84. India contends that the contents of the EIA make clear that the dam site was accounted for in its entirety. With respect to best practices, India argues that its EIA covered all the most important aspects of an EIA: that it be in writing, be conducted sufficiently early to be taken account in decision-making, include an opportunity for public comment, and be comprehensive.

[323] India's Rejoinder, para. 3.103. India also rejects Pakistan's classifications of fish species and of impact zones, as well as the socio-economic impacts in the region, as arbitrary and subjective. India's Rejoinder, para. 3.118.

[324] India's Rejoinder, para. 2.151.

[325] India's Rejoinder, para. 2.159.

[326] India's Rejoinder, paras. 2.172–2.177.

[327] India's Rejoinder, paras. 1.69–1.70.

[328] Hearing Tr., (Day 6), 27 August 2012, at 33:2–20.

guaranteed that an "environmental flow will continue throughout the year."[329] According to the Agent, there would be no dry period below the KHEP, in accordance with Indian laws. The Agent indicated that the exact amount of the flow was under consideration by the Indian Ministry of Environment and Forests, but that it would not be less than "the minimum observed flow of 3.94 [cumecs] at the site."[330]

B. The Permissibility of Reservoir Depletion under the Treaty

263. As stated in Pakistan's Request for Arbitration and Memorial, the Second Dispute relates to the following question:

> Whether under the Treaty, India may deplete or bring the reservoir level of a run-of-river Plant below Dead Storage Level in any circumstances except in the case of an unforeseen emergency.[331]

264. Pakistan's concern with reservoir depletion arises out of the KHEP's design as a Run-of-River Plant, as described in the Indian Commissioner's letter of 19 June 2006, notifying Pakistan of the KHEP's re-configured design, and in the appendices to India's Counter-Memorial. As set forth therein, the KHEP includes a spillway with a design flood of 2,000 m3/s and three gated openings located at an elevation of 2,370 metres—that is, with the base of the gates 10 metres above the riverbed and 14.5 metres below the KHEP's Dead Storage Level.[332] India indicates that the spillway will perform the dual function of flood discharge and sediment removal and, in particular, signals its

[329] Hearing Tr., (Day 9), 30 August 2012, at 114:13–15.

[330] Hearing Tr., (Day 9), 30 August 2012, at 115:4–15.

[331] Request for Arbitration, para. 4; Pakistan's Memorial, para. 1.12.

[332] *See* Indian Commissioner's letter to the Pakistani Commissioner, 19 June 2006, (Annex PK-163); India's Counter-Memorial, Appendix 2, paras. 12, 17; India's Counter-Memorial, Annex I, n.3 (*see* "MDDL"); *see also* Pakistan's Memorial, paras. 3.17, 6.19; India's Rejoinder, Report, Prof. Dr. Anton J. Schleiss, Laboratory of Hydraulic Constructions (LCH), EPFL, Switzerland: "Note on Second Dispute regarding Drawdown Flushing," 7 May 2012, (IN-Tab I) (the "Schleiss Report"), p. 4.

Dead Storage is defined by the Treaty as "that portion of the storage which is not used for operational purposes"; Dead Storage Level "means the level corresponding to Dead Storage." In practice, the Dead Storage Level is calculated by reference to the surface of the reservoir at its maximum ordinary capacity (its "Full Pondage Level"). The storage between Full Pondage Level and the Dead Storage Level is termed the "Operating Pool," and its volume is regulated by Annexure D. The Dead Storage then extends from the riverbed to the lower limit of the Operating Pool, once the latter's capacity is determined under the Treaty. Pursuant to Paragraph 8(*c*) of Annexure D, the volume of the Operating Pool may not exceed twice the capacity required to meet fluctuations in the daily and weekly generating loads of the Plant when generating "Firm Power"—the electricity it can produce year round on the basis of the minimum average discharge at the site. In other words, the Dead Storage Level is a calculation based on the hydrological data for the minimum flow at the site and the engineer's determination of the storage capacity required to meet the planned daily and weekly variation in the generation of electricity.

intention to use the spillway for drawdown flushing.[333] A dam with a low-level spillway can be represented schematically as follows:

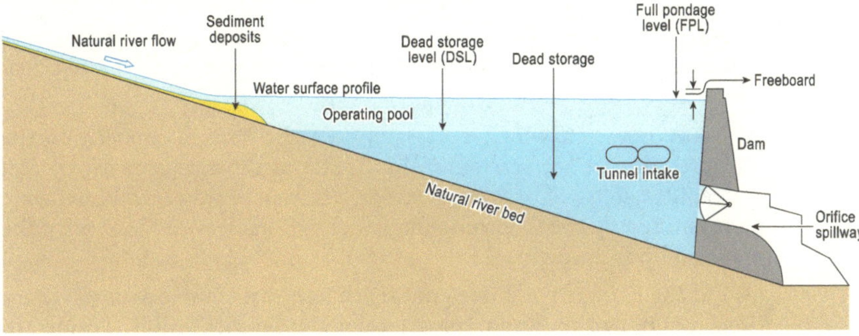

Source: Pakistan's Memorial, Volume 2, Figure 12.

265. The specific design of the KHEP, including the location of the spillway and gated openings, can be seen in the following technical diagrams, provided by India.*

266. Drawdown flushing is a technique for the removal of sediment from the reservoir of a hydro-electric plant. The procedure consists of drawing the water in the reservoir down to a level close to that of the riverbed by releasing the water through low-level outlets in the dam. When the water is drawn down during drawdown flushing, its velocity through the reservoir approximates the river's natural flow and its increased capacity to transport sediment lifts accumulated deposits from the riverbed, expelling sediment from the reservoir through the outlets in the dam.[334] In the case of the KHEP, drawdown flushing would entail drawing down the water to the level of the spillway gates and therefore below Dead Storage Level.[335]

267. In this context, the Parties disagree as to whether, under the Treaty, India may bring the reservoir level of a Run-of-River Plant such as the KHEP below Dead Storage Level in circumstances other than unforeseen emergencies and, in particular, for the purpose of drawdown flushing. Pakistan submits that drawdown flushing is prohibited by specific provisions of the Treaty. India argues that it is permitted under the "state-of-the-art concept" enshrined in the Treaty, as confirmed by the *Baglihar* expert determination. India moreover objects to the admissibility of the Second Dispute for determination by the Court.

268. This Part summarizes the Parties' arguments regarding the Second Dispute, beginning with India's objection to admissibility and followed by the Parties' substantive arguments.

---

[333] Indian Commissioner's letter to the Pakistani Commissioner, 25 May 2007, (Annex PK-174); India's Counter-Memorial, Appendix 2, paras. 12, 18, 35–37.

* Secretariat note: Located in the front pocket of this volume.

[334] Pakistan's Memorial, para. 6.20.

[335] India's Counter-Memorial, Appendix 2, para. 37.

1. The Parties' arguments on the admissibility of the Second Dispute

269. Article IX of the Treaty provides for the settlement of differences and disputes that may arise in respect of the Treaty. Paragraphs (1) and (2) of Article IX read as follows:

> (1) Any question which arises between the Parties concerning the interpretation or application of this Treaty or the existence of any fact which, if established, might constitute a breach of this Treaty shall first be examined by the Commission, which will endeavour to resolve the question by agreement.
>
> (2) If the Commission does not reach agreement on any of the questions mentioned in Paragraph (1), then a difference will be deemed to have arisen, which shall be dealt with as follows:
>
> (*a*) Any difference which, in the opinion of either Commissioner, falls within the provisions of Part 1 of Annexure F shall, at the request of either Commissioner, be dealt with by a Neutral Expert in accordance with the provisions of Part 2 of Annexure F;
>
> (*b*) If the difference does not come within the provisions of Paragraph (2) (*a*), or if a Neutral Expert, in accordance with the provisions of Paragraph 7 of Annexure F, has informed the Commission that, in his opinion, the difference, or a part thereof, should be treated as a dispute, then a dispute will be deemed to have arisen which shall be settled in accordance with the provisions of Paragraphs (3), (4) and (5):
>
> Provided that, at the discretion of the Commission, any difference may either be dealt with by a Neutral Expert in accordance with the provisions of Part 2 of Annexure F or be deemed to be a dispute to be settled in accordance with the provisions of Paragraphs (3), (4) and (5), or may be settled in any other way agreed upon by the Commission.

270. Paragraphs (3), (4) and (5) of Article IX establish the procedure for the Governments of India and Pakistan to resolve disputes by agreement or, should such efforts fail, for the constitution of a court of arbitration.

271. Article IX classifies issues that may arise between the Parties concerning the interpretation or application of the Treaty (or concerning the existence of a fact which, if established, might constitute a breach of the Treaty) as "questions," "differences," or "disputes." Any such issue will first be considered a "question." "Questions" are examined by the Commission, which endeavours to resolve them by agreement. If the Commission fails to reach agreement in respect of a question, the Treaty provides for some questions to be considered and resolved as "differences," while others proceed to become "disputes." Although the Parties remain free to employ any mode of settlement to deal with any disagreement between them, distinct procedures may apply in default of such agreement. "Differences" may be resolved in an expedited fashion by a neutral expert—a "highly qualified engineer" appointed following the proce-

dure set out in Annexure F to the Treaty.[336] "Disputes," on the other hand, must be resolved either by agreement of the Governments of India and Pakistan or, if no settlement can be reached, by a court of arbitration.

272. India submits that the Second Dispute is not admissible for determination by the Court, because it should first have been submitted to a neutral expert and because there is, accordingly, at present no "dispute" within the meaning of Article IX of the Treaty.[337] Specifically, India argues that: (1) the consideration of the Second Dispute by the Court is premature, as Pakistan has failed to follow the procedure envisaged by Article IX of the Treaty for the submission of "disputes" to a court of arbitration;[338] and (2) the Second Dispute is a technical question that falls within Part 1 of Annexure F to the Treaty and should therefore be classified as a "difference" and resolved by a neutral expert.[339] Pakistan disputes both propositions.

(a) Whether Pakistan has followed the procedure of Article IX for the submission of disputes to the Court

India's arguments

273. India's first objection to the admissibility of the Second Dispute concerns the procedure by which a dispute may be brought before a court of arbitration. According to India, Pakistan did not follow the procedural steps required by the Treaty for a "dispute" to be deemed to have arisen. In India's view, given the absence of agreement within the Commission on the disposition of the Second Dispute, Pakistan should have requested the appointment of a neutral expert and should have asked that expert to decide whether the Second Dispute constitutes a "difference" or a "dispute." Only, India argues, if a neutral expert were to determine that the Second Dispute was not a technical question within Part 1 of Annexure F to the Treaty could it be brought before a court of arbitration.

274. India accepts that any issue in respect of the Treaty raised by a Party would first be considered a "question" for the Commission to examine.[340] Indeed, India notes that Article VIII(4) of the Treaty obliges the Commission to "make every effort" to settle such questions promptly.[341] In India's view, however, this is more than a perfunctory obligation. India considers that "serious efforts must be made in the Permanent Indus Commission to resolve any 'Question' raised by either party under what may be referred to as the

[336] Treaty, Annexure F, Para. 4.

[337] India's Counter-Memorial, para. 7.2; India's Rejoinder, paras. 4.2, 4.4.

[338] India's Rejoinder, paras. 4.1, 4.4, 4.34.

[339] India's Counter-Memorial, para. 1.16; India's Rejoinder, paras. 4.35, 4.41.

[340] India's Rejoinder, para. 4.7.

[341] India's Rejoinder, para. 4.7.

co-operative 'umbrella' of the Commission."[342] Members of the Commission must be highly qualified engineers, and "the Commissioners ... carry a significant responsibility in scrupulously implementing the stage-wise mechanism provided under the Treaty."[343]

275. In the event that the Commission's efforts fail, however, India considers that there is only one path that a Commissioner may initiate unilaterally: the referral of the resulting difference to a neutral expert.[344] Article IX(2)(*a*), India notes, expressly empowers a Commissioner to request a neutral expert if—in that Commissioner's opinion—a difference is technical and within the ambit of Part 1 of Annexure F. If, however, the Commissioners disagree in this respect, India argues that reference must be had to Annexure F itself, and to its Paragraph 7, which provides for the neutral expert to decide on the procedure applicable to a difference in the event of a disagreement in the Commission.[345]

276. In contrast to Article IX(2)(*a*), India argues, Article IX(2)(*b*) includes no provision for a single Commissioner to deem a "dispute" to have arisen.[346] Instead, Article IX(2)(*b*) applies only if Article IX(2)(*a*) does not—in other words, if neither Commissioner considers the difference to be a technical matter for a neutral expert—or if a neutral expert, having considered the matter, determines that the difference falls outside his competence. Accordingly, India submits, in the event of a disagreement as to how to proceed, neither Party can simply initiate arbitration: "it has to go back to a neutral expert to decide whether or not [the difference] is a dispute" that can be taken to a court of arbitration.[347] In India's view, this priority in favour of the Commission and the neutral expert is understandable in light of the key role that the Treaty gives to engineers in interpreting its most important provisions[348] and the need for the Parties to be able to proceed quickly to a neutral expert in respect of the engineering questions arising from the Commission's day-to-day work.[349]

277. In the present case, India considers that this procedure was not followed. The Commissioners never agreed that the difference was not a technical matter for a neutral expert, nor was any neutral expert ever requested to pass upon the proper disposition of the difference. On the contrary, India submits, its Commissioner "was of the opinion that the 'difference' fell within the provisions of [P]aragraph 2(*a*)," a position with which the Pakistani Commissioner disagreed.[350] This disagreement was clear, India argues, notwithstanding its

[342] India's Rejoinder, para. 4.8.

[343] India's Rejoinder, paras. 4.16–4.17.

[344] India's Rejoinder, para. 4.21.

[345] Hearing Tr., (Day 6), 27 August 2012, at 109:8 to 110:11, 110:22 to 111:7.

[346] Hearing Tr., (Day 6), 27 August 2012, at 111:8–12.

[347] Hearing Tr., (Day 6), 27 August 2012, at 111:24 to 112:5.

[348] India's Rejoinder, para. 4.14.

[349] Hearing Tr., (Day 6), 27 August 2012, at 116:9–24.

[350] India's Rejoinder, para. 4.19; *see also* Hearing Tr., (Day 9), 30 August 2012, at 100:3–8 ("The Pakistan Commissioner in the present case did not accept that the difference fell within

position that the matter could be resolved even without recourse to a neutral expert. Far from attempting to forestall discussion within the Commission or denying that the Second Dispute constituted at least a "question,"[351] India submits that its position recognized the importance of such discussions and of the Commission. India considers its consistent position to have been that the Commission should resolve these questions by agreement and that it was unnecessary to address the issue outside the Commission—in particular because the authoritative precedent of the *Baglihar* expert determination was available to assist the Commission in understanding the substance of the Second Dispute.[352]

278. Given the Commissioners' disagreement on how to proceed, India argues that it was incumbent upon the Pakistani Commissioner to submit the Second Dispute to a neutral expert and for that expert to determine that Dispute's proper disposition.[353] In India's view, the Pakistani Commissioner's decision not to make such a request and to instead unilaterally qualify the Second Dispute as a "dispute" in the 11 March 2009 Letter "usurp[ed] the role of the Commission and the Neutral Expert" and caused the premature submission of the Second Dispute for consideration by this Court.[354]

Pakistan's arguments

279. Pakistan submits that the Second Dispute is properly before the Court.[355] First, Pakistan notes that the Court's jurisdiction over both disputes is not contested.[356] Second, Pakistan argues that it made extensive efforts to resolve the Second Dispute through negotiation and has fulfilled the procedural requirements of Article IX of the Treaty.[357]

280. In Pakistan's view, Article IX(2)(*a*) permits either Party to insist on the appointment of a neutral expert. If a request for such an appointment is made, it falls to the neutral expert to determine whether the question put to him is within his competence. But a request for the appointment of a neutral

paragraph 2(*a*), that is within the [23] items of Part 1 of Annexure F to go to a Neutral Expert. The Indian Commissioner held the contrary view …").

[351] India's Rejoinder, paras. 4.6–4.7, 4.11. According to India, the substance of the Second Dispute was raised by Pakistan in the form of "*Questions*" during the 100th meeting of the Commission. India's Rejoinder, para. 4.11. In accordance with Arts. VIII(4)(*b*) and IX(1) of the Treaty, the Commission discussed and attempted to resolve these questions at its 100th, 101st and 103rd meetings held respectively in May-June 2008, July 2008 and May 2009. India's Rejoinder, paras. 4.11–4.12, 4.25, 4.32, referring to Record of the 100th Meeting of the Commission, Lahore, 31 May–4 June 2008, (Annex PK-34), pp. 147–185, and Record of the 103rd Meeting of the Commission, New Delhi, 31 May–5 June 2009, (Annex PK-36), pp. 227–228.

[352] India's Rejoinder, para. 4.13.

[353] India's Counter-Memorial, para. 7.6; India's Rejoinder, paras. 1.84, 4.18–4.19, 4.21, 4.33.

[354] India's Counter-Memorial, para. 1.16; India's Rejoinder, paras. 1.84, 4.1, 4.4, 4.26, 4.32, 4.34.

[355] Pakistan's Memorial, paras. 4.8–4.9.

[356] Hearing Tr., (Day 10), 31 August 2012, at 41:17–19 ("this Court has jurisdiction—indeed, it is not contested that this Court has jurisdiction—over both disputes").

[357] Pakistan's Memorial, para. 4.8.

expert must in fact be made, and in the absence of such a request, this Court is competent to evaluate and decide the Second Dispute itself. In other words, "if the Commissioner doesn't trigger the Neutral Expert procedure under Article IX(2)(*a*) prior to the establishment of the Court of Arbitration, that priority is never triggered and the Court of Arbitration has jurisdiction under Article IX(5) of the Treaty."[358]

281. According to Pakistan, prior to its submissions in these proceedings, India had never argued that the Second Dispute was a matter for a neutral expert or that it constituted a "difference" under the Treaty. Moreover, Pakistan argues, India has "consistently denied the existence even of a question for the purposes of Article IX(1) of the Treaty."[359] Turning to the record of the Commission, Pakistan observes that India repeatedly sought to characterize matters relating to the Second Dispute as "issues," rather than "questions," and objected to any reference to the terminology of Article IX of the Treaty.[360] Against this background, Pakistan submits, it is not now open to India to "backtrack" through multiple years—during which Pakistan submitted the Second Dispute to this Court—and argue that there is in fact a "difference" to be resolved by a neutral expert.[361]

282. Not only did India reject the applicability of Article IX, Pakistan observes, but India never sought the appointment of a neutral expert.[362] Had such a request been made, Pakistan acknowledges that "the question whether the difference did fall within Part 1 of Annexure F would have been a matter for the Neutral Expert."[363] However, Pakistan argues, "as neither party made such a request—and indeed the Indian Commissioner expressly took the position that there was no difference—Article IX(2)(*a*) does not apply in this case."[364] Pakistan therefore considers that it correctly initiated proceedings before this Court.[365] Having determined not to request a neutral expert at the

[358] Hearing Tr., (Day 4), 23 August 2012, at 172:20–24.

[359] Hearing Tr., (Day 4), 23 August 2012, at 155:13–15; *see also* Hearing Tr., (Day 4), 23 August 2012, at 157:13–15; Hearing Tr., (Day 8), 29 August 2012, at 78:2–7.

[360] Hearing Tr., (Day 4), 23 August 2012, at 161:17 to 172:3; *see also* Record of the 100th Meeting of the Commission, Lahore, 31 May–4 June 2008, (Annex PK-34), pp. 3, 26–29; Record of the 101st Meeting of the Commission, New Delhi, 25–28 July 2008, (Annex PK-35), pp. 12–14; Record of the 103rd Meeting of the Commission, New Delhi, 31 May–5 June 2009, (Annex PK-36), pp. 12–22.

[361] Pakistan's Memorial, para. 4.9(*d*)–(*f*); Pakistan's Reply, paras. 1.39–1.41, referring to Record of the 100th Meeting of the Commission, Lahore, 31 May–4 June 2008, (Annex PK-34); Record of the 101st Meeting of the Commission, New Delhi, 25–28 July 2008, (Annex PK-35); Record of the 103rd Meeting of the Commission, New Delhi, 31 May–5 June 2009, (Annex PK-36); Pakistani Commissioner's letter to the Indian Commissioner, 11 March 2009, (Annex PK-194); India's Note Verbale, 20 August 2009, (Annex PK-214).

[362] Pakistan's Memorial, para. 4.11; Pakistan's Reply, para. 1.41.

[363] Hearing Tr., (Day 10), 31 August 2012, at 40:21–24.

[364] Hearing Tr., (Day 4), 23 August 2012, at 158:16–20.

[365] Hearing Tr., (Day 8), 29 August 2012, at 78:8–12.

appropriate juncture, India is no longer free to insist that a neutral expert determine the disposition of the Second Dispute in the first instance.[366]

283. According to Pakistan, it is now for the Court to decide whether the Second Dispute before it is a "dispute" within the meaning of the Treaty. Pakistan points to Paragraph 16 of Annexure G to the Treaty, which provides that the Court "shall decide all questions relating to its competence."[367] Once a dispute is referred to the Court, Pakistan argues, "the Court has the power to make a final determination on all questions of competence and procedure."[368] Accepting India's admissibility argument to the contrary, Pakistan submits, would amount to permitting India to frustrate the working of the Treaty's dispute resolution provisions, first in the Commission and now before the Court.[369]

(b) Whether the Second Dispute is a technical matter that falls within Part 1 of Annexure F and should therefore be classified as a "difference" to be decided by a neutral expert

India's arguments

284. India's second objection to admissibility is that, irrespective of the procedure followed, the Second Dispute is a matter for a neutral expert. The Second Dispute relates to the design of the KHEP and the location of outlets for sediment control below Dead Storage Level pursuant to Paragraph 8(*d*) of Annexure D.[370] Questions concerning the conformity of a Plant with this provision are consigned by the Treaty to the determination of a neutral expert.[371] Moreover, India observes, Pakistan has itself committed to referring the question of low-level outlets to a neutral expert—the same issue it now seeks to bring before the Court.

285. India recalls that, at the 100th meeting of the Commission in May–June 2008, Pakistan raised the following two questions:

> (4) Whether the design of the [KHEP] is in conformity with Paragraph 8(*d*) of Annexure D to the Treaty?
>
> [...]
>
> (6) Whether under the Treaty, India may deplete or bring the reservoir level of a run-of-river Plant below dead storage level in any circumstances except in the case of an unforeseen emergency?[372]

---

[366] Hearing Tr., (Day 4), 23 August 2012, at 155:3–6; Hearing Tr., (Day 8), 29 August 2012, at 78:12–14.

[367] Pakistan's Memorial, para. 4.7, quoting Para. 16 of Annexure G.

[368] Pakistan's Memorial, paras. 4.7, 4.10.

[369] Hearing Tr., (Day 4), 23 August 2012, at 172:6–12.

[370] India's Counter-Memorial, para. 7.2.

[371] India's Counter-Memorial, para. 7.8.

[372] India's Rejoinder, para. 4.11, quoting Record of the 100th Meeting of the Commission, Lahore, 31 May–4 June 2008, (Annex PK-34), p. 183.

286. When questioned on the appropriateness of including Question 6 in the Commission's discussions of the KHEP, India notes, Pakistan explicitly accepted that the questions are a "single composite issue," stating that "while Question No. 6 may be general in scope, the need for its examination arises directly out of Pakistan's objections to the current design of the Kishenganga Project."[373] At the same time, Pakistan outlined its objections, pursuant to Paragraph 8(*d*), to the low-level orifice spillways contemplated for the KHEP. By the 11 March 2009 Letter, Pakistan then notified India of its intention to seek the appointment of a neutral expert with respect to the following difference concerning low-level orifice spillways:

> Pakistan is of the considered view that the orifice spillway provided in the current design of the [KHEP] constitutes an outlet below Dead Storage Level which is not in accordance with the criteria contained in Paragraph 8(*d*) of Annexure D to the Treaty. India does not agree with Pakistan's position.[374]

287. In India's view, "Pakistan is thus on record as having confirmed a direct connection, as a matter of design, between the questions referred to the Court as the subject-matter of the second Dispute and the difference in regard to the design of the Kishenganga Project covered by Paragraph 8(*d*) of Annexure D, which Pakistan has notified should be dealt with by a Neutral Expert."[375] According to India, the question of conformity with Paragraph 8(*d*) relates to the use of orifice spillways for sediment control. Pakistan's own view, India argues, is that such spillways can only contribute to sediment control through drawdown flushing, which requires the depletion of the reservoir.[376] The question of depletion is thus intrinsically linked to the question Pakistan has proposed to refer to a neutral expert.

288. However, even had Pakistan not committed to refer the question to a neutral expert, India submits that the Second Dispute is inherently technical and "concerns a matter of design which [pursuant to the Treaty] has to be resolved by a Neutral Expert."[377] Under the Treaty, questions "as to whether or not the design of KHEP conforms to the criteria set out in Paragraph 8(*d*)" are within the competence of the neutral expert and—as Pakistan itself accepts—the need to consider drawdown flushing arises directly

---

[373] Pakistani Commissioner's letter to the Indian Commissioner, 29 April 2009, (Annex PK-202), p. 5; *see also* India's Rejoinder, para. 4.28.

[374] India's Counter-Memorial, paras. 7.3–7.4, quoting Pakistani Commissioner's letter to the Indian Commissioner, 11 March 2009, (Annex PK-194).

[375] Hearing Tr., (Day 6), 27 August 2012, at 127:13–20.

[376] Hearing Tr., (Day 6), 27 August 2012, at 124:8–16; *see also* Pakistani Commissioner's letter to the Indian Commissioner, 29 April 2009, (Annex PK-202), p. 4 ("Orifice spillways will only provide any incremental sediment control benefits (as compared to either an ungated spillway or crest gated spillways) if India is able to carry out drawdown flushing with the level of the reservoir below dead storage level").

[377] India's Counter-Memorial, para. 7.8.

out of that provision.[378] Additionally, India considers the Second Dispute to be "demonstrably technical,"[379] noting in particular the technical examination of the question in the expert report by Professor Dr. Anton J. Schleiss submitted by India (the "Schleiss Report"), the expert report by Dr. Gregory L. Morris submitted by Pakistan (the "Morris Report"), and the minutes of the 100th, 101st and 103rd meetings of the Commission.[380] India also points to the *Baglihar* determination, noting that the neutral expert in that case treated a "similar question" as technical and proceeded to render a determination on that basis. In India's view, it would be appropriate for another neutral expert to decide the Second Dispute.[381]

Pakistan's arguments

289. In Pakistan's view, the Second Dispute is "manifestly ... not a technical argument"[382] and does not fall within the list of technical questions for referral to a neutral expert.[383] On the contrary, Pakistan considers the Second Dispute to be "an important legal argument about the correct interpretation of certain specific provisions of the treaty,"[384] in particular the meaning of Paragraphs 2 and 14 of Annexure D to the Treaty, and the question of the weight to be given to the *Baglihar* expert determination.[385]

290. Moreover, Pakistan submits, it never notified India of any intention to refer the Second Dispute to a neutral expert.[386] The permissibility of orifice spillways is a distinct question and "there is no composite issue."[387] Rather, Pakistan argues, "[t]here is a series of separate questions, two of which Pakistan has identified as suitable for a Court of Arbitration and four of which Pakistan has identified as suitable for determination by a Neutral Expert."[388] India's use of drawdown flushing to justify a certain type of low-level outlet at the KHEP does not subsume the underlying legal question of "whether drawdown flushing is permitted at all."[389]

---

[378] India's Rejoinder, para. 4.35.

[379] India's Rejoinder, para. 4.24.

[380] India's Rejoinder, paras. 4.35–4.39, referring to Schleiss Report; Pakistan's Reply, Tab E, Gregory L. Morris, "Response to Items A, B and C in Chapter 7, Counter-Memorial of the Government of India" (18 February 2012).

[381] India's Counter-Memorial, paras. 7.12–7.14; India's Rejoinder, para. 4.43.

[382] Hearing Tr., (Day 4), 23 August 2012, at 173:12.

[383] Pakistan's Memorial, para. 4.11.

[384] Hearing Tr., (Day 4), 23 August 2012, at 173:13–15.

[385] Pakistan's Reply, paras. 1.42, 6.4.

[386] Pakistan's Reply, para. 1.41, referring to India's Counter-Memorial, para. 1.16.

[387] Hearing Tr., (Day 8), 29 August 2012, at 79:15–16.

[388] Hearing Tr., (Day 8), 29 August 2012, at 79:16–20.

[389] Hearing Tr., (Day 8), 29 August 2012, at 80:1–7.

2. The Parties' arguments on the permissibility of reservoir depletion below Dead Storage Level

291. Pakistan is concerned that permitting drawdown flushing would allow India to exercise control over the waters of the Western Rivers by allowing the design of larger and lower outlets for reservoirs on those rivers. Such outlets would, in practice, increase India's physical ability to control the flow of the Western Rivers. With this concern in mind, it is Pakistan's case that drawdown flushing is prohibited by specific provisions of the Treaty restricting India's ability to deplete the reservoir of a Run-of-River Plant.[390] India opposes Pakistan's interpretation of the relevant provisions and argues that drawdown flushing is permitted under the Treaty's "state-of-the-art" concept, which permits the Treaty to be interpreted in light of technological advances. The Parties also disagree on the weight to be given by the Court to the *Baglihar* expert determination.

(a) *The permissibility of reservoir depletion generally*

Pakistan's arguments

292. As is the case for the permissibility of the KHEP in the First Dispute, Pakistan submits that the question of whether India may deplete reservoirs on the Western Rivers—for drawdown flushing or otherwise—concerns the basic issue of "the permitted extent of Indian interference with the flow of the Western Rivers."[391]

293. According to Pakistan, "if India were permitted to deplete reservoirs as it saw fit, it would have very important rights in terms of interference with flow: first in terms of increasing the flow so as to deplete a given reservoir, and then in terms of reducing or halting the flow entirely when the reservoir is being refilled."[392] Given the significant number of Indian hydro-electric projects on the upper reaches of the Western Rivers, permitting India to use low-level outlets without restriction would enable it to have a "major impact on the timing of flows into Pakistan."[393]

294. The Treaty addresses this concern, Pakistan argues, by permitting India to generate hydro-electric power on the Western Rivers only to the extent permitted by Annexure D. Annexure D, in turn, contains specific provisions (discussed in detail below) that both prohibit India from lowering the water level of a reservoir below Dead Storage Level and restrict the design of Indian

[390] Pakistan's Reply, paras. 6.12–6.13.

[391] Hearing Tr., (Day 4), 23 August 2012, at 153:23–24; *see also* Pakistan's Memorial, para. 6.2.

[392] Hearing Tr., (Day 4), 23 August 2012, at 154:2–8; *see also* Pakistan's Memorial, paras. 6.2–6.4, 6.32.

[393] Pakistan's Memorial, para. 6.31, quoting J. Briscoe, "War or Peace on the Indus?" *The News*, 3 April 2010, (Annex PK-229).

dams on the Western Rivers to limit India's ability to effect such depletion.[394] As presented to the Court, the Second Dispute is thus general in nature; it concerns the permissible operation, and by extension design, of any hydro-electric plant on the Western Rivers—not merely the KHEP.[395]

295. According to Pakistan, physical restrictions on India's ability to alter the flow of the Western Rivers were part of the bargain enshrined in the Treaty. Quoting Professor John Briscoe, former Senior Water Advisor at the World Bank, Pakistan submits that it "would agree [to the Treaty] only if limitations on India's capacity to manipulate the timing of flows was hard-wired into the treaty."[396] This was done even though the Parties were aware of the need to control sediment accumulation,[397] as well as the practice of using low-level outlets to flush sediments from a reservoir.[398] Paragraph 8(*d*) of Annexure D, Pakistan observes, refers to the need for "sediment control" even as it imposes restrictions on the size and placement of outlets.[399] And according to Pakistan's expert, Dr. Morris, "flushing and sluicing techniques were recognized and employed prior to the treaty," although their use in storage reservoirs was comparatively new.[400] As evidence of the state of sediment control knowledge in 1960, Pakistan points to a 1951 paper (published in the proceedings of the 1951 Congress in New Delhi of the International Commission on Large Dams (the "ICOLD")) on the design of the Mera Dam in Italy's Villa di Chiavenna valley and the planned use of drawdown flushing in the operation of those works.[401] Dr. Morris also noted the well-known use of flushing in the operation of the Old Aswan Dam.[402]

296. Finally, Pakistan observes, India acknowledged the existence of the prohibition on depletion and drawdown flushing for most of the life of the Treaty, stating in the course of Commission meetings in 1995 that "restrictions imposed by the Treaty not to lower the water level in the reservoir below [Dead Storage Level], even though the same may be necessary for effective flushing of the reservoir, is a major handicap in efficient operation of sediment sluices."[403]

---

[394] Pakistan's Memorial, para. 6.32.

[395] Hearing Tr., (Day 10), 31 August 2012, at 42:15–17; Hearing Tr., (Day 4), 23 August 2012, at 154:16–18.

[396] Hearing Tr., (Day 4), 23 August 2012, at 176:17–19, quoting J. Briscoe, "War or Peace on the Indus?" *The News*, 3 April 2010, (Annex PK-229).

[397] Hearing Tr., (Day 4), 23 August 2012, at 184:4–6.

[398] Hearing Tr., (Day 2), 21 August 2012, at 124:6–7 (Court examination of Dr. Morris) ("I could say that the technique was already known").

[399] Pakistan's Reply, para. 6.19; Morris Report, p. 5.

[400] Morris Report, p. 18.

[401] Hearing Tr., (Day 2), 21 August 2012, at 94:12 to 95:12 (direct examination of Dr. Morris); C. Marcello, *Le Barrage du Mera à Villa di Chiavenna*, Communication of the Quatrieme Congrès de Grands Barrages, New Delhi, 1951, (Annex PK-251).

[402] Hearing Tr., (Day 2), 21 August 2012, at 124:6 to 125:3 (Court examination of Dr. Morris).

[403] Pakistan's Memorial, para. 6.12, quoting Record of the 96th Meeting of the Commission, New Delhi, 1–2 June 2005, (Annex PK-31), p. 4; Pakistan's Reply, para. 6.13.

India's arguments

297. According to India, Pakistan's fear that drawdown flushing will be used to control the flow of the Western Rivers and deprive Pakistan of water is unfounded.[404] Moreover, India submits that the intense focus Pakistan places on this possibility ignores the Treaty's concern that India be able effectively to generate hydro-electric power on the Western Rivers, a concern reflected in the Treaty's flexible accommodation of an evolving technological state of the art.[405] Drawdown flushing, India argues, was not known or accepted as a sediment management practice in 1960, but has since become the state of the art.[406]

298. With respect to the flow of the Western Rivers, India submits that Pakistan is adequately protected under the Treaty even if the KHEP is equipped with outlets intended for drawdown flushing. Under any circumstances, India argues, the flushing and refilling of the KHEP reservoir would be limited by the Treaty to the prescribed flood period of the year—that is, from 21 June to 20 August—unless the Parties agreed otherwise.[407] Moreover, it would be "wholly unrealistic" to deplete and refill the Dead Storage on an *ad hoc* basis, or during the lean season. Such operation requires a complete stop in power generation, which for the KHEP would cause a loss of power worth some 30 million rupees (approximately USD 560,000) per day;[408] during the lean season this process would extend unacceptably over many weeks, instead of the few days that would be required during the high flow season.[409]

299. At the same time, India considers that Pakistan ignores the Treaty's accommodation of evolving technology. According to India, "the framers of the Treaty were mindful of the rapid evolution of the technology and therefore enshrined the 'state of the art' concept in the Treaty."[410] Design criteria are required to be "consistent with sound and economical design and satisfactory construction and operation,"[411] India notes, and "in the absence of any prohibition under the Treaty, India is entitled to use state-of-the-art maintenance processes and measures, including drawdown flushing, to ensure long-term sustainability of the KHEP."

300. For India, the Treaty drafters cannot have intended to prohibit drawdown flushing insofar as knowledge of the technique was limited in the 1960s. India endorses the review of the historical record undertaken in the *Baglihar* determination for the following proposition:

> Before 1960, the theoretical aspects of sediment transport were generally known, with the exception of the turbidity currents. The removal pro-

[404] India's Counter-Memorial, paras. 7.43–7.44, 7.95.

[405] India's Counter-Memorial, para. 7.56.

[406] India's Rejoinder, para. 1.85.

[407] India's Counter-Memorial, paras. 7.43–7.44, 7.95.

[408] India's Counter-Memorial, paras. 7.45, 7.95.

[409] India's Counter-Memorial, para. 7.96.

[410] India's Counter-Memorial, para. 7.56.

[411] India's Counter-Memorial, para. 7.52.

> cesses of deposited sediment by flushing and dredging, and the routing by sluicing and venting were also known and applied, but only in some cases. It was after 1970 that these processes of flushing, sluicing, and venting became more generally developed.[412]

301. Similarly, India argues, the risks of sedimentation were less thoroughly appreciated in 1960 than they are today: "it was only 20 years later, in 1980, that the concept of an integrated reservoir sedimentation management began to be clear and coherent."[413] In light of this level of awareness—and in light of the fact that the "provision of gates at low elevation in the 1960s would have been very difficult because [the] technologies related to gate operation were not developed at that time"[414]—India considers it reasonable that the Treaty would not expressly address drawdown flushing and would continue to require outlets at the highest level "consistent with sound and economical design."[415] Nevertheless, India considers flushing permissible in light of the evolving nature of this standard.[416]

302. Finally, with respect to its prior position on drawdown flushing, India accepts that "for a considerable period up to the time the Baglihar case came up before the Neutral Expert, it was assumed by the Indian and Pakistani engineers that in terms of the definition of Dead Storage, drawdown below Dead Storage Level was not allowed for flushing or otherwise."[417] However, India notes, the questions in *Baglihar* led to a re-examination of the Treaty by India and the adoption of a revised legal interpretation.[418]

(b) The Treaty's definition of "Dead Storage"

303. Paragraph 2(*a*) of Annexure D to the Treaty defines "Dead Storage" as follows:

> "Dead Storage" means that portion of the storage which is not used for operational purposes and "Dead Storage Level" means the level corresponding to Dead Storage.

Pakistan's arguments

304. In Pakistan's view, the definition of Dead Storage in Annexure D should be seen in light of the obligation on India to let flow the waters of the

---

412 Hearing Tr., (Day 6), 27 August 2012, at 150:13–20, quoting *Baglihar* Determination, (Annex PK-230), p. 42.

413 Hearing Tr., (Day 6), 27 August 2012, at 150:23 to 151:1, quoting *Baglihar* Determination, (Annex PK-230), p. 42.

414 Hearing Tr., (Day 3), 22 August 2012, at 102:12–15 (cross-examination of Dr. Rangaraju).

415 Hearing Tr., (Day 3), 22 August 2012, at 95:13 to 96:4 (cross-examination of Dr. Rangaraju).

416 India's Rejoinder, para. 1.85.

417 India's Counter-Memorial, para. 7.22.

418 India's Counter-Memorial, para. 7.23.

Western Rivers.[419] Restrictions on storage, including through this definition, represent "one of the techniques," agreed upon by the Parties, "to restrict the scope for interference with flow."[420] For Pakistan, the definition acts as a prohibition: because Dead Storage is not used for operational purposes, it "cannot just be drawn down as India see fit" in the course of operating a Run-of-River Plant.[421]

305. According to Pakistan, this restriction "cannot be sidestepped" by labelling the flushing of reservoir storage a "maintenance" activity and attempting to distinguish it from "operation."[422] Despite India's efforts to the contrary, Pakistan argues, "the fine distinction ... that India seeks to draw is nowhere supported by the language of the Treaty."[423] On the contrary, at least two of the sources invoked by India in fact support the opposite interpretation, treating sediment removal as an aspect of the operation of a reservoir.[424] Paragraph 8(*d*) of Annexure D provides that "outlets ... necessary for sediment control ... shall be of the minimum size, and located at the highest level, consistent with sound and economical design and with satisfactory operation of the works." In this provision, Pakistan argues, "[s]ediment control is seen as a matter of operation, not some separate concept of maintenance."[425] Similarly, the ICOLD Code of Ethics invoked by India addresses sediment management as a matter of operation.[426]

306. Not only, Pakistan argues, is there no textual basis for the confined understanding of "operational purposes" advocated by India, but other aspects of the Treaty are incompatible with such a view as well. The restrictions on the flow below a Plant in the course of "operation," for instance, cannot be viewed as applying only to the generation of hydro-electric power.[427] Pakistan would be offered "no practical protection" if India could obviate such flow restrictions simply by claiming to engage in "maintenance" rather than "operations."[428]

India's arguments

307. India submits that, by its explicit terms, the definition of "Dead Storage" at Paragraph 2(*a*) of Annexure D to the Treaty—"that portion of storage which *is not* used for operational purposes"—describes the actual practice of

[419] Pakistan's Memorial, para. 6.8.

[420] Hearing Tr., (Day 4), 23 August 2012, at 176:9–11.

[421] Pakistan's Memorial, para. 6.9; *see also* Pakistan's Memorial, para. 6.21.

[422] Hearing Tr., (Day 4), 23 August 2012, at 177:20–23.

[423] Pakistan's Reply, para. 6.17; *see also* Hearing Tr., (Day 4), 23 August 2012, at 178:3–4.

[424] Hearing Tr., (Day 8), 29 August 2012, at 85:18–24.

[425] Pakistan's Reply, para. 6.17.

[426] Pakistan's Reply, para. 6.18; Hearing Tr., (Day 4), 23 August 2012, at 180:15–25; Hearing Tr., (Day 8), 29 August 2012, at 85:20–23.

[427] Pakistan's Memorial, para. 6.30.

[428] Pakistan's Memorial, para. 6.30.

using Dead Storage.[429] According to India, the definition does not incorporate a prohibition: "there are no words of obligation, such as 'shall,' in the definition."[430] Had the framers of the Treaty intended to prohibit the use of Dead Storage for operational purposes, the definition would have described that "portion of the storage *which cannot/may not* be used for operational purposes."[431]

308. Although the Treaty does not define "operational purposes," India submits that drawdown flushing is not an operational purpose. For India, "operational purposes" are confined to power generation and do not include the maintenance of the reservoir[432] and, in particular, activities that make use of the "operating pool"—a term defined in the Treaty. According to India, "if dead storage is depleted for purposes of sediment control, this cannot be an operational purpose… . For such purposes, the operating pool is used."[433] In fact, during drawdown flushing, Dead Storage is not used at all, but is rather "disused or discharged."[434]

309. In India's view, drawdown flushing, like "lubrication of bearings, maintaining the requisite cleanliness, painting of gates, removal of weeds, plastering of worn concrete, replacement of chains, pulleys, etc.," is inherently a maintenance operation and ancillary to the generation of power.[435] Importantly, India observes, "[t]here is no prohibition in Annexure D against maintenance."[436] On the contrary, "maintenance is implicitly contemplated in [P]aragraph 8(*d*)'s recognition that sediment control may be necessary."[437] This interpretation, India notes, was also endorsed by the Neutral Expert in the *Baglihar* determination[438] and by Dr. Schleiss in his expert report in these proceedings.[439]

(c) *The Treaty's provisions on the filling of reservoirs*

310. Paragraph 14 of Annexure D provides as follows:

> The filling of Dead Storage shall be carried out in accordance with the provisions of Paragraph 18 or 19 of Annexure E.

311. In turn, Paragraphs 18 and 19 of Annexure E provide, in relevant part:

> 18. The initial filling below Dead Storage Level, at any site, shall be carried out at such times and in accordance with such rules as may be

[429] India's Counter-Memorial, paras. 7.23, 7.46, quoting Treaty, Annexure D, Para. 2(*d*) (emphasis added by India); India's Rejoinder, paras. 4.55, 4.57, 4.87, 4.94.

[430] Hearing Tr., (Day 6), 27 August 2012, at 145:4–5.

[431] India's Rejoinder, para. 4.59.

[432] India's Counter-Memorial, paras. 7.50, 7.94.

[433] Hearing Tr., (Day 6), 27 August 2012, at 145:13–16.

[434] India's Counter-Memorial, para. 7.50.

[435] India's Rejoinder, para. 4.89.

[436] Hearing Tr., (Day 6), 27 August 2012, at 145:16–17.

[437] Hearing Tr., (Day 6), 27 August 2012, at 145:18–20.

[438] India's Counter-Memorial, paras. 7.25, 7.26; India's Rejoinder, para. 4.94.

[439] India's Counter-Memorial, paras. 4.87–4.88, referring to Schleiss Report, pp. 6–7.

> agreed upon. In case the Commissioners are unable to reach agreement, India may carry out the filling as follows:
>
> [...]
>
> 19. The Dead Storage shall not be depleted except in an unforeseen emergency. If so depleted, it will be re-filled in accordance with the conditions of its initial filling.

Pakistan's arguments

312. In Pakistan's submission, Paragraph 14 of Annexure D, through its reference to the provisions for Storage Works in Annexure E, imposes on Run-of-River Plants the restriction that Dead Storage "shall not be depleted except in an unforeseen emergency." According to Pakistan, the need for removal of accumulated sediment cannot constitute an "unforeseen emergency," given that this need has already been anticipated by India, as well as by the Treaty at Paragraph 8(*d*) of Annexure D.[440] Accordingly, Pakistan argues, the depletion of Dead Storage for drawdown flushing is prohibited by Paragraph 14.

313. In interpreting the incorporation from Annexure E, Pakistan submits that the ordinary meaning of Paragraph 14 is a reference to all of Paragraphs 18 and 19 of Annexure E—including the prohibition on reservoir depletion.[441] According to Pakistan, "the second sentence of paragraph 19 of Annexure E follows on—and only follows on—from the rule on depletion in the first sentence of paragraph 19."[442] The second sentence begins with the words "if so depleted"; grammatically it "makes no sense"[443] without the preceding sentence. In Pakistan's view, the provision "cannot be interpreted and applied as if it established a rule for 'filling' that applied in other circumstances."[444] Moreover, Pakistan asks, given that the schedule for filling is contained in Paragraph 18, if the Parties' concern was related only to filling (and not to depletion), "why would there be the reference to paragraph 19 of Annexure E at all? Why not just refer to paragraph 18?"[445]

314. In Pakistan's consideration, the prohibition on depletion resulting from Paragraph 14 is also logical in the context of the Treaty's overall effort to limit storage and restrict India's ability to control the flow of the Western Rivers.[446] The Parties were aware that sediment would be a problem.[447] Yet sedimentation, Pakistan argues, is a greater problem for Storage Works than for Run-of-River installations, for which the techniques for sediment manage-

[440] Pakistan's Memorial, para. 6.21.

[441] Pakistan's Reply, paras. 6.23–6.25; *see also* Hearing Tr., (Day 4), 23 August 2012, at 185:13–18.

[442] Hearing Tr., (Day 4), 23 August 2012, at 186:9–12.

[443] Hearing Tr., (Day 4), 23 August 2012, at 186:12–15.

[444] Pakistan's Reply, para. 6.25.

[445] Hearing Tr., (Day 8), 29 August 2012, at 82:11–16; Hearing Tr., (Day 8), 29 August 2012, at 82:17–22.

[446] Hearing Tr., (Day 4), 23 August 2012, at 184:17–23.

[447] Hearing Tr., (Day 4), 23 August 2012, at 184:4–6.

ment were well-developed in 1960. Annexure E expressly prohibits the depletion of Storage Works for sediment control and provides instead that, as such works fill with sediment, India is entitled to construct additional, replacement storage on the Western Rivers.[448] It would be counter-intuitive for concerns over sedimentation to have resulted in greater flexibility precisely for those run-of-river installations where sediment is actually a lesser problem.[449]

315. Finally, Pakistan observes, the KHEP is not typical of the type of Run-of-River Plant that may have been contemplated by Annexure D. After its re-design from a Storage Work in 2006, the KHEP retained many characteristics of an Annexure E Storage Work,[450] in particular, a Dead Storage volume far greater than is characteristic of typical Run-of-River Plants.[451] Considering its design and the large hydrological size of its reservoir,[452] Pakistan suggests that the KHEP could be better characterized as an Annexure E Storage Work. Viewed as a Storage Work in terms of Annexure E, Pakistan considers that the express prohibition on depletion in Paragraph 19 would unquestionably apply.[453]

India's arguments

316. In India's view, Paragraph 14 of Annexure D, and its reference to the relevant provisions of Annexure E, restricts the filling and refilling of the reservoirs of Run-of-River Plants—but not the depletion of such reservoirs. Depletion, India notes, "isn't mentioned at all in Annexure D."[454]

317. In drafting the Treaty, India argues, the Parties employed cross-references as a matter of economy and consistency.[455] Paragraph 14 of Annexure D addresses the filling of the reservoir of a Run-of-River Plant by reference to Paragraphs 18 and 19 of Annexure E. The scope of the reference, however, is established by its own terms: Paragraph 14 refers only to the "filling" of Dead Storage—not to its depletion. Accordingly, for India, only the portions of Paragraphs 18 and 19 dealing with filling are relevant to the reference.[456] In India's view, such an interpretation is consistent with other provisions of the Treaty[457]

[448] Hearing Tr., (Day 4), 23 August 2012, at 187:1–3.

[449] Hearing Tr., (Day 4), 23 August 2012, at 187:5–8.

[450] Pakistan's Reply, paras. 6.27, 6.30.

[451] Pakistan's Reply, para. 6.27, referring to Morris Report, p. 13.

[452] Pakistan argues that the relatively small overall reservoir capacity of the KHEP (in comparison with other, much-larger dams) is "irrelevant" because it is based on gross volume only. Instead, the relevant metric should be the relationship between reservoir capacity and annual watershed runoff volume (inflow)—the reservoir's "hydrologic size." Pakistan's Reply, para. 6.28, citing Morris Report, p. 11. Viewed in such terms, the KHEP reservoir is not small; indeed in hydrological terms it is 20 times larger than the reservoir of the NJHEP. Pakistan's Reply, para. 6.29, quoting Morris Report, p. 12.

[453] Pakistan's Reply, paras. 6.30–6.31.

[454] Hearing Tr., (Day 6), 27 August 2012, at 139:24–25.

[455] Hearing Tr., (Day 6), 27 August 2012, at 140:9–20.

[456] India's Counter-Memorial, paras. 7.40–7.41.

[457] Paragraph 17 of Annexure D, India notes, refers to the reservoir of a Run-of-River Plant "being filled in accordance with ... Paragraph 14." India's Rejoinder, para. 4.63, quoting Treaty,

and with the practice elsewhere of making prohibitions explicit.[458] Had the drafters contemplated a prohibition on depletion, India argues, it would have been expressly stated.[459]

318. According to India, the existence of distinct rules on depletion for Storage Works (Annexure E), and Run-of-River Plants (Annexure D) is consistent with the different nature of such projects. Run-of-River Plants such as the KHEP require the impoundment of a significantly smaller quantity of water than Storage Works. In the KHEP's design, the volume of water between Dead Storage Level and the spillway gates is small and would require only a few hours to refill with average minimum daily flows.[460] In view of the reduced capacity for Run-of-River Plants to impact downstream flows, India argues, the Treaty allows for greater flexibility in the depletion of the reservoirs of such Plants.[461] Further, India notes, the absence of a rule on depletion in Annexure D is consistent with the Treaty's approach to lost storage capacity. Annexure E prohibits the use of flushing on Storage Works, but Paragraph 23 of that Annexure permits India to construct additional replacement storage.[462] No equivalent provision for Run-of-River Plants exists, suggesting that the Treaty intended the flushing of storage, rather than its replacement, for such Plants.[463]

319. Finally, India rejects Pakistan's allegation that the KHEP is actually an Annexure E Storage Work. The Treaty, India notes, defines a Run-of-River Plant as "a hydro-electric power plant that develops power without the use of Live Storage as an integral part of the Plant, except for Pondage and Surcharge Storage." According to India, this definition does not depend on the overall volume of water impounded by a project, but only on the relationship between Live Storage and the volume of water used in regular power generation.[464] In India's view, the KHEP conforms to that definition.[465] Moreover, the re-design of the KHEP from a Storage Work greatly reduced both the overall and Live Storage volumes of the Plant,[466] and with a capacity to inflow ratio of 0.59 percent, India considers the KHEP consistent with other Run-of-River Plant designs.[467]

Annexure D, Para. 17 (emphasis added by India).

[458] India notes the practice in Paragraph 8 of Annexure D, which provides that "[t]here shall be no outlets below the Dead Storage Level" except under the prescribed conditions. India's Rejoinder, para. 4.64.

[459] India's Rejoinder, para. 4.65.

[460] India's Counter-Memorial, paras. 7.31–7.32, 7.35; India's Rejoinder, para. 4.72, referring to the Schleiss Report.

[461] India's Counter-Memorial, paras. 7.33, 7.42; Hearing Tr., (Day 6), 27 August 2012, at 142:6–21.

[462] Hearing Tr., (Day 6), 27 August 2012, at 143:6 to 144:2.

[463] India's Counter-Memorial, para. 7.38.

[464] India's Rejoinder, para. 4.74.

[465] India's Rejoinder, paras. 4.67–4.68, referring to Pakistan's Memorial, para. 3.9.

[466] The KHEP's design as a Storage Work included 220 MCM of Gross Storage and 173.75 MCM of Live Storage. As a Run-of-River Plant, the KHEP's current design envisages respectively only 18.35 MCM and 7.55 MCM.

[467] India's Rejoinder, para. 4.73.

India also observes that Pakistan itself has "treated, described and objected to aspects of [the] KHEP since 2006 on the basis it is a run-of-river plant."[468]

(d) The Treaty's provisions on low-level outlets

320. Paragraph 8 of Annexure D requires the design of any new Run-of-River Plant to conform to the following criteria:

> [...]
>
> (*d*) There shall be no outlets below the Dead Storage Level, unless necessary for sediment control or any other technical purpose; any such outlet shall be of the minimum size, and located at the highest level, consistent with the sound and economical design and with satisfactory operation of the works.
>
> [...]

Pakistan's arguments

321. Pakistan considers that the references to "sediment control" and to "outlets below the Dead Storage Level" in Paragraph 8(*d*) of Annexure D are "not a permission to deplete below dead storage level; it's simply a permission to have outlets below dead storage level."[469] This distinction is important, because such outlets can—and in Pakistan's view must—be used to control sediment "without drawing down below the dead storage level."[470] Although Pakistan acknowledges that the provision operates with reference to "sound and economical design," Pakistan submits that this cannot "entirely remove the general rule that is in the first part of the provision: minimum size, located at the highest level."[471]

India's arguments

322. According to India, the relevance of Paragraph 8(*d*) is that it "expressly contemplates two things: both control of sedimentation and outlets below the dead storage level … for sediment control."[472] Nowhere in the provision is there any mention of a prohibition on depletion or a requirement of an unforeseen emergency.[473] On the contrary, because "depletion of dead storage would in fact occur for sediment control," and because Paragraph 8(*d*) expressly permits sediment control, depletion is implicitly permitted by Annexure D.[474] This being the case, India argues, the control of sediment

[468] India's Rejoinder, para. 4.84.

[469] Hearing Tr., (Day 10), 31 August 2012, at 43:10–15.

[470] Hearing Tr., (Day 8), 29 August 2012, at 83:21–22.

[471] Hearing Tr., (Day 4), 23 August 2012, at 190:18–20.

[472] Hearing Tr., (Day 6), 27 August 2012, at 138:11–15; *see also* India's Rejoinder, para. 4.49.

[473] Hearing Tr., (Day 6), 27 August 2012, at 138:16–17.

[474] Hearing Tr., (Day 6), 27 August 2012, at 141:5–9.

through drawdown flushing "cannot be deemed to be an 'exercise of control over the waters of the Western Rivers.'"[475]

(e) The Treaty's provisions on water flow

323. The chapeau of Paragraph 15 of Annexure D restricts the flow that may be released below a Plant in the following terms:

> Subject to the provisions of Paragraph 17 [excluding periods of filling], the works connected with a Plant shall be so operated that (*a*) the volume of water received in the river upstream of the Plant during any period of seven consecutive days, shall be delivered into the river below the Plant during the same seven-day period, and (*b*) in any one period of 24 hours within that seven-day period, the volume delivered into the river below the Plant shall not be less that 30%, and not more than 130%, of the volume received in the river above the Plant during the same 24-hour period.

Pakistan's arguments

324. Pakistan submits that, although Paragraph 15 does not expressly address the release of water from Dead Storage, the practical impact of the flow restrictions is such that "[d]rawdown flushing is ... severely curtailed (if not prohibited)."[476] According to Pakistan, the rapid depletion of the reservoir to flush it "would contravene paragraph 15 of Annexure D, insofar as 130% or more of the volume received in the river above the Plant within a given 24 hour period was being delivered into the river below the Plant."[477] Pakistan considers this concern to be present irrespective of the season in which drawdown flushing is carried out, and notes that the Treaty does not limit the restrictions on the release of water to any particular season.[478]

India's arguments

325. India accepts that the restrictions under Paragraph 15 of Annexure D on the release of water below a Plant remain applicable, but submits that these restrictions do not prevent drawdown flushing. According to India, given that drawdown flushing would be effected in the high flow season, "the question of any reduced flow does not arise."[479]

(f) The necessity of drawdown flushing

Pakistan's arguments

326. In Pakistan's view, the permissibility of drawdown flushing turns on the interpretation of the specific Treaty provisions discussed in the preceding

[475] India's Rejoinder, para. 4.49.
[476] Pakistan's Memorial, para. 6.30.
[477] Pakistan's Reply, para. 6.32.
[478] Pakistan's Reply, para. 6.32.
[479] India's Counter-Memorial, para. 7.51.

sections and not on any general test of necessity. Nevertheless, Pakistan briefly addresses India's arguments concerning the necessity of drawdown flushing.[480]

327. Pakistan does not dispute the need for effective sediment management of reservoirs of hydro-electric projects.[481] However, in Pakistan's view, effective sediment management at Run-of-River Plants, including the KHEP, can be accomplished without recourse to drawdown flushing. Relying on the Morris Report, Pakistan explains that sediment management in Run-of-River Plants is routinely achieved by sluicing high sediment loads downstream:

> sediment management in run-of-river facilities was worked out many decades ago by providing large gate capacity which allows sediment to be sluiced through the impounded river during high flow periods. This is achieved by opening the large gates and allowing the river to flow through the impounded river reach at a high velocity.[482]

328. According to Pakistan, these well-established procedures do not change if a Run-of-River facility is designed to include a high dam rather than a low barrage: "A run-of-river project, ... if properly designed, would operate as a typical run-of-river facility once the large dead storage volume has become filled with sediment."[483] In the words of Pakistan's expert, the distinction between a barrage and a dam "rests a little bit on semantics"; provided that gates are in place to scour sediment from in front of the intake area, the process of controlling sediment will be the same.[484]

329. In Pakistan's view, the emphasis that India places on drawdown flushing is appropriate only for storage reservoirs.[485] India's case relies primarily on examples of storage reservoirs rather than Run-of-River Plants.[486] The ICOLD recommendations on which India places heavy reliance were developed primarily with the problem of storage dams in mind.[487] Moreover, Pakistan argues, India has understated the substantial environmental impact of flushing.[488] According to Dr. Morris, the heavily concentrated sediments released in the course of flushing "can have very large impacts a very long way downstream," as a consequence of which, flushing is restricted or prohibited

---

[480] Pakistan's Reply, paras. 6.10–6.12.

[481] Pakistan's Reply, para. 6.10.

[482] Morris Report, p. 3; Hearing Tr., (Day 2), 21 August 2012, at 113:18–24 (cross-examination of Dr. Morris). Pakistan's expert discussed, in particular, the effective use of sluicing at the Kali Gandaki hydro-electric project in Nepal, a run-of-river facility which, like the KHEP, features a high dam design. *See* Hearing Tr., (Day 2), 21 August 2012, at 108:15 to 110:1 (cross-examination of Dr. Morris).

[483] Morris Report, p. 3.

[484] Hearing Tr., (Day 2), 21 August 2012, at 107:7–12 (cross-examination of Dr. Morris).

[485] Pakistan's Reply, para. 6.11; Morris Report, pp. 9, 19.

[486] Pakistan's Reply, para. 6.11.

[487] Morris Report, pp. 3, 9, 18.

[488] Hearing Tr., (Day 8), 29 August 2012, at 87:8–13.

by regulation in many areas of the world.[489] In Pakistan's view, such negative impacts would need to be assessed in any evaluation of the necessity of drawdown flushing, were it permitted by the Treaty.[490]

330. Turning to the KHEP and the Treaty, Pakistan does not accept that flushing constitutes the only viable means of controlling sediment.[491] As stated by Dr. Morris, sluicing would also present "a very viable option to examine" for the KHEP that "could function well."[492] With respect to protecting the KHEP intake from sediment, Dr. Morris testified that the same result could be achieved with intakes and outlets placed at a higher level (as required by Paragraph 8 of Annexure D to the Treaty). As coarse and abrasive particles tend to be concentrated near the bottom of a reservoir, a Run-of-River Plant will typically use a high-level intake by "establishing a weir running parallel to the flow path which allows only the water from the upper portion of the water column to be withdrawn from the river."[493] For the KHEP, however, India has chosen to use a "deeper orifice-type intake design which also requires significant submergence depth to control the effect of vortices."[494] The Morris Report illustrates the difference between the high level intakes of typical Run-of-River Plants and the KHEP's deep orifice-type intakes by the following diagram:

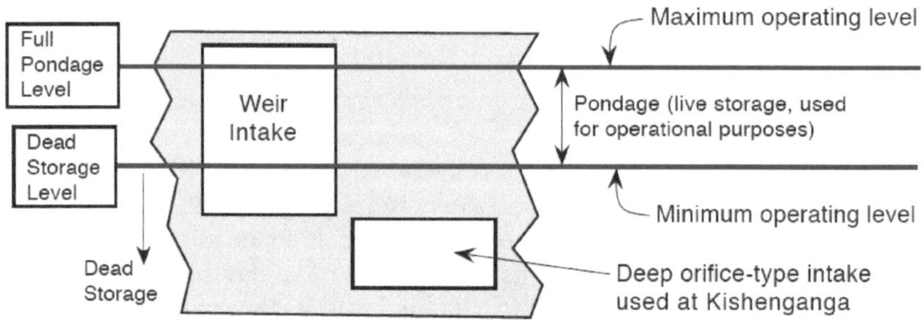

[489] Hearing Tr., (Day 2), 21 August 2012, at 131:14–16 (Court examination of Dr. Morris). Specifically, Dr. Morris states that flushing will have a significant impact on downstream aquatic life by clogging the gills of fish, clogging the loose gravel in the bed material, and depleting oxygen levels. *See* Hearing Tr., (Day 2), 21 August 2012, at 132:24–25 (Court examination of Dr. Morris); *see also* Hearing Tr., (Day 2), 21 August 2012, at 100:13–15 (cross-examination of Dr. Morris).

[490] *See* Hearing Tr., (Day 8), 29 August 2012, at 87:8–13.

[491] Hearing Tr., (Day 8), 29 August 2012, at 90:9–12 ("Pakistan does challenge any conclusion that only drawdown flushing would work at KHEP."); *see also* Hearing Tr., (Day 8), 29 August 2012, at 87:19–21. Pakistan further notes that even India's submissions indicate that excluding flushing would only marginally increase the problem of sedimentation in the KHEP reservoir. *See* Hearing Tr., (Day 8), 29 August 2012, at 88:2–4.

[492] Hearing Tr., (Day 2), 21 August 2012, at 126:22–24 (Court examination of Dr. Morris). Under cross-examination, Dr. Morris accepted that flushing was also technically feasible and could be considered as an alternative where permitted. *See* Hearing Tr., (Day 2), 21 August 2012, at 100:24–25, 104:11–13, 117:9–10 (cross-examination of Dr. Morris).

[493] Morris Report, p. 15.

[494] Morris Report, p. 15.

In effect, having chosen an atypically deep intake design, India then justifies an even deeper outlet by the need to clear sediment from the area of the intake.[495]

India's arguments

331. India submits that no provisions of the Treaty were intended specifically to prohibit the use of drawdown flushing for reservoirs of Run-of-River Plants; the framers of the Treaty did not intend to "freeze" the construction of hydro-electric projects to the technology of 1960. On the contrary, they enshrined a "state-of-the-art" concept in the Treaty through the use of provisions relating to the "sound and economical design and satisfactory construction and operation of the works" and "customary and accepted practice of design."[496] As such, the relevant question for India is whether drawdown flushing in fact represents the state of the art, and whether such techniques are necessary for the KHEP.[497]

332. In India's view, "the state of art today is that '... [f]or the control of reservoir sedimentation, bottom outlets should be designed (and operated) to preserve reservoir storage in the long term.'"[498] At the KHEP, India considers that "drawdown flushing is the only effective measure which can ensure sustainability of the pondage."[499] Although technical aspects of the KHEP—in particular the practice of assigning spillways the dual function of flood control and sediment management—are relatively new, India considers that they are in keeping with the provision for low-level outlets included in the Treaty.[500]

333. Elaborating on this argument, India notes that sediment management is essential for the sustainability of any hydro-electric project. The absence of effective sediment management rapidly leads to the loss of capacity of reservoirs and the abandonment of hydro-electric projects,[501] and conservation of storage is especially crucial in light of the "diminishing availability of suitable, environmentally acceptable and economically viable sites."[502] Thus, the ICOLD Code of Ethics enjoins engineers to "take great care, during operation of the scheme, to extend the life to the maximum extent possible and especially as regards the management (prevention of removal) of sedimenta-

---

[495] Morris Report, pp. 14, 15.

[496] India's Counter-Memorial, para. 7.52; India's Rejoinder, paras. 4.94–4.95.

[497] India's Counter-Memorial, para. 7.59.

[498] India's Counter-Memorial, para. 7.59, quoting ICOLD, Bulletin 115, "Dealing with reservoir sedimentation," 1999, (Annex IN-TX-1), p. 79.

[499] Hearing Tr., (Day 6), 27 August 2012, at 161:24 to 162:1, quoting Schleiss Report, p. 7.

[500] India's Rejoinder, para. 4.100.

[501] India's Counter-Memorial, paras. 7.60–7.63, referring to Alessandro Palmieri, *Sustainability of Dams—Reservoir Sedimentation Management and Safety Implications* (World Bank, 1998), (Annex IN-TX-2); Yang Xiaoqing, "Manual on Sediment Management and Measurement," World Meteorological Organization Operational Hydrology Report No. 47, WMO-No. 948 (2003), (Annex IN-TX-3), para. 7.76; India's Rejoinder, para. 4.88, referring to Schleiss Report, pp. 6–7.

[502] India's Counter-Memorial, para. 7.64.

tion."[503] India and Pakistan, as members of ICOLD, are in India's view "morally committed" to following this tenet.[504] Controlling sediment is also essential to ensure that the water drawn in by the intake is free from sediments to avoid damage to the turbines and sediment deposits in the head-race tunnel.[505]

334. According to India, drawdown flushing, when it involves bringing the water level of the reservoir close to the original riverbed level, is an effective and internationally recognized method for sediment management.[506] This is confirmed in modern literature,[507] as well as by ICOLD Bulletin 115[508] and the experience of a variety of hydro-electric projects across the world.[509] In India's view, the ICOLD recommendations are not limited to Storage Works, but expressly apply to any dams exceeding 15 metres in height, regardless of whether they involve storage or Run-of-River projects; this includes the KHEP, with its 37-metre dam design.[510] Accordingly, India considers the Morris Report incorrect in stating that drawdown flushing is required in Storage Works only. Drawdown flushing is also necessary in high-head Run-of-River Plants because the latter are often built in mountain regions on steep rivers that are endangered by sedimentation.[511] In fact, India notes, drawdown flushing is considered particularly efficient for small reservoirs with a low capacity/inflow ratio.[512]

---

[503] India's Counter-Memorial, para. 7.65, quoting ICOLD Code of Ethics, adopted at the 74th Executive Meeting, Sitges, June 2006, (Annex IN-TX-4).

[504] India's Counter-Memorial, para. 7.66.

[505] India's Counter-Memorial, para. 7.85; Schleiss Report, p. 5.

[506] India's Counter-Memorial, para. 7.81; *see also* Hearing Tr., (Day 3), 22 August 2012, at 67:21–68:6, 78:19–25, 82:21–25.

[507] India's Counter-Memorial, paras. 7.98, 7.81, referring to W.R. White, "World Water: Resources, Usage and the Role of Man-Made Reservoirs" (March 2010), (Annex IN-TX-7), and to R. White, "Evacuation of sediment from reservoirs," (Annex IN-TX-8).

[508] ICOLD, Bulletin 115, "Dealing with reservoir sedimentation," 1999, (Annex IN-TX-1), paras. 4.1.2, 7.1.

[509] According to India, successful drawdown flushing operations were carried out at the Baira (India), Gebidem (Switzerland), Gmund (Austria), Hengshan (China), Honglinggjin (China), Mangahao (New Zealand), Naodehai (China), Palagneda (Switzerland), Santo Domingo (Venezuela), Cherry Creek (U.S.A.), Dashidaira (Japan), Roseires (Sudan), Three Gorges (China), and Welbedacht (South Africa) reservoirs. India's Counter-Memorial, paras. 7.81–7.82, referring to E. Atkinson, The Feasibility of Flushing Sediment from Reservoirs, Report OD137 (November 1996), (Annex IN-TX-10), p. 2; para. 7.82, referring to Record of the 96th Meeting of the Commission, New Delhi, 1–2 June 2005, (Annex PK-31), p. 5; para. 7.102. India also mentions that the NJHEP envisages drawdown flushing on a "much larger scale" than the KHEP. India's Counter-Memorial referring to the Pakistani Water and Power Development Authority (WAPDA), (Annex IN-79).

[510] India's Rejoinder, para. 4.77.

[511] Schleiss Report, p. 2.

[512] India's Rejoinder, paras. 4.75–4.78, referring to W. Rodney White, "Flushing of Sediments from Reservoirs," Contributing Paper to the World Commission on Dams, (Annex IN-TX-9), p. vi; Schleiss Report, p. 5; K.G. Rangaraju, "Critical Appraisal of the Report of Dr. Morris," 14 May 2012.

335. With respect to the KHEP, India notes that sedimentation problems are particularly acute in the Himalayan rivers such as the Kishenganga/Neelum, due to climatic, tectonic and geological factors.[513] Contrary to the suggestions made in the Morris Report,[514] India does not accept that a Run-of-River project will operate without adverse effect once the Dead Storage has filled with sediment. In India's view, this assertion ignores the fact that sediments do not accumulate along a horizontal plane, but settle simultaneously in the Dead and Live Storage, a fact Dr. Morris acknowledges in another document.[515]

336. Based on its calculations, India submits that "it is imperative to carry out regular flushing [at the KHEP] to minimize sedimentation and loss of storage capacity as well as to maintain the favourable sediment environment near the power intake."[516] Modelling exercises carried out by both India and Pakistan[517] illustrate the benefits drawdown flushing would have for the KHEP.[518] In contrast, India argues, the use of non-drawdown methods of sediment management such as sluicing through an ungated or crest-gated spillway would present difficulties—both technically and in terms of conformity with the Treaty.[519] In India's view, this would not change with a higher level of intake and outlets, or with the use of a small barrage/weir intake.[520] The latter method is used exclusively at low-head Run-of-River Plants with limited storage.[521] Effective sediment management requires that the spillway be as close as possible to the riverbed to create river-like flow conditions allowing the maximal displacement of sediments. The intake must, on the one hand, be above the level of the spillway to avoid being affected by sediments. At the same time, the intake

---

[513] India's Counter-Memorial, paras. 7.67–7.68.

[514] Morris Report, p. 3.

[515] India's Rejoinder, para. 4.96, referring to Gregory L. Morris and Jiahua Fan, *Reservoir Sedimentation Handbook: Design and Management of Reservoirs, Dams, and Watersheds for Sustainable Use*, Electronic version 1.01, September 2009, (Annex IN-135). For example, in 31 years of operation, the Tarbela reservoir in Pakistan lost 33.30 percent of its Dead Storage and 27.22 percent of its Live Storage. India's Counter-Memorial, paras. 7.72–7.73, referring to Izhar-ul-Haq & S. Tanveer Abbas, "Sedimentation of Tarbela & Mangla Reservoirs," Paper No. 659, Pakistan Engineering Congress, 70th Annual Session Proceedings, 2006, (Annex IN-TX-6), p. 28.

[516] India's Counter-Memorial, para. 7.92.

[517] Pakistan's Memorial, Hagler Bailly Pakistan, Water Matters, Southern Waters & Beuster, Clarke and Associates, "Kishenganga/Neelum Water Diversion: Environmental Assessment," May 2011, pp. 334–336. India's Counter-Memorial, paras. 7.88–7.91.

[518] India's Counter-Memorial, paras. 7.86–7.91.

[519] The Indian Commissioner explained at the 100th and 101st meetings of the Commission that an ungated spillway was not an option due to the site conditions, including the narrowness of the Gurez Valley, the geology, and the design flood and sediment. With a crest-gated spillway, the outlets in the dam would have had to be placed lower than those of the KHEP and the gates would have had a discharge capacity of 140 percent of the river flow. These features could have invited Pakistan's objections under the Treaty. India's Counter-Memorial, paras. 7.83–7.84, referring to Record of the 100th Meeting of the Commission, Lahore, 31 May–4 June 2008, (Annex PK-34), p. 24; Record of the 101st Meeting of the Commission, New Delhi, 25–28 July 2008, (Annex PK-35), p. 10; India's Rejoinder, paras. 4.98, 4.106.

[520] India's Rejoinder, paras. 4.107–4.108, referring to the Schleiss Report, pp. 4–5.

[521] Schleiss Report, p. 2.

must be sufficiently submerged to avoid vortex formation and air entrainment into the intake as well as to ensure pressure flow in the head-race tunnel.[522]

337. In evaluating its design options, India accepts that, as the upstream State, it must examine any design options submitted to it by the downstream State. Nevertheless, India is entitled to "give preference to the solution contained in its own scheme provided that it takes into consideration in a reasonable manner the interests of the [downstream] State."[523] For India, the KHEP's spillway outlets, as currently designed and located, are consistent with sound and economical design.[524]

(g) The Baglihar expert determination

338. The *Baglihar* expert determination, issued on 12 February 2007 by Professor Raymond Lafitte, a neutral expert appointed under Annexure F to the Treaty, addressed a number of differences between the Parties with respect to the Baglihar hydro-electric project located on the Chenab River. Among other issues, the Neutral Expert considered the conformity of the design of the Baglihar project's low-level sluice spillway with Paragraph 8(*d*) of Annexure D to the Treaty.[525]

339. In this context, the Neutral Expert stated the following:

> Sound operation of the outlets will necessitate carrying out maintenance of the reservoir with drawdown sluicing each year during the monsoon season. The reservoir level should be drawn down to a level of about 818 m asl, that is to say 17 m below that of the Dead Storage Level. For this level, the free flow discharge is the annual flood of the order of 2,500 m3/s. This is in conformity with Annexure D, Part 1, 2(*a*) of the Treaty, which provides that "'Dead Storage' means that portion of the storage which is not used for *operational purpose*". Operational purpose refers to power generation (and this is impossible for the Dead Storage because of the high level of the power intake). The reservoir drawdown below the Dead Storage Level will be done for *maintenance purposes*. It is commonly agreed in practice that maintenance is an absolute necessity, with its ultimate objective of ensuring the *sustainability of the scheme*.[526]

340. The Parties disagree as to the relevance of this section of *Baglihar* to the Court's consideration of the Second Dispute.

---

[522] Schleiss Report, pp. 3–4.

[523] India's Counter-Memorial, para. 7.92, referring to *Lake Lanoux*, (Annex IN-14), para. 23.

[524] Schleiss Report, p. 4.

[525] *Baglihar* Determination, (Annex PK-230), pp. 92–100. Paragraph 8(*d*) of Annexure D to the Treaty provides as follows:

> There shall be no outlets below the Dead Storage Level, unless necessary for sediment control or any other technical purpose; any such outlet shall be of the minimum size, and located at the highest level, consistent with sound and economical design and with satisfactory operation of the works.

[526] *Baglihar* Determination, (Annex PK-230), p. 100.

Pakistan's arguments

341. At the outset, Pakistan submits that it is not seeking to appeal *Baglihar*, but only to show that this Expert determination is not binding upon the Court with respect to the Second Dispute.[527] For Pakistan, *Baglihar* could have no more than persuasive value although, for the reasons stated in the preceding sections, Pakistan disagrees with the reasoning of the Neutral Expert.[528]

342. Pakistan points out that, pursuant to the explicit terms of Paragraph 11 of Annexure F to the Treaty, the decision of a neutral expert is "final and binding" on the Parties and a court of arbitration only "in respect of the particular matter on which the decision is made." *Baglihar* concerned a different matter from the one presently before the Court as it involved a different hydro-electric project (the Baglihar project rather than the KHEP) on a different river (the Chenab rather than the Kishenganga/Neelum).[529]

343. While acknowledging that the issue of the Neutral Expert's competence "is not a matter for this Court to decide," Pakistan nevertheless asserts that, in deciding on the permissibility of drawdown flushing under the Treaty, the Neutral Expert exceeded his competence.[530] Pakistan's principal complaints are that the Parties did not refer to the Neutral Expert any difference concerning drawdown flushing and that Pakistan did not have an opportunity to address the issue. In support, Pakistan provides a brief account of *Baglihar*'s procedural history, which it submits is confirmed by India's own narrative of the course of those proceedings.[531]

344. According to Pakistan, the Parties made their submissions on the basis that the Baglihar project would be operated without drawdown flushing, assuming that the Treaty prohibited this technique.[532] The Neutral Expert's draft determination, which was communicated to the Parties for their comments prior to the issuance of the final determination, also proceeded on the basis that drawdown flushing was prohibited under the Treaty.[533] India for the first time asserted that drawdown flushing was permitted in its written comments on the draft determination, which were not communicated to Pakistan, and in the oral hearing that followed.[534] At the hearing, India only outlined

[527] Pakistan's Memorial, para. 6.24; Pakistan's Reply, para. 6.6.

[528] Hearing Tr., (Day 4), 23 August 2012, at 195:1–8.

[529] Pakistan's Memorial, para. 6.25; Pakistan's Reply, para. 6.6.

[530] Pakistan's Memorial, para. 6.28; Pakistan's Reply, para. 6.7.

[531] Pakistan's Reply, para. 6.7, referring to India's Counter-Memorial, paras. 7.19–7.26; Hearing Tr., (Day 4), 23 August 2012, at 196:13 to 197:14.

[532] Pakistan's Memorial, para. 6.26, referring to *Baglihar* Determination, (Annex PK-230), p. 96, which excerpts the Parties' respective memorial and counter-memorial in that case; *Baglihar* transcript, 28 May 2006, (Annex PK-233), pp. 138–139; *Baglihar* transcript, 19 October 2006, (Annex PK-232), p. 33; Hearing Tr., (Day 4), 23 August 2012, at 179:17–25; Hearing Tr., (Day 8), 29 August 2012, at 92:14 to 93:15.

[533] Pakistan's Memorial, para. 6.27, referring to Raymond Lafitte, *Baglihar*, "Final Draft Determination by the Neutral Expert," 30 October 2006, (Annex PK-231), pp. 88–89.

[534] Pakistan's Memorial, para. 6.27, fn. 232, referring to *Baglihar* transcript, 8 November 2006 (Annex PK-234), p. 264; Hearing Tr., (Day 8), 29 August 2012, at 93:16–24.

the arguments "it would have made" were the question of drawdown flushing before the Neutral Expert. Pakistan therefore correctly did not seek to respond to these arguments immediately, but reserved its position on the matter.[535] Nevertheless, the Neutral Expert reversed his conclusion on drawdown flushing in his final determination, without giving Pakistan the opportunity to respond to the positive case made by India.[536]

345. Pakistan concludes that being outside the Neutral Expert's competence, the *Baglihar* determination cannot be properly regarded as "final and binding," nor given any weight.[537]

346. In any event, Pakistan submits that the Neutral Expert's reasoning is unpersuasive and his conclusion with regard to the permissibility of drawdown flushing under the Treaty— erroneous.[538] In particular, the Neutral Expert erred in according priority to India's concerns about sedimentation over the wording of the Treaty.[539]

India's arguments

347. In its Counter-Memorial, India argues that the Second Dispute constitutes an appeal of the *Baglihar* determination and, as such, is not admissible for consideration by the Court. India points out that Pakistan challenges the Neutral Expert's competence and the correctness of his decision.[540]

348. In its Rejoinder, India submits that it seeks to rely on *Baglihar* not as a "binding" precedent, but as only "a relevant and applicable precedent … dealing with similar facts and law; and therefore one that obviously sheds authoritative light … on the interpretation of the provisions in question."[541] In this regard, India contends that relying on precedents is a "desirable and universally accepted practice."[542] At the hearing, India referred to *Baglihar* as an "authoritative precedent."[543]

349. With regard to the procedure in *Baglihar*, India explains that the Neutral Expert invited the Parties' comments on a draft of his determination "as

[535] Pakistan's Memorial, para. 6.27, fn. 232; Pakistan's Reply, para. 6.8; Hearing Tr., (Day 8), 29 August 2012, at 93:23 to 94:7, referring to *Baglihar* transcript of 8 November 2006 (Annex PK-234).

[536] Pakistan's Memorial, para. 6.27.

[537] Pakistan's Memorial, para. 6.28, fn. 233; Hearing Tr., (Day 8), 29 August 2012, at 96:20–21.

[538] Pakistan's Memorial, paras. 6.29–6.33; Hearing Tr., (Day 4), 23 August 2012, at 195:7–15.

[539] Pakistan's Memorial, para. 6.31, referring to J. Briscoe, "War or Peace on the Indus?" *The News*, 3 April 2010, (Annex PK-229), pp. 1–2; Hearing Tr., (Day 4), 23 August 2012, at 195:16 to 196:5.

[540] India's Counter-Memorial, paras. 7.17, 7.27.

[541] India's Rejoinder, paras. 4.44.

[542] India's Rejoinder, para. 4.44.

[543] Hearing Tr., (Day 6), 27 August 2012, at 126:14–22.

a courtesy" and "[a]s is usual in the relationship between engineers."[544] His draft determination prompted India to re-examine its position on the interpretation of Paragraph 2(*a*) of Annexure D to the Treaty and submit its new views to the Neutral Expert by way of comments.[545] Pakistan chose not to reply to India's new argument.[546] The Neutral Expert then issued his final determination, deciding without referring to any of the submissions made before him by the Parties, "in the light of his own experience and understanding of the modern technical processes of generating power from hydroelectric projects."[547] The Neutral Expert's conclusions reflected his concern that without drawdown flushing, the Baglihar project would by all accounts last no more than two decades.[548]

C. The Relevance of Territorial Claims

350. The Parties disagree as to whether Pakistan, in the course of this arbitration, has improperly invoked the Treaty in support of any territorial claims it may have in Pakistan-administered Jammu and Kashmir, thus violating Article XI(1) of the Treaty.

351. Article XI(1) of the Treaty provides:

> (1) It is expressly understood that
>
> (*a*) this Treaty governs the rights and obligations of each Party in relation to the other with respect only to the use of the waters of the Rivers and matters incidental thereto; and
>
> (*b*) nothing contained in this Treaty, and nothing arising out of the execution thereof, shall be construed as constituting a recognition or waiver (whether tacit, by implication or otherwise) of any rights or claims whatsoever of either of the Parties other than those rights or claims which are expressly recognized or waived in this Treaty.
>
> Each of the Parties agrees that it will not invoke this Treaty, anything contained therein, or anything arising out of the execution thereof, in support of any of its own rights or claims whatsoever or in disputing any of the rights or claims whatsoever of the other Party, other than those rights or claims which are expressly recognized or waived in this Treaty.

Pakistan's arguments

352. In Pakistan's submission, Article XI of the Treaty was adopted so as to allow the Treaty to regulate the rights and obligations of the Parties

[544] India's Counter-Memorial, para. 7.19, quoting *Baglihar* Determination, (Annex PK-230), p. 4.

[545] India's Counter-Memorial, paras. 7.20–7.23.

[546] India's Counter-Memorial, para. 7.24.

[547] India's Counter-Memorial, paras. 7.25–7.26.

[548] Hearing Tr., (Day 9), 30 August 2012, at 109:12 to 111:6.

with respect to the use of the waters of the *entire* relevant area of the Indus system of rivers, including those parts of it located in Pakistan-administered and India-administered Jammu and Kashmir, while avoiding the underlying dispute over these territories.[549]

353. Pakistan agrees with India that Article XI(1) of the Treaty prevents the Parties from invoking the Treaty in support of any territorial claims that they may have over Pakistan-administered or India-administered Jammu and Kashmir, and submits that it has complied with this provision.[550] Specifically, in presenting arguments concerning the alleged adverse impact of the KHEP on the territory of Pakistan-administered Jammu and Kashmir, Pakistan has not invoked the Treaty improperly.[551] This is because the Parties' rights and obligations under the Treaty with respect to the use of the waters of the Indus system of rivers extend to uses made in territories, such as Pakistan-administered and India-administered Jammu and Kashmir, that are under the factual control of one of the Parties.[552] The opposite interpretation would create a gap in the Treaty.[553] During the negotiation of the Treaty, this interpretation was confirmed by the World Bank, advised by an English barrister, Sir John Foster. Pakistan put the following question to the Bank:

> It is the intent that –
>
> (*a*) The rights and obligations of India under the Treaty shall extend to acts and omissions in, or affecting, that portion of Jammu and Kashmir that is under the control of India.
>
> (*b*) The rights and obligations of Pakistan under the Treaty shall extend to acts and omissions in, or affecting, the remainder of Jammu and Kashmir.
>
> (*c*) The Treaty shall not affect the respective positions taken by the Parties in the dispute over Jammu and Kashmir.
>
> Question: Does the present draft accomplish the foregoing?[554]

[549] Hearing Tr., (Day 1), 20 August 2012, at 25:18–27:10; Hearing Tr., (Day 3), 22 August 2012, at 162:1–11, 166:2–12, quoting Niranjan Das Gulhati, *Indus Waters Treaty: an exercise in international mediation* (Allied Publishers, 1973), p. 263 ("In the light of the disagreement between India and Pakistan on the status of Jammu and Kashmir, it was agreed that effort be made to write the treaty in such manner as to bypass the problem of Jammu and Kashmir"); Hearing Tr., (Day 7), 28 August 2012, at 1:22–4:15.

[550] Pakistan's Reply, paras. 2.15–2.17.

[551] Pakistan's Reply, paras. 2.18–2.20a.

[552] Pakistan's Reply, para. 2.20b. Pakistan adds that in any event it represents Pakistan-administered Kashmir for purposes of the Treaty, and that such representation is opposable to India. Hearing Tr., (Day 3), 23 August 2012, at 167:14 to 169:18.

[553] Hearing Tr., (Day 1), 20 August 2012, at 25:25 to 26:4; Hearing Tr., (Day 7), 28 August 2012, at 13:7–21.

[554] Pakistan's Reply, para. 2.20c, quoting Memorandum Regarding Questions to be put to John Foster Esq. (Annex PK-241).

354. In response to this question, Pakistan was assured that its fears were "ill-founded."[555] Pakistan therefore submits that it is entitled to argue that the KHEP will have an adverse impact on areas located in Pakistan-administered Jammu and Kashmir.[556]

355. Finally, Pakistan submits that in accordance with Article XI(1) of the Treaty, India's arguments concerning the validity of Pakistan's and India's claims over Pakistan-administered Jammu and Kashmir are not a proper subject for adjudication by the Court.[557] In any event, Pakistan rejects all of India's arguments regarding the juridical status of Pakistan-administered Jammu and Kashmir.[558]

India's arguments

356. India claims that there is "an important territorial element" in the present case.[559] It points out that all the areas which would, according to Pakistan, be adversely affected by the KHEP, whether in terms of hydro-electric or agricultural use, or environmentally, are located in Pakistan-administered Jammu and Kashmir.[560] It further contends that Pakistan-administered Jammu and Kashmir is not legally a part of Pakistan.[561] On this basis, India argues that Pakistan is invoking the Treaty to support its claims in the territory of Pakistan-administered Jammu and Kashmir and to dispute India's claims in the same territory. In so doing, Pakistan is in direct violation of Article XI(1) (*b*) of the Treaty.[562]

357. In addition, in India's view, it has no obligation under the Treaty to avoid adverse impact on territories that do not form part of Pakistan, as the Treaty does not apply to regions that are only under Pakistan's *de facto* control.[563] India recalls that during the negotiation of the Treaty, Pakistan proposed a provision that would have extended the application of the Treaty to "all of the territories which at the time are under [a Party's actual control]" and that this provision was rejected by India and excluded from the final text of the

[555] Pakistan's Reply, para. 2.20c, quoting Telegram from G. Mueenuddin, Pakistan's chief negotiator, to "Foreign Rawalpindi," 15 April 1960, (Annex PK-242).

[556] Pakistan's Reply, paras. 2.18–2.20a.

[557] Pakistan's Reply, para. 2.22.

[558] Hearing Tr., (Day 7), 28 August 2012, at 11:16–22.

[559] India's Counter-Memorial, para. 1.32.

[560] India's Counter-Memorial, paras. 1.34, 2.65–2.66.

[561] India's Counter-Memorial, paras. 1.34–1.38, 1.42; India's Rejoinder, paras. 1.94–1.95; Hearing Tr., (Day 5), 24 August 2012, at 46:1–21.

[562] India's Counter-Memorial, paras. 1.33, 6.49; India's Rejoinder, paras. 1.93, 1.99; Hearing Tr., (Day 5), 24 August 2012, at 47: 4–22, 48:14 to 49:17.

[563] India's Counter-Memorial, paras. 1.43, 2.66; India's Rejoinder, para. 1.105; Hearing Tr., (Day 5), 24 August 2012, at 48:8–13, referring to VCLT, Art. 29. India adds that Pakistan-administered Kashmir is not a party to the Treaty and is not represented in the Treaty by Pakistan. Hearing Tr., (Day 5), 24 August 2012, at 45:12–18; Hearing Tr., (Day 9) 30 August 2012, at 3:23 to 7:11.

Treaty.[564] While Pakistan alleges that it received confirmation from the World Bank that the Treaty would apply to Pakistan-administered and India-administered Jammu and Kashmir, India notes that in support of this allegation, Pakistan mostly cites internal correspondence of Pakistan, which does not form part of the *travaux préparatoires* of the Treaty. In addition, Pakistan appears to be relying on an interpretation made not by the World Bank, but by Sir John Foster, retained to answer certain questions of the World Bank.[565]

IV. Analysis of the Court

358. At the outset of its analysis, the Court considers it appropriate to note the extraordinary contribution of the World Bank to the conception, mediation, negotiation, drafting and financing of the Indus Waters Treaty, an instrument critical to the life and well-being of hundreds of millions of people of India and Pakistan. The conclusion of the Indus Waters Treaty in 1960, in which the leaders and staff of the World Bank lent vital support to the Parties, was and remains a great achievement of international cooperation.

A. The Territorial Scope of the Treaty

359. In the course of these proceedings, the Parties have advanced arguments concerning the status of Pakistan-administered and India-administered Jammu and Kashmir and have differed over whether and how this Partial Award may bear upon the question of sovereignty over Jammu and Kashmir. Before engaging in an analysis of the two disputes at hand, the Court considers it important to clarify at the outset the scope of its inquiry—and of the Indus Waters Treaty itself—as it relates to the question of sovereignty over Jammu and Kashmir.

360. The Treaty was negotiated and concluded amid difficulties in the relations between India and Pakistan. One of the most profound and sensitive issues between the Parties was (and remains) the question of sovereignty over Jammu and Kashmir. While negotiating the Treaty, the danger that unresolved questions of sovereignty could stand in the way of agreement on the allocation of the waters of the Indus river system was plain to the representatives of the World Bank and the Parties, who clearly sought to craft the Treaty so as to avoid those difficulties. The Court thus has no doubt that the manner in which the Treaty expresses the Parties' respective rights and obligations represents a conscious effort to reach a definitive apportionment of the use of the waters of the Indus system of rivers, while avoiding entirely the matter of sovereignty over the areas through which those waters flow. To this end, the Treaty focuses

---

[564] India's Counter-Memorial, paras. 1.39–1.40, 2.63–2.64, quoting World Bank's list of riders proposed by India and Pakistan for inclusion in draft text, rider No. 11 (Pakistan), 24 November 1959, (Annex IN-49); India's Rejoinder, paras. 1.96–1.98.

[565] India's Rejoinder, paras. 1.102–1.103.

on the right of each Party to the *use* of some of the waters of the Indus system of rivers without going into the question of sovereignty over the territory of Jammu and Kashmir through which some of those rivers transit.

361. Article XI(1) of the Treaty embodies this approach:[566] although its phrasing makes no reference to any territorial dispute between India and Pakistan, its purpose was precisely to assure the Parties that their respective rights in or claims to disputed territories would remain unaffected by the Treaty.[567] The Treaty "governs the rights and obligations of each Party in relation to the other with respect *only* to the *use of the waters* of the Rivers" and, further, provides that nothing therein "shall be construed as constituting a recognition or waiver … of any rights or claims whatsoever of either of the Parties *other than those rights or claims which are expressly recognized or waived in this Treaty*."[568] These terms preclude any effect on the rights or claims of the Parties with respect to anything but the use of the waters.

362. In keeping with the terms and intentions of Article XI(1), this Partial Award does not—and cannot—have any bearing on the rights or claims that either Party may maintain to sovereignty over the territory of Jammu and Kashmir. Nor are such putative rights or claims relevant to the resolution of the disputes placed before this Court. The Court thus finds it unnecessary to set out in detail the arguments put forth by the Parties on the status of Jammu and Kashmir.

363. Having established that this Partial Award can have no bearing on the Parties' territorial dispute over Jammu and Kashmir, the remaining con-

---

[566] In full, Article XI(1) of the Treaty reads as follows:

(1) It is expressly understood that

(*a*) this Treaty governs the rights and obligations of each Party in relation to the other with respect only to the use of the waters of the Rivers and matters incidental thereto; and

(*b*) nothing contained in this Treaty, and nothing arising out of the execution thereof, shall be construed as constituting a recognition or waiver (whether tacit, by implication or otherwise) of any rights or claims whatsoever of either of the Parties other than those rights or claims which are expressly recognized or waived in this Treaty.

Each of the Parties agrees that it will not invoke this Treaty, anything contained therein, or anything arising out of the execution thereof, in support of any of its own rights or claims whatsoever or in disputing any of the rights or claims whatsoever of the other Party, other than those rights or claims which are expressly recognized or waived in this Treaty.

[567] *See* Letter from William A.B. Iliff, the most senior of the World Bank's negotiators, to Niranjan D. Gulhati, India's chief negotiator, 16 June 1959, (Annex PK-246): "My recollection of the understanding reached in the course of our conversations with the Indian authorities in Delhi is that … India was concerned that the actual construction by Pakistan of a reservoir at Mangla should not carry any implication that India's sovereign rights in Jammu and Kashmir were in any way or to any degree eroded. India therefore wished to find some formula that would protect her in this respect … The general principle underlying the Bank approach was that neither party should, on the one hand, seek to gain, in or from the Water Treaty, any support for its own general position on the Kashmir issue, or, on the other hand, should seek to erode the general position of the other party."

[568] Emphasis added.

sideration for the Court in this regard is whether the Parties' rights and obligations under the Treaty regarding the use of the waters of the Indus system of rivers extend to those portions of the rivers that flow in disputed territory, including the area in which India is building the KHEP and those reaches of the Neelum Valley that Pakistan contends will be adversely affected by the KHEP's operation.

364. In addressing this question, each Party refers to a different portion of the documentary record of the negotiations preceding the Treaty. Arguing that disputed territories are covered by the Treaty, Pakistan relies on the opinion of Sir John Foster, an eminent English barrister, whose views were sought by the World Bank to reassure the Parties that "the text of the draft of [the] Treaty expresses clearly and correctly [their] intent,"[569] namely, to avoid any indication that the Treaty would affect disputes over sovereign rights in Jammu and Kashmir. For its part, India emphasizes the omission from the final Treaty text of a proposed rider that would have provided that the rights and obligations of each Party under the Treaty "apply to all the territories which at the time were under its actual control."[570] The Court finds the spare negotiating record on this matter to be inconclusive; insofar as Foster did not represent the Parties, his opinion is not determinative of the meaning of Article XI. Nonetheless, the Parties' agreement to the text of this provision in full knowledge of Foster's interpretation may be construed as acceptance of his view. As for the Parties' rejection of the proposed rider, it may be that the Parties simply wished to avoid overt reference to the divisions between them. But it is clear that the Parties shared the view of the World Bank that the Treaty should not and did not affect questions of sovereignty over Jammu and Kashmir.

---

[569] Memorandum Regarding Questions to be put to John Foster Esq., (Annex PK-241). Foster opined that the text of Article XI (then Article X) expressed clearly and correctly the following stated intent of Pakistan:

(*a*) The rights and obligations of India under the Treaty shall extend to acts and omissions in, or affecting, that portion of Jammu and Kashmir that is under the control of India.

(*b*) The rights and obligations of Pakistan under the Treaty shall extend to acts and omissions in, or affecting, the remainder of Jammu and Kashmir.

(*c*) The Treaty shall not affect the respective positions taken by the Parties in the dispute over Jammu and Kashmir.

See also Telegram from G. Mueenuddin, Pakistan's chief negotiator, to "Foreign Rawalpindi," 15 April 1960, (Annex PK-242): "In general Foster's opinion was that our fears were ill-founded and the Draft of the Treaty (*a*) accomplished the common intent and (*b*) excluded all other matters."

[570] World Bank's list of riders proposed by India and Pakistan for inclusion in the draft text of 24 November 1959, rider No. 11 (Pakistan), (Annex IN-49). The proposal reads, in full:

> The rights and obligations of each of the Parties under this Treaty apply to all the territories which at the time are under its actual control; but neither the provisions of this Treaty nor any steps taken as permitted in this Treaty, or to promote compliance therewith, shall be construed as affecting in any way the positions of the Parties as to the right to exercise such control.

365. The Court recognizes that the text of the Treaty itself, read in context and in light of its object and purpose, is paramount in resolving the disputes brought before it. The Preamble of the Treaty refers to the Parties' desire to attain the "most complete and satisfactory utilisation of the waters of the Indus system of rivers" and states further that the Treaty fixes the rights and obligations of the Parties concerning the use of "these waters." These words are emblematic of the Treaty's intent to apply to the aggregate of the Indus river system and not only to those waters flowing through uncontested territory. The Parties have not pointed to—and the Court has not found—any provision that would exclude from the scope of the Treaty any portion of the waters of the Indus system of rivers that flow through Pakistan and India. Moreover, four of the rivers governed by the Treaty (the Indus, the Jhelum, the Chenab and the Ravi) flow partly through the territory of Jammu and Kashmir. Were the Treaty to exclude these watercourses during their transit of the region, it would fall significantly short of providing the comprehensive solution sought by the Parties for the development and allocation of the waters of the Indus system.

366. For these reasons, the Court finds that the rights and obligations of the Parties under the Treaty extend to their use of those waters of the Indus system that flow through Pakistan and India, including those waters flowing through either Pakistan-administered or India-administered Jammu and Kashmir. Pakistan is therefore entitled to invoke the Treaty, as it does here, to object to the construction of the KHEP as a hydro-electric project located in India-administered territory, by arguing that it will impermissibly affect the flow of the river and uses of the waters thereof (including future uses by the NJHEP) in Pakistan-administered territory.[571]

B. The First Dispute: the Permissibility of Delivering the Waters of the Kishenganga/Neelum River into Another Tributary Through the KHEP

367. The Court now turns to the First Dispute. In essence, the Court has been asked to decide whether India is permitted under the Treaty to deliver the waters of the Kishenganga/Neelum River into another tributary in the course of the operation of the KHEP. Pakistan maintains that the KHEP is not in conformity with the Treaty; the Court's analysis of the specific objections set out by Pakistan follows.

[571] Similar considerations apply in relation to the area of Azad Jammu and Kashmir ("AJK"), where the NJHEP is located and many of the KHEP's adverse effects alleged by Pakistan would occur. India has argued that AJK is a self-governing state and not part of Pakistan under its constitution. Following the Treaty's logic, however, the Court observes that Pakistan has uses of water belonging to the Indus system of rivers in AJK. It is not for the Court to pass upon the relationship between Pakistan and AJK.

1. India's general obligations under Articles III and IV(6)

368. Pakistan argues that the Treaty contains a number of provisions that restrict Indian uses of the Western Rivers in general, regardless of whether they involve hydro-electric power generation. It invokes Article III of the Treaty, which sets out both India's fundamental obligation to "let flow" the waters of the Western Rivers and its right to employ those waters, under certain conditions, for hydro-electric power generation and other uses. Specifically, Pakistan contends that the KHEP does not conform to Article III(2) of the Treaty, which in its view restricts India's use of the Western Rivers (including for hydro-electric power generation) to "the drainage basin thereof." Insofar as the electricity generated by the KHEP would be contributed to India's whole northern grid, Pakistan maintains that such a use will not be restricted to the drainage basin of the Jhelum.[572]

369. In the Court's view, however, Article III(2) restricts what India may do with the waters of the Western Rivers, and not with the products that may be generated from their use. There is no indication in the Treaty that a geographic restriction on the use of electricity or any other product of the use of the waters was intended.

370. Pakistan also invokes India's general obligation to "use its best endeavours to maintain the natural channels of the Rivers" as stipulated in Article IV(6) of the Treaty. Article IV(6) provides as follows:

> Each Party will use its best endeavours to maintain the natural channels of the Rivers, as on the Effective Date, in such condition as will avoid, as far as practicable, any obstruction to the flow in these channels likely to cause material damage to the other Party.

371. As set forth above,[573] Pakistan maintains that by failing to assess adequately the environmental impact of the KHEP's inter-tributary transfer, India has breached its Article IV(6) obligation. Arguing that a thorough assessment of the KHEP's downstream environmental impact is necessary to comply with the "best endeavours" obligation of Article IV(6), Pakistan seeks to demonstrate that the diversion of water at the KHEP will, by significantly reducing the flow in the Kishenganga/Neelum, cause material environmental damage below the Line of Control.

372. The Court considers that this provision, which is worded in "best endeavours" terms, is obligatory and not merely aspirational in nature. Where the Parties contemplated the latter, they specified so expressly, such as in paragraphs 9 and 10 of Article IV of the Treaty, which provide that "[e]ach Party declares its *intention*."[574] In contrast, the phrase "[e]ach Party *will use its best endeavours*"[575] expresses a stronger commitment.

---

[572] *See* paras. 194–196 of this Partial Award.

[573] *See* paras. 256–256 of this Partial Award.

[574] Emphasis added.

[575] Emphasis added.

373. Nonetheless, Article IV(6) bears no direct relevance to inter-tributary transfer as such. On the plain meaning of its terms, Article IV(6) concerns the maintenance of the physical condition of the *channels* of the rivers, and not the maintenance of the volume and timing of the flow of water in these channels. The Court understands the term "channel" in Article IV(6) in its common usage, i.e., to denote the bed of the river, which may or may not be filled with water.[576] Accordingly, the Court sees this provision as mandating the preservation of the natural paths of the rivers (what India calls the "geometry of the channels")[577] in an effort to conserve the rivers' capacity to carry water, thereby protecting the Parties from dry spells and floods. This interpretation is confirmed by the Treaty's *travaux préparatoires*.[578]

374. Further, Article IV(6) does not require the maintenance of the condition of the channels so as to avoid any type of riverbed degradation, but bears more precisely on the avoidance of "any obstruction to the flow in these channels likely to cause material damage to the other Party."[579] While Pakistan has emphasized that by trapping sediment in its reservoir and releasing "sediment hungry" water below the dam, the KHEP may contribute to the erosion of the riverbed,[580] it has not adequately explained what specific *obstructions* to the flow of waters in the Kishenganga/Neelum downstream of the KHEP would be created as a result of its construction and operation.

375. Nor can the KHEP itself be considered an "obstruction" of the kind foreseen by Article IV(6). The general obligation upon both India and Pakistan covering all uses of the Western and the Eastern Rivers under Article IV(6) must yield to the specific Treaty rights of the Parties. The Court cannot accept that Article IV(6) debars the construction and operation of works specifically contemplated by the Treaty. The KHEP was designed and is intended to be operated under the regime of Annexure D, to which the Court now turns.[581]

---

[576] *See* the relevant definition of "channel" in *Webster's Third New International Dictionary of the English Language*, unabridged (G & C Merriam Co., 1981): "1 a: the hollow bed where a natural body or stream of water runs or may run"); *Oxford English Dictionary*, online (http://oxforddictionaries.com): "a hollow bed for a natural or artificial waterway: *the river is confined in a narrow channel*" (emphasis in the original). "Riverbed" is defined by Webster's Dictionary as "the channel occupied or formerly occupied by a river" and by the Oxford English Dictionary as "the bed or channel in which a river flows."

[577] India's Counter-Memorial, para. 4.155.

[578] A December 1959 draft of the Treaty shows that Article IV(6) initially provided for the avoidance of obstructions to "the natural flow in the Rivers." Treaty, draft of 9 December 1959, Art. IV(4), (Annex PK-12). This early phrasing could have been taken to refer to the volume of water normally passing through at any given time of year, but was replaced by the present text.

[579] Treaty, Art. IV(6).

[580] Pakistan's Memorial, Tab D, Hagler Bailly Pakistan, Water Matters, Southern Waters & Beuster, Clarke and Associates, "Kishenganga/Neelum Water Diversion: Environmental Assessment," May 2011, p. 2–4.

[581] The Court would however note that the reference in Article IV(6) to the avoidance of material damage to the other Party, a reference which reappears in Article IV(9), has environmental connotations and lends a measure of support to Pakistan's invocation of contemporary environmental jurisprudence. Article IV(9) provides:

2. The requirements for Run-of-River Plants under Annexure D

376. The right to generate hydro-electric power (provided that such generation is conducted in accordance with Annexures D or E) is an express exception to India's obligation to let flow the waters of the Western Rivers.[582] Annexure D provides comprehensive criteria for the design and operation of new Run-of-River Plants.

377. As set out in greater detail above,[583] Pakistan submits, first, that Annexure D does not permit the permanent diversion of a tributary of the Jhelum; second, that even if Annexure D does permit such diversion, the KHEP does not qualify as a Plant under Paragraph 15(iii); and, third, that even if the KHEP does qualify as such a Plant, it fails the test of necessity provided in that Paragraph. India counters that the KHEP is permissible and consistent with Paragraph 15 in all respects. The Court will address each issue in turn.

(a) The permissibility of inter-tributary transfers in general

378. Whether Annexure D permits inter-tributary transfers is answered by the plain text of Paragraph 15(iii). This Paragraph provides that "where a Plant is located on a Tributary of The Jhelum ..., the water released below the Plant may be delivered ... into another Tributary ...," thus allowing the diversion of water from one tributary to another, provided that the works in question fall within the terms of that Paragraph.

379. With respect to the scope of permissible diversion, the Court is not convinced that Paragraph 15(iii) was intended only to permit the occasional diversion of water in the course of operation, rather than diversion as an integral part of the design and operation of a Plant.[584] No such distinction is evident from the text itself. Moreover, whether effected by tunnel or canal, any release of water from one tributary into another will be a major undertaking, involving substantial engineering works constructed at great expense. The Court can see no purpose that would be served by investing in the extensive infrastructure required for transfer, only to carry out such transfers on an occasional basis and in a manner ancillary to the *raison d'être* of a Plant—power generation.

380. This interpretation is consistent with the letter from the Chairman of India's Central Water and Power Commission to India's Ministry for Irrigation and Power dated 16 May 1960, which shows that India was contemplating,

---

Each Party declares its intention to operate its storage dams, barrages and irrigation canals in such manner, consistent with the normal operations of its hydraulic systems, as to avoid, as far as feasible, material damage to the other Party.

[582] Treaty, Art. III(2)(*d*). Pursuant to Paragraph 1 of Annexure D, however, where a new hydro-electric plant is incorporated within a Storage Work, its design, construction, and operation are governed by the provisions of Annexure E to the Treaty.

[583] *See* paras. 199–227 of this Partial Award.

[584] *See* Hearing Tr., (Day 1), 20 August 2012, at 15:10 to 16:1.

at the time the Treaty was concluded, a diversion scheme on the Kishenganga/ Neelum River similar to the KHEP as now presented.[585] Although there is no indication in the record that India's projections were shared with Pakistan or raised in the course of negotiations,[586] the CWPC Letter demonstrates that one Party to the Treaty was fully aware of and interested in the power to be generated by such an inter-tributary diversion.[587]

(b) *The KHEP as a Run-of-River Plant located on a tributary to the Jhelum*

381. Paragraph 15(iii) of Annexure D provides:

> Subject to the provisions of Paragraph 17, the works connected with a Plant shall be so operated that (*a*) the volume of water received in the river upstream of the Plant, during any period of seven consecutive days, shall be delivered into the river below the Plant during the same seven-day period, and (*b*) in any one period of 24 hours within that seven-day period, the volume delivered into the river below the Plant shall be not less than 30%, and not more than 130%, of the volume received in the river above the Plant during the same 24-hour period: Provided however that:

[585] The CWPC Letter (Annex IN-54) provided the comments of the Power Wing of India's CWPC with respect to the draft of the Treaty under consideration as at 16 May 1960. With respect to the draft of Annexure E and the construction of Storage Works on the Jhelum, the CWPC Letter states in relevant part as follows (emphasis in the original):

> (*b*) JHELUM (excluding JHELUM main): A note on the preliminary hydro-electric survey for the Indus basin in India was forwarded to Shri R. R. Bahl, the then Joint Secretary, Ministry of Irrigation & Power under my D.O. letter No. 20/1/58-HE, dated the 13th January, 1958. This was also then seen by Shri Gulati and other officers connected with the Canal Water Dispute. As pointed out therein, the only tributary of the Jhelum where storage is required for generation of power is Kishenganga. A 200 ft. high dam at Nail with a catchment area of about 770 sq. miles with a storage of about 0.25 maft. would afford a regulated power draft of 1,000 cusecs which can then be conveyed across the ridge and dropped into lake Wular utilising a total drop of 2740 ft. and yielding a power potential of the order of 300,000 kw at 60% load factor. This regulated power draft can be further utilised, along with the natural flows of the main Jhelum in three power stations at a total head of about 1700 ft. below Baramula. In view of this, a minimum storage of *0.3 million aft* should be secured on the tributaries of the Jhelum for power generation.

[586] In this context, the Court notes that Article 32 of the VCLT was not meant to close the category of supplementary means that may be utilized in treaty interpretation to those enumerated therein. *See HICEE B.V.* v. *the Slovak Republic*, PCA Case No. 2009–11, Partial Award, 23 May 2011, at paras. 117 and 135.

[587] In light of the significance that the Court accords to the CWPC Letter, the Court does not consider it important that, in 1960, the CWPC apparently contemplated a diversion scheme based on a Storage Work (and raised the issue in the context of its comments on Annexure E), while the Treaty's only express provision on diversion concerns Run-of-River Plants under Annexure D. The relevance of the CWPC Letter is not as a comment on any specific treaty provision, which was part of the draft or was developed thereafter, but rather as an indication of India's interest, as early as 1960, in producing hydro-electricity through the diversion of the Kishenganga River.

[…]

(iii) where a Plant is located on a Tributary of The Jhelum on which Pakistan has any Agricultural use or hydro-electric use, the water released below the Plant may be delivered, if necessary, into another Tributary but only to the extent that the then existing Agricultural Use or hydro-electric use by Pakistan on the former Tributary would not be adversely affected.

382. For India to take advantage of the possibility of inter-tributary transfer provided for in Paragraph 15(iii), the KHEP must meet the following three conditions: (1) it must be a Run-of-River Plant; (2) it must be located on a tributary of the Jhelum; and (3) the inter-tributary transfer must be within the terms laid down in Paragraph 15(iii). The Court will consider these three requirements in turn.

383. As to condition (1), "Run-of-River Plant" is a term of art under the Treaty. Following the definition in Paragraph 2(*g*) of Annexure D, a Run-of-River Plant is "a hydro-electric plant that develops power without Live Storage as an integral part of the plant, except for Pondage and Surcharge Storage." Live Storage, Pondage and Surcharge Storage are themselves defined in Paragraph 2 of the Annexure, and it is not the volume of water impounded, but the volume of water stored for hydro-electric power generation that establishes whether a project constitutes a Run-of-River Plant pursuant to the definition.[588] Bearing these provisions in mind, the Court does not doubt that, although originally conceived as a Storage Work, the KHEP has been designed and notified to Pakistan as a Run-of-River Plant within the meaning of that definition. Pakistan has drawn the Court's attention to documents that have described Run-of-River Plants in other ways, but these descriptions cannot stand against the formal definition given in Annexure D for the purposes of that Annexure.

384. As to condition (2), the comprehensive definition of "Tributary" in Article I(2) of the Treaty encompasses the Kishenganga/Neelum River.[589] There

[588] In Annexure D, "Surcharge Storage" is defined as "uncontrollable storage occupying space above the Full Pondage Level" and essentially describes the margin of safety between the maximum ordinary capacity of the reservoir and the parapet of the dam, designed to prevent the dam from being overtopped during extreme floods or in the face of strong wind and wave action (Para. 2(*e*)). "Pondage" is storage intended to meet variations in the daily and weekly generating loads of the Plant and is regulated by the Treaty by reference to the designed generating capacity of the Plant (*see* Para. 2(*c*)). Accordingly, for the purposes of the Treaty a "Run-of-River Plant" is any Plant that is not designed to generate power from stored water beyond the volume expressly permitted to be stored and utilized as "Pondage."

[589] Article I(2) of the Treaty reads as follows:

The term "Tributary" of a river means any surface channel, whether in continuous or intermittent flow and by whatever name called, whose waters in the natural course would fall into that river, e.g. a tributary, a torrent, a natural drainage, an artificial drainage, a *nadi*, a *nallah*, a *nai*, a *khad*, a *cho*. The term also includes any subtributary or branch or subsidiary channel, by whatever name called, whose waters, in the natural course, would directly or otherwise flow into that surface channel.

is no dispute between the Parties that the Kishenganga/Neelum is a tributary of the Jhelum. The question is therefore whether the KHEP is "located on" the Kishenganga. On this issue, the Parties have taken very different views.[590] For India, it suffices if part of the works is situated on the river itself, and the decisive criterion is the origin of the water that will be used for the operation of the Plant. For Pakistan, the crux is that the generation of hydro-electricity in the KHEP will take place at a substantial distance (23 kilometres) from the Kishenganga/Neelum River.

385. The arguments raised by Pakistan are serious ones. They put into question whether the KHEP conforms to the natural understanding of what would constitute a Run-of-River Plant. As the Court has pointed out, however, "Run-of-River Plant" is the subject of a specific Treaty definition, so that for all purposes under Annexure D it must be given a "special meaning" of the kind foreseen in Article 31(4) of the Vienna Convention on the Law of Treaties (the "VCLT") in place of its "ordinary meaning."[591]

386. The Court notes that, while the terms "Plant" and "works" are both repeatedly used in the Treaty, neither is the subject of a specific Treaty definition either in Annexure D or more generally. The variety of provisions in which the term "Plant" appears, however, shows that the term was intended to cover all aspects of a hydro-electric installation and not merely those components involved in the actual generation of electricity (such as the powerhouse). Paragraph 8 of Annexure D, for instance, expressly deals with the design of a "Plant" and includes restrictions, ranging from the dam and spillway to the need for a regulating basin, that are in no way limited to a particular element of the works. Similarly, Appendix II to Annexure D, which identifies the information that must be shared for any new Run-of-River Plant, requires the provision of a plan "showing dam spillway, intake and outlet works, diversion works, head-race and forebay, powerhouse, tail-race and Regulating Basin." This demonstrates, in the view of the Court, that the term "Plant," as employed in Annexure D, is apt to describe the entirety of an installation such as the KHEP.

387. That being so, the Court sees no warrant under the Treaty for disaggregating the elements that comprise an installation such as the KHEP, designed to operate as an integrated whole and to serve a single purpose, namely, the generation of hydro-electricity. The works that trap and channel the water feeding the KHEP are *a fortiori* located on the Kishenganga. While the Court would not go so far as to endorse the argument that any Plant must necessarily be regarded as "located on" the watercourse from which it draws water, it has no hesitation in reaching the conclusion that, for the specific purposes of Paragraph 15(iii) of Annexure D, the KHEP must be regarded as "located on" the Kishenganga, which is in turn a tributary of the Jhelum.

[590] *See* paras. 210–218 of this Partial Award.

[591] Article 31(4) of the VCLT provides: "A special meaning shall be given to a term if it is established that the parties so intended."

388. Turning now to condition (3), the Court observes that the requirement that inter-tributary transfer must be within the terms of Paragraph 15(iii) comprises two elements: the criterion of "necessity" (which will be dealt with in the following section) and the place into which the water delivered from the Kishenganga/Neelum is released after passing through the KHEP powerhouse. Pakistan submits that, in delivering water from the turbines into the Bonar Nallah, the KHEP is not delivering the "water released below the Plant" "into another Tributary" as foreseen in Paragraph 15(iii).

389. The Court is unconvinced by Pakistan's argument that this water must first be released back into the Kishenganga/Neelum below the dam before it may permissibly be delivered into another tributary of the Jhelum. The additional restriction would make no operational sense. Paragraph 15(iii), moreover, refers to water "released below the Plant," not to water "released below the dam." In the Court's understanding of the term "Plant," water released from the KHEP tail-race into the Bonar Nallah is undoubtedly released below the Plant. It is simply the case that here, there is not one watercourse but two flowing below (or downstream of) the Plant into which water may be released. Similarly, the Court cannot accept that the phrase "into another Tributary" was intended to mean anything other than another tributary of the Jhelum. There is no textual basis for concluding that the second use of the term "Tributary" in Paragraph 15(iii) differs from the first and refers exclusively, as Pakistan suggests, to tributaries of the Kishenganga/Neelum itself.

(c) The criterion that inter-tributary transfers must be "necessary"

390. Having concluded that Paragraph 15(iii) permits diversion, and that the KHEP is generally in keeping with the type of scheme envisaged therein, the Court turns to the question of whether such diversion is "necessary." This analysis initially raises a further question: necessary for what? Before proceeding, the Court finds it useful for the light it may throw on the Parties' underlying intention to recall how the term entered into the draft of the Treaty.

391. The record put before the Court shows that the word "necessary" was added at a very late stage. In the World Bank's draft of 6 June 1960, inter-tributary transfer was dealt with in the following terms:

> (*c*) where a Plant is located on a Tributary of The Jhelum on which Pakistan has any Agricultural Use or hydro-electric use the water released below the Plant may not be delivered into another Tributary if the then existing Agricultural Use or hydro-electric use by Pakistan on the former Tributary would be adversely affected.[592]

392. In the final text of the Treaty, the language had become the following:

> (iii) where a Plant is located on a Tributary of The Jhelum on which Pakistan has any Agricultural use or hydro-electric use, the water

[592] Treaty, draft of 6 June 1960, (Annex PK-22), Annexure D, para. 15(iii).

> released below the Plant may ~~not~~ be delivered, if necessary, into another Tributary *but only to the extent that* ~~if~~ the then existing Agricultural Use or hydro-electric use by Pakistan on the former Tributary would *not* be adversely affected.[593]

393. The record shows that this change was proposed by India, but does not indicate the reasons underlying the change. The Court feels justified in assuming, all the same, that India's purpose was to underline that it had a right (albeit not an unlimited one) to undertake inter-tributary transfers; this would explain why the provision was changed from a negative construction into a positive one.

394. The change of form entailed certain drafting problems, however. In the first place, there was the question of the tributaries to which the provision would apply. Here the drafters left the wording unchanged: "where a Plant is located on a Tributary of The Jhelum on which Pakistan has any Agricultural Use or hydro-electric use." The literal effect of this phrase might now appear to be—to the eyes of a reader coming fresh to the final text—that India's right to make inter-tributary transfers at all only came into being once Pakistan had established some use on the downstream reaches of that tributary. Such a result would be so contrary to plain common sense that the Court would in any case rule it out *in limine*. Once the negotiating background described above is considered, it becomes plain that a description of the relevant tributaries which made perfect sense as part of a provision in negative form cannot have been intended to have a radically restrictive effect when the provision was recast in positive form. The very purpose of changing into the positive form was to emphasize the right, not to curtail it.

395. The second drafting problem arising out of the change of form was evidently one to which the drafters did pay specific attention. The change from a provision constructed as a double negative, i.e., a prohibition qualified by an exception, into a permission seems to have been thought to require the introduction of some kind of qualification to indicate that the permission was not an absolute one. The device chosen was the limiting phrase "if necessary." It served to indicate that the change to the positive, permissive form was not intended to turn inter-tributary transfer into the rule, but to leave it as something that had to be justified by the exigencies of each particular case. Once this is understood, it becomes easier to attribute the proper meaning to the words chosen.

396. Paragraph 15(iii) thus provides that "the water released below the Plant may be delivered, if necessary, into another Tributary." In this formulation, the relevant action for which necessity is to be determined is the delivery of water—not the act of constructing a new Run-of-River Plant. As no specific purpose is identified against which necessity could be evaluated, the Court concludes that necessity is to be determined by reference to the purpose for which the water is to be delivered into another tributary; in the case of the

---

[593] Modifications from the 6 June 1960 draft indicated.

KHEP, this purpose is the generation of hydro-electric power. The Court therefore concludes that the relevant question for the interpretation of this element of Paragraph 15(iii) is whether the delivery of water into another Tributary is necessary to generate hydro-electric power.

397. Turning to the threshold for necessity, the Court sees no need to associate this term with indispensability or emergency action, as argued by Pakistan. The concept of necessity appears elsewhere in the Treaty without such connotations, including the provisions of Annexure G interpreted by the Court in its Order on Interim Measures.[594] The Court sees no reason, for purposes of the Treaty, to ascribe to it any special meaning beyond the normal use of the term to describe action that is "required, needed or essential for a particular purpose."[595] The Court considers inapposite the concepts of necessity developed in international trade law, investment law and other special areas. Likewise, the Court finds it inappropriate to import the understanding of necessity as a circumstance precluding wrongfulness under the law of State responsibility.

398. The Court has little difficulty in holding that the delivery of water from the Kishenganga/Neelum to another tributary is required to achieve the purpose of generating hydro-electricity through the KHEP. If, as the Court has decided, the Treaty confers a right on a Party (in this case, India's right to the use of the waters for the purpose of generating hydro-electricity in conformity with Annexure D), it must be taken to be a right that can meaningfully be exercised. It is true that some hydro-electricity can be generated from the natural flow of the Kishenganga/Neelum at Gurez, but in the Court's understanding, no Run-of-River Plant operating without making use of the difference in elevation between the two tributaries of the Jhelum would begin to approach the power-generating capacity of the KHEP. Therefore, diversion is necessary for any attempt to generate hydro-electric power on the scale contemplated by India, and Annexure D imposes no limit on the amount of electric power that India may generate through Run-of-River Plants.[596] This interpretation does not, however, reduce necessity to a mere test of what is desirable, nor does it become a self-judging matter for India alone to evaluate. The Court can imagine situations in which the benefits of including the diversion of water within the scheme of a Run-of-River Plant would be so marginal that such a diversion could not fairly be termed "necessary." In the present case, however, the Court concludes, on the basis of its understanding of the KHEP and its

[594] Order on Interim Measures, para. 139.

[595] *Ibid.* The Oxford English Dictionary defines "necessary" as a synonym of "required to be done, achieved, or present; needed" (Concise, 11th ed., 2008). Similarly, the New Oxford American Dictionary provides the following synonyms for "necessary": "required to be done, achieved, or present; needed; essential" (3rd ed., 2010).

[596] Indeed, the Treaty provides in Paragraph 1 of Annexure D that "subject to the provisions of this Annexure," the use by India of the waters of the Western Rivers to generate hydro-electricity "shall be unrestricted."

appreciation of the Gurez site, that diversion from that site is, in fact, "necessary" for India to generate significant power.

399. The Court's conclusion on this matter should not be taken to mean that potential downstream harm is irrelevant to the analysis. On the contrary, the Court considers that adverse effects on downstream uses are a central element of Paragraph 15(iii), but one that operates in a different manner from the proportionality test advanced by Pakistan. Where necessity is invoked under customary international law as a circumstance precluding the international wrongfulness of State action, proportionality may properly be considered. In that case, the claim being made is not simply that the acts in question were necessary to protect an essential State interest, but also that such interest is of paramount importance—and therefore sufficient to override the rights and interests of the State that would otherwise be wronged.[597] Viewed in terms of its ordinary meaning, however, "necessary" lacks this additional connotation. As a matter of common sense, it is apparent that certain actions may be necessary to accomplish even very modest purposes, and that such actions do not become any less necessary to their intended purpose if it happens that they also inflict ancillary harm.

3. The interpretation of the "then existing Agricultural Use or hydro-electric use by Pakistan" in Paragraph 15(iii)

400. As the Parties have emphasized,[598] the essence of the First Dispute is a difference of views between the Parties as to the proper interpretation of Paragraph 15(iii) of Annexure D, particularly this provision's requirement that any Indian inter-tributary Run-of-River Plant operate "only to the extent that the then existing Agricultural Use or hydro-electric use by Pakistan on the former Tributary would not be adversely affected." What exactly constitutes a "*then existing* Agricultural Use or hydro-electric use" lies at the very centre of the First Dispute.

401. In seeking the proper meaning of Paragraph 15, the Court is guided by the fundamental rules of treaty interpretation as set out in Article 31(1) of the VCLT: "[a] treaty shall be interpreted in good faith and in accordance with the ordinary meaning to be given to the terms of the treaty in their context and in the light of its object and purpose."

---

[597] For this reason, Article 25 of the International Law Commission's Articles on State Responsibility requires both an "essential interest" of the State invoking necessity and consideration of the essential interests of other affected States. *See* Responsibility of States for International Wrongful Acts, UN Doc. A/RES/56/83, 12 December 2001, Art. 25.

[598] Hearing Tr., (Day 1), 20 August 2012, at 14:24 to 15:1 (Counsel for Pakistan): "[T]he case comes down to the interpretation and application of Annexure D, paragraph 15 (iii), which by the end of this case will be engraved on your hearts."

(a) The text

402. The Court's interpretation begins with the text of Paragraph 15, and specifically with the ordinary meaning of the terms there used.[599] The provision is reprinted below:

> 15. Subject to the provisions of Paragraph 17, the works connected with a Plant shall be so operated that (*a*) the volume of water received in the river upstream of the Plant, during any period of seven consecutive days, shall be delivered into the river below the Plant during the same seven-day period, and (*b*) in any one period of 24 hours within that seven-day period, the volume delivered into the river below the Plant shall be not less than 30%, and not more than 130%, of the volume received in the river above the Plant during the same 24-hour period: Provided however that:
>
> (i) where a Plant is located at a site on the Chenab Main below Ramban, the volume of water received in the river upstream of the Plant in any one period of 24 hours shall be delivered into the river below the Plant within the same period of 24 hours;
>
> (ii) where a Plant is located at a site on the Chenab Main above Ramban, the volume of water delivered into the river below the Plant in any one period of 24 hours shall not be less than 50% and not more than 130%, of the volume received above the Plant during the same 24-hour period; and
>
> (iii) where a Plant is located on a Tributary of The Jhelum on which Pakistan has any Agricultural use or hydro-electric use, the water released below the Plant may be delivered, if necessary, into another Tributary but only to the extent that the then existing Agricultural Use or hydro-electric use by Pakistan on the former Tributary would not be adversely affected.

403. Read on its own, Paragraph 15 seems to be operational in character. The text leading to sub-paragraph (iii) delineates a number of operational constraints for new Run-of-River Plants. To begin with, the first sentence of Paragraph 15 states, quite plainly, that "the works connected with a Plant shall be so *operated* that ..."[600] The remaining part of Paragraph 15's chapeau lays out

---

[599] *Polish Postal Service in Danzig, Advisory Opinion*, [1925] P.C.I.J. Series B, No. 11 (May 16), p. 39 ("It is a cardinal principle of interpretation that words must be interpreted in the sense which they would normally have in their context, unless such interpretation would lead to something unreasonable or absurd."); *Arbitral Award of* 31 *July 1989 (Guinea-Bissau* v. *Senegal), I.C.J. Reports 1991*, p. 53 at p. 69, quoting *Competence of the General Assembly for the Admission of a State to the United Nations, Advisory Opinion, I.C.J. Reports 1950*, p. 4 at p. 8 ("the first duty of a tribunal which is called upon to interpret and apply the provisions of a treaty, is to endeavour to give effect to them in their natural and ordinary meaning, in the context in which they occur."); *Abyei Arbitration (The Government of Sudan/The People's Liberation Army/Movement)*, Final Award, 22 July 2009, *PCA Award Series* (2012), para. 575 ("In accordance with Article 31 of the [VCLT], the Tribunal must interpret the text of the Formula by initially looking at the ordinary meaning of the terms used.").

[600] Emphasis added.

the operational constraints on a new Run-of-River Plant when it delivers water below the Plant over "any one period" of 24 hours and "any period" of seven consecutive days. Finally, sub-paragraphs (i) and (ii) modify the operational constraints on a Plant located on the Chenab Main above or below Ramban.

404. In the same vein, sub-paragraph (iii) is phrased as an operational provision: its function is to qualify the general operational constraints found in the chapeau of Paragraph 15 where a Plant "is located on a Tributary of The Jhelum on which Pakistan has any Agricultural Use or hydro-electric use." The present tense structure ("*is* located"; "*has*" any agricultural or hydro-electric use)[601] suggests that the determination whether Pakistan has any agricultural or hydro-electric uses should take place throughout the operational life of a Run-of-River Plant, whenever India diverts water through an inter-tributary transfer.

405. Sub-paragraph (iii) then continues with the words "the water released below the Plant may be delivered, if necessary, into another Tributary but only to the extent that the then existing Agricultural Use or hydro-electric use by Pakistan on the former Tributary would not be adversely affected." Here again, the choice of the words "*then existing* Agricultural Use or hydro-electric use"[602] suggests that the sub-paragraph is to be given an operational meaning, as any delivery of water by the KHEP for purposes of power generation can occur "only to the extent" that Pakistan's "then existing" agricultural or hydro-electric uses "would not be adversely affected." The formulation of Paragraph 15(iii) thus lends credence to what has been termed in these proceedings an "ambulatory" interpretation of Paragraph 15.

(b) The context

406. Under Article 31(1) of the VCLT, "context" comprises other parts of the Treaty's text, including its Preamble and Annexures.[603] Paragraph 15 cannot be interpreted in a textual vacuum—its location within Part 3 of Annexure D ("New Run-of-River Plants") and, indeed, within the entirety of Annexure D ("Generation of Hydro-Electric Power by India on the Western Rivers") must be taken into account.

407. A review of the context of Paragraph 15 makes clear that the provision is placed within a continuum of design, construction and operation that

---

601 Emphasis added.

602 Emphasis added.

603 Under Article 31(2) of the VCLT,

> [t]he context for the purpose of the interpretation of a treaty shall comprise, in addition to the text, including its preamble and annexes:
>
> (*a*) any agreement relating to the treaty which was made between all the parties in connection with the conclusion of the treaty;
>
> (*b*) any instrument which was made by one or more parties in connection with the conclusion of the treaty and accepted by the other parties as an instrument related to the treaty.

cannot properly be separated into watertight compartments. Within the context of Part 3 of Annexure D ("New Run-of-River Plants"), Paragraph 15(iii) comes toward the end of an orderly progression beginning with the design restrictions with which India must comply if it wishes to build and operate a new Run-of-River Plant (Paragraph 8). India is required to provide detailed design information to Pakistan (Paragraph 9). Pursuant to Paragraph 9 of Annexure D, for example, India must provide at least six months' advance notice of the design of a new Run-of-River Plant before construction is permitted. This advance notice must be given in writing with the information specified in Appendix II to Annexure D. Appendix II, in turn, requires India to provide Pakistan with key information on the contemplated Plant, including "Particulars of Design" that go into great detail about the Plant and its power-generating capacity. Required disclosure includes "[d]ischarge proposed to be passed through the Plant, initially and ultimately, and expected variations in the discharge on account of the daily and weekly load fluctuations,"[604] and "[m]aximum aggregate capacity of power units (exclusive of standby units) for Firm Power and Secondary Power."[605] India is also required to provide the "[e]stimated effect of proposed development on the flow pattern below the last plant downstream."[606] The Court has no doubt that the foregoing details were placed in these sections of the Treaty to put Pakistan on notice not only in respect of the *design details* of a new Plant but also in respect of its intended *operational modalities*. Thus, as is clear from early on in Part 3 of Annexure D, a single paragraph can encompass both design and operational provisions.[607]

408. Following Paragraph 9, Pakistan may object to any aspect of the proposed design within three months of receipt of India's information (Paragraph 10). If a question regarding the permissibility of the proposed design arises, "either Party may proceed to have the question resolved" pursuant to the dispute resolution mechanism provided in Article IX(1) and (2) (Paragraph 11). This is the time at which the legality of a particular design can properly be challenged. The following two paragraphs confirm this: in the event of any alteration to the design before or after the Plant comes into operation (Paragraph 12), or should an emergency arise requiring immediate repairs or alterations (Par-

---

604 Treaty, Annexure D, Appendix II, para. 4(*h*).

605 Treaty, Annexure D, Appendix II, para. 4(i).

606 Treaty, Annexure D, Appendix II, para. 5(*a*).

607 Beyond Annexure D, the intermingling of design and operational provisions continues. For example, Annexure F, which deals with the competence of the neutral expert, supports the view that Part 3 of Annexure D (of which Paragraph 15 forms part) contemplates both the construction and operational phases in the life of a Run-of-River Plant. Annexure F, Part 1 ("Questions to be Referred to a Neutral Expert") states, in part:

> 1. Subject to the provisions of Paragraph 2, either Commissioner may, under the provisions of Article IX(2)(*a*), refer to a Neutral Expert any of the following questions:
>
> [...]
>
> (12) Whether or not the operation by India of any plant constructed in accordance with the provisions of Part 3 of Annexure D conforms to the criteria set out in Paragraphs 15, 16 and 17 of that Annexure.

agraph 13), Pakistan has the express right to question the design changes contemplated or made in accordance with Paragraph 11 and the dispute resolution mechanism set forth in Article IX. Paragraph 13 also marks the point where Annexure D moves into the operational restrictions on new Run-of-River Plants; the operational provisions then continue through to Paragraph 17.[608] Notably, at no point does the sequence of Paragraphs 8 to 12 specify Pakistan's "then existing Agricultural Use or hydro-electric use" as a factor.

409. In the Court's view, the various paragraphs contained in Part 3 of Annexure D must be interpreted in a mutually reinforcing manner to avoid forbidding with one provision what is permitted by others. It would make little sense, and cannot have been the Parties' intention, to read the Treaty as permitting new Run-of-River Plants to be designed and built in a certain manner, but then prohibiting the operation of such a Plant in the very manner for which it was designed. Such an interpretation of the various paragraphs of Part 3 in isolation from one another would render ineffective those provisions that specifically permit the development of hydro-electric power in accordance with the design constraints of Annexure D.

(c) The object and purpose of the Treaty

410. Turning to the object and purpose of the Treaty, the Court notes that the Treaty establishes a regime of qualified rights and priorities in respect of specific uses, which governs the interpretation of Paragraph 15. The Treaty recognizes Pakistan's right to "unrestricted" use of all the waters of the Western Rivers, including the Kishenganga/Neelum.[609] The deliberate division and allocation of the six main watercourses of the Indus system of rivers between the Parties is a defining characteristic of the Treaty. The inevitable conclusion is that Pakistan is given priority in the use of the waters of the Western Rivers, just as India has priority in the use of the waters of the Eastern Rivers.[610]

411. Pakistan's right to the Western Rivers is not absolute since it relates only to those waters of the Western Rivers "which India is under an obligation to let flow under the provisions of [Article III(2) of the Treaty]." The right is subject to expressly enumerated Indian uses on the Western Rivers, including the generation of hydro-electric power to the extent permitted by the Treaty.

412. Article III(1) of the Treaty states:

> Pakistan shall receive for unrestricted use all those waters of the Western Rivers which India is under obligation to let flow under the provisions of Paragraph (2).

[608] Paragraphs 18 to 23 of Annexure D concern "Small Plants," which are not directly relevant to this dispute.

[609] Treaty, Art. III(1).

[610] For India's "unrestricted use" of the waters of the Eastern Rivers, *see* Treaty, Art. II(1).

In turn, Paragraph (2) provides:

> India shall be under an obligation to let flow all the waters of the Western Rivers, and shall not permit any interference with these waters, *except* for the following uses, restricted … in the case of each of the rivers, The Indus, The Jhelum and The Chenab, to the drainage basin thereof:
>
> [...]
>
> (*d*) *Generation of hydro-electric power*, as set out in Annexure D.[611]

Similarly, although the chapeau of Annexure D confirms India's right to generate hydro-electric power on the Western Rivers in language similar to that of Pakistan's unrestricted "let flow" right, it is circumscribed by the terms of Annexure D itself:

> 1. The provisions of this Annexure shall apply with respect to the use by India of the waters of the Western Rivers for the generation of hydro-electric power under the provisions of Article III(2)(*d*) and, *subject to the provisions of this Annexure*, such use shall be *unrestricted*: … [612]

413. Thus, on the one hand, the Treaty establishes that Pakistan enjoys unrestricted use of those waters of the Western Rivers which it is entitled to receive. On the other hand, the Treaty's specifications in respect of India's hydro-electric uses on the Western Rivers are inconsistent with denying to India the capacity to generate electricity from power plants built in conformity with the Treaty. Any interpretation of Paragraph 15 the logical result of which would be to allow Pakistan unilaterally to curtail the ability of such Indian Plants to operate would subvert an important element of the object and purpose of the Treaty.

4. Challenges of the application of Paragraph 15(iii) to the KHEP

414. The Court now turns to the application of Paragraph 15(iii) to the specific case of the KHEP, the first occasion on which India has undertaken to build a Plant the power-generating capacity of which is derived from an inter-tributary transfer between two tributaries of the Jhelum River.

(a) The Parties' approaches to "then existing" uses as applied to the KHEP

415. As discussed at some length above,[613] the *text* of Paragraph 15(iii) lends a measure of support to an ambulatory interpretation—one which would subject the regular operation of Plants to any "then existing" agricultural or hydro-electric use Pakistan may have. However, in the *context* of the KHEP, that analysis requires a measure of qualification: under the overall structure

[611] Emphasis added.

[612] Emphasis added.

[613] *See* paras. 402–405 of this Partial Award.

of Annexure D, the general permissibility of any new Run-of-River Plant's design is determined prior to the commencement of that Plant's construction.[614] Once a Plant's design is accepted or acquiesced in as being consistent with the requirements of Paragraph 8 of Annexure D—or is found to be so consistent by a neutral expert or court of arbitration, in the event that one Party challenges the legality of the design[615]—the construction of that Plant can proceed as designed. Paragraph 9 requires India to communicate to Pakistan in writing the specific information detailed in Appendix II to Annexure D, "[t]o enable Pakistan to satisfy itself that the design of a Plant conforms to the criteria mentioned in Paragraph 8." Pakistan is thus effectively put on notice, at the time the design is communicated to it, of India's intended uses.

416. Part 3 of Annexure D sets out a deliberate sequence of design restrictions (Paragraphs 8 to 12) and operational constraints (Paragraphs 13 to 17) consistent with the natural cycle of development for hydro-electric (indeed, any large-scale) infrastructure projects: by defining the point at which proposed designs can be fixed, Annexure D gives the State, its creditors, its contractors and all others involved in such projects the stability and predictability that are indispensable for such projects to proceed to construction and operation over a period of years.

417. A strictly ambulatory approach to Paragraph 15(iii) would undermine the progression of design and operations provisions of Annexure D. The several sub-paragraphs of Paragraph 8 would not encompass all the design requirements necessary for India to consider and communicate to Pakistan, and Paragraphs 9–11 would not provide a mechanism that leads to certainty as to the legality of a Plant's design, construction and operation. Notably, as opposed to the clear mechanism provided by Paragraphs 9–11, no such mechanism is found in Annexure D for Pakistan to provide, on an ongoing basis, information as to its "then existing" agricultural and hydro-electric uses of which India would need to take account. Moreover, a fixed point after which a particular design would create a right upon which India could rely would never emerge. Fixing such a point, however, is the evident purpose of the progression of necessary steps set out in Paragraphs 8 to 17 of Annexure D.

418. Looking at the question more broadly by reference to the object and purpose of the Treaty, the Court cannot accept in full the interpretation proffered by either Party. As discussed above, Article III and Annexure D of the Treaty speak of the right of Pakistan to the "unrestricted" use of the waters of the Jhelum and its tributaries and of India's corresponding obligation to "let flow" the waters of the Jhelum. The Treaty allocates the use of the waters

[614] *See* Treaty, Annexure D, Paras. 8–12.

[615] Under Paragraph 11 of Annexure D, "[i]f a question arises as to whether or not the design of a Plant conforms to the criteria set out in Paragraph 8, then either Party may proceed to have the question resolved in accordance with the provisions of Article IX(1) and (2)." In turn, Article IX(1) and (2) outlines the various dispute settlement options—Commission, neutral expert, court of arbitration—available to the Parties to resolve a question, difference or dispute.

of the Western Rivers (including the Jhelum and its tributaries) to Pakistan, curtailing, sometimes quite severely, India's freedom to utilize the waters of the Western Rivers for the generation of hydro-electric power and limiting, for the most part, the use of those waters to certain agricultural uses, and to domestic and non-consumptive uses.[616]

419. On that basis, Pakistan has argued that an ambulatory interpretation of Paragraph 15(iii) of Annexure D is merely an extension of this preference, inherent in the Treaty, with respect to the Western Rivers. Following that line of argument, Pakistan's "then existing" downstream agricultural and hydro-electric uses would be privileged even if, as a result, the KHEP could only be operated during half of the year or less to accommodate the operational requirements of the NJHEP or, equally, the requirements of other subsequent hydro-electric plants to be constructed by Pakistan further downstream. India would enjoy no effective rights to the use of the waters of the Western Rivers for power generation *vis-à-vis* Pakistan, just as Pakistan has no effective rights to the use of the waters of the Eastern Rivers.[617]

420. However, India points to equally weighty considerations of object and purpose in support of its position. India relies on its express right to use the waters of the Western Rivers, including the Jhelum and its tributaries, to generate hydro-electric power. Under Article III(2) of the Treaty, the generation of hydro-electric power as set out in Annexure D is one of the specified exceptions to the "let flow" principle. And Annexure D's opening paragraph speaks of the "unrestricted" right of India to generate hydro-electric power so long as it is in a manner consistent with Annexure D as a whole.[618] Given the significant rights enjoyed by India as the upstream riparian under customary international law, as well as the natural advantages enjoyed by the upstream riparian, the Court recognizes, in view of the acute need both of India and Pakistan for hydro-electric power, that India might not have entered into the Treaty at all had it not been accorded significant rights to the use of those waters to develop hydro-electric power on the Western Rivers.

421. The Preamble magnifies this tension in the object and purpose of the Treaty: each Party can claim one part of the Preamble to buttress its argument, as the Treaty is "equally desirous" of (1) "attaining the most complete and satisfactory utilization of the waters of the Indus system of rivers," and "the need, therefore," of (2) "fixing and delimiting, in a spirit of goodwill and friendship, the rights and obligations of each in relation to the other concerning the use of these waters."

---

[616] Treaty, Art. III(2).

[617] *See* Treaty, Art. II(1): "[a]ll the waters of the Eastern Rivers shall be available for the unrestricted use of India, except as otherwise expressly provided in this Article."

[618] Treaty, Annexure D, Para. 1. For the full text of this provision, *see* para. 413 of this Partial Award.

(b) Implications of adopting the "ambulatory" approach

422. If the Court were to adopt Pakistan's "ambulatory" approach, a new inter-tributary Run-of-River Plant could be cleared for construction when its design was consistent with Paragraph 8 of Annexure D; but India would nonetheless be required to yield whenever Pakistan subsequently sought to use the waters. Such an interpretation would have a chilling effect on the undertaking of any inter-tributary project on the Kishenganga/Neelum River as no responsible project proponent, financing creditor or government agency would incur the expense or make the effort to construct a Plant the viability of which would be subject to the unilateral will and action of another party.

423. In the case of the KHEP, its operation—and thus its power-generating capacity and its economic viability—would be perpetually subject to the sword of Damocles. A strictly ambulatory approach might well require the KHEP to shut down for the drier months of the year, given the significantly larger throughput of water at the NJHEP.[619] The future establishment of Pakistani agricultural and hydro-electric uses could require India to direct most or even all of the river's water downstream without being able to reserve any for use by the KHEP during a large part of the year. Hypothetically, were a new Plant to be built by Pakistan at, say, Dudhnial (or at any other point on the Kishenganga/Neelum between the Line of Control and the NJHEP), the KHEP would need to release as much of the Kishenganga/Neelum's water as would be necessary to allow such new Pakistani plants to operate. The upshot is that, under Pakistan's approach, the KHEP could quite easily be rendered inert—or, at the very least, reduced to generating only a small fraction of its design capacity. Such a result would deprive India of a key benefit recognized by the Treaty: the generation of hydro-electric power through an inter-tributary transfer from one tributary of the Jhelum to another.

424. The lack of stability, potential for wastage of resources and incompatibility of Pakistan's approach with the design and construction approval requirements of Annexure D lead the Court to conclude that the strictly ambulatory approach is not reconcilable with the context of Paragraph 15(iii) and the object and purpose of the Treaty when applied to the KHEP. No sound reading of the Treaty's framework for Indian hydro-electric uses on the Western Rivers can foreclose entirely India's ability to generate electricity from a power plant built in accordance with Annexure D.

(c) Implications of adopting the "critical period" approach

425. If Pakistan's preferred approach to Paragraph 15(iii) calls for a dynamic assessment by India of the agricultural and hydro-electric uses of

[619] *See* India's Counter-Memorial, para. 5.10 ("With a design discharge of 280 cumec to generate 969 [megawatts], the N-JHEP will require a minimum daily flow of 47 cumec (one-sixth) to cater to four hours (one-sixth of a day) of peaking power.").

Pakistan whenever water is released by the KHEP, India's competing approach is comparatively static, focusing only on a key moment, or critical date. Simply put, for India, the phrase "then existing use" means that any new development by India is limited by such downstream uses of waters by Pakistan as are demonstrated to exist on the date when India communicates to Pakistan its "firm intention" to proceed with a project.[620]

426. The question of when a particular set of facts concerning a project crystallizes into a "firm intention" is therefore a key consideration in ascertaining the reasonableness of this approach. India maintains that this moment of "firm intention" can be determined by reference to Paragraph 9 of Annexure D (requiring that India provide Pakistan with complete information about its intended design at least six months before beginning construction). Accordingly, India argues that Pakistan's agricultural and hydro-electric uses must be "frozen at the stage when the design is being finalized."[621]

427. The Court has discussed Part 3 of Annexure D, including Paragraph 9, elsewhere in this Partial Award,[622] and agrees that under Annexure D, the date when India proposes its design is an important moment. But as the succeeding paragraphs of Annexure D make clear, notification of design is insufficient to exhibit a "firm intention" to proceed; the three-month period following such notice within which Pakistan may object must be taken into account, as well as the time it may take for questions of the Plant's conformity with the criteria in Paragraph 8 to be resolved through the Treaty's dispute resolution mechanisms (Paragraphs 10–11). Annexure D also acknowledges the possibility of design changes during the construction phase of a Plant, prior to it coming into operation (Paragraph 12(*a*)). Alterations in the configuration of the Plant may equally occur after it comes into operation (Paragraph 12(*b*)) or in response to emergencies (Paragraph 13).

428. Put in more general terms, the sequence of Paragraphs 9–13 may not in practice reflect the vast and often contradictory record that can attend large infrastructure projects of this nature, with different changes and evolutions in the Plant's design specifications, unforeseen discoveries in the areas to be excavated and tunnelled, and the vagaries of securing proper financing and government approvals. Thus, when faced with an actual project, the moment at which a "firm intention" crystallizes can be very difficult to pinpoint.[623] It

[620] India's Counter-Memorial, para. 4.139.

[621] India's Counter-Memorial, para. 4.123.

[622] *See* paras. 407–409 of this Partial Award.

[623] This critical date or period could be situated at various points in the life of a project: design, public tender, government approvals, securing of financing, breaking of ground for construction, completion of construction. Crucially, apart from the progress being made toward design, approval, construction and completion of the project, the *communication* of each step to the other Party in the manner envisaged by the Treaty is essential, because the other Party must be able to rely on the information provided through the Treaty process in order for the Treaty itself to work as envisaged. One must therefore analyze both the "facts on the ground" and which facts were formally notified to the other Party under the Treaty.

would not be wise for the Court to identify *ex ante* any one fact or formula to make this determination. The Court appreciates the difficulty of determining the critical date at any one stage in this continuum of design, financing, government approval, construction, completion and operation. Each project will be unique; its progressive crystallization can be linear or, more often than not, episodic, with redesigns, stops and restarts, changes in contractors and sources of financing, and the like.

429. That said, finding a particular period during which India's right to construct and operate a Run-of-River Plant became vested would be consistent with the framework of Paragraphs 8 to 11 of Annexure D. Rather than focusing on a moment of "firm intention" on the part of India, the Court considers it more appropriate to speak of a "critical period," wherein a cumulation of facts—tenders, financing secured, government approvals in place and construction underway—has achieved a level of certitude indicating that a project will proceed "firmly" as proposed.

430. In identifying the critical period prior to the completion of construction, the Court has deliberately ruled out two other possible points at which crystallization could be said to occur. One moment that could provide near certainty as to when a particular project crystallizes is the date on which construction of a Plant is completed. But setting the critical date at completion of construction could lead to undesirable results by encouraging both States to proceed to build their respective plants in the hopes of winning the race to completion, but with no guarantee that what is being built will be able to be operated as designed. This could lead to an extreme waste in resources and exacerbation of international tensions. At the opposite end of the spectrum between design and operation, selecting as the critical date the time at which design plans are communicated to the other Party is also unsatisfactory. While at this point in time it is possible to give notice to the other Party of an intention to build a Plant, there is no guarantee that that Plant will be completed within the time projected (or ever).

431. Having clarified what the Court considers an appropriate critical reference period in which a Party's intention to proceed with a project becomes established, the Court can now consider the key issue: just as the Court has examined whether a strictly ambulatory approach would lead to unreasonable results (which the Court has concluded it does), the Court must examine the implications of adopting a critical period interpretation for the Parties' respective rights to the use of the waters of the Kishenganga/Neelum. Such an analysis exposes a basic concern in relation both to the text of Paragraph 15(iii) of Annexure D and to the Treaty's object and purpose.

432. Inherent in the critical period approach is the requirement that any new Indian Run-of-River Plant take account of Pakistan's existing agricultural

and hydro-electric uses, pursuant to Paragraph 15(iii) of Annexure D.[624] This is a point India does not contest; it believes that at the time India's project crystallized, Pakistan did not—and still does not—have any *existing* hydro-electric uses nor any significant agricultural uses. But such a view begs the question of when a "then existing" agricultural or hydro-electric use crystallizes for Pakistan. Pakistan's uses need to be judged in the same manner as India's. Accordingly, crystallization of Pakistani hydro-electric design plans may create a "freeze" on additional Indian upstream hydro-electric uses. Sustaining an unqualified critical period approach could thus result in a race in which each Party would seek to create uses that would freeze out those by the other. The Court considers that its interpretation of Annexure D (including Paragraph 15(iii)) must minimize, to the greatest extent possible, the implications of a regime for the Kishenganga/Neelum's waters that would result in such a race, in which the first Party reaching the critical period would have the ability to freeze upstream or downstream uses (as the case may be, depending on who the "winner" is).

(d) The Treaty's balance between the rights of both Parties

433. The Court considers that neither of the two approaches to interpretation discussed above—the ambulatory and critical period approaches—is fully satisfactory. Rather, the proper interpretation of Paragraph 15(iii) of Annexure D combines certain elements of both approaches. The Court is guided by the need to reflect the equipoise which the Treaty sets out between Pakistan's right to the use of the waters of the Western Rivers (including the Jhelum and its tributary, the Kishenganga/Neelum) and India's right to use the waters of those rivers for hydro-electric generation once a Plant complies with the provisions of Annexure D.

434. Pakistan's relevant uses in this context are, in the Court's view, essentially its hydro-electric uses. As for agricultural uses, the Court notes the observation of India—not contradicted by Pakistan—that there are no significant existing agricultural uses of the Kishenganga/Neelum's main river.[625] It appears to the Court that agricultural uses in the Neelum Valley are largely met by the tributary streams that feed the river.[626]

435. Accordingly, the Court considers that its interpretative task consists of two principal elements. The Court must first establish the critical period at which the KHEP crystallized. Consistent with Part 3 of Annexure D (particularly the notice provisions of Paragraph 9), and using the same critical

[624] Presumably, pre-existing agricultural and hydro-electric uses would be one of the objections Pakistan can make to any Indian Plant design brought to it under Paragraph 9 of Annexure D.

[625] Hearing Tr., (Day 5), 24 August 2012, at 77:22 to 78:1.

[626] *See* Pakistan's Reply, paras. 4.52–4.57 (discussing the rainfall and snowmelt waters used for agricultural purposes).

period criteria, the Court must then determine whether the NJHEP was an "existing use" that India needed to take into account at the time the KHEP crystallized. As shown below, the Court's determination of the critical period leads to the conclusion that the KHEP preceded the NJHEP, such that India's right to divert the waters of the Kishenganga/Neelum for power generation by the KHEP is protected under the Treaty.

436. Second, India's right to divert the waters of the Kishenganga/ Neelum cannot be absolute. The premise underlying Paragraph 15(iii)—that Pakistan's existing uses are to be taken into account in the operation of India's Plants—remains a guiding principle (albeit not to the preclusive extent of the ambulatory approach). Paragraph 15(iii) protects Pakistan's right to a portion of the waters of the Kishenganga/Neelum throughout the year for its existing agricultural and hydro-electric uses.

5. The import of the Court's interpretation for the construction and operation of the KHEP

(a) India's vested right to build and operate the KHEP

437. The Court faces a difficult task: it must determine which Party has demonstrated not only that it planned its respective hydro-electric project "first," but also that it was the first to take concrete steps toward the realization of those plans. The Court has meticulously reviewed the evidence submitted by both Parties, including internal correspondence, letters between the Parties, the records of the meetings of the Commission and environmental impact assessments.[627] What emerges for both projects is a succession of stops and starts, of plans communicated and plans revised, of permits given but not implemented, of financing purportedly obtained and withheld, of tenders on particular project plans that are not consistent with the final design, and other vagaries. Nonetheless, a decision must be made, and having weighed the totality of the record, the Court concludes that India has a stronger claim to having coupled intent with action at the KHEP earlier than Pakistan achieved the same at the NJHEP, resulting in the former's priority in right over the latter with respect to the use of the waters of the Kishenganga/Neelum for hydro-electric power generation.

438. The Parties differ sharply as to which facts are determinative for this purpose. For Pakistan, India's plans to build a hydro-electric project in accordance with the Treaty must take account of any "planned uses" of the waters at a specific location, once Pakistan is "firmly committed."[628] Pakistan maintains that such a commitment occurred as early as December 1988, when

[627] The Court's review resulted in consideration of some 120 of the documents offered by the Parties as evidence that it considers relevant; these are mostly found in Volumes 5 and 6 of Pakistan's Memorial and in Volumes 3A and 3B of India's Counter-Memorial.

[628] Pakistan's Reply, para. 5.15.

India was made aware that Pakistan was engaged in planning the NJHEP.[629] Pakistan also points to India having requested details about the NJHEP in 1989—"specifically in the context of the determination of 'existing … uses'"—which Pakistan then provided in March 1990.[630] For its part, India traces the first mention of the "Kishenganga Hydroelectric Project" to a document produced in 1971,[631] which well pre-dates the initial contemplation of the NJHEP that occurred, in India's view, in 1989.[632] India submits that it had taken steps to demonstrate its "firm intention" to proceed with the KHEP by no later than June 1994, when the finalized information about the KHEP's design (as a Storage Work) was provided to Pakistan.[633] Although Pakistan was only notified in 2005–2006 that the KHEP would proceed as a Run-of-River Plant, India maintains that this change was made to take account of Pakistan's objections to the design as a Storage Work, and that the revised design remains the same in significant respects;[634] thus, India considers this revision irrelevant in determining the point at which its firm intention to proceed was formed.

439. For the Court, however, the critical period cannot be placed in the 1980s and 1990s, as no significant steps beyond the thicket of project plans, intentions and communications occurred within those decades; indeed, from the present vantage point it is quite clear that subsequent developments and changes to the scale of the KHEP and NJHEP plans contradict many aspects of the original plans communicated to the other Party. Whatever factors are involved in determining the critical period *post hoc* and with the benefit of hindsight, this Court cannot endorse the fixing of that period based on any set of plans that, according to the established facts, are not currently under construction at Gurez or Nauseri.

---

[629] Pakistan's Memorial, paras. 2.12–2.13, referring to the Pakistani Commissioner's letter to the Indian Commissioner, 22 April 1989, (Annex PK-40): "The waters of [the] Neelum (Kishenganga) River [stand] committed to [the NJHEP]." Pakistan's Reply, para. 3.32.

[630] Pakistan's Reply, para. 3.36.

[631] Hearing Tr., (Day 9), 30 August 2012, at 51:13–21, referring to Letter from the CWPC to the Under Secretary of the Indian Ministry of Irrigation and Power, 13 May 1971, (Annex IN-55); Letter from the Under Secretary of the Power Department of the Government of Jammu & Kashmir to the Indian Ministry of Irrigation and Power, 3 April 1973, (Annex IN-56).

[632] Hearing Tr., (Day 5), 24 August 2012, at 148:15.

[633] India's Counter-Memorial, para. 4.148.

[634] India communicated to Pakistan at the time that "neither the axis of the dam, the location and layout of the project, nor its installed capacity or diversion works have changed… [nor has the] delivery of water to Bonar-Madmati Nallah" (India's Counter-Memorial, para. 3.50, quoting Record of the 99th Meeting of the Commission, New Delhi, 30 May to 4 June 2007, (Annex PK-33)).

440. Instead of the periods offered by either Party, the Court considers the period after the year 2000 to be the most relevant period. That is when plans and intent began to coalesce in respect of both the KHEP and NJHEP, as they are currently being constructed. The years 2004–2006 were critical for the KHEP as seen from the following chronology:

(1) By July 2000, India's National Hydroelectric Power Corporation (NHPC) had published a notice of tender ("International Competitive Bidding (ICB) Notice Inviting Tenders") for the execution of the "Kishenganga Hydroelectric Project (3 x 110 [megawatts])" over the KHEP, which was then conceived as a Storage Work.[635]

(2) By 2002, Pakistan had complained of construction at the KHEP.[636]

(3) In November 2002, an EIA of the KHEP had been completed by India.[637]

(4) By September 2003, a public hearing by the State Pollution Control Border had been conducted to solicit public attitudes to the KHEP project.[638]

(5) By April 2004, India's Ministry of Environment and Forests had provided environmental clearance to the KHEP (as originally designed).[639]

(6) By July 2004, India's Planning Commission had issued "in principle approval" for the KHEP.[640]

(7) In November 2004 and February 2005, the Permanent Indus Commission met specifically on the subject of the KHEP and Pakistan's objections to the project. India also updated Pakistan on the pro-

---

[635] *See* Pakistani Commissioner's letter to the Indian Commissioner, 11 November 2000, enclosing a copy of a Notice Inviting Tenders, *The Tribune*, 27 July 2000, (Annex IN-95/PK-94).

[636] *See* Pakistani Commissioner's letter to the Indian Commissioner, 10 April 2002, (Annex PK-100), stating that Pakistan has learned that India has "started construction" and requesting that India stop construction until the matter is resolved by the Commission.

[637] India's Counter-Memorial, vol. 2B, Tab D, Centre for Inter-Disciplinary Studies of Mountain & Hill Environment (CISMHE), University of Delhi, "Environmental Impact Assessment (EIA) of Kishenganga H.E. Project," November 2002.

[638] *See* Indian Ministry of Power's letter to the Government of Jammu & Kashmir, 5 May 2005, (Annex IN-72) ("During the public hearing conducted by the State Pollution Control Board at Gurez on 6.9.2003 almost all the public representatives, senior citizens and the public in general opposed the proposed construction of dam for the power project as in their opinion the varied bio-diversity along with ethnic and cultural identity of the inhabitants of the Gurez valley will be totally lost if they are made to migrate to other places.").

[639] Indian Ministry of Environment & Forests' letter to the National Hydroelectric Power Corporation (NHPC), 19 April 2004, (Annex IN-103) ("The Environmental Management Plan submitted by NHPC has been examined. The Ministry of Environment and Forests hereby accords environmental clearance as per the provisions of the Environmental Impact Assessment Notification, 1994, subject to strict compliance [with] the terms and conditions as follows …").

[640] *See* Indian Ministry of Power's letter to the Government of Jammu & Kashmir, 5 May 2005, (Annex IN-72) ("While according in-principle approval for the project in July 2004, the Planning Commission had observed that the specific per mega watt capital investment on the project is much higher than other hydel projects and on account first 5 years, 8% free power will be provided … ").

gress of works, particularly at the Bandipura site.[641] The Commission toured the KHEP site in November 2005.[642]

(8) In the period up to April and May 2005, India revised the KHEP's design, obtained approval for the revised design, and brought the revised design to both India's Cabinet Committee on Economic Affairs and the State Government of Jammu and Kashmir.[643]

(9) In March 2006, the Indian Ministry of Environment and Forests issued a clearance for the KHEP's revised design as a Run-of-River Plant.[644]

(10) In April and then June of 2006, India first notified Pakistan about the reconfiguration of the KHEP and then conveyed the revised design information for the KHEP as a Run-of-River Plant. [645]

441. Juxtaposing the KHEP's progression with developments at the NJHEP, it is clear that the NJHEP was well behind in key aspects of planning and implementation. Approvals for the NJHEP from Pakistan's Water

---

[641] Record of the 92nd Meeting of the Commission, Lahore, 27–29 November 2004, para. 70, (Annex PK-28). During the 93rd meeting, India's update on the status of the various components of the KHEP included a statement that, as to the Bandipura works, "[e]xcavation for underground works (Power House Complex and adjoining reaches) is in progress. The enabling works related to HRT are also going on" and, as to the Gurez works, that the "diversion tunnel work [was] held up due to climatic reasons and would be resumed in May. The interfering activities (construction activities related to dam and power intake) are yet to be taken up." Record of the 93rd Meeting of the Commission, New Delhi, 9–13 February 2005, (Annex PK-29). Further updates on the KHEP's project were conveyed at the 94th and 96th meetings of the Commission. *See* Record of the 94th Meeting of the Commission, Lahore, 7–12 May 2005, para. 53, (Annex PK-30); Record of the 96th Meeting of the Commission, New Delhi, 1–2 June 2005, (Annex PK-31).

[642] Record of the 104th Tour of Inspection by the Commission, 7–10 November 2005, (Annex PK-37).

[643] *See* Indian Ministry of Power's letter to the Government of Jammu & Kashmir, 5 May 2005, (Annex IN-72) ("In a meeting taken by Principal Secretary to Prime Minister on 19.4.2005, the revised proposal for implementation of Kishenganga HEP was discussed in detail and it was decided that the revised proposal may be taken to PIB/CCEA quickly after obtaining the concurrence of the State Government." Also, "I would request you to kindly consider the revised proposal and convey the concurrence of the State Government at the earliest so that the investment approval of Kishenganga HEP could be expedited.").

[644] Indian Ministry of Environment and Forests' letter to the National Hydroelectric Power Corporation (NHPC), 9 March 2006, (Annex IN-104) ("It is now noted by the Ministry that NHPC propose to reduce the dam height from 77 to 37m, as a result of which the length of reservoir would get reduced from 11.2 km to 4.5 km and area of submergence would get reduced from 7.65 sq.km to 2 sq.km. Only one village would now get affected. As such this revised environment clearance letter is issued in supersession of the earlier environment clearance letter dated 19.4.2004.").

[645] *See* Indian Commissioner's letter to the Pakistani Commissioner, 20 April 2006, (Annex IN-96) ("The Kishenganga Project has now been reconfigured, on the lines mentioned during the 97th meeting as a Run-of-River Hydroelectric Plant with a height of 36m and pondage of 7.6MCM … The information about the design of the project is under compilation and will be communicated to you shortly."); Indian Commissioner's letter to the Pakistani Commissioner, 19 June 2006, (Annex IN-97).

Resources and Power Development Authority (WAPDA),[646] Pakistan's Economic Coordination Committee[647] and the Pakistani Cabinet were not received until 2007.[648] Funding was still being sought in early that year.[649] And only in January 2008 was a letter of commencement issued[650] with implementation apparently set to start in the second quarter of that year.[651]

442. Thus, within the critical period of 2004–2006, India demonstrated a serious intent to move ahead with the project and took steps to make the KHEP a reality (through a combination of design, tender, financing, public consultations, environmental assessments and, crucially, national and local government approvals) of which Pakistan was aware (either through communications by India at the Commission level or through evidence that the Pakistani Commissioner had obtained independently). This suffices to convince the Court that the KHEP had progressed to a stage of firm intention to proceed before that same point was reached with respect to the NJHEP. While it is clear that there were many "bumps in the road" in the progression of the KHEP—the ineffectiveness of the Commission process in arriving at an orderly resolution of questions in this case being particularly striking to this Court—it is clear that, by 2004–2006, the plans for the KHEP were being finalized. The same cannot be said for the NJHEP.

443. In rendering its decision on this matter, the Court acknowledges that it has the benefit of hindsight and is thus able to establish precedence for

[646] "Cabinet Approves 969MW Neelum-Jhelum hydropower project," *Daily Times*, 13 December 2007, (Annex IN-76) ("Water and Power Development Authority (WAPDA) has already approved award of the contract to the lowest bidder i.e. CGGC-CMEC a joint venture on March 9, 2007 at the contract price of Rs 90.885 billion including foreign exchange of $785 million. The Project Director office is established and is operational at Muzaffarabad to execute the project in the site."); Entry for NJHEP on the website of the Pakistan Electric Power Corporation (PEPCO), (Annex IN-78) ("Construction Contract was awarded on July 07, 2007, to M/s CGGC-CMEC Consortium China for implementation of the project at a cost of Rs 90.90 billion including Rs. 46.499 Billions foreign component"); *see also* Entry for the NJHEP on the website of the Pakistani Water and Power Development Authority (WAPDA), (Annex IN-79).

[647] "Cabinet Approves 969MW Neelum-Jhelum hydropower project," *Daily Times*, 13 December 2007, (Annex IN-76) ("Economic Coordination Committee (ECC) of the cabinet had earlier approved the project in April during the current year.").

[648] *Ibid.* ("Federal cabinet on Wednesday formally approved the strategically important Neelum-Jhelum Hydropower project at a revised cost of Rs 128.4 billion with a foreign exchange component of Rs 46.5 billion. The formal approval was made in the federal cabinet meeting chaired by the caretaker Prime Minister Muhammadmian Soomro. The approval cleared the way for the long-awaited construction of the project.").

[649] *Ibid.* ("In order to arrange foreign exchange component of $785 million the government made a presentation to Kuwait Fund management delegation on March 21, 2007 and a formal request has been sent to Economic Affairs division for a further submission to Kuwait Fund.").

[650] Entry for NJHEP on the website of the Pakistan Electric Power Corporation (PEPCO), (Annex IN-78); Entry for the NJHEP on the website of the Pakistani Water and Power Development Authority (WAPDA), (Annex IN-79).

[651] Ijaz Kakakhel, "Financing Neelum-Jhelum hydropower project: Kuwait Fund signs $40.8m loan agreement with Pakistan," *Daily Times*, 26 November 2010, (Annex IN-77) ("The project implementation started in the second quarter of 2008 and was expected to be completed by the end of 2015. However, the formal (official) completion period was 2016.").

the KHEP based on both Plants having already gone through virtually the entire process of a large infrastructure project to the point of ongoing construction. When the Parties stand at an earlier phase of this process and actual construction has not yet begun, the picture will be more opaque. Should similar questions arise in the future concerning a given project or set of projects, the Treaty prescribes a formal procedure designed to bring a measure of order and certainty in the resolution of competing claims, and to questions of propriety of Plant design, *before* construction commences.[652]

444. Article IX foresees that the Parties may reach a bilateral, negotiated solution through the Commission (Art. IX(1)), or (if the Commission cannot resolve the matter) may put a matter before either a neutral expert or court of arbitration (Art. IX(2)). These procedures are designed to achieve resolution before construction of a Project commences; adherence to this process is the best way to avoid the invidious idea that the Parties are in a race to design, construct and operate a hydro-electric plant "first." Indeed, the Court notes that strict and timely adherence to the anticipated process for the resolution of differences and disputes would likely preclude such a race from occurring, as the dispute settlement mechanism would be triggered prior to the expenditure of immense resources for the construction of a Plant.

(b) The preservation of downstream flows

445. India's right under the Treaty to divert the waters of the Kishenganga/Neelum to operate the KHEP is subject to the constraints specified by the Treaty, including Paragraph 15(iii) of Annexure D as discussed above and, in addition, by the relevant principles of customary international law to be applied by the Court pursuant to Paragraph 29 of Annexure G when interpreting the Treaty. As discussed in the following paragraphs, both of these limitations require India to operate the KHEP in a manner that ensures a min-

[652] That procedure is found in Part 3 of Annexure D, and specifically in Paragraphs 9–11 thereof: Under Paragraph 9, India is under the obligation to "communicate to Pakistan, in writing" its project plans for new Run-of-River Plants, as specified in Appendix II to Annexure D. This is explicitly done "[t]o enable Pakistan to satisfy itself that the design of a Plant conforms to the criteria mentioned in Paragraph 8." This is also the point at which objections to the construction and operation of any new inter-tributary Plant on the grounds of adverse effect to the "then existing Agricultural Use or hydro-electric use by Pakistan" ought to be made pursuant to Paragraph 15(iii) of Annexure D. Under Paragraph 10, "[w]ithin three months of the receipt by Pakistan of the information specified in Paragraph 9, Pakistan shall communicate to India, in writing, any objection that it may have with regard to the proposed design on the ground that it does not conform to the criteria mentioned in Paragraph 8." As with Paragraph 9, this three-month period is also the time for Pakistan to lay out, in clear terms, what it considers to be its then existing agricultural and hydro-electric uses. Critically, under Paragraph 11, "[i]f a question arises as to whether or not the design of a Plant conforms to the criteria set out in Paragraph 8, then either Party may proceed to have the question resolved in accordance with the provisions of Article IX(1) and (2)." Thus, should the Parties reach an impasse regarding the existence of agricultural or hydro-electric uses by Pakistan that would require India to re-design or even halt the construction of a Plant (at least as originally proposed), either Party would be able to seek a definitive solution through the Treaty's dispute settlement mechanism.

imum flow of water in the riverbed of the Kishenganga/Neelum downstream of the Plant.

446. Accepting that the KHEP crystallized prior to the NJHEP under the critical period analysis set out above, Pakistan nonetheless retains the right to receive a minimum flow of water from India in the Kishenganga/Neelum riverbed. That right stems in part from Paragraph 15(iii) of Annexure D, which gives rise to India's right to construct and operate hydro-electric projects involving inter-tributary transfers but obliges India to operate those projects in such a way as to avoid adversely affecting Pakistan's "then existing" agricultural and hydro-electric uses.[653] The requirement to avoid adverse effects on Pakistan's agricultural and hydro-electric uses of the waters of the Kishenganga/Neelum cannot, however, deprive India of its right to operate the KHEP—a right that vested during the critical period of 2004–2006. Both Parties' entitlements under the Treaty must be made effective so far as possible: India's right to divert water for the operation of the KHEP is tempered by Pakistan's right to hydro-electric and agricultural uses of the waters of the Western Rivers, just as Pakistan's right to these uses is tempered by India's right to divert the waters for the KHEP's operation. Any interpretation that disregards either of these rights would read the principles of Paragraph 15(iii) out of the Treaty, to one or the other Party's injury.

447. India's duty to ensure that a minimum flow reaches Pakistan also stems from the Treaty's interpretation in light of customary international law. Under Paragraph 29 of Annexure G of the Treaty,

> [e]xcept as the Parties may otherwise agree, the law to be applied by the Court shall be this Treaty and, whenever necessary for its interpretation or application, but only to the extent necessary for that purpose, the following in the order in which they are listed:
>
> (*a*) International conventions establishing rules which are expressly recognized by the Parties.
>
> (*b*) Customary international law.[654]

[653] The Court notes that it is quite possible, in view of the particular topography of the region, that the KHEP lies at the only location on the Kishenganga/Neelum where an inter-tributary transfer is economically viable (*see* India's Counter-Memorial, paras. 4.23, 4.70; Pakistan's Reply, paras. 1.4–1.10; India's Rejoinder, paras. 2.42). If this is true, the KHEP may be the only instance in which Paragraph 15(iii) becomes problematic, as any other inter-tributary transfer that may be contemplated on other tributaries of the Jhelum would result in returning waters to the Jhelum Main before crossing the Line of Control, thereby causing no adverse effect to any uses that Pakistan may have.

[654] In addition to Paragraph 29 of Annexure G to the Treaty, customary rules on treaty interpretation (codified in the VCLT) require that the Court take account of relevant customary international law—including international environmental law—when interpreting the Treaty. *See* VCLT, Art. 31(3)(*c*) ("There shall be taken into account, together with the context: … (*c*) any relevant rules of international law applicable in the relations between the parties.").

448. Well before the Treaty was negotiated, a foundational principle of customary international environmental law had already been enunciated in the *Trail Smelter* arbitration. There, the Tribunal held that

> no State has the right to use or permit the use of its territory in such a manner as to cause injury by fumes in or to the territory of another or the properties or persons therein, when the case is of serious consequence and the injury is established by clear and convincing evidence.[655]

A broader restatement of the duty to avoid transboundary harm is embodied in Principle 21 of the 1972 Stockholm Declaration, pursuant to which States, when exploiting natural resources, must "ensure that activities within their jurisdiction or control do not cause damage to the environment of other States or of areas beyond the limits of national jurisdiction."[656]

449. There is no doubt that States are required under contemporary customary international law to take environmental protection into consideration when planning and developing projects that may cause injury to a bordering State. Since the time of *Trail Smelter*, a series of international conventions,[657] declarations[658] and judicial and arbitral decisions have addressed the need to manage natural resources in a sustainable manner. In particular, the International Court of Justice expounded upon the principle of "sustainable development" in *Gabčíkovo-Nagymaros*, referring to the "need to reconcile economic development with protection of the environment."[659]

450. Applied to large-scale construction projects, the principle of sustainable development translates, as the International Court of Justice recently put it in *Pulp Mills*, into "a requirement under general international law

---

[655] 16 April 1938 and 11 March 1941, 13 R.I.A.A. 1905, at 1965. This approach was reaffirmed in subsequent decisions including the *Legality of the Threat or Use of Nuclear Weapons*, Advisory Opinion, *I.C.J. Reports 1996*, p. 226, p. 242.

[656] *See also* Principle 13, which, however, is phrased in more hortatory terms. Stockholm Declaration of the United Nations Conference on the Human Environment, 16 June 1972, UN Doc. A/CONF.48/14/Rev.1, 3.

[657] *See* the International Convention for the Regulation of Whaling, 2 December 1946, 161 U.N.T.S. 72; the Convention on Fishing and Conservation of Living Resources of the High Seas, 29 April 1958, 559 U.N.T.S. 285; the African Convention on the Conservation of Nature and Natural Resources, 15 September 1968, 1001 U.N.T.S. 0; the United Nations Convention on the Law of the Sea, 10 December 1982, 1833 U.N.T.S. 397; the ASEAN Agreement on the Conservation of Nature and Natural Resources (not in force), opened for signature 9 July 1985; and the Treaty on European Union, 7 February 1992, 1757 U.N.T.S. 3. The preamble of the 1994 General Agreement on Tariffs and Trade (WTO Agreement), 1867 U.N.T.S. 187, also makes reference to the objective of sustainable development.

[658] The Stockholm Declaration as well as the subsequent Rio Declaration on Environment and Development provide that "environmental protection shall constitute an integral part of the development process and cannot be considered in isolation from it." Rio Declaration on Environment and Development, 1992, UN Doc. A/CONF.151/26/Rev.1 vol. I, 3. More recently, the Johannesburg Declaration on Sustainable Development reaffirmed these values and elaborated on the importance of "sustainable development." World Summit on Sustainable Development (Johannesburg Summit) Report, 26 August–4 September 2002, UN Doc. A/CONF.199/20.

[659] *Case concerning the Gabčíkovo-Nagymaros Project (Hungary/Slovakia)*, Judgment, *I.C.J. Reports 1997*, p. 7, p. 78.

to undertake an environmental impact assessment where there is a risk that the proposed industrial activity may have a significant adverse impact in a transboundary context, in particular, on a shared resource." The International Court of Justice affirmed that "due diligence, and the duty of vigilance and prevention which it implies, would not be considered to have been exercised, if a party planning works liable to affect the regime of the river or the quality of its waters did not undertake an environmental impact assessment on the potential effects of such works."[660] Finally, the International Court of Justice emphasized that such duties of due diligence, vigilance and prevention continue "once operations have started and, where necessary, throughout the life of the project."[661]

451. Similarly, this Court recalls the acknowledgement by the Tribunal in the *Iron Rhine* arbitration of the "principle of general international law" that States have "a duty to prevent, or at least mitigate" significant harm to the environment when pursuing large-scale construction activities.[662] As the *Iron Rhine* Tribunal determined, this principle "applies not only in autonomous activities but also in activities undertaken in implementation of specific treaties,"[663] such as, it may be said, the present Treaty.

452. It is established that principles of international environmental law must be taken into account even when (unlike the present case) interpreting treaties concluded before the development of that body of law. The *Iron Rhine* Tribunal applied concepts of customary international environmental law to treaties dating back to the mid-nineteenth century, when principles of environmental protection were rarely if ever considered in international agreements and did not form any part of customary international law. Similarly, the International Court of Justice in *Gabčíkovo-Nagymaros* ruled that, whenever necessary for the application of a treaty, "new norms have to be taken into consideration, and ... new standards given proper weight."[664] It is therefore incumbent upon this Court to interpret and apply this 1960 Treaty in light of the customary international principles for the protection of the environment in force today.

453. In this context, the Court takes note of India's commitment to ensure a minimum environmental flow downstream of the KHEP at all times. As India's Agent, Secretary to the Government of India's Ministry of Water Resources, declared before this Court during the hearing on the merits:

---

[660] *Pulp Mills on the River Uruguay (Argentina* v. *Uruguay)*, Judgment, *I.C.J. Reports 2010*, p. 14, p. 83.

[661] *Ibid.*, at pp. 83–84.

[662] *Arbitration Regarding the Iron Rhine* ("Ijzeren Rijn") *Railway between the Kingdom of Belgium and the Kingdom of the Netherlands*, Award, 24 May 2005, *PCA Award Series* (2007), para. 59.

[663] *Ibid.*

[664] *Case concerning the Gabčíkovo-Nagymaros Project (Hungary/Slovakia)*, Judgment, *I.C.J. Reports 1997*, p. 7, p. 78.

> So I would like to first assure the court that there will be a minimum environmental flow, and that will be in accordance with our laws.
>
> Number 2: there have been questions of the quantum, how much is India going to release? The NHPC—which is building the KHEP actually—as been in discussion with the Ministry of Environment and Forests on the quantum. Of course, the Ministry of Environment and Forests would like the maximum; there is a discussion going on. But I'd like to assure the court—this is an assurance I am giving—that the minimum environmental flow would not be less than the minimum observed flow of 3.94 [cumecs] at the site.
>
> As per the NESPAK figures which we've analysed, the average flow between the KHEP and [the Line of Control] is 4.1 cumecs. So even if I said 3.9 for the minimum, and I add this 4.1, at the [Line of Control] you would have sufficient flow. There would not be a dry period or any time when there is no water in the river.
>
> I assure the honourable court that we can't leave our territory dry; and since we can't do that, by consequence we can't leave any of Pakistani territory, which comes later on, dry.[665]

454. Similarly, the Court takes note of the statement in Pakistan's Reply that:

> India's contention [that Pakistan is applying a double standard as between its criticism of the KHEP's environmental flow and Pakistan's plans for an environmental flow below the NJHEP] is incorrect because the releases downstream of NJHEP have yet to be fixed, and a further consideration of environmental impacts is now being carried through by the same international team, applying the same methodology, as with respect to Pakistan's Environmental Assessment of the downstream impacts of the KHEP.[666]

This is an acknowledgment that hydro-electric projects (including Pakistan's projects) must be planned, built and operated with environmental sustainability in mind.

(c) The insufficiency of the data on record to determine a precise minimum downstream flow; the Court's request for further data

455. There is thus no disagreement between the Parties that the maintenance of a minimum flow downstream of the KHEP is required in response to considerations of environmental protection. The Parties differ, however, as to the quantity of water that would constitute an appropriate minimum; thus, the precise amount of flow to be preserved remains to be determined by the Court. The evidence presented by the Parties does not provide an adequate basis for such a determination, lacking sufficient data with respect to the relationship between flows and (1) power generation, (2) agricultural uses, and (3) environ-

[665] Hearing Tr., (Day 9), 30 August 2012, at 115:3–25.

[666] Pakistan's Reply, para. 4.48.

mental factors downstream of the KHEP below the Line of Control.[667] Accordingly, the Court finds itself unable, on the basis of the information presently at its disposal, to make an informed judgment as to whether a minimum flow of 3.94 m3/s (said to correspond to the lowest recorded flow over a 30-year period), which India committed to maintain in its operation of the KHEP, is sufficient to accommodate Pakistan's right under the Treaty and customary international law to the avoidance or mitigation of environmental harm.

456. The Court therefore defers its determination of the appropriate minimum flow downstream of the KHEP to a further, Final Award, to be issued after it has had the benefit of considering further written submissions on the matter from the Parties.

457. In the Final Award, the precise rate of the minimum flow will be fixed. The Parties' use of the waters for hydro-electric and agricultural uses, and the environmental conditions, will never be static, of course; but stability and predictability in the availability of the waters of the Kishenganga/Neelum for each Party's use are vitally important for the effective utilization of rights accorded to each Party by the Treaty (including its incorporation of customary international environmental law).

458. The Parties are requested to provide further data concerning the impacts of a range of minimum flows to be discharged at the KHEP dam on the following:

For India:

a) power generation at the KHEP;

b) environmental concerns from the dam site at Gurez to the Line of Control;

For Pakistan:

a) power generation at the NJHEP;

b) agricultural uses of water downstream of the Line of Control to Nauseri; and

c) environmental concerns at and downstream of the Line of Control to Nauseri.

459. In compiling these further data, the Parties are required to incorporate a sufficient range of minimum flows so as to give the Court a full picture of the sensitivity of the river system.

460. These data should be accompanied by full information on the assumptions underlying these analyses, including those for power gener-

[667] The Court recognizes that the Parties have provided significant data, in particular with respect to the generation of hydro-electric power and environmental impacts of the KHEP. These data, however, have been put before the Court only for scenarios in which the KHEP would be allowed to withdraw water either to the maximum possible extent, or not at all. This data analysis does not enable the Court to appreciate the effect of any potential intermediate flow.

ation and environmental concerns, and the associated uncertainty in the Parties' estimates.

461. In addition, the Court would welcome receiving more detailed information on the estimates already put before it by each Party of historical flows at the KHEP dam site, at the Line of Control and at the NJHEP dam site.[668]

462. Finally, the Court would also welcome provision by the Parties of any relevant legislation, regulatory pronouncements or decisions that the Governments of Pakistan and India may have respectively issued concerning environmental flow requirements for hydro-electric or similar projects and, in particular, the Government of India for the KHEP.[669]

463. The Parties are requested to provide the foregoing information to the Court by no later than 120 days from the issuance of this Partial Award (i.e., by 19 June 2013). Each Party is invited to then comment on the information submitted by the other Party no later than 60 days thereafter (i.e., by 19 August 2013). After considering these submissions, the Court will issue its Final Award setting forth its decision on this matter, and will exert its best effort to do so by no later than the end of 2013.

C. The Second Dispute: The Permissibility of Reservoir Depletion Under the Treaty

1. The scope of the Second Dispute

464. In the Second Dispute placed before this Court, the Parties disagree as to whether India may, within the terms of the Treaty, periodically lower the water level in the reservoir at a Run-of-River Plant on the Western Rivers for purposes of sediment control through the procedure known as drawdown flushing.

465. As formulated by Pakistan in its Request for Arbitration and Memorial, the Court is asked to determine:

> Whether under the Treaty, India may deplete or bring the reservoir level of a run-of-river Plant below Dead Storage Level (DSL) in any circumstances except in the case of unforeseen emergency?[670]

[668] In the case of Pakistan, these are the daily flow data corresponding to Annexes 3, 4 and 9 of Pakistan's Memorial, vol. 3, Tab B, National Engineering Services Pakistan Limited, "Kishenganga/Neelum River: Hydrology and Impact of Kishenganga Hydroeletric Plant on Energy Generation in Pakistan," April 2011 (covering the period from 1971 to 2004). In the case of India these are daily flow estimates from the KHEP and the Line of Control for the same period. These data should be provided electronically, in Excel format.

[669] In this regard, the Court recalls the Agent of India's statement at the hearing on the merits that the Indian National Hydroelectric Power Corporation (NHPC) and the Ministry of Environment and Forests had undertaken to cooperate to select an appropriate quantum for a minimum environmental flow at the KHEP. Hearing Tr., (Day 9), 30 August 2012, at 115:7–12.

[670] Pakistan's Request for Arbitration, para. 4; Pakistan's Memorial, para. 1.12.

466. The terms of the Second Dispute could be understood to relate to the permissibility of reservoir depletion in the abstract.[671] The record, however, both in the Commission and before this Court, indicates that Pakistan's core concern is that India's planned operation of the reservoirs at the KHEP and other, future hydro-electric projects will include depletion below Dead Storage Level for the purpose of flushing accumulated sediment from the reservoir. India, in turn, has confirmed its intention to employ drawdown flushing with respect to the KHEP.[672] Within this context, the Parties' pleadings with respect to the Second Dispute, as well as the relief requested by Pakistan, focus on the permissibility of this procedure.[673] The question facing the Court is therefore whether the Treaty prohibits drawdown flushing by India at the KHEP and at other, future Run-of-River Plants on the Western Rivers.

467. The question presented by the Second Dispute touches upon issues of fundamental concern to both Parties. For Pakistan, because the drawdown flushing of a reservoir necessarily affects the rate and timing of the flow below the dam (increasing the flow as water is released from the reservoir and reducing the flow when the reservoir is subsequently refilled), its prohibition in the Treaty is essential to securing Pakistan's uninterrupted use of the flow of water in the downstream stretches of the Western Rivers, an objective that Pakistan considers to be one of the Treaty's vital aims.[674] In addition, Pakistan is concerned about the impact of the release of sediment into the downstream river environment.[675] In Pakistan's view, the restrictions on India's ability to

---

[671] The use of the phrase "except in case of unforeseen emergency" could also be understood to indicate a specific concern with the paragraph of Annexure E (concerning Storage Works) that provides that "[t]he Dead Storage shall not be depleted except in an unforeseen emergency." It may be asked whether this provision applies equally to Run-of-River Plants. The Parties' pleadings make clear, however, that the dispute concerns whether any provision of the Treaty prevents the depletion of the reservoirs at Run-of-River Plants on the Western Rivers below Dead Storage Level for the purpose of drawdown flushing.

[672] India's Counter-Memorial, Appendix 2, paras. 35–37 ("Envisaged Procedure for Carrying Out Drawdown Flushing").

[673] *See* Pakistan's Memorial, para. 6.21 ("... the legality of drawdown flushing ... constitutes a central aspect of the [Second Dispute] ... the central feature of drawdown flushing is that the reservoir will be depleted (drawn down) below the Dead Storage Level"); *see also* the relief sought by Pakistan in relation to the Second Dispute, Pakistan's Memorial, chapter 7 ("Submissions"):

i. a determination that under the Treaty, the water level of the reservoir of a Run-of-River Plant may not be reduced below Dead Storage Level except in the case of an unforeseen emergency, and

ii. a determination that drawdown flushing for the purpose of sediment removal does not constitute an unforeseen emergency, and

iii. a mandatory and permanent injunction restraining India from reducing the water level of the reservoir of the KHEP except in the event of an unforeseen emergency.

[674] Hearing Tr., (Day 4), 23 August 2012, at 154:2–9; *see also* Pakistan's Memorial, paras. 6.2–6.3, 6.22, 6.32; Pakistan's Reply, para. 6.33.

[675] *See* Hearing Tr., (Day 2), 21 August 2012, at 131:17 to 132:7 (Court examination of Dr. Morris) ("there are two principal mechanisms by which the sediments released by flushing do create problems. One is oxygen depletion. The sediment has an oxygen demand which is depleted in the water column. Number 2, it has a function of clogging the gills of aquatic organisms, fish

fill and deplete reservoirs give concrete expression to India's obligation under Article III to "let flow" and "not permit any interference with" the waters of the Western Rivers.[676] In India's view, by contrast, the availability of drawdown flushing is central to the meaningful exercise of its right under the Treaty to generate hydro-electric power on the Western Rivers. According to India, drawdown flushing is the most effective sediment management technique available for the KHEP, and the outcome of the Second Dispute will determine India's ability to achieve maximal longevity (and therefore value) for this and other hydro-electric projects.

468. These concerns are heightened by the broad scope of the Second Dispute. While the Parties' disagreement has taken shape in the context of the KHEP's design and India's intention to use drawdown flushing for that reservoir, the Second Dispute, as framed by Pakistan and argued by both Parties, is not limited to the KHEP alone: it concerns India's right to use drawdown flushing at any Run-of-River Plant that India may construct on the Western Rivers in the future.[677] Accordingly, the Court's decision on the Second Dispute will apply to other Run-of-River Plants to be built, as well as to the KHEP.

469. Although it is the Court's duty to decide, as a matter of law, upon the permissibility of drawdown flushing generally under the Treaty, the Court must emphasize that its decision will have no effect on the Parties' rights and obligations in respect of the Baglihar hydro-electric project, as determined by the Neutral Expert in *Baglihar*. In the time since that determination, India has finalized the design of the project and completed construction in reliance upon the Neutral Expert's determination, which it was fully entitled to do. The Neutral Expert's determination has thus quite literally been realized in concrete at Baglihar, and it is not for this Court to revisit fundamental aspects of the design and operation of that Plant. Nor could Pakistan so ask: Annexure F expressly provides that the decision of a neutral expert shall be final and binding "in respect of the particular matter on which the decision is made."[678] Indeed, Pakistan itself has not sought a reversal of the *Baglihar* determina-

---

and whatever other organisms that require that. And I should say there is a third one: when you release sediment like this, you can get clogging of the gravels on the riverbed. Many species of fish—I'm not familiar with the species in Kishenganga *per se*, but typically a fish in mountain streams lays eggs in gravels and sands in the bottom, and this deposition of fine material will clog the gravels. It's a tremendous problem throughout the Pacific Northwest with the salmon, for instance. And they have this impact on the composition of the bed itself."); *see generally* Hearing Tr., (Day 2), 21 August 2012, at 129:17 to 134:2 (Court examination of Dr. Morris).

[676] Pakistan's Memorial, para. 6.3c.

[677] *See* Hearing Tr., (Day 10), 31 August 2012, at 44:9–11 (Pakistan's Closing Statement): "I stress again: the key point is that the Second [Dispute] is not about [the Kishenganga River]; it's about all the dams that India may build on the Western Rivers."

[678] Treaty, Annexure F, Para. 11. Paragraph 11 provides in full: "The decision of the Neutral Expert on all matters within his competence shall be final and binding, in respect of the particular matter on which the decision is made, upon the Parties and upon any Court of Arbitration established under the provisions of Article IX(5)."

tion,[679] nor has it asked for the dismantling of the Baglihar hydro-electric plant.[680] Pakistan has made it clear that it does not purport to appeal the *Baglihar* determination.

470. The effect of a neutral expert's determination is restricted to the elements of the design and operation of the specific hydro-electric plant considered by that Expert.[681] Although India has urged the Court to consider the Second Dispute to have been effectively resolved by *Baglihar*,[682] the Court does not see in Annexure F any indication that the Parties intended a neutral expert's determination to have a general precedential value beyond the scope of the particular matter before him. *Baglihar* is binding for the Parties in relation to the Baglihar project; the present decision, by contrast, is binding in respect of the general question presented in these proceedings.

471. As India has objected to the admissibility of the Second Dispute, the Court will first address India's objections.

2. The admissibility of the Second Dispute

472. The Court begins its analysis of India's objection to the admissibility of the Second Dispute by reference to Article IX of the Treaty, which provides for the settlement of differences and disputes arising in relation to the Treaty as follows:

> (1) Any question which arises between the Parties concerning the interpretation or application of this Treaty or the existence of any fact which, if established, might constitute a breach of this Treaty shall first be examined by the Commission, which will endeavour to resolve the question by agreement.
>
> (2) If the Commission does not reach agreement on any of the questions mentioned in Paragraph (1), then a difference will be deemed to have arisen, which shall be dealt with as follows:
>
> (*a*) Any difference which, in the opinion of either Commissioner, falls within the provisions of Part 1 of Annexure F shall, at the request of either Commissioner, be dealt with by a Neutral Expert in accordance with the provisions of Part 2 of Annexure F;
>
> (*b*) If the difference does not come within the provisions of Paragraph (2) (*a*), or if a Neutral Expert, in accordance with the

[679] Pakistan's Memorial, para. 6.24; Pakistan's Reply, para. 6.5. Pakistan also acknowledges that the *Baglihar* Neutral Expert's competence "is not a matter for this Court to decide." Pakistan's Memorial, para. 6.28.

[680] *See* the relief sought by Pakistan at note 673 above.

[681] Treaty, Annexure F, Para. 11.

[682] As characterized by India, the *Baglihar* determination is not legally binding on this Court—in India's words, "reliance is not sought as binding precedent"—but an "authoritative interpretation" of the question presented here that "should be respected by the Parties in a way that would eliminate repetitive examination of the same issue." India's Rejoinder, para. 4.44.

> provisions of Paragraph 7 of Annexure F, has informed the Commission that, in his opinion, the difference, or a part thereof, should be treated as a dispute, then a dispute will be deemed to have arisen which shall be settled in accordance with the provisions of Paragraphs (3), (4) and (5):

473. The purpose of Article IX is to provide a comprehensive framework for the resolution of disagreements between the Parties arising from the Treaty, either by negotiation (both within the Commission and at the inter-governmental level) or by submitting disagreements to one of two forms of third-party settlement. In this respect, the Court recalls the importance placed in the Preamble of the Treaty on the need to make "provision for the settlement, in a cooperative spirit, of all such questions as may hereafter arise in regard to the interpretation or application of the provisions agreed upon herein."[683]

474. Under Article IX, certain technical differences between the Parties, identified in a defined list in Annexure F of the Treaty, may be referred to a neutral expert, who must be a highly qualified engineer. In general, such technical questions relate either to the application of the Treaty to particular factual circumstances or to the compliance of individual projects with the terms of the Treaty. A matter may also become a "dispute" as defined in Article IX, in which case it may be referred to a court of arbitration, unless it is resolved at the inter-governmental level. Once appointed or constituted, neutral experts and courts of arbitration are both empowered to decide upon their own competence, the former pursuant to Paragraph 7 of Annexure F[684] and the latter pursuant to Paragraph 16 of Annexure G.[685]

475. As set forth above,[686] India raises two objections to the admissibility of the Second Dispute. First, India submits that, except when the Commissioners are in agreement to pursue an alternative course, the Treaty requires a neutral expert to make the initial determination of whether a matter arising

---

[683] Treaty, Preamble.

[684] Paragraph 7 of Annexure F provides as follows:

> Should the Commission be unable to agree that any particular difference falls within Part 1 of this Annexure, the Neutral Expert shall, after hearing both Parties, decide whether or not it so falls. Should he decide that the difference so falls, he shall proceed to render a decision on the merits; should he decide otherwise, he shall inform the Commission that, in his opinion, the difference should be treated as a dispute. Should the Neutral Expert decide that only a part of the difference so falls, he shall, at his discretion, either:
>
> (*a*) proceed to render a decision on the part which so falls, and inform the Commission that, in his opinion, the part which does not so fall should be treated as a dispute, or
>
> (*b*) inform the Commission that, in his opinion, the entire difference should be treated as a dispute.

[685] Paragraph 16 of Annexure G provides as follows:

> Subject to the provisions of this Treaty and except as the Parties may otherwise agree, the Court shall decide all questions relating to its competence and shall determine its procedure...

[686] *See* paras. 269–287 of this Partial Award.

between the Parties is a technical difference to be referred to a neutral expert or a dispute to be referred to a court of arbitration, and that Pakistan did not request the appointment of such a neutral expert in this instance. Second, India submits that the subject-matter of the Second Dispute is objectively among the questions consigned to a neutral expert by the list in Annexure F and, moreover, that Pakistan has itself expressed the intention to submit the same issue to a neutral expert. The Court will examine each objection to the admissibility of the Second Dispute in turn.

(a) Whether Pakistan has complied with the procedure of Article IX of the Treaty

476. The Parties' disagreement on the procedure to be followed hinges on the interpretation of Article IX(2)(*a*), which establishes the circumstances in which a neutral expert is authorized to resolve a "difference" between the Parties. In contrast to that provision, the conditions for the establishment of a court of arbitration are expressed largely in the negative. Except where a neutral expert decides that a matter should instead be referred to a court of arbitration, a difference is deemed to be a "dispute" only if it has not been referred to a neutral expert under the provisions of Article IX(2)(*a*). In other words, to establish whether it is properly seized of the Second Dispute, the Court must determine whether it was incumbent on either the Indian or the Pakistani Commissioner to refer the matter to a neutral expert.

477. Under Article IX(2)(*a*), the respective Commissioners exercise two distinct functions: (1) a Commissioner may have an opinion as to whether a difference falls among those that may be referred to a neutral expert; and (2) a Commissioner may request that a difference be referred to such an expert. Viewed in terms of the former function, a Commissioner's opinion as to the proper treatment of the difference can be read to create a procedural requirement: a difference must be referred to a neutral expert if "in the opinion of either Commissioner" it falls within the relevant portion of Annexure F. Alternatively, and viewed in terms of the Commissioners' latter function, the Commissioner's request could be read to act only as a triggering mechanism: a difference that is objectively within the enumerated list shall be referred to a neutral expert "at the request of either Commissioner." The two roles potentially played by these provisions can be seen even more clearly in the 9 December 1959 draft of the Treaty, in which the phrases that now make up Article IX(2) *a*) were expressed as successive paragraphs within then-draft Article IX.[687] In making their arguments, however, the Parties have emphasized only the aspects of Article IX(2)(*a*) that align with the role they respectively ascribe to it.

---

[687] Draft Article IX as at 9 December 1959 provided as follows:

(2) If the Commission does not reach agreement, then a difference will be deemed to have arisen, and it shall be dealt with as follows:

478. In the Court's view, the conjunction within Article IX(2)(*a*) of both references manifests the Parties' intention for the Commissioners to exercise a dual role under that Article, both as the initiators of the neutral expert process and a part of a mechanism that requires recourse to a neutral expert in certain circumstances. Article IX(2)(*a*) thus requires that a difference be referred to a neutral expert if either Commissioner believes that it relates to one of the identified technical matters and prefers that it be resolved by a neutral expert. This requirement only becomes effective, however, if a request for the appointment of a neutral expert is actually made. It is insufficient for a Commissioner merely to express the view that a difference would, at some point, be an appropriate matter for a neutral expert.

479. For the Court, this is the natural consequence of the combination, within a single sentence, of the two elements of Article IX(2)(*a*), and is the only interpretation to give full effect to the words of the Article. The phrase "in the opinion of either Commissioner" serves to guarantee either Party's ability to empower a neutral expert in respect of the many critical technical questions identified in Annexure F. Under Article IX(2)(*a*), a disagreement regarding the competence of a neutral expert is not a hurdle to appointment; any objection will simply be resolved by the Expert himself. At the same time, the requirement of an actual request is necessary, in the Court's view, to avoid the procedural impasse that could arise, for example, under the formulation recalled in the December 1959 draft: a Commissioner could express the view that a difference fell within Annexure F, thereby unequivocally foreclosing access to a court of arbitration, and yet decline to request a neutral expert to resolve the difference. Such a "pathological clause" (to use the parlance of international arbitration) was commendably avoided in the final version of Article IX.

480. It is undisputed that neither the Indian nor the Pakistani Commissioner requested the appointment of a neutral expert in respect of the subject-matter of the Second Dispute.[688] That suffices to dispense with India's first objection to admissibility. The Court also considers it relevant, however, to note that at no point prior to the commencement of these proceedings did the Indian Commissioner ever express the view that the Second Dispute—nor indeed any of the six questions raised by Pakistan—constituted a difference

(*a*) any difference which, in the opinion of either Commissioner, relates to one or more of the subjects specified in Annexure F shall be dealt with as provided in Paragraph (3) of this Article;

[...]

(3) A difference to be dealt with under this Paragraph shall, at the request of either Commissioner, be settled in accordance with the following provisions: –

[...]

[688] The Court notes that a Commissioner's request must be made through the procedure set out in Paragraph 5(*c*) of Annexure F of the Treaty. Where no joint appointment is possible, such a request takes the form of a letter from one of the Parties to the World Bank (in default of agreement between the Parties on the selection of another appointing authority), requesting the appointment of a neutral expert. *See* Hearing Tr., (Day 9), 30 August 2012, at 111:14 to 113:4.

within the competence of a neutral expert. On the contrary, a review of the records of the 100th, 101st, and 103rd Commission meetings reveals that India variously advanced the positions that the "issues" raised by Pakistan could be the subject of further discussion within the Commission;[689] that "there can be no differences as the design of the KHEP is consistent with the provisions of the treaty";[690] and that, insofar as depletion below Dead Storage Level is a general issue and not specifically related to the KHEP, "there is no scope for considering that any difference has arisen."[691] With respect to whether the permissibility of depletion below Dead Storage Level fell within the competence of a neutral expert, however, the Indian Commissioner was consistently silent.

481. In light of this record, sustaining the position India has advanced in these proceedings would require the Court to accept either (1) that the provision for a neutral expert to be appointed where a Commissioner considers such an expert competent operates, in fact, to disable any other procedure (such as resort to a court of arbitration) in the absence of express agreement within the Commission, or (2) that India's current embrace of the neutral expert process suffices to disempower the present Court. In the Court's view, the first interpretation is not sustainable. As confirmed by the Preamble of the Treaty, the purpose of Article IX is to provide for the settlement, "in a cooperative spirit," of differences and disputes through the various specified procedures. In keeping with that goal, Article IX(2)(*a*) ensures the appointment of a neutral expert where a Party actually requests the appointment of the same. It does not serve to impose—for its own sake—an additional procedural hurdle to access to a court of arbitration. Nor can the Court accept that India's current position in these proceedings, to the effect that the Second Dispute is a matter for a neutral expert, would be relevant under Article IX(2)(*a*)—even if India were now to request the appointment of such an expert. The Court considers that, having consistently maintained in the Commission that no difference between the Parties existed, India cannot now assert that the Second Dispute is, in fact, a difference after all.

482. In the absence of any indication by India during the key period prior to the commencement of these proceedings that the subject-matter of the Second Dispute was a matter for a neutral expert, and of any request—by either Party—for the appointment of such an Expert, the Court dismisses India's first objection to the admissibility of the Second Dispute.

---

[689] Record of the 100th Meeting of the Commission, Lahore, 31 May to 4 June 2008, (Annex PK-34), p. 19.

[690] Record of the 101st Meeting of the Commission, New Delhi, 25–28 July 2008, (Annex PK-35), p. 11.

[691] *Ibid.*, p. 14.

(b) Whether the subject matter of the Second Dispute can properly be heard by the Court

483. In its second objection to admissibility, India submits that the Second Dispute involves "highly technical issues of a kind prescribed in the Treaty to be dealt with by a Neutral Expert."[692] In approaching India's objection, the Court will first examine its underlying premise—namely, that a technical question listed within Part 1 of Annexure F *must* be submitted to a neutral expert.

484. In the Court's view, nothing in the Treaty requires that a technical question listed in Part 1 of Annexure F be decided by a neutral expert rather than a court of arbitration—*except* where a Party so requests (and then only if the neutral expert considers himself competent). With the exception of Article IX(2)(*a*), which the Court has considered and discussed in the context of India's first objection, recourse to a neutral expert is expressed throughout the Treaty in permissive—not mandatory—terms. Paragraph 1 of Annexure F, which sets forth the questions for which a neutral expert is competent, states that a "Commissioner *may* … refer to a Neutral Expert any of the following questions."[693] But nowhere does the Treaty stipulate that only a neutral expert may consider such matters. Instead, Paragraph 2 of Annexure F expressly limits the competence of a neutral expert over technical questions that are joined with a claim for financial compensation,[694] while Paragraph 13 requires that any matter not within his competence that may arise from a neutral expert's decision be resolved as a dispute under Article IX.[695] It is therefore apparent that the Treaty contemplates that technical matters can be dealt with by mechanisms other than that of the neutral expert.

485. Similarly, the Court can identify no Treaty provision that would bar it from considering a technical question, unless a Party had in fact requested the appointment of a neutral expert. Article IX(2)(*b*), establishing the circumstances in which a "difference" will be deemed a "dispute," operates by reference to the provision preceding it and the existence of a request for the appointment of an expert—and not by reference to Part 1 of Annexure F. Had the Parties so desired, the establishment of a Court could readily have been conditioned on a purely objective test of whether a dispute fell outside the list

[692] India's Rejoinder, para. 4.41.

[693] Treaty, Annexure F, para. 1 (emphasis added).

[694] Paragraph 2 of Annexure F provides as follows:

If a claim for financial compensation is raised with respect to any question specified in Paragraph 1, that question shall not be referred to a Neutral Expert unless the two Commissioners are agreed that it should be so referred.

[695] Paragraph 13 of Annexure F provides as follows:

Without prejudice to the finality of the Neutral Expert's decision, if any question (including a claim to financial compensation) which is not within the competence of a Neutral Expert should arise out of his decision, that question shall, if it cannot be resolved by agreement be settled in accordance with the provisions of Article IX (3), (4) and (5).

of identified technical questions; yet the Treaty does not adopt this approach.[696] Similarly, whereas Annexure F includes Paragraph 7 (directing a neutral expert to evaluate his competence against the list of technical questions), no comparable provision is found in Annexure G. The Court is not required to conduct an analysis of its competence or, potentially, to inform the Commission that a dispute involving technical matters should, in fact, be referred to a neutral expert.

486. The very composition of a court of arbitration also points to its competence in technical matters. In general, the skills or qualifications required of the members of a commission or tribunal represent a probative indication of the role the Parties intended that body to perform.[697] Here, one of the Court's umpires is required to be a "highly qualified engineer," and, indeed, nothing would stop the Parties from appointing engineers as their Party-appointed arbitrators or as the Chairman of the Court.[698]

487. In sum, the Court concludes that, although a neutral expert is competent only with respect to the technical questions identified in Annexure F, a duly constituted court of arbitration can consider any question "concerning the interpretation or application of [the] Treaty or the existence of any fact which, if established, might constitute a breach of this Treaty."[699] Accordingly, the Court considers that no dispute brought before a court of arbitration could be rendered inadmissible merely on the grounds that it involved a technical question.

488. The Court will now examine whether any further issue of admissibility arises from India's assertion that Pakistan has committed itself to submit the Second Dispute to a neutral expert. As the Court understands it, the significance of Pakistan's 11 March 2009 Letter and its pronounced intention to submit the question of orifice spillways at the KHEP to a neutral expert[700]

---

[696] The Court also notes that many of the provisions of Annexures D and E of the Treaty, including those relating to questions of the design of hydro-electric and storage facilities that are unquestionably within the list of questions in Part 1 of Annexure F, provide for disputes to be resolved "in accordance with the provisions of Article IX (1) and (2)." *See* Treaty, Annexure D, Paras. 7, 11, 21; Treaty, Annexure E, Paras. 6, 14, 16, 25. In the Court's view, this anticipates the possibility that such questions could be addressed through any of the modes of settlement contained in Article IX, rather than pursuant only to Article IX(2)(*a*).

[697] *See, e.g., Abyei Arbitration (The Government of Sudan/The People's Liberation Army/Movement)*, Final Award, 22 July 2009, *PCA Award Series* (2012), para. 468 ("The skill set of the Experts appointed to the [Abyei Boundary Commission] is also an important indicator of the procedural expectations of the Parties.").

[698] Annexure G of the Treaty imposes no qualifications on the individuals who may be appointed by a Party as arbitrator. *See* Treaty, Annexure G, Paras. 4(*a*) and 6.

[699] Treaty, Art. IX(1).

[700] Pakistan's 11 March 2009 Letter formulated the question of orifice spillways as follows:

> Pakistan is of the considered view that the orifice spillway provided in the current design of the [KHEP] constitutes an outlet below Dead Storage Level which is not in accordance with the criteria contained in Paragraph 8(*d*) of Annexure D to the Treaty. India does not agree with Pakistan's position.

is two-fold. Insofar as the Second Dispute may involve the same question, the 11 March 2009 Letter could arguably have triggered Article IX(2)(*a*) and committed the Parties to refer the difference to a neutral expert. In the Court's view, however, only an actual request for the appointment of an expert would activate the neutral expert process and preclude such a difference from submission to a court of arbitration.[701] Alternatively, the 11 March 2009 Letter and Pakistan's consideration that spillway design and sediment control are technical matters appropriate for a neutral expert could be seen as evidence that the Second Dispute is in fact technical in nature. But this would not alter the Court's view that the presence of potentially technical issues does not affect the admissibility of the Second Dispute.

489. For these reasons, no issue of admissibility follows from Pakistan's 11 March 2009 Letter. The Court nevertheless wishes to emphasize that, in its view, the difference concerning the permissibility of low-level orifice spillways that Pakistan has proposed to refer to a neutral expert is not identical with the Second Dispute now put before the Court. The former concerns whether the orifice spillway outlets contemplated for the KHEP are necessary for sediment control and are "of the minimum size and located at the highest level, consistent with sound and economical design and with satisfactory operation of the works."[702] The Second Dispute, by contrast, concerns the permissible modes of operation of low-level outlets generally and, in particular, whether India may employ drawdown flushing for sediment control. These are certainly related questions—as Pakistan itself has accepted before the Commission[703]—and the Court recalls in this regard its observations, in its analysis on the First Dispute, on the interlaced nature of design and operation.[704] Indeed, in the Court's view, it is not possible to evaluate whether the inclusion of a particular type of outlet is necessary, or whether such outlets are of an appropriate size and location, without first knowing how (or even whether) the Treaty anticipates that such outlets could actually be operated.

---

[701] The Court notes that Paragraph 5 of Annexure F distinguishes between the notice of intention to submit a difference to a neutral expert (Para. 5(*a*)), specifying the difference and how it falls within the neutral expert's competence under Annexure F, and the request for the appointment of a neutral expert (Para. 5(*c*)). In the Court's view, Pakistan's 11 March 2009 Letter is a notification under Paragraph 5(*a*). For the Court, however, an actual request for the appointment of an Expert under Paragraph 5(*c*) would be required to commit the Parties under Article IX(2)(*a*) to the neutral expert process.

[702] Treaty, Annexure D, Para. 8(*d*).

[703] Record of the 101st Meeting of the Commission, New Delhi, 25–28 July 2008, (Annex PK-35), p. 13 ("[I]t was stated by the PCIW [Pakistan Commissioner for Indus Waters] that while the issue was general in nature, it arose directly out of the design of KGHP [KHEP] and its discussion in the previous meetings and correspondence of the parties. PCIW noted specifically that the discussion with respect to sediment control and spillway design under Paragraphs 8(*d*) and 8(*e*) of Annexure D would not be meaningful unless the legality of drawdown flushing was first determined.").

[704] *See* paras. 407–409 of the Final Award.

490. It does not follow, however, that the two questions are a "single composite issue" that must be decided in a single forum, much less that the antecedent legal question of permissible operation becomes subsumed within questions relating to the design of a particular project. As the Court understands it, Pakistan has not objected to drawdown flushing on the grounds that it is technically unfeasible at the KHEP (or elsewhere); rather, Pakistan's position is that, irrespective of its technical merits or demerits, drawdown flushing is precluded by the Treaty. This is a legal question and, in the Court's view, not an indispensable part of the question of "whether or not the design of a Plant conforms to the criteria set out in Paragraph 8," for which a neutral expert would be competent. The Court accepts, of course, that such an expert may have to interpret the Treaty in the process of rendering a determination on the matters put before him. But where a legal issue (such as the permissibility of reservoir depletion) is contested and does not fall within a question identified for the neutral expert, the Court considers that it would be incumbent on such an expert to refer the matter back to the Commission to be handled as a dispute.

491. For the foregoing reasons, India's second objection to admissibility cannot be upheld. The Court holds that the Second Dispute is admissible and will proceed to consider the merits.

3. The permissibility of drawdown flushing

492. To resolve the Second Dispute, the Court must determine whether the Treaty permits drawdown flushing for sediment control at Indian Run-of-River Plants located on the Western Rivers. As detailed above,[705] Pakistan contends that an express prohibition on the depletion of reservoirs—which would effectively render drawdown flushing impossible—is incorporated by reference from Annexure E, which regulates the operation of Storage Works. Pakistan further submits that, within Annexure D itself, the combined effect of: (1) the definition of Dead Storage; (2) the restrictions on the low-level outlets that effective flushing would require; and (3) the limits imposed on the release of water below a dam, operates to prohibit drawdown flushing. Conversely, India contends that not only do these provisions not prohibit the use of drawdown flushing, but that the Treaty was purposely drafted with a flexible state-of-the-art principle to take full advantage of advances in technical knowledge, including in sediment control.

493. The Court will begin by considering the processes available for the control of sediment in hydro-electric installations. It will then turn to the background to the Treaty and the scope of India's right to develop storage and generate hydro-electric power on the Western Rivers. Thereafter, the Court will examine the specific Treaty provisions invoked by the Parties for and

[705] *See* paras. 291–337 of this Partial Award.

against the permissibility of drawdown flushing, as well as the need for such flushing at the KHEP.

494. The KHEP is a Run-of-River Plant and the question posed to the Court by Pakistan concerns the permissibility of reservoir depletion only for Run-of-River Plants. Indeed, despite assertions on several occasions that the KHEP maintains the features of a Storage Work,[706] the Court does not consider that the nature of India's project is seriously in dispute between the Parties. Pakistan has consistently described—and objected to—the KHEP by reference to Annexure D of the Treaty and, for its part, the Court considers that Pakistan's description of the KHEP is essentially correct: the KHEP employs a high dam and thus impounds a significantly larger volume of water than many run-of-river installations; it also utilizes an intake design more commonly seen in storage reservoirs. Nevertheless, because the Treaty defines a Run-of-River Plant solely by reference to the volume of storage designed to be used in the generation of power,[707] the total volume of storage behind the dam is not relevant in the classification of the works. In any event, the dispute presented to the Court is not limited to sediment control at the KHEP; rather, it concerns the permissibility generally of reservoir depletion at any future Run-of-River Plant on the Western Rivers. Accordingly, in the following analysis, the Court will review the question in terms of Annexure D to the Treaty, which governs the design, construction and operation of new Run-of-River Plants on the Western Rivers.

(a) Reservoir sedimentation and sediment control

495. Although ultimately legal in nature, the Second Dispute as presented by the Parties involves extensive reference to the processes of sedimentation and sediment management, the comparative effectiveness of different approaches and the environmental impact of sediment released from reservoirs. The resolution of the Second Dispute requires an understanding of how sediment is deposited in reservoirs and the techniques that are available to control its accumulation. Accordingly, before turning to the Treaty provisions relevant to this subject, it is appropriate to review, in general terms, the behaviour of sediment in rivers and reservoirs, as presented by the experts of both Parties.[708]

---

[706] *See, e.g.*, Pakistan's Reply, paras. 6.27–6.31.

[707] *See* para. 383 of this Partial Award and the accompanying footnotes. For the purposes of the Treaty a "Run-of-River Plant" is any Plant that is not designed to generate power from stored water beyond the volume expressly permitted to be stored and utilized as "Pondage." The potential presence of even large volumes of Dead Storage below the Pondage is irrelevant to this definition, provided that such storage cannot be used to generate electricity.

[708] The following discussion is drawn from the testimony of the Parties' experts as well as the following sources in the record: ICOLD, Bulletin 115, "Dealing with reservoir sedimentation," 1999, (Annex IN-TX-1); Alessandro Palmieri, *Sustainability of Dams—Reservoir Sedimentation Management and Safety Implications* (World Bank, 1998), (Annex IN-TX-2); Yang Xiaoqing, "Manual on Sediment Management and Measurement," World Meteorological

496. Sediment is an element of any watercourse or river system and enters the water as a result of erosion within the watershed of the river in question, as well as from the banks and bed of the river itself. Quantities of sediment can vary dramatically between river systems as a result of differences in the geology, climate, and vegetation of the catchment area, as well as human activities such as agriculture. Within a particular river system, the quantities of sediment entering the water will also vary substantially over time as a result of seasonal factors such as snowmelt and monsoon rains, as well as discrete events such as earthquakes and landslides that may push large quantities of soil into the water. In many rivers, peak sediment loads may be many times the average concentration, and in extreme cases, quantities of sediment greater than the entire average annual load may enter a river within the space of a few days.

497. Once in the water, sediment travels progressively downstream, either along the river bottom in the case of coarser sands and gravel (or even larger rocks and boulders during extreme floods), or in suspension in the case of finer particles. The capacity of a river to transport sediment is directly related to both the amount of sediment entering the river system and to its flow. For coarser sands and gravel from the riverbed, the greater the velocity of the water, the more sediment will be put into motion by the river's hydraulic energy. Quantities of sediment in excess of a river's transport capacity will be deposited along the river bottom and banks; such concentrations may subsequently be eroded and transported downstream when the transport capacity of the river increases.

498. Because the capacity of a river to transport sediment is directly linked to the velocity of the flow, it will vary over the reach of a river. In particular, any body of still water, such as a pool, lake, or reservoir will have the effect of slowing the flow and reducing its transport capacity, thereby causing suspended sediment to settle to the bottom. Coarse particles will typically be deposited at the upstream end where the flow first enters a reservoir, while finer sediments will settle further into the reservoir as the dispersal of the incoming water progressively reduces its flow. As a result of these dynamics, sedimentation is a concern at any reservoir where the long-term maintenance

Organization Operational Hydrology Report No. 47, WMO-No. 948, (2003), (Annex IN-TX-3); Durga Prasad Sangroula, "Sediment Management for Sustainability of Storage Projects in Himalayas: A Case Study of the Kulekhani Reservoir in Nepal," International Conference on Small Hydropower: Hydro Sri Lanka, October 2007, (Annex IN-TX-5); Izhar-ul-Haq & S. Tanveer Abbas, "Sedimentation of Tarbela & Mangla Reservoirs," Paper No. 659, Pakistan Engineering Congress, 70th Annual Session Proceedings, 2006, (Annex IN-TX-6); W.R. White, "World Water: Resources, Usage and the Role of Man-Made Reservoirs," March 2010, (Annex IN-TX-7); W. Rodney White, "Flushing of Sediments from Reservoirs," Contributing Paper to the World Commission on Dams, (Annex IN-TX-9); E. Atkinson, The Feasibility of Flushing Sediment from Reservoirs, Report OD137, November 1996, (Annex IN-TX-10); Gregory L. Morris and Jiahua Fan, *Reservoir Sedimentation Handbook: Design and Management of Reservoirs, Dams, and Watersheds for Sustainable Use*, Electronic version 1.01, September 2009, (Annex IN-135); Gregory L. Morris, "Reservoir Sedimentation and Sustainable Development in India: Problem Scope and Remedial Strategies," Proceedings of the 6th International Symposium on Reservoir Sedimentation, 1995, (Annex IN-137).

of a significant storage volume is an objective. Simply put, any reservoir will eventually fill with sediment, reducing its utility and eventually rendering it inoperable if this process is left uncontrolled.

499. In broad terms, the accumulation of sediment in a reservoir can be controlled by reducing the quantity of sediment entering the reservoir, by passing sediment loads through the reservoir without allowing significant quantities to settle out of suspension, or by periodically removing accumulated sediment after it has been allowed to deposit in the reservoir. Each approach has advantages and limitations and may be either more or less effective in the context of particular watersheds and particular reservoir sites. A combination of approaches is often the most effective method of managing sediment.

500. Reducing the volume of sediment entering a reservoir is typically attempted through efforts to control erosion in the watershed upstream of the reservoir, generally by reducing agricultural run-off and by planting soil-retaining vegetation. Erosion control, however, has shown limited effectiveness in reducing sediment concentrations, for example over large watersheds, in tectonically unstable areas and on rivers with high variability in annual peak flows. Alternatively, sediment can be prevented from entering a reservoir by constructing a bypass channel, such that heavy sediment concentrations are routed around the reservoir, or by locating a reservoir off the main channel of the river, permitting only relatively clear water to be drawn into the reservoir and stored. Such reservoir designs, however, require a particular topography in the area surrounding the planned reservoir and may only be feasible at certain sites.

501. Passing sediment through a reservoir without permitting its deposition is typically carried out through the process known as sluicing. During peak sediment loads, the incoming flow (and its sediment) is allowed to pass freely through the reservoir, thus minimizing the retention of such silt-laden water. The water level of the reservoir may also be partially drawn down to increase the velocity of the flow through the reservoir and maintain its corresponding capacity to transport sediment. Additionally, in certain reservoirs, a highly concentrated flow of sediment into the reservoir may form what is known as a density or turbidity current, in which the flow of sediment-laden water maintains its concentration and velocity while travelling along the bottom of the reservoir. Provided that the density current reaches the dam without significant dilution and that appropriate outlets are available, the sediment in a density current may be vented or sluiced downstream without any need for drawdown. In either case, because sluicing delivers sediment downstream at the same time and in the same concentrations that would naturally occur, its environmental impact is generally limited.

502. Finally, the accumulation of sediment in a reservoir may be controlled by removing such sediment after it has been allowed to deposit. Although this may be done mechanically, through dredging or siphoning, the limits on the volumes of sediment that can be removed by such techniques is

such that sediment removal is typically approached in terms of flushing—the process at issue in these proceedings—in which the river flow itself is used to remove accumulated sediment. In a flushing operation, sediment deposits are eroded and expelled by the flow of water through the reservoir, typically by drawing the water level in the reservoir down to a level at (or near) the reservoir bottom. Drawn down to such an extent, the river is largely restored to its natural flow velocity, which maximizes the capacity of the water to erode and transport deposited sediment. Although both sluicing and flushing operations may involve reservoir drawdown and will operate more efficiently at lower water levels, the extent of the required drawdown is typically greater for flushing operations; the velocity through the reservoir required to scour accumulated sediment is greater than that required to maintain the suspension of sediment in the incoming flow. Although flushing may be attempted with only partial depletion of a reservoir, this technique is not as efficient as flushing after a complete drawdown and—in light of the need for frequent repetition—is not commonly used. The effects of flushing without any drawdown of the reservoir are generally limited to a narrow cone in the immediate vicinity of the outlet and such an approach is typically used only to clear the area surrounding the intake of a hydro-electric plant.[709] Considering the heavy concentrations of sediment released in flushing, it may have significant environmental impacts on the water quality and other aspects of the downstream reaches of the river, particularly in the area immediately below the dam.

(b) *The context of the Treaty with respect to drawdown flushing*

503. The permissibility of depletion below Dead Storage Level is regulated explicitly by specific provisions in Annexure D (and, through incorporation by reference, Annexure E). These provisions are, however, to be interpreted within the context of the Treaty as a whole—in particular, against the background of permissible uses and the allocation of rights on the Western Rivers. The Court will begin its analysis of the Treaty with a number of contextual aspects that bear upon all of the specific provisions identified by the Parties in respect of the question of reservoir depletion.

504. First, one of the primary objectives of the Treaty is to limit the storage of water by India on the Western Rivers (and, correspondingly, to prohibit entirely the storage of water by Pakistan on the upper reaches of the Eastern Rivers). Annexure E to the Treaty strictly limits the volume of General Storage, Power Storage, and Flood Storage that India may develop on each of the Western Rivers.[710] For new Run-of-River Plants, Annexure D likewise restricts the permissible volume of pondage, and pegs this limit to power generation

[709] ICOLD, Bulletin 115, "Dealing with reservoir sedimentation," 1999, (Annex IN-TX-1), p. 49.

[710] Treaty, Annexure E, Para. 7.

at the *minimum* mean discharge calculated at the site.[711] These are not generous limits—the volume of storage permitted to India on the Jhelum Main, for instance, is zero—and even the limited available record of the Treaty's negotiating history suggests that these amounts of storage were a key point of contention between the Parties.[712] The outcome was significant in that it achieved a careful balance between the Parties' respective negotiating positions, allowing India hydro-electric use of the waters of the Western Rivers while protecting Pakistan against the possibility of water storage on the upstream reaches of those Rivers having an unduly disruptive effect on the flow of water to Pakistan.

505. In contrast, Dead Storage is the only category of storage, under either Annexure D or E, that is unrestricted in volume. India may include Dead Storage in the design of any Run-of-River Plant or Storage Work and may provide for Dead Storage of any capacity. This fact is consistent with the other restrictions on storage on the Western Rivers only if Dead Storage is somehow qualitatively different and was understood to be truly "dead"—an area to be filled once, and not thereafter subject to manipulation. The absence of limits on the volume of Dead Storage cannot, of course, itself impose a restriction on how such storage may used. But it is suggestive of the mindset of the Parties in providing for storage of this type.

506. Second, the Court notes that in many instances the Treaty does not simply restrict the Parties from taking certain actions, but also constrains their entitlement to construct works that would enable such actions to be taken. Thus, India is not only restricted in storing water on the Western Rivers; it is also prohibited from constructing Storage Works except within the limited capacity permitted by the Treaty.[713] Annexure D, in turn, sets out the permissible operation of a Run-of-River Plant, and also includes in Paragraph 8 restrictions on the design of such Plants.[714] In particular, Paragraph 8(*d*) prohibits outlets from a reservoir below the Dead Storage Level, "unless necessary for sediment control or any other technical purpose." Any outlets that may be necessary must be of the "minimum size and located at the highest level" that

---

[711] Treaty, Annexure D, Paras. 2(*i*), 8(*c*).

[712] *See, e.g.*, Note to Files from W.A.B. Iliff, 19 April 1960, (Annex IN-50) ("After Mr. Gulhati and Mr. Mueenuddin had handed me their respective figures for ... the amount of storage which India might be permitted to build on the Western Rivers, I informed each of them in a joint meeting that the gap between the positions of the two sides was so wide that there was no possible hope that the Bank could bring them together by a 'good offices' technique... . I went on to request that each of them should ask his Government to reconsider their positions and to present to the Bank ... a revised figure moving in the direction of closing the gap.").

[713] Article III(4) of the Treaty provides that "[e]xcept as provided in Annexure D and E, India shall not store any water of, or construct any storage works on, the Western Rivers."

[714] Paragraph 11 of Annexure E includes similar physical restrictions on the design of any Storage Works that India may construct on the Western Rivers. As a matter of general approach, the Treaty appears to routinely reinforce operational limits on the conduct of the Parties with physical restrictions on the development of infrastructure.

would be "consistent with sound and economical design and with satisfactory operation of the works."[715]

507. In their submissions, the Parties have advanced sharply divergent views of the meaning of Paragraph 8(*d*), Pakistan characterizing the provision as a constructive prohibition on drawdown flushing and India, as an express authorization to design the dam as necessary for effective sediment management. In the Court's view, however, Paragraph 8(*d*) is neither. This Paragraph does not prohibit flushing, even in a roundabout fashion, by prohibiting the necessary outlets. Outlets below Dead Storage Level are permitted if "necessary for sediment control." Nor does Paragraph 8(*d*) evidence the Parties' intention to permit drawdown flushing. Outlets below Dead Storage Level can be used to control sediment accumulation through sluicing, without significantly reducing the level of water in the reservoir. Thus, no rule either permitting or proscribing drawdown flushing follows from the terms of Paragraph 8(*d*).

508. The relevance of this provision is contextual. Design restrictions on the availability of outlets from Dead Storage make sense only against a background assumption that the uses to which Dead Storage could be put are also somehow constrained. If depletion of Dead Storage was intended, whether for flushing or otherwise, the Court can see no obvious purpose that would be served by limiting the size and placement of outlets from Dead Storage. This is all the more so, considering that the preferred location for outlets intended for flushing would be at the riverbed or, in other words, at the lowest level of the reservoir—not the highest. The existence of a restriction on outlets thus strongly suggests that some limitation on the use and depletion of Dead Storage was also intended.

509. Finally, as the Court considered in detail above, it is beyond debate that the intention behind the Treaty was to allow India to develop the hydro-electric potential of the Western Rivers, largely through the use of Run-of-River Plants. This is an important aspect of the Treaty context with respect to drawdown flushing. The Court does not accept that, in serious negotiations extending over the course of years, India and Pakistan would have wasted time on the allocation of rights that could not, in fact, be used productively. In this respect, the Court concurs with the idea that "anything you build needs to work."[716] If a prohibition on drawdown flushing would render any sustainable hydro-electric development impossible, the Court would consider this relevant in approaching any Treaty provision seeming to suggest such a prohibition. In light, however, of the variety of approaches available to manage sediment—not all of which would require the depletion of reservoirs below Dead Storage Level—the Court considers this a matter for further examination in its discussion of the necessity of drawdown flushing.

---

[715] Treaty, Annexure D, Para. 8(*d*).

[716] Hearing Tr., (Day 2), 21 August 2012, at 121:16,18 (cross-examination of Dr. Morris).

(c) *The specific provisions of the Treaty*

510. Turning from the Treaty's context to its specifics, the Court considers that two provisions—concerning the release of water below a Plant and the restrictions on reservoir filling—directly bear on the permissibility of drawdown flushing. The Court will address each of these provisions in turn.

511. The chapeau of Paragraph 15 of Annexure D establishes the flow that may be released below a Run-of-River Plant in the following terms:

> Subject to the provisions of Paragraph 17 [excluding periods of filling], the works connected with a Plant shall be so operated that (*a*) the volume of water received in the river upstream of the Plant during any period of seven consecutive days, shall be delivered into the river below the Plant during the same seven-day period, and (*b*) in any one period of 24 hours within that seven-day period, the volume delivered into the river below the Plant shall not be less than 30%, and not more than 130%, of the volume received in the river above the Plant during the same 24-hour period. [...][717]

512. Although Pakistan argues that drawdown flushing would be "severely curtailed (if not prohibited)" by the flow restrictions in Paragraph 15,[718] such is not necessarily the case: depending upon the flow at and hydrological size of a particular reservoir, drawdown flushing may or may not conform with these restrictions. In general, drawdown flushing would be incompatible with Paragraph 15 at hydrologically large reservoirs and at most reservoirs during the low flow season. Insofar, however, as hydrologically small reservoirs could still be flushed within seven days while complying with the daily limits on the permissible delivery of water below the Plant, the flow restrictions in Paragraph 15 will not prohibit drawdown flushing. However, as currently envisaged by India, the use of drawdown flushing at the KHEP would in all probability not comply with the flow restrictions of Paragraph 15.[719]

513. The decisive prohibition on the depletion of a reservoir below Dead Storage Level stems from Paragraph 14 of Annexure D, through its incorporation by reference of Paragraph 19 of Annexure E. Paragraph 14 provides as follows:

> The filling of Dead Storage shall be carried out in accordance with the provisions of Paragraph 18 or 19 of Annexure E.

In turn, Paragraphs 18 and 19 of Annexure E provide as follows:

---

[717] Paragraph 16 further elaborates the applicable 24-hour and 7-day periods as follows:

> For the purpose of Paragraph 15, the period of 24 hours shall commence at 8 a.m. daily and the period of 7 consecutive days shall commence at 8 a.m. on every Saturday. The time shall be Indian Standard Time.

[718] Pakistan's Memorial, para. 6.30(*c*); *see also* Pakistan's Reply, para. 6.32.

[719] *See* India's Counter-Memorial, p. 269–270. While the KHEP reservoir could, under certain flow conditions, be flushed through more gradual depletion and refilling while observing the limits of Paragraph 15, the Court's ultimate conclusion on the permissibility of drawdown flushing does not hinge on this provision.

> 18. The annual filling of Conservation Storage and the initial filling below Dead Storage Level, at any site, shall be carried out at such times and in accordance with such rules as may be agreed upon between the Commissioners. In case the Commissioners are unable to reach agreement, India may carry out the filling as follows:
>
> [...]
>
> (*b*) if the site is on The Jhelum, between 21st June and 20th August; and
>
> [...]
>
> 19. The Dead Storage shall not be depleted except in an unforeseen emergency. If so depleted, it will be re-filled in accordance with the conditions of its initial filling.

514. In approaching these provisions, the Court cannot separate the prohibition on depletion in Paragraph 19 from the provisions on refilling. By referring to Paragraph 19 as well as Paragraph 18 (containing the schedule for initial filling), the drafters of Annexure D evidently intended to provide for a situation of refilling. Far from being irrelevant, however, the circumstances in which a reservoir can be depleted are directly related to the need to refill it. This is all the more true insofar as the second sentence of Paragraph 19 begins with the words "[i]f so depleted" and is grammatically incoherent if incorporated without the preceding text. It therefore follows that Annexure D transposes Paragraph 19 of Annexure E in its entirety—including the prohibition on the depletion of Dead Storage. Further, it is undisputed between the Parties that sediment accumulation would not constitute an unforeseen emergency.[720]

515. Having identified at least one operative provision of Annexure D that prohibits the depletion of Dead Storage for drawdown flushing, the Court considers it sufficient to note that the definition of Dead Storage in Annexure D—"that portion of the storage which is not used for operational purposes"—is consistent with this outcome. The Court considers it unnecessary, under the circumstances, to decide whether the definition alone would constitute a prohibition. The Court does, however, consider it appropriate to emphasize that a distinction between "operation" and "maintenance" (advanced by India primarily in reference to the definition of Dead Storage) would not permit India to carry out drawdown flushing in the face of the restrictions the Court has identified in Paragraphs 14 and 15.[721] In an instrument as detailed and comprehensive as the present Treaty, the Court cannot

---

[720] It is undisputed between the Parties that Paragraph 19 of Annexure E, insofar as it applies, constitutes a prohibition on drawdown flushing (the need for sediment management not being an unforeseen emergency). *See* Pakistan's Memorial, para. 6.21; India's Counter-Memorial, para. 737 (accepting that Paragraph 19 prohibits drawdown flushing in the context of Annexure E).

[721] With respect to the limits on flow in Paragraph 15, India has in fact conceded that they would remain applicable during any flushing operation. India's Counter-Memorial, para. 7.51. Although this would ordinarily suffice to dispense with the matter, the Court notes certain statements by India's expert to the effect that categorizing flushing as maintenance would disable any restriction, including those on flow and even the express prohibition on depletion in Annexure E.

accept that a category of "maintenance purposes" nowhere specified in the Treaty can be invoked to free a party from restrictions that are explicitly laid down in the Treaty.

(d) *The necessity of drawdown flushing for power generation on the Western Rivers*

516. To complete its analysis, the Court turns to the key factor that bears further consideration in light of the prohibition on flushing apparent in the text: the question of whether drawdown flushing is indispensable to any sustainable generation of hydro-electric power on the Western Rivers.[722] Such an inquiry requires an examination of the impact any proscription of drawdown flushing would have on the viability of Indian Run-of-River Plants on the Western Rivers.

517. Having reviewed the technical documentation submitted by the Parties[723] and in reliance on the opinions of the experts presented by them, the Court concludes that the constraints imposed by the Treaty should not condemn the KHEP or other Indian hydro-electric projects on the Western Rivers to an impractical and uneconomically short project life.[724] While the prohibition on reservoir depletion will preclude India from having recourse to flushing with drawdown below Dead Storage Level, the Court recalls that flushing is but one of a number of techniques available for sediment control.[725]

518. With respect to the KHEP, the Court accepts Dr. Morris's opinion that sediment sluicing offers a feasible alternative to drawdown flushing. Sluicing, the Court recalls, is the technique whereby sediment-laden inflows

---

See Hearing Tr., (Day 3), 22 August 2012, at 90:2 to 94:18. In light of this suggestion in the record, the Court considers it appropriate to address this question expressly.

[722] In the Court's view, the Parties' discussion of whether drawdown flushing was understood and was within the expectation of the Treaty drafters in 1960 is subsumed within the question of whether such flushing is necessary at the KHEP and other Run-of-River installations today. The Court accepts that the Treaty is to be interpreted in light of technological developments and that the Parties are not bound to the technology of 1960. Nevertheless, any general "state-of-the-art" principle cannot serve to override the essential equilibrium on water use and flow agreed to by the Parties in the Treaty. This may well mean that some techniques that would be considered state-of-the-art will be unavailable to India in the future; so long as other methods are available and can be made effective, however, India is bound by the constraints of the Treaty.

[723] *See* the sources listed above at note 708 in this Partial Award.

[724] India has both stated that drawdown flushing is "one of the effective techniques" for maintaining the sustainability of reservoirs (India's Counter-Memorial, para. 7.81), and asserted that drawdown flushing is "essential" or "necessary" to the sustainability of the KHEP (India's Counter-Memorial, para. 7.89), comparing its projected lifespan with and without drawdown flushing (India's Counter-Memorial, para. 7.88).

[725] *See* paras. 495–502 of this Partial Award. *See also* Hearing Tr., (Day 2), 21 August 2012, at 101:14 to 104:13 (cross-examination of Dr. Morris); Hearing Tr., (Day 3), 22 August 2012, at 78:3–20; 105:22 to 107:6 (cross-examination of Dr. Rangaraju); for a short list of sediment management options, *see* ICOLD, Bulletin 115, "Dealing with reservoir sedimentation," 1999, (Annex IN-TX-1), pp. 13, 15.

are released through the dam before the sediment particles can settle in the reservoir. As the Court understands it, the basis for Dr. Morris's opinion is the historically well-established record of effective sediment control at run-of-river installations through the use of a high-level intake to the power turbines and of sediment sluices in the immediate vicinity of the intake.[726] In Dr. Morris's opinion—which the Court also accepts—no significant difference follows from the fact that the KHEP is a Run-of-River Plant located on top of the reservoir created by a high dam, rather than at a low barrage. Where a high dam is being used to raise the elevation of the intake and the corresponding generating capacity—and not to create usable storage behind the dam—the Dead Storage can fill with sediment without consequence. Once the Dead Storage is filled with sediment, the upper reaches of the reservoir would operate identically to a low barrage[727] and could be cleared of sediment through sluicing, without a need to draw down the reservoir.[728] According to Dr. Morris, it is the KHEP's current intake design—rather than anything inherent in the height of the dam or the size of the reservoir—that prevents the KHEP from simply sluicing sediment like a barrage.[729]

519. The essence of Dr. Morris's opinion on the feasibility of sluicing at the KHEP site has not been contradicted by India's experts. Despite Dr. Rangaraju's view that drawdown flushing is "essential," the Court considers his testimony to establish that drawdown flushing is an appropriate (and perhaps preferable) technique, but not the only possible one.[730] With reference to drawdown flushing, Dr. Rangaraju stated that "nobody can claim that this is the only technique possible"[731] and further acknowledged that he had not examined whether sluicing would suffice to control sediment at the KHEP.[732]

520. Similarly, the Court understands the report of Dr. Schleiss to state that drawdown flushing is essential for the sustained operation of the KHEP *as currently designed*, but not to exclude other possible designs that could operate on a different basis. Dr. Schleiss's principal concern involves the encroachment of coarse sediment from the delta at the upper end of the reservoir on the KHEP's submerged power intake; other sediments would be controlled through "normal spillway operation" (i.e., operation not requiring drawdown) and by venting turbidity currents containing a "high amount of suspended fine

[726] Morris Report, p. 10.

[727] Hearing Tr., (Day 2), 21 August 2012, at 108:2 to 110:3 (cross-examination of Dr. Morris).

[728] Because significantly lower water velocities are required to remove suspended sediment from the reservoir than to dislodge accumulated sediment (which is the purpose of drawdown flushing), sluicing, unlike flushing, can be carried out without or with only partial drawdown. *See* ICOLD, Bulletin 115, "Dealing with reservoir sedimentation," 1999, (Annex IN-TX-1), § 3.1.1.

[729] Morris Report, pp. 14–15.

[730] Hearing Tr., (Day 3), 22 August 2012, at 105:22 to 107:6 (cross-examination of Dr. Rangaraju); *see also* India's Counter-Memorial, para. 7.81.

[731] Hearing Tr., (Day 3), 22 August 2012, at 78:19–20 (cross-examination of Dr. Rangaraju).

[732] Hearing Tr., (Day 3), 22 August 2012, at 82 to 83 (cross-examination of Dr. Rangaraju).

sediment."[733] In the Court's view, this is not in fact fundamentally inconsistent with the testimony of Dr. Morris, who asserts sluicing is feasible on the basis of alternative intake designs. Ultimately, the Court considers that Dr. Schleiss has not established to its satisfaction that another intake design that could operate without drawdown flushing would be technically unworkable.[734]

521. The Court's view that India's right to generate hydro-electric power on the Western Rivers can meaningfully be exercised without drawdown flushing extends beyond the specifics of the KHEP to other, future Run-of-River Plants. Based on the evidence provided to it, the Court notes that, in general, sluicing is recommended for narrow, hydrologically small[735] reservoirs located on rivers where surplus inflow is available for discharging sediment,[736] and that sluicing with little drawdown is particularly effective in regions where a significant percentage of the annual sediment load is carried by the river in short and predictable periods.[737] While acknowledging that the potential impact of sediment must be evaluated and modelled in relation to each particular site and dam design, the Court presently sees no reason why the factors favouring the feasibility of a sluicing mode of operation at the KHEP site would not apply

[733] Schleiss Report, p. 6.

[734] Dr. Schleiss states that a submerged intake is required at the KHEP in light of the need to maintain water pressure throughout the head-race tunnel. *See* Schleiss Report, p. 4 ("the intake has to have sufficient submergence from the operation level of the reservoir in order to avoid vortex formation and consequently air entrainment into the intake as well as to ensure pressure flow in the headrace tunnel under all operation conditions"). He further states, without elaboration, that the topographical conditions at the site require the intake to draw water directly from the reservoir itself, rather than by way of a separate weir and desilting basin. *See ibid.*, p. 5 ("Under the local topographic condition of the KHEP it is technically not feasible to design free surface desilting basins."). For the Court, this suffices to establish that the current design of the KHEP may well be the simplest alternative and the use of drawdown flushing the most economical approach to sediment management; it does not establish that these approaches are the only ones available.

[735] The hydrological size of the reservoir is computed as the ratio of total reservoir volume to mean annual inflow. From a sediment management perspective, it is more significant than a reservoir's absolute size. Reservoirs with a capacity inflow ratio exceeding 30 or 50 percent are considered hydrologically large. *See* Gregory L. Morris and Jiahua Fan, *Reservoir Sedimentation Handbook: Design and Management of Reservoirs, Dams, and Watersheds for Sustainable Use*, Electronic version 1.01, September 2009, (Annex IN-135), § 3.3.1; W. Rodney White, "Flushing of Sediments from Reservoirs," Contributing Paper to the World Commission on Dams, (Annex IN-TX-9), p. vi.

[736] ICOLD, Bulletin 115, (Annex IN-TX-1), §§ 3.1.2, 3.1.3; Gregory L. Morris and Jiahua Fan, *Reservoir Sedimentation Handbook: Design and Management of Reservoirs, Dams, and Watersheds for Sustainable Use*, Electronic version 1.01, September 2009, (Annex IN-135), § 13.1.3.

[737] Hearing Tr., (Day 2), 21 August 2012, at 127:15–25 (cross-examination of Dr. Morris); Durga Prasad Sangroula, "Sediment Management for Sustainability of Storage Projects in Himalayas: A Case Study of the Kulekhani Reservoir in Nepal," International Conference on Small Hydropower: Hydro Sri Lanka, October 2007, (Annex IN-TX-5), pp. 7–8; Gregory L. Morris, "Reservoir Sedimentation and Sustainable Development in India: Problem Scope and Remedial Strategies," Proceedings of the 6th International Symposium on Reservoir Sedimentation, 1995, (Annex IN-137), p. 59.

equally to other sites on the Western Rivers at which India would be likely to construct Run-of-River Plants.

522. In carrying out this evaluation, the Court emphasizes that it is not considering whether the development of hydro-electric power without recourse to drawdown flushing is preferable for India. It is not for the Court to apply "best practices" in resolving this dispute. India has quite understandably argued in these proceedings for a right to the optimal design and operation of its hydro-electric installations on the upstream stretches of the Western Rivers. However, any exercise of design involves consideration of a variety of factors—not all of them technical. Hydrologic, geologic, social, economic, environmental and regulatory considerations are all directly relevant,[738] and the Court considers the Treaty restraints on the construction and operation by India of reservoirs to be such a regulatory factor.[739] For the Court, the optimal design and operation of a hydro-electric plant is that which can practically be achieved within the constraints imposed by the Treaty.

* * *

523. The Court is conscious of the fact that the issues of reservoir construction and operation raised by the Second Dispute come before it at a time at which the process of harnessing the potential for the generation of hydro-electricity on the Western Rivers, as foreseen by the Treaty, is already under way. This does not alter the duty of the Court to interpret and apply the Treaty in the manner required by Paragraph 29 of Annexure G. It would not be in accordance with the governing principles enunciated in this Partial Award for the interpretation of the Treaty, and its application, to cast doubt retrospectively on any Run-of-River Plants already in operation on the Western Rivers. For the same reasons, the Court wishes to make plain that this Partial Award may not be so interpreted as to affect retrospectively any such Plant already under construction (although not yet in operation) the design of which, having been duly communicated by India under the provisions of Annexure D, had not been objected to by Pakistan as provided for in Annexure D. That is plainly not the case for the Kishenganga Hydro-Electric Project itself.

---

[738] *See* Hearing Tr., (Day 2), 21 August 2012, at 100:13 to 101:4, 118:7 to 119:12 (cross-examination of Dr. Morris); *see also* Alessandro Palmieri, *Sustainability of Dams—Reservoir Sedimentation Management and Safety Implications* (World Bank, 1998), (Annex IN-TX-2), p. 4.

[739] In the case of the KHEP, the Court is cognizant that changes to the design of the project may be required to optimize the management of sediment in light of this Partial Award. In this respect, it is provident for the Court to note that its *Order on Interim Measures* has temporarily restrained the construction of "permanent works on or above the Kishenganga/Neelum riverbed," a development that may now serve to facilitate any changes in design that India may need to implement in light of the Court's decision on drawdown flushing.

V. Decision

Having considered the Parties' written and oral submissions, the Court of Arbitration unanimously decides:

A. In relation to the First Dispute,

(1) The Kishenganga Hydro-Electric Project, as described to the Court by India, constitutes a Run-of-River Plant for the purpose of Paragraph 15 of Annexure D to the Indus Waters Treaty, and in particular sub-paragraph (iii) thereof.

(2) India may accordingly divert water from the Kishenganga/Neelum River for power generation by the Kishenganga Hydro-Electric Plant and may deliver the water released below the power station into the Bonar Nallah.

(3) India is however under an obligation to construct and operate the Kishenganga Hydro-Electric Plant in such a way as to maintain a minimum flow of water in the Kishenganga/Neelum River, at a rate to be determined by the Court in a Final Award.

B. In relation to the Second Dispute,

(1) Except in the case of an unforeseen emergency, the Treaty does not permit reduction below Dead Storage Level of the water level in the reservoirs of Run-of-River Plants on the Western Rivers.

(2) The accumulation of sediment in the reservoir of a Run-of-River Plant on the Western Rivers does not constitute an unforeseen emergency that would permit the depletion of the reservoir below Dead Storage Level for drawdown flushing purposes.

(3) Accordingly, India may not employ drawdown flushing at the reservoir of the Kishenganga Hydro-Electric Plant to an extent that would entail depletion of the reservoir below Dead Storage Level.

(4) Paragraphs B(1) and B(2) above do not apply to Run-of-River Plants that are in operation on the date of issuance of this Partial Award. Likewise, Paragraphs B(1) and B(2) do not apply to Run-of-River Plants already under construction on the date of issuance of this Partial Award, the design of which, having been duly communicated by India under the provisions of Annexure D, had not been objected to by Pakistan as provided for in Annexure D.

C. This Partial Award imposes no further restrictions on the construction and operation of the Kishenganga Hydro-Electric Plant, which remain subject to the provisions of the Treaty as interpreted in this Partial Award.

D. To enable the Court to determine the minimum flow of water in the Kishenganga/Neelum River referred to in paragraph A(3) above, the Parties are required to submit to the Court the information specified in paragraphs 458 to 462 within the time periods set out in paragraph 463 of this Partial Award.

E. The interim measures indicated by the Court in its 23 September 2011 *Order on the Interim Measures Application of Pakistan dated June 6, 2011* are hereby lifted.

F. The costs of the proceedings to be awarded by the Court pursuant to Paragraph 26 of Annexure G to the Treaty shall be determined in the Court's Final Award.

Done at The Hague, this 18th of February 2013.

[*Signed*]
Professor Lucius Caflich

[*Signed*]
Professor Jan Paulsson

[*Signed*]
Judge Bruno Simma

[*Signed*]
H.E. Judge Peter Tomka

[*Signed*]
Professor Howard S. Wheater FREng

[*Signed*]
Sir Franklin Berman KCMG QC

[*Signed*]
Judge Stephen M. Schwebel, Chairman

[*Signed*]
Mr. Aloysius Llamzon, Registrar

ADDENDUM

The Indus Waters Treaty 1960[740] between the Government of India, the Government of Pakistan and the International Bank for Reconstruction and Development.

Signed at Karachi, on 19 September 1960

Preamble

The Government of India and the Government of Pakistan, being equally desirous of attaining the most complete and satisfactory utilisation of the waters of the Indus system of rivers and recognising the need, therefore, of fixing and delimiting, in a spirit of goodwill and friendship, the rights and obligations of each in relation to the other concerning the use of these waters and of making provision for the settlement, in a cooperative spirit, of all such questions as may hereafter arise in regard to the interpretation or application of the provisions agreed upon herein, have resolved to conclude a Treaty in furtherance of these objectives, and for this purpose have named as their plenipotentiaries:

The Government of India:

Shri Jawaharlal Nehru, Prime Minister of India, and

The Government of Pakistan:

Field Marshal Mohammad Ayub Khan, H.P., H.J., President of Pakistan;

who, having communicated to each other their respective Full Powers and having found them in good and due form, have agreed upon the following Articles and Annexures:

Article I

Definitions

As used in this Treaty:

(1) The terms "Article" and "Annexure" mean respectively an Article of, and an Annexure to, this Treaty. Except as otherwise indicated, references to Paragraphs are to the paragraphs in the Article or in the Annexure in which the reference is made.

(2) The term "Tributary" of a river means any surface channel, whether in continuous or intermittent flow and by whatever name called, whose waters in the natural course would fall into that river, e.g. a tributary, a torrent, a natural drainage, an artificial drainage, a *nadi*,

[740] Came into force on 12 January 1961, upon the exchange of the instruments of ratification at New Delhi, with retroactive effect from 1 April 1960, in accordance with article XII (2).

The text printed herein incorporates the corrections effected by the Protocol signed on 27 November, 2 and 23 December 1960 (*see* 419 U.N.T.S 290).

a *nallah*, a *nai*, a *khad*, a *cho*. The term also includes any subtributary or branch or subsidiary channel, by whatever name called, whose waters, in the natural course, would directly or otherwise flow into that surface channel.

(3) The term "The Indus," "The Jhelum," "The Chenab," "The Ravi," "The Beas" or "The Sutlej" means the named river (including Connecting Lakes, if any) and all its Tributaries: Provided however that

(i) none of the rivers named above shall be deemed to be a Tributary;

(ii) The Chenab shall be deemed to include the river Panjnad; and

(iii) the river Chandra and the river Bhaga shall be deemed to be Tributaries of The Chenab,

(4) The term "Main" added after Indus, Jhelum, Chenab, Sutlej, Beas or Ravi means the main stem of the named river excluding its Tributaries, but including all channels and creeks of the main stem of that river and such Connecting Lakes as form part of the main stem itself. The Jhelum Main shall be deemed to extend up to Verinag, and the Chenab Main up to the confluence of the river Chandra and the river Bhaga,

(5) The term "Eastern Rivers" means The Sutlej, The Beas and The Ravi taken together.

(6) The term "Western Rivers" means The Indus, The Jhelum and The Chenab taken together.

(7) The term "the Rivers" means all the rivers, The Sutlej, The Beas, The Ravi, The Indus, The Jhelum and The Chenab.

(8) The term "Connecting Lake" means any lake which receives water from, or yields water to, any of the Rivers; but any lake which occasionally and irregularly receives only the spill of any of the Rivers and returns only the whole or part of that spill is not a Connecting Lake.

(9) The term "Agricultural Use" means the use of water for irrigation, except for irrigation of household gardens and public recreational gardens.

(10) The term "Domestic Use" means the use of water for:

(*a*) drinking, washing, bathing, recreation, sanitation (including the conveyance and dilution of sewage and of industrial and other wastes), stock and poultry, and other like purposes;

(*b*) household and municipal purposes (including use for household gardens and public recreational gardens); and

(*c*) industrial purposes (including mining, milling and other like purposes);

but the term does not include Agricultural Use or use for the generation of hydro-electric power.

(11) The term "Non-Consumptive Use" means any control or use of water for navigation, floating of timber or other property, flood protection or flood control, fishing or fish culture, wild life or other like beneficial purposes, provided that, exclusive of seepage and evaporation of water incidental to the control or use, the water (undiminished in volume within the practical range of measurement) remains in, or is returned to, the same river or its Tributaries; but the term does not include Agricultural Use or use for the generation of hydro-electric power.

(12) The term "Transition Period" means the period beginning and ending as provided in Article II (6).

(13) The term "Bank" means the International Bank for Reconstruction and Development.

(14) The term "Commissioner" means either of the Commissioners appointed under the provisions of Article VIII (1) and the term "Commission" means the Permanent Indus Commission constituted in accordance with Article VIII (3).

(15) The term "interference with the waters" means:

(*a*) Any act of withdrawal therefrom; or

(*b*) Any man-made obstruction to their flow which causes a change in the volume (within the practical range of measurement) of the daily flow of the waters: Provided however that an obstruction which involves only an insignificant and incidental change in the volume of the daily flow, for example, fluctuations due to afflux caused by bridge piers or a temporary by-pass, etc., shall not be deemed to be an interference with the waters.

(16) The term "Effective Date" means the date on which this Treaty takes effect in accordance with the provisions of Article XII, that is, the first of April 1960.

Article II

Provisions Regarding Eastern Rivers

(1) All the waters of the Eastern Rivers shall be available for the unrestricted use of India, except as otherwise expressly provided in this Article.

(2) Except for Domestic Use and Non-Consumptive Use, Pakistan shall be under an obligation to let flow, and shall not permit any interference with, the waters of the Sutlej Main and the Ravi Main in the reaches where these rivers flow in Pakistan and have not yet finally

crossed into Pakistan. The points of final crossing are the following: (*a*) near the new Hasta Bund upstream of Suleimanke in the case of the Sutlej Main, and (*b*) about one and a half miles upstream of the syphon for the B-R-B-D Link in the case of the Ravi Main.

(3) Except for Domestic Use, Non-Consumptive Use and Agricultural Use (as specified in Annexure B), Pakistan shall be under an obligation to let flow, and shall not permit any interference with, the waters (while flowing in Pakistan) of any Tributary which in its natural course joins the Sutlej Main or the Ravi Main before these rivers have finally crossed into Pakistan.

(4) All the waters, while flowing in Pakistan, of any Tributary which, in its natural course, joins the Sutlej Main or the Ravi Main after these rivers have finally crossed into Pakistan shall be available for the unrestricted use of Pakistan: Provided however that this provision shall not be construed as giving Pakistan any claim or right to any releases by India in any such Tributary. If Pakistan should deliver any of the waters of any such Tributary, which on the Effective Date joins the Ravi Main after this river has finally crossed into Pakistan, into a reach of the Ravi Main upstream of this crossing, India shall not make use of these waters; each Party agrees to establish such discharge observation stations and make such observations as may be necessary for the determination of the component of water available for the use of Pakistan on account of the aforesaid deliveries by Pakistan, and Pakistan agrees to meet the cost of establishing the aforesaid discharge observation stations and making the aforesaid observations.

(5) There shall be a Transition Period during which, to the extent specified in Annexure H, India shall

(i) limit its withdrawals for Agricultural Use,
(ii) limit abstractions for storages, and
(iii) make deliveries to Pakistan from the Eastern Rivers.

(6) The Transition Period shall begin on 1st April1960 and it shall end on 31st March 1970, or, if extended under the provisions of Part 8 of Annexure H, on the date up to which it has been extended. In any event, whether or not the replacement referred to in Article IV (1) has been accomplished, the Transition Period shall end not later than 31st Match 1973.

(7) If the Transition Period is extended beyond 31st March 1970, the provisions of Article V (5) shall apply.

(8) If the Transition Period is extended beyond 31st March 1970, the provisions of Paragraph (5) shall apply during the period of extension beyond 31st March 1970.

(9) During the Transition Period, Pakistan shall receive for unrestricted use the waters of the Eastern Rivers which are to be released by India in accordance with the provisions of Annexure H. After the end of the Transition Period, Pakistan shall have no claim or right to releases by India of any of the waters of the Eastern Rivers. In case there are any releases, Pakistan shall enjoy the unrestricted use of the waters so released after they have finally crossed into Pakistan: Provided that in the event that Pakistan makes any use of these waters, Pakistan shall not acquire any right whatsoever, by prescription or otherwise, to a continuance of such releases or such use.

Article III

Provisions Regarding Western Rivers

(1) Pakistan shall receive for unrestricted use all those waters of the Western Rivers which India is under obligation to let flow under the provisions of Paragraph (2).

(2) India shall be under an obligation to let flow all the waters of the Western Rivers, and shall not permit any interference with these waters, except for the following uses, restricted (except as provided in item (*c*) (ii) of Paragraph 5 of Annexure C) in the case of each of the rivers, The Indus, The Jhelum and The Chenab, to the drainage basin thereof:

- (*a*) Domestic Use;
- (*b*) Non-Consumptive Use;
- (*c*) Agricultural Use, as set out in Annexure C; and
- (*d*) Generation of hydro-electric power, as set out in Annexure D.

(3) Pakistan shall have the unrestricted use of all waters originating from sources other than the Eastern Rivers which are delivered by Pakistan into The Ravi or The Sutlej, and India shall not make use of these waters. Each Party agrees to establish such discharge observation stations and make such observations as may be considered necessary by the Commission for the determination of the component of water available for the use of Pakistan on account of the aforesaid deliveries by Pakistan.

(4) Except as provided in Annexures D and E, India shall not store any water of, or construct any storage works on, the Western Rivers.

Article IV

Provisions Regarding Eastern Rivers and Western Rivers

(1) Pakistan shall use its best endeavours to construct and bring into operation, with due regard to expedition and economy, that part of a system of works which will accomplish the replacement, from the Western Rivers and other sources, of water supplies for irrigation canals in Pakistan which, on 15th August 1947, were dependent on water supplies from the Eastern Rivers.

(2) Each Party agrees that any Non-Consumptive Use made by it shall be so made as not to materially change, on account of such use, the flow in any channel to the prejudice of the uses on that channel by the other Party under the provisions of this Treaty. In executing any scheme of flood protection or flood control each Party will avoid, as far as practicable, any material damage to the other Party, and any such scheme carried out by India on the Western Rivers shall not involve any use of water or any storage in addition to that provided under Article III.

(3) Nothing in this Treaty shall be construed as having the effect of preventing either Party from undertaking schemes of drainage, river training, conservation of soil against erosion and dredging, or from removal of stones, gravel or sand from the beds of the Rivers: Provided that

(*a*) in executing any of the schemes mentioned above, each Party will avoid, as far as practicable, any material damage to the other Party;

(*b*) any such scheme carried out by India on the Western Rivers shall not involve any use of water or any storage in addition to that provided under Article III;

(*c*) except as provided in Paragraph (5) and Article VII (1) (*b*), India shall not take any action to increase the catchment area, beyond the area on the Effective Date, of any natural or artificial drainage or drain which crosses into Pakistan, and shall not undertake such construction or remodelling of any drainage or drain which so crosses or falls into a drainage or drain which so crosses as might cause material damage in Pakistan or entail the construction of a new drain or enlargement of an existing drainage or drain in Pakistan; and

(*d*) should Pakistan desire to increase the catchment area, beyond the area on the Effective Date, of any natural or artificial drainage or drain, which receives drainage waters from India, or, except in an emergency, to pour any waters into it in excess of the quantities received by it as on the Effective Date, Pakistan shall, before undertaking any work for these purposes, increase the capacity of that drainage or drain to the extent necessary so as not to impair its efficacy for dealing with drainage waters received from India as on the Effective Date.

(4) Pakistan shall maintain in good order its portions of the drainages mentioned below with capacities not less than the capacities as on the Effective Date:

(i) Hudiara Drain
(ii) Kasur Nala
(iii) Salimshah Drain
(iv) Fazilka Drain.

(5) If India finds it necessary that any of the drainages mentioned in Paragraph (4) should be deepened or widened in Pakistan, Pakistan agrees to undertake to do so as a work of public interest, provided India agrees to pay the cost of the deepening or widening.

(6) Each Party will use its best endeavours to maintain the natural channels of the Rivers, as on the Effective Date, in such condition as will avoid, as far as practicable, any obstruction to the flow in these channels likely to cause material damage to the other Party.

(7) Neither Party will take any action which would have the effect of diverting the Ravi Main between Madhopur and Lahore, or the Sutlej Main between Harike and Suleimanke, from its natural channel between high banks.

(8) The use of the natural channels of the Rivers for the discharge of flood or other excess waters shall be free and not subject to limitation by either Party, and neither Party shall have any claim against the other in respect of any damage caused by such use. Each Party agrees to communicate to the other Party, as far in advance as practicable, any information it may have in regard to such extraordinary discharges of water from reservoirs and flood flows as may affect the other Party.

(9) Each Party declares its intention to operate its storage dams, barrages and irrigation canals in such manner, consistent with the normal operations of its hydraulic systems, as to avoid, as far as feasible, material damage to the other Party.

(10) Each Party declares its intention to prevent, as far as practicable, undue pollution of the waters of the Rivers which might affect adversely uses similar in nature to those to which the waters were put on the Effective Date, and agrees to take all reasonable measures to ensure that, before any sewage or industrial waste is allowed to flow into the Rivers, it will be treated, where necessary, in such manner as not materially to affect those uses: Provided that the criterion of reasonableness shall be the customary practice in similar situations on the Rivers.

(11) The Parties agree to adopt, as far as feasible, appropriate measures for the recovery, and restoration to owners, of timber and other property floated or floating down the Rivers, subject to appropriate charges being paid by the owners.

(12) The use of water for industrial purposes under Articles II (2), II (3) and III (2) shall not exceed:

(*a*) in the case of an industrial process known on the Effective Date, such quantum of use as was customary in that process on the Effective Date;

(*b*) in the case of an industrial process not known on the Effective Date:

(i) such quantum of use as was customary on the Effective Date in similar or in any way comparable industrial processes; or

(ii) if there was no industrial process on the Effective Date similar or in any way comparable to the new process, such quantum of use as would not have a substantially adverse effect on the other Party.

(13) Such part of any water withdrawn for Domestic Use under the provisions of Articles II (3) and III (2) as is subsequently applied to Agricultural Use shall be accounted for as part of the Agricultural Use specified in Annexure B and Annexure C respectively; each Party will use its best endeavours to return to the same river (directly or through one of its Tributaries) all water withdrawn therefrom for industrial purposes and not consumed either in the industrial processes for which it was withdrawn or in some other Domestic Use.

(14) In the event that either Party should develop a use of the waters of the Rivers which is not in accordance with the provisions of this Treaty, that Party shall not acquire by reason of such use any right, by prescription or otherwise, to a continuance of such use.

(15) Except as otherwise required by the express provisions of this Treaty, nothing in this Treaty shall be construed as affecting existing territorial rights over the waters of any of the Rivers or the beds or banks thereof, or as affecting existing property rights under municipal law over such waters or beds or banks.

Article V

Financial Provisions

(1) In consideration of the fact that the purpose of part of the system of works referred to in Article IV (1) is the replacement, from the Western Rivers and other sources, of water supplies for irrigation canals in Pakistan which, on 15th August 1947, were dependent on water supplies from the Eastern Rivers, India agrees to make a

fixed contribution of Pounds Sterling 62,060,000 towards the costs of these works. The amount in Pounds Sterling of this contribution shall remain unchanged irrespective of any alteration in the par value of any currency.

(2) The sum of Pounds Sterling 62,060,000 specified in Paragraph (1) shall be paid in ten equal annual instalments on the 1st of November of each year. The first of such annual instalments shall be paid on 1st November 1960, or if the Treaty has not entered into force by that date, then within one month after the Treaty enters into force.

(3) Each of the instalments specified in Paragraph (2) shall be paid to the Bank for the credit of the Indus Basin Development Fund to be established and administered by the Bank, and payment shall be made in Pounds Sterling, or in such other currency or currencies as may from time to time be agreed between India and the Bank.

(4) The payments provided for under the provisions of Paragraph (3) shall be made without deduction or set-off on account of any financial claims of India on Pakistan arising otherwise than under the provisions of this Treaty: Provided that this provision shall in no way absolve Pakistan from the necessity of paying in other ways debts to India which may be outstanding against Pakistan.

(5) If, at the request of Pakistan, the Transition Period is extended in accordance with the provisions of Article II (6) and of Part 8 of Annexure H, the Bank shall thereupon pay to India out of the Indus Basin Development Fund the appropriate amount specified in the Table below:

Table	
Period of Aggregate Extension of Transition Period	*Payment to India £ Stg.*
One year	3,125,000
Two years	6,406,250
Three years	9,850,000

(6) The provisions of Article IV (1) and Article V (1) shall not be construed as conferring upon India any right to participate in the decisions as to the system of works which Pakistan constructs pursuant to Article IV (1) or as constituting an assumption of any responsibility by India or as an agreement by India in regard to such works.

(7) Except for such payments as are specifically provided for in this Treaty, neither Party shall be entitled to claim any payment for

observance of the provisions of this Treaty or to make any charge for water received from it by the other Party.

Article VI

Exchange of Data

(1) The following data with respect to the flow in, and utilisation of the waters of, the Rivers shall be exchanged regularly between the Parties:

(*a*) Daily (or as observed or estimated less frequently) gauge and discharge data relating to flow of the Rivers at all observation sites.

(*b*) Daily extractions for or releases from reservoirs.

(*c*) Daily withdrawals at the heads of all canals operated by government or by a government agency (hereinafter in this Article called canals), including link canals.

(*d*) Daily escapages from all canals, including link canals.

(*e*) Daily deliveries from link canals.

These data shall be transmitted monthly by each Party to the other as soon as the data for a calendar month have been collected and tabulated, but not later than three months after the end of the month to which they relate: Provided that such of the data specified above as are considered by either Party to be necessary for operational purposes shall be supplied daily or at less frequent intervals, as may be requested. Should one Party request the supply of any of these data by telegram, telephone, or wireless, it shall reimburse the other Party for the cost of transmission.

(2) If, in addition to the data specified in Paragraph (1) of this Article, either Party requests the supply of any data relating to the hydrology of the Rivers, or to canal or reservoir operation connected with the Rivers, or to any provision of this Treaty, such data shall be supplied by the other Party to the extent that these are available.

Article VII

Future Co-operation

(1) The two Parties recognize that they have a common interest in the optimum development of the Rivers, and, to that end, they declare their intention to co-operate, by mutual agreement, to the fullest possible extent. In particular:

(*a*) Each Party, to the extent it considers practicable and on agreement by the other Party to pay the costs to be incurred, will, at the request of the other Party, set up or install such hydrologic observation stations within the drainage basins of the Rivers, and set up or install such meteorological observation stations relating thereto and carry out such observations thereat, as may be requested, and will supply the data so obtained.

(*b*) Each Party, to the extent it considers practicable and on agreement by the other Party to pay the costs to be incurred, will, at the request of the other Party, carry out such new drainage works as may be required in connection with new drainage works of the other Party.

(*c*) At the request of either Party, the two Parties may, by mutual agreement, co-operate in undertaking engineering works on the Rivers.

The formal arrangements, in each case, shall be as agreed upon between the Parties.

(2) If either Party plans to construct any engineering work which would cause interference with the waters of any of the Rivers and which, in its opinion, would affect the other Party materially, it shall notify the other Party of its plans and shall supply such data relating to the work as may be available and as would enable the other Party to inform itself of the nature, magnitude and effect of the work. If a work would cause interference with the waters of any of the Rivers but would not, in the opinion of the Party planning it, affect the other Party materially, nevertheless the Party planning the work shall, on request, supply the other Party with such data regarding the nature, magnitude and effect, if any, of the work as may be available.

Article VIII

Permanent Indus Commission

(1) India and Pakistan shall each create a permanent post of Commissioner for Indus Waters, and shall appoint to this post, as often as a vacancy occurs, a person who should ordinarily be a high-ranking engineer competent in the field of hydrology and water-use. Unless either Government should decide to take up any particular question directly with the other Government, each Commissioner will be the representative of his Government for all matters arising out of this Treaty, and will serve as the regular channel of communication on all matters relating to the implementation of the Treaty, and, in particular, with respect to

(*a*) the furnishing or exchange of information or data provided for in the Treaty; and

(*b*) the giving of any notice or response to any notice provided for in the Treaty.

(2) The status of each Commissioner and his duties and responsibilities towards his Government will be determined by that Government.

(3) The two Commissioners shall together form the Permanent Indus Commission.

(4) The purpose and functions of the Commission shall be to establish and maintain co-operative arrangements for the implementation of this Treaty, to promote co-operation between the Parties in the development of the waters of the Rivers and, in particular,

(*a*) to study and report to the two Governments on any problem relating to the development of the waters of the Rivers which may be jointly referred to the Commission by the two Governments: in the event that a reference is made by one Government alone, the Commissioner of the other Government shall obtain the authorization of his Government before he proceeds to act on the reference;

(*b*) to make every effort to settle promptly, in accordance with the provisions of Article IX (1) any question arising thereunder;

(*c*) to undertake, once in every five years, a general tour of inspection of the Rivers for ascertaining the facts connected with various developments and works on the Rivers;

(*d*) to undertake promptly, at the request of either Commissioner, a tour of inspection of such works or sites on the Rivers as may be considered necessary by him for ascertaining the facts connected with those works or sites; and

(*e*) to take, during the Transition Period, such steps as may be necessary for the implementation of the provisions of Annexure H.

(5) The Commission shall meet regularly at least once a year, alternately in India and Pakistan. This regular annual meeting shall be held in November or in such other month as may be agreed upon between the Commissioners. The Commission shall also meet when requested by either Commissioner.

(6) To enable the Commissioners to perform their functions in the Commission, each Government agrees to accord to the Commissioner of the other Government the same privileges and immunities as are accorded to representatives of member States to the principal and subsidiary organs of the United Nations under Sections 11, 12 and 13 of Article IV of the Convention on the Privileges and Immunities of the United Nations (dated 13th February, 1946) during the periods specified in those Sections. It is understood and agreed that these privileges and immunities are accorded to the Commissioners not for the personal benefit of the individuals themselves but in order to safeguard the independent exercise of their functions in connection with the Commission; consequently, the Government appointing the Commissioner not only has the right but is under a duty to waive the immunity of its Commissioner in any case where, in the opinion of the appointing Government, the immunity would

impede the course of justice and can be waived without prejudice to the purpose for which the immunity is accorded.

(7) For the purposes of the inspections specified in Paragraph (4) (*c*) and (*d*), each Commissioner may be accompanied by two advisers or assistants to whom appropriate facilities will be accorded.

(8) The Commission shall submit to the Government of India and to the Government of Pakistan, before the first of June of every year, a report on its work for the year ended on the preceding 31st of March, and may submit to the two Governments other reports at such times as it may think desirable.

(9) Each Government shall bear the expenses of its Commissioner and his ordinary staff. The cost of any special staff required in connection with the work mentioned in Article VII (1) shall be borne as provided therein.

(10) The Commission shall determine its own procedures.

Article IX

Settlement of Differences and Disputes

(1) Any question which arises between the Parties concerning the interpretation or application of this Treaty or the existence of any fact which, if established, might constitute a breach of this Treaty shall first be examined by the Commission, which will endeavour to resolve the question by agreement.

(2) If the Commission does not reach agreement on any of the questions mentioned in Paragraph (1), then a difference will be deemed to have arisen, which shall be dealt with as follows:

(*a*) Any difference which, in the opinion of either Commissioner, falls within the provisions of Part 1 of Annexure F shall, at the request of either Commissioner, be dealt with by a Neutral Expert in accordance with the provisions of Part 2 of Annexure F;

(*b*) If the difference does not come within the provisions of Paragraph (2) (*a*), or if a Neutral Expert, in accordance with the provisions of Paragraph 7 of Annexure F, has informed the Commission that, in his opinion, the difference, or a part thereof, should be treated as a dispute, then a dispute will be deemed to have arisen which shall be settled in accordance with the provisions of Paragraphs (3), (4) and (5):

Provided that, at the discretion of the Commission, any difference may either be dealt with by a Neutral Expert in accordance with the provisions of Part 2 of Annexure F or be deemed to be a dispute to be settled in accordance with the provisions of Paragraphs (3), (4) and (5), or may be settled in any other way agreed upon by the Commission.

(3) As soon as a dispute to be settled in accordance with this and the succeeding paragraphs of this Article has arisen, the Commission shall, at the request of either Commissioner, report the fact to the two Governments, as early as practicable, stating in its report the points on which the Commission is in agreement and the issues in dispute, the views of each Commissioner on these issues and his reasons therefor.

(4) Either Government may, following receipt of the report referred to in Paragraph (3), or if it comes to the conclusion that this report is being unduly delayed in the Commission, invite the other Government to resolve the dispute by agreement. In doing so it shall state the names of its negotiators and their readiness to meet with the negotiators to be appointed by the other Government at a time and place to be indicated by the other Government. To assist in these negotiations, the two Governments may agree to enlist the services of one or more mediators acceptable to them.

(5) A Court of Arbitration shall be established to resolve the dispute in the manner provided by Annexure G

(*a*) upon agreement between the Parties to do so; or

(*b*) at the request of either Party, if, after negotiations have begun pursuant to Paragraph (4), in its opinion the dispute is not likely to be resolved by negotiation or mediation; or

(*c*) at the request of either Party, if, after the expiry of one month following receipt by the other Government of the invitation referred to in Paragraph (4), that Party comes to the conclusion that the other Government is unduly delaying the negotiations.

(6) The provisions of Paragraphs (3), (4) and (5) shall not apply to any difference while it is being dealt with by a Neutral Expert.

Article X

Emergency Provision

If, at any time prior to 31st March 1965, Pakistan should represent to the Bank that, because of the outbreak of large-scale international hostilities arising out of causes beyond the control of Pakistan, it is unable to obtain from abroad the materials and equipment necessary for the completion, by 31st March 1973, of that part of the system of works referred to in Article IV (1) which relates to the replacement referred to therein, (hereinafter referred to as the "replacement element") and if, after consideration of this representation in consultation with India, the Bank is of the opinion that

(*a*) these hostilities are on a scale of which the consequence is that Pakistan is unable to obtain in time such materials and equipment as must be procured from abroad for the completion, by 31st March 1973, of the replacement element, and

(*b*) since the Effective Date, Pakistan has taken all reasonable steps to obtain the said materials and equipment and, with such resources of materials and equipment as have been available to Pakistan both from within Pakistan and from abroad, has carried forward the construction of the replacement element with due diligence and all reasonable expedition,

the Bank shall immediately notify each of the Parties accordingly. The Parties undertake, without prejudice to the provisions of Article XII (3) and (4), that, on being so notified, they will forthwith consult together and enlist the good offices of the Bank in their consultation, with a view to reaching mutual agreement as to whether or not, in the light of all the circumstances then prevailing, any modifications of the provisions of this Treaty are appropriate and advisable and, if so, the nature and the extent of the modifications.

Article XI

General Provisions

(1) It is expressly understood that

(*a*) this Treaty governs the rights and obligations of each Party in relation to the other with respect only to the use of the waters of the Rivers and matters incidental thereto; and

(*b*) nothing contained in this Treaty, and nothing arising out of the execution thereof, shall be construed as constituting a recognition or waiver (whether tacit, by implication or otherwise) of any rights or claims whatsoever of either of the Parties other than those rights or claims which are expressly recognized or waived in this Treaty.

Each of the Parties agrees that it will not invoke this Treaty, anything contained therein, or anything arising out of the execution thereof, in support of any of its own rights or claims whatsoever or in disputing any of the rights or claims whatsoever of the other Party, other than those rights or claims which are expressly recognized or waived in this Treaty.

(2) Nothing in this Treaty shall be construed by the Parties as in any way establishing any general principle of law or any precedent.

(3) The rights and obligations of each Party under this Treaty shall remain unaffected by any provisions contained in, or by anything arising out of the execution of, any agreement establishing the Indus Basin Development Fund.

Article XII

Final Provisions

(1) This Treaty consists of the Preamble, the Articles hereof and Annexures A to H hereto, and may be cited as "The Indus Waters Treaty 1960".

(2) This Treaty shall be ratified and the ratifications thereof shall be exchanged in New Delhi. It shall enter into force upon the exchange of ratifications, and will then take effect retrospectively from the first of April 1960.

(3) The provisions of this Treaty may from time to time be modified by a duly ratified treaty concluded for that purpose between the two Governments.

(4) The provisions of this Treaty, or the provisions of this Treaty as modified under the provisions of Paragraph (3), shall continue in force until terminated by a duly ratified treaty concluded for that purpose between the two Governments.

IN WITNESS WHEREOF the respective Plenipotentiaries have signed this Treaty and have hereunto affixed their seals.

Done in triplicate in English at Karachi on this Nineteenth day of September 1960.

For the Government of India:

[*Signed*]
JAWAHARLAL NEHRU

For the Government of Pakistan:

[*Signed*]
MOHAMMAD AYUB KHAN, FIELD MARSHAL, H.P., H.J.

For the International Bank for Reconstruction and Development for the purposes specified in Articles V and X and Annexures F, G and H:

[*Signed*]
W. A. B. ILIFF

Annexure A—Exchange of Notes between Government of India and Government of Pakistan

[...]

Annexure B—Agricultural use by Pakistan from certain tributaries of the Ravi

[...]

Annexure C—Agricultural use by India from the Western Rivers

(Article III (2) (c))

1. The provisions of this Annexure shall apply with respect to the Agricultural Use by India from the Western Rivers under the provisions of Article III (2) (*c*) and, subject to the provisions of this Annexure, such use shall be unrestricted.

2. As used in this Annexure, the term "Irrigated Cropped Area" means the total area under irrigated crops in a year, the same area being counted twice if it bears different crops in *kharif* and *rabi*. The term shall be deemed to exclude small blocks of *ghair mumkim* lands in an irrigated field, lands on which cultivation is dependent on rain or snow and to which no irrigation water is applied, areas naturally inundated by river flow and cultivated on *sailab* thereafter, any area under floating gardens or *demb* lands in and along any lakes, and any area under waterplants growing within the water-spread of any lake or in standing water in a natural depression.

3. India may withdraw from the Chenab Main such waters as India may need for Agricultural Use on the following canals limited to the maximum withdrawals noted against each:

Name of Canal	*Maxiumum Withdrawals for Agricultural Use*
(*a*) Ranbir Canal	1,000 cusecs from 15th April to 14th October, and 350 cusecs from 15th October to 14th April.
(*b*) Pratap Canal	400 cusecs from 15th April to 14th October, and 100 cusecs from 15th October to 14th April.

Provided that:

(i) The maximum withdrawals shown above shall be exclusive of any withdrawals which may be made through these canals for purposes of silt extraction on condition that the waters withdrawn for silt extraction are returned to The Chenab.

(ii) India may make additional withdrawals through the Ranbir Canal up to 250 cusecs for hydro-electric generation on condition that the waters so withdrawn are returned to The Chenab.

(iii) If India should construct a barrage across the Chenab Main below the head regulators of these two canals, the withdrawals to be then made, limited to the amounts specified in (*a*) and (*b*) above, during each 10-day period or subperiod thereof, shall be as determined by the Commission in accordance with sound irrigation practice and, in the absence of agreement between the Commissioners, by a Neutral Expert in accordance with the provisions of Annexure F.

4. Apart from the irrigation from the Ranbir and Pratap Canals under the provisions of Paragraph 3, India may continue to irrigate from the Western Rivers those areas which were so irrigated as on the Effective Date.

5. In addition to such withdrawals as may be made in accordance with the provisions of Paragraphs 3 and 4, India may, subject to the provisions of Paragraphs 6, 7, 8 and 9, make further withdrawals from the Western Rivers to the extent India may consider necessary to meet the irrigation needs of the areas specified below:

Particulars	*Maximum Irrigated Cropped Area (over and above the cropped area irrigated under the provisions of Paragraphs 3 and 4)—(acres)*
(*a*) From The Indus, in its drainage basin	70,000
(*b*) From The Jhelum, in its drainage basin	400,000
(*c*) From The Chenab	
(i) in its drainage basin	225,000 of which not more than 100,000 acres will be in the Jammu District.
(ii) outside its drainage basin in the area west of the Deg Nadi (also called Devak River), the aggregate capacity of irrigating channels leading out of the drainage basin of the Chenab to this area not to exceed 120 cusecs.	6,000

Provided that

(i) in addition to the maximum Irrigated Cropped Area specified above, India may irrigate road-side trees from any source whatever;

(ii) the maximum Irrigated Cropped Area shown against items (*a*), (*b*) and (*c*) (i) above shall be deemed to include cropped areas, if any, irrigated from an open well, a tube-well, a spring, a lake (other than a Connecting lake) or a tank, in excess of the areas so irrigated as on the Effective Date; and

(iii) the aggregate of the areas specified against items (*a*), (*b*) and (*c*) (i) above may be re-distributed among the three drainage basins in such manner as may be agreed upon between the Commissioners.

6. (*a*) Within the limits of the maximum Irrigated Cropped Areas specified against items (*b*) and (*c*) (i) in Paragraph 5, there shall be no restriction on the development of such of these areas as may be irrigated from an open well, a tube-well, a spring, a lake (other than a Connecting Lake) or a tank.

(*b*) Within the limits of the maximum Irrigated Cropped Areas specified against items (*b*) and (*c*) in Paragraph 5, there shall be no restriction on the development of such of these areas as may be irrigated from General Storage (as defined in Annexure E): the areas irrigated from General Storage may, however, receive irrigation from river flow also, but, unless the Commissioners otherwise agree, only in the following periods: –

(i) from The Jhelum: 21st June to 20th August
(ii) from The Chenab: 21st June to 31st August:

Provided that withdrawals for such irrigation, whether from General Storage or from river flow, are controlled by Government.

7. Within the limits of the maximum Irrigated Cropped Areas specified against items (*b*) and (*c*) in Paragraph 5, the development of these areas by withdrawals from river flow (as distinct from withdrawals from General Storage *cum* river flow in accordance with Paragraph 6 (*b*)) shall be regulated as follows:

(*a*) Until India can release water from Conservation Storage (as defined in Annexure E) in accordance with sub-paragraphs (*b*) and (*c*) below, the new area developed shall not exceed the following:

(i) from The Jhelum: 150,000 acres
(ii) from The Chenab: 25,000 acres during the Transition Period and 50,000 acres after the end of the Transition Period.

(*b*) In addition to the areas specified in (*a*) above, there may be developed from The Jhelum or The Chenab an aggregate area of 150,000 acres if there is released annually from Conservation Storage, in accordance with Paragraph 8, a volume of 0.2 MAF into The Jhelum and a volume of 0.1 MAF into The Chenab; provided that India shall have the option to store on and release into The Chenab the whole or a part of the volume of 0.2 MAF specified above for release into The Jhelum.

(*c*) Any additional areas over and above those specified in (*a*) and (*b*) above may be developed if there is released annually from

Conservation Storage a volume of 0.2 MAF into The Jhelum or The Chenab, in accordance with Paragraph 8, in addition to the releases specified in (*b*) above.

8. The releases from Conservation Storage, as specified in Paragraphs 7 (*b*) and 7 (*c*), shall be made in accordance with a schedule to be determined by the Commission which shall keep in view, first, the effect, if any, on Agricultural Use by Pakistan consequent on the reduction in supplies available to Pakistan as a result of the withdrawals made by India under the provisions of Paragraph 7 and, then, the requirements, if any, of hydro-electric power to be developed by India from these releases. In the absence of agreement between the Commissioners, the matter may be referred under the provisions of Article IX (2) (*a*) for decision to a Neutral Expert.

9. On those Tributaries of The Jhelum on which there is any Agricultural Use or hydro-electric use by Pakistan, any new Agricultural Use by India shall be so made as not to affect adversely the then existing Agricultural Use or hydro-electric use by Pakistan on those Tributaries.

10. Not later than 31st March 1961, India shall furnish to Pakistan a statement showing, for each of the Districts and Tehsils irrigated from the Western Rivers, the Irrigated Cropped Area as on the Effective Date (excluding only the area irrigated under the provisions of Paragraph 3), arranged in accordance with items (*a*), (*b*) and (*c*) (i) of Paragraph 5: Provided that, in the case of areas in the Punjab, the date may be extended to 30th September 1961.

11. (*a*) As soon as the statistics for each crop year (commencing with the beginning of *kharif* and ending with the end of the following *rabi*) have been compiled at the District Headquarters, but not later than the 30th November following the end of that crop year, India shall furnish to Pakistan a statement showing for each of the Districts and Tehsils irrigated from the Western Rivers, the total Irrigated Cropped Areas (excluding the area irrigated under the provisions of Paragraph 3) arranged in accordance with items (*a*), (*b*), (*c*) (i) and (*c*) (ii) of Paragraph 5: Provided that, in the case of areas in the Punjab, the 30th November date specified above may be extended to the following 30th June in the event of failure of communications.

(*b*) If the limits specified in Paragraph 7 (*a*) or 7 (*b*) are exceeded for any crop year, the statement shall also show the figures for Irrigated Cropped Areas falling under Paragraph 6 (*a*) and 6 (*b*) respectively, unless appropriate releases from Conservation Storage under the provisions of Paragraph 8 have already begun to be made.

Annexure D—Generation of hydro-electric power by India on the Western Rivers

(Article III (2) (d))

1. The provisions of this Annexure shall apply with respect to the use by India of the waters of the Western Rivers for the generation of hydro-electric power under the provisions of Article III (2) (*d*) and, subject to the provisions of this Annexure, such use shall be unrestricted: Provided that the design, construction and operation of new hydro-electric plants which are incorporated in a Storage Work (as defined in Annexure E) shall be governed by the relevant provisions of Annexure E.

Part 1—Definitions

2. As used in this Annexure:

(*a*) "Dead Storage" means that portion of the storage which is not used for operational purposes and "Dead Storage Level" means the level corresponding to Dead Storage.

(*b*) "Live Storage" means all storage above Dead Storage.

(*c*) "Pondage" means Live Storage of only sufficient magnitude to meet fluctuations in the discharge of the turbines arising from variations in the daily and the weekly loads of the plant.

(*d*) "Full Pondage Level" means the level corresponding to the maximum Pondage provided in the design in accordance with Paragraph 8 (*c*).

(*e*) "Surcharge Storage" means uncontrollable storage occupying space above the Full Pondage Level.

(*f*) "Operating Pool" means the storage capacity between Dead Storage level and Full Pondage Level.

(*g*) "Run-of-River Plant" means a hydro-electric plant that develops power without Live Storage as an integral part of the plant, except for Pondage and Surcharge Storage.

(*h*) "Regulating Basin" means the basin whose only purpose is to even out fluctuations in the discharge from the turbines arising from variations in the daily and the weekly loads of the plant.

(*i*) "Firm Power" means the hydro-electric power corresponding to the minimum mean discharge at the site of a plant, the minimum mean discharge being calculated as follows:

The average discharge for each 10-day period (1st to 10th, 11th to 20th and 21st to the end of the month) will be worked out for each year for which discharge data, whether observed or estimated, are proposed to be studied for purposes of design. The mean of the yearly values for each 10-day period will then be worked out. The lowest of the mean values thus obtained will be taken as the minimum mean discharge. The studies will be based on data for as long a period as available but may be limited to the latest 5 years in the case of Small Plants (as defined in Paragraph 18) and to the latest 25 years in the case of other Plants (as defined in Paragraph 8).

(*j*) "Secondary Power" means the power, other than Firm Power, available only during certain periods of the year.

Part 2—Hydro-electric Plants in Operation, or under Construction, as on the Effective Date

3. There shall be no restriction on the operation of the following hydro-electric plants which were in operation as on the Effective Date:

Name of Plant	*Capacity (exclusive of standby units) (kilowatts)*
(i) Pahalgam	186
(ii) Bandipura	30
(iii) Dachhigam	40
(iv) Ranbir Canal	1,200
(v) Udhampur	640
(vi) Poonch	160

4. There shall be no restriction on the completion by India, in accordance with the design adopted prior to the Effective Date, or on the operation by India, of the following hydro-electric plants which were actually under construction on the Effective Date, whether or not the plant was on that date in partial operation:

Name of Plant	*Designed capacity (exclusive of standby units) (kilowatts)*
(i) Mahora	12,000
(ii) Ganderbal	15,000
(iii) Kupwara	150
(iv) Bhadarwah	600
(v) Kishtwar	350
(vi) Rajouri	650
(vii) Chinani	14,000
(viii) Nichalani Banihal	600

5. As soon as India finds it possible to do so, but not later than 31st March 1961, India shall communicate to Pakistan the information specified in Appendix I to this Annexure for each of the plants specified in Paragraphs 3 and 4. If any such information is not available or is not pertinent to the design of the plant or to the conditions at the site, it will be so stated.

6. (*a*) If any alteration proposed in the design of any of the plants specified in Paragraphs 3 and 4 would result in a material change in the information furnished to Pakistan under the provisions of Paragraph 5, India shall, at least 4 months in advance of making the alteration, communicate particulars of the change to Pakistan in writing and the provisions of Paragraph 7 shall then apply.

(*b*) In the event of an emergency arising which requires repairs to be undertaken to protect the integrity of any of the plants specified in Paragraphs 3 and 4, India may undertake immediately the necessary repairs or alterations and, if these repairs or alterations result in a change in the information furnished to Pakistan under the provisions of Paragraph 5, India shall as soon as possible communicate particulars of the change to Pakistan in writing. The provisions of Paragraph 7 shall then apply.

7. Within three months of the receipt of the particulars specified in Paragraph 6, Pakistan shall communicate to India in writing any objection it may have with regard to the proposed change on the ground that the change involves a material departure from the criteria set out in Paragraph 8 or 18 of this Annexure or Paragraph 11 of Annexure E as the case may be. If no objection is received by India from Pakistan within the specified period of three months, then Pakistan shall be deemed to have no objection. If a question arises as to whether or not the change involves a material departure from such of the criteria mentioned above as may be applicable, then either Party may proceed to have the question resolved in accordance with the provisions of Article IX (1) and (2).

Part 3—New Run-of-River Plants

8. Except as provided in Paragraph 18, the design of any new Run-of-River Plant (hereinafter in this Part referred to as a Plant) shall conform to the following criteria:

(*a*) The works themselves shall not be capable of raising artificially the water level in the Operating Pool above the Full Pondage Level specified in the design.

(*b*) The design of the works shall take due account of the requirements of Surcharge Storage and of Secondary Power.

(*c*) The maximum Pondage in the Operating Pool shall not exceed twice the Pondage required for Firm Power.

(*d*) There shall be no outlets below the Dead Storage Level, unless necessary for sediment control or any other technical purpose; any such outlet shall be of the minimum size, and located at the highest level, consistent with sound and economical design and with satisfactory operation of the works.

(*e*) If the conditions at the site of a Plant make a gated spillway necessary, the bottom level of the gates in normal closed position shall be located at the highest level consistent with sound and economical design and satisfactory construction and operation of the works.

(*f*) The intakes for the turbines shall be located at the highest level consistent with satisfactory and economical construction and operation of the Plant as a Run-of-River Plant and with customary and accepted practice of design for the designated range of the Plant's operation.

(*g*) If any Plant is constructed on the Chenab Main at a site below Kotru (Longitude 74°-59' East and Latitude 33°-09' North), a Regulating Basin shall be incorporated.

9. To enable Pakistan to satisfy itself that the design of a Plant conforms to the criteria mentioned in Paragraph 8, India shall, at least six months in advance of the beginning of construction of river works connected with the Plant, communicate to Pakistan, in writing, the information specified in Appendix II to this Annexure. If any such information is not available or is not pertinent to the design of the Plant or to the conditions at the site, it will be so stated.

10. Within three months of the receipt by Pakistan of the information specified in Paragraph 9, Pakistan shall communicate to India, in writing, any objection that it may have with regard to the proposed design on the ground that it does not conform to the criteria mentioned in Paragraph 8. If no objection is received by India from Pakistan within the specified period of three months, then Pakistan shall be deemed to have no objection.

11. If a question arises as to whether or not the design of a Plant conforms to the criteria set out in Paragraph 8, then either Party may proceed to have the question resolved in accordance with the provisions of Article IX (1) and (2).

12. (*a*) If any alteration proposed in the design of a Plant before it comes into operation would result in a material change in the information furnished to Pakistan under the provisions of Paragraph 9, India shall immediately communicate particulars of the change to Pakistan in writing and the provisions of Paragraphs 10 and 11 shall then apply, but the period of three months specified in Paragraph 10 shall be reduced to two months.

(*b*) If any alteration proposed in the design of a Plant after it comes into operation would result in a material change in the information furnished to Pakistan under the provisions of Paragraph 9, India shall, at least four months in advance of making the alteration, communicate particulars of the change to Pakistan in writing and the provisions of Paragraphs 10 and 11 shall then apply, but the period of three months specified in Paragraph 10 shall be reduced to two months.

13. In the event of an emergency arising which requires repairs to be undertaken to protect the integrity of a Plant, India may undertake immediately the necessary repairs or alterations; if these repairs or alterations result in a change in the information furnished to Pakistan under the provisions of Paragraph 9, India shall, as soon as possible, communicate particulars of the change to Pakistan in writing to enable Pakistan to satisfy itself that after such change the design of the Plant conforms to the criteria specified in Paragraph 8. The provisions of Paragraphs 10 and 11 shall then apply.

14. The filling of Dead Storage shall be carried out in accordance with the provisions of Paragraph 18 or 19 of Annexure E.

15. Subject to the provisions of Paragraph 17, the works connected with a Plant shall be so operated that (*a*) the volume of water received in the river upstream of the Plant, during any period of seven consecutive days, shall be delivered into the river below the Plant during the same seven-day period, and (*b*) in any one period of 24 hours within that seven-day period, the volume delivered into the river below the Plant shall be not less than 30%, and not more than 130%, of the volume received in the river above the Plant during the same 24-hour period: Provided however that:

(i) where a Plant is located at a site on the Chenab Main below Ramban, the volume of water received in the river upstream of the Plant in any one period of 24 hours shall be delivered into the river below the Plant within the same period of 24 hours;

(ii) where a Plant is located at a site on the Chenab Main above Ramban, the volume of water delivered into the river below the Plant in any one period of 24 hours shall not be less than 50% and not more than 130%, of the volume received above the Plant during the same 24-hour period; and

(iii) where a Plant is located on a Tributary of The Jhelum on which Pakistan has any Agricultural use or hydro-electric use, the water released below the Plant may be delivered, if necessary, into another Tributary but only to the extent that the then existing Agricultural Use or hydro-electric use by Pakistan on the former Tributary would not be adversely affected.

16. For the purpose of Paragraph 15, the period of 24 hours shall commence at 8 a.m. daily and the period of 7 consecutive days shall commence at 8 a.m. on every Saturday. The time shall be Indian Standard Time.

17. The provisions of Paragraph 15 shall not apply during the period when the Dead Storage at a Plant is being filled in accordance with the provisions of Paragraph 14. In applying the provisions of Paragraph 15:

(*a*) a tolerance of 10% in volume shall be permissible; and (*b*) Surcharge Storage shall be ignored.

18. The provisions of Paragraphs 8, 9, 10, 11, 12 and 13 shall not apply to a new Run-of-River Plant which is located on a Tributary and which conforms to the following criteria (hereinafter referred to as a Small Plant):

(*a*) the aggregate designed maximum discharge through the turbines does not exceed 300 cusecs;

(*b*) no storage is involved in connection with the Small Plant, except the Pondage and the storage incidental to the diversion structure; and

(*c*) the crest of the diversion structure across the Tributary, or the top level of the gates, if any, shall not be higher than 20 feet above the mean bed of the Tributary at the site of the structure.

19. The information specified in Appendix III to this Annexure shall be communicated to Pakistan by India at least two months in advance of the beginning of construction of the river works connected with a Small Plant. If any such information is not available or is not pertinent to the design of the Small Plant or to the conditions at the site, it will be so stated.

20. Within two months of the receipt by Pakistan of the information specified in Appendix III, Pakistan shall communicate to India, in writing, any objection that it may have with regard to the proposed design on the ground that it does not conform to the criteria mentioned in Paragraph 18. If no objection is received by India from Pakistan within the specified period of two months, then Pakistan shall be deemed to have no objection.

21. If a question arises as to whether or not the design of a Small Plant conforms to the criteria set out in Paragraph 18, then either Party may proceed to have the question resolved in accordance with the provisions of Article IX (1) and (2).

22. If any alteration in the design of a Small Plant, whether during the construction period or subsequently, results in a change in the information furnished to Pakistan under the provisions of Paragraph 19, then India shall immediately communicate the change in writing to Pakistan.

23. If, with any alteration proposed in the design of a Small Plant, the design would cease to comply with the criteria set out in Paragraph 18, then the provisions of Paragraphs 18 to 22 inclusive shall no longer apply and, in lieu thereof, the provisions of Paragraphs 8 to 13 inclusive shall apply.

Part 4—New Plants on Irrigation Channels

24. Notwithstanding the foregoing provisions of this Annexure, there shall be no restriction on the construction and operation by India of new hydro-electric plants on any irrigation channel taking off the Western Rivers, provided that

(*a*) the works incorporate no storage other than Pondage and the Dead Storage incidental to the diversion structure, and

(*b*) no additional supplies are run in the irrigation channel for the purpose of generating hydro-electric power.

Part 5—General

25. If the change referred to in Paragraphs 6 (*a*) and 12 is not material, India shall communicate particulars of the change to Pakistan, in writing, as soon as the alteration has been made or the repairs have been undertaken. The provisions of Paragraph 7 or Paragraph 23, as the case may be, shall then apply.

Appendix I to Annexure D

(Paragraph 5)

1. Location of Plant

General map showing the location of the site; if on a Tributary, its situation with respect to the main river.

2. Hydraulic Data

(*a*) Stage-area and stage-capacity curves of the reservoir, forebay and Regulating Basin.

(*b*) Full Pondage Level, Dead Storage Level and Operating Pool.

(*c*) Dead Storage capacity.

3. Particulars of Design

(*a*) Type of spillway, length and crest level; size, number and top level of spillway gates.

(*b*) Outlet works: function, type, size, number, maximum designed capacity and sill levels.

(*c*) Aggregate designed maximum discharge through the turbines.

(*d*) Maximum aggregate capacity of power units (exclusive of standby units) for Firm Power and Secondary Power.

(*e*) Regulating Basin and its outlet works: dimensions and maximum discharge capacity.

4. General

Probable date of completion of river works, and dates on which various stages of the plant would come into operation.

Appendix II to Annexure D

(Paragraph 9)

1. Location of Plant

General map showing the location of the site; if on a Tributary, its situation with respect to the main river.

2. Hydrologic Data

(*a*) General map (Scale: ¼ inch or more = 1 mile) showing the discharge observation site or sites or rainfall gauge stations on whose data the design is based. In case of a Plant on a Tributary, this map should also show the catchment area of the Tributary above the site.

(*b*) Observed or estimated daily river discharge data on which the design is based (observed data will be given for as long a period as available; estimated data will be given for as long a period as possible; in both cases data may be limited to the latest 25 years).

(*c*) Flood data, observed or estimated (with details of estimation).

(*d*) Gauge-discharge curve or curves for site or sites mentioned in (*a*) above.

3. Hydraulic Data

(*a*) Stage-area and stage-capacity curves of the reservoir, forebay and Regulating Basin, with contoured survey maps on which based.

(*b*) Full Pondage Level, Dead Storage Level and Operating Pool together with the calculations for the Operating Pool.

(*c*) Dead Storage capacity.

(*d*) Estimated evaporation losses in the reservoir, Regulating Basin, head-race, forebay and tail-race.

(*e*) Maximum designed flood discharge, discharge-capacity curve for spillway and maximum designed flood level.

(*f*) Designated range of operation.

4. Particulars of Design

(*a*) Dimensioned plan showing dam, spillway, intake and outlet works, diversion works, head-race and forebay, powerhouse, tail-race and Regulating Basin.

(*b*) Type of dam, length and height above mean bed of river.

(*c*) Cross-section of the river at the site; mean bed level.

(*d*) Type of spillway, length and crest level; size, number and top level of spillway gates.

(*e*) Type of intake, maximum designed capacity, number and size, sill levels; diversion works.

(*f*) Head-race and tail-race: length, size, maximum designed capacity.

(*g*) Outlet works: function, type, size, number, maximum designed capacity and sill levels.

(*h*) Discharge proposed to be passed through the Plant initially and ultimately, and expected variations in the discharge on account of the daily and the weekly load fluctuations.

(*i*) Maximum aggregate capacity of power units (exclusive of standby units) for Firm Power and Secondary Power.

(*j*) Regulating Basin and its outlet works: type, number, size, sill levels and designed maximum discharge capacity.

5. General

(*a*) Estimated effect of proposed development on the flow pattern below the last plant downstream (with details of estimation).

(*b*) Probable date of completion of river works, and dates on which various stages of the Plant would come into operation.

Appendix III to Annexure D

(Paragraph 19)

1. Location of Small Plant

General map showing the location of the site on the Tributary and its situation with respect to the main river.

2. Hydrologic Data

(*a*) Observed or estimated daily Tributary discharge (observed data will be given for as long a period as available; estimated data will be given for as long a period as possible; in both cases, data may be limited to the latest five years).

(*b*) Flood data, observed or estimated (with details of estimation).

(*c*) Gauge-discharge curve relating to discharge site.

3. Hydraulic Data

(*a*) Stage-area and stage-capacity curves of the forebay with survey map on which based.

(*b*) Full Pondage Level, Dead Storage Level and Operating Pool together with the calculations for the Operating Pool.

4. Particulars of Design

(*a*) Dimensioned plan showing diversion works, outlet works, head-race and forebay, powerhouse and tail-race.

(*b*) Type of diversion works, length and height of crest or top level of gates above the mean bed of the Tributary at the site.

(*c*) Cross-section of the Tributary at the site; mean bed level.

(*d*) Head-race and tail-race: length, size and designed maximum capacity.

(*e*) Aggregate designed maximum discharge through the turbines.

(*f*) Spillway, if any: type, length and crest level; size, number and top level of gates.

(*g*) Maximum aggregate capacity of power units (exclusive of standby units) for Firm Power and Secondary Power.

ANNEXURE E—STORAGE OF WATERS BY INDIA ON THE WESTERN RIVERS

(Article III (4))

1. The provisions of this Annexure shall apply with respect to the storage of water on the Western Rivers, and to the construction and operation of Storage Works thereon, by India under the provisions of Article III (4).

2. As used in this Annexure:

(*a*) "Storage Work" means a work constructed for the purpose of impounding the waters of a stream; but excludes

(i) a Small Tank,

(ii) the works specified in Paragraphs 3 and 4 of Annexure D, and

(iii) a new work constructed in accordance with the provisions of Annexure D.

(*b*) "Reservoir Capacity" means the gross volume of water which can be stored in the reservoir.

(*c*) "Dead Storage Capacity" means that portion of the Reservoir Capacity which is not used for operational purposes, and "Dead Storage" means the corresponding volume of water.

(*d*) "Live Storage Capacity" means the Reservoir Capacity excluding Dead Storage Capacity, and "Live Storage" means the corresponding volume of water.

(*e*) "Flood Storage Capacity" means that portion of the Reservoir Capacity which is reserved for the temporary storage of flood waters in order to regulate downstream flows, and "Flood Storage" means the corresponding volume of water.

(*f*) "Surcharge Storage Capacity" means the Reservoir Capacity between the crest of an uncontrolled spillway or the top of the crest gates in normal closed position and the maximum water elevation above this level for which the dam is designed, and "Surcharge Storage" means the corresponding volume of water.

(*g*) "Conservation Storage Capacity" means the Reservoir Capacity excluding Flood Storage Capacity, Dead Storage Capacity and Surcharge Storage Capacity, and "Conservation Storage" means the corresponding volume of water.

(*h*) "Power Storage Capacity" means that portion of the Conservation Storage Capacity which is designated to be used for generating electric energy, and "Power Storage" means the corresponding volume of water.

(*i*) "General Storage Capacity" means the Conservation Storage Capacity excluding Power Storage Capacity, and "General Storage" means the corresponding volume of water.

(*j*) "Dead Storage Level" means the level of water in a reservoir corresponding to Dead Storage Capacity, below which level the reservoir does not operate.

(*k*) "Full Reservoir Level" means the level of water in a reservoir corresponding to Conservation Storage Capacity.

(*l*) "Multi-purpose Reservoir" means a reservoir capable of and intended for use for more than one purpose.

(*m*) "Single-purpose Reservoir" means a reservoir capable of and intended for use for only one purpose.

(*n*) "Small Tank" means a tank having a Live Storage of less than 700 acre-feet and fed only from a non-perennial small stream: Provided that the Dead Storage does not exceed 50 acre-feet.

3. There shall be no restriction on the operation as heretofore by India of those Storage Works which were in operation as on the Effective Date or on the construction and operation of Small Tanks.

4. As soon as India finds it possible to do so, but not later than 31st March 1961, India shall communicate to Pakistan in writing the information specified in the Appendix to this Annexure for such Storage Works as were in operation as on the Effective Date. If any such information is not available or is not pertinent to the design of the Storage Work or to the conditions at the site, it will be so stated.

5. (*a*) If any alteration proposed in the design of any of the Storage Works referred to in Paragraph 3 would result in a material change in the information furnished to Pakistan under the provisions of Paragraph 4, India shall, at least 4 months in advance of making the alteration, communicate particulars of the change to Pakistan in writing and the provisions of Paragraph 6 shall then apply.

(*b*) In the event of an emergency arising which requires repairs to be undertaken to protect the integrity of any of the Storage Works referred to in Paragraph 3, India may undertake immediately the necessary repairs or alterations and, if these repairs or alterations result in a change in the information furnished to Pakistan under the provisions of Paragraph 4, India shall as soon as possible communicate particulars of the change to Pakistan in writing. The provisions of Paragraph 6 shall then apply.

6. Within three months of the receipt of the particulars specified in Paragraph 5, Pakistan shall communicate to India in writing any objection it may have with regard to the proposed change on the ground that the change involves a material departure from the criteria set out in Paragraph 11. If no objection is received by India from Pakistan within the specified period of three months, then Pakistan shall be deemed to have no objection. If a question arises as to whether or not the change involves a material departure from such of the criteria mentioned above as may be applicable, then either Party may proceed to have the question resolved in accordance with the provisions of Article IX (1) and (2).

7. The aggregate storage capacity of all Single-purpose and Multi-purpose Reservoirs which may be constructed by India after the Effective Date on each of the River Systems specified in Column (2) of the following table shall not exceed, for each of the categories shown in Columns (3), (4) and (5), the quantities specified therein:

		Conservation Storage Capacity		
	River System	*General Storage Capacity*	*Power Storage Capacity*	*Flood Storage Capacity*
(1)	(2)	(3)	(4)	(5)
		million acre-feet		
(*a*)	The Indus	0.25	0.15	Nil
(*b*)	The Jhelum (excluding the Jhelum Main)	0.50	0.25	0.75
(*c*)	The Jhelum Main	Nil	Nil	As provided in Paragraph 9
(*d*)	The Chenab (excluding the Chenab Main)	0.50	0.60	Nil
(*e*)	The Chenab Main	Nil	0.60	Nil

Provided that

(i) the storage specified in Column (3) above may be used for any purpose whatever, including the generation of electric energy;

(ii) the storage specified in Column (4) above may also be put to Non-Consumptive Use (other than flood protection or flood control) or to Domestic Use;

(iii) India shall have the option to increase the Power Storage Capacity specified against item (*d*) above by making a reduction by an equal amount in the Power Storage Capacity specified against items (*b*) or (*e*) above; and

(iv) Storage Works to provide the Power Storage Capacity on the Chenab Main specified against item (*e*) above shall not be constructed at a point below Naunut (Latitude 33° 19' N. and Longitude 75° 59' E.).

8. The figures specified in Paragraph 7 shall be exclusive of the following:

(*a*) Storage in any Small Tank.

(*b*) Any natural storage in a Connecting Lake, that is to say, storage not resulting from any man-made works.

(*c*) Waters which, without any man-made channel or works, spill into natural depressions or borrow-pits during floods.

(*d*) Dead Storage.

(*e*) The volume of Pondage for hydro-electric plants under Annexure D and under Paragraph 21 (*a*).

(*f*) Surcharge Storage.

(*g*) Storage in a Regulating Basin (as defined in Annexure D).

(*h*) Storage incidental to a barrage on the Jhelum Main or on the Chenab Main not exceeding 10,000 acre-feet.

9. India may construct on the Jhelum Main such works as it may consider necessary for flood control of the Jhelum Main and may complete any such works as were under construction on the Effective Date: Provided that

(i) any storage which may be effected by such works shall be confined to off-channel storage in side valleys, depressions or lakes and will not involve any storage in the Jhelum Main itself; and

(ii) except for the part held in lakes, borrow-pits or natural depressions, the stored waters shall be released as quickly as possible after the flood recedes and returned to the Jhelum Main lower down.

These works shall be constructed in accordance with the provisions of Paragraph 11 (*d*).

10. Notwithstanding the provisions of Paragraph 7, any Storage Work to be constructed on a Tributary of The Jhelum on which Pakistan has any Agricultural Use or hydro-electric use shall be so designed and operated as not to adversely affect the then existing Agricultural Use or hydro-electric use on that Tributary.

11. The design of any Storage Work (other than a Storage Work falling under Paragraph 3) shall conform to the following criteria:

(*a*) The Storage Work shall not be capable of raising artificially the water level in the reservoir higher than the designed Full Reservoir Level except to the extent necessary for Flood Storage, if any, specified in the design.

(*b*) The design of the works shall take due account of the requirements of Surcharge Storage.

(*c*) The volume between the Full Reservoir Level and the Dead Storage Level of any reservoir shall not exceed the Conservation Storage Capacity specified in the design.

(*d*) With respect to the Flood Storage mentioned in Paragraph 9, the design of the works on the Jhelum Main shall be such that no water can spill from the Jhelum Main into the off-channel storage except when the water level in the Jhelum Main rises above the low flood stage.

(*e*) Outlets or other works of sufficient capacity shall be provided to deliver into the river downstream the flow of the river received upstream of the Storage Work, except during freshets or floods. These outlets or works shall be located at the highest level consistent with sound and economical design and with satisfactory operation of the Storage Work.

(*f*) Any outlets below the Dead Storage Level necessary for sediment control or any other technical purpose shall be of the minimum size, and located at the highest level, consistent with sound and economical design and with satisfactory operation of the Storage Work.

(*g*) If a power plant is incorporated in the Storage Work, the intakes for the turbines shall be located at the highest level consistent with satisfactory and economical construction and operation of the plant and with customary and accepted practice of design for the designated range of the plant's operation.

12. To enable Pakistan to satisfy itself that the design of a Storage Work (other than a Storage Work falling under Paragraph 3) conforms to the criteria mentioned in Paragraph 11, India shall, at least six months in advance of the beginning of construction of the Storage Work, communicate to Pakistan in writing the information specified in the Appendix to this Annexure; if any such information is not available or is not pertinent to the design of the Storage Work or to the conditions at the site, it will be so stated:

Provided that, in the case of a Storage Work falling under Paragraph 9,

(i) if the work is a new work, the period of six months shall be reduced to four months, and

(ii) if the work is a work under construction on the Effective Date, the information shall be furnished not later than 31st December 1960.

13. Within three months (or two months, in the case of a Storage Work specified in Paragraph 9) of the receipt by Pakistan of the information specified in Paragraph 12, Pakistan shall communicate to India in writing any objection that it may have with regard to the proposed design on the ground that the design does not conform to the criteria mentioned in Paragraph 11. If no objection is received by India from Pakistan within the specified period of three months (or two months, in the case of a Storage Work specified in Paragraph 9), then Pakistan shall be deemed to have no objection.

14. If a question arises as to whether or not the design of a Storage Work (other than a Storage Work falling under Paragraph 3) conforms to the criteria set out in Paragraph 11, then either Party may proceed to have the question resolved in accordance with the provisions of Article IX (1) and (2).

15. (*a*) If any alteration proposed in the design of a Storage Work (other than a Storage Work falling under Paragraph 3) before it comes into operation would result in a material change in the information furnished to Pakistan under the provisions of Paragraph 12, India shall immediately communicate particulars of the change to Pakistan in writing and the provisions of Paragraphs 13 and 14 shall then apply, but where a period of three months is specified in Paragraph 13, that period shall be reduced to two months.

(*b*) If any alteration proposed in the design of a Storage Work (other than a Storage Work falling under Paragraph 3), after it comes into operation would result in a material change in the information furnished to Pakistan under the provisions of Paragraph 12, India shall, at least four months in advance of making the alteration, communicate particulars of the change to Pakistan in writing and the provisions of Paragraphs 13 and 14 shall then apply, but where a period of three months is specified in Paragraph 13, that period shall be reduced to two months.

16. In the event of an emergency arising which requires repairs to be undertaken to protect the integrity of a Storage Work (other than a Storage Work falling under Paragraph 3), India may undertake immediately the necessary repairs or alterations; if these repairs or alterations result in a change in the information furnished to Pakistan under the provisions of Paragraph 12, India shall, as soon as possible, communicate particulars of the change to Pakistan in writing to enable Pakistan to satisfy itself that after such change the design of the work conforms to the criteria specified in Paragraph 11. The provisions of Paragraphs 13 and 14 shall then apply.

17. The Flood Storage specified against item (*b*) in Paragraph 7 may be effected only during floods when the discharge of the river exceeds the amount specified for this purpose in the design of the work; the storage above Full Reservoir Level shall be released as quickly as possible after the flood recedes.

18. The annual filling of Conservation Storage and the initial filling below the Dead Storage Level, at any site, shall be carried out at such times and in accordance with such rules as may be agreed upon between the Commissioners. In case the Commissioners are unable to reach agreement, India may carry out the filling as follows:

(*a*) if the site is on The Indus, between 1st July and 20th August;

(*b*) if the site is on The Jhelum, between 21st June and 20th August; and (*c*) if the site is on The Chenab, between 21st June and 31st August at such rate as not to reduce, on account of this filling, the flow in the Chenab Main above Merala to less than 55,000 cusecs.

19. The Dead Storage shall not be depleted except in an unforeseen emergency. If so depleted, it will be refilled in accordance with the conditions of its initial filling.

20. Subject to the provisions of Paragraph 8 of Annexure C, India may make releases from Conservation Storage in any manner it may determine.

21. If a hydro-electric power plant is incorporated in a Storage Work (other than a Storage Work falling under Paragraph 3), the plant shall be so operated that:

(*a*) the maximum Pondage (as defined in Annexure D) shall not exceed the Pondage required for the firm power of the plant, and the water-level in the reservoir corresponding to maximum Pondage shall not, on account of this Pondage, exceed the Full Reservoir Level at any time; and

(*b*) except during the period in which a filling is being carried out in accordance with the provisions of Paragraph 18 or 19, the volume of water delivered into the river below the work during any period of seven consecutive days shall not be less than the volume of water received in the river upstream of the work in that seven-day period.

22. In applying the provisions of Paragraph 21 (*b*):

(*a*) the period of seven consecutive days shall commence at 8 a.m. on every Saturday and the time shall be Indian Standard Time;

(*b*) a tolerance of 10% in volume shall be permissible and adjusted as soon as possible; and

(*c*) any temporary uncontrollable retention of water due to variation in river supply will be accounted for.

23. When the Live Storage Capacity of a Storage Work is reduced by sedimentation, India may, in accordance with the relevant provisions of this Annexure, construct new Storage Works or modify existing Storage Works so as to make up the storage capacity lost by sedimentation.

24. If a power plant incorporated in a Storage Work (other than a Storage Work falling under Paragraph 3) is used to operate a peak power plant and lies on any Tributary of The Jhelum on which there is any Agricultural Use by Pakistan, a Regulating Basin (as defined in Annexure D) shall be incorporated.

25. If the change referred to in Paragraph 5 (*a*) or 15 is not material, India shall communicate particulars of the change to Pakistan, in writing, as soon as the alteration has been made or the repairs have been undertaken. The provisions of Paragraph 6 or Paragraphs 13 and 14, as the case may be, shall then apply.

Appendix to Annexure E

(Paragraphs 4 and 12)

1. Location of Storage Work

General map showing the location of the site; if on a Tributary, its situation with respect to the main river.

2. Hydrologic Data

(*a*) General map (Scale: ¼ inch or more = 1 mile) showing the discharge observation site or sites or rainfall gauge stations, on whose data the design is based. In case of a work on a Tributary, this map should also show the catchment area of the Tributary above the site.

(*b*) Observed or estimated daily river discharge data on which the design is based (observed data will be given for as long a period as available; estimated data will be given for as long a period as possible; in both cases data may be limited to the latest 25 years).

(*c*) Flood data, observed or estimated (with details of estimation).

(*d*) Gauge-discharge curve or curves for site or sites mentioned in (*a*) above.

(*e*) Sediment data.

3. Hydraulic Data

(*a*) Stage-area and stage-capacity curves of the reservoir with contoured survey maps on which based.

(*b*) Reservoir Capacity, Dead Storage Capacity, Flood Storage Capacity, Conservation Storage Capacity, Power Storage Capacity, General Storage Capacity and Surcharge Storage Capacity.

(*c*) Full Reservoir Level, Dead Storage Level and levels corresponding to Flood Storage and Surcharge Storage.

(*d*) Estimated evaporation losses in the reservoir.

(*e*) Maximum designed flood discharge and discharge-capacity curve for spillway.

(*f*) If a power plant is incorporated in a Storage Work:

(*i*) Stage-area and stage-capacity curves of forebay and Regulating Basin, with contoured survey maps on which based.
(ii) Estimated evaporation losses in the Regulating Basin, head-race, forebay and tail-race.
(iii) Designated range of operation.

4. Particulars of Design

(*a*) Dimensioned plan showing dam, spillway, diversion works and outlet works.

(*b*) Type of dam, length and height above mean bed of the river.

(*e*) Cross-section of the river at the site and mean bed level.

(*d*) Type of spillway, length and crest level; size, number and top level of spillway gates.

(*e*) Type of diversion works, maximum designed capacity, number and size; sill levels.

(*f*) Outlet works: function, type, size, number, maximum designed capacity and sill levels.

(*g*) If a power plant is incorporated in a Storage Work,

(i) Dimensioned plan showing head-race and forebay, powerhouse, tail-race and Regulating Basin.

(ii) Type of intake, maximum designed capacity, size and sill level.

(iii) Head-race and tail-race, length, size and maximum designed capacity.

(iv) Discharge proposed to be passed through the plant, initially and ultimately, and expected variations in the discharge on account of the daily and the weekly load fluctuations.

(v) Maximum aggregate capacity of power units (exclusive of standby units) for firm power and secondary power.

(vi) Regulating Basin and its outlet works: type, number, size, sill levels and designed maximum discharge capacity.

5. General

(*a*) Probable date of completion of river works and probable dates on which various stages of the work would come into operation.

(*b*) Estimated effect of proposed Storage Work on the flow pattern of river supplies below the Storage Work or, if India has any other Storage Work or Run-of-River Plant (as defined in Annexure D) below the proposed Storage Work, then on the flow pattern below the last Storage Work or Plant.

Annexure F—Neutral Expert

(Article IX (2))

Part 1—Questions to be referred to a Neutral Expert

1. Subject to the provisions of Paragraph 2, either Commissioner may, under the provisions of Article IX (2) (*a*) refer to a Neutral Expert any of the following questions:

(1) Determination of the component of water available for the use of Pakistan

(*a*) in the Ravi Main, on account of the deliveries by Pakistan under the provisions of Article II (4), and

(*b*) at various points on The Ravi or The Sutlej, on account of the deliveries by Pakistan under the provisions of Article III (3).

(2) Determination of the boundary of the drainage basin of The Indus or The Jhelum or The Chenab for the purposes of Article III (2).

(3) Whether or not any use of water or storage in addition to that provided under Article III is involved in any of the schemes referred to in Article IV (2) or in Article IV (3) (*b*) and carried out by India on the Western Rivers.

(4) Questions relating to

(*a*) obligations with respect to construction or remodelling of, or pouring of waters into, any drainage or drain as provided in Article IV (3) (*e*) and Article IV (3) (*d*); and

(*b*) maintenance of drainages specified in Article IV (4).

(5) Questions arising under Article IV (7) as to whether any action taken by either Party is likely to have the effect of diverting the Ravi Main between Madhopur and Lahore, or the Sutlej Main between Harike and Suleimanke, from its natural channel between high banks.

(6) Determination of facts relating to questions arising under Article IV (11) or Article IV (12).

(7) Whether any of the data requested by either Party falls outside the scope of Article VI (2).

(8) Determination of withdrawals to be made by India under proviso (iii) to Paragraph 3 of Annexure C.

(9) Determination of schedule of releases from Conservation Storage under the provisions of Paragraph 8 of Annexure C.

(10) Whether or not any new Agricultural Use by India, on those Tributaries of The Jhelum on which there is any Agricultural Use or hydro-electric use by Pakistan conforms to the provisions of Paragraph 9 of Annexure C.

(11) Questions arising under the provisions of Paragraph 7, Paragraph 11 or Paragraph 21 of Annexure D.

(12) Whether or not the operation by India of any plant constructed in accordance with the provisions of Part 3 of Annexure D conforms to the criteria set out in Paragraphs 15, 16 and 17 of that Annexure.

(13) Whether or not any new hydro-electric plant on an irrigation channel taking off the Western Rivers conforms to the provisos to Paragraph 24 of Annexure D.

(14) Whether or not the operation of a Storage Work which was in operation as on the Effective Date substantially conforms to the provisions of Paragraph 3 of Annexure E.

(15) Whether or not any part of the storage in a Connecting Lake is the result of man-made works constructed after the Effective Date (Paragraph 8 (*b*) of Annexure E).

(16) Whether or not any flood control work constructed on the Jhelum Main conforms to the provisions of Paragraph 9 of Annexure E.

(17) Whether or not any Storage Work to be constructed on a Tributary of The Jhelum on which Pakistan has any Agricultural Use or hydro-electric use conforms to the provisions of Paragraph 10 of Annexure E.

(18) Questions arising under the provisions of Paragraph 6 or 14 of Annexure E.

(19) Whether or not the operation of any Storage Work constructed by India after the Effective Date, conforms to the provisions of Paragraphs 17, 18, 19, 21 and 22 of Annexure E and, to the extent necessary, to the provisions of Paragraph 8 of Annexure C.

(20) Whether or not the storage capacity proposed to be made up by India under Paragraph 23 of Annexure E exceeds the storage capacity lost by sedimentation.

(21) Determination of modifications to be made in the provisions of Parts 2, 4 or 5 of Annexure H in accordance with Paragraphs 11, 31 or 38 thereof when the additional supplies referred to in Paragraph 66 of that Annexure become available.

(22) Modification of Forms under the provisions of Paragraph 41 of Annexure H.

(23) Revision of the figure for the conveyance loss from the head of the Madhopur Beas Link to the junction of the Chakki Torrent with the Beas Main under the provisions of Paragraph 45 (*c*) (ii) of Annexure H.

2. If a claim for financial compensation has been raised with respect to any question specified in Paragraph 1, that question shall not be referred to a Neutral Expert unless the two Commissioners are agreed that it should be so referred.

3. Either Commissioner may refer to a Neutral Expert under the provisions of Article IX (2) (*a*) any question arising with regard to the determination of costs under Article IV (5), Article IV (11), Article VII (l) (*a*) or Article VII (1) (*b*).

Part 2—Appointment and Procedure

4. A Neutral Expert shall be a highly qualified engineer, and, on the receipt of a request made in accordance with Paragraph 5, he shall be appointed, and the terms of his retainer shall be fixed, as follows:

(*a*) During the Transition Period, by the Bank.

(*b*) After the expiration of the Transition Period,

(i) jointly by the Government of India and the Government of Pakistan, or

(ii) if no appointment is made in accordance with (i) above

within one month after the date of the request, then by such person or body as may have been agreed upon between the two Governments in advance, on an annual basis, or, in the absence of such agreement, by the Bank.

Provided that every appointment made in accordance with (*a*) or (*b*) (ii) above shall be made after consultation with each of the Parties.

The Bank shall be notified of every appointment, except when the Bank is itself the appointing authority.

5. If a difference arises and has to be dealt with in accordance with the provisions of Article IX (2) (*a*), the following procedure will be followed:

(*a*) The Commissioner who is of the opinion that the difference falls within the provisions of Part 1 of this Annexure (hereinafter in this paragraph referred to as "the first Commissioner") shall notify the other Commissioner of his intention to ask for the appointment of a Neutral Expert. Such notification shall clearly state the paragraph or paragraphs of Part 1 of this Annexure under which the difference falls and shall also contain a statement of the point or points of difference.

(*b*) Within two weeks of the receipt by the other Commissioner of the notification specified in (*a*) above, the two Commissioners will endeavour to prepare a joint statement of the point or points of difference.

(*c*) After expiry of the period of two weeks specified in (*b*) above, the first Commissioner may request the appropriate authority specified in Paragraph 4 to appoint a Neutral Expert; a copy of the request shall be sent at the same time to the other Commissioner.

(*d*) The request under (*c*) above shall be accompanied by the joint statement specified in (*b*) above; failing this, either Commissioner may send a separate statement to the appointing authority and, if he does so, he shall at the same time send a copy of the separate statement to the other Commissioner.

6. The procedure with respect to each reference to a Neutral Expert shall be determined by him, provided that:

(*a*) he shall afford to each Party an adequate hearing;

(*b*) in making his decision, he shall be governed by the provisions of this Treaty and by the *compromis*, if any, presented to him by the Commission; and

(*c*) without prejudice to the provisions of Paragraph 3, unless both Parties so request, he shall not deal with any issue of financial compensation.

7. Should the Commission be unable to agree that any particular difference falls within Part 1 of this Annexure, the Neutral Expert shall, after hearing both Parties, decide whether or not it so falls. Should he decide that the difference so falls, he shall proceed to render a decision on the merits; should

he decide otherwise, he shall inform the Commission that, in his opinion, the difference should be treated as a dispute. Should the Neutral Expert decide that only a part of the difference so falls, he shall, at his discretion, either:

(*a*) proceed to render a decision on the part which so falls, and inform the Commission that, in his opinion, the part which does not so fall should be treated as a dispute, or

(*b*) inform the Commission that, in his opinion, the entire difference should be treated as a dispute.

8. Each Government agrees to extend to the Neutral Expert such facilities as he may require for the discharge of his functions.

9. The Neutral Expert shall, as soon as possible, render a decision on the question or questions referred to him, giving his reasons. A copy of such decision, duly signed by the Neutral Expert, shall be forwarded by him to each of the Commissioners and to the Bank.

10. Each Party shall bear its own costs. The remuneration and the expenses of the Neutral Expert and of any assistance that he may need shall be borne initially as provided in Part 3 of this Annexure and eventually by the Party against which his decision is rendered, except as, in special circumstances, and for reasons to be stated by him, he may otherwise direct. He shall include in his decision a direction concerning the extent to which the costs of such remuneration and expenses are to be borne by either Party.

11. The decision of the Neutral Expert on all matters within his competence shall be final and binding, in respect of the particular matter on which the decision is made, upon the Parties and upon any Court of Arbitration established under the provisions of Article IX (5).

12. The Neutral Expert may, at the request of the Commission, suggest for the consideration of the Parties such measures as are, in his opinion, appropriate to compose a difference or to implement his decision.

13. Without prejudice to the finality of the Neutral Expert's decision, if any question (including a claim to financial compensation) which is not within the competence of a Neutral Expert should arise out of his decision, that question shall, if it cannot be resolved by agreement, be settled in accordance with the provisions of Article IX (3), (4) and (5).

Part 3—Expenses

14. India and Pakistan shall, within 30 days after the Treaty enters into force, each pay to the Bank the sum of U.S. $5,000 to be held in trust by the Bank, together with any income therefrom and any other amounts payable to the Bank hereunder, on the terms and conditions hereinafter set forth in this Annexure.

15. The remuneration and expenses of the Neutral Expert, and of any assistance that he may need, shall be paid or reimbursed by the Bank from

the amounts held by it hereunder. The Bank shall be entitled to rely upon the statement of the Neutral Expert as to the amount of the remuneration and expenses of himself (determined in accordance with the terms of his retainer) and of any such assistance utilized by him.

16. Within 30 days of the rendering of a decision by the Neutral Expert, the Party or Parties concerned shall, in accordance with that decision, refund to the Bank the amounts paid by the Bank pursuant to Paragraph 15.

17. The Bank will keep amounts held by it hereunder separate from its other assets, in such form, in such banks or other depositories and in such accounts as it shall determine. The Bank may, but it shall not be required to, invest these amounts. The Bank will not be liable to the Parties for failure of any depository or other person to perform its obligations. The Bank shall be under no obligation to make payments hereunder of amounts in excess of those held by it hereunder.

18. If at any time or times the amounts held by the Bank hereunder shall in its judgment be insufficient to meet the payments provided for in Paragraph 15, it will so notify the Parties, which shall, within 30 days thereafter, pay to the Bank, in equal shares, the amount specified in such notice as being the amount required to cover the deficiency. Any amounts so paid to the Bank may, by agreement between the Bank and the Parties, be refunded to the Parties.

Annexure G—Court of Arbitration

(Article IX (5))

1. If the necessity arises to establish a Court of Arbitration under the provisions of Article IX, the provisions of this Annexure shall apply.

2. The arbitration proceeding may be instituted

(*a*) by the two Parties entering into a special agreement (*compromis*) specifying the issues in dispute, the composition of the Court and instructions to the Court concerning its procedures and any other matters agreed upon between the Parties; or

(*b*) at the request of either Party to the other in accordance with the provisions of Article IX (5) (*b*) or (*c*). Such request shall contain a statement setting forth the nature of the dispute or claim to be submitted to arbitration, the nature of the relief sought and the names of the arbitrators appointed under Paragraph 6 by the Party instituting the proceeding.

3. The date of the special agreement referred to in Paragraph 2 (*a*), or the date on which the request referred to in Paragraph 2 (*b*) is received by the other Party, shall be deemed to be the date on which the proceeding is instituted.

4. Unless otherwise agreed between the Parties, a Court of Arbitration shall consist of seven arbitrators appointed as follows:

(*a*) Two arbitrators to be appointed by each Party in accordance with Paragraph 6; and

(*b*) Three arbitrators (hereinafter sometimes called the umpires) to be appointed in accordance with Paragraph 7, one from each of the following categories:

(i) Persons qualified by status and reputation to be Chairman of the Court of Arbitration who may, but need not, be engineers or lawyers.
(ii) Highly qualified engineers.
(iii) Persons well versed in international law.

The Chairman of the Court shall be a person from category (*b*) (i) above.

5. The Parties shall endeavour to nominate and maintain a Standing Panel of umpires (hereinafter called the Panel) in the following manner:

(*a*) The Panel shall consist of four persons in each of the three categories specified in Paragraph 4 (*b*).

(*b*) The Panel will be selected, as soon as possible after the Effective Date, by agreement between the Parties and with the consent of the persons whose names are included in the Panel.

(*c*) A person may at any time be retired from the Panel at the request of either Party: Provided however that he may not be so retired

(i) during the period after arbitration proceedings have been instituted under Paragraph 2 (*b*) and before the process described in Paragraph 7 (*a*) has been completed; or
(ii) during the period after he has been appointed to a Court and before the proceedings are completed.

(*d*) If a member of the Panel should die, resign or be retired, his successor shall be selected by agreement between the Parties.

6. The arbitrators referred to in Paragraph 4 (*a*) shall be appointed as follows:

The Party instituting the proceeding shall appoint two arbitrators at the time it makes a request to the other Party under Paragraph 2 (*b*). Within 30 days of the receipt of this request, the other Party shall notify the names of the arbitrators appointed by it.

7. The umpires shall be appointed as follows:

(*a*) If a Panel has been nominated in accordance with the provisions of Paragraph 5, each umpire shall be selected as follows from the Panel, from his appropriate category, provided that the category has, at that time, at least three names on the Panel:

The Parties shall endeavour to agree to place the names of the persons in each category in the order in which they shall be invited to serve on the Court. If such agreement cannot be reached within 30 days of the date on which the proceeding is instituted, the Parties shall promptly establish such an order by drawing lots. If, in any category, the person whose name is placed first in the order so established, on receipt of an invitation to serve on the Court, declines to do so, the person whose name is next on the list shall be invited. The process shall be repeated until the invitation is accepted or all names in the category are exhausted.

(*b*) If a Panel has not been nominated in accordance with Paragraph 5, or if there should be less than three names on the Panel in any category or if no person in a category accepts the invitation referred to in Paragraph 7 (*a*), the umpires, or the remaining umpires or umpire, as the case may be, shall be appointed as follows:

(i) By agreement between the Parties.

(ii) Should the Parties be unable to agree on the selection of any or all of the three umpires, they shall agree on one or more persons to help them in making the necessary selection by agreement; but if one or more umpires remain to be appointed 60 days after the date on which the proceeding is instituted, or 30 days after the completion of the process described in sub-paragraph (*a*) above, as the case may be, then the Parties shall determine by lot for each umpire remaining to be appointed, a person from the appropriate list set out in the Appendix to this Annexure, who shall then be requested to make the necessary selection.

(iii) A national of India or Pakistan, or a person who is, or has been, employed or retained by either of the Parties shall be disqualified from selection under sub-paragraph (ii) above:

Provided that

(1) the person making the selection shall be entitled to rely on a declaration from the appointee, before his selection, that he is not disqualified on any of the above grounds; and

(2) the Parties may by agreement waive any or all of the above disqualifications in the case of any individual appointee.

(iv) The lists in the Appendix to this Annexure may, from time to time, be modified or enlarged by agreement between the Parties.

8. In selecting umpires pursuant to Paragraph 7, the Chairman shall be selected first, unless the Parties otherwise agree.

9. Should either Party fail to participate in the drawing of lots as provided in Paragraphs 7 and 10, the other Party may request the President of the Bank to nominate a person to draw the lots, and the person so nominated shall do so after giving due notice to the Parties and inviting them to be represented at the drawing of the lots.

10. In the case of death, retirement or disability from any cause of one of the arbitrators or umpires his place shall be filled as follows:

(*a*) In the case of one of the arbitrators appointed under Paragraph 6, his place shall be filled by the Party which appointed him. The Court shall, on request, suspend the proceedings but for not longer than 15 days pending such replacement.

(*b*) In the case of an umpire, a new appointment shall be made by agreement between the Parties or, failing such agreement, by a person determined by lot from the appropriate list set out in the Appendix to this Annexure, who shall then be requested to make the necessary selection subject to the provisions of Paragraph 7 (*b*) (iii). Unless the Parties otherwise agree, the Court shall suspend the proceedings pending such replacement.

11. As soon as the three umpires have accepted appointment, they together with such arbitrators as have been appointed by the two Parties under Paragraph 6 shall form the Court of Arbitration. Unless the Parties otherwise agree, the Court shall be competent to transact business only when all the three umpires and at least two arbitrators are present.

12. Each Party shall be represented before the Court by an Agent and may have the assistance of Counsel.

13. Within 15 days of the date of institution of a proceeding, each Party shall place sufficient funds at the disposal of its Commissioner to meet in equal shares the initial expenses of the umpires to enable them to attend the first meeting of the Court. If either Party should fail to do so, the other Party may initially meet the whole of such expenses.

14. The Court of Arbitration shall convene, for its first meeting, on such date and at such place as shall be fixed by the Chairman.

15. At its first meeting the Court shall

(*a*) establish its secretariat and appoint a Treasurer;

(*b*) make an estimate of the likely expenses of the Court and call upon each Party to pay to the Treasurer half of the expenses so estimated: Provided that, if either Party should fail to make such payment, the other Party may initially pay the whole of the estimated expenses;

(*c*) specify the issues in dispute;

(*d*) lay down a programme for submission by each side of legal pleadings and rejoinders; and

(*e*) determine the time and place of reconvening the Court.

Unless special circumstances arise, the Court shall not reconvene until the pleadings and rejoinders have been closed. During the intervening period, at the request of either Party, the Chairman of the Court may, for sufficient reason, make changes in the arrangements made under (*d*) and (*e*) above.

16. Subject to the provisions of this Treaty and except as the Parties may otherwise agree, the Court shall decide all questions relating to its competence and shall determine its procedure, including the time within which each Party

must present and conclude its arguments. All such decisions of the Court shall be by a majority of those present and voting. Each arbitrator, including the Chairman, shall have one vote. In the event of an equality of votes, the Chairman shall have a casting vote.

17. The proceedings of the Court shall be in English.

18. Two or more certified copies of every document produced before the Court by one Party shall be communicated by the Court to the other Party; the Court shall not take cognizance of any document or paper or fact presented by a Party unless so communicated.

19. The Chairman of the Court shall control the discussions. The discussions shall not be open to the public unless it is so decided by the Court with the consent of the Parties. The discussions shall be recorded in minutes drawn up by the Secretaries appointed by the Chairman. These minutes shall be signed by the Chairman and shall alone have an authentic character.

20. The Court shall have the right to require from the Agents of the Parties the production of all papers and other evidence it considers necessary and to demand all necessary explanations. In case of refusal, the Court shall take formal note of it.

21. The members of the Court shall be entitled to put questions to the Agents and Counsel of the Parties and to demand explanations from them on doubtful points. Neither the questions put nor the remarks made by the members of the Court during the discussions shall be regarded as an expression of an opinion of the Court or any of its members.

22. When the Agents and Counsel of the Parties have, within the time allotted by the Court, submitted all explanations and evidence in support of their case, the Court shall pronounce the discussions closed. The Court may, however, at its discretion re-open the discussions at any time before making its Award. The deliberations of the Court shall be in private and shall remain secret.

23. The Court shall render its Award, in writing, on the issues in dispute and on such relief, including financial compensation, as may have been claimed. The Award shall be accompanied by a statement of reasons. An Award signed by four or more members of the Court shall constitute the Award of the Court. A signed counterpart of the Award shall be delivered by the Court to each Party. Any such Award rendered in accordance with the provisions of this Annexure in regard to a particular dispute shall be final and binding upon the Parties with respect to that dispute.

24. The salaries and allowances of the arbitrators appointed pursuant to Paragraph 6 shall be determined and, in the first instance, borne by their Governments; those of the umpires shall be agreed upon with them by the Parties or by the persons appointing them, and (subject to Paragraph 13) shall be paid, in the first instance, by the Treasurer. The salaries and allowances of

the secretariat of the Court shall be determined by the Court and paid, in the first instance, by the Treasurer.

25. Each Government agrees to accord to the members and officials of the Court of Arbitration and to the Agents and Counsel appearing before the Court the same privileges and immunities as are accorded to representatives of members states to the principal and subsidiary organs of the United Nations under Sections 11, 12 and 13 of Article IV of the Convention on the Privileges and Immunities of the United Nations (dated 13th February 1946) during the periods specified in these Sections. The Chairman of the Court, with the approval of the Court, has the right and the duty to waive the immunity of any official of the Court in any case where the immunity would impede the course of justice and can be waived without prejudice to the interests of the Court. The Government appointing any of the aforementioned Agents and Counsel has the right and the duty to waive the immunity of any of its said appointees in any case where in its opinion the immunity would impede the course of justice and can be waived without prejudice to the effective performance of the functions of the said appointees. The immunities and privileges provided for in this paragraph shall not be applicable as between an Agent or Counsel appearing before the Court and the Government which has appointed him.

26. In its Award, the Court shall also award the costs of the proceedings, including those initially borne by the Parties and those paid by the Treasurer.

27. At the request of either Party, made within three months of the date of the Award, the Court shall re-assemble to clarify or interpret its Award. Pending such clarification or interpretation the Court may, at the request of either Party and if in the opinion of the Court circumstances so require, grant a stay of execution of its Award. After furnishing this clarification or interpretation, or if no request for such clarification or interpretation is made within three months of the date of the Award, the Court shall be deemed to have been dissolved.

28. Either Party may request the Court at its first meeting to lay down, pending its Award, such interim measures as, in the opinion of that Party, are necessary to safeguard its interests under the Treaty with respect to the matter in dispute, or to avoid prejudice to the final solution or aggravation or extension of the dispute. The Court shall, thereupon, after having afforded an adequate hearing to each Party, decide, by a majority consisting of at least four members of the Court, whether any interim measures are necessary for the reasons hereinbefore stated and, if so, shall specify such measures: Provided that

> (*a*) the Court shall lay down such interim measures only for such specified period as, in its opinion, will be necessary to render the Award: this period may, if necessary, be extended unless the delay in rendering the Award is due to any delay on the part of the Party which requested the interim measures in supplying such information as may be required by the other Party or by the Court in connection with the dispute; and

(*b*) the specification of such interim measures shall not be construed as an indication of any view of the Court on the merits of the dispute.

29. Except as the Parties may otherwise agree, the law to be applied by the Court shall be this Treaty and, whenever necessary for its interpretation or application, but only to the extent necessary for that purpose, the following in the order in which they are listed:

(*a*) International conventions establishing rules which are expressly recognized by the Parties.

(*b*) Customary international law.

Appendix to Annexure G

(Paragraph 7 (b))

List I *for selection of Chairman*	*List II* *for selection of Engineer Member*	*List III* *for selection of Legal Member*
(i) The Secretary-General of the United Nations	(i) The President of Massachusetts Institute of Technology, Cambridge, Mass., U.S.A.	(i) The Chief Justice of the United States
(ii) The President of the International Bank for Reconstruction and Development	(ii) The Rector of the Imperial College of Science and Technology, London, England	(ii) The Lord Chief Justice of England

Annexure H—Transitional Arrangements

[...]

* * *

In the Matter of
the Indus Waters Kishenganga Arbitration

-before-

The Court of Arbitration constituted
in accordance with the Indus Waters Treaty 1960
between the Government of India
and the Government of Pakistan
Signed on 19 September, 1960

-between-

The Islamic Republic of Pakistan

-and-

The Republic of India

Decision on India's Request for Clarification or Interpretation Dated 20 May 2013

Court of Arbitration:

Judge Stephen M. Schwebel (Chairman)
Sir Franklin Berman KCMG QC
Professor Howard S. Wheater FREng
Professor Lucius Caflisch
Professor Jan Paulsson
Judge Bruno Simma
H.E. Judge Peter Tomka

Secretariat:

The Permanent Court of Arbitration

20 December 2013

I. Introduction

1. On 17 May 2010, the Government of Pakistan initiated the present proceedings against the Government of India under the Indus Waters Treaty of 1960 (the "Treaty"). On 18 February 2013, the Court of Arbitration (the "Court") issued its *Partial Award*. A detailed history of the proceedings through that date is set out in that award. The present decision answers a request for clarification or interpretation of the *Partial Award* made by India.

II. Background to the request

2. Paragraph 27 of Annexure G to the Indus Waters Treaty sets out the scope of the Court of Arbitration's duty to clarify or interpret its Award. Paragraph 27 states that:

> At the request of either Party, made within three months of the date of the Award, the Court shall reassemble to clarify or interpret its Award. Pending such clarification or interpretation the Court may, at the request of either Party and if in the opinion of the Court circumstances so require, grant a stay of execution of its Award. After furnishing this clarification or interpretation, or if no request for such clarification or interpretation is made within three months of the date of the Award, the Court shall be deemed to have been dissolved.

3. Invoking Paragraph 27, India, on 20 May 2013, filed a *Request for Clarification or Interpretation* (the "Request") in which it sought "clarification or interpretation with respect to paragraph B.1" of the Court's *Partial Award*. Paragraph B of the "Decision" section (Part V) in the Court's *Partial Award* (the "Decision") relates to the Second Dispute, in which Pakistan requested the Court to determine

> Whether under the Treaty, India may deplete or bring the reservoir level of a run-of-river Plant below Dead Storage Level (DSL) in any circumstances except in the case of an unforeseen emergency?[1]

4. Paragraph B of the Decision provides as follows:

> In relation to the Second Dispute,
>
> (1) Except in the case of an unforeseen emergency, the Treaty does not permit reduction below Dead Storage Level of the water level in the reservoirs of Run-of-River Plants on the Western Rivers.
>
> (2) The accumulation of sediment in the reservoir of a Run-of-River Plant on the Western Rivers does not constitute an unforeseen emergency that would permit the depletion of the reservoir below Dead Storage Level for drawdown flushing purposes.
>
> (3) Accordingly, India may not employ drawdown flushing at the reservoir of the Kishenganga Hydro-Electric Plant to an extent that would entail depletion of the reservoir below Dead Storage Level.

[1] Pakistan's Request for Arbitration, para. 4.

(4) Paragraphs B(1) and B(2) above do not apply to Run-of-River Plants that are in operation on the date of issuance of this Partial Award. Likewise, Paragraphs B(1) and B(2) do not apply to Run-of-River Plants already under construction on the date of issuance of this Partial Award, the design of which, having been duly communicated by India under the provisions of Annexure D, had not been objected to by Pakistan as provided for in Annexure D.

5. At the invitation of the Court, Pakistan filed a *Submission in Response to India's Request for Interpretation or Clarification* on 19 July 2013. India in turn presented a *Reply on the Request for Clarification or Interpretation* on 2 September 2013. Finally, Pakistan submitted its *Rejoinder to India's Reply dated 2 September 2013 in the matter of India's Request for Clarification or Interpretation* on 30 September 2013.

6. The Court has considered the submissions of each Party carefully. In accordance with Paragraph 27 of Annexure G and Article 19 of the Court's Supplemental Rules of Procedure (the "Supplemental Rules"), the Court hereby issues its *Decision on India's Request for Clarification or Interpretation.*

III. The Parties' Arguments

7. In its Request, India takes issue with the Court's decision in its *Partial Award* that "[e]xcept in the case of an unforeseen emergency, the Treaty does not permit reduction below Dead Storage Level of the water level in the reservoirs of Run-of-River Plants on the Western Rivers."[2]

8. India asks the Court to "clarify that the permissibility of depletion or reduction below Dead Storage Level of the water level in the reservoirs of future Indian Run-of-River plants on the Western Rivers depends on a site-specific analysis of the feasibility of methods of sediment control other than drawdown flushing."[3] In response, Pakistan submits that "there is no shadow of ambiguity in paragraph B.1" of the Court's Decision and that India's Request "is an attempt to have the Court's unambiguous reasoning and determinations in respect of the Second Dispute replaced by quite different reasoning and determinations in favour of India."[4]

9. Before turning to its analysis, the Court will summarize the Parties' arguments in respect of the admissibility of India's Request as well as of the necessity of clarification or interpretation.

[2] *Ibid.*, at para. B(1).

[3] India's Request for Clarification or Interpretation, para. 2 ("India's Request").

[4] Pakistan's Submission in Response to India's Request for Interpretation or Clarification, para. 3 ("Pakistan's Response").

A. The Timeliness and Admissibility of India's Request

Pakistan's Argument

10. As an initial matter, Pakistan argues that India's Request is untimely. In Pakistan's view, 20 May 2013 is not within three months of 18 February 2013, the date of the *Partial Award.*[5]

11. Pakistan further submits that the Request is inadmissible because "in fact it is not seeking interpretation, but rather a new decision."[6] Following the practice of the International Court of Justice (the "ICJ"), Pakistan argues that the object of a request for interpretation "must be solely to obtain clarification of the meaning and the scope of what the Court has decided with binding force, and not to obtain an answer to questions not so decided."[7] Against this standard, Pakistan contends that the Request should be dismissed: the language of the *Partial Award* being unambiguous, India has no basis for seeking clarification.[8]

India's Argument

12. India maintains that its Request was filed in a timely manner, as India acted in accordance with the Supplemental Rules, which specify that any request for interpretation made pursuant to Paragraph 27 of Annexure G must be filed within 90 days of the Award.[9] The method for calculating periods of time is also contained in the Supplemental Rules. As the 90-day limit fell on Sunday, 19 May 2013, India contends that when it submitted its request on 20 May 2013, the next working day, it did so in a timely manner.[10]

13. India further submits that its Request relates to "genuine ambiguity" in Paragraph B.1 of the Court's Decision in light of the reasoning in other sections of the *Partial Award.* In India's view, the Award "must be interpreted as requiring a site-specific analysis for future projects that come within the ambit of the Treaty;"[11] but this proposition is said not to be apparent in the Court's decision. According to India, "[i]t is precisely to clarify this point of interpretation, and to avoid future disputes on the issue, that India has submitted its Request."[12]

---

[5] *Ibid.*, para. 5.

[6] *Ibid.*, para. 6.

[7] *Ibid.*, para. 6, *quoting Request for Interpretation of the Court's Judgment of* 20 *November 1950 in the Asylum Case (Colombia/Peru), I.C.J. Reports 1950*, p. 402.

[8] *Ibid.*, para. 6.

[9] Article 19(1) of the Supplemental Rules provides: "Any request for interpretation of the Award, in accordance with Paragraph 27 of Annexure G to the Treaty, shall be made within 90 days after the receipt of the Award, by giving notice to the Court and the other Party."

[10] India's Reply on the Request for Clarification or Interpretation, paras. 6–7 ("India's Reply").

[11] *Ibid.*, para. 4.

[12] *Ibid.*, para. 5.

B. The Necessity of Clarification or Interpretation

India's Argument

14. India submits that a clarification or interpretation of the Court's *Partial Award* is required because Paragraph B(1) of the Court's Decision could be read—incorrectly, in India's view—"as categorically prohibiting India from reducing the water level below Dead Storage Level during drawdown flushing for sediment control in all future Run-of-River plants."[13] India requests the Court to clarify that, rather than a categorical prohibition, "the permissibility of depletion or reduction below Dead Storage Level of the water level in the reservoirs of future Indian Run-of-River plants on the Western Rivers depends on a site-specific analysis of the feasibility of methods of sediment control other than drawdown flushing."[14]

15. India argues that clarification is required for two reasons. First, in India's view, the Parties presented and argued the Second Dispute in the context of the Kishenganga Hydro-Electric Project (the "KHEP"), not in terms of the general permissibility of drawdown flushing. According to India, "Pakistan did not argue that alternatives to such drawdown flushing exist, and thus that depleting or reducing water level below Dead Storage Level during drawdown flushing is not necessary and not allowed, at any site other than the KHEP dam site."[15] As a corollary to this point, India contends that, consistent with the manner in which the Parties submitted the question, the Parties "did not present any evidence regarding the existence of a feasible and effective alternative to depleting or reducing water level below Dead Storage Level during drawdown flushing at any site other than the KHEP dam site or on any other Western River or tributary thereof."[16]

16. Second, India submits that the Court's reasoning on the impermissibility of drawdown flushing is dependent on the availability of effective alternative methods for flushing sediment, which need to be established on a case-by-case basis: "[t]he Court reasoned that the permissibility of depleting or reducing the water level below Dead Storage Level during drawdown flushing ultimately depends on the availability of an alternative effective method of sediment control."[17] According to India, the availability of such alternative means must therefore be established for each site before a prohibition on drawdown flushing could apply.[18]

---

[13] India's Request, para. 3.

[14] *Ibid.*, para. 2.

[15] *Ibid.*, para. 22.

[16] *Ibid.*, para. 24.

[17] *Ibid.*, para. 30.

[18] *Ibid.*, para. 38.

Pakistan's Argument

17. Pakistan submits that "[t]here is no shadow of ambiguity in paragraph B.1 of the Court's dispositive, whether viewed in isolation or together with the underlying reasoning of the Court."[19]

18. According to Pakistan, the Court's decision on the Second Dispute corresponds to the broad manner in which the question was presented and argued. In Pakistan's view, the Second Dispute "is a question of obvious breadth in that it goes to what the Treaty permits. It is not a question that is in any way confined to operations at the KHEP."[20] The Parties' arguments were similarly broad and "in its pleadings India sought to address the issues of sedimentation and sedimentation control in notable breadth."[21] India, Pakistan argues, "of course understood the case it had to meet."[22] Similarly, in Pakistan's view, the Parties introduced no shortage of evidence on sedimentation, and India's "contentions are based on India portraying discrete elements of the argument and evidence as if these were the sole elements before the Court."[23] It was for India to make site-specific arguments if it wished to do so and, according to Pakistan, the "suggestion that it was somehow for Pakistan to introduce all the evidence and to persuade the Court that drawdown flushing was not essential at other [hydro-electric project] sites on the Western Rivers is ... to turn the case on its head." [24]

19. Based on this record of evidence and argument, Pakistan argues that the Court issued a clear, categorical prohibition. The decision does not, however, "negate India's right to develop hydro-electric power through the use of Run-of-River Plants provided for elsewhere in the Treaty" as India has argued.[25] Rather, in Pakistan's view, "[t]he general prohibition on drawdown flushing limits India's right to develop hydro-electric power through the use of Run-of-River Plants: it does not negate it."[26] According to Pakistan, the prohibition is precisely the type of regulatory limit on the development of hydro-electric power identified and discussed by the Court in its Partial Award.

IV. Analysis of the Court

20. The Court begins its analysis with the preliminary matters raised by the Parties and concludes that India's Request was timely. The 90-day deadline specified in the Supplemental Rules adds further precision to the Treaty's

[19] Pakistan's Response, para. 3.*a*.

[20] *Ibid.*, para. 13.

[21] *Ibid.*, para. 16.*c*.

[22] *Ibid.*, para. 16.*c*.

[23] *Ibid.*, para. 16.*a*.

[24] *Ibid.*, para. 26(*e*).

[25] Pakistan's Rejoinder to India's Reply dated 2 September 2013 in the matter of India's Request for Clarification or Interpretation, para. 8 ("Pakistan's Rejoinder").

[26] Pakistan's Rejoinder, para. 8.

requirement that a request be submitted "within three months." As noted correctly by India, the final day of the 90-day period following the Court's issuance of the *Partial Award* was a Sunday. Because Article 2(2) of the Supplemental Rules states that when the last day of a period for filing is a non-workday, the period is extended until the next workday, the Parties were free to submit any request for clarification or interpretation of the *Partial Award* until Monday, 20 May 2013. India filed its Request on that day.

21. On the admissibility of India's Request, the Court recalls Paragraph 27 of Annexure G:

> At the request of either Party, made within three months of the date of the Award, the Court shall reassemble to clarify or interpret its Award. Pending such clarification or interpretation the Court may, at the request of either Party and if in the opinion of the Court circumstances so require, grant a stay of execution of its Award. After furnishing this clarification or interpretation, or if no request for such clarification or interpretation is made within three months of the date of the Award, the Court shall be deemed to have been dissolved.

22. Although the Parties have referred to the case law of the ICJ on the admissibility of a request for interpretation, this Court notes that the body of ICJ practice on the matter is based specifically on the ICJ Statute and the ICJ Rules of Court, which include substantive preconditions to the exercise of the ICJ's interpretative power.[27] By contrast, neither the Treaty nor the Supplemental Rules set any condition, except the filing deadline, for a Party requesting interpretation or clarification. Once a timely request is made by a Party, the Court, in accordance with Paragraph 27 of Annexure G, "shall reassemble to clarify or interpret its Award."

23. That said, the Court's mandate to clarify or interpret its Award remains limited. It is a well established principle of international law—accepted by both Parties[28]—that it is not the function of the Court, when asked to interpret or clarify its prior decision, to revise that decision.[29] The Court "con-

[27] *See* I.C.J. Statute, Article 60 ("In the event of dispute as to the meaning or scope of the judgment, the Court shall construe it upon the request of any party."); I.C.J. Rules of the Court, Article 98.

[28] India's Reply, paras. 2–3; Pakistan's Response, paras. 7–9.

[29] Ethiopia-Eritrea Boundary Commission, Decision Regarding the 'Request for Interpretation, Correction and Consultation' submitted by the Federal Democratic Republic of Ethiopia on 13 May 2002, para. 16 (24 June 2002)("The concept of interpretation does not open up the possibility of appeal against a decision or the reopening of matters clearly settled by a decision."), available at http://www.pca-cpa.org/showpage.asp?pag_id=1150; *Arbitration on the Delimitation of the Continental Shelf (France-United Kingdom)*, Decision of 14 March 1978, para. 29, RIAA, Vol. XVIII, p. 3, at pp. 295–296 ("'Interpretation' is a process that is merely auxiliary, and may serve to explain but may not change what the Court has already settled with binding force as *res judicata*."). Similarly, the ICJ recently explained that when interpreting its judgment it "must keep strictly within the limits of the original judgment and *cannot question matters that were settled therein with binding force.*" *Request for Interpretation of the Judgment of 1962 in the Case concerning the Temple of Preah Vihear (Cambodia* v. *Thailand)*, Judgment of 11 November 2013, para. 66 (emphasis added).

fines itself to explaining, by an interpretation, that upon which it has already passed judgment."[30] The Court now turns to the question of whether its Partial Award requires or admits the clarification or interpretation requested by India.

24. In its Request, India posits that two aspects of the Court's *Partial Award* warrant clarification or interpretation. First, India argues that the Court's general decision on the permissibility of reservoir depletion for drawdown flushing exceeds the scope of the question presented to it and discussed by the Parties, and the scope of the evidence on record. Second, India notes the Court's general consideration of the feasibility of alternative methods of sediment control and contends that, in light of the scope of the question submitted, the permissibility of drawdown flushing at future Run-of-River Plants, other than the KHEP, must depend on the conduct of a further, site-specific analysis. The Court will address each proposition in turn.

25. With respect to the scope of the question submitted and discussed by the Parties, this Court considers it to be beyond doubt that the permissibility of drawdown flushing was put before the Court as a general issue. As noted in the *Partial Award*, Pakistan's Request for Arbitration was formulated in general terms, and was not limited to the KHEP:

> Whether under the Treaty, India may deplete or bring the reservoir level of a run-of-river Plant below Dead Storage Level in any circumstances except in the case of an unforeseen emergency.[31]

26. The Court mentioned and further discussed the "broad scope of the Second Dispute" in the following terms:

> The terms of the Second Dispute could be understood to relate to the permissibility of reservoir depletion in the abstract.[671] The record, however, both in the Commission and before this Court, indicates that Pakistan's core concern is that India's planned operation of the reservoirs at the KHEP and other, future hydro-electric projects will include depletion below Dead Storage Level for the purpose of flushing accumulated sediment from the reservoir. India, in turn, has confirmed its intention to employ drawdown flushing with respect to the KHEP.[672] Within this context, the Parties' pleadings with respect to the Second Dispute, as well as the relief requested by Pakistan, focus on the permissibility of this procedure.[673] The question facing the Court is therefore whether the Treaty prohibits drawdown flushing by India at the KHEP and at other, future Run-of-River Plants on the Western Rivers.
>
> [...]
>
> While the Parties' disagreement has taken shape in the context of the KHEP's design and India's intention to use drawdown flushing for that reservoir, the Second Dispute, as framed by Pakistan and argued by

[30] *Interpretation of Judgments Nos. 7 & 8 (The Chorzów Factory) (Germany* v. *Poland)*, P.C.I.J., Series A, No. 13, at p. 21 (16 December 1927).

[31] Partial Award, para. 263, *quoting* Request for Arbitration, para. 4, and Pakistan's Memorial, para. 1.12.

both Parties, is not limited to the KHEP alone: it concerns India's right to use drawdown flushing at any Run-of-River Plant that India may construct on the Western Rivers in the future.[677] Accordingly, the Court's decision on the Second Dispute will apply to other Run-of-River Plants to be built, as well as to the KHEP.

---

671 The use of the phrase "except in case of unforeseen emergency" could also be understood to indicate a specific concern with the paragraph of Annexure E (concerning Storage Works) that provides that "[t]he Dead Storage shall not be depleted except in an unforeseen emergency." It may be asked whether this provision applies equally to Run-of-River Plants. The Parties' pleadings make clear, however, that the dispute concerns whether any provision of the Treaty prevents the depletion of the reservoirs at Run-of-River Plants on the Western Rivers below Dead Storage Level for the purpose of drawdown flushing.

672 India's Counter-Memorial, Appendix 2, paras. 35–37 ("Envisaged Procedure for Carrying Out Drawdown Flushing").

673 *See* Pakistan's Memorial, para. 6.21 ("... the legality of drawdown flushing ... constitutes a central aspect of the [Second Dispute] ... the central feature of drawdown flushing is that the reservoir will be depleted (drawn down) below the Dead Storage Level"); *see also* the relief sought by Pakistan in relation to the Second Dispute, Pakistan's Memorial, chapter 7 ("Submissions"):
i. a determination that under the Treaty, the water level of the reservoir of a Run-of-River Plant may not be reduced below Dead Storage Level except in the case of an unforeseen emergency, and
ii. a determination that drawdown flushing for the purpose of sediment removal does not constitute an unforeseen emergency, and
iii. a mandatory and permanent injunction restraining India from reducing the water level of the reservoir of the KHEP except in the event of an unforeseen emergency.

677 *See* Hearing Tr., (Day 10), 31 August 2012, at 44:9–11 (Pakistan's Closing Statement): "I stress again: the key point is that the Second [Dispute] is not about [the Kishenganga River]; it's about all the dams that India may build on the Western Rivers."[32]

27. Faced in the Second Dispute with a question of interpretation centred on the general meaning and application of a particular provision of the Indus Waters Treaty and its relationship with the Treaty as a whole, the Court's answer to it was general as well and not limited to the KHEP. Indeed, the Court itself indicated the limits of its Decision, stating in Paragraph B(4) that:

> Paragraphs B(1) and B(2) above do not apply to Run-of-River Plants that are in operation on the date of issuance of this Partial Award. Likewise, Paragraphs B(1) and B(2) do not apply to Run-of-River Plants already under construction on the date of issuance of this Partial Award, the design of which, having been duly communicated by India under the

---

32 Partial Award, paras. 466, 468.

> provisions of Annexure D, had not been objected to by Pakistan as provided for in Annexure D.[33]

The inclusion of such an express limitation makes clear that—except where so limited—the Court's Decision applies to Run-of-River Plants generally.

28. This conclusion does not fully dispose of India's Request, however. India argues that even if the Court's decision is not limited to the KHEP, the reasoning behind that decision suggests that India must conduct a site-specific evaluation of the feasibility of alternative methods of sediment control at its other, future Run-of-River Plants before the Court's prohibition on drawdown flushing would apply. While India's underlying concerns are understandable, the argument proceeds from a misapprehension of the place of alternative methods within the Court's interpretation of the Treaty.

29. The interpretative process of the Court began with an examination of the text of the Treaty, read in its context and in light of the Treaty's object and purpose.[34] In its *Partial Award*, the Court examined the text of the Treaty and found that "[t]he decisive prohibition on the depletion of a reservoir below Dead Storage Level stems from Paragraph 14 of Annexure D, through its incorporation by reference of Paragraph 19 of Annexure E."[35]

30. The Court also considered the context of the Treaty. In doing so, the Court identified two aspects of the Treaty context consistent with a prohibition on the depletion of Dead Storage for drawdown flushing. First, the Court noted that the existence of strict limits on all types of storage other than Dead Storage is consistent "only if Dead Storage is somehow qualitatively different and was understood to be truly 'dead'—an area to be filled once and not thereafter subject to manipulation."[36] Second, the Court observed that the Treaty's restrictions on low-level outlets from Dead Storage "make sense only against a background assumption that the uses to which Dead Storage could be put are also somehow constrained. If depletion of Dead Storage was intended, whether

[33] *See also* Partial Award, paras. 469–470 (regarding the *Baglihar* expert determination); Partial Award, para. 521 (regarding the extension of the Court's view on India's right to "other, future Run-of-River Plants"); Partial Award, para. 523 (regarding other plants in operation or "already under construction (although not yet in operation) the design of which, having been duly communicated by India under the provisions of Annexure D, had not been objected to by Pakistan as provided for in Annexure D").

[34] *See, e.g.*, Vienna Convention on the Law of Treaties, 23 May 1969, 1155 U.N.T.S. 331, Art. 31(1). Although neither India nor Pakistan is a party to the Vienna Convention, the Court recalls that India acknowledged that the principles of that Convention are part of customary international law. *See* Partial Award, para. 174, n. 101. In *Kasikili/Sedudu Island (Botswana/Namibia), I.C.J. Reports 1999*, p. 1059, para.18, the ICJ stated that it "has already had occasion in the past to hold that customary international law found expression in Article 31 of the Vienna Convention .... Article 4 of the Convention which provides that it 'applies only to treaties which are concluded after its entry into force ... with regards to such States' does not, therefore prevent the Court from interpreting the 1890 Treaty in accordance with the rules in Article 31 of the Convention."

[35] Partial Award, para. 513.

[36] *Ibid.*, para. 505.

for flushing or otherwise, the Court can see no obvious purpose that would be served by limiting the size and placement of outlets from Dead Storage."[37]

31. It was in the course of the examination of the Treaty's context that the Court considered alternative methods of managing sediment. As the Court noted, "it is beyond debate that the intention behind the Treaty was to allow India to develop the hydro-electric potential of the Western Rivers, largely through the use of Run-of-River Plants."[38] Therefore, "[i]f a prohibition on drawdown flushing would render any sustainable hydro-electric development impossible, the Court would consider this relevant in approaching any Treaty provision seeming to suggest such a prohibition."[39]

32. The Court's consideration of alternative methods of controlling sediment thus formed part of its interpretation of the Treaty, not the application of that interpretation to a particular site. The Court's primary interest was not in establishing whether alternative methods were feasible at the KHEP or any other particular site. Rather, its interest lay in establishing whether run-of-river hydro-electric power generation without the use of drawdown flushing was so unfeasible as to effectively negate India's right to generate hydro-electric power on the Western Rivers. If so, such a result would call into question a prohibition specified in the Treaty text and elsewhere in the Treaty context. Based upon the evidence presented by the Parties, however, the Court found this not to be the case.[40]

33. In its Request, India relies upon paragraph 521 of the *Partial Award* and what it considers to be the Court's qualified language with respect to the prohibition on drawdown flushing.[41] In particular, India highlights the Court's acknowledgment that "the potential impact of sediment must be evaluated and modelled in relation to each particular site and dam design" to argue that a site-specific analysis was an intended condition to the prohibition. This argument, however, overlooks the context in which this aspect of the Court's analysis was made. Faced with a Treaty applicable throughout the tributary

---

[37] *Ibid.*, para. 508.

[38] *Ibid.*, para. 509.

[39] *Ibid.*, para. 509 (emphasis added).

[40] *Ibid.*, paras. 517, 521.

[41] Paragraph 521 of the Partial Award states as follows:

> The Court's view that India's right to generate hydro-electric power on the Western Rivers can meaningfully be exercised without drawdown flushing extends beyond the specifics of the KHEP to other, future Run-of-River Plants. Based on the evidence provided to it, the Court notes that, in general, sluicing is recommended for narrow, hydrologically small reservoirs located on rivers where surplus inflow is available for discharging sediment, and that sluicing with little drawdown is particularly effective in regions where a significant percentage of the annual sediment load is carried by the river in short and predictable periods. While acknowledging that the potential impact of sediment must be evaluated and modelled in relation to each particular site and dam design, the Court presently sees no reason why the factors favouring the feasibility of a sluicing mode of operation at the KHEP site would not apply equally to other sites on the Western Rivers at which India would be likely to construct Run-of-River Plants. (footnotes omitted)

system of the Western Rivers, the Court's evaluation of alternative methods of sediment control was necessarily general, and not dependent upon the characteristics of particular sites—although as the Court also recognized, the actual impact of sediment at any particular site can only be evaluated in the context of that site. Rather than limiting the application of the Treaty's prohibition on drawdown flushing, however, this fact goes to the question of whether a particular site will be available as a practical matter to India for hydro-electric development. In short, the Court's analysis in paragraph 521 does not—and was not intended to—qualify the overall conclusion reached by the Court.

34. In respect of the realization of specific hydro-electric projects, particularly future projects, the Court noted that "[h]ydrologic, geologic, social, economic, environmental and regulatory considerations are all directly relevant" and that the prohibition on drawdown flushing constitutes one such regulatory consideration.[42] As the Court made clear in its *Partial Award*, it is for India to secure appropriate locations and to draw appropriate designs for its Run-of-River Plants, bearing in mind that the Indus Waters Treaty has foreclosed the depletion of Dead Storage for drawdown flushing.[43] That prohibition is based on constraints that are part of the Treaty's essential bargain, as is evident from the *Partial Award*'s analysis of the text and context of the Treaty. It follows that the prohibition in question is not dependent on the particulars of a given site or project; that is, to use India's term, the prohibition is not "site-specific" but general.

V. DECISION

Having considered the Parties' written submissions, the Court of Arbitration unanimously decides that:

A. India's Request for Clarification or Interpretation of the Court's Partial Award of 18 February 2013 is timely and admissible.

B. Subject to Paragraph B(4) of the "Decision" section (Part V) in the *Partial Award* of 18 February 2013, the prohibition on the reduction below Dead Storage Level of the water in the reservoirs of Run-of-River Plants on the Western Rivers, except in the case of unforeseen emergency, is of general application.

Done at the Peace Palace, The Hague

Dated: 20 December 2013

[*Signed*]
PROFESSOR LUCIUS CAFLICH

[*Signed*]
PROFESSOR JAN PAULSSON

---

[42] Partial Award, para. 522.

[43] *Ibid.*, paras. 521, 522.

[*Signed*]
Judge Bruno Simma

[*Signed*]
H.E. Judge Peter Tomka

[*Signed*]
Professor Howard S. Wheater FREng

[*Signed*]
Sir Franklin Berman KCMG QC

[*Signed*]
Judge Stephen M. Schwebel, Chairman

[*Signed*]
Mr. Aloysius Llamzon, Registrar

IN THE MATTER OF
THE INDUS WATERS KISHENGANGA ARBITRATION

-before-

THE COURT OF ARBITRATION CONSTITUTED
IN ACCORDANCE WITH THE INDUS WATERS TREATY 1960
BETWEEN THE GOVERNMENT OF INDIA
AND THE GOVERNMENT OF PAKISTAN
SIGNED ON 19 SEPTEMBER, 1960

-between-

THE ISLAMIC REPUBLIC OF PAKISTAN

-and-

THE REPUBLIC OF INDIA

FINAL AWARD

Court of Arbitration:

Judge Stephen M. Schwebel (Chairman)
Sir Franklin Berman KCMG QC
Professor Howard S. Wheater FREng
Professor Lucius Caflisch
Professor Jan Paulsson
Judge Bruno Simma
H.E. Judge Peter Tomka

Secretariat:

The Permanent Court of Arbitration

20 December 2013

Agents, Counsel, and other Representatives of the Parties

Agent for Pakistan:

— Mr. Saif Ullah Chattha, Secretary, Ministry of Water and Power

Agent for India:

— Mr. Alok Rawat, Secretary, Ministry of Water Resources

Co-Agents for Pakistan:

— Mr. Mirza Asif Baig, Pakistan Commissioner for Indus Waters
— Mr. Mohammad Karim Khan Agha Prosecutor General, National Accountability Bureau

Co-Agents for India:

— Mr. Rudrendra Tandon, Joint Secretary (PAI), Ministry of External Affairs
— Dr. Neeru Chadha, Joint Secretary & The Legal Adviser, Ministry of External Affairs
— Mr. G. Aranganathan, Member, Central Water Commission & Indian Commissioner for Indus Waters

Counsel for Pakistan:

— Professor James Crawford SC, University of Cambridge, Matrix Chambers
— Professor Vaughan Lowe QC, University of Oxford, Essex Court Chambers
— Mr. Samuel Wordsworth QC, Essex Court Chambers
— Ms. Shamila Mahmood, Senior Legal Consultant, Government of Pakistan

Counsel for India:

— Mr. Fali S. Nariman, Senior Advocate, Supreme Court of India
— Mr. R.K.P. Shankardass, Senior Advocate, Supreme Court of India
— Mr. Rodman Bundy, Eversheds LLP, Singapore
— Professor Stephen C. McCaffrey, McGeorge School of Law, University of the Pacific
— Professor Daniel Barstow Magraw, Johns Hopkins University
— Mr. S.C. Sharma, Advocate, Supreme Court of India

Representatives for Pakistan:

— Mr. Aamir Shoukat, Chargé d'affaires, Embassy of Pakistan
— Mr. Faris Qazi, Deputy Commissioner for Indus Waters

Representatives for India:

— H.E. Rajesh Nandan Prasad, Ambassador of India to the Netherlands
— Mr. Darpan Talwar, Director, Central Water Commission & former Senior Joint Commissioner (Indus), Ministry of Water Resources, Technical Adviser
— Mr. P.K. Saxena, Senior Joint Commissioner, Ministry of Water Resources & former Director, Central Water, Commission, Technical Adviser
— Mr. Balraj Joshi, General Manager, NHPC Ltd., Project Representative
— Mr. Shahid Ali Khan, Chief (Environment), NHPC Ltd., Technical Advisor
— Mr. Rajeev Baboota, Chief Engineer, NHPC Ltd., Technical Advisor
— Dr. Alka Upadhyay, DHI (India) Ltd., Technical Advisor

Representative for the Government of Azad Jammu and Kashmir:

— Mr. Sardar Raheem, Secretary of Irrigation and Agriculture

Expert Witnesses for Pakistan:

— Dr. Gregory L. Morris, GLM Engineering COOP
— Dr. Jackie King, River Ecology & Environmental Flow Specialist, Southern Waters
— Mr. Syed Muhammad Mehr Ali Shah, Principal Engineer, NESPAK
— Mr. Vaqar Zakaria, Managing Director, Hagler Bailly Pakistan

Expert Witnesses for India:

— Dr. K.G. Rangaraju, Hydraulic Engineering Consultant & Former Head of Civil Engineering, IIT, Roorkee
— Dr. S. Sathyakumar, Scientist, Wildlife Institute of India, Dehra Dun
— Mr. Jesper Goodley Dannisøe, Senior Project Manager, DHI (Water & Environment), Denmark
— Dr. Niels Th. Jepsen, Senior Scientist, Section for Freshwater Fisheries Ecology, Technical University of Denmark

Technical Experts for Pakistan:

— Professor Jens Christian Refsgaard, Geological Survey of Denmark and Greenland (GEUS)

— Dr. Cate Brown, River Ecology & Environmental Flow Specialist, Southern Waters

— Mr. Hans Beuster, Hydrologist, Beuster, Clarke and Associates

— Mr. Saleem Warsi, Flow Measurement Expert, Water and Power Development Authority

— Mr. Manzar Naeem Qureshi, Power Economics Expert, Hagler Bailly Pakistan

Technical Experts for India:

— Dr. George W. Annandale, Principal, Golder Associates Inc., Denver, Colorado

— Dr. Michael J.B. Green, Partner, Roots—For Life, U.K.

— Prof. Dr. Anton J. Schleiss, Laboratory of Hydraulic Constructions (LCH), EPFL, Switzerland

— Dr. Edmund D. Andrews, Tenaya Water Resources, LLC, Boulder, Colorado, USA

— Dr. G. Mathias Kondolf, Professor of Environmental Planning and Geography, University of California, Berkeley, USA

— Dr. John S. Richardson, Professor and Head of Department, University of British Columbia

TABLE OF CONTENTS

GLOSSARY OF DEFINED TERMS

Court	The Court of Arbitration in these proceedings as constituted pursuant to Article IX(5) and Annexure G of the Treaty
KHEP	Kishenganga Hydro-Electric Project
GWh	Gigawatt hours
India's Comments, CEA Report, August 2013	India's Comments on the Information Supplied by Pakistan on 21 June 2013, Vol. 2, Tab B, Central Electricity Authority, "Further Submissions on Impact of Minimum Releases from KHEP on Power Generation at KHEP," August 2013
India's Comments, CWC Report, August 2013	India's Comments on the Information Supplied by Pakistan on 21 June 2013, Vol. 2, Tab A, Central Water Commission (CWC), Government of India, "Hydrology Report," August 2013
India's Comments, Kondolf Report, August 2013	India's Comments on the Information Supplied by Pakistan on 21 June 2013, Tab C, G Mathias Kondolf, "Environmental Flows for the Kishenganga River Below KHEP," 13 August 2013
India's Data Submission, CEA Report, June 2013	India's Submission on the Information Requested by the Court in its Partial Award dated 18 February 2013, Vol. 2, Tab B, Central Electricity Authority, "Impact of Minimum Releases from KHEP on Power Generation at KHEP," June 2013
India's Data Submission, CWC Report, June 2013	India's Submission on the Information Requested by the Court in its Partial Award dated 18 February 2013, Vol. 2, Tab A, Central Water Commission (CWC), Government of India, "Hydrology Report," June 2013
India's Data Submission, DHI Report, 2013	India's Submission on the Information Requested by the Court in its Partial Award dated 18 February 2013, Tab F, DHI (India) Water & Environment, "Environmental Studies for Assessment of Impacts of Minimum Flow Releases," June 2013
NJHEP	Neelum-Jhelum Hydro-Electric Project
Order on Interim Measures	Order on the Interim Measures Application of Pakistan issued by the Court on 6 June 2011
Pakistan's Comments, NESPAK Hydrology Report, August 2013	Pakistan's Comments on India's Response dated 21 June 2013 to the Court's Request for Further Information (Made Pursuant to Paragraph 463 of the Partial Award), Annex A, National Engineering Services Pakistan (Pvt.) Limited, "Kishenganga Dam Partial Award: NESPAK's Comments on India's CWC Hydrology Report of June 2013," August 2013

Pakistan's Comments, NESPAK Power Generation Report, August 2013	Pakistan's Comments on India's Response dated 21 June 2013 to the Court's Request for Further Information (Made Pursuant to Paragraph 463 of the Partial Award), Annex C, National Engineering Services Pakistan (Pvt.) Limited, "Kishenganga Dam Partial Award: NESPAK Comments on India's 'CEA' Report on Impact of Minimum Release from KHEP on Power Generation by KHEP," August 2013
Pakistan's Data Submission, Environmental Report, June 2013	Pakistan's Data and Information Submitted in Accordance with the Partial Award (Paragraphs 458–462), Tab A, Water Matters, Southern Waters, Hagler Bailly Pakistan, Beuster, Clarke & Associates: "Kishenganga Dam Partial Award, Data Sought: Environmental Flows," 6 June 2013
Pakistan's Data Submission, NESPAK Hydrology Report, June 2013	Pakistan's Data and Information Submitted in Accordance with the Partial Award (Paragraphs 458–462), Tab C, National Engineering Services Pakistan (Pvt.) Limited, "Kishenganga Dam Partial Award: Detailed Information on Hydrological Estimates," June 2013 (including peer review by Professor Jens Christian Refsgaard in Appendix V)
Pakistan's Data Submission, NESPAK Power Generation Report, June 2013	Pakistan's Data and Information Submitted in Accordance with the Partial Award (Paragraphs 458–462), Tab B, National Engineering Services Pakistan (Pvt.) Limited, "Kishenganga Dam Partial Award: Power Generation at Neelum-Jhelum Hydroelectric Project," June 2013
Pakistan's Memorial, Environmental Report, April 2011	Pakistan's Memorial, Vol. 3, Tab D, Hagler Bailly Pakistan, Water Matters, Southern Waters & Beuster, Clarke and Associates, "Kishenganga/Neelum River Water Diversion: Environmental Assessment," May 2011
Pakistan's Memorial, NESPAK Report, April 2011	Pakistan's Memorial, Vol. 3, Tab B, National Engineering Services Pakistan (Pvt.) Limited, "Kishenganga/Neelum River, Hydrology and Impact of Kishenganga Hydroelectric Plant on Energy Generation in Pakistan," April 2011
Pakistan's Reply, NESPAK Report, February 2012	Pakistan's Reply, Vol. II, Tab B, National Engineering Services Pakistan (Pvt.) Limited, "NESPAK Consideration of India's Hydrology Report," February 2012
Partial Award	Partial Award issued by the Court on 18 February 2013
Parties	The Islamic Republic of Pakistan and the Republic of India
Treaty	Indus Waters Treaty 1960 Between the Government of India, the Government of Pakistan and the International Bank for Reconstruction and Development signed at Karachi on 19 September 1960, 419 U.N.T.S. 126
World Bank	International Bank for Reconstruction and Development

I. Procedural History

1. A detailed history of this arbitration is set out in the Court's Partial Award of 18 February 2013 (the "*Partial Award*"). In the present procedural summation, the Court records key developments subsequent to the issuance of its *Partial Award*.

A. The Indus Waters Treaty and the Initiation of this Arbitration

2. On 19 September 1960, the Governments of the Republic of India and the Islamic Republic of Pakistan (the "Parties") signed the Indus Waters Treaty (the "Treaty").[1] The Treaty was also signed by the International Bank for Reconstruction and Development (the "World Bank") in respect of the World Bank's role under certain provisions of the Treaty. Instruments of ratification were exchanged between the Parties on 12 January 1961; the Treaty entered into force on that date with retroactive effect to 1 April 1960, as stated in Article XII(2).

3. Through a *Request for Arbitration* dated 17 May 2010, Pakistan initiated proceedings against India pursuant to Article IX and Annexure G of the Treaty.

4. In its Request for Arbitration, Pakistan stated that the Parties had failed to resolve the "Dispute" concerning the Kishenganga Hydro-Electric Project (the "KHEP") by agreement pursuant to Article IX(4) of the Treaty. Pakistan identified "two questions that are at the centre" of the dispute in the following terms:

> *a.* Whether India's proposed diversion of the river Kishenganga (*Neelum*) into another Tributary, i.e. the Bonar-Madmati Nallah, being one central element of the Kishenganga Project, breaches India's legal obligations owed to Pakistan under the Treaty, as interpreted and applied in accordance with international law, including India's obligations under Article III(2) (let flow all the waters of the Western rivers and not permit any interference with those waters) and Article IV(6) (maintenance of natural channels)?
>
> *b.* Whether under the Treaty, India may deplete or bring the reservoir level of a run-of-river Plant below Dead Storage Level (DSL) in any circumstances except in the case of an unforeseen emergency?[2]

5. As of 17 December 2010, a Court of Arbitration (the "Court") was constituted, comprising: Judge Stephen M. Schwebel (Chairman), Sir Franklin

[1] *Indus Waters Treaty 1960 Between the Government of India, the Government of Pakistan and the International Bank for Reconstruction and Development*, 19 September 1960, 419 U.N.T.S. 126 ("Treaty").

[2] Pakistan's Request for Arbitration, para. 4.

Berman, Professor Howard S. Wheater, Professor Lucius Caflisch, Professor Jan Paulsson, Judge Bruno Simma, and H.E. Judge Peter Tomka.

B. The Proceedings on Interim Measures and the Merits

6. On 23 September 2011, further to a request from Pakistan and after receiving the written and oral submissions of both Parties, the Court issued its *Order on the Interim Measures Application of Pakistan dated 6 June 2011* (the "Order on Interim Measures"). The operative provisions of the Order read:

> 152. Having found that it is necessary to lay down certain interim measures in order to "avoid prejudice to the final solution ... of the dispute" as provided under Paragraph 28 of Annexure G to the Indus Waters Treaty, the Court unanimously rules that:
>
> (1) For the duration of these proceedings up until the rendering of the Award,
>
> (*a*) It is open to India to continue with all works relating to the Kishenganga Hydro-Electric Project, except for the works specified in (*c*) below;
>
> (*b*) India may utilize the temporary diversion tunnel it is said to have completed at the Gurez site, and may construct and complete temporary cofferdams to permit the operation of the temporary diversion tunnel, such tunnel being provisionally determined to constitute a "temporary by-pass" within the meaning of Article I(15)(*b*) as it relates to Article III(2) of the Treaty;
>
> (*c*) Except for the sub-surface foundations of the dam stated in paragraph 151(iv) above, India shall not proceed with the construction of any permanent works on or above the Kishenganga/Neelum River riverbed at the Gurez site that may inhibit the restoration of the full flow of that river to its natural channel; and
>
> (2) Pakistan and India shall arrange for periodic joint inspections of the dam site at Gurez in order to monitor the implementation of sub-paragraph 1(*c*) above. The Parties shall also submit, by no later than December 19, 2011, a joint report setting forth the areas of agreement and any points of disagreement that may arise between the Parties concerning the implementation of this Order.
>
> 153. The Court shall remain actively seized of this matter, and may revise this Order or issue further orders at any time in light of the circumstances then obtaining.

7. Between May 2011 and May 2012, the Parties made written submissions to the Court. From 20 to 31 August 2012, the Court held a two-week hearing in The Hague.

8. On 18 February 2013, the Court issued its *Partial Award* in which it decided as follows:

> Having considered the Parties' written and oral submissions, the Court of Arbitration unanimously decides:

A. In relation to the First Dispute,

(1) The Kishenganga Hydro-Electric Project, as described to the Court by India, constitutes a Run-of-River Plant for the purpose of Paragraph 15 of Annexure D to the Indus Waters Treaty, and in particular sub-paragraph (iii) thereof.

(2) India may accordingly divert water from the Kishenganga/Neelum River for power generation by the Kishenganga Hydro-Electric Plant and may deliver the water released below the power station into the Bonar Nallah.

(3) India is however under an obligation to construct and operate the Kishenganga Hydro-Electric Plant in such a way as to maintain a minimum flow of water in the Kishenganga/Neelum River, at a rate to be determined by the Court in a Final Award.

B. In relation to the Second Dispute,

(1) Except in the case of an unforeseen emergency, the Treaty does not permit reduction below Dead Storage Level of the water level in the reservoirs of Run-of-River Plants on the Western Rivers.

(2) The accumulation of sediment in the reservoir of a Run-of-River Plant on the Western Rivers does not constitute an unforeseen emergency that would permit the depletion of the reservoir below Dead Storage Level for drawdown flushing purposes.

(3) Accordingly, India may not employ drawdown flushing at the reservoir of the Kishenganga Hydro-Electric Plant to an extent that would entail depletion of the reservoir below Dead Storage Level.

(4) Paragraphs B(1) and B(2) above do not apply to Run-of-River Plants that are in operation on the date of issuance of this Partial Award. Likewise, Paragraphs B(1) and B(2) do not apply to Run-of-River Plants already under construction on the date of issuance of this Partial Award, the design of which, having been duly communicated by India under the provisions of Annexure D, had not been objected to by Pakistan as provided for in Annexure D.

C. This Partial Award imposes no further restrictions on the construction and operation of the Kishenganga Hydro-Electric Plant, which remain subject to the provisions of the Treaty as interpreted in this Partial Award.

D. To enable the Court to determine the minimum flow of water in the Kishenganga/Neelum River referred to in paragraph A(3) above, the Parties are required to submit to the Court the information specified in paragraphs 458 to 462 within the time periods set out in paragraph 463 of this Partial Award.

E. The interim measures indicated by the Court in its 23 September 2011 *Order on the Interim Measures Application of Pakistan dated 6 June 2011* are hereby lifted.

F. The costs of the proceedings to be awarded by the Court pursuant to Paragraph 26 of Annexure G to the Treaty shall be determined in the Court's Final Award.

9. Paragraphs 458 to 463 of the *Partial Award*, referenced in Section D of the Court's Decision, provide:

> 458. The Parties are requested to provide further data concerning the impacts of a range of minimum flows to be discharged at the KHEP dam on the following:
>
> *For India:*
>
> *a*) power generation at the KHEP;
>
> *b*) environmental concerns from the dam site at Gurez to the Line of Control;
>
> *For Pakistan:*
>
> *a*) power generation at the NJHEP [Neelum-Jhelum Hydro-Electric Project];
>
> *b*) agricultural uses of water downstream of the Line of Control to Nauseri; and
>
> *c*) environmental concerns at and downstream of the Line of Control to Nauseri.
>
> 459. In compiling these further data, the Parties are required to incorporate a sufficient range of minimum flows so as to give the Court a full picture of the sensitivity of the river system.
>
> 460. These data should be accompanied by full information on the assumptions underlying these analyses, including those for power generation and environmental concerns, and the associated uncertainty in the Parties' estimates.
>
> 461. In addition, the Court would welcome receiving more detailed information on the estimates already put before it by each Party of historical flows at the KHEP dam site, at the Line of Control and at the NJHEP dam site.[668]
>
> 462. Finally, the Court would also welcome provision by the Parties of any relevant legislation, regulatory pronouncements or decisions that the Governments of Pakistan and India may have respectively issued concerning environmental flow requirements for hydro-electric or similar projects and, in particular, the Government of India for the KHEP.[669]
>
> 463. The Parties are requested to provide the foregoing information to the Court by no later than 120 days from the issuance of this Partial Award (i.e., by 19 June 2013). Each Party is invited to then comment on the information submitted by the other Party no later than 60 days thereafter (i.e., by 19 August 2013). After considering these submissions, the Court will issue its Final Award setting forth its decision on this matter, and will exert its best effort to do so by no later than the end of 2013.

---

668 In the case of Pakistan, these are the daily flow data corresponding to Annexes 3, 4 and 9 of Pakistan's Memorial, vol. 3, Tab B, National Engineering Services Pakistan Limited, "Kishenganga/Neelum River: Hydrology and Impact of Kishenganga Hydroeletric Plant on Energy Generation in Pakistan," April 2011 (covering

the period from 1971 to 2004). In the case of India these are daily flow estimates from the KHEP and the Line of Control for the same period. These data should be provided electronically, in Excel format.

669 In this regard, the Court recalls the Agent of India's statement at the hearing on the merits that the Indian National Hydroelectric Power Corporation (NHPC) and the Ministry of Environment and Forests had undertaken to cooperate to select an appropriate quantum for a minimum environmental flow at the KHEP. Hearing Tr., (Day 9), 30 August 2012, at 115:7-12.

C. Proceedings on India's Request for Clarification or Interpretation

10. On 20 May 2013, India submitted to the Court *a Request for Clarification or Interpretation*, pursuant to paragraph 27 of Annexure G to the Treaty, in which it requested "clarification or interpretation with respect to paragraph B.1 of the Court's Decision" in the *Partial Award*.

11. Paragraph 27 of Annexure G provides:

> At the request of either Party, made within three months of the date of the Award, the Court shall reassemble to clarify or interpret its Award. Pending such clarification or interpretation the Court may, at the request of either Party and if in the opinion of the Court circumstances so require, grant a stay of execution of its Award. After furnishing this clarification or interpretation, or if no request for such clarification or interpretation is made within three months of the date of the Award, the Court shall be deemed to have been dissolved.

12. At the invitation of the Court, Pakistan presented a *Submission in Response to India's Request for Interpretation or Clarification* on 19 July 2013. India submitted a *Reply on the Request for Clarification or Interpretation* on 2 September 2013. Pakistan presented its *Rejoinder to India's Reply dated 2 September 2013 in the matter of India's Request for Clarification or Interpretation* on 30 September 2013.

13. On 20 December 2013, the Court issued its *Decision on India's Request for Clarification or Interpretation*, the operative portion of which states as follows:

> Having considered the Parties' written submissions, the Court of Arbitration unanimously decides that:
>
> A. India's Request for Clarification or Interpretation of the Court's *Partial Award* of 18 February 2013 is timely and admissible.
>
> B. Subject to Paragraph B(4) of the Decision in the *Partial Award* of 18 February 2013, the prohibition on the reduction below Dead Storage Level of the water in the reservoirs of Run-of-River Plants on the Western Rivers, except in the case of unforeseen emergency, is of general application.

D. Proceedings on the Matter of the Minimum Flow

14. On 21 June 2013, Pakistan transmitted its *Data and Information Submitted in Accordance with the Partial Award (Paragraphs 458–462)*, accompanied by (1) two expert reports by National Engineering Services Pakistan (Pvt) Limited; (2) an expert report by Water Matters, Southern Waters, Hagler Bailly Pakistan and Beuster Clarke & Associates; and (3) three supporting reports, submitted electronically, by Southern Waters Ecological Research and Consulting CC in association with Hagler Bailly Pakistan, Beuster, Clarke & Associates, and Streamflow Solutions CC. On the same day, India transmitted its *Submission on the Information Requested by the Court in its Partial Award dated 18 February 2013*, together with expert reports by: (1) the Indian Central Water Commission; (2) the Indian Central Electricity Authority; (3) DHI (India) Water & Environment; (4) Dr. Michael J.B. Green; (5) Dr. Niels Jepsen; (6) Professor G. Mathias Kondolf; (7) Dr. John S. Richardson; and (8) Dr. Edmund D. Andrews. After receiving both submissions, the Registry transmitted copies simultaneously to the Parties and to the Court of Arbitration.

15. On 13 August 2013, the Court granted both Parties a one-week extension of the deadline for the submission of the Parties' comments fixed in paragraph 463 of the *Partial Award.*

16. On 26 August 2013, Pakistan submitted its *Comments on India's Response dated 21 June 2013 to the Court's Request for Further Information (Made Pursuant to Paragraph 463 of the Partial Award)*, accompanied by expert reports by: (1) National Engineering Services Pakistan (Pvt.) Limited; (2) Professor Jens Christian Refsgaard; (3) Dr. Gregory L. Morris; (4) Water Matters, Southern Waters, Hagler Bailly Pakistan, Streamflow Solutions, Beuster, Clarke & Associates, and Fluvius; and (5) Dr. Ian Campbell. On the same day, India presented its *Comments on the Information Supplied by Pakistan on 21 June 2013,* accompanied by expert reports by: (1) the Indian Central Water Commission, (2) the Indian Central Electricity Authority, (3) Professor G. Mathias Kondolf, (4) Dr. Edmund D. Andrews, and (5) Dr. Niels Jepsen. After receiving both submissions, the Registry transmitted copies simultaneously to the Parties and to the Court of Arbitration.

II. Arguments of the Parties

A. Admissibility of the Parties' Submissions

Pakistan's Arguments

17. Pakistan objects to the scope of India's Submission of 21 June 2013 on the ground that India "seek[s] to overturn or revise decisions that have been taken, with final and binding effect, in the Partial Award."[3] According to

[3] Pakistan's Comments on India's Response dated 21 June 2013 to the Court's Request for Further Information (Made Pursuant to Paragraph 463 of the Partial Award), para. 2.

Pakistan, "India has used the occasion of the Court's request to submit data and information as an opportunity to put forward further, new, arguments and to adduce further, new, expert evidence."[4] Pakistan requests the Court to "extract from the submissions of each Party the data that it requires, and … disregard extraneous material."[5]

India's Arguments

18. India objects that the "constellation of environmental material" accompanying Pakistan's submissions goes well beyond the Court's request for data and is "pervaded by what amounts to advocacy."[6] India criticizes the scope and content of Pakistan's submissions but makes no request to the Court, stating that "India is confident that the Court will see this strategy for what it is."[7]

B. The Parties' Submissions on Hydrology

19. In paragraph 461 of its *Partial Award*, the Court had invited the Parties to provide "more detailed information on the estimates already put before it by each Party of historical flows at the KHEP dam site, at the Line of Control and at the [Neelum-Jhelum Hydro-Electric Project ("NJHEP")] dam site." The accompanying footnote specified that

> [i]n the case of Pakistan, these are the daily flow data corresponding to Annexes 3, 4 and 9 of Pakistan's Memorial, vol. 3, Tab B, National Engineering Services Pakistan Limited, "Kishenganga/Neelum River: Hydrology and Impact of Kishenganga Hydroeletric Plant on Energy Generation in Pakistan," April 2011 (covering the period from 1971 to 2004). In the case of India these are daily flow estimates from the KHEP and the Line of Control for the same period.

20. In the reports submitted in response to the Court's order,[8] Pakistan provides daily flow estimates at the KHEP dam site, the Line of Control and

---

[4] *Ibid.*, para. 4.

[5] *Ibid.*, para. 13.

[6] India's Comments on the Information Supplied by Pakistan on 21 June 2013, para. 1.3.

[7] *Ibid.*, para. 1.3.

[8] Pakistan's Data and Information Submitted in Accordance with the Partial Award (Paragraphs 458–462), Tab C, National Engineering Services Pakistan (Pvt.) Limited, "Kishenganga Dam Partial Award: Detailed Information on Hydrological Estimates," June 2013 (including peer review by Professor Jens Christian Refsgaard in Appendix V) ("Pakistan's Data Submission, NESPAK Hydrology Report, June 2013"); Pakistan's Comments on India's Response dated 21 June 2013 to the Court's Request for Further Information (Made Pursuant to Paragraph 463 of the Partial Award), Annex A, National Engineering Services Pakistan (Pvt.) Limited, "Kishenganga Dam Partial Award: NESPAK's Comments on India's CWC Hydrology Report of June 2013," August 2013 ("Pakistan's Comments, NESPAK Hydrology Report, August 2013"); Pakistan's Comments on India's Response dated 21 June 2013 to the Court's Request for Further Information (Made Pursuant to Paragraph 463 of the Partial Award), Annex B, Jens Christian Refsgaard, "Comments to CWC's Hydrology Report of June 2013," August 2013 ("Pakistan's Comments, Refsgaard Report, August 2013").

the NJHEP dam site, which substantially reproduce figures previously submitted.[9] India gives ten-daily flow estimates at the KHEP dam site and the Line of Control, and monthly flow estimates at the Line of Control and the NJHEP dam site.[10] Each Party then uses its figures to evaluate the potential impact of a range of minimum flows on the environment and power generation at the KHEP and NJHEP.[11]

21. The Parties' methodologies for estimating flow are not dissimilar. Both Parties use flow data from measuring stations located near the targeted location, if such data are available for the relevant years (1971 to 2004).[12] Both Parties fill in gaps in these data by correlating the available data from the selected measuring stations with those of a reference station and by conducting a regression analysis.[13] Both Parties use the Muzzafarabad measuring station as their reference station on the Kishenganga/Neelum River.[14] For locations where there are no nearby measuring stations, such as at the Line of Control,

---

[9] Pakistan's Data Submission, NESPAK Hydrology Report, June 2013, Appendices I–III.

[10] India's Submission on the Information Requested by the Court in its Partial Award dated 18 February 2013, Vol. 2, Tab A, Central Water Commission (CWC), Government of India, "Hydrology Report," June 2013 ("India's Data Submission, CWC Report, June 2013"), Annexes II–V. Pakistan emphasizes that, contrary to the "Court's express request," India has failed to provide daily flow estimates, while India explains that reliable daily flow series could not be constructed as "a good amount of statistical approximations have already been performed in view of the uncertainties in observed flows" and any further estimation would be "artificial" and "unrealistic" (Pakistan's Comments on India's Response dated 21 June 2013 to the Court's Request for Further Information (Made Pursuant to Paragraph 463 of the Partial Award), paras. 16–17; India's Data Submission, CWC Report, June 2013, paras. 13.1, 13.5, 14.1). India also submits a second report: India's Comments on the Information Supplied by Pakistan on 21 June 2013, Vol. 2, Tab A, Central Water Commission (CWC), Government of India, "Hydrology Report," August 2013 ("India's Comments, CWC Report, August 2013").

[11] *See* India's Submission on the Information Requested by the Court in its Partial Award dated 18 February 2013, paras. 2.4–2.5, 3.12, 3.19; Pakistan's Data and Information Submitted in Accordance with the Partial Award (Paragraphs 458–462), Tab A, Water Matters, Southern Waters, Hagler Bailly Pakistan, Beuster, Clarke and Associates, "Kishenganga Dam Partial Award, Data Sought: Environmental Flows," June 6, 2013, s. 3.5.2; Pakistan's Data and Information Submitted in Accordance with the Partial Award (Paragraphs 458–462), Tab B, National Engineering Services Pakistan (Pvt.) Limited, "Kishenganga Dam Partial Award: Power Generation at Neelum-Jhelum Hydroelectric Project," June 2013 ("Pakistan's Data Submission, NESPAK Power Generation Report, June 2013"), s. 2.1.

[12] Thus, for the KHEP dam site, both Parties rely on data collected at the Gurez and Wampora gauging stations, which are located 2 km and 5 km respectively from the dam site. Pakistan (but not India) also relies on data obtained at the Nauseri gauging station for its flow estimates at the NJHEP dam site. *See* Pakistan's Memorial, Vol. 3, Tab B, National Engineering Services Pakistan (Pvt.) Limited, "Kishenganga/Neelum River: Hydrology and Impact of Kishenganga Hydroelectric Plant on Energy Generation in Pakistan," April 2011 ("Pakistan's Memorial, NESPAK Report, April 2011"), s. 1.3; India's Submission on the Information Requested by the Court in its Partial Award dated 18 February 2013, paras. 2.7–2.8, 2.20–2.21.

[13] Pakistan's Memorial, NESPAK Report, April 2011, pp. 17–32; India's Submission on the Information Requested by the Court in its Partial Award dated 18 February 2013, para. 2.9.

[14] Pakistan's Memorial, NESPAK Report, April 2011, p. 17; India's Counter-Memorial dated 23 November 2011, Vol. 2A, Tab A, Central Water Commission (CWC), Government of India, "Hydrology Report on Kishenganga Hydro-Electric Project," October 2011, pp. 37–38.

both Parties estimate flow using data from stations situated elsewhere along the Kishenganga/Neelum.[15]

22. Despite these methodological similarities, the Parties disagree as to: (i) whether data previously exchanged under the Treaty or "corrected" data should be used for calculating the minimum flow; (ii) whether data from the Nauseri gauging station are reliable and sound; and (iii) whether to use Pakistan's or India's regression analysis for filling in gaps in the observed data. The Parties also disagree (iv) about the appropriate framework of analysis, and the resultant availability of flow, at the Line of Control.

1. Data previously exchanged under the Treaty vs. "corrected" data

Pakistan's Arguments

23. With respect to the data it collected at its Muzzafarabad measuring station, Pakistan uses what it calls "corrected" or "quality-assured" data.[16] While Pakistan provides "raw" data to India pursuant to the data exchange requirements of Article VI(1) of the Treaty, these data are subsequently evaluated by Pakistan's Surface Water Hydrology Directorate to account for variations in the level or stage over the course of the day (in particular during the high-flow season) and to adjust the rating curve between the stage and the river discharge on the basis of an annual analysis of potential changes.[17] Pakistan considers such quality assurance to be standard practice,[18] although such data are not, and according to Pakistan cannot be, shared with India within the three-month period required by the Treaty.[19] However, Pakistan submits that India could have accessed these corrected data by consulting, for a fee, the yearbooks of Pakistan's Surface Water Hydrology Directorate.[20]

24. Pakistan submits that, for the purpose of determining the minimum flow, the Court should use the most reliable data, in accordance with

---

[15] Pakistan's Memorial, NESPAK Report, April 2011, pp. 35-40; India's Data Submission, CWC Report, June 2013, para. 10.2.

[16] Pakistan's Reply, Vol. II, Tab B, National Engineering Services Pakistan (Pvt.) Limited, "NESPAK Consideration of India's Hydrology Report," February 2012 ("Pakistan's Reply, NESPAK Report, February 2012"), p. 3, s. ES.4.

[17] Pakistan explains that the data provided to India under Article VI(1) were the current measurements taken at Muzzafarabad. However, these measurements were sporadic, and the gaps in the data could not accurately be filled by correlating the current measurements and the daily water level (stage) measurements taken at Muzzafarabad because the current and stage measurements were taken at different times of day. Pakistan further explains that, for the corrected data, discharge values were computed from stage measurements taken at Muzzafarabad by applying rating curves based on additional data. *See* Pakistan's Data Submission, NESPAK Hydrology Report, June 2013, Appendix IV, pp. 112–115.

[18] Pakistan's Data Submission, NESPAK Hydrology Report, June 2013, Appendix V, pp. 131–33.

[19] *Ibid.*, Appendix IV, p. 112; Appendix V, p. 132.

[20] Hearing Tr., (Day 1), 20 August 2012, at 83:12 to 84:6 (Cross-Examination of Mr. Mehr Ali Shah).

good scientific practice, regardless of whether the data in question were originally exchanged pursuant to the Treaty.[21]

25. Pakistan contends that India's argument that Pakistan tampered with its Muzzafarabad data is baseless, as is evident from the small difference between the Parties' data and the fact that the alleged discrepancies occur during the high-flow periods. Pakistan would derive no benefit from changing the values for discharges that exceed the combined capacity of the KHEP and NJHEP, as such high flows are irrelevant to the Court's minimum flow determination.[22]

India's Arguments

26. India submits that, in making its minimum flow determination, the Court should rely solely on data contemporaneously exchanged by the Parties pursuant to Article VI(1) of the Treaty, for three reasons.[23] First, Pakistan has failed to explain why it did not supply India with the corrected data prior to this arbitration.[24] Second, according to India, the Parties' intent was that data exchanged pursuant to the Treaty be used in the Treaty's implementation.[25] Third, India argues that Pakistan's "corrected" data contain numerous inconsistencies[26] and cannot be verified because Pakistan has failed to explain how it arrived at its corrections.[27]

27. India argues that, as a result of these unexplained corrections of the data, Pakistan underestimates dry season flows at Muzzafarabad and overestimates flows at the KHEP dam site. The effect is thereby to exaggerate the adverse effect of reduced flows on power generation by the NJHEP and to underestimate the adverse effects of any minimum flow on power generation at the KHEP.[28]

---

[21] Pakistan's Comments on India's Response dated 21 June 2013 to the Court's Request for Further Information (Made Pursuant to Paragraph 463 of the Partial Award), paras. 21–22; *see also* Pakistan's Comments, Refsgaard Report, August 2013, p. 50.

[22] Pakistan's Data Submission, NESPAK Hydrology Report, June 2013, Appendix IV, s. 2.1(*d*).

[23] India's Comments on the Information Supplied by Pakistan on 21 June 2013, para. 2.34.

[24] *Ibid.*, para. 2.15.

[25] India's Submission on the Information Requested by the Court in its Partial Award dated 18 February 2013, paras. 2.15–2.16.

[26] For example, India notes that Pakistan's corrected data indicate that measurements are missing for certain days for which observed data was actually communicated to India under the Treaty and vice versa, and that there are discrepancies between the data provided by Pakistan in this arbitration and the Surface Water Hydrology Directorate's published data. *See* India's Comments on the Information Supplied by Pakistan on 21 June 2013, para. 2.18; India's Data Submission, CWC Report, June 2013, para. 9.10; India's Comments, CWC Report, August 2013, para. 14.

[27] India's Submission on the Information Requested by the Court in its Partial Award dated 18 February 2013, paras. 2.17–2.19; India's Comments on the Information Supplied by Pakistan on 21 June 2013, para. 2.17.

[28] India's Submission on the Information Requested by the Court in its Partial Award dated 18 February 2013, para. 2.13; India's Comments on the Information Supplied by Pakistan on 21 June 2013, para. 2.19.

28. India also takes issue with Pakistan's use of the data for the Gurez and Wampora gauging stations previously transmitted by India under the Treaty. India notes that while both Parties have described the high-flow data from the Gurez station and the low-flow data from the Wampora station as unreliable (and both were discarded by India), Pakistan appears to have made use of the low-flow data from Wampora and has otherwise not explained which of India's data it used in calculating the flow at the KHEP and which it discarded.[29]

2. Reliability and integrity of data from the Nauseri gauging station

Pakistan's Arguments

29. In estimating daily flows at the NJHEP dam site, Pakistan relies, *inter alia*, on data collected during an 18-month period (July 1990 to December 1991) at the Nauseri gauging station, from which it derives a 34-year time-series covering 1971 to 2004 through a correlation to the flows at Muzzafarabad.

30. Pakistan submits that the Nauseri data from this 18-month period are reliable because the Nauseri and Muzzafarabad data are highly correlated for that time.[30] A high correlation is not surprising, given that the two measuring stations are only 35 kilometres apart and have similar catchment areas.[31]

India's Arguments

31. India submits that data collected at the Nauseri gauging station should not be used because they were not communicated to India pursuant to Article VI(1) of the Treaty and because a period of 18 months is too short to determine whether information obtained at a gauging station is reliable.[32] India adds that the correlation between the Nauseri and Muzzafarabad data is unusually high, which suggests that the Nauseri data were not observed but rather fully derived from the Muzzafarabad data.[33]

---

[29] India's Comments on the Information Supplied by Pakistan on 21 June 2013, paras. 2.5–2.12; India's Data Submission, CWC Report, June 2013, para. 9.11.

[30] Pakistan's Reply, NESPAK Report, February 2012, s. 5.1.4.

[31] Pakistan's Data Submission, NESPAK Hydrology Report, June 2013, Appendix IV, s. 2.2(*c*).

[32] India's Submission on the Information Requested by the Court in its Partial Award dated 18 February 2013, paras. 2.21–2.23; India's Comments on the Information Supplied by Pakistan on 21 June 2013, paras. 2.23(i)&(ii), 2.35; India's Data Submission, CWC Report, June 2013, para. 9.7.

[33] India's Rejoinder, Vol. II, Tab A, Central Water Commission (CWC), "Response to the Replies of NESPAK on CWC's Hydrology Report," April 2012, s. 4.1.

3. Regression analysis

Pakistan's Arguments

32. Pakistan submits that, to fill in gaps in the observed data, a single annual regression equation using monthly discharges should be used to correlate data from the various gauging stations on the Kishenganga/Neelum.[34] According to Pakistan, India's use of seasonal regression equations (that is, different equations for different groups of months) is less reliable because such equations are based on fewer data points and ignore outliers.[35] According to Pakistan, the quantity of data points is a particular concern in light of the "inherent uncertainties" in India's data for the sites at Gurez and Wampora, and the large variation between individual data points and the regression line.[36]

India's Arguments

33. India uses a seasonal regression analysis, applying three distinct correlation equations for the periods from November to February (the low flow season), March to June (the snow-melt season), and July to October (the high flow season).[37] According to India, this analysis is preferable because it takes into account "the vastly different flow patterns associated with the different seasons affecting the river system."[38]

34. India submits that Pakistan's use of an annual regression analysis may explain why Pakistan's flow series indicates that flows were greater at the KHEP dam site than at the Line of Control in some months, despite the contribution of tributaries between these two locations.[39]

4. Flow at the Line of Control

Pakistan's Arguments

35. Pakistan objects to India's use of a 90-percent reliable (i.e., dry) year for its analysis. In Pakistan's view, values from such years ignore extreme conditions that occur from time to time and such an approach "distorts the

---

[34] Pakistan's Data Submission, NESPAK Hydrology Report, June 2013, Appendix IV, pp. 124–125.

[35] Pakistan's Data Submission, NESPAK Hydrology Report, June 2013, Appendix IV, p. 124; Pakistan's Reply, Vol. II, Tab A, Jens Christian Refsgaard, "Review of NESPAK Consideration of India's Hydrology Report," 15 February 2012, p. 4.

[36] Pakistan's Comments, NESPAK Hydrology Report, August 2013, para. 5.25.

[37] India's Submission on the Information Requested by the Court in its Partial Award dated 18 February 2013, paras. 2.25–2.27; India's Data Submission, CWC Report, June 2013, para. 6.2, 7.1.

[38] India's Submission on the Information Requested by the Court in its Partial Award dated 18 February 2013, para. 2.29; India's Data Submission, CWC Report, June 2013, paras. 7.1–7.5, 9.6; India's Comments on the Information Supplied by Pakistan on 21 June 2013, para. 2.25.

[39] India's Data Submission, CWC Report, June 2013, paras. 9.14–9.16; India's Comments on the Information Supplied by Pakistan on 21 June 2013, para. 2.31.

picture of the hydrology of the river."[40] According to Pakistan, the Court's minimum flow determination should be based on "an understanding of the *actual* existing flow regime, not a flow regime ironed out [to] exclude extreme hydrological conditions that have in fact occurred, and that will continue to reoccur, leading to actual impacts on the riverine ecosystem."[41]

36. According to Pakistan, "India's presentation seems oriented to depict that there is ample water availability in the form of flow contributions from the intermediate catchment between KHEP dam site and the Line of Control."[42] In fact, Pakistan argues, in natural conditions, flows below 10 cumecs at the KHEP occur only 0.7 percent of the time, yet with a minimum flow release of 4.25 cumecs as proposed by India, such low flows would occur 55 percent of the time.[43] On India's own figures, Pakistan contends, India's proposed release would create flows at the Line of Control that are lower than the lowest ever recorded flow 18.5 percent of the time.[44]

India's Arguments

37. India bases its analysis of the flow available at the Line of Control on a 90-percent reliable year (in other words, a flow that will be available in 90 percent of years), arguing that this is the basis on which Indian Run-of-River Plants are designed.[45] Examining the intermediate flow between the KHEP and the Line of Control under both Indian and Pakistani data, India calculates that intervening tributaries add between 2.1 and 3.31 cumecs with 90 percent reliability.[46] Combined with even the 3.94-cumec minimum promised by India's Agent at the merits hearing, the flow at the Line of Control would be more than 6 cumecs—and likely more than 7 cumecs—90 percent of the time.[47] With the addition of a further 3 cumecs from a tributary just 4 kilometres downstream of the Line of Control, India submits that a substantial flow would be available under any minimum release from the KHEP.[48]

---

[40] Pakistan's Comments on India's Response dated 21 June 2013 to the Court's Request for Further Information (Made Pursuant to Paragraph 463 of the Partial Award), para. 20(*e*)&(*g*).

[41] *Ibid.*, para. 17 (emphasis in original); Pakistan's Comments, NESPAK Hydrology Report, August 2013, para. 5.34. Pakistan also notes that India's use of a hydrological year beginning in June is not in accordance with best practices (Pakistan's Comments, NESPAK Hydrology Report, August 2013, para. 5.30).

[42] Pakistan's Comments, NESPAK Hydrology Report, August 2013, para. 5.33.

[43] Pakistan's Comments on India's Response dated 21 June 2013 to the Court's Request for Further Information (Made Pursuant to Paragraph 463 of the Partial Award), para. 18; Pakistan's Comments, NESPAK Hydrology Report, August 2013, paras. 5.51–5.52.

[44] Pakistan's Comments, NESPAK Hydrology Report, August 2013, para. 5.56.

[45] India's Submission on the Information Requested by the Court in its Partial Award dated 18 February 2013, paras. 2.51, 2.53, 3.11.

[46] India's Data Submission, CWC Report, June 2013, paras. 15.2–15.8.

[47] *Ibid.*, para. 15.9.

[48] *Ibid.*, para. 15.10.

C. The Parties' Submissions on the Effect of Minimum Flow on Power Generation and the Economics of the KHEP

38. As requested by the Court, both Pakistan and India have presented data on the effect of a range of flows on power generation at their respective hydro-electric plants—Pakistan with respect to the NJHEP and India with respect to the KHEP. Each Party has also commented on the other's presentation of effects on power generation at its plant.

Pakistan's Arguments

39. For the NJHEP, Pakistan outlines the lost energy that would result from 17 different scenarios for a minimum release from the KHEP. These scenarios present a reduction in energy generation at the NJHEP ranging from 0 to 13.6 percent. Among these, the minimum flow of 3.94 cumecs promised by India during the merits hearing would result in a loss at the NJHEP of 635 gigawatt hours ("GWh") or 12.3 percent of capacity.[49] Pakistan also calculates the revenue lost on the basis of "replacement energy by means of energy from fuel oil and high speed diesel power generation" and contends that a 3.94-cumec release would result in an annual loss for Pakistan of USD 130,400,000.[50] Although the losses vary substantially across the outlined scenarios, Pakistan contends that a minimum flow of less than 80 cumecs at the KHEP would cause a significant loss in energy at the NJHEP.[51]

40. Turning to India's submission on power generation at the KHEP, Pakistan argues that India's data are misleading and that India's submission amounts to an attempt to "re-litigate an issue that was exhaustively addressed during the hearing on the merits."[52] Pakistan argues that India incorrectly assumes that "the Partial Award gives priority to India's needs and thus concludes that Pakistan's entitlement to downstream flows should be 'limited to a minimum.'"[53] According to Pakistan, India then structures its presentation of data accordingly and considers minimum flows only between 0 to 10 cumecs. Pakistan submits that India, in doing so, has neglected the actual finding of the *Partial Award* that "[b]oth Parties' entitlements under the Treaty must be made effective so far as possible"[54] and has also failed to "fulfil the Court's requirement of incorporating a sufficient range of minimum flows to be dis-

[49] Pakistan's Data and Information Submitted in Accordance with the Partial Award (Paragraphs 458–462), para. 19.

[50] *Ibid.*, paras. 19–20.

[51] *Ibid.*, para. 21.

[52] Pakistan's Comments on India's Response dated 21 June 2013 to the Court's Request for Further Information (Made Pursuant to Paragraph 463 of the Partial Award), paras. 23–24.

[53] *Ibid.*, para. 24.

[54] *Ibid.*, para. 25, *quoting* Partial Award, para. 446.

charged below the KHEP so as to give the Court a 'full picture' of the sensitivity of the river system."[55]

41. Pakistan further criticizes India's presentation of data that, in Pakistan's view, follows from India's assumption of priority. First, Pakistan disputes the idea that power plants are designed on the basis of dry-year flows and argues that "India is using a dry year as the base scenario for analysis because the effect of downstream releases is magnified in percentage terms when examined in the context of the reduced water flows in a dry year."[56] Second, Pakistan objects to the fact that India has presented energy losses only for December, the lowest flow month. In Pakistan's view, "the point to be examined is the magnitude of those losses in the context of the average annual energy production at KHEP, not the magnitude of those losses in the context of the driest month of a dry year."[57] Finally, Pakistan objects that India has exaggerated energy losses at the KHEP by comparing them against a scenario of no downstream release, notwithstanding that its own laws already mandate a 4.25-cumec minimum.[58]

42. In presenting its data, Pakistan maintains that India has invoked the threat to the economic viability of the KHEP posed by higher minimum releases, but "has not put before the Court the data that would be needed for any detailed and reliable assessment of the economic viability of KHEP."[59] Pakistan accordingly has constructed its own economic analysis, using the cost of the KHEP published in 2011, the cost of energy from other sources in India, and prevailing interest rates.[60] Based on this analysis, Pakistan concludes that the KHEP would generate an economic internal rate of return ranging from 20.2 percent with no minimum release to 10.9 percent with a 100-cumec minimum release. As even this last figure is well above the 6 percent interest rate prevailing in India at the time the project was approved, Pakistan concludes that the "KHEP remains economically viable for all of the scenarios formulated and tested by Pakistan in its submission of 21 June 2013."[61]

India's Arguments

43. As context for its data on energy generation at the KHEP, India submits that "the Partial Award makes it clear that the KHEP and NJHEP are not

[55] Pakistan's Comments on India's Response dated 21 June 2013 to the Court's Request for Further Information (Made Pursuant to Paragraph 463 of the Partial Award), Annex C, National Engineering Services Pakistan (Pvt.) Limited, "Kishenganga Dam Partial Award: NESPAK Comments on India's 'CEA' Report on Impact of Minimum Release from KHEP on Power Generation by KHEP," August 2013 ("Pakistan's Comments, NESPAK Power Generation Report, August 2013"), para. 4.2.

[56] Pakistan's Comments on India's Response dated 21 June 2013 to the Court's Request for Further Information (Made Pursuant to Paragraph 463 of the Partial Award), para. 28.

[57] *Ibid.*, para. 29.

[58] *Ibid.*, para. 30.

[59] *Ibid.*, para. 32.

[60] *See* Pakistan's Comments, NESPAK Power Generation Report, August 2013, paras. 5.1–5.10.

[61] *Ibid.*, paras. 5.10–5.11.

to be treated on a basis of equality."[62] According to India, the Court's reasoning in the *Partial Award* was such that the "obligation to release a 'minimum flow' should indeed be limited to a minimum."[63] India also recalls its arguments that Pakistan has much more water available to it at the NJHEP site, that each cumec of water generates significantly more energy at the KHEP than it would at the NJHEP, and that India's losses are compounded because releases from the KHEP will also reduce energy generation at India's Uri-I and Uri-II projects on the lower Jhelum.[64]

44. In response to the Court's request for data, India outlines the effect on power generation during dry (90-percent dependable), average (50-percent dependable), and wet (10-percent dependable) years. India calculates the losses at a range of minimum flows between 0 and 10 cumecs and provides both annual and dry season (October-March) figures for percentage loss of generating capacity.[65] Based on these data, India reaches the following conclusions:

> - For every cumec of minimum release below KHEP dam, there is a definite loss in power generation at KHEP.
>
> - The winter months from the October to March are associated with low flows and the power generation will be adversely affected during these months on account of minimum releases from KHEP dam. This reduction would be almost Linear in nature.
>
> - The average annual loss in energy generation at KHEP is the maximum in 90% Dependable Year (Dry Year) viz. about 16% [with a 10-cumec minimum release] which works out as around 32 MU per cumec.
>
> - On monthly basis, the loss in energy on account of minimum release below KHEP dam would be significant in Dry Year (90% dependable year) with the loss being as high as 80.2% in percentage terms in the month of December corresponding to minimum release of 10 cumec.[66]

45. Turning to Pakistan's flow data regarding the NJHEP, India considers Pakistan's seventeen minimum flow scenarios to be "grossly inflated."[67]

---

[62] India's Submission on the Information Requested by the Court in its Partial Award dated 18 February 2013, para. 3.5.

[63] *Ibid.*, para. 3.7.

[64] *Ibid.*, para. 3.7.

[65] India's Submission on the Information Requested by the Court in its Partial Award dated 18 February 2013, Vol. 2, Tab B, Central Electricity Authority, "Impact of Minimum Releases from KHEP on Power Generation at KHEP," June 2013 ("India's Data Submission, CEA Report, June 2013").

[66] India's Data Submission, CEA Report, June 2013, s. 6.

[67] India's Comments on the Information Supplied by Pakistan on 21 June 2013, para. 4.3. India also objects to the fact that Pakistan's submission presents power losses that are higher than those indicated in its Memorial and Reply submissions as a result of a design change at the NJHEP in April 2012. According to India, "it is inadmissible for Pakistan to augment its alleged losses in this manner at such a late stage of the proceedings, particularly when no evidence supporting how the increase was arrived at has been furnished. Even though the amount of increase is relatively modest—702 GWh vs. 695 GWh—this still represents a 1% increase [and] ... each

In India's view, the releases proposed by Pakistan "would cause the KHEP to be completely shut down for months of the year, and ... are contrary to the Court's statements in the Partial Award regarding India's right under the Treaty to proceed with the KHEP in a manner that makes the project viable."[68]

46. According to India, any minimum flow greater than 4.25 cumecs would seriously compromise the economic viability of the KHEP.[69] Examining a 90-percent dependable (dry) year (on the basis of which the KHEP was designed), India submits that a minimum release of 20 cumecs would render the KHEP inoperable for three months of the year, while Pakistan's 100-cumec release would prevent the KHEP from operating for 10 months of the year.[70] On the whole, India argues, "Pakistan's minimum release scenarios of 10 cumecs and above would cause the KHEP to operate below its design discharge for between 60% and 95% of the time, a result that simply would not respect India's priority of right to the waters."[71]

47. Even with a minimum flow of 10 cumecs, India submits that during a 90-percent dependable (dry) year, the KHEP would suffer a significantly larger percentage loss of generating capacity than would the NJHEP. "Given that the Court has ruled that the KHEP has priority in right over the NJHEP with respect to the use of the waters of the river for hydro-electric power generation," India argues, "it is impossible to justify a 10 cumec minimum release, let alone higher releases."[72]

48. With a minimum release of 7.2 cumecs during a 90-percent dependable (dry) year, India notes, the percentage loss at the two plants would be equal (at 11.2 percent). Nevertheless, in India's view,

> even this 7.2 cumec scenario would result in the KHEP being able to operate at its design discharge for only four months of the year—a result that would run counter to the Court's admonition that the KHEP must not be made to operate at only a small fraction of its design capacity. Moreover, a minimum release of 7.2 cumec would also not reflect the Court's finding that the KHEP has priority in right to the waters, a factor which strongly militates in favour of a lower minimum release, and the fact that Pakistan's losses have been overstated as a result of its new claim and the use of non-Treaty flow data.[73]

---

percentage point is important." India's Comments on the Information Supplied by Pakistan on 21 June 2013, para. 4.20.

[68] India's Comments on the Information Supplied by Pakistan on 21 June 2013, para. 4.3.

[69] *Ibid.*, para. 4.8; *see generally* India's Comments on the Information Supplied by Pakistan on 21 June 2013, Vol. 2, Tab B, Central Electricity Authority, "Further Submissions on Impact of Minimum Releases from KHEP on Power Generation at KHEP," August 2013 ("India's Comments, CEA Report, August 2013").

[70] India's Comments on the Information Supplied by Pakistan on 21 June 2013, para. 4.4.

[71] India's Comments on the Information Supplied by Pakistan on 21 June 2013, para. 4.17.

[72] *Ibid.*, para. 4.31.

[73] *Ibid.*, para. 4.31 (footnotes omitted).

D. The Parties' Submissions on Agricultural Uses in the Neelum Valley

Pakistan's Arguments

49. Pakistan observes that agriculture in the Neelum Valley is "almost entirely dependent on rain" rather than on water from the Kishenganga/Neelum.[74] This is, however, a system of "subsistence farming as water is often unavailable to meet crop needs."[75] According to Pakistan, improvements in agricultural productivity will depend on the introduction of lift irrigation, using solar, high-speed diesel, or small-scale hydro-electric powered pumps. Looking to the future, Pakistan concludes that "[a]ny future development in the agricultural sector, and hence the possibility of breaking the cycle of poverty, is predicated upon the uninterrupted flow of water which, if ensured, will make a substantial difference to the quality of life of the inhabitants of the Neelum Valley."[76]

50. Pakistan acknowledges the difficulty of providing data with respect to future agricultural uses. It nevertheless maintains that "[a]gricultural uses are ... expressly protected by paragraph 15(iii) of Annexure D,"[77] and submits that "some allowance must be made for future development in striking the balance to which the Court has referred in its Partial Award."[78]

India's Arguments

51. India submits that for agricultural uses "to be taken into account in calculating a minimal flow that India must release through the Kishenganga dam, Pakistan must establish two facts: (1) that there was river-dependent agricultural use on the stretch between the LOC [Line of Control] and Nauseri during the critical period established by the Court, and (2) that such use will be adversely affected by the KHEP."[79] In India's view, despite initially claiming large areas under cultivation, Pakistan "has failed to show that there is any such agriculture."[80] India further notes the Court's observation in the *Partial Award* that "[i]t appears to the Court that agricultural uses in the Neelum Valley are largely met by the tributary streams that feed the river."[81]

---

[74] Pakistan's Reply, para. 4.52.

[75] *Ibid.*, para. 4.52.

[76] *Ibid.*, para. 4.61; Pakistan's Data and Information Submitted in Accordance with the Partial Award (Paragraphs 458–462), para. 22.

[77] Pakistan's Data and Information Submitted in Accordance with the Partial Award (Paragraphs 458–462), para. 22.

[78] *Ibid.*, para. 23.

[79] India's Submission on the Information Requested by the Court in its Partial Award dated 18 February 2013, para. 5.15.

[80] *Ibid.*, para. 5.15.

[81] *Ibid.*, para. 5.15 fn. 155, *quoting* Partial Award, para. 434.

52. As India interprets the Court's *Partial Award*, any submission with respect to current or future agricultural uses "would not be timely, since it would be beyond the time-frame established in the Treaty, as interpreted in the Partial Award. It would thus be simply too late to be considered in calculating minimum flow, and in fact is irrelevant to such a calculation."[82] In India's view, the Court rejected "Pakistan's contention that 'then existing' means 'future'" with respect to uses in the context of Paragraph 15(iii) of Annexure D to the Treaty.[83] In any event, India considers future uses by Pakistan to be "unidentified, unplanned and unsubstantiated"[84] and submits that Pakistan has ample water for any such development, as "roughly two-thirds of the water at Nauseri enters the river after the KHEP dam site."[85]

E. The Parties' Submissions on the Environmental Impact of the KHEP

53. As requested by the Court, both Pakistan and India have presented data on the effect of a range of flows on the environment below the KHEP. Each Party has also commented on the other Party's environmental submissions.

Pakistan's Arguments

54. Pakistan presents its data on environmental concerns through a revised submission based on the DRIFT methodology ("Downstream Implications of Flow Transformation") employed in its expert submissions earlier in these proceedings.[86] This approach endeavours to estimate the effect of chang-

[82] *Ibid.*, para. 5.15.

[83] India's Comments on the Information Supplied by Pakistan on 21 June 2013, paras. 3.14, 3.16.

[84] *Ibid.*, para. 3.13.

[85] *Ibid.*, para. 3.17.

[86] *See generally* Pakistan's Data and Information Submitted in Accordance with the Partial Award (Paragraphs 458–462), Tab A, Water Matters, Southern Waters, Hagler Bailly Pakistan, Beuster, Clarke & Associates: "Kishenganga Dam Partial Award, Data Sought: Environmental Flows," June 6, 2013 ("Pakistan's Data Submission, Environmental Report, June 2013"). As described by Pakistan,

> [DRIFT] is a holistic approach that employs a multidisciplinary team to analyse the likely effects of a range of flow scenarios. Its aim is to produce predictions of change in the form of three streams of information—ecological, economic and social—that represent the three pillars of sustainable development. It incorporates a custom-built Decision Support System (DSS) that holds all the relevant data, understanding and local wisdom about the river provided by the team of river and social specialists. DRIFT has been used in many transboundary or basin-wide water development investigations over the last 15 years, including the Orange/Senqu (Lesotho and South Africa); the Mekong (Cambodia, Lao PDR, Thailand, Viet Nam); the Pangani Basin (Tanzania); the Zambezi Delta (Mozambique); the Okavango (Angola, Namibia, Botswana); the Cunene (Angola, Namibia); as well as numerous applications in its country of origin, South Africa. It was designed to meet the needs and realities of water-resource planning in developing countries.

Pakistan's Memorial, Vol. 3, Tab D, Hagler Bailly Pakistan, Water Matters, Southern Waters & Beuster, Clarke and Associates, "Kishenganga/Neelum River Water Diversion: Envies to the flow regime through the integrated examination of a large number of indicators related to the hydrology, sediments, hydraulics, geomorphology, water quality, vegetation, macroinvertebrates, and fish of the river.[87] As described by Pakistan's experts, the objective of the analysis is to address the Court's observation that "hydro-electric projects (including Pakistan's projects) must be planned, built and operated with environmental sustainability in mind" and offer guidance on the flow regime that would be environmentally sustainable in the Kishenganga/Neelum.[88]

55. By comparison with its earlier submissions, Pakistan has expanded its team of experts to include a hydraulics specialist and specialists in sedimentology and geomorphology and has increased its range of indicators in light of the Court's ruling on drawdown flushing in its *Partial Award*.[89] Pakistan's experts have also developed 17 flow scenarios (corresponding to those discussed above in relation to power generation). In addition to the current baseline condition, a maximum diversion scenario, and the 3.94-cumec release identified by India during the merits hearing, Pakistan's experts have evaluated minimum releases between 10 and 100 cumecs (in increments of 10 cumecs),[90] percentage-based scenarios in which between 10 and 90 percent of the flow at the KHEP would be passed downstream,[91] and two variable release scenarios in which the downstream release would vary by season and between dry and normal years.[92] As in previous submissions, each scenario was evaluated for effects at the Line of Control, at the NJHEP site at Nauseri, and at Dudhnial (halfway between the Line of Control and Nauseri).

56. In keeping with the DRIFT methodology and based on the predicted response of the indicators to various flow regimes, Pakistan's experts graded the resultant ecological condition of the Kishenganga/Neelum under the 17 scenarios on a scale from A to F, ranging from pristine to critically modi-

ronmental Assessment," May 2011 ("Pakistan's Memorial, Environmental Report, May 2011"), pp. 2–12.

[87] For the full list of indicators, see Pakistan's Data Submission, Environmental Report, June 2013, p. 9.

[88] *Ibid.*, p. 3, *quoting* Partial Award, para. 454.

[89] *Ibid.*, p. 8. Previously, in light of the significant uncertainty as to whether the flushing of sediments from the KHEP reservoir would be permitted, Pakistan's experts had dealt with the effects of sediment separately.

[90] Using the nomenclature of Pakistan's expert report, in scenario K10 the minimum flow would be 10 cumecs. In scenario K40, the minimum flow would be 40 cumecs.

[91] Using the nomenclature of Pakistan's expert report, in scenario KH1E9, 10 percent of the flow would be diverted and 90 percent passed downstream. In scenario KH7E3, 70 percent would be diverted and 30 percent passed downstream.

[92] Under scenario KVT1, the dry season release between 11 October and 13 March would be 16 cumecs (or 13 cumecs in a dry year). Under scenario KVT2, the dry season release between 11 October and 13 March would be 14 cumecs (or 11 cumecs in a dry year). Under both scenarios, the shoulder season release between 14 March and 9 April and between 29 August and 10 October would be 52 cumecs (or 39 cumecs in a dry year). Between 10 April and 28 August (when flow in the river is abundant), neither scenario would mandate a minimum release. *See* Pakistan's Data Submission, Environmental Report, June 2013, p. 20.

fied.[93] The results show that the current baseline condition of the Kishenganga/Neelum at the Line of Control is in low category B (near pristine). Various high release scenarios, for example a 20-cumec minimum flow and above, would maintain the river in category C (moderately modified from natural). Other scenarios, including a 10-cumec minimum flow, would achieve high category D conditions (significantly modified from natural), while a minimum flow of 3.94 cumecs and a maximum diversion scenario would reduce the river to low category D.

57. Evaluating these results against international practice, Pakistan maintains that

> The UK, the USA and Australia vary slightly in the numbers they give, but generally they recommend that for the maintenance of good ecological condition in high-gradient rivers, daily flows should never fall below about 70% of natural. This number should increase to 80–90% in the dry season, with the percentage of flow remaining in the river being higher the lower the flow is. African studies suggest that 60–70% or more of natural dry season daily flow is needed to maintain a Category B river while more than 40% is needed for a Category C river.... African studies tend to recommend lower percentages than those of the UK, Australia and the USA.
>
> All of the scenarios would meet these recommended standards for wet season flows. K40 to K100, and KH1E9 and KH2E8 would meet the UK, USA and Australian recommendations for dry season flows ... and K20, KH3E7 and KVT1 would be somewhat below them .... These latter three would also meet or come close to meeting the African recommendations for Category B rivers, while K10, KH5E5. KH7E3 and KVT2 .... would meet the recommendation for a Category C river. The remaining three

---

[93] In detail, the A to F categories, which Pakistan considers are "intuitively understood by river specialists," are described as follows:

> Category A: pristine; natural. No development in the basin, or none that affects the river.
>
> Category B: near-pristine; near-natural. There may be areas of slight deterioration, but these are mostly localised and could easily be reversed with better catchment management. An example would be mild sewage pollution from a small village or town.
>
> Category C: moderately modified from natural. Changes will be noticeable, with the loss of some sensitive species, communities and/or habitats. The river could still appear quite attractive but would not be functioning as an optimally efficient ecosystem. If the deterioration was due to water quality changes, for instance, the river would probably not be attaining the level of health expected for recreational use.
>
> Category D: significantly modified from natural. This is a 'working river'. The emphasis could be on the use of the river water for other purposes (e.g. crop irrigation) and so little is available for river maintenance, or it could simply be an ecosystem that has not been considered in urban and rural development plans and so has declined due to lack of care. This would be seen as the lowest level that any river should ever fall to, and would be unacceptable in many areas and under many circumstances.
>
> Category E/F: critically modified. This would be seen as a very degraded and unhealthy river, unacceptable as a future state and requiring urgent remedial action. Alternatively, it could be a canalised or similarly unnatural one.

See Pakistan's Data Submission, Environmental Report, June 2013, pp. 40–41.

scenarios ... would be well below any of the internationally recognised standards reviewed here for high-altitude, high-gradient, scenic rivers.[94]

58. Pakistan concludes as follows:

> Scenarios K40–100, while offering the best prospects for river condition (high C), provide the lowest amounts of water for diversion to KHEP ....
>
> Scenarios KVT1, KVT2, KH3E7 and K20 offer slightly higher levels of diversion and a lower Category C river condition. This condition is lower than would generally be considered appropriate for such a river.
>
> The other scenarios would not generally be seen among river scientists as offering an acceptable condition for such a river.[95]

59. Turning to India's environmental submission, Pakistan is critical. First, in Pakistan's view, India's decision to analyse minimum flows only below 10 cumecs is inconsistent with the Court's request.[96] Second, Pakistan notes that the release of 4.25 cumecs mandated by the Indian Ministry of Environment & Forests "is not supported by any reasoning, either in the October 2012 decision of India's Ministry of Environment and Forests or in India's submission."[97] Finally, Pakistan considers that India's most recent environmental analysis suffers from the same problematic absence of methodology that, in Pakistan's view, characterized India's earlier environmental reports and failed to stand up to scrutiny during the cross-examination of India's experts.[98] Rather than provide new data, Pakistan argues that India has simply tried to "retrieve this situation" through a further report from the same experts, accompanied by additional peer reviews.[99]

60. Examining the results of India's environmental analysis, Pakistan's experts conclude that although India's experts adopted "a sound way to approach the assessment, as far as we can ascertain they do not carry this through into practice."[100] As the first step, Pakistan considers that the Indian model for flows in the Kishenganga/Neelum is ill-suited to assessing low flows and ignores standard practices in the field of ecohydraulics.[101] According to

---

[94] *Ibid.*, p. 42.

[95] *Ibid.*, p. 43.

[96] Pakistan's Comments on India's Response dated 21 June 2013 to the Court's Request for Further Information (Made Pursuant to Paragraph 463 of the Partial Award), para. 35.

[97] *Ibid.*, para. 36.

[98] *Ibid.*, para. 37.

[99] *Ibid.*, para. 37.

[100] Pakistan's Comments on India's Response dated 21 June 2013 to the Court's Request for Further Information (Made Pursuant to Paragraph 463 of the Partial Award), Annex E, Water Matters, Southern Waters, Hagler Bailly Pakistan, Streamflow Solutions, Beuster, Clarke & Associates, Fluvius "Kishenganga Dam Partial Award: Comment on the Environmental aspects of the Indian submission of 21 June 2013" (August 2013) (Pakistan's Comments, Environmental Report, August 2013), p. 25.

[101] According to Pakistan's report, India "uses a well-established and useful hydrodynamic model called MIKE 11, which is commendable. Execution of the modelling, however, is in our opinion not fit for purpose. First, it appears to be an application more suited for engineering

Pakistan, India's experts then consider only the survival of three fish species, and only on the basis of undocumented minimum (rather than optimum) depths for each species.[102] India's experts then proceed to link "maximum water depths with minimum fish depth requirements" in an approach that Pakistan's experts consider "obscure, simplistic and misleading."[103]

61. In sum, Pakistan submits that India's

> argument that a release of 4.25 m3/s will be adequate to avoid serious adverse impacts on the river is based upon selective references to a couple of parameters that give results favourable to India, completely ignoring the recognized methodologies for addressing these questions, and ignoring the obviously dramatic impact on the flows along the river at the LOC [Line of Control].[104]

India's Arguments

62. In approaching the question of the environmental effects of the KHEP, India first notes that the Indian Ministry of Environment & Forests has fixed a minimum flow of 4.25 cumecs for the KHEP.[105] According to India, this figure was set after a process that considers "all the relevant environmental and socio-economic factors" leading to results that vary from project to project.[106]

---

investigation of high and medium flows than an ecohydraulics investigation of low flows." *Ibid.*, p. 25. Pakistan's experts further note that "[i]n terms of conditions that the aquatic life would face through their 30 scenarios, DHI predicts maximum depths of questionable validity; DHI predicts velocities that are not subsequently used; and DHI does not predict at all how much wetted river bed would be left for the organisms to live in." *Ibid.*, p. 12.

[102] Pakistan's experts conclude that

> DHI uses one of their own data sets from 2012 and one other reference to define the habitat needs of three fish species. They do not specify the habitat needs of any other aquatic organisms. Their conclusions that a minimum depth of 0.5 m for trout and 0.25 m for loach are sufficient for survival are not supported by the data they present. Even if they are, DHI's targeting of the lowest depths fish were found at, rather than analysing their data to produce optimum depths, is not appropriate and would not promote fish survival.

Ibid., p. 25.

[103] According to Pakistan's Report,

> The terms 'sustain', 'maintain' and 'protect' the river ecosystem appear throughout the reports by DHI and some of their reviewers, linked to the recommended flow of 2.0 m3 s-1 or proposed one of 4.25 m3 s-1, but these are inappropriate conclusions for an ecosystem that would, under a release of about 4 m3 s-1 lose more than 60% of its flow in the dry season; that would experience a dry season that was several weeks to months longer; and that would lose more than a third of the wetted bed in the dry season and more than a third of that remaining would be unsuitable for trout. These would be such profound physical changes that it is unimaginable that there will be only a minimal response from the ecosystem.

Ibid., p. 25.

[104] Pakistan's Comments on India's Response dated 21 June 2013 to the Court's Request for Further Information (Made Pursuant to Paragraph 463 of the Partial Award), para. 42.

[105] India's Submission on the Information Requested by the Court in its Partial Award dated 18 February 2013, para. 4.6.

[106] *Ibid.*, para. 4.5.

India further notes that the 4.25-cumec minimum was fixed before India was aware that the Court would request further environmental data.[107]

63. India submits that the Parties are substantially in agreement with respect to the effects (or non-effects) that the diversion of the Kishenganga/Neelum at the KHEP would have. According to India, the Parties are in agreement that the KHEP (1) will not have an impact on any threatened species; (2) will not have any significant impact on mammals or birds; (3) will not have any significant impact on other terrestrial flora or fauna; (4) will not increase the risk of any human disease; and (5) will not have a significant impact on tourism.[108] In India's view,

> The only questions that remain, therefore, are whether the KHEP will cause significant adverse effects on fish and macro-invertebrates below the LOC, and possibly: whether the KHEP will have any significant adverse effects on the Musk Deer National Park if the effects of Pakistan's proposed dams are not considered; and whether the KHEP will cause significant degradation of the aquatic environment in certain stretches of the river (which Pakistan argued and India refuted in earlier pleadings) other than with respect to the alleged impact on fish and macro-invertebrates.[109]

64. In respect of these questions, India's experts conclude that neither changes in the sediment transport patterns nor in the water temperature will be significant enough to affect aquatic life. Although the KHEP will alter the flow of sediment in the Kishenganga/Neelum, the sluicing regime imposed by the Court's *Partial Award* will continue to pass approximately two-thirds of the river's sediment load downstream, and tributaries below the dam will also add sediments. In the view of India's experts, "[t]he reduction in sediment downstream of the KHEP dam resulting from sediment trapping will be minor," and in any event "native species have evolved in a dynamic environment, in which they periodically take refuge from high mainstem sediment concentrations by migrating up tributaries."[110] Similarly, India's experts conclude that because the KHEP has limited pondage and retains water for only a short period of time, "alteration in temperature and its impact becomes negligible."[111]

65. Having eliminated sedimentation and temperature as relevant factors, India's experts proceed to evaluate the flow regime in the reach between the KHEP and the Line of Control under a variety of scenarios. India's experts examined the riverbed profile at 12 sites at one kilometre intervals from the

---

[107] *Ibid.*, para. 4.6.

[108] *Ibid.*, para. 4.18; *see also ibid.*, paras. 4.9–4.17.

[109] *Ibid.*, para. 4.19.

[110] India's Submission on the Information Requested by the Court in its Partial Award dated 18 February 2013, Tab F, DHI (India) Water & Environment, "Environmental Studies for Assessment of Impacts of Minimum Flow Releases," June 2013 ("India's Data Submission, DHI Environmental Report, June 2013"), p. 21.

[111] *Ibid.*, p. 22.

KHEP to the Line of Control. At each site, India estimated the water level for minimum flows from 0 to 3 cumecs (at increments of 1 cumec), at 3.94 cumec, and from 4 to 10 cumecs (at increments of 0.25 cumecs), and replicated each calculation across the 99.99-percent, 90-percent, 75-percent, 50-percent, 25-percent and 10-percent dependable flow values.[112] India's experts then compared these depths to the minimum depths required by three umbrella species of fish: brown trout, snow trout and Tibetan stone loach. Based on these calculations, India's experts conclude that

> The reach between the dam and the first tributary is the most vulnerable to reductions in flow and the site at 6km downstream show the 90th and 99.9th percentile flows as dropping below the minimum 0.5 m depth specified for brown and snow trout. However, *Triplophysa* [Tibetan stone loach] would have sufficient depths even with a minimum flow of 2.0 m3/s. Thus, the analysis indicates depths would drop below minimum depth requirements for trout species about 10 percent of the time in the upper 5.7-km reach below the dam. Downstream of this point, contribution of runoff from the tributaries will dilute the effects of the dam on flow regime.[113]

66. Given these limited effects, India argues that "a minimum flow of 2.0 cumec will suffice to protect the three umbrella species in the stretch down to the LOC [Line of Control]."[114]

67. As to Pakistan's environmental submission, India argues "that Pakistan is urging the Court to require a far greater minimum environmental flow than is actually necessary to protect the riverine environment below the Line of Control."[115] At the broadest level, India objects to the attention that Pakistan devotes to concepts of sustainable development and "development space."[116] In India's view, this goes well beyond anything in the Treaty and attempts to arrogate to the Court an inappropriate and indeterminate role that cannot be reconciled with the precise balancing of rights in the Treaty. According to India, "the Court does not have the mandate to define the development future of India. The test that Pakistan proposes is one for planners and policy-makers of India, not for judges or arbitrators."[117]

68. India similarly objects to the use of the DRIFT methodology, which in its view, is an element of this expansive conception of the Court's role: "[DRIFT] is thus designed as a planning tool, not as a normative instrument."[118] India considers DRIFT to be "inappropriate for the purposes in ques-

---

[112] See cross-section depth charts at *ibid.*, pp. 73–102.

[113] *Ibid.*, p. 37.

[114] India's Submission on the Information Requested by the Court in its Partial Award dated 18 February 2013, para. 4.35.

[115] India's Comments on the Information Supplied by Pakistan on 21 June 2013, para. 6.4.

[116] *Ibid.*, paras. 6.5–6.7.

[117] *Ibid.*, para. 6.8.

[118] *Ibid.*, para. 6.9.

tion here" and considers it significant that DRIFT has not been used extensively in Asia, in light of the importance of local knowledge and expertise in the analytic process.[119] According to India, the DRIFT process employs too many indicators, including some that are not a concern,[120] on the basis of "unsubstantiated" response curves, to generate a single assessment of the river on the basis of "amorphously and arbitrarily described"[121] categories of "ecosystem integrity," a term which is never defined and which has no accepted scientific definition.[122] In India's view, "[e]nvironmental impacts cannot be combined in some sort of environmental cost-benefit analysis," and "summing cumulative impacts based on parameters whose relationships are not defined and unsupported by data is not a statistically, let alone ecologically, valid approach"—in particular in a trans-boundary context.[123] Finally, given the lack of instances in which the DRIFT approach has been previously tested and validated, in particular in Himalayan rivers, India submits that Pakistan's DRIFT software is a "work in progress."[124]

69. Beyond the question of whether DRIFT is an appropriate methodology for application to the Kishenganga/Neelum, India takes issue with a number of aspects of Pakistan's implementation of the approach. First, India objects to Pakistan's consideration of a mix of minimum release, percentage release, and variable release scenarios. As Pakistan makes use of a constant minimum flow on its own dams, India views this as the only permissible approach at the KHEP for, in its view, the Treaty limits the obligations on the Parties to "customary practices followed in similar situations" when assessing what measures must reasonably be taken (for instance, with respect to such

---

[119] *Ibid.*, paras. 6.9, 6.11. India's expert, Dr. Kondolf notes that

> DRIFT assessments are based largely on expert opinion. However, experts require actual data for the river in question, or their expertise may be irrelevant to the questions posed. If the data are sufficient and of good quality and the experts' training and experience are relevant to the river in question, the assessment may be good, but if experts are not experienced in the river system, and/or, most importantly, if data are lacking on which to base expert judgments, there is no reason to expect the assessment to be accurate.

India's Comments on the Information Supplied by Pakistan on 21 June 2013, Tab C, G. Mathias Kondolf, "Environmental Flows for the Kishenganga River Below KHEP," 13 August 2013, p. 5 ("India's Comments, Kondolf Report, August 2013"). In his view, in Pakistan's attempt to implement the methodology, "[t]he specialists who developed the 'response curves' relating habitat conditions to flow levels were not knowledgeable about the Kishenganga system (which is utterly different from the South African rivers on which DRIFT was developed), and had to work in the absence of adequate data on the river." India's Comments, Kondolf Report, August 2013, pp. 17-18.

[120] India notes, in particular, Pakistan's continued inclusion of otter populations and tourism in the DRIFT model, notwithstanding the Parties' agreement that these are not issues of concern. *See* India's Comments on the Information Supplied by Pakistan on 21 June 2013, para. 6.53.

[121] India's Comments on the Information Supplied by Pakistan on 21 June 2013, para. 6.12.

[122] *Ibid.*, para. 6.13.

[123] *Ibid.*, paras. 6.16, 6.21.

[124] *Ibid.*, para. 6.22.

matters as environmental pollution).[125] Second, India is of the view that the DRIFT model neglects important factors, including the significant role of tributaries in the ecosystem[126] and additional dams that Pakistan may construct downstream of the Line of Control.[127] Third, India submits that Pakistan's study was carried out with inadequate observation and lacked sufficient data to generate reliable response curves, in particular with respect to fish prevalence,[128] sediment transport,[129] and geomorphology.[130] India concludes that "Pakistan had almost no information on which to base a DRIFT approach, not to mention to evaluate it over time."[131]

70. Finally, apart from these shortcomings, India submits that "Pakistan's DRIFT study in fact supports MoEF [the Ministry of Environment & Forests]'s determination that a minimum flow of 4.25 is more than adequate."[132] If one looks not immediately at the Line of Control, but downstream at Pakistan's sites at Dudhnial and Nauseri, India argues, "a minimum flow of 3.94 cumec would result in no substantial impact on fish or macro-invertebrates at either site."[133]

F. Monitoring the Minimum Flow

Pakistan's Arguments

71. Pakistan submits that "[w]hatever flow regime is ordered by the Court, it is vital that it be accompanied by an adequate monitoring regime."[134] Pakistan therefore requests

> an order from the Court that the flow regime be supported by India providing to Pakistan, on a real time basis, (i) daily flow data from gauges recording the inflow into the KHEP reservoir and the outflow below

[125] *Ibid.*, paras. 6.33–6.34. Although the Treaty does not, of course, address the question of minimum flows, India submits that "[t]here is no reason to believe that this understanding of reasonableness would not also have been adopted by the Parties in relation to minimum flows if they had foreseen that minimum flow releases would be required." India's Comments on the Information Supplied by Pakistan on 21 June 2013, para. 6.34. India also submits that anything other than a constant minimum flow would place excessive administrative burdens on India, which would "inevitably require India to respond to Pakistani requests to justify its measurements, calculations and actual releases." India's Comments on the Information Supplied by Pakistan on 21 June 2013, para. 6.36.

[126] India's Comments on the Information Supplied by Pakistan on 21 June 2013, para. 6.52.

[127] *Ibid.*, paras. 6.42–6.43.

[128] *Ibid.*, para. 6.45.

[129] *Ibid.*, para. 6.46.

[130] *Ibid.*, para. 6.47.

[131] *Ibid.*, para. 6.48.

[132] *Ibid.*, para. 6.55.

[133] *Ibid.*, para. 6.56.

[134] Pakistan's Data and Information Submitted in Accordance with the Partial Award (Paragraphs 458–462), para. 30.

the KHEP dam, as well as (ii) the reservoir level, and (iii) with regular inspections permitted to Pakistan of the gauging stations.[135]

India's Arguments

72. India objects to Pakistan's request and submits that "such inspection on the territory of another State is unprecedented and beyond the scope of the inspection regime agreed by the Parties in the Treaty."[136]

73. In India's view, an additional inspection regime would be unwarranted and unnecessary. According to India, the Indus Waters Commission already serves the monitoring role that Pakistan seeks. India notes that "[t]here is no reason to believe on the basis of the historical record that this 'communication within the Commission cannot be relied upon as a means for transmitting accurate data in a timely manner'."[137]

74. The only basis for such a regime, in India's view, would be an assumption of bad faith that is neither justified under the circumstances nor permitted by international law.[138] Far from smoothing relations, the introduction of an additional mechanism "would risk exacerbating tensions between [the Parties]," as it would "override the cooperation mechanisms made available under the Treaty."[139]

75. India maintains that the Parties' exchange of data on flows and water utilization through the Commission under Articles VI and VIII of the Treaty has proceeded regularly and smoothly since its inception.[140]

III. Analysis OF the Court

A. Scope of the Parties' Submissions

76. As set out above (see paragraphs 17 and 18), each Party has voiced concerns regarding the scope and content of the other's response to the Court's request for the submission of additional data. The Court nevertheless considers both Parties' submissions to be reasonable and appropriate in light of the Court's request. Within the substantive areas laid out in Paragraphs 458–462 of the *Partial Award*, the scope of the data requested by the Court was deliberately left unrestrained, and it was to be expected that the Parties would wish to emphasize and draw attention to different aspects in light of their differing views on the issues remaining for the Court.

---

135 *Ibid.*, para. 32.

136 India's Comments on the Information Supplied by Pakistan on 21 June 2013, para. 7.3.

137 *Ibid.*, para. 7.7.

138 *Ibid.*, para. 7.21 citing *Affaire du Lac Lanoux (France v. Spain)*, Award of 16 November 1957, RIAA Vol. 12, p. 281 (French original), 1974 Yearbook of the International Law Commission, vol. 2, part 2, p. 194 (1976) (English translation) (Annex IN-LX-2).

139 India's Comments on the Information Supplied by Pakistan on 21 June 2013, para. 7.22.

140 *Ibid.*, para. 7.7.

77. Thus, the Court does not consider any part of the Parties' submissions made following the *Partial Award* to be inadmissible.

B. Determination of the Minimum Flow

1. Introduction

78. As indicated in paragraphs 455–457 of the *Partial Award*, the purpose of this Final Award is to fix the precise rate of the minimum flow to be preserved downstream of the KHEP.

79. The Court will approach this question by initially recalling the matters already decided in its *Partial Award*. It will then address the Parties' differences regarding the hydrologic data record for the Kishenganga/Neelum. Thereafter, the Court will assess, on the basis of the evidence before it, the effects that the KHEP is likely to have on agricultural and hydro-electric uses by Pakistan and on the downstream environment. The Court will then determine, taking into account these effects, the minimum flow. Finally, the Court will address Pakistan's request that the Court establish a monitoring regime.

2. The Court's *Partial Award* and its present task

80. The Court initially considers it appropriate to recall the key elements of its reasoning as set forth in the *Partial Award*.

81. Paragraph 15(iii) of Annexure D to the Treaty provides that:

> where a Plant is located on a Tributary of The Jhelum on which Pakistan has any Agricultural use or hydro-electric use, the water released below the Plant may be delivered, if necessary, into another Tributary but only to the extent that the then existing Agricultural Use or hydro-electric use by Pakistan on the former Tributary would not be adversely affected.

The Parties differed as to the meaning of this provision and, in particular, as to what would constitute a "then existing Agricultural Use or hydro-electric use by Pakistan." After considering each Party's interpretation of the phrase, the Court considered that the proper interpretation required elements of each Party's approach to be given effect:

> 433. The Court considers that neither of the two approaches to interpretation discussed above—the ambulatory and critical period approaches—is fully satisfactory. Rather, the proper interpretation of Paragraph 15(iii) of Annexure D combines certain elements of both approaches. The Court is guided by the need to reflect the equipoise which the Treaty sets out between Pakistan's right to the use of the waters of the Western Rivers (including the Jhelum and its tributary, the Kishenganga/Neelum) and India's right to use the waters of those rivers for hydro-electric generation once a Plant complies with the provisions of Annexure D.

> 434. Pakistan's relevant uses in this context are, in the Court's view, essentially its hydro-electric uses. As for agricultural uses, the Court notes the observation of India—not contradicted by Pakistan—that there are no significant existing agricultural uses of the Kishenganga/Neelum's main river. It appears to the Court that agricultural uses in the Neelum Valley are largely met by the tributary streams that feed the river.
>
> 435. Accordingly, the Court considers that its interpretative task consists of two principal elements. The Court must first establish the critical period at which the KHEP crystallized. Consistent with Part 3 of Annexure D (particularly the notice provisions of Paragraph 9), and using the same critical period criteria, the Court must then determine whether the NJHEP was an "existing use" that India needed to take into account at the time the KHEP crystallized. As shown below, the Court's determination of the critical period leads to the conclusion that the KHEP preceded the NJHEP, such that India's right to divert the waters of the Kishenganga/Neelum for power generation by the KHEP is protected under the Treaty.
>
> 436. Second, India's right to divert the waters of the Kishenganga/Neelum cannot be absolute. The premise underlying Paragraph 15(iii)—that Pakistan's existing uses are to be taken into account in the operation of India's Plants—remains a guiding principle (albeit not to the preclusive extent of the ambulatory approach). Paragraph 15(iii) protects Pakistan's right to a portion of the waters of the Kishenganga/Neelum throughout the year for its existing agricultural and hydro-electric uses.[141]

82. Pursuant to this interpretation, Pakistan's agricultural and hydro-electric uses are relevant at two distinct times: first, at the time the KHEP crystallized; and, second, on an ongoing basis throughout the operation of India's Plant.

83. With respect to the first point in time, the Court examined the actions and communications of the Parties from 2004–2006 and concluded that "India has a stronger claim to having coupled intent with action at the KHEP earlier than Pakistan achieved the same at the NJHEP, resulting in the former's priority in right over the latter with respect to the use of the waters of the Kishenganga/Neelum for hydro-electric power generation."[142]

84. With respect to the second relevant time and the ongoing accommodation of Pakistan's agricultural and hydro-electric uses in the operation of India's Plants, the Court reasoned as follows:

> 445. India's right under the Treaty to divert the waters of the Kishenganga/Neelum to operate the KHEP is subject to the constraints specified by the Treaty, including Paragraph 15(iii) of Annexure D as dis-

[141] Partial Award, paras. 433–436 (internal citations omitted).

[142] *Ibid.*, para. 437.

> cussed above and, in addition, by the relevant principles of customary international law to be applied by the Court pursuant to Paragraph 29 of Annexure G when interpreting the Treaty. As discussed in the following paragraphs, both of these limitations require India to operate the KHEP in a manner that ensures a minimum flow of water in the riverbed of the Kishenganga/Neelum downstream of the Plant.
>
> 446. Accepting that the KHEP crystallized prior to the NJHEP under the critical period analysis set out above, Pakistan nonetheless retains the right to receive a minimum flow of water from India in the Kishenganga/Neelum riverbed. That right stems in part from Paragraph 15(iii) of Annexure D, which gives rise to India's right to construct and operate hydro-electric projects involving inter-tributary transfers but obliges India to operate those projects in such a way as to avoid adversely affecting Pakistan's "then existing" agricultural and hydro-electric uses.[653] The requirement to avoid adverse effects on Pakistan's agricultural and hydro-electric uses of the waters of the Kishenganga/Neelum cannot, however, deprive India of its right to operate the KHEP—a right that vested during the critical period of 2004–2006. Both Parties' entitlements under the Treaty must be made effective so far as possible: India's right to divert water for the operation of the KHEP is tempered by Pakistan's right to hydro-electric and agricultural uses of the waters of the Western Rivers, just as Pakistan's right to these uses is tempered by India's right to divert the waters for the KHEP's operation. Any interpretation that disregards either of these rights would read the principles of Paragraph 15(iii) out of the Treaty, to one or the other Party's injury.[143]
>
> 653 The Court notes that it is quite possible, in view of the particular topography of the region, that the KHEP lies at the only location on the Kishenganga/Neelum where an inter-tributary transfer is economically viable (*see* India's Counter-Memorial, paras. 4.23, 4.70; Pakistan's Reply, paras. 1.4–1.10; India's Rejoinder, paras. 2.42). If this is true, the KHEP may be the only instance in which Paragraph 15(iii) becomes problematic, as any other inter-tributary transfer that may be contemplated on other tributaries of the Jhelum would result in returning waters to the Jhelum Main before crossing the Line of Control, thereby causing no adverse effect to any uses that Pakistan may have.

85. The Court further reasoned that "India's duty to ensure that a minimum flow reaches Pakistan also stems from the Treaty's interpretation in light of customary international law."[144] It discussed the role of customary international law, specifically principles of customary international environmental law, as follows:

> 452. It is established that principles of international environmental law must be taken into account even when (unlike the present case) interpreting treaties concluded before the development of that body of

143 *Ibid.*, paras. 445–446.

144 *Ibid.*, para. 447.

> law. The *Iron Rhine* Tribunal applied concepts of customary international environmental law to treaties dating back to the mid-nineteenth century, when principles of environmental protection were rarely if ever considered in international agreements and did not form any part of customary international law. Similarly, the International Court of Justice in *Gabčíkovo-Nagymaros* ruled that, whenever necessary for the application of a treaty, "new norms have to be taken into consideration, and ... new standards given proper weight."[664] It is therefore incumbent upon this Court to interpret and apply this 1960 Treaty in light of the customary international principles for the protection of the environment in force today.[145]
>
> 664 *Case concerning the Gabčíkovo-Nagymaros Project (Hungary/Slovakia)*, Judgment, *I.C.J. Reports 1997*, p. 7, p. 78.

86. The Court then noted both Parties' recognition of the need for a minimum flow of water downstream of the KHEP for environmental sustainability and concluded:

> 455. There is thus no disagreement between the Parties that the maintenance of a minimum flow downstream of the KHEP is required in response to considerations of environmental protection. The Parties differ, however, as to the quantity of water that would constitute an appropriate minimum; thus, the precise amount of flow to be preserved remains to be determined by the Court.[146]

87. Taken as a whole, the task facing the Court—now having the benefit of significantly more information and analysis from the Parties—is to determine a minimum flow that will mitigate adverse effects to Pakistan's agricultural and hydro-electric uses throughout the operation of the KHEP, while preserving India's right to operate the KHEP and maintaining the priority it acquired from having crystallized prior to the NJHEP. At the same time, in fixing this minimum flow, the Court must give due regard, in keeping with Paragraph 29 of Annexure G, to the customary international law requirements of avoiding or mitigating trans-boundary harm and of reconciling economic development with the protection of the environment.

88. Finally, as the Court emphasized in its *Partial Award*, the need for "stability and predictability in the availability of the waters of the Kishenganga/Neelum for each Party's use" [147] calls for the Court to fix the precise rate of the minimum flow, even though the operation of the KHEP and the development of Pakistan's agricultural and hydro-electric uses will likely not remain static, possibly changing over time.

145 *Ibid.*, para. 452.

146 *Ibid.*, para. 455.

147 *Ibid.*, para. 457.

3. The Parties' submissions on hydrology

89. Before turning to the place of agriculture, hydro-electric power and the environment in the Court's determination of the minimum flow, the Court must first recall the Parties' submissions on the hydrology of the Kishenganga/Neelum, as these estimates of the river's flow under different conditions underpin all other calculations.

90. Although the Parties have submitted extensive evidence highlighting the differences in methodology between them, what is striking for the Court is how similar the Parties' hydrologic estimates actually are. During the low-flow season, in particular, the Parties' estimates for average monthly flows rarely differ by a significant amount, and indeed Pakistan's data for flows at the Line of Control during the driest months of the year are slightly higher than India's own data. However, significant differences in estimated flows at the Line of Control occur for the very lowest flows. This is not unexpected, given the lack of observations at this point and the limited flow data from nearby sites, and the Court has borne these differences in mind in its determination.[148]

91. At this point, the Court finds it important to comment on one aspect of the Parties' method of gathering hydrological data. The Parties have disagreed as to the appropriateness of using data exchanged monthly (and not later than within three months of measurement) under Article VI of the Treaty, or data subsequently subjected to statistical analysis and quality control, as was done by Pakistan's Surface Water Hydrology Directorate. In the Court's view, there is no requirement that decisions by the Commission, the Neutral Expert, or Courts of Arbitration rendered in relation to the Treaty be based solely on data exchanged pursuant to Article VI(2). Indeed, the Court considers that quality assurance, if done in a transparent manner, is consonant with best practices in the field of hydrology. At the same time, the Court notes that after undertaking such analysis, Pakistan made no effort to share the published, quality-assured data for the Indus basin with India. In this respect, the Court is not satisfied with the suggestion that India can, for a fee, consult the published data in Pakistan's hydrologic yearbooks. The Court commends to the Parties the practice of undertaking quality assurance on hydrologic data collected on tributaries of the Indus and of sharing such data (together with sufficient elaboration to explain variations from data exchanged under Article VI) through the mechanisms of the Permanent Indus Commission.

---

[148] Taking the monthly average across the full 34-year range submitted by the Parties, India's data indicate average flows in the driest months of October through March of 46.57, 28.24, 22.63, 22.1, 26.14, and 53.72 cumecs, respectively. *See* India's Data Submission, CWC Report, June 2013, Annex IV. Over the same period, Pakistan's data indicate averages in the same months of 45.3, 30.9, 24.4, 23.3, 28.3, and 60.4 cumecs, respectively. *See* Pakistan's Data Submission, NESPAK Power Generation Report, June 2013, Appendix II.

As the task before the Court involves a limitation on a plant being built by India, the Court has elected to use India's flow data in subsequent calculations. For the avoidance of doubt, the Court wishes to make clear that this determination of the minimum flow does not depend on which flow data set is employed.

4. The downstream effects of the KHEP

92. The Court now turns, on the basis of the Parties' submissions, to the effects that the KHEP may have on Pakistan's agricultural and hydro-electric uses and on the environment downstream and past the Line of Control. In the subdivision thereafter, the Court reviews the interplay of those effects with India's rights under the Treaty as laid down in the *Partial Award*. The Court thus adopts a two-step approach: it will first consider the downstream effects of the KHEP in the light of the responses to its request for additional data, and will then decide how the Treaty, as interpreted in its *Partial Award*, should be applied to these facts.

(a) Pakistan's agricultural uses

93. Pakistan has submitted no data on current or anticipated agricultural uses of water from the Kishenganga/Neelum. Pakistan has, however, stated that future development in the Neelum Valley will be contingent on the increased use of lift irrigation from the river and on a move away from subsistence agriculture. The Parties disagree as to whether such potential future uses are relevant to the determination of the minimum flow.

94. As is shown by the passages in the *Partial Award* set out above (see paragraphs 81 to 84), the Court has already decided that—although no Pakistani agricultural use has been established as of the time at which the KHEP crystallized and acquired priority—Pakistan's Treaty rights in this regard will remain relevant to the continuing operation of the KHEP in conformity with Paragraph 15(iii). In now setting a fixed minimum flow, anticipated future agricultural uses would ordinarily feature in the Court's determination. However, as Pakistan has not submitted even an estimate of the likely scope of such development, much less evidence upon which the Court could rely, the Court is unable to take account of such potential uses and has reached its determination of the minimum flow on the basis of hydro-electric and environmental factors alone. Having done so, the Court is nevertheless confident that the minimum flow it prescribes below on the basis of other factors will ensure sufficient water in the river so as not to curtail significantly agricultural development in the Neelum Valley. In this connection, the Court recognizes the flow contribution to the main river of tributaries that lie downstream from the KHEP and past the Line of Control.

(b) Pakistan's hydro-electric uses

95. On the basis of the data submitted by Pakistan, it is apparent that the operation of the KHEP will reduce the potential energy generated by the NJHEP under nearly any minimum flow scenario. According to Pakistan's figures, even a 100-cumec minimum release at the KHEP would lead to a reduc-

tion in energy generation of 2 GWh at the NJHEP.[149] India does not challenge these calculations, but objects to Pakistan's flow scenarios, arguing that each would substantially reduce power generation at the KHEP and undermine the priority accorded to the KHEP in the Court's *Partial Award*.[150]

96. The Court will consider India's observation subsequently when discussing the implications of the priority accorded to the KHEP. With respect to the effects of the KHEP, the Court notes only that the NJHEP would be affected by any prescribed minimum flow and that the relationship between flow and energy generation is direct and approximately linear.

(c) *The downstream environment*

97. The Parties have submitted markedly different assessments of the environmental changes that would occur downstream of the KHEP. As set out in detail above (see paragraphs 54 to 70), Pakistan has undertaken a holistic assessment of the interaction of a range of environmental indicators and predicts moderate to serious changes in the ecosystem at the Line of Control, with the degree of change dependent on the rate of flow in the river.[151] India, in contrast, has based its assessment on the anticipated water depth and its effect on three umbrella species of fish, and concludes that there would be no effect on the aquatic environment with a flow of as low as 2 cumecs.

98. In the Court's view, the differences between the Parties must be viewed in light of the evolving science of predicting the environmental changes that would result from altered flow conditions. Pakistan has undertaken a far more extensive analysis, attempting to capture complex interactions within the river ecosystem. The Court notes that assessments of this nature are increasingly used by scientists and policymakers to bring a deeper understanding of ecology to bear on the management and development of river

[149] Pakistan's Data Submission, NESPAK Power Generation Report, June 2013, p. 12.

[150] *See generally* India's Comments on the Information Supplied by Pakistan on 21 June 2013, paras. 4.1 to 4.41; India's Comments, CEA Report, August 2013.

[151] In this Final Award, the Court refers at various points to a "minimum flow" and to an "environmental flow." For the sake of clarity, the Court notes the differences between these terms: an environmental flow is not necessarily a fixed minimum, affecting only the dry season, but is rather the flow regime anticipated to maintain environmental change resulting from infrastructure and development within the range considered acceptable under the circumstances of the river in question. Environmental flows may therefore be higher or lower, depending on those circumstances, and may include requirements affecting the high flow seasons of a river that cannot reasonably be described as a "minimum." Indeed, Pakistan's proposals of percentage or variable release flow regimes are examples of such environmental flows. It is only the particular characteristics of the Kishenganga/Neelum and the fact that low-season flows appear to be the principal drivers of ecological change that permit the Court to discuss environmental flows in terms of a fixed minimum. At the same time, because the Court's ultimate flow determination is based not solely on the environment, but also on hydro-electric power generation as required under the Treaty, the Court's decision fixes a "minimum flow." Insofar as this minimum flow serves to mitigate significant environmental harm, it also serves as an environmental flow without being synonymous with that term.

systems.[152] In contrast, India has carried out a simpler assessment, drawing its conclusions essentially from a single indicator—the habitat available for selected fish species.

99. The Court accepts that there is no single "correct" approach to such environmental assessments. For any given river or project, the correct approach will depend upon the existing state of the river, the magnitude of anticipated changes, the importance of the proposed project, and the availability of time, funding, and local expertise. For some situations, a simple assessment may indeed be preferred.

100. Nevertheless, for a project of the magnitude of the KHEP, the Court is of the view that an in-depth assessment of the type that Pakistan has attempted for these proceedings is a more appropriate tool for estimating potential changes in the downstream environment. This does not mean, however, that all of the critiques levelled at Pakistan's assessment are invalid. Certainly, the availability of additional data, more time, and more extensive local familiarity with the Kishenganga/Neelum would have produced a more instructive assessment. But, for the Court, these criticisms go to the degree of certainty to be ascribed to Pakistan's specific results, not to the general value of the attempt to apply contemporary international practices in a challenging setting. In contrast, the Court is not wholly satisfied that India's consideration of the water depths available for fish and its associated analysis offer adequate assurances in light of the complexity of the ecosystem in the Kishenganga/Neelum.

101. The Court acknowledges India's point that the environmental sensitivity that Pakistan urges in these proceedings does not match Pakistan's own historical practices, where the environmental flow has often been set at a low minimum, apparently using a "rule of thumb" approach. The Court will address the issue of the balance to be achieved between the environment and other uses of the Kishenganga/Neelum in subsequent subdivisions. With respect to the information brought to bear on decision-making, however, the Court sees no reason to remain wedded to past practices. On the contrary, more comprehensive and accurate information on the likely impacts of infrastructure projects can only benefit decision-making in both Pakistan and India. The Court urges both Parties to continue or expand their attention to environmental considerations at other projects, including the NJHEP. In the Court's view, such an approach is consistent with the acute need of both Parties for increased production of hydro-power. Indeed, the Court's ultimate decision on the minimum flow is informed by a deep awareness of the critical importance (and shortage) of electricity in both India and Pakistan. Meaningful development in this area need not be at odds with careful consideration of environmental effects.

---

[152] See the assessments discussed in Pakistan's Memorial, Environmental Report, May 2011, p. 2-12; and in Pakistan's Data Submission, Environmental Report, June 2013, pp. 27–30.

102. Turning to the results of Pakistan's assessment, the Court notes Pakistan's conclusion that an environmental flow of 40 cumecs or more would offer the "best prospects" for maintaining the river in the "high C" category (in terms of the condition categories discussed above at paragraph 56 and note 93), while a flow of 20 cumecs or a 70-percent release (or one of Pakistan's variable release scenarios) would produce a "lower Category C river condition." In Pakistan's view, "[t]he other scenarios would not generally be seen among river scientists as offering an acceptable condition for such a river."[153] In the Court's view, the grading of the condition of the Kishenganga/Neelum into categories, while helpful as shorthand, has the potential to suggest mathematical precision, and the Court recalls its earlier comments on the degree of uncertainty inherent in such an exercise. It nevertheless accepts that, if the aim is to moderate changes to the environment at or below the Line of Control, that would require an environmental flow in the Kishenganga/Neelum substantially higher than that which India has proposed in these proceedings.

103. Examining the Parties' hydrological tables alone, the Court also notes the sensitivity of the hydrograph at the Line of Control and, in particular, the flow duration curve to flow releases from the KHEP. For example, based on India's 1971–2004 10-day flow estimates, under current conditions, a flow of 12 cumecs at the Line of Control represents an exceptional event, with just nine occurrences of lower 10-day flows in 34 years. As the release from the KHEP drops below 12 cumecs, however, this exceptional condition would become more common, rising to 16 percent of the time with a release of 9 cumecs, and 30 percent of the time with an 8-cumec release. In other words, as the release falls below 12 cumecs, the lowest flows at the Line of Control progressively become the norm for a significant part of the dry season.

104. The Court provisionally concludes that an approach that takes exclusive account of environmental considerations—assessed in the absence of other considerations—would suggest an environmental flow of some 12 cumecs. The Court so estimates despite its appreciation of the uncertainties inherent in environmental projections in this case, based in part as they are on modelling and expert analysis, supported by limited local data. Since the Parties' data indicate that the effect of the KHEP on dry-season flows is the principal determinant of ecological change, the Court sees no reason to consider a percentage or variable release regime.[154]

---

[153] Pakistan's Data Submission, Environmental Report, June 2013, p. 43.

[154] This would, of course, not necessarily be the case with other river conditions, and the Court's decision in this respect should not be interpreted to equate an environmental flow with a fixed minimum flow. Under other circumstances, in particular where the difficulties of cooperation between the multiple State bureaucracies are not present, the appropriate environmental flow could well involve a regime of variable releases.

5. Maintaining the priority accorded to the KHEP in the *Partial Award*

105. As set out in the preceding section, the effects of the KHEP on the environment and on power generation by Pakistan (including at the NJHEP) both suggest the need for a higher minimum flow than India proposes, though one markedly less than what Pakistan appears to espouse. Taking environmental considerations alone, in the appreciation of the Court, would appear to suggest releasing a flow of some 12 cumecs downstream of the KHEP at all times. And if Pakistan's hydro-electric uses alone were to be taken into account, moderating the KHEP's effect on the NJHEP might entail even higher releases.

106. Assessing the effects of the KHEP, however, is only the first step of the task facing the Court. Two additional factors must be given effect in its determination of the minimum flow.

107. First, as India correctly observes,[155] the *Partial Award* accorded priority to the KHEP, stating as follows:

> having weighed the totality of the record, the Court concludes that India has a stronger claim to having coupled intent with action at the KHEP earlier than Pakistan achieved the same at the NJHEP, resulting in the former's priority in right over the latter with respect to the use of the waters of the Kishenganga/Neelum for hydro-electric power generation.[156]

108. While the Court also held that the KHEP must be operated in such a manner that "[b]oth Parties' entitlements under the Treaty must be made effective so far as possible," it stated clearly that "[t]he requirement to avoid adverse effects on Pakistan's agricultural and hydro-electric uses of the waters of the Kishenganga/Neelum cannot, however, deprive India of its right to operate the KHEP." [157] The right to operate the KHEP is a right to operate it effectively.

109. In balancing India's right to operate the KHEP effectively with the needs of the downstream environment, the Court has decided that, on the basis of the evidence currently available, India should have access to at least half of the average flow at the KHEP site during the driest months. In the Court's view, it would not be in conformity with the Treaty to fix a minimum release above half the minimum monthly average flow for the purpose of avoiding adverse effects on the NJHEP.

110. The Court's *Partial Award* did not make the operation of the KHEP immune from environmental considerations. Here, however, the Court consid-

[155] India's Submission on Information Requested by the Court in its Partial Award dated 18 February 2013, paras. 3.14, 5.5, 5.10, 5.29, 6.5, 6.11; India's Comments on the Information Supplied by Pakistan on 21 June 2013, paras. 1.15, 1.23, 1.29. 1.33–1.38, 4.8, 4.17, 4.31, 4.37, 6.88.

[156] Partial Award, para. 437.

[157] *Ibid.*, para. 446.

ers that a second factor becomes relevant. As India has recalled to the Court,[158] recourse to customary international law is conditioned by Paragraph 29 of Annexure G to the Indus Waters Treaty, which provides as follows:

> Except as the Parties may otherwise agree, the law to be applied by the Court shall be this Treaty and, whenever necessary for its interpretation or application, but only to the extent necessary for that purpose, the following in the order in which they are listed:
>
> (*a*) International conventions establishing rules which are expressly recognized by the Parties.
>
> (*b*) Customary international law.[159]

111. As the Court noted with approval in its *Partial Award*, the Tribunal in the *Iron Rhine Arbitration*, building on the judgment of the International Court of Justice in the *Case concerning the Gabčíkovo-Nagymaros Project*, held that principles of international environmental law must be taken into account even when interpreting treaties concluded before the development of that body of law.[160] In implementing this holding, the Court notes that the place of customary international law in the interpretation or application of the Indus Waters Treaty remains subject to Paragraph 29. Unlike the treaty at issue in *Iron Rhine*, this Treaty expressly limits the extent to which the Court may have recourse to, and apply, sources of law beyond the Treaty itself.

112. As the Court held in its *Partial Award*, "States have 'a duty to prevent, or at least mitigate' significant harm to the environment when pursuing large-scale construction activities."[161] In light of this duty, the Court has no difficulty concluding that the requirement of an environmental flow (without prejudice to the level of such flow) is necessary in the application of the Treaty. At the same time, the Court does not consider it appropriate, and certainly not "necessary," for it to adopt a precautionary approach and assume the role of policymaker in determining the balance between acceptable environmental change and other priorities, or to permit environmental considerations to override the balance of other rights and obligations expressly identified in the Treaty—in particular the entitlement of India to divert the waters of a tributary of the Jhelum. The Court's authority is more limited and extends only to mitigating significant harm. Beyond that point, prescription by the Court is not only unnecessary, it is prohibited by the Treaty. If customary international law were applied not to circumscribe, but to negate rights expressly granted

---

[158] India's Counter-Memorial, paras. 6.97, 6.104; India's Rejoinder, paras. 1.11–1.12, 2.9, 2.180.

[159] Treaty, Annexure G, para. 29.

[160] Partial Award, para. 452, *citing Arbitration Regarding the Iron Rhine* ("Ijzeren Rijn") *Railway between the Kingdom of Belgium and the Kingdom of the Netherlands*, Award, 24 May 2005, *PCA Award Series* (2007), para. 59; *Case concerning the Gabčíkovo-Nagymaros Project (Hungary/Slovakia)*, Judgment, *I.C.J. Reports 1997*, p. 7, p. 78.

[161] Partial Award, para. 451, *quoting Arbitration Regarding the Iron Rhine* ("Ijzeren Rijn") *Railway between the Kingdom of Belgium and the Kingdom of the Netherlands*, Award, 24 May 2005, *PCA Award Series* (2007), para. 59.

in the Treaty, this would no longer be "*interpretation or application*" *of* the Treaty but the substitution of customary law *in place of* the Treaty. Echoing the Court's caution in the *Partial Award*, the prioritization of the environment above all other considerations would effectively "read the principles of Paragraph 15(iii) [of Annexure D] out of the Treaty."[162] That Paragraph 29 does not permit.

113. The Court has also examined India's flow estimates, and has noted (see above at paragraph 103) the extreme sensitivity of low flows at the Line of Control to the release from the KHEP. The most severe winter in the 34-year record used by both India and Pakistan to assess impacts was 1974–75. The Court notes that, based on India's data, a minimum flow criterion of 9 cumecs at KHEP is a relatively severe criterion with respect to environmental flow, but would nevertheless be sufficient to maintain the natural flows through the December, January, February period of that winter.[163]

114. Examining the effect that a 9-cumec minimum would have on the KHEP, the Court notes that this would, on average, accord India 51.9 percent of the flow at the KHEP dam site during the month of January, and that India's portion of the flow would increase to more than 60 percent in November and February, and well over 75 percent in October and March. Preserving a minimum flow of 9 cumecs would result in a monthly reduction in energy generation at the KHEP of, on average, 19.5 GWh from October to March.[164] Although such a reduction is quite significant—in percentage terms—during the driest month of January, over the dry season as a whole it would amount to a 19.2 percent average reduction in energy generation.[165] On an annual basis, the average reduction in energy generation at the KHEP would be 5.7 percent. While India has not included an economic model for the KHEP in its submis-

[162] Partial Award, para. 446.

[163] The Court notes that Pakistan's environmental analysis, using Pakistan's flow estimates, is based on a classification of 'ecosystem integrity', with categories from A to E, as defined in paragraph 56, above. Pakistan summarises its estimated effects of different flow regimes in Figure 6.1 of its June 2013 submission and argues, based on environmental considerations, that category C (moderately modified from normal) is appropriate. *See* Pakistan's Data and Information Submitted in Accordance with the Partial Award (Paragraphs 458–462) at p. 7. The Court agrees that if environmental considerations were the sole consideration, category C would be desirable, and has noted above that a flow of 12 cumecs would be appropriate. However, given the right of India to develop hydropower, and the associated right to operate KHEP effectively, the Court considers that a high category D ('significantly modified from normal') represents an appropriate balance between the needs of the environment and India's rights for power generation.

[164] According to the formula for energy generation at the KHEP provided by India, *see* India's Submission on the Information Requested by the Court in its Partial Award dated 18 February 2013 at para. 3.10, and an average of India's flow data across the full 34-year range in which data is available, a 9-cumec minimum flow would reduce the KHEP's daily energy generation by 641,250 kWh in comparison with the 4.25-cumec minimum required by Indian law, resulting in a monthly average reduction of 19,451,250 kWh between October and March.

[165] The Court's figures for the net and percentage reduction in energy generation are calculated as against the 4.25-cumec minimum flow ordered by the Indian Ministry of Environment & Forests, which the Court takes as the baseline for its determination and for the purposes of this Award.

sions in these proceedings, the evidence before the Court does not establish that a 5.7 percent reduction in annual energy generation would render the KHEP economically unviable.

115. The Court therefore concludes that a minimum flow criterion of 9 cumecs is consistent with Pakistan's analysis of environmental flows, given the need to balance power generation with environmental and other downstream uses, and, based on India's data, would maintain the natural flow regime in the most severe winter conditions.

116. For all these reasons, the Court fixes the minimum flow to be released downstream from the KHEP dam at 9 cumecs.[166]

C. Review Mechanism

117. As the Court noted in its discussion of Pakistan's environmental submission, a degree of uncertainty is inherent in any attempt to predict environmental responses to changing conditions. In addition, flows at the Line of Control are un-gauged, and understandably subject to estimates which differ between the Parties, at least for the lowest flows. Uncertainty is also present in attempts to predict future flow conditions, and the Court is cognizant that flows in the Kishenganga/Neelum may come to differ, perhaps significantly, from the historical record as a result of factors beyond the control of either Party, including climate change.

118. In its *Partial Award*, the Court stated that "stability and predictability in the availability of the waters of the Kishenganga/Neelum for each Party's use are vitally important for the effective utilization of rights accorded to each Party by the Treaty (including its incorporation of customary international environmental law)."[167] This remains true. Indeed, the Court rejected a fully ambulatory interpretation of Paragraph 15(iii) of the Treaty for this reason. At the same time, the Court considers it important not to permit the doctrine of *res judicata* to extend the life of this Award into circumstances in which its reasoning no longer accords with reality along the Kishenganga/Neelum. The minimum flow will therefore be open to reconsideration as laid down in the following paragraph.

119. The KHEP should be completed in such a fashion as to accommodate possible future variations in the minimum flow requirement. If, beginning seven years after the diversion of the Kishenganga/Neelum through the KHEP, either Party considers that reconsideration of the Court's determination of the minimum flow is necessary, it will be entitled to seek such reconsideration through the Permanent Indus Commission and the mechanisms of the Treaty.

[166] For the avoidance of doubt, if at any time the flow in the Kishenganga/Neelum immediately upstream of the KHEP dam is below 9 cumecs, India is only required to release an amount equivalent to 100 percent of the inflow, until such time as the flow upstream of the KHEP dam again exceeds 9 cumecs.

[167] Partial Award, para. 457.

D. Monitoring

120. As recounted in greater detail above (see above at paragraph 71), Pakistan has requested that the Court establish a monitoring regime to permit it to evaluate India's compliance with the minimum flow fixed in this Award.

121. In the Court's view, the appropriate mechanism for the exchange of data and for the monitoring of the Parties' uses on tributaries of the Indus River is the Permanent Indus Commission. The Court recalls, in particular, that Article VI(1) of the Treaty already requires the Parties to exchange "(*a*) Daily (or as observed or estimated less frequently) gauge and discharge data relating to flow of the Rivers at all observation sites" and "(*b*) Daily extractions for or releases from reservoirs."[168] The Court is confident that the Parties will continue to do so, and that the data provided by India will include the necessary data relating to the KHEP. The Court further recalls that Article VIII(4) calls for the Commission to "undertake promptly, at the request of either Commissioner, a tour of inspection of such works or sites on the Rivers as may be considered necessary by him for ascertaining the facts connected with those works or sites."[169]

122. In light of the foregoing provisions, it is neither necessary, nor within the Court's purview, to instruct the Commission as to the manner in which it carries out its responsibilities or to mandate a special monitoring regime in implementation of this Award.

IV. Costs

123. Paragraph 26 of Annexure G to the Treaty provides as follows:

> In its Award, the Court shall also award the costs of the proceedings, including those initially borne by the Parties and those paid by the Treasurer.

124. In the Court's view, this arbitration presents difficult issues of treaty interpretation disputed by the Parties. The Parties' legal arguments were carefully considered, whether or not they prevailed, and the Parties acted with skill, dispatch, and economy in presenting their respective cases. The Court can therefore see no reason to depart from the principle, common in public international law proceedings, that each Party shall bear its own costs. The costs of the Court will also be shared equally.

---

[168] Treaty, Art. VI(1)(*a*)–(*b*).

[169] *Ibid.*, Art. VIII(4)(*d*).

V. Decision

Having considered the Parties' submissions, the Court of Arbitration unanimously decides:

A. In the operation of the KHEP:

(1) Subject to paragraph (2) below, India shall release a minimum flow of 9 cumecs into the Kishenganga/Neelum River below the KHEP at all times at which the daily average flow in the Kishenganga/Neelum River immediately upstream of the KHEP meets or exceeds 9 cumecs.

(2) At any time at which the daily average flow in the Kishenganga/Neelum River immediately upstream of the KHEP is less than 9 cumecs, India shall release 100 percent of the daily average flow immediately upstream of the KHEP into the Kishenganga/Neelum River below the KHEP.

B. Beginning 7 years after the diversion of water from the Kishenganga/Neelum River for power generation by the KHEP, either Party may seek reconsideration of the minimum flow in paragraph (A) above through the Permanent Indus Commission and the mechanisms of the Treaty.

C. This Final Award imposes no further restrictions on the operation of the KHEP, which remains subject to the provisions of the Treaty as interpreted in this Final Award and in the Court's *Partial Award*.

D. Each Party shall bear its own costs. The costs of the Court will be shared equally by the Parties.

Done at the Peace Palace, The Hague

Dated: 20 December 2013

[*Signed*]
Professor Lucius Caflich

[*Signed*]
Professor Jan Paulsson

[*Signed*]
Judge Bruno Simma

[*Signed*]
H.E. Judge Peter Tomka

[*Signed*]
Professor Howard S. Wheater FREng

[*Signed*]
Sir Franklin Berman KCMG QC

[*Signed*]
Judge Stephen M. Schwebel, Chairman

[*Signed*]
Mr. Aloysius Llamzon, Registrar

PART II

Award in the Arbitration regarding the Chagos Marine Protected Area between Mauritius and the United Kingdom of Great Britain and Northern Ireland

Award of 18 March 2015

PARTIE II

Sentence arbitrale relative au différend entre Maurice et le Royaume-Uni de Grande-Bretagne et d'Irlande du Nord concernant l'aire marine protégée des Chagos

Sentence du 18 mars 2015

Award in the Arbitration regarding the Chagos Marine Protected Area between Mauritius and the United Kingdom of Great Britain and Northern Ireland

Sentence arbitrale relative au différend entre Maurice et le Royaume-Uni de Grande-Bretagne et d'Irlande du Nord concernant l'aire marine protégée des Chagos

Jurisdiction over First Submission—Part XV, Articles 286 and 288 of United Nations Convention on the Law of the Sea ("UNCLOS")—challenge to UK declaration of marine protected area ("MPA") in parts of Chagos Archipelago, as UK not "coastal state" as defined by UNCLOS—dispute properly characterized as relating to territorial sovereignty over Chagos Archipelago—Article 298(*a*)(i) of UNCLOS indicates drafters' sensitivity to compulsory settlement of disputes for delimitation of maritime boundaries—question of sovereignty over land central to the dispute, not ancillary—Tribunal without jurisdiction to address sovereignty dispute, no jurisdiction over First Submission.

Jurisdiction over Third Submission—Mauritius submission to Commission on the Limits of the Continental Shelf—willingness by both Parties to proceed under "sovereignty umbrella"—no dispute, Tribunal need not rule on jurisdiction or merits.

Jurisdiction over Fourth Submission—compatibility of MPA with UK's obligations under UNCLOS and 1995 Fish Stocks Agreement—interpretation of Article 297 of UNCLOS and characterisation of MPA determinative of Tribunal's jurisdiction—undertakings made by UK to Mauritius on 23 September 1965 ("undertakings"), as per Articles 2(3) and 56(2) of UNCLOS, justify provisional conclusion of binding obligations subject to Tribunal's jurisdiction—neither MPA nor rights asserted by Mauritius limited to living resources of exclusive economic zone ("EEZ"), but relate broadly to preservation of marine environment and legal regime applicable to Chagos Archipelago and surrounding waters—Articles 63 and 64 of UNCLOS and 1995 Fish Stocks Agreement subject to jurisdictional exclusions in Article 297(3)(*a*) of UNCLOS.

Jurisdiction over Second Submission—Mauritius' rights as a coastal State under UNCLOS—for same reasons stated for First Submission, Tribunal without jurisdiction over Second Submission.

Obligation to exchange views under Article 283 of UNCLOS as challenge to jurisdiction—obligation concerning the means to resolve dispute, not an obligation to engage in negotiations or other forms of peaceful dispute resolution—should be applied without undue formalism as to manner and precision of views exchanged—conditions satisfied by Mauritius.

Merits—Mauritius' rights in the territorial sea, EEZ and continental shelf areas affected by the MPA—Parties' intent at conclusion of undertakings was a firm commitment—matter of international law upon Mauritian independence—agreements reaffirmed in correspondence between parties in decades following independence—general principle of international law of estoppel applicable—UK made repeated representations in respect of undertakings on: eventual return of Chagos Archipelago;

benefits of any minerals or oil discovered; existence and obligation of fishing rights—Mauritius reliance on undertakings—legitimate reliance on representation need not require binding unilateral declaration—UK estopped from denying binding effects of these commitments.

Interpretation and application of relevant UNCLOS articles—balance of authentic language versions of Article 2(3) of UNCLOS favours reading text as obligation—confirmed by object and purpose and negotiating history of UNCLOS—obligation limited to exercising sovereignty subject to general rules of international law, including to act in good faith.

Interpretation of 'due regard' under Article 56(2) of UNCLOS—interpreted as such regard for rights as is called for by the circumstances and the nature of the rights at issue—no universal rule of conduct—record shows lack of adequate consultation with Mauritius and a lack of appropriate balancing exercise of rights and interests arising from undertakings—UK in breach of Articles 2(3) and 56(2) of UNCLOS—MPA proclamation incompatible with UNCLOS.

Article 194 of UNCLOS applicable to MPA—obligation in Article 194(1) is purely prospective, no violation found by UK—Article 194(4) obligation to 'refrain from unjustifiable interference' functionally equivalent to 'due regard' or good faith—declaration of MPA incompatible with Article 194(4) and Mauritius' fishing activities in the territorial sea.

Tribunal finding relates to the manner of MPA establishment, not substance—open to Parties to enter into negotiations for mutually satisfactory arrangement.

Compétence pour statuer sur le premier moyen – Partie XV, articles 286 et 288 de la Convention des Nations Unies sur le droit de la mer (« Convention ») – contestation de la proclamation par le Royaume-Uni d'une aire marine protégée dans certaines parties de l'archipel des Chagos, le Royaume-Uni n'étant pas « l'État côtier » au sens de la Convention – le différend est dûment qualifié comme étant lié à la souveraineté territoriale sur l'archipel des Chagos – le sous-alinéa a) i) du paragraphe 1 de l'article 298 de la Convention montre que les rédacteurs étaient attachés au règlement obligatoire des différends en matière de délimitation maritime – la question de la souveraineté sur le territoire n'est pas accessoire, mais bien au cœur du différend – le Tribunal n'est pas compétent pour connaître des différends relatifs à la souveraineté et est dès lors inhabile à statuer sur le premier moyen.

Compétence relative au troisième moyen – demande déposée par Maurice auprès de la Commission des limites du plateau continental – volonté des deux parties d'aborder la question dans la perspective de la souveraineté – en l'absence de différend, le Tribunal n'a à statuer ni sur la compétence ni sur le fond.

Compétence relative au quatrième moyen – compatibilité de l'établissement de l'aire marine protégée avec les obligations qui incombent au Royaume-Uni au titre de la Convention et de l'Accord sur les stocks de poissons de 1995 – l'interprétation de l'article 297 de la Convention et la qualification de l'aire marine protégée déterminent la compétence du Tribunal – les engagements pris par le Royaume-Uni envers Maurice le 23 septembre 1965 (« les engagements »), conformément aux articles 2, paragraphe 3, et 56, paragraphe 2, de la Convention, justifient la conclusion provisoire relative à la présence d'obligations contraignantes relevant de la compétence du Tribunal – ni la question de l'aire marine protégée, ni les droits revendiqués par Maurice ne se limitent aux ressources biologiques de la zone économique exclusive (ZEE), mais se rapportent de façon générale à la préservation de l'environnement marin et au régime juridique applicable à l'archipel des Chagos et aux eaux environnantes – les articles 63 et 64 de la Convention et l'Accord sur les stocks de poissons de 1995 sont assujettis aux exclusions juridictionnelles prévues au paragraphe 3 a) de l'article 297 de la Convention.

Compétence relative au deuxième moyen – droits de Maurice en tant qu'État côtier au sens de la Convention – pour les raisons évoquées en ce qui concerne le premier moyen, le Tribunal n'est pas compétent pour statuer sur le deuxième.

Obligation de procéder à des échanges de vues, conformément à l'article 283 de la Convention, invoquée à titre d'exception d'incompétence – il s'agit d'une obligation concernant les moyens de régler un différend, et non d'une obligation d'engager des négociations ou d'autres formes de règlement pacifique des différends – cette obligation devrait être appliquée sans formalisme excessif quant à la manière et à la précision des vues échangées – Maurice a satisfait à ces conditions.

Fond – droits de Maurice sur sa mer territoriale, sa ZEE et les parties du plateau continental comprises dans l'aire marine protégée – lors de la conclusion des engagements, l'intention des parties était de conclure un accord ferme – la question relève du droit international depuis l'indépendance de Maurice – accords confirmés dans la correspondance échangée entre les parties au cours des décennies qui ont suivi l'indépendance – le principe général de droit international de l'estoppel s'applique – le Royaume-Uni a réitéré à maintes reprises ses engagements relatifs à la restitution de l'archipel des Chagos, aux avantages découlant de la découverte de minerais ou de pétrole, et à l'existence de droits de pêche opposables – Maurice a fait fond sur ces engagements – une déclaration n'a pas besoin d'être unilatérale et formelle pour qu'il soit légitime de s'y fier – le Royaume-Uni est irrecevable à nier le caractère contraignant de ces engagements.

Interprétation et application des dispositions de la Convention – les différentes versions linguistiques officielles du paragraphe 3 de l'article 2 de la Convention tendent à en confirmer le caractère obligatoire – l'objet et le but de la Convention et l'historique des négociations y afférentes confirment cette interprétation – obligation limitée à l'exercice de la souveraineté dans les conditions prévues par les règles générales du droit international, y compris celle d'agir de bonne foi.

Interprétation de l'expression « tient dûment compte » au paragraphe 2 de l'article 56 de la Convention – expression interprétée comme évoquant la prise en considération des droits dans la mesure justifiée par les circonstances et la nature des droits en question – absence de règle de conduite universelle – le dossier révèle l'insuffisance des consultations effectuées auprès de Maurice et un déséquilibre dans l'exercice des droits et des avantages découlant des engagements – le Royaume-Uni a contrevenu aux articles 2, paragraphe 3, et 56, paragraphe 2, de la Convention – la proclamation de l'aire marine protégée était contraire à la Convention.

Application de l'article 194 de la Convention à la proclamation de l'aire marine protégée – l'obligation énoncée au paragraphe 1 de l'article 194 est purement prospective et n'a pas été violée par le Royaume-Uni – l'obligation de « s'abstenir de toute ingérence injustifiable », énoncée au paragraphe 4 de l'article 194, s'apparente, sur le plan fonctionnel, à celle de « tenir dûment compte » ou d'agir de bonne foi – la proclamation de l'aire marine protégée était incompatible avec l'article 194, paragraphe 4, de la Convention et les activités de pêche menées par Maurice dans sa mer territoriale.

La conclusion du Tribunal a trait à la façon dont l'aire marine protégée a été établie et non au fond – il est loisible aux parties d'entamer des négociations en vue de trouver une solution satisfaisante pour l'une et l'autre.

* * * * *

---

* Professor James Crawford ceased to act as Counsel for Mauritius on 9 November 2014.

** Dominic Grieve QC, MP held the office of Attorney General until 15th July 2014.

IN THE MATTER OF THE CHAGOS MARINE PROTECTED AREA ARBITRATION

-before-

AN ARBITRAL TRIBUNAL CONSTITUTED UNDER ANNEX VII OF THE UNITED NATIONS CONVENTION ON THE LAW OF THE SEA

-between-

THE REPUBLIC OF MAURITIUS

-and-

THE UNITED KINGDOM OF GREAT BRITAIN AND NORTHERN IRELAND

AWARD

The Arbitral Tribunal:

Professor Ivan Shearer AM, President
Judge Sir Christopher Greenwood CMG, QC
Judge Albert Hoffmann
Judge James Kateka
Judge Rüdiger Wolfrum

Registry:

Permanent Court of Arbitration

18 March 2015

*** Mr. Suresh Chandre Seeballuck and Dr. Jaya Nyamrajsing Meetarbhan are no longer in the public service since January 2015.

Agents, Counsel, and other Representatives of the Parties

Agent of Mauritius:

— Mr. Dheerendra Kumar Dabee GOSK, SC, Solicitor-General of Mauritius

Agent of the United Kingdom

— Ms. Alice Lacourt, Legal Counsellor, Foreign and Commonwealth Office *Replacing* Mr. Christopher Whomersley CMG, Deputy Legal Adviser, Foreign and Commonwealth Office

Deputy Agent of Mauritius:

— Ms. Aruna Devi Narain, Parliamentary Counsel

Deputy Agent of the United Kingdom

— Ms. Nicola Smith, Assistant Legal Adviser, Foreign and Commonwealth Office *Replacing* Ms. Margaret Purdasy, Assistant Legal Adviser, Foreign and Commonwealth Office

Counsel for Mauritius

— Professor James Crawford AC, SC, FBA[*], University of Cambridge

— Professor Philippe Sands QC, Matrix Chambers

— Ms. Alison Macdonald, Matrix Chambers

— Mr. Paul Reichler, Foley Hoag LLP

— Mr. Andrew Loewenstein, Foley Hoag LLP

Counsel for the United Kingdom

— The Rt. Hon. Dominic Grieve QC, MP[**], Her Majesty's Attorney General

— Professor Alan Boyle, University of Edinburgh and Essex Court Chambers

— Ms. Penelope Nevill, 20 Essex Street Chambers

— Ms. Amy Sander, Essex Court Chambers

— Sir Michael Wood KCMG, 20 Essex Street Chambers

— Mr. Samuel Wordsworth QC, Essex Court Chambers

Junior Counsel for the United Kingdom

— Mr. Eran Sthoeger

Representatives of Mauritius

— Mr. Suresh Chandre Seeballuck GOSK***

— H.E. Dr. Jaya Nyamrajsing Meetarbhan GOSK***, Ambassador and Permanent Representative of the Republic of Mauritius to the United Nations

— Ms. Shiu Ching Young Kim Fat, Ministry of Foreign Affairs, Regional Integration and International Trade

Representatives of the United Kingdom

— Ms. Jo Bowyer, Foreign and Commonwealth Office

— Ms. Mina Patel, Foreign and Commonwealth Office

— Ms. Neelam Rattan, Foreign and Commonwealth Office

— Ms. Rebecca Raynsford, Attorney General's Office

— Mr. Douglas Wilson, Attorney General's Office

Advisers to Mauritius

— Ms. Elizabeth Wilmshurst CMG, Doughty Street Chambers

— Dr. Douglas Guilfoyle, University College London

Junior Counsel for Mauritius

— Mr. Yuri Parkhomenko, Foley Hoag, LLP

— Mr. Remi Reichhold, Legal Assistant, Matrix Chambers

— Mr. Fernando L. Bordin

Assistants to Mauritius

— Mr. Rodrigo Tranamil, Foley Hoag, LLP

— Ms. Nancy Lopez, Foley Hoag, LLP

TABLE OF CONTENTS

TABLE OF MAPS

Glossary of Defined Terms / List of Abbreviations

1965 Agreement	The agreement between the United Kingdom and the Mauritius Council of Ministers in 1965 to the detachment of the Chagos Archipelago
1995 Fish Stocks Agreement	The Agreement for the Implementation of the Provisions of the United Nations Convention on the Law of the Sea of 10 December 1982 Relating to the Conservation and Management of Straddling Fish Stocks and Highly Migratory Fish Stocks of 4 August 1995
BIOT	The British Indian Ocean Territory
CHOGM	The Commonwealth Heads of Government Meeting
CLCS	The Commission on the Limits of the Continental Shelf
Conference	The Third UN Conference on the Law of the Sea
Convention	The 1982 United Nations Convention on the Law of the Sea
EPPZ	Environmental Protection and Preservation Zone
FCMZ	Fisheries Conservation and Management Zone
FCO	The Foreign and Commonwealth Office of the United Kingdom
ICJ	The International Court of Justice
ILC	The International Law Commission
ILC Guiding Principles	The International Law Commission's Guiding Principles Applicable to Unilateral Declarations of States Capable of Creating Legal Obligation
IOTC	The Indian Ocean Tuna Commission
IOTC Agreement	The Agreement for the Establishment of the Indian Ocean Tuna Commission
ITLOS	The International Tribunal for the Law of the Sea
Lancaster House Meeting	The meeting held at Lancaster House on the afternoon of 23 September 1965
Lancaster House Undertakings	Points (i) through (viii) of paragraph 22 of the final record of the Lancaster House Meeting of 23 September 1965
Mauritius	The Republic of Mauritius
MLP	The Mauritius Labour Party
MPA	Marine Protected Area
PCA	The Permanent Court of Arbitration

Public Consultation	The public consultation process carried out by the United Kingdom regarding the potential creation of the MPA
UNCLOS	The 1982 United Nations Convention on the Law of the Sea
United Kingdom	The United Kingdom of Great Britain and Northern Ireland

Chapter I. Introduction

A. The Parties

1. The Applicant is the Republic of Mauritius ("Mauritius"). Mauritius became an independent State on 12 March 1968, prior to which it was a colony of the United Kingdom of Great Britain and Northern Ireland (the "United Kingdom"). Mauritius was previously a French colony from 1715 until 1814, at which time France ceded it to the United Kingdom.

2. The Respondent is the United Kingdom, which exercised colonial rule over Mauritius until its independence. The United Kingdom continues to administer the Chagos Archipelago, previously a dependency of the colony of Mauritius, as the British Indian Ocean Territory ("BIOT"). The BIOT was established on 8 November 1965.

3. Mauritius is represented in these proceedings by its Agent, Mr. Dheerendra Kumar Dabee GOSK, SC, Solicitor-General of the Republic of Mauritius and its Deputy Agent, Ms. Aruna Devi Narain.

4. The United Kingdom is represented in these proceedings by its Agent, Ms. Alice Lacourt, Legal Counsellor at the Foreign and Commonwealth Office (the "FCO"), who replaced Mr. Christopher A. Whomersley CMG, Deputy Legal Adviser, as Agent on 5 June 2014. The United Kingdom is further represented by its Deputy Agent, Ms. Nicola Smith, who replaced Ms. Margaret Purdasy in this position on 21 January 2015.

B. The Dispute

5. The dispute between the Parties concerns a decision of the United Kingdom, taken on 1 April 2010, by which it established a Marine Protected Area ("MPA") around the Chagos Archipelago, which is administered by the United Kingdom as the BIOT. The MPA extends to a distance of 200 nautical miles from the baselines of the Chagos Archipelago and covers an area of more than half a million square kilometres.

6. According to Mauritius, the establishment of the MPA by the United Kingdom violates the 1982 United Nations Convention on the Law of the Sea (the "Convention" or "UNCLOS"), to which Mauritius and the United Kingdom are party, and other rules of international law.

7. Mauritius contends that the United Kingdom is not entitled to declare an MPA or other maritime zones because it is not the "coastal State" within the meaning of, *inter alia*, Articles 2, 55, 56 and 76 of the Convention. Alternatively, Mauritius contends that the United Kingdom is not entitled unilaterally to declare an MPA over the objections of Mauritius in light of the undertakings made by the United Kingdom at the time of the detachment of the Chagos Archipelago, insofar as Mauritius has been endowed with certain rights of a "coastal State".

8. Mauritius further contends that the MPA is fundamentally incompatible with the rights and obligations provided for by the Convention, including the fishing rights of Mauritius in regard to the Chagos Archipelago and its surrounding waters. Mauritius alleges that the United Kingdom has also breached its obligations under the Convention and international law with respect to consultation and co-operation.

9. In its final submissions, Mauritius also contends that it was entitled to file Preliminary Information regarding the continental shelf surrounding the Chagos Archipelago with the United Nations Commission on the Limits of the Continental Shelf ("CLCS") and that the United Kingdom should not be permitted to prevent the CLCS from making recommendations in respect of any further submissions that Mauritius may make regarding the Chagos Archipelago.

10. In bringing these proceedings Mauritius has invoked Articles 286 and 287 of the Convention.

11. The United Kingdom challenges the Tribunal's jurisdiction over all aspects of the dispute. The United Kingdom first raised this challenge in its Preliminary Objections and at a hearing before the Tribunal on 11 January 2013 regarding the procedure to consider jurisdictional objections. By Order of 15 January 2013, the Tribunal rejected the United Kingdom's request for a separate procedural phase and decided that jurisdictional objections would be considered together with the proceedings on the merits.

12. According to the United Kingdom, these proceedings are an attempt by Mauritius to construct a case under the Convention in order to bring a dispute concerning sovereignty over the Chagos Archipelago within the jurisdiction of the Tribunal, which is "artificial and baseless."[1] Furthermore, the United Kingdom contends that Mauritius has failed to meet its obligation to consult with the United Kingdom concerning the violations of the Convention of which Mauritius complains.

13. With respect to the merits of Mauritius' claims, the United Kingdom asserts that it acquired sovereignty over the Chagos Archipelago in 1814, continued to exercise sovereignty at all relevant times, and is therefore unquestionably the coastal State for the purposes of the Convention. The United Kingdom also denies that the MPA is incompatible with the rights of Mauritius under the Convention. Finally, the United Kingdom contends that it has complied fully with its obligations under the Convention and international law to consult and co-operate.

* * *

[1] The United Kingdom's Counter-Memorial, para. 1.10.

CHAPTER II. PROCEDURAL HISTORY

A. The Initiation of this Arbitration

14. By its *Notification and Statement of Claim* dated 20 December 2010, Mauritius initiated arbitration proceedings against the United Kingdom pursuant to Article 287 of the Convention and in accordance with Article 1 of Annex VII to the Convention.

B. The Constitution of the Arbitral Tribunal

15. In its *Notification and Statement of Claim*, Mauritius appointed Judge Rüdiger Wolfrum, a German national, as a member of the Tribunal in accordance with Article 3(*b*) of Annex VII to the Convention. On 19 January 2011, the United Kingdom appointed Judge Sir Christopher Greenwood CMG, QC, a British national, as a member of the Tribunal in accordance with Article 3(*c*) of Annex VII to the Convention.

16. Owing to disagreement between the Parties regarding the appointment of the remaining three members of the Tribunal, Mauritius sent a letter dated 21 February 2011 to the President of the International Tribunal for the Law of the Sea ("ITLOS"). Therein, Mauritius requested that the President of ITLOS appoint the remaining three members of the Tribunal in accordance with Article 3(*e*) of Annex VII to the Convention.

17. On 25 March 2011, the President of ITLOS appointed Judge James Kateka, a Tanzanian national, and Judge Albert Hoffmann, a South African national, as arbitrators, and Professor Ivan Shearer AM, an Australian national, as arbitrator and President of the Tribunal.

18. On 31 March 2011, the President of the Tribunal wrote to the Permanent Court of Arbitration (the "PCA") to ascertain whether the PCA was willing to serve as Registry for the proceedings. The PCA responded affirmatively by letter of the same date. By communications dated 4 and 6 April 2011, respectively, the United Kingdom and Mauritius confirmed that they had no objection to the PCA serving as Registry for the proceedings. The PCA's appointment was subsequently formalized on 21 March 2012 by the conclusion of Terms of Appointment.

C. The Challenge to the Appointment of Judge Greenwood and its Dismissal

19. On 2 May 2011, the PCA transmitted to the Parties the Declarations of Acceptance and Statements of Impartiality and Independence of the five arbitrators. An additional Disclosure Statement submitted by Judge Greenwood was also transmitted under the same cover.

20. On 19 May 2011, Mauritius requested further disclosure from Judge Greenwood concerning his relationship with the Government of the United Kingdom. Judge Greenwood provided a Further Disclosure Statement on 20 May 2011, in which he reiterated his independence and commitment to act with complete impartiality.

21. On 23 May 2011, Mauritius conveyed its intention to challenge the appointment of Judge Greenwood. On 30 May 2011, the Tribunal communicated to the Parties a proposed procedure and timetable for resolving the challenge to Judge Greenwood, in which the remaining members of the Tribunal would decide the challenge. The United Kingdom and Mauritius indicated their consent to this approach on 3 and 8 June 2011, respectively.

22. Between June and August 2011, Mauritius and the United Kingdom made submissions in respect of the challenge, in accordance with the agreed procedure.

23. On 4 October 2011, the Tribunal held a hearing on the challenge at the Peace Palace in The Hague, the Netherlands. On 13 October 2011, the Tribunal issued its decision (without reasons) to dismiss the challenge to the appointment of Judge Greenwood. The Tribunal subsequently provided written reasons in respect of its decision on 30 November 2011.

D. The Adoption of the Terms of Appointment and Rules of Procedure

24. On 6 January 2012, the Tribunal circulated draft Terms of Appointment for the proceedings and invited the Parties' comments. The Tribunal also invited the Parties to seek agreement on the procedural rules and on a schedule for the further conduct of the proceedings.

25. Following an exchange of correspondence, the Parties and the Tribunal reached agreement on the Terms of Appointment, which were finalized and signed on 21 March 2012.

26. Between January and March 2012, the Parties and the Tribunal exchanged correspondence concerning the draft Rules of Procedure, in particular with respect to the hearing venue and the procedure in the event of a request to consider objections to the Tribunal's jurisdiction in a preliminary procedural phase. Following consultation with the Parties, the Tribunal finalized and adopted the Rules of Procedure on 29 March 2012.

27. On 13 December 2012, following consultation with the Parties, the Tribunal issued Procedural Order N° 1, specifying in greater detail the procedure to be followed with respect to submissions.

E. The United Kingdom's Application for the Bifurcation of the Proceedings and the Parties' Written Submissions

28. On 1 August 2012, Mauritius submitted its *Memorial.*

29. On 31 October 2012, the United Kingdom submitted its *Preliminary Objections to Jurisdiction*, in which it requested, among other things, the bifurcation of proceedings to address its jurisdictional objections as a preliminary matter and a separate hearing on the question of bifurcation. On 21 November 2012, Mauritius submitted its *Written Observations on the Question of Bifurcation*, in which it opposed the bifurcation of the proceedings.

30. On 21 December 2012, the United Kingdom submitted a *Written Reply of the United Kingdom to the Written Observations of Mauritius* on the question of bifurcation.

31. On 11 January 2013, the Tribunal held a hearing on the question of bifurcation in Dubai, United Arab Emirates. On 15 January 2013, following the hearing, the Tribunal issued Procedural Order N° 2, in which it rejected the United Kingdom's request for bifurcation and decided that jurisdictional objections would be considered with the proceedings on the merits.

32. On 17 January 2013, the United Kingdom requested an extension of time for the submission of its *Counter-Memorial.* The Parties subsequently agreed to an amended schedule for written submissions, which was conveyed to the Tribunal by a letter dated 30 January 2013. In accordance with this amended schedule, the United Kingdom submitted its *Counter-Memorial* on 15 July 2013.

33. On 15 November 2013, Mauritius requested an extension of time until 18 November 2013 to file its *Reply.* The Tribunal granted this request on 16 November 2013 on the basis that an equivalent extension was granted to the United Kingdom with respect to the filing of its *Rejoinder.* Mauritius submitted its *Reply* on 18 November 2013.

34. On 17 March 2014, the United Kingdom submitted its *Rejoinder.*

F. Redactions to Documents in Annex 185 to Mauritius' Reply

35. In its *Reply*, Mauritius noted that certain documents set out in Annex 185 thereto contained redactions. These documents had originally been disclosed by the United Kingdom in the course of separate judicial proceedings in the English courts to which Mauritius was not a party. Mauritius invited the United Kingdom to confirm that it would "submit, along with its

Rejoinder, unredacted copies of the documents at Annex 185" and reserved its right to make an application to the Tribunal in this respect.[2]

36. On 30 November 2013, the United Kingdom responded to Mauritius' invitation and indicated that it would revert in due course regarding the appropriateness of additional disclosure. The United Kingdom confirmed, in any event, that no redactions had been made for the purpose of suppressing evidence which might be unhelpful to it in these proceedings. The United Kingdom further asserted that it had "fully complied with international law practices and the applicable Rules of Procedure" in its production of documents.

37. On 13 December 2013, Mauritius invited the United Kingdom to confirm the basis on which it had made redactions to the documents in Annex 185 to Mauritius' *Reply* and whether it maintained any or all of those redactions in the present proceedings. On 19 December 2013, the United Kingdom repeated the contents of its letter of 30 November 2013 and stated that it would consider the extent to which any redactions could be removed in the course of drafting its *Rejoinder*.

38. On 9 January 2014, the Tribunal wrote to the Parties, recalling the Parties' correspondence and urging the United Kingdom to remove "all redactions that are not strictly required on grounds of irrelevancy or legal professional privilege" and to indicate the basis for each redaction that it wished to maintain.

39. On 11 February 2014, Mauritius wrote to the Tribunal, requesting an indication from the United Kingdom regarding the status of its review of the redacted documents. In response, on 14 February 2014, the United Kingdom noted that "there are a large number of redactions to be considered, and the process needs to be carried out in consultation with the counsel who represented the Government in the proceedings in the United Kingdom courts" and indicated that it would revert as soon as possible. On 19 February 2014, the Tribunal requested the United Kingdom to complete its review of all of the redacted documents by 3 March 2014.

40. On 3 March 2014, the United Kingdom provided a version of the documents contained in Annex 185 with some redactions removed, while maintaining a number of redactions "principally on the grounds of legal professional privilege, relationships with third countries and national security." By the same letter, the United Kingdom requested Mauritius to confirm that it had conducted a review of its own internal documents and that all relevant documents had been disclosed.

41. On 14 March 2014, Mauritius invited the United Kingdom to indicate the basis for each remaining redaction, recalling the Tribunal's letter of 9 January 2014. Mauritius also confirmed, with respect to the United Kingdom's request, that "Mauritius considers that it has fully pleaded its case, including by way of disclosure of appropriate documentation."

[2] Mauritius' Reply, para. 1.21.

42. On 18 March 2014, the Tribunal confirmed its intention for the United Kingdom to indicate the basis for each redaction it sought to maintain and requested that the United Kingdom comment on Mauritius' proposal for the Tribunal or a document master to review the unredacted texts and confirm in each instance that non-disclosure was justified. By the same letter, the Tribunal requested that Mauritius respond to the United Kingdom concerning the disclosure of its own internal documents.

43. On 25 March 2014, the United Kingdom submitted a version of the documents contained in Annex 185 with the grounds of each redaction indicated and noted that it was willing to accommodate discussions with the Tribunal on an *ex parte* basis regarding the rationale for any particular redaction.

44. On 7 April 2014, Mauritius set out its concerns regarding the United Kingdom's stated grounds for the remaining redactions and invited the Tribunal to request the United Kingdom to provide unredacted copies of the documents for *ex parte* review to ensure that the redactions were justified. With respect to Mauritius' internal documents, Mauritius noted that no order for document production had been sought, but indicated that, in any case, it had reviewed its own internal documents to the fullest extent possible and disclosed all relevant documents.

45. On 8 April 2014, the Tribunal requested the United Kingdom to make available unredacted copies of the documents in Annex 185 for examination by the Tribunal in Istanbul in advance of the hearing. By letter dated 9 April 2014, the United Kingdom confirmed its arrangements to transport the documents to Istanbul and invited the Tribunal to attend at the British Consulate-General in Istanbul on 21 April 2014.

46. On 14 April 2014, the Tribunal proposed a procedure in respect of the redacted documents, providing for a preliminary review by the Presiding Arbitrator of unredacted copies of the documents themselves, followed by a review by the Tribunal as a whole, "unless considered unnecessary in light of the Presiding Arbitrator's preliminary review."

47. On 20 April 2014, following a further exchange of correspondence with the Parties, the President informed the Parties that he would attend an *ex parte* meeting at the British Consulate-General on 21 April 2014 and that this meeting would be "limited to confirming that the contents of each redaction qualify for non-disclosure on grounds recognized by the Tribunal."

48. On 21 April 2014, the President of the Tribunal, together with the Registrar, attended the *ex parte* meeting at the British Consulate-General in Istanbul. Thereafter, the President reported his findings to the Tribunal as a whole.

49. On 22 April 2014, the Tribunal wrote to the Parties, confirming the President's finding that each redaction was justified and conveying the Tribunal's decision that the redacted passages should not be subject to disclosure.

G. The Hearing on Jurisdiction and the Merits

50. On 22 November 2013, the Tribunal, following consultations with the Parties and the PCA, confirmed that the hearing would take place in Istanbul, Turkey.

51. On 22 April 2014, the Tribunal, with the Parties' consent, confirmed the change in the place of the hearing by a formal amendment to Article 9(2) of the Rules of Procedure.

52. The hearing on jurisdiction and the merits took place from 22 April to 9 May 2014 at the facilities of the Pera Palace Hotel, Istanbul, Turkey. The following individuals participated on behalf of the Parties:

Mauritius

Agent

— Mr. Dheerendra Kumar Dabee GOSK, SC

Deputy Agent

— Ms. Aruna Devi Narain

Counsel

— Professor James Crawford AC, SC, FBA

— Professor Philippe Sands QC

— Ms. Alison MacDonald

— Mr. Paul S. Reichler

— Mr. Andrew Loewenstein

Representatives

— Mr. Suresh Chandre Seeballuck GOSK

— H.E. Dr. Jaya Nyamrajsigh Meetarbhan GOSK

— Ms. Shiu Ching Young Kim Fat

Advisers

— Ms. Elizabeth Wilmshurst CMG

— Dr. Douglas Guilfoyle

Junior Counsel

— Mr. Yuri Parkhomenko

— Mr. Remi Reichhold

— Mr. Fernando L. Bordin

Assistants

— Mr. Rodrigo Tranamil

— Ms. Nancy Lopez

United Kingdom

Agent

— Mr. Christopher Whomersley CMG

Deputy Agent

— Ms. Margaret Purdasy

Counsel

— The Rt. Hon. Dominic Grieve QC, MP

— Professor Alan Boyle

— Ms. Penelope Nevill

— Ms. Amy Sander

— Sir Michael Wood KCMG

— Mr. Samuel Wordsworth QC

Junior Counsel

— Mr. Eran Sthoeger

Representatives

— Ms. Jo Bowyer

— Ms. Mina Patel

— Ms. Neelam Rattan

— Ms. Rebecca Raynsford

— Mr. Douglas Wilson

53. On 16 May 2014, the PCA issued a press release on the conclusion of the hearing on jurisdiction and the merits.

* * *

Chapter III. Factual Background

A. Geography

54. Mauritius is composed of a group of islands,[3] situated in the south-western part of the Indian Ocean.[4] In addition to one main island, the Island of Mauritius, the territory of Mauritius includes the islands of Cargados Carojos Shoals (the St Brandon Group of 16 Islands and Islets);[5] Rodrigues Island; and Agalega.[6] Pursuant to Section 111 of its Constitution (as amended with effect from 1992), Mauritius also claims the territory of Tromelin Island (disputed by the French Republic) and the Chagos Archipelago (disputed by the United Kingdom).[7] The location of Mauritius and the Chagos Archipelago is shown in Map 1 on page 385[*].

55. The Chagos Archipelago comprises a number of coral atolls,[8] located in the middle of the Indian Ocean, some of which are above sea level and form islands.[9] The largest island of the Chagos Archipelago, Diego Garcia, is situated in the south-west of the archipelago.[10] The Chagos Archipelago is shown in Map 2 on page 386[**].

B. Historical Background

56. Beginning in the late 15th century, Portuguese explorers began to venture into the Indian Ocean and recorded the location of Mauritius and the other Mascarene Islands, Rodrigues and Réunion (the latter presently a French overseas department). In the 16th century, the Portuguese were joined by Dutch and English sailors, both nations having established East India Companies to exploit the commercial opportunities of the Indian Ocean and the Far East. Although Mauritius was used as a stopping point in the long voyages to and from the Indian Ocean, no attempt was made to establish a permanent settlement.[11]

57. The first permanent colony in Mauritius was established by the Dutch East India Company in 1638.[12] The Dutch maintained a small presence

---

[3] Mauritius' Memorial, para. 2.3.

[4] The United Kingdom's Counter-Memorial, para. 2.13.

[5] Mauritius' Memorial, para. 2.3.

[6] Mauritius' Memorial, para. 2.3; The United Kingdom's Counter-Memorial, para. 2.13.

[7] Mauritius' Memorial, para. 2.3.

[*] Secretariat note: The page number has been modified.

[8] Final Transcript, 81:3–4.

[9] The United Kingdom's Counter-Memorial, paras. 2.3, 2.9.

[10] Mauritius' Memorial, para. 2.6; The United Kingdom's Counter-Memorial, 2.11.

[**] Secretariat note: The page number has been modified.

[11] Mauritius' Memorial, paras. 2.7–2.10.

[12] Mauritius' Memorial, paras. 2.7, 2.10.

on Mauritius, with a brief interruption, until 1710 at which point the Dutch East India Company abandoned the island.[13] Following the Dutch departure, the French government took possession of Mauritius in 1715, renaming it the *Ile de France*.[14]

58. The Chagos Archipelago was known during this period, appearing on Portuguese charts as early as 1538, but remained largely untouched.[15] France progressively claimed and surveyed the Archipelago in the mid-18th century and granted concessions for the establishment of coconut plantations, leading to permanent settlement. Throughout this period, France administered the Chagos Archipelago as a dependency of the *Ile de France*.[16]

59. In 1810, the British captured the *Ile de France*[17] and renamed it Mauritius.[18] By the Treaty of Paris of 30 May 1814, France ceded the *Ile de France* and all its dependencies (including the Chagos Archipelago) to the United Kingdom.[19]

60. These early historical events are not in dispute between the Parties.[20]

C. The British Administration of Mauritius and the Chagos Archipelago

61. From the date of the cession by France until 8 November 1965, when the Chagos Archipelago was detached from the colony of Mauritius, the Archipelago was administered by the United Kingdom as a Dependency of Mauritius.[21] During this period, the economy of the Chagos Archipelago was primarily driven by the coconut plantations and the export of copra (dried coconut flesh) for the production of oil, although other activities developed as the population of the Archipelago expanded.[22] British administration over the Chagos Archipelago was exercised by various means, including by visits to the Chagos Archipelago made by Special Commissioners and Magistrates from Mauritius.[23]

---

[13] Mauritius' Memorial, para. 2.10.

[14] Mauritius' Memorial, para. 2.10.

[15] Mauritius' Memorial, paras. 2.8, 2.11.

[16] Mauritius' Memorial, para. 2.16.

[17] Mauritius' Memorial, para. 2.15; The United Kingdom's Counter-Memorial, para. 2.17.

[18] Mauritius' Memorial, para. 2.18.

[19] Mauritius' Memorial, paras. 2.15–2.16; The United Kingdom's Counter-Memorial, paras. 2.16–2.18.

[20] Final Transcript, 98:10–13.

[21] Mauritius' Memorial, paras. 2.17, 2.22; The United Kingdom's Counter-Memorial, paras. 2.16, 2.19, 2.32.

[22] Mauritius' Reply, para. 2.20.

[23] Mauritius' Memorial, para. 2.22; The United Kingdom's Counter-Memorial, paras. 2.16, 2.24.

THE LOCATION OF THE CHAGOS ARCHIPELAGO

Map 1

Projection / Datum: Mercator / WGS84

The base map is taken from Natural Earth. This map is for illustrative purposes only.

62. Although the broad outlines of British Administration of the colony during this period are not in dispute, the Parties disagree as to the extent of economic activity in the Chagos Archipelago and its significance for Mauritius, and on the significance of the Archipelago's status as a dependency.[24]

[24] Mauritius' Memorial, para. 2.17; The United Kingdom's Counter-Memorial, para. 2.19.

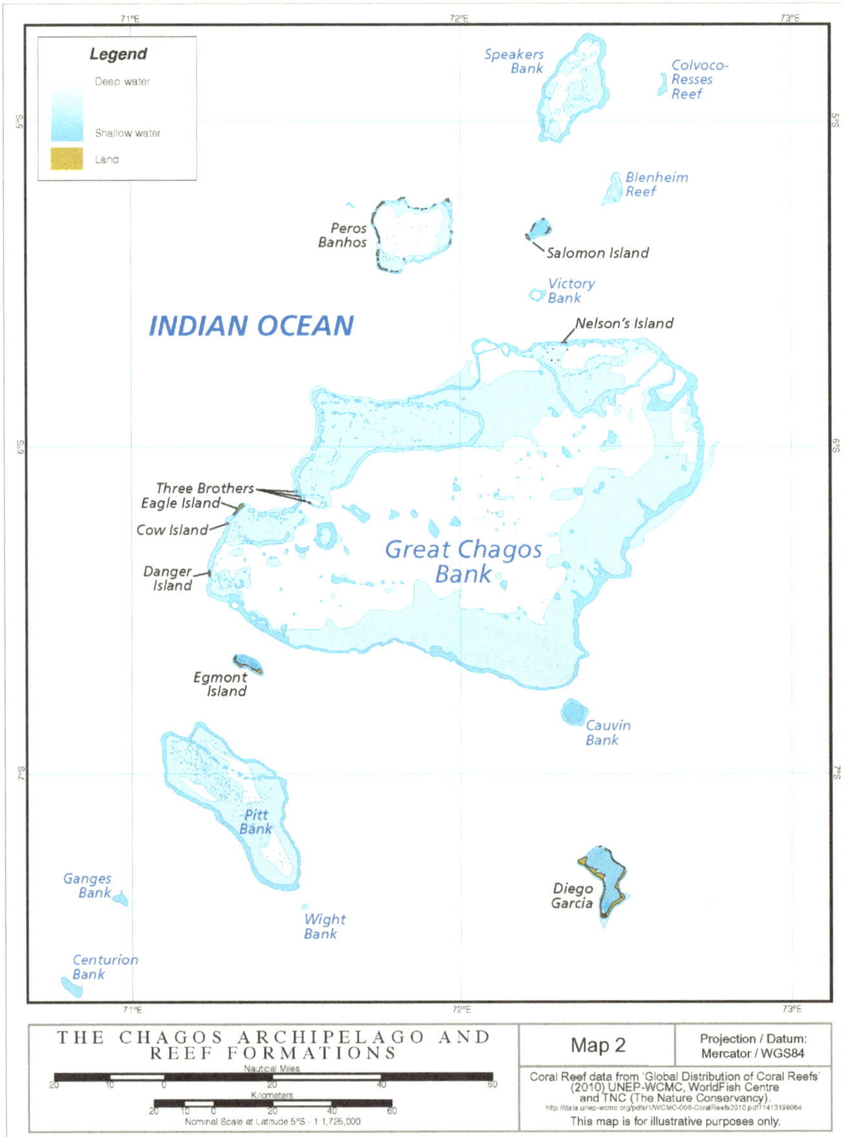

THE CHAGOS ARCHIPELAGO AND REEF FORMATIONS

Mauritius contends that there were "close economic, cultural and social links between Mauritius and the Chagos Archipelago"[25] and that "the administration of the Chagos Archipelago as a constituent part of Mauritius continued without interruption throughout that period of British rule".[26] The Unit-

[25] Mauritius' Reply, para. 2.18.

[26] Mauritius' Memorial, para. 2.17.

ed Kingdom, in contrast, submits that the Chagos Archipelago was only "very loosely administered from Mauritius"[27] and "in law and in fact quite distinct from the Island of Mauritius."[28] The United Kingdom further contends that "[t]he islands had no economic relevance to Mauritius, other than as a supplier of coconut oil"[29] and that, in any event, economic, social and cultural ties between the Chagos Archipelago and Mauritius during this period are irrelevant to the Archipelago's legal status.[30]

D. The Independence of Mauritius

63. Beginning in 1831, the administration of the British Governor of Mauritius was supplemented by the introduction of a Council of Government, originally composed of *ex-officio* members and members nominated by the Governor.[31] The composition of this Council was subsequently democratized through the progressive introduction of elected members.[32] In 1947, the adoption of a new Constitution for Mauritius replaced the Council of Government with separate Legislative and Executive Councils.[33] The Legislative Council was composed of the Governor as President, 19 elected members, 12 members nominated by the Governor and 3 *ex-officio* members.[34]

64. The first election of the Legislative Council took place in 1948, and the Mauritius Labour Party (the "MLP") secured 12 of the 19 seats available for elected members.[35] The MLP strengthened its position in the 1953 election by securing 14 of the available seats, although the MLP lacked an overall majority in the Legislative Council because of the presence of a number of members appointed by the Governor.[36]

65. The 1953 election marked the beginning of Mauritius' move towards independence.[37] Following that election, Mauritian representatives began to press the British Government for universal suffrage, a ministerial system of government and greater elected representation in the Legislative Council. By 1959, the MLP-led government had openly adopted the goal of complete independence.

[27] The United Kingdom's Counter-Memorial, para. 2.19.

[28] The United Kingdom's Counter-Memorial, para. 2.32.

[29] The United Kingdom's Counter-Memorial, para. 2.19.

[30] The United Kingdom's Rejoinder, para. 2.21.

[31] Mauritius' Memorial, para. 2.30.

[32] Mauritius' Memorial, para. 2.30.

[33] Mauritius' Memorial, para. 2.31; Final Transcript, 99:11–15.

[34] Mauritius' Memorial, para. 2.31.

[35] Mauritius' Memorial, para. 2.32; Final Transcript, 99:16–17.

[36] Mauritius' Memorial, para. 2.32; Final Transcript, 99:20 to 100:2.

[37] Mauritius' Memorial, para. 2.32; The United Kingdom's Counter-Memorial, para. 2.42.

66. Constitutional Conferences were held in 1955, 1958, 1961, and 1965,[38] resulting in a new constitution in 1958 and the creation of the post of Chief Minister in 1961 (renamed as the Premier after 1963).[39] In 1962, Dr. Seewoosagur Ramgoolam (later Sir Seewoosagur Ramgoolam) became the Chief Minister[40] within a Council of Ministers chaired by the Governor and, following the 1963 election, formed an all-party coalition government to pursue negotiations with the British on independence.[41]

67. The final Constitutional Conference was held in London in September 1965 and was principally concerned with the debate between those Mauritian political leaders favouring independence and those preferring some form of continued association with the United Kingdom.[42] On 24 September 1965, the final day of the conference, the Secretary of State for the Colonies, the Rt. Hon. Anthony Greenwood MP,[43] who was the minister in the United Kingdom Government with responsibility for Mauritius, announced that the United Kingdom Government intended that Mauritius would proceed to full independence.[44]

68. Mauritius became independent on 12 March 1968.[45]

E. The Detachment of the Chagos Archipelago

69. In conjunction with the move toward Mauritian independence, the United Kingdom formulated a proposal to separate the Chagos Archipelago from the remainder of the colony of Mauritius, and to retain the Archipelago under British control. According to Mauritius, the proposal to separate the Chagos Archipelago stemmed from a decision by the United Kingdom in the early 1960s to "accommodate the United States' desire to use certain islands in the Indian Ocean for defence purposes."[46]

70. The record before the Tribunal sets out a series of bilateral talks between the United Kingdom and the United States in 1964 at which the two

[38] Mauritius' Memorial, paras. 2.33–2.40; The United Kingdom's Counter-Memorial, paras. 2.42–2.44; Final Transcript, 100:3–19.

[39] The United Kingdom's Counter-Memorial, para. 2.43.

[40] Mauritius' Memorial, para. 2.36; Final Transcript, 100:15–16.

[41] Mauritius' Memorial, paras. 2.37–2.38; The United Kingdom's Counter-Memorial, para. 2.43.

[42] Mauritius' Memorial, para. 2.40; The United Kingdom's Counter-Memorial, para. 2.44.

[43] At the first session of the hearings in Istanbul, counsel for Mauritius stated for the record that Mr. Anthony Greenwood was not related to Sir Christopher Greenwood; Final Transcript, 18:12.

[44] Mauritius Constitutional Conference 1965, presented to Parliament by the Secretary of State for the Colonies by Command of Her Majesty, Command Paper 2797 at para. 20 (October 1965) (Annex UKCM-11).

[45] Mauritius Independence Act 1968 (Annex UKCM-19); The Mauritius Independence Order 1968 (Annex UKCM-20).

[46] Mauritius' Memorial, para. 3.3.

States decided that, in order to execute the plans for a defence facility in the Chagos Archipelago, the United Kingdom would "provide the land, and security of tenure, by detaching islands and placing them under direct U.K. administration."[47]

71. The suitability of Diego Garcia as the site of the planned defence facility was determined following a joint survey of the Chagos Archipelago and certain islands of the Seychelles in 1964.[48] Following the survey, the United States sent its proposals to the United Kingdom, identifying Diego Garcia as its first preference as the site for the defence facility.[49] The United Kingdom and the United States conducted further negotiations between 1964 and 1965 regarding the desirability of "detachment of the entire Chagos Archipelago,"[50] as well as the islands of Aldabra, Farquhar and Desroches (then part of the colony of the Seychelles).[51] They further discussed the terms of compensation that would be required "to secure the acceptance of the proposals by the local Governments."[52]

72. On 19 July 1965, the Governor of Mauritius was instructed to communicate the proposal to detach the Chagos Archipelago to the Mauritius Council of Ministers and to report back on the Council's reaction.[53] The initial reaction of the Mauritian Ministers, conveyed by the Governor's report of 23 July 1965, was a request for more time to consider the proposal. The report also noted that Sir Seewoosagur Ramgoolam expressed "dislike of detachment".[54] At the next meeting of the Council on 30 July 1965, the Mauritian Ministers indicated that detachment would be "unacceptable to public opinion in Mauritius" and proposed the alternative of a long-term lease, coupled with safeguards for mineral rights and a preference for Mauritius if fishing or agri-

---

[47] "British Indian Ocean Territory" 1964–1968, Chronological Summary of Events relating to the Establishment of the "B.I.O.T." in November, 1965 and subsequent agreement with the United States concerning the Availability of the Islands for Defence Purposes at p. 9, FCO 32/484 (Annex MM-3).

[48] Mauritius' Memorial, paras. 3.7 to 3.9; Robert Newton, *Report on the Anglo-American Survey in the Indian Ocean* at para. 20, 1964, CO 1036/1332 (Annex MM-2).

[49] Letter dated 14 January 1965 from the Counselor for Politico-Military Affairs at the US Embassy in London to the Head of the Permanent Under-Secretary's Department, UK Foreign Office (Annex-MM-5); *see also* Letter dated 15 January 1965 from the British Embassy, Washington to the UK Foreign Office (Annex MM-6).

[50] Letter dated 10 February 1965 from the Counselor for Politico-Military Affairs at the US Embassy in London to the Head of the Permanent Under-Secretary's Department, UK Foreign Office (Annex MM-7).

[51] Foreign Office Telegram No. 3582 to Washington, 30 April 1965, FO 371/184523 (Annex MM-9).

[52] Foreign Office Telegram No. 3582 to Washington, 30 April 1965, FO 371/184523 (Annex MM-9); *see also* Permanent Under-Secretary's Department (Foreign Office), Secretary of State's Visit to Washington and New York, 21–24 March, Defence Interests in the Indian Ocean, Brief No. 14, 18 March 1965, FO 371/184524 (Annex MM-8).

[53] Colonial Office Telegram No. 198 to Mauritius, No. 219 to Seychelles, 19 July 1965, FO 371/184526 (Annex MM-10).

[54] Mauritius Telegram No. 170 to the Colonial Office, 23 July 1965, FO 371/184526 (Annex MM-10).

cultural rights were ever granted.[55] The Parties differ in their understanding of the strength of, and motivation for, the Mauritian reaction.[56] In any event, on 13 August 1965, the Governor of Mauritius informed the Mauritian Ministers that the United States objected to the proposal of a lease.[57]

73. Discussions over the detachment of the Chagos Archipelago continued in a series of meetings between certain Mauritian political leaders, including Sir Seewoosagur Ramgoolam,[58] and the Secretary of State for the Colonies, Anthony Greenwood, coinciding with the Constitutional Conference of September 1965 in London.[59] Over the course of three meetings, the Mauritian leaders pressed the United Kingdom with respect to the compensation offered for Mauritian agreement to the detachment of the Archipelago, noting the involvement of the United States in the establishment of the defence facility and Mauritius' need for continuing economic support (for example through a higher quota for Mauritius sugar imports into the United States), rather than the lump sum compensation being proposed by the United Kingdom.[60] The United Kingdom took the firm position that obtaining concessions from the United States was not feasible; the United Kingdom did, however, increase the level of lump sum compensation on offer from £1 million to £3 million and introduced the prospect of a commitment that the Archipelago would be returned to Mauritius when no longer needed for defence purposes.[61] The Mauritian leaders also met with the Economic Minister at the U.S. Embassy in London on the question of sugar quotas,[62] and Sir Seewoosagur Ramgoolam met privately with Prime Minister Harold Wilson on the morning of 23 September 1965.[63] The

[55] Mauritius Telegram No. 175 to the Colonial Office, 30 July 1965, FO 371/184526 (Annex MM-13).

[56] *See* Final Transcript, 168:12–24; 599:16 to 600:12; 924:17–20.

[57] Mauritius Telegram No. 188 to the Colonial Office, 13 August 1965, FO 371/184526 (Annex MM-15).

[58] In addition to Sir Seewoosagur Ramgoolam, the Mauritian leaders involved in these discussions were Attorney General Jules Koenig (*Parti Mauricien Social Democrate*), Minister Sookdeo Bissoondoyal (Independent Forward Bloc) and Minister Abdool Razack Mohamed (Muslim Committee of Action) and Minister Maurice Paturau (independent). *See* Mauritius' Memorial, para. 3.22 n. 120.

[59] The need for defence issues to be kept separate from the Constitutional Conference was first raised in a private meeting between Sir Seewoosagur Ramgoolam and the Secretary of State on 3 September 1965. *See* Note of a meeting with the Secretary of State at 10 a.m. on 3 September 1965 (Annex UKR-5).

[60] For the records of the meetings on 13 and 20 September 2014, see Mauritius—Defence Matters: record of a meeting in the Secretary of State's room in the Colonial Office at 10.30 a.m. on Monday 13 September 1965 (Annex UKR-6); Record of a Meeting in the Colonial Office at 9.00 a.m. on Monday, 20th September, 1965, Mauritius—Defence Issues, FO 371/184528 (Annex MM-16).

[61] *Ibid.*

[62] Note of a Meeting held at the Embassy of the U.S.A., London, at 11.30 a.m. on Wednesday 15 September 1965 (Annex UKR-7).

[63] Record of a Conversation between the Prime Minister and the Premier of Mauritius, Sir Seewoosagur Ramgoolam, at No. 10, Downing Street, at 10 a.m. on Thursday, 23 September 1965, FO 371/184528 (Annex MM-18). For the briefing documents prepared in advance of the Prime

United Kingdom's record of this conversation records Prime Minister Wilson having told Sir Seewoosagur Ramgoolam that –

> in theory, there were a number of possibilities. The Premier and his colleagues could return to Mauritius either with Independence or without it. On the Defence point, Diego Garcia could either be detached by order in Council or with the agreement of the Premier and his colleagues. The best solution of all might be Independence and detachment by agreement, although he could not of course commit the Colonial Secretary at this point.[64]

74. The meetings culminated in the afternoon of 23 September 1965 (the "Lancaster House Meeting") in a provisional agreement on the part of Sir Seewoosagur Ramgoolam and his colleagues[65] to agree in principle to the detachment of the Archipelago in exchange for the Secretary of State recommending certain actions by the United Kingdom to the Cabinet.[66] The draft record of the Lancaster House Meeting set out the following:

> Summing up the discussion, the SECRETARY OF STATE asked whether he could inform his colleagues that Dr. [Seewoosagur] Ramgoolam, Mr. Bissoondoyal and Mr. Mohamed were prepared to agree to the detachment of the Chagos Archipelago on the understanding that he would recommend to his colleagues the following:–
>
> (i) negotiations for a defence agreement between Britain and Mauritius;
>
> (ii) in the event of independence an understanding between the two governments that they would consult together in the event of a difficult internal security situation arising in Mauritius;
>
> (iii) compensation totalling up to [illegible] Mauritius Government over and above direct compensation to landowners and the cost of resettling others affected in the Chagos Islands;
>
> (iv) the British Government should use its good offices with the United States Government in support of Mauritius' request for concessions over sugar imports and the supply of wheat and other commodities;
>
> (v) that the British Government would do their best to persuade the American Government to use labour and materials from Mauritius for construction work in the islands;
>
> (vi) that if the need for the facilities on the islands disappeared the islands should be returned to Mauritius.

Minister's meeting, see Colonial Office, Note for the Prime Minister's Meeting with Sir Seewoosagur Ramgoolam, Premier of Mauritius, 22 September 1965, PREM 13/3320 (Annex MM-17).

[64] Record of a Conversation between the Prime Minister and the Premier of Mauritius, Sir Seewoosagur Ramgoolam, at No. 10, Downing Street, at 10 a.m. on Thursday, 23 September 1965, FO 371/184528 at p. 3 (Annex MM-18).

[65] Mr. Koenig of the *Parti Mauricien Social Democrate* was not present for this final meeting.

[66] The draft record of this meeting is set out at Records relating to meetings on 23 September 1965 (Annex UKR-8).

> SIR S. RAMGOOLAM said that this was acceptable to him and Messrs. Bissoondoyal and Mohamed in principle but he expressed the wish to discuss it with his other ministerial colleagues.

75. Thereafter, Sir Seewoosagur Ramgoolam addressed a handwritten note to the Under-Secretary of State at the Colonial Office, Mr. Trafford Smith, setting out further conditions relating to navigational and meteorological facilities on the Archipelago, fishing rights, emergency landing facilities, and the benefit of mineral or oil discoveries. Sir Seewoosagur Ramgoolam's note provided as follows:

> Dear Mr. Trafford Smith,
>
> I and Mr. Mohamed have gone through the enclosed paper on the question of Diego Garcia and another near island (i.e. two altogether) and we wish to point out the amendments that should be effected on page 4 of this document. The matters to be added formed part of the original requirements submitted to H.M.G. We think that these can be incorporated in any final agreement.
>
> With kind regards,
> S. Ramgoolam
>
> P.S. The two copies handed over to me are herewith enclosed.[67]

76. The third page to Sir Seewoosagur Ramgoolam's note set out the following items:

(vii) Navigational & Meteorological facilities
(viii) Fishing rights
(ix) Use of Air Strip for Emergency Landing and if required for development of the other islands
(x) Any mineral or oil discovered on or near islands to revert to the Mauritius Government.[68]

77. These additions were incorporated into paragraph 22 of the final record of the Lancaster House Meeting, which the Tribunal considers to warrant quotation in full:

Record of a Meeting held in Lancaster House at 2.30 p.m. on Thursday 23rd September Mauritius Defence Matters

Present: The Secretary of State (in the Chair)

- Lord Taylor
- Sir Hilton Poynton

[67] Manuscript letter of 1 October 1965 (Annex UKCM-9).

[68] Manuscript letter of 1 October 1965 (Annex UKCM-9).

- Sir John Rennie
- Mr. P. R. Noakes
- Mr. J. Stacpoole
- Sir S. Ramgoolam
- Mr. S. Bissoondoyal
- Mr. J. M. Paturau
- Mr. A. R. Mohamed

THE SECRETARY OF STATE expressed his apologies for the unavoidable postponements and delays which some delegations at the Constitutional Conference had met with earlier in the day. He explained that he was required to inform his colleagues of the outcome of his talks with Mauritian Ministers about the detachment of the Chagos Archipelago at 4 p.m. that afternoon and was therefore anxious that a decision should be reached at the present meeting.

2. He expressed his anxiety that Mauritius should agree to the establishment of the proposed facilities, which besides their usefulness for the defence of the free world, would be valuable to Mauritius itself by ensuring a British presence in the area. On the other hand it appeared that the Chagos site was not indispensable and there was therefore a risk that Mauritius might lose this opportunity. In the previous discussions he had found himself caught between two fires: the demands which the Mauritius Government had made, mainly for economic concessions by the United States, and the evidence that the United States was unable to concede these demands. He had throughout done his best to ensure that whatever arrangements were agreed upon should secure the maximum benefit for Mauritius. He was prepared to recommend to his colleagues if Mauritius agreed to the detachment of the Chagos Archipelago:–

(i) negotiations for a defence agreement between Britain and Mauritius;

(ii) that if Mauritius became independent, there should be an understanding that the two governments would consult together in the event of a difficult internal security situation arising in Mauritius;

(iii) that the British Government should use its good offices with the United States Government in support of Mauritius request for concessions over the supply of wheat and other commodities;

(iv) that compensation totalling up to £3m. should be paid to the Mauritius Government over and above direct compensation to landowners and others affected in the Chagos Islands.

This was the furthest the British Government could go. They were anxious to settle this matter by agreement but the other British Ministers concerned were of course aware that the islands were distant from Mauritius, that the link with Mauritius was an accidental one and that it would be possible for the British Government to detach them from Mauritius by Order in Council.

3. SIR S. RAMGOOLAM replied that the Mauritius Government were anxious to help and to play their part in guaranteeing the defence of the free world. He asked whether the Archipelago could not be leased, (THE SECRETARY OF STATE said that this was not acceptable). MR. BISSOONDOYAL enquired whether the Islands would revert to Mauritius if the need for defence facilities there disappeared. THE SECRETARY OF STATE said that he was prepared to recommend this to his colleagues.

4. MR. PATURAU said that he recognised the value and importance of an Anglo-Mauritius defence agreement, and the advantage for Mauritius if the facilities were established in the Chagos Islands, but he considered the proposed concessions a poor bargain for Mauritius.

5. MR. BISSOONDOYAL asked whether there could be an assurance that supplies and manpower from Mauritius would be used so far as possible. THE SECRETARY OF STATE said that the United States Government would be responsible for construction work and their normal practice was to use American manpower but he felt sure the British Government would do their best to persuade the American Government to use labour and materials from Mauritius.

6. SIR S. RAMGOOLAM asked the reason for Mr. Koenig's absence from the meeting and MR. BISSOONDOYAL asked whether the reason was a political one, saying that if so this might affect the position.

7. MR. MOHAMED made an energetic protest against repeated postponements of the Secretary of State's proposed meeting with the M.C.A. [Muslim Committee of Action], which he regarded as a slight to his party.

8. THE SECRETARY OF STATE repeated the apology with which he had opened the meeting, explaining that it was often necessary in such conferences to concentrate attention on a delegation which was experiencing acute difficulties, while he himself had been obliged to devote much time to a crisis in another part of the world.

9. MR. MOHAMED then handed the Secretary of State a recent private letter from Mauritius which disclosed that extensive misrepresentations about the course of the Conference had been published in a Parti Mauricien newspaper. THE SECRETARY OF STATE commented that such misrepresentations should be disregarded, and that MR. MOHAMED had put forward the case for his community with great skill and patience.

10. MR. MOHAMED said that his party was ready to leave the bases question to the discretion of H.M.G. and to accept anything which was for the good of Mauritius. Mauritius needed a guarantee that defence help would be available nearby in case of need.

11. At SIR S. RAMGOOLAM's request the Secretary of State repeated the outline he had given at a previous meeting of the development

aid which would be available to Mauritius between 1966–1968, viz. a C.D. & W. [Commonwealth Development & Welfare] allocation totalling £2.4 million (including carryover) thus meaning that £800,000 a year would be available by way of grants in addition Mauritius would have access to Exchequer loans, which might be expected to be of the order of £1m. a year, on the conditions previously explained. He pointed out that Diego Garcia was not an economic asset to Mauritius and that the proposed compensation of £3m. would be an important contribution to Mauritius development. There was no chance of raising this figure.

12. SIR S. RAMGOOLAM said that there was a gap of some £4m. per year between the development expenditure which his government considered necessary in order to enable the Mauritian economy to "take off" and the resources in sight, and enquired whether it was possible to provide them with additional assistance over a 10 year period to bridge this gap.

13. THE SECRETARY OF STATE mentioned the possibility of arranging for say £2m. of the proposed compensation to be paid in 10 instalments annually of £200,000.

14. SIR S. RAMGOOLAM enquired about the economic settlement with Malta on independence and was informed that these arrangements had been negotiated in the context of a special situation for which there was no parallel in Mauritius.

15. SIR H. POYNTON pointed out that if Mauritius did not become independent within three years, the Colonial Office would normally consider making a supplementary allocation of C.D. & W. grant money to cover the remainder of the life of the current C.D. & W. Act, i.e. the period up to 1970. He added that if Mauritius became independent, they would normally receive the unspent balance of their C.D. & W. allocation in a different form and it would be open to them after the three year period to seek further assistance such as Britain was providing for a number of independent Commonwealth countries.

16. SIR S. RAMGOOLAM said that he was prepared to agree in principle to be helpful over the proposals which H.M.G. had put forward but he remained concerned about the availability of capital for development in Mauritius and hoped that the British Government would be able to help him in this respect.

17. MR. BISSOONDOYAL said that while it would have been easier to reach conclusions if it had been possible to obtain unanimity among the party leaders, his party was prepared to support the stand which the Premier was taking. They attached great importance to British assistance being available in the event of a serious emergency in Mauritius.

18. MR. PATURAU asked that his disagreement should be noted. The sum offered as compensation was too small and would provide only temporary help for Mauritius economic needs. Sums as large as £25m. had been mentioned in the British press and Mauritius needed a substantial contribution to close the gap of £4–5m. in the development

budget. He added that since the decision was not unamimous [*sic*], he foresaw serious political trouble over it in Mauritius.

19. THE SECRETARY OF STATE referred to his earlier suggestion that payment of the monetary compensation should be spread over a period of years.

20. SIR S. RAMGOOLAM said that he was hoping to come to London for economic discussions in October. The Mauritius Government's proposals for development expenditure had not yet been finalised, but it was already clear that there would be a very substantial gap on the revenue side.

21. SIR H. POYNTON said that the total sum available for C.D. & W. assistance to the dependent territories was a fixed one and it would not be possible to increase the allocation for one territory without proportionately reducing that of another.

22. Summing up the discussion, the SECRETARY OF STATE asked whether he could inform his colleagues that Dr. [Sir Seewoosagur] Ramgoolam, Mr. Bissoondoyal and Mr. Mohamed were prepared to agree to the detachment of the Chagos Archipelago on the understanding that he would recommend to his colleagues the following:–

(i) negotiations for a defence agreement between Britain and Mauritius;

(ii) in the event of independence an understanding between the two governments that they would consult together in the event of a difficult internal security situation arising in Mauritius;

(iii) compensation totalling up to £3m. should be paid to the Mauritius Government over and above direct compensation to landowners and the cost of resettling others affected in the Chagos Islands;

(iv) the British Government would use their good offices with the United States Government in support of Mauritius' request for concessions over sugar imports and the supply of wheat and other commodities;

(v) that the British Government would do their best to persuade the American Government to use labour and materials from Mauritius for construction work in the islands;

(vi) the British Government would use their good offices with the U.S. Government to ensure that the following facilities in the Chagos Archipelago would remain available to the Mauritius Government as far as practicable:

(*a*) Navigational and Meteorological facilities;

(*b*) Fishing Rights;

(*c*) Use of Air Strip for emergency landing and for refuelling civil planes without disembarkation of passengers.

(vii) that if the need for the facilities on the islands disappeared the islands should be returned to Mauritius;

(viii) that the benefit of any minerals or oil discovered in or near the Chagos Archipelago should revert to the Mauritius Government.

23. SIR S. RAMGOOLAM said that this was acceptable to him and Messrs. Bissoondoyal and Mohamed in principle but he expressed the wish to discuss it with his other ministerial colleagues.

24. THE SECRETARY OF STATE pointed out that he had to leave almost immediately to convey the decision to his own colleagues and LORD TAYLOR urged the Mauritian Ministers not to risk losing the substantial sum offered and the important assurance of a friendly military presence nearby.

25. SIR S. RAMGOOLAM said that Mr. Paturau had urged him to make a further effort to secure a larger sum by way of compensation, but the Secretary of State said there was no hope of this.

26. SIR J. RENNIE said that while he had hoped that Mauritius would be able to obtain trading concessions in these negotiations, this was now ruled out. It was in the interest of Mauritius to take the opportunity offered to ensure a friendly military presence in the area. What was important about the compensation was the use to which the lump sum was put.

27. SIR S. RAMGOOLAM mentioned particular development projects, such as a dam and a land settlement scheme, and expressed the hope that Britain would make additional help available in an independence settlement.

28. SIR H. POYNTON said that the Mauritius Government should not lose sight of the possibility of securing aid for such purposes from the World Bank, the I.D.A. and from friendly governments. While Mauritius remained a colony such powers as Western Germany regarded Mauritius economic problems as a British responsibility but there was the hope that after independence aid would be available from these sources. When Sir S. Ramgoolam suggested that he had said that grants could be extended for up to 10 years, Sir H. Poynton pointed out that he had only indicated that when the period for which the next allocation had been made expired, it would be open to the Mauritius Government to seek further assistance, from Britain, even though Mauritius had meanwhile become independent. It would not be possible to reach any understanding at present beyond saying that independence did not preclude the possibility of negotiating an extension of Commonwealth aid.

29. At this point the SECRETARY OF STATE left for 10, Downing Street [*sic*], after receiving authority from Sir S. Ramgoolam and Mr. Bissoondoyal to report their acceptance in principle of the proposals outlined above subject to the subsequent negotiation of details.

> Mr. Mohamed gave the same assurance, saying that he spoke also for his colleague Mr. Osman. Mr. Paturau said he was unable to concur.[69]

Collectively, the Tribunal will refer to points (i) through (viii) of paragraph 22 of the record of this meeting as the "Lancaster House Undertakings".

78. On 6 October 1965, instructions were sent to the Governor of Mauritius to secure "early confirmation that the Mauritius Government is willing to agree that Britain should now take the necessary legal steps to detach the Chagos Archipelago from Mauritius on the conditions enumerated in (i)–(viii) in paragraph 22 of the enclosed record [of the Lancaster House Meeting]."[70] The Secretary of State went on to note that –

> 5. As regards points (iv), (v) and (vi) the British Government will make appropriate representation to the American Government as soon as possible. You will be kept fully informed of the progress of these representations.
>
> 6. The Chagos Archipelago will remain under British sovereignty, and Her Majesty's Government have taken careful note of points (vii) and (viii).[71]

79. On 5 November 1965, the Governor of Mauritius informed the Colonial Office as follows:

> Council of Ministers today confirmed agreement to the detachment of Chagos Archipelago on conditions enumerated, on the understanding that
>
> (1) statement in paragraph 6 of your despatch "H.M.G. have taken careful note of points (vii) and (viii)" means H.M.G. have in fact agreed to them.
>
> (2) As regards (vii) undertaking to Legislative Assembly excludes
>
> (*a*) sale or transfer by H.M.G. to third party or
>
> (*b*) any payment or financial obligation by Mauritius as condition of return.
>
> (3) In (viii) "on or near" means within area within which Mauritius would be able to derive benefit but for change of sovereignty. I should be grateful if you would confirm this understanding is agreed.[72]

80. The Governor also noted that "[Parti Mauricien Social Démocrate] Ministers dissented and (are now) considering their position in the government."[73] The Parties differ regarding the extent to which Mauritian consent to the detachment was given voluntarily.[74]

---

[69] Record of a Meeting held in Lancaster House at 2.30 p.m. on Thursday 23rd September [1965], Mauritius Defence Matters, CO 1036/1253 at paras. 22–23 (Annex MM-19).

[70] Colonial Office Despatch No. 423 to the Governor of Mauritius, 6 October 1965, FO 371/184529 (Annex MM-21).

[71] *Ibid.*

[72] Mauritius Telegram No. 247 to the Colonial Office, 5 November 1965, FO 371/184529 (Annex MM-25).

[73] *Ibid.*

[74] *See* Final Transcript, 148:3–10; 248:24 to 249:3; 523:7 to 524:13.

81. The detachment of the Chagos Archipelago was effected by the establishment of the BIOT on 8 November 1965 by Order in Council.[75] Pursuant to the Order in Council, the governance of the newly created BIOT was made the responsibility of the office of the BIOT Commissioner, appointed by the Queen upon the advice of the United Kingdom FCO. The BIOT Commissioner is assisted in the day-to-day management of the territory by a BIOT Administrator.

82. On the same day, the Secretary of State cabled the Governor of Mauritius as follows:

> As already stated in paragraph 6 of my despatch No. 423, the Chagos Archipelago will remain under British sovereignty. The islands are required for defence facilities and there is no intention of permitting prospecting for minerals or oils on or near them. The points set out in your paragraph 1 should not therefore arise but I shall nevertheless give them further consideration in view of your request.[76]

83. On 12 November 1965, the Governor of Mauritius cabled the Colonial Office, querying whether the Mauritian Ministers could make public reference to the items in paragraph 22 of the record of the Lancaster House Meeting and adding "[i]n this connection I trust further consideration promised … will enable categorical assurances to be given."[77]

84. On 19 November 1965, the Colonial Office cabled the Governor of Mauritius as follows:

> U.K./U.S. defence interests.
>
> 1. There is no objection to Ministers referring to points contained in paragraph 22 of enclosure to Secret despatch No. 423 of 6th October so long as qualifications contained in paragraphs 5 and 6 of the despatch are borne in mind.
>
> 2. It may well be some time before we can give final answers regarding points (iv), (v) and (vi) of paragraph 22 and as you know we cannot be at all hopeful for concessions over sugar imports and it would therefore seem unwise for anything to be said locally which would raise expectations on this point.
>
> 3. As regards point (vii) the assurance can be given provided it is made clear that a decision about the need to retain the islands must rest entirely with the United Kingdom Government and that it would not (repeat not) be open to the Government of Mauritius to raise the matter, or press for the return of the islands on its own initiative.

---

[75] British Indian Ocean Territory Order 1965 (S.I. 1965/1920) (Annex MM-32) (Annex UKCM-10).

[76] Colonial Office Telegram No. 298 to Mauritius, 8 November 1965, FO 371/184529 (Annex MM-29).

[77] Text of cable reproduced in Note on Mauritius and Diego Garcia (Annex UKR-13).

> 4. As stated in paragraph 2 of my telegram No. 298 there is no intention of permitting prospecting for minerals and oils. The question of any benefits arising therefrom should not [...] [illegible][78]

85. On 21 December 1965, in response to questions in the Mauritius Legislative Assembly regarding the obligations agreed to by the United Kingdom, Mr. Forget (on behalf of the Premier and Minister of Finance) identified the following agreements (among other points):

> [...]
>
> (*e*) If the British Government decides that the Chagos Archipelago is no longer required for defence purposes, the islands will be returned to Mauritius. The question what would happen in such circumstances to any installations in the Chagos Archipelago is, of course, a hypothetical one, and would no doubt be discussed between the interested Governments in light of practical requirements and considerations at the time.
>
> [...]
>
> (*i*) The Honourable Member's question is, again, a hypothetical one and I should make clear that there has never been any indication of minerals in the Chagos Archipelago, which is a string of coral atolls. The British Government has no intention of allowing prospecting for minerals while the islands are being used for defence purposes. For the position thereafter, I would refer the Honourable Member to the first sentence of the reply to Question (*e*).[79]

86. Following the public announcement of the detachment of the Chagos Archipelago, the matter was raised in the Special Committee on the Situation with regard to the Implementation of the Declaration on the Granting of Independence to Colonial Countries and Peoples. On 16 December 1965, the Generally Assembly adopted Resolution 2066(XX) as follows:

> 2066 (XX). Question of Mauritius
>
> *The General Assembly,*
>
> *Having considered* the question of Mauritius and other islands composing the Territory of Mauritius,
>
> *Having examined* the chapters of the reports of the Special Committee on the Situation with regard to the Implementation of the Declaration on the Granting of Independence to Colonial Countries and Peoples relating to the Territory of Mauritius,
>
> *Recalling* its resolution 1514 (XV) of 14 December 1960 containing the Declaration on the Granting of Independence to Colonial Countries and Peoples,

[78] Colonial Office Telegram 313, 19 November 1965, *reproduced in* Note on Mauritius and Diego Garcia (Annex UKR-13).

[79] Debate in Mauritius' Legislative Assembly of 21 December 1965 (Annex UKCM-15).

> *Regretting* that the administering Power has not fully implemented resolution 1514 (XV) with regard to that Territory,
>
> *Noting with deep concern* that any step taken by the administering Power to detach certain islands from the Territory of Mauritius for the purpose of establishing a military base would be in contravention of the Declaration, and in particular of paragraph 6 thereof,
>
> 1. *Approves* the chapters of the reports of the Special Committee on the Situation with regard to the Implementation of the Declaration on the Granting of Independence to Colonial Countries and Peoples relating to the Territory of Mauritius, and endorses the conclusions and recommendations of the Special Committee contained therein;
>
> 2. *Reaffirms* the inalienable right of the people of the Territory of Mauritius to freedom and independence in accordance with General Assembly resolution 1514 (XV);
>
> 3. *Invites* the Government of the United Kingdom of Great Britain and Northern Ireland to take effective measures with a view to the immediate and full implementation of resolution 1514 (XV);
>
> 4. *Invites* the administering Power to take no action which would dismember the Territory of Mauritius and violate its territorial integrity;
>
> 5. *Further invites* the administering Power to report to the Special Committee and to the General Assembly on the implementation of the present resolution;
>
> 6. *Requests* the Special Committee to keep the question of the Territory of Mauritius under review and to report thereon to the General Assembly at its twenty-first session.
>
> *1398th plenary meeting,*
> *16 December 1965.*[80]

The status of Mauritius was also raised, along with that of other non-self-governing territories, in General Assembly resolutions adopted on 20 December 1966[81] and 19 December 1967.[82]

87. In 1975, in anticipation of the transition of the Seychelles to independence the following year, the United Kingdom and the United States entered into discussions on the possibility of returning Aldabra, Farquhar and Desroches to the Seychelles. Neither the United Kingdom nor the United States saw any defence need for the islands, and the United Kingdom considered that the return would facilitate a smooth transition.[83] It was also recog-

---

[80] United Nations General Assembly Resolution 2066 (XX) (Annex MM-38).

[81] United Nations General Assembly Resolution 2232 (XXI) (Annex MM-45).

[82] United Nations General Assembly Resolution 2357 (XXII) (Annex MM-51).

[83] For a partial record of the U.S./U.K. review of the potential return of Aldabra, Farquhar and Desroches to the Seychelles, see Memorandum by the UK Secretary of State for Foreign and Commonwealth Affairs, "British Indian Ocean Territory: The Ex-Seychelles Islands", 4 July 1975 (Annex MM-72); Briefing note dated 14 July 1975 from John Hunt to the UK Prime Minister (Annex MM-73); Office of International Security Operations Bureau, Politico-Military

nized that the islands remained populated and that the political repercussions of the resettlement of the Chagossians[84] (discussed below) would render it impractical to take similar steps on the other BIOT islands. On 18 March 1976, the United States, United Kingdom, and Seychelles reached an agreement to return the islands, with effect from the independence of the Seychelles on 29 June 1976, in exchange for a commitment by the Seychelles not to permit military access to the islands by third States and to continue a policy of strict nature conservancy, in particular with respect to Aldabra.[85] The agreement was given effect by the adoption on 9 June 1976 of an Order in Council.[86]

F. The Removal of the Chagossian Population

88. At the time of the detachment of the Chagos Archipelago in 1965, there were approximately 1,360 persons resident on the islands.[87] Including those born on the islands, the total Chagossian population may be considered to have been between 1,500 and 1,750 persons.[88]

89. On 30 December 1966, the United Kingdom and the United States concluded an Agreement Concerning the Availability for Defense Purposes of the British Indian Ocean Territory which provided for "the islands [to] be available to meet the needs of both Governments for defense" and that "required sites [for defence facilities] shall be made available to the United States authorities without charge".[89] Pursuant to a further exchange of notes, kept secret at the time, the United States agreed to contribute £5 million to

Affairs, United States Department of State, "Disposition of the Seychelles Islands of the BIOT", 31 October 1975 (Annex MM-74); Anglo/US Consultations on the Indian Ocean: November 1975, Agenda Item III, Brief No. 4: Future of Aldabra, Farquhar and Desroches, November 1975 (Annex MM-75); British Embassy, Washington, November 1975, Minutes of Anglo-US Talks on the Indian Ocean held on 7 November 1975 (Extract) (Annex MM-76).

[84] The term "Chagossian" refers to the inhabitants of the Chagos Archipelago. At various points in the record before the Tribunal, the term "Ilois" is also used to refer to this population.

[85] Heads of Agreement between the Government of the United Kingdom of Great Britain and Northern Ireland, the Administration of the "British Indian Ocean Territory" and the Government of Seychelles Concerning the Return of Aldabra, Desroches and Farquhar to Seychelles to be Executed on Independence Day, FCO 40/732 (Annex MM-79).

[86] The British Indian Ocean Territory Order 1976 (S.I. 1976/893) (Annex UKCM-32).

[87] *See* Robert Newton, *Report on the Anglo-American Survey in the Indian Ocean* at para. 7, 1964, CO 1036/1332 (Annex MM-2).

[88] Final Transcript, 392:23 to 393:8, *citing* R. Gifford & R.P. Dunne, "A Dispossessed People: the Depopulation of the Chagos Archipelago 1965–1973" 20 *Population, Space and Place*, pp. 37–49 (2014).

[89] Exchange of Notes Constituting an Agreement between the Government of the United Kingdom of Great Britain and Northern Ireland and the Government of the United States of America concerning the Availability for Defence Purposes of the British Indian Ocean Territory, London, 30 December 1966, 603 UNTS 273 (Annex MM-46).

the costs of establishing the BIOT, to be paid by waiving United Kingdom payments in respect of joint missile development programmes.[90]

90. Between 1968 and 1973, the United Kingdom proceeded to arrange for the purchase of privately held land and to remove the Chagossian population from the Archipelago. On 16 April 1971, the BIOT Commissioner passed Immigration Ordinance, 1971, which provided in section 4 that "[n]o person shall enter the Territory or, being in the Territory, shall be present or remain in the Territory, unless he is in possession of a permit or his name is endorsed on a permit in accordance with the provisions of … this Ordinance".[91] The record indicates that the resettlement and compensation of the Chagossian population had been contemplated in discussions with the United States as early as January 1964,[92] and the Lancaster House Undertakings (see above at paragraph 77) included reference to "direct compensation to landowners and the cost of resettling others affected in the Chagos Islands."[93]

91. Further to talks conducted in early 1972, the United Kingdom agreed to pay Mauritius the sum of £650,000 as compensation for the costs of resettling persons displaced from the Chagos Archipelago.[94]

92. In 1975, a former resident of the Chagos Archipelago, Mr. Michel Vencatassen, initiated a claim for compensation in the courts of England and Wales against the British Government. This was settled in 1982 with an agreement in which the United Kingdom would pay £4 million into a fund for the former residents of the Archipelago.[95] On 7 July 1982, Mauritius and the United Kingdom concluded an agreement pursuant to which –

> The Government of the United Kingdom shall *ex gratia* with no admission of liability pay to the Government of Mauritius for and on behalf

[90] For British correspondence relating to the U.S. contribution, see Minute dated 12 May 1967 from the Secretary of State for Defence to the Foreign Secretary, FO 16/226 (Annex MM-48); Minute dated 22 May 1967 from a Colonial Office official, A. J. Fairclough, to a Minister of State, with a Draft Minute appended for signature by the Secretary of State for Commonwealth Affairs addressed to the Foreign Secretary, FCO 16/226 (Annex MM-49).

[91] Reproduced in *R (Bancoult)* v. *Secretary of State for Foreign and Commonwealth Affairs (No. 1)* [2001] QB 1067 (Laws LJ and Gibbs J).

[92] *See* "British Indian Ocean Territory" 1964–1968, Chronological Summary of Events relating to the Establishment of the "B.I.O.T." in November, 1965 and subsequent agreement with the United States concerning the Availability of the Islands for Defence Purposes at p. 5, FCO 32/484 (Annex MM-3).

[93] Record of a Meeting held in Lancaster House at 2.30 p.m. on Thursday 23rd September [1965], Mauritius Defence Matters, CO 1036/1253 (Annex MM-19).

[94] For correspondence relating to the United Kingdom's payment in respect of resettlement costs, see Letter dated 26 June 1972 from the British High Commission, Port Louis, to the Prime Minister of Mauritius (Annex MM-66); Letter dated 4 September 1972 from Prime Minister of Mauritius to British High Commissioner, Port Louis (Annex MM-67); Letter dated 24 March 1973 from Prime Minister of Mauritius to the British High Commissioner, Port Louis (Annex MM-69).

[95] Mauritius' Memorial, para. 3.75; summarized in *R (Bancoult)* v. *Secretary of State for Foreign and Commonwealth Affairs (No. 2)* [2009] 1 AC 453, para. 12.

> of the Ilois[96] and the Ilois community in Mauritius in accordance with Article 7 of this Agreement the sum of £4 million which, taken together with the payment of £650,000 already made to the Government of Mauritius, shall be in full and final settlement of all claims [arising from the removal or resettlement of the population of the Chagos Archipelago].[97]

The 1982 agreement was then implemented in Mauritius by the Ilois Trust Fund Act of 30 July 1982.[98]

93. In 1998, another former resident of the Chagos Archipelago, Mr. Olivier Bancoult, sought judicial review in the courts of England and Wales of section 4 of the BIOT Immigration Ordinance, 1971 (see paragraph 90 above). On 3 November 2000, the High Court held that "there is no principled basis upon which s.4 of the Ordinance can be justified as having been empowered by s.11 of the BIOT Order",[99] insofar as the removal of the Chagossian population did not fall within the Commissioner's power to "make laws for the peace, order and good government of the Territory".[100]

94. On 3 November 2000, the Commissioner enacted the BIOT Immigration Ordinance, 2000, which restricted access to the Archipelago, but included an exception allowing Chagossians entry, except with respect to Diego Garcia.

95. In April 2002, a group of 4,959 former residents of the Chagos Archipelago and their descendants brought a claim against the Attorney General of England and Wales and the BIOT Commissioner for compensation and restoration of property rights. On 9 October 2003, the High Court dismissed this action on the grounds that no tort at common law was committed by the removal of the Chagossian population and that further compensation for property loss was precluded by the Limitation Act, 1980 and the Claimants' renunciation of claims in exchange for the compensation provided in 1982.[101]

96. On 10 June 2004, the United Kingdom adopted, by Order in Council, the British Indian Ocean Territory (Constitution) Order, 2004, which provided in section 9 as follows:

> No right of abode in the Territory

[96] The term "Ilois" refers to the same population of former residents of the Archipelago as the term "Chagossians".

[97] Agreement between the Government of the United Kingdom of Great Britain and Northern Ireland and the Government of Mauritius concerning the Ilois, Port Louis, 7 July 1982, with amending Exchange of Notes, Port Louis, 26 October 1982, Cmnd. 8785, 1316 UNTS 128.

[98] Ilois Trust Fund Act 1982, Act No 6 of 1982, 30 July 1982.

[99] *R (Bancoult)* v. *Secretary of State for Foreign and Commonwealth Affairs (No. 1)* [2001] QB 1067 at para. 57 (Laws LJ and Gibbs J).

[100] Immigration Ordinance 1971 s. 11, as reproduced in *R (Bancoult)* v. *Secretary of State for Foreign and Commonwealth Affairs (No. 1)* [2001] QB 1067 at para. 57 (Laws LJ and Gibbs J).

[101] *Chagos Islanders* v. *Attorney General* [2003] EWHC 2222 at paras. 737–747 (Ouseley J). The Court of Appeal denied leave to appeal on 22 July 2004. *See Chagos Islanders* v. *Attorney General* [2004] EWCA Civ 997, per Sedley LJ.

> 9. (1) Whereas the Territory was constituted and is set aside to be available for the defence purposes of the Government of the United Kingdom and the Government of the United States of America, no person has the right of abode in the Territory.
>
> (2) Accordingly, no person is entitled to enter or be present in the Territory except as authorised by or under this Order or any other law for the time being in force in the Territory.[102]

On the same day, the United Kingdom adopted, by Order in Council, the British Indian Ocean Territory (Immigration) Order, 2004, replacing BIOT Immigration Ordinance, 2000 and removing the exception allowing Chagossians entry, except with respect to Diego Garcia. The Order also created a penal offence of unlawful entry into the territory.[103]

97. In August 2004, Mr. Bancoult initiated proceedings seeking judicial review of the 2004 Orders in Council. After decisions in the High Court[104] and Court of Appeal[105] quashing section 9 of the (Constitution) Order, 2004 as irrational insofar as it was unconnected to the well-being of the Chagossian population, the House of Lords (by three votes to two) allowed an appeal by the Secretary of State. In so doing, the House of Lords held (per Lord Hoffmann) that "Her Majesty exercises her powers of prerogative legislation for a non-self-governing colony on the advice of her ministers in the United Kingdom and will act in the interests of her undivided realm, including both the United Kingdom and the colony"[106] and that, in light of the assessment that resettlement was economically unviable and the Chagossian interest in funded resettlement, it was "impossible to say, taking fully into account the practical interests of the Chagossians, that the decision to reimpose immigration control on the islands was unreasonable or an abuse of power."[107]

98. Thereafter, Mr. Bancoult and other Chagossians pursued their claims before the European Court of Human Rights. In December 2012, the European Court held in *Chagos Islanders* v. *The United Kingdom* that the claim was inadmissible, on the grounds that –

> in settling their claims in the Ventacassen litigation and in accepting and receiving compensation, those applicants have effectively renounced further use of these remedies. They may no longer, in these circumstances, claim to be victims of a violation of the [European Convention on Human Rights], within the meaning of Article 34 of the [European

[102] British Indian Ocean Territory (Constitution) Order 2004 (Annex UKCM-77).

[103] British Indian Ocean Territory (Immigration) Order 2004 (Authority MM-53).

[104] *R (Bancoult)* v. *Secretary of State for Foreign and Commonwealth Affairs (No. 2)* [2006] EWHC 1038 (Admin).

[105] *R (Bancoult)* v. *Secretary of State for Foreign and Commonwealth Affairs (No. 2)* [2008] QB 365.

[106] *R (Bancoult)* v. *Secretary of State for Foreign and Commonwealth Affairs (No. 2)* [2009] 1 AC 453 at para. 47 (Hoffmann LJ).

[107] *Ibid.* at para. 58.

> Convention on Human Rights]. Those applicants who were not party to the proceedings but who could at the relevant time have brought their claims before the domestic courts have, for their part, failed to exhaust domestic remedies as required by Article 35 § 1 of the [European Convention on Human Rights].[108]

99. In the course of the proceedings before the present Tribunal, the Attorney-General of England and Wales, the Rt. Hon. Dominic Grieve QC MP made the following statement regarding the Chagossian population:

> we regret very much the circumstances in which they were removed from the islands and recognise that what was done then should not have happened. A substantial sum in compensation was paid to the former inhabitants in the 1980s—a point that was recognised by the European Court of Human Rights in their recent decision. When in Opposition, the political party of which I'm a member said that we would look again at our current policy for BIOT. When we first came into Government, we were constrained by the proceedings in the European Court of Human Rights. But immediately after those proceedings were concluded, my colleague, the Foreign Secretary, announced that we would be looking again at the question of the United Kingdom's policy towards BIOT. As part of that review we are looking again at the question of resettlement. And we hope to be able to reach conclusions in the early part of next year in respect of that.[109]

G. Subsequent Relations between Mauritius and the United Kingdom Concerning the Chagos Archipelago

100. Between 1968 and 1980, Mauritius generally did not raise the question of the Chagos Archipelago in public fora and diplomatic communications. The Parties differ as to the significance of the absence of public claims by Mauritius. In Mauritius' view, this silence must be understood in light of the "difficult socio-economic situation" and Mauritius' heavy reliance on the United Kingdom in the years following independence.[110] According to the United Kingdom, the silence indicates that "until 1980, the then Government of Mauritius did not question the obvious fact that at independence the BIOT was not part of the territory of the Republic of Mauritius."[111]

101. On 7 July 1982, following elections and a change of government, the Parliament of Mauritius adopted the Interpretation and General Clauses (Amendment) Act, 1982, which incorporated the Chagos Archipelago into the definition of Mauritius for the purposes of Mauritian law as follows:

---

[108] *Chagos Islanders* v. *the United Kingdom*, No. 35622/04, para. 81, 12 December 2012.

[109] Final Transcript, 43:9–19.

[110] Mauritius' Reply, para. 2.94.

[111] The United Kingdom's Rejoinder, para. 2.61.

Section 2(*b*) of the [Interpretation and General Clauses Act] is amended in the definition of "State of Mauritius" or "Mauritius" by deleting the words "Tromelin and Cargados Carajos" and replacing them by the words "Tromelin, Cargados Carajos and the Chagos Archipelago, including Diego Garcia".[112]

102. On 21 July 1982, the Parliament of Mauritius established a Select Committee on the Excision of the Chagos Archipelago to examine the circumstances of the detachment of the islands. The Select Committee interviewed surviving participants of the events of 1965, although their recollections were inconsistent and differed in material respects from the documentary record set out above (see paragraphs 69–85). The Select Committee's Report was published on 1 June 1983 and was strongly critical of the detachment of the Archipelago, the lack of transparency with which the pre-independence Government of Mauritius handled the matter, and the lack of candour of a number of the participants in their testimony to the Committee. The Select Committee also identified what it described as a "blackmail element" in the way in which the question of detachment had been presented by the United Kingdom and concluded that detachment had represented a violation of the UN Charter.[113]

103. Since 1980, Mauritius contends that "[i]t has consistently asserted its rights [to sovereignty over the Chagos Archipelago] in statements to the UN General Assembly".[114] According to Mauritius, it "has also consistently asserted its sovereignty over the Chagos Archipelago in bilateral communications with the UK".[115] The Parties differ as to whether Mauritius' statements to the United Nations indicate a claim of current sovereignty or simply a claim to the eventual return of the islands, pursuant to the United Kingdom's undertaking, when no longer required for defence purposes. In either event, the

[112] Interpretation and General Clauses (Amendment) Act 1982 (Annex UKR-26).

[113] Report of the Select Committee of the Mauritius Assembly on the Excision of the Chagos Archipelago, June 1983 (Annex UKCM-46).

[114] Mauritius' Reply, para. 2.85; *see also* Extracts from Annual Statements Made by Mauritius to the United Nations General Assembly (Chagos Archipelago) (Annex MM-95).

[115] Mauritius' Reply, para. 2.86; see also Letter dated 9 January 1998 from the Prime Minister of Mauritius to the UK Secretary of State for Foreign and Commonwealth Affairs (Annex MM-106); Note Verbale dated 5 July 2000 from the Ministry of Foreign Affairs and International Trade, Mauritius to the British High Commission, Port Louis, No. 52/2000 (1197) (Annex MM-111); Note Verbale dated 6 November 2000 from the Ministry of Foreign Affairs and Regional Cooperation, Mauritius to the British High Commission, Port Louis, No. 97/2000 (1197/T4) (Annex MM-113); Letter dated 30 December 2009 from the Minister of Foreign Affairs, Regional Integration and International Trade, Mauritius to the UK Secretary of State for Foreign and Commonwealth Affairs (Annex MM-157); Letter dated 19 February 2010 from the Secretary to Cabinet and Head of the Civil Service, Mauritius to the British High Commissioner, Port Louis (Annex MM-162); Note Verbale dated 2 April 2010 from the Ministry of Foreign Affairs, Regional Integration and International Trade, Mauritius to the British High Commission, Port Louis, No. 11/2010 (1197/28/10) (Annex MM-167); Letter dated 20 October 2011 from the Minister of Foreign Affairs, Regional Integration and International Trade, Mauritius to the UK Secretary of State for Foreign and Commonwealth Affairs (Annex MM-172); Letter dated 21 March 2012 from the Minister of Foreign Affairs, Regional Integration and International Trade, Mauritius to the UK Secretary of State for Foreign and Commonwealth Affairs (Annex MM-173).

United Kingdom has consistently responded by maintaining its view that the Chagos Archipelago remains British.[116]

104. In its 1992 Constitution, Mauritius incorporated the following definition of Mauritius:

> 'Mauritius' includes –
>
> (*a*) the Islands of Mauritius, Rodrigues, Agalega, Tromelin, Cargados Carajos and the Chagos Archipelago, including Diego Garcia and any other island comprised in the State of Mauritius;
>
> (*b*) the territorial sea and the air space above the territorial sea and the islands specified in paragraph (*a*);
>
> (*c*) the continental shelf; and
>
> (*d*) such places or areas as may be designated by regulations made by the Prime Minister, rights over which are or may become exercisable by Mauritius.[117]

105. On 31 May 1977, Mauritius adopted its Maritime Zones Act, 1977.[118] On 27 December 1984, Mauritius adopted the Maritime Zones (Exclusive Economic Zones) Regulations, 1984, setting out, *inter alia*, the coordinates of the exclusive economic zone surrounding the Chagos Archipelago.[119] The United Kingdom protested against this action on 18 February 1985.[120]

106. On 25 July 1997, the United Kingdom acceded to the Convention, with an Instrument of Accession extending to the BIOT. Mauritius did not object. According to Mauritius, limited resources inhibit its ability to track all accessions to multilateral treaties that may implicate the Chagos Archipelago, but "[w]henever Mauritius has noted that a multilateral convention has been so extended, it has not failed to protest."[121] Mauritius did object to the extension of the Agreement for the Implementation of the Provisions of the United Nations Convention on the Law of the Sea of 10 December 1982 Relating to the Conservation and Management of Straddling Fish Stocks and Highly Migratory Fish Stocks of 4 August 1995 (the "1995 Fish Stocks Agreement")[122] and has stated in these proceedings that "Mauritius does not accept that the United Kingdom is entitled to extend the territorial scope of its treaty obligations to the Archipelago."[123]

---

[116] The United Kingdom's Counter-Memorial, paras. 2.84–2.88.

[117] The Constitution of Mauritius (Amendment No. 3) Act 1991, section 19 (Annex UKR-32).

[118] Final Transcript, 423:5–8.

[119] *See* The United Kingdom's Counter-Memorial, para. 2.102.

[120] United Kingdom's Note Verbale of 18 February 1985 (Annex UKCM-50).

[121] Final Transcript, 141:7–8.

[122] Final Transcript, 141:8–10; *see also* Declarations to the Agreement for the Implementation of the Provisions of the United Nations Convention on the Law of the Sea of 10 December 1982 relating to the Conservation and Management of Straddling Fish Stocks and Highly Migratory Fish Stocks, *available at* <http://www.un.org/depts/los/convention_agreements/fish_stocks_agreement_declarations.htm>.

[123] Final Transcript, 141:5–7.

107. On 28 February 2005, Mauritius adopted the Maritime Zones Act, 2005, replacing earlier legislation.[124] Pursuant to this Act, on 5 August 2005, Mauritius adopted the Maritime Zones (Baselines and Delineating Lines) Regulations, 2005, setting out the geographical coordinates for the baselines of, *inter alia*, the Chagos Archipelago.[125] On 26 July 2006, Mauritius conveyed these geographical coordinates to the UN Secretary-General.[126] On 27 June 2008, Mauritius made a further deposit of charts and geographical coordinates with the United Nations.[127] On 19 March 2009, the United Kingdom protested against Mauritius' deposit of information in respect of the Chagos Archipelago.[128] On 9 June 2009, Mauritius reiterated its non-recognition of the BIOT to the United Nations.[129]

108. On 14 January 2009, in talks (conducted under a sovereignty umbrella) between the United Kingdom and Mauritius concerning the Chagos Archipelago, the United Kingdom indicated that it was not interested in making a submission to the Commission on the Limits of the Continental Shelf, but was open to the possibility of a joint submission with Mauritius in light of the impending deadlines for States Parties to submit preliminary information.[130] The content of these discussions is set out in detail below in connection with the Tribunal's consideration of its jurisdiction over Mauritius' Third Submission (see paragraphs 331–343).

---

[124] Maritime Zones Act 2005 (Annex MM-131).

[125] Final Transcript, 423:9–20.

[126] Note Verbale dated 26 July 2006 from the Permanent Mission of the Republic of Mauritius to the United Nations, New York, to the UN Secretary General, No. 4678/06 (Annex MM-134).

[127] *See* Deposit by the Republic of Mauritius of charts and lists of geographical coordinates of points, pursuant to article 16, paragraph 2, and article 47, paragraph 9, of the Convention, M.Z.N. 63. 2008. LOS (Maritime Zone Notification) 27 June 2008, *available at* http://www.un.org/depts/los/LEGISLATIONANDTREATIES/losic/losic28e.pdf.

[128] Final Transcript, 509:1–4; *see also* Note Verbale dated 19 March 2009 from the Permanent Mission of the United Kingdom of Great Britain and Northern Ireland to the Secretary-General to the United Nations concerning a deposit of charts and lists of geographical coordinates by the Republic of Mauritius, reproduced in United Nations, Law of the Sea Bulletin No. 69, available at http://www.un.org/depts/los/doalos_publications/LOSBulletins/bulletinpdf/bulletin69e.pdf.

[129] Note Verbale dated 9 June 2009 from Permanent Mission of the Republic of Mauritius to the United Nations, New York to the Secretary General of the United Nations, No. 107853/09 (Annex MM-147).

[130] There is no agreed record of this meeting. The United Kingdom's record is set out in UK Foreign and Commonwealth Office, Overseas Territories Directorate, "British Indian Ocean Territory: UK/Mauritius Talks", 14 January 2009 (Annex MR-128). Mauritius' record is set out in Ministry of Foreign Affairs, Regional Integration and International Trade, Mauritius, "Meeting of Officials on the Chagos Archipelago/British Indian Ocean Territory held at the Foreign and Commonwealth Office, London, Wednesday 14 January 2009, 10 a.m.", 23 January 2009 (Annex MR-129). The Joint Communqué issued at the close of the meeting mentions only a "mutual discussion" concerning "the continental shelf". Joint communiqué of meeting of 14 January 2009 (Annex UKCM-93).

109. On 6 May 2009, Mauritius submitted preliminary information concerning the outer limits of the continental shelf in the Chagos Archipelago to the CLCS.[131]

110. On 21 July 2009, a second round of Mauritius–United Kingdom talks took place (again under a sovereignty umbrella), in which submissions to the CLCS were discussed. The United Kingdom did not object to Mauritius' submission of preliminary information to the CLCS, and the Parties agreed to move forward with the joint preparation of a full submission.[132] The Joint Communiqué issued after the talks stated as follows:

> Both delegations were of the view that it would be desirable to have a coordinated submission for an extended continental shelf in the Chagos Archipelago/British Indian Ocean Territory region to the UN Commission on the Limits of the Continental Shelf, in order not to prejudice the interest of Mauritius in that area and to facilitate its consideration by the Commission. It was agreed that a joint technical team would be set up with officials from both sides to look into possibilities and modalities of such a coordinated approach, with a view to informing the next round of talks.[133]

A third round of joint talks was proposed for November 2009 or January 2010,[134] but did not take place in light of developments discussed below (see paragraphs 131–141).

111. In its *Rejoinder* in these proceedings, submitted on 14 March 2014, the United Kingdom commented on Mauritius' submission of preliminary information to the CLCS as follows:

> Mauritius cannot alter the status of the BIOT continental shelf by making its own submission to the CLCS with respect to BIOT. [...] In accordance with the terms of article 76(7), only the coastal State may delineate the outer limits of the continental shelf. In accordance with article 76(8), only the coastal State may submit information to the CLCS on the limits of the shelf beyond 200 nautical miles. Mauritius is not the coastal State in respect of BIOT and as such it has no standing before the CLCS with respect to BIOT.[135]

---

[131] Preliminary Information Submitted by the Republic of Mauritius Concerning the Extended Continental Shelf in the Chagos Archipelago Region Pursuant to the Decision Contained in SPLOS/183 (Annex MM-144).

[132] Again, there is no agreed record of this meeting. The United Kingdom's record is set out in UK Foreign and Commonwealth Office, Overseas Territories Directorate, "UK/Mauritius Talks on the British Indian Ocean Territory", 24 July 2009 (Annex MR-143). Mauritius' record is set out in Information Paper by the Prime Minister of Mauritius, Second Meeting at Senior Officials' Level between Mauritius and UK on the Chagos Archipelago, CAB(2009) 624, 12 August 2009 (Annex MR-144).

[133] Joint Communiqué, Second round of bilateral talks between Mauritius and the UK on the Chagos Archipelago, 21 July 2009, Port Louis, Mauritius (Annex MM-148).

[134] Note Verbale dated 5 November 2009 from Ministry of Foreign Affairs, Regional Integration and International Trade, Mauritius to the British High Commission, Port Louis, No. 46/2009 (1197/28/4) (Annex MM-150).

[135] The United Kingdom's Rejoinder, para. 8.39.

H. Subsequent Relations between Mauritius and the United Kingdom Concerning Fishing Rights

112. Following the detachment of the Chagos Archipelago, the Colonial Office cabled the Governor of Mauritius on 10 November 1965, seeking details of the nature and extent of fishing around the islands.[136] On 17 November 1965, the Governor replied as follows:

> (*a*) Nature fishing practised: mainly handline with some basket and net fishing by local population for own consumption.
>
> (*b*) Use of international waters: nil, though vessels from Seychelles and occasionally Mauritius use anchorage facilities.
>
> (*c*) Extent territorial waters: unknown. Area covered by banks (up to 80 fathoms) about 6,000 square miles.
>
> (*d*) Value as source of fish: best reference report Wheeler Ommaney, Mauritius Seychelles Fisheries Survey. Fishable area roughly 2,433 square miles. Available potential: fish 95,000 tons, shark 147,000 tons.[137]

113. Following correspondence exchanged with the Governor of Mauritius,[138] BIOT officials,[139] and officials in the United States[140] regarding the form of fishing limits, the BIOT Commissioner established a fisheries zone contiguous to the territorial sea of the BIOT on 10 July 1969. This fisheries zone extended from the outer limit of the (then) 3 nautical mile territorial sea to 12 nautical miles from the low waterline (or otherwise from the baselines from which the territorial sea was measured).[141]

114. On 17 April 1971, the BIOT Commissioner enacted the Fisheries Limits Ordinance, 1971. The ordinance imposed a general prohibition of commercial fishing within the 12 nautical mile limit set out therein. Section 4 empowered the Commissioner "for the purpose of enabling fishing traditionally carried on in any area within the contiguous zone" to designate countries whose nationals would be exempted from the prohibition.[142]

---

[136] Colonial Office Telegram No. 305 to Mauritius, 10 November 1965 (Annex MM-34).

[137] Mauritius Telegram (unnumbered) to the Secretary of State for the Colonies, 17 November 1965 (Annex MM-37).

[138] *See* Letter dated 12 July 1967 from the UK Commonwealth Office to the Governor of Mauritius, FCO 16/226 (Annex MM-50).

[139] Despatch dated 28 April 1969 from J. W. Ayres, Foreign and Commonwealth Office to J. R. Todd, Administrator, BIOT, FCO 31/2763 (Annex MM-52).

[140] In respect of the United Kingdom's consultation with the United States, see Letter dated 6 September 1968 from A. Brooke Turner, UK Foreign Office to K.M. Wilford, British Embassy, Washington, FCO 31/134 (Annex MR-68); Telegram No. 3129 dated 22 October 1968 from British Embassy Washington to UK Foreign and Commonwealth Office, FCO 141/1437 (Annex MR-69).

[141] "British Indian Ocean Territory" Proclamation No. 1 of 1969 (Annex MM-53).

[142] "British Indian Ocean Territory" Ordinance No. 2 of 1971 (Annex MM-60).

115. On 2 July 1971, the British High Commission in Port Louis was directed in the following terms to inform Mauritius that Mauritian fishermen would be exempted from the ordinance:

> Included within the BIOT fishing zone are certain waters which have been traditionally fished by vessels from Mauritius. [...] the Commissioner of BIOT will use his powers under Section 4 of BIOT Ordinance No 2/1971, to enable Mauritian fishing boats to continue fishing in the 9-mile contiguous zone in the waters of the Chagos Archipelago. This exemption stems from the understanding on fishing rights reached between HMG and the Mauritius Government, at the time of the Lancaster House Conference in 1965 [...]. We would be most grateful if you would inform the Mauritius Government of the foregoing at whatever level you consider appropriate.[143]

116. Although the record does not indicate any order formally designating Mauritius pursuant to Section 4 of the ordinance, the BIOT Administrator reported in 1972 that "Mauritians have been declared as traditional fishermen in BIOT as the islands formerly formed part of Mauritius."[144] The Parties are, in any event, agreed that the "understanding was that Mauritian-flagged vessels were designated to fish in the 3nm–12nm contiguous zone."[145]

117. By July 1983, the United Kingdom had noted the absence of an order formally designating Mauritius for the purposes of the 1971 Ordinance and was considering steps to "regularise the position."[146] Shortly thereafter, the discovery in August 1983 that several Mauritian fishing vessels were operating in the territorial sea around the Chagos Archipelago without the knowledge of British officials, and were also gathering coconuts on the outlying islands, prompted the United Kingdom to "look afresh at [its] policy on access by Mauritian vessels to BIOT".[147]

118. On 12 August 1984, the BIOT Commissioner adopted the Fishery Limits Ordinance, 1984 and repealed the 1971 Ordinance.[148] The new ordinance provided for the designation of particular States as eligible to fish in the territorial sea and contiguous zone surrounding the Chagos Archipelago. Following designation, vessels from such States were required to comply with

---

[143] Despatch dated 2 July 1971 from M. Elliott, UK Foreign and Commonwealth Office to R. G. Giddens, British High Commission, Port Louis, FCO 31/2763 (Annex MM-63).

[144] Despatch dated 26 May 1972 from J. R. Todd, BIOT Administrator to P. J. Walker, UK Foreign and Commonwealth Office, FCO 31/2763 (Annex MM-65).

[145] The United Kingdom's Counter-Memorial, para. 2.98; *see also* Mauritius' Reply, para. 2.100.

[146] Minute dated 5 August 1983 from Maritime, Aviation and Environment Department to East Africa Department, UK Foreign and Commonwealth Office, "BIOT: Fishing Ordinance" (Annex MR-88).

[147] Letter from W.N. Wenban-Smith, East Africa Department to PS/Mr. Rifkind, 23 August 2014, Redacted documents from the Judicial Review Proceedings (*Bancoult* v. *Secretary of State for Foreign and Commonwealth Affairs*) (Annex MR-185).

[148] BIOT Ordinance No. 11 of 1984 (Annex UKCM-49).

a licensing regime to specify the type of fishing and areas in which it could be carried out. On 21 February 1985, Mauritius was formally designated pursuant to the Fisheries Limit Ordinance, 1984 "for the purpose of enabling fishing traditionally carried on in any area within the fishery limits to be continued by fishing boats registered in Mauritius".[149]

119. On 23 July 1991, the United Kingdom wrote to Mauritius, providing advance notice that the Commissioner would shortly declare a 200 nautical mile Fisheries Conservation and Management Zone ("FCMZ") in the waters surrounding the Chagos Archipelago. The United Kingdom explained the measure in the following terms:

> There are good environmental reasons for this action. Tuna stocks migrate around the Indian Ocean, large numbers passing through the area to be included in the 200 mile zone. In the view of the British Government on the advice of technical experts, it is important that these waters are subject to regulatory control through licensing. If we fail to exercise our responsibilities stocks will dwindle to the detriment of other Indian Ocean states and territories. It is important also that we conserve the stock position and so protect the future fishing interests of the Chagos group. An extension of the zone will allow the application of regulations relating to types of net and fishing gear.
>
> In view of the traditional fishing interests of Mauritius in the waters surrounding British Indian Ocean Territory, a limited number of licences free of charge have been offered to artisanal fishing companies for inshore fishing. We shall continue to offer a limited number of licences free of charge on this basis.[150]

Mauritius responded to this communication by reiterating its claim to sovereignty over the Chagos Archipelago.[151]

120. On 1 October 1991, the BIOT Commissioner issued a Proclamation establishing the FCMZ.[152] On the same day, the BIOT Commissioner adopted the Fisheries (Conservation and Management) Ordinance, 1991, replacing the Fisheries Limit Ordinance, 1984.[153] The 1991 Ordinance extended the licensing regime of the 1984 Ordinance, but no longer required the prior designation of a State as a criteria for licensing.

121. On 1 July 1992, the United Kingdom informed Mauritius in the following terms that it would continue to issue fishing licenses for Mauritian vessels free of charge:

---

[149] British Indian Ocean Territory Notice No. 7 of 1985 (Annex MM-98).

[150] Note Verbale dated 23 July 1991 from British High Commission, Port Louis, to Government of Mauritius, No. 043/91 (Annex MM-99).

[151] Note Verbale dated 7 August 1991 from Ministry of External Affairs, Mauritius to British High Commission, Port Louis, No. 35(91) 1311 (Annex MM-100).

[152] British Indian Ocean Territory Proclamation No. 1 of 1991 (Annex MM-101).

[153] British Indian Ocean Territory Ordinance No. 1 of 1991 (Annex MM-102).

> There are no plans to establish an exclusive economic zone around the Chagos islands. HMG takes seriously its obligations to ensure the conservation of the resources of the Archipelago and declared a 200 mile exclusive fishing zone on 1 October 1991 as its contribution to safeguarding the tuna and other fish stocks of the Indian Ocean. The British Government has honoured the commitments entered into in 1965 to use its good offices with the United States Government to ensure that fishing rights would remain available to Mauritius as far as practicable. It has issued free licences for Mauritius fishing vessels to enter both the original 12 mile fishing zone of the territory and now the wider waters of the exclusive fishing zone. It will continue to do so, provided that the Mauritian vessels respect the licence conditions laid down to ensure proper conservation of local fishing resources.[154]

122. On 27 January 1994, Mauritius and the United Kingdom established the British-Mauritian Fisheries Commission to address the conservation of fish stocks. In the Joint Statement setting out the creation of the Commission, the Parties agreed to a comprehensive "sovereignty umbrella" pursuant to which neither the creation of the Commission nor any activity carried out pursuant to it would be understood to prejudice the Parties' respective positions regarding the Chagos Archipelago.[155]

123. On 13 August 2003, the United Kingdom informed Mauritius in the following terms that it intended to establish an Environmental Protection and Preservation Zone ("EPPZ") encompassing the same geographical area of the FCMZ:

> The Government of Mauritius will wish to be aware that in order to help preserve and protect the environment of the Great Chagos Bank, the British Government proposes to issue a similar Proclamation [to the FCMZ] by the Commissioner for BIOT, but this time establishing an Environmental (Protection and Preservation) Zone. This will be defined so as to have the same geographical extent as BIOT's FCMZ. It will not involve any change in the land areas comprised within BIOT. A copy of the Proclamation, together with copies of the relevant charts and co-ordinates, will be deposited with the UN under Article 75 of UNCLOS later this year.[156]

124. On 17 September 2003, the BIOT Commissioner issued British Indian Ocean Territory Proclamation No. 1 of 2003, establishing the EPPZ.[157]

---

[154] Letter dated 1 July 1992 from the British High Commissioner, Port Louis, to the Prime Minister of Mauritius (Annex MM-103).

[155] Joint Statement on the Conservation of Fisheries under a 'sovereignty umbrella', 27 January 1994 (Annex UKCM-62).

[156] Letter dated 13 August 2003 from the Director of Overseas Territories Department, UK Foreign and Commonwealth Office, to the Mauritius High Commissioner, London (Annex MM-120).

[157] British Indian Ocean Territory Proclamation No. 1 of 2003 (Annex MM-121).

In response to concerns raised by Mauritius over the EPPZ,[158] the United Kingdom stated that the nature of the FCMZ/EPPZ was not a full exclusive economic zone for all purposes.[159] The United Kingdom deposited the geographical coordinates for the EPPZ with the UN Secretary-General on 12 March 2004.[160] Mauritius protested against this deposit on 14 and 20 April 2004.[161]

125. The Parties differ regarding the scale and significance of the fishing conducted by Mauritian vessels pursuant to the foregoing regime. The United Kingdom looks at the number of licences issued by the BIOT administration and concludes that "the take-up of commercial fishing licenses by Mauritian-flagged vessels was very low, in some years nil".[162] Mauritius relies on the catch data of its Ministry of Fisheries to conclude that "there have been catches by Mauritian fishing vessels in Chagos Archipelago since at least 1977. The mean annual catch is 164 tons."[163]

I. The Marine Protected Area

1. Initial Steps regarding the MPA and the United Kingdom's Consultations with Mauritius

126. On 9 February 2009, the London newspaper *The Independent* reported that a giant marine park was planned for the Chagos Archipelago.[164] This publication prompted the Mauritian Ministry of Foreign Affairs, Regional Integration and International Trade, the following month, to reiterate its view on sovereignty over the Chagos Archipelago:

> both under Mauritian law and international law, the Chagos Archipelago is under the sovereignty of Mauritius [...] The creation of any Marine Park in the Chagos Archipelago will therefore require, on the part of all parties that have genuine respect for international law, the consent of Mauritius.[165]

[158] Letter dated 7 November 2003 from the Minister of Foreign Affairs and Regional Cooperation, Mauritius to the UK Secretary of State for Foreign and Commonwealth Affairs (Annex MM-122).

[159] Letter dated 12 December 2003 from the Minister responsible for Overseas Territories, UK Foreign and Commonwealth Office to the Minister of Foreign Affairs and Regional Cooperation, Mauritius (Annex MM-124).

[160] Law of the Sea Bulletin No. 54 (2004) at p. 128.

[161] *See* Note Verbale dated 14 April 2004 from the Permanent Mission of the Republic of Mauritius to the United Nations, New York, to the Secretary General of the United Nations, No. 4780/04 (NY/UN/562) (Annex MM-126); Note Verbale dated 20 April 2004 from the Mauritius High Commission, London to the UK Foreign and Commonwealth Office, Ref. MHCL 886/1/03 (Annex MM-127).

[162] The United Kingdom's Counter-Memorial, para. 2.111.

[163] Mauritius' Reply, para. 2.124.

[164] S. Gray, "Giant marine park plan for Chagos", *The Independent*, 9 February 2009 (Annex MM-138).

[165] Note Verbale dated 5 March 2009 from the Ministry of Foreign Affairs, Regional Integration and International Trade, Mauritius to the UK Foreign and Commonwealth Office, No. 2009(1197/28) (Annex MM-139).

127. In response, the United Kingdom FCO reiterated that it had no doubts regarding the United Kingdom's sovereignty over the BIOT and stated further as follows:

> the proposal for a marine park in the Chagos Archipelago (BIOT) is the initiative of the Chagos Environment Network and not of the Government of the United Kingdom of Great Britain and Northern Ireland. However, the Government of the United Kingdom of Great Britain and Northern Ireland welcomes and encourages recognition of the global importance of the British Indian Ocean Territory and notes the very high standards of preservation there that have been made possible by the absence of human settlement in the bulk of the territory and the environmental stewardship of the BIOT Administration and the US military.[166]

128. During the second round of Mauritius–United Kingdom joint talks on 21 July 2009 (see paragraph 110 above), the issue of a potential marine protected area was raised. The United Kingdom's account of the meeting records the following:

> 8. The UK delegation explained that environmental law had been strengthened in BIOT over the last 15 years with the establishment of strict nature reserves, Ramsar designation in [Diego Garcia] and the establishment of an EPPZ. The Territory and its environs had become one of the most valuable sites in the world for coral biodiversity and also had the cleanest oceans and was a valuable scientific resource. This was due to lack of inhabitants. The UK derived no commercial benefit from resources. The fishery was a loss-making venture and heavily subsidised by HMG. Looking ahead, the value of BIOT as a reserve/sanctuary for marine life and coral would only increase. It was better to invest available resources in a higher level of environmental protection. There was a proposal from the Chagos Environment Network (CEN). One of the ideas being mooted was that the whole of the EEZ be a no-take zone for fishing. The scientific basis had not yet been fully established but the idea merited consideration. An alternative route would be a more gradual process, i.e., to designate the reefs as no take or another proposal of a different / larger area than that of the closure of reef areas extending 12 n miles from the 200m depth contour and leave the rest of the fishery open.
>
> 9. There were powerful arguments in the UK to establish a marine protected area. However, many questions still needed to be worked through. The UK delegation explained the advantage to Mauritius that through a marine protected area, the value of the Territory would be raised and this resource would eventually be ceded to Mauritius. No decisions had yet been taken. The UK was discussing issues with the US: BIOT was

[166] Note Verbale dated 13 March 2009 from the UK Foreign and Commonwealth Office to the Ministry of Foreign Affairs, Regional Integration and International Trade, Mauritius, No. OTD 04/03/09 (Annex MM-140).

created for defence purposes and the environmental agenda must not overcome that purpose.

10. The Mauritian delegation explained that they had taken exception to the proposal from the CEN but on the basis that it implied that the Mauritians had no interest in the environment. They had also found it necessary to protest on sovereignty grounds. There was a general agreement that scientific experts should be brought together. However, the Mauritians welcomed the project but would need to have more details and understand the involvement of the Mauritian government. The UK delegation explained that not many details were available as the UK wanted to talk to Mauritius before proposals were developed. If helpful the UK could, for the purposes of discussion, produce a proposal with variations on paper for the Mauritians to look at.

11. The UK delegation added that the Foreign Secretary was minded to go towards a consultative process and that would be a standard public consultation, However, the UK had wanted to speak to Mauritius about the ideas beforehand. Also, we needed to bear in mind the case before the [European Court of Human Rights]. Any ideas proposed would be without prejudice to any judgment by the Court.[167]

129. The Mauritian account records the same exchanges in the following terms:

(v) Establishment of Marine Protected Area

This item was included at the request of the British side. It explained that the UK Government wished to start dialogue on a proposal made by a British Non-Governmental Organisation to establish a marine protected area in the region of the Chagos Archipelago.

The British side supports the proposal for the following reasons:

(*a*) the region is still pristine as a result of non-settlement; and should remain one of the very few such rare areas in the world;

(*b*) the benefits out of fishing activities accrue mostly to developed countries rather than to those of the region; and

(*c*) the conservation and preservation of the pristine environment outweighs, by far, the benefits derived from fishing activities.

In reply, the Mauritian side while expressing concern that the matter was not a subject of prior discussions with Mauritius, welcomed the proposal, since it concerns the protection of the environment, the moreso that it is in line with the policy of Government to promote sustainable development.

The Mauritius side asked for additional details in respect of the proposed project.

[167] UK Foreign and Commonwealth Office, Overseas Territories Directorate, "UK/Mauritius Talks on the British Indian Ocean Territory", 24 July 2009 (Annex MR-143).

> The Mauritian side agreed that a team of officials and marine scientists from both sides meet to examine the implications of the concept with a view to informing the next round of talks. The British side made it clear that any proposal for the establishment of the marine protected area would be without prejudice to the outcome of the decision at the European Court of Human Rights.[168]

130. The Joint Communiqué issued following the talks stated:

> The British delegation proposed that consideration be given to preserving the marine biodiversity in the waters surrounding the Chagos Archipelago/British Indian Ocean Territory by establishing a marine protected area in the region. The Mauritian side welcomed, in principle, the proposal for environmental protection and agreed that a team of officials and marine scientists from both sides meet to examine the implications of the concept with a view to informing the next round of talks. The UK delegation made it clear that any proposal for the establishment of the marine protected area would be without prejudice to the outcome of the proceedings at the European Court of Human Rights.[169]

131. On 10 November 2009, the United Kingdom initiated a public consultation process regarding the potential creation of the MPA (the "Public Consultation"). On the same day, the British High Commissioner provided the Foreign Minister of Mauritius, Dr. Arvin Boolell, with a copy of the Public Consultation document[170] and the United Kingdom's Foreign Secretary placed a call to the Prime Minister of Mauritius, Dr. Navinchandra Ramgoolam.[171] The United Kingdom's record of this telephone call read as follows:

> The Foreign Secretary said that he understood that UK and Mauritian officials had been talking very productively about a marine protected area being created during the bilateral discussions on areas of mutual cooperation on BIOT. He wanted to reassure PM Ramgoolam that the public consultation being launched was on the *idea* of an MPA and it was only an *idea* at this point. Going out to consultation was the right thing to do before making any decisions. We would talk to Mauritius before we made any final decision. Mauritian views were important. We were arranging a facilitator to travel out to Port Louis and to Victoria in January to hold meetings with all interested parties. While the focus would be on the Chagossian community, the facilitator would also listen to other peoples' views.

---

[168] Information Paper by the Prime Minister of Mauritius, Second Meeting at Senior Officials' Level between Mauritius and UK on the Chagos Archipelago, CAB(2009) 624, 12 August 2009 (Annex MR-144).

[169] Joint Communiqué, Second round of bilateral talks between Mauritius and the UK on the Chagos Archipelago, 21 July 2009, Port Louis, Mauritius (Annex MM-148).

[170] UK Foreign and Commonwealth Office, Consultation on Whether to Establish a Marine Protected Area in the "British Indian Ocean Territory", November 2009 (Annex MM-152).

[171] Prime Minister of Mauritius, December 1995 to September 2000 and from July 2005 to December 2014. Dr. Navinchandra Ramgoolam is the son of Sir Seewoosagur Ramgoolam.

The Foreign Secretary reassured PM Ramgoolam that there would be no impact on the UK commitment to cede the Territory to Mauritius when it was no longer needed for defence purposes. In the meantime, an MPA provided a demonstration of our bilateral relationship of trust and would make something of the remarkable features that exist in BIOT. He hoped the UK and Mauritius could work closely together on this.

PM Ramgoolam responded that environmental protection was an important subject for him. He had a few problems with the consultation document which he had only just seen and would be sending a Note Verbale on this. His first problem was on page 12 "we {Mauritius} have agreed in principle to the establishment of an MPA". This was not the case. Could we amend the consultation document?

In addition Mr. Ramgoolam said that the consultation document completely overlooked the issue of resettlement. A total ban on fishing would not be conducive to resettlement. Neither was there any mention of the sovereignty issue. PM Ramgoolam did not want the MPA consultation to take place outside of the bilateral talks between the UK and Mauritius on Chagos.

The Foreign Secretary said he hoped there had been no misunderstanding. He understood that the discussions between the UK and Mauritius had been positive. He would ask officials to look at page 12 of the consultation document. *Comment: we have amended the language in page 12 to reflect more closely the wording in the communiqué.* He added that while the bilateral talks were an important forum, the purpose of the consultation was to bring the idea of an MPA to a wider public. Neither the consultation nor any decision would prejudice the court cases or any of the issues PM Ramgoolam referred to. He hoped PM Ramgoolam would see that the consultation was a positive thing.

PM Ramgoolam repeated his point that a ban on fishing would be incompatible with resettlement. The Foreign Secretary suggested he make that point in the consultation but there were all sorts of ways of organising sustainable fishing. Resettlement was a different question and would take enormous resources regardless of which Government did this. He knew that PM Ramgoolam was aware of the Government's strong position on this issue.

PM Ramgoolam said he had a problem with the consultation document saying that the BIOT Commissioner would make the declaration of an MPA. They wanted it to be declared by the UK Government as Mauritius did not recognise BIOT. He pointed out that he had elections next year. *Comment: this should not be an insurmountable problem. The Foreign Secretary might instruct the BIOT Commissioner to declare an MPA and make this clear in any press release.*

The Foreign Secretary said he believed that there was nothing in the document that weakened the Mauritian claim on sovereignty. There was no reason for Mauritius to criticise Ramgoolam on that score. The UK commitment to cede the Territory was as before. He added that he had a

> lot of respect for PM Ramgoolam's political skills and could not see the consultation being a problem for PM Ramgoolam.
>
> PM Ramgoolam said he would take up the issue with Gordon Brown at CHOGM. He asked if the subject could be brought up at the next bilateral talks. The Foreign Secretary agreed that it could be.[172]

132. On the same day, Mauritius wrote to the British High Commission regarding the consultation document's representation of Mauritian support for the MPA:

> The Ministry of Foreign Affairs, Regional Integration and International Trade wishes to inform the High Commission that the Government of the Republic of Mauritius has not welcomed the establishment of a marine protected area during the bilateral talks on the Chagos Archipelago held in Mauritius last July, contrary to what is stated at page 12 of the Consultation Document.
>
> In that regard, the Ministry of Foreign Affairs, Regional Integration and International Trade would like to point out that what was stated in the Joint Communiqué issued following the bilateral talks of last July was that the Mauritian side had welcomed, in principle, the proposal for environmental protection and agreed that a team of officials and marine scientists from both sides would meet to examine the implications of the concept with a view to informing the next round of talks.
>
> The Ministry of Foreign Affairs, Regional Integration and International Trade therefore requests that the Foreign and Commonwealth Office accordingly amend its Consultation Document to accurately reflect the position of the Government of the Republic of Mauritius.[173]

133. The United Kingdom indicated in the following terms that it would correct the consultation document:

> The British High Commission would like to underline that the purpose of the consultation is to gain views on a proposal made by an environmental NGO: the Chagos Conservation Trust. No policy decision has been made on the issue in hand. Our approach aims to be consultative and inclusive: the Chagos Conservation Trust's MPA proposal was discussed with the Government of Mauritius in bilateral talks on BIOT/Chagos Islands prior to the launch of the public consultation. We anticipate further discussion in the next round of bilateral talks, which we had hoped to hold this month, but which now look likely to be held in early 2010.
>
> In light of this constructive and ongoing dialogue, the British High Commission would like to reassure the Ministry of Foreign Affairs, Regional Integration and International Trade that no offence was intended by the wording on page 12 of the draft consultation document

[172] Record of telephone call between Foreign Secretary and Mauritian Prime Minister, 10 November 2009 (Annex UKCM-106).

[173] Note Verbale dated 10 November 2009 from the Ministry of Foreign Affairs, Regional Integration and International Trade, Mauritius to the British High Commission, Port Louis, No. 48/2009 (1197/28/10) (Annex MM-153).

> that was shared with you on 10 November. We were, therefore, happy to amend the wording of the final document (released later that day on the following site: (http://www.ukinmauritius.fco.gov.uk) to reflect the views expressed in your Note Verbale.[174]

134. On 23 November 2009, Mauritius wrote further to the United Kingdom as follows:

> The Ministry of Foreign Affairs, Regional Integration and International Trade, whilst welcoming the amendment at page 12 of the Consultation Document, regrets to note that the precise stand of the Mauritian side on the MPA project, as stated in the Joint Communiqué issued following the bilateral talks of last July and in its Note Verbale of 10 November 2009, has not been fully reflected in the amended Consultation Document. That stand, as per the Joint Communiqué, reads as follows:–
>
> "The Mauritian side welcomed, in principle, the proposal for environmental protection and agreed that a team of officials and marine scientists from both sides meet to examine the implications of the concept with a view to informing the next round of talks".
>
> Furthermore, the Ministry of Foreign Affairs, Regional Integration and International Trade would like to state that since there is an on-going bilateral Mauritius-UK mechanism for talks and consultations on issues relating to the Chagos Archipelago and a third round of talks is envisaged early next year, the Government of the Republic of Mauritius believes that it is inappropriate for the consultation on the proposed marine protected area, as far as Mauritius is concerned, to take place outside this bilateral framework.
>
> The Government of Mauritius considers that an MPA project in the Chagos Archipelago should not be incompatible with the sovereignty of the Republic of Mauritius over the Chagos Archipelago and should address the issues of resettlement, access to the fisheries resources, and the economic development of the islands in a manner which would not prejudice an eventual enjoyment of sovereignty. A total ban on fisheries exploitation and omission of those issues from any MPA project would not be compatible with the long-term resolution of, or progress in the talks, on the sovereignty issue.
>
> The stand of the Government of Mauritius is that the existing framework for talks on the Chagos Archipelago and the related environmental issues should not be overtaken or bypassed by the consultation launched by the British Government on the proposed MPA.[175]

[174] Note Verbale dated 11 November 2009 from the British High Commission, Port Louis, to the Ministry of Foreign Affairs, Regional Integration and International Trade, Mauritius, No. 54/09 (Annex MM-154).

[175] Note Verbale dated 23 November 2009 from the Ministry of Foreign Affairs, Regional Integration and International Trade, Mauritius to the UK Foreign and Commonwealth Office, No. 1197/28/10 (Annex MM-155).

2. The Commonwealth Heads of Government Meeting and its Aftermath

135. On 27 November 2009, the Parties' respective Prime Ministers, Dr. Navinchandra Ramgoolam, GCSK, MP, FRCP and the Rt. Hon. Gordon Brown MP were present at the Commonwealth Heads of Government Meeting ("CHOGM") in Trinidad and Tobago. The Parties agree that the Prime Ministers had a separate discussion regarding the MPA, but disagree as to its contents.

136. Mauritius' contemporaneous record of the conversation is as follows:

> 33. A tête-à-tête meeting took place between the British Prime Minister and myself in the morning of Friday 27 November 2009. Two main subjects were covered:
>
> (*a*) Mauritian Sovereignty over the Chagos Archipelago; and
>
> (*b*) the Marine Protected Area.
>
> 34. I explained to the British Prime Minister that the bilateral talks which we have engaged with the British side are going on in a positive atmosphere and that it is imperative that the issue of sovereignty continues to be addressed.
>
> 35. I stated that Mauritius does not recognize the British Indian Ocean Territory and therefore, we cannot even discuss the issue of a Marine Protected Area with them. I emphasized that the issue of resettlement remains a pending issue and Mauritian fishing rights have to be taken into consideration. I therefore indicated that since bilateral talks were intended to deal with all the issues concerning Chagos progressively, this is the venue we should continue to use to further our discussions.
>
> 36. The British Prime Minister paid tribute to the leadership role played by Mauritius in the deliberations of the meeting particularly on the issue of Climate Change from the perspective of Small Island Developing Countries. On the issue of Marine Protected Area, he assured me that nothing would be done to undermine resettlement and the sovereignty claim of Mauritius over the Chagos Archipelago and that he would put a hold on this project.[176]

137. In the present proceedings, Dr. Ramgoolam recalls the conversation further in the following terms:

> 10. [...] I [...] took the opportunity to convey to Mr. Brown the deep concern of Mauritius over the proposal of the United Kingdom to establish a 'marine protected area' around the Chagos Archipelago and the launching of a public consultation by the UK Foreign and Commonwealth Office on 10 November 2009, just two weeks earlier, in this regard. That announcement had been the subject of media attention. I

[176] Extract of Information Paper CAB (2009) 953—Commonwealth Heads of Government Meeting, 9 December 2009 (Annex MR-148).

indicated to Mr. Brown that when the British High Commissioner in Mauritius had called on me on 22 October 2009 to announce the UK's proposal, I had expressed surprise that he was not able to offer me any document in relation to that proposal and told him that I would raise the matter with the British Prime Minister during the forthcoming CHOGM in Port of Spain. I had made very clear the objection of Mauritius to the UK's proposal.

11. I also conveyed to Mr. Brown that since the bilateral talks between Mauritius and the United Kingdom were intended to deal with all issues relating to the Chagos Archipelago, they were the only proper forum in which there should be further discussions on the proposed 'marine protected area'.

12. I further pointed out that the issues of sovereignty and resettlement remained pending and that the rights of Mauritius in the Chagos Archipelago waters had to be taken into consideration.

13. In response, Mr. Brown asked me once again: "What would you like me to do?" I remember these words clearly.

14. I replied: "You must put a stop to it". There could have been no doubt that I was referring to the proposed 'marine protected area'.

15. Mr. Brown then said: "I will put it on hold". He told me that he would speak to the British Foreign Secretary. He also assured me that the proposed 'marine protected area' would be discussed only within the framework of the bilateral talks between Mauritius and the UK.[177]

138. The United Kingdom's account of the same conversation differs. Based on internal United Kingdom correspondence, by 8 December 2009 the British High Commission became aware of Dr. Ramgoolam's understanding of his exchange with Mr. Brown and sought clarification from London. The Foreign and Commonwealth Office then approached the Prime Minister's Office whose account, as relayed, was to the effect that "the PM did not say that the consultation/MPA proposal was over or that the issue had finished. What we are told the PM said is that were Ramgoolam to be haemorrhaging support in the run up to Mauritian elections, then the PM would do what he could to be helpful—this leading in to the question around delaying any decision until after the Mauritian election."[178] As presented in these proceedings, the United Kingdom's view of this conversation is that "Gordon Brown did not say what the Mauritian Prime Minister understood him to have said".[179]

[177] Statement of Dr. the Honourable Navinchandra Ramgoolam, Prime Minister of the Republic of Mauritius, 6 November 2013 (Annex MR-183).

[178] E-mail from Andrew Allen, Head of Southern Oceans Team, Overseas Territories Directorate, Foreign and Commonwealth Office to Ewan Ormiston, Deputy High Commissioner Mauritius, 8 December 2009 (UK Arbitrator's Folder, Tab 75).

[179] Final Transcript, 502:13–14.

139. On 15 December 2009, the UK Foreign Secretary, David Miliband, wrote to the Mauritius Foreign Minister, Dr. Arvin Boolell, recalling their parallel discussions at the CHOGM:

> I very much welcomed the opportunity to meet you at CHOGM. We had a useful discussion on the proposal for a Marine Protected Area in the British Indian Ocean Territory. I believe we both agree that without prejudice to wider political issues, discussed below, there is an opportunity to protect an area of outstanding natural beauty which contains islands, reef systems and waters which in terms of preservation and biodiversity are among the richest on the planet. As we agreed at the time, both the UK and Mauritius now need to reflect on next steps and work to bridge any differences in approach.
>
> At our meeting, you mentioned your concerns that the UK should have consulted Mauritius further before launching the consultation exercise. I regret any difficulty this has caused you or your Prime Minister in Port Louis. I hope you will recognize that we have been open about the plans and that the offer of further talks has been on the table since July.
>
> I would like to reassure you again that the public consultation does not in any way prejudice or cut across our bilateral intergovernmental dialogue with Mauritius on the proposed Marine Protected Area. The purpose of the public consultation is to seek the views of the wider interested community, including scientists, NGOs, those with commercial interests and other stakeholders such as the Chagossians.
>
> The consultations and our plans for an MPA do not in any way impact on our commitment to cede the territory when it is no longer needed for defence purposes. Our ongoing bilateral talks are an excellent forum for your Government to express its views on the MPA. We welcome the prospect of further discussion in the context of these talks, the next round of which now look likely to happen in January.
>
> As well as the MPA there are, of course, many other issues for bilateral discussion. My officials remain ready to continue the talks and I hope that Mauritius will take up the opportunity to pursue this bilateral dialogue.
>
> [...][180]

140. Dr. Boolell responded to the Foreign Secretary on 30 December 2009 as follows:

> During our recent meeting in the margins of the Commonwealth Heads of Government Meeting, I had expressed the concerns of the Government of Mauritius about the Marine Protected Area project. I had stated that it was inappropriate for the British authorities to embark on consultations on the matter outside the bilateral Mauritius-United Kingdom mechanism for talks on issues relating to the Chagos Archipelago.

[180] Letter dated 15 December 2009 from the UK Secretary of State for Foreign and Commonwealth Affairs to the Minister of Foreign Affairs, Regional Integration and International Trade, Mauritius (Annex MM-156).

> On the substance of the proposal, I had conveyed to you that the Government of Mauritius considers that the establishment of a Marine Protected Area around the Chagos Archipelago should not be incompatible with the sovereignty of Mauritius over the Chagos Archipelago. As you are aware, the Mauritian position, as also endorsed at various multilateral fora, is that the Chagos Archipelago was illegally excised by the British Government from the territory of Mauritius prior to the grant of independence to Mauritius. The Government of Mauritius has repeatedly informed the British Government that it does not recognize the so-called British Indian Ocean Territory and deplores the fact that Mauritius is still not in a position to exercise effective control over the Chagos Archipelago as a result of the illegal excision of its territory.
>
> Moreover, the issues of resettlement in the Chagos Archipelago, access to the fisheries resources and the economic development of the islands in a manner that would not prejudice the effective exercise by Mauritius of its sovereignty over the Chagos Archipelago are matters of high priority to the Government of Mauritius. The exclusion of such important issues in any discussion relating to the proposed establishment of a Marine Protected Area would not be compatible with resolution of the issue of sovereignty over the Chagos Archipelago and progress in the ongoing talks between Mauritius and the United Kingdom.
>
> In these circumstances, as I have mentioned, Mauritius is not in a position to hold separate consultations with the team of experts of the UK on the proposal to establish a Marine Protected Area.
>
> You will no doubt be aware that, in the margins of the last CHOGM, our respective Prime Ministers agreed that the Marine Protected Area project be put on hold and that this issue be addressed during the next round of Mauritius-United Kingdom bilateral talks.[181]

141. On the same day, Mauritius dispatched a Note Verbale to the United Kingdom, stating as follows:

> The Ministry of Foreign Affairs, Regional Integration and International Trade wishes to inform the Foreign and Commonwealth Office that the Government of Mauritius considers that the next round of bilateral talks between the two Governments cannot take place during the month of January 2010, in the absence of satisfactory clarification and reassurances on the part of the Government of the United Kingdom on issues raised by the Government of Mauritius in the above-mentioned Note Verbale [of 23 November 2009] in relation to the Marine Protected Area project and in view of the continuation by the Government of the United Kingdom of the initial consultation process it had embarked upon.
>
> The Government of Mauritius trusts that it will receive, within a reasonable period, adequate clarification and reassurances on the part

[181] Letter dated 30 December 2009 from the Minister of Foreign Affairs, Regional Integration and International Trade, Mauritius to the UK Secretary of State for Foreign and Commonwealth Affairs (Annex MM-157).

> of the Government of the United Kingdom on the issues raised in the above-mentioned Note Verbale.[182]

142. On 13 January 2010, Foreign Minister Boolell called on the British High Commissioner, Mr. John Murton. The conversation that ensued covered the differing understandings of the Prime Ministers' meeting at CHOGM and potential ways forward. The High Commissioner's record is as follows:

> By far the biggest issue was the outcome of the PM Brown/PM Ramgoolam tête-à-tête. Ramgoolam had briefed Cabinet following the meeting at CHOGM and told them that Brown had agreed to 'drop' the consultation. He was very (and unusually) clear and definitive about this and had clearly expected Brown to make some sort of statement to this effect. Ramgoolam also briefed the press on the matter and took pride in pointing to this result as stemming from his good relationship with Brown (Boolell noted he had a 'soft spot' for him). As the days wore on after the summit without a statement, Ramgoolam became increasingly frustrated. When Miliband's letter arrived (which we had written thinking it was very conciliatory), Ramgoolam took this as a kick in the teeth. Ramgoolam's anger triggered the notes of 30 December and, upon Ramgoolam's instructions, the press briefing by Boolell earlier this month.
>
> Some of these points are manageable, but the discord between Ramgoolam's readout of the PM's meeting and the readout from Brown is clearly large and, in many ways, insurmountable. I detected no sense that the Mauritians are playing a game on this. Ramgoolam clearly believes Brown promised him what he had wanted and that, somehow, Miliband has sought to circumvent this. I assured Boolell this wasn't the case and showed him the readout we had received from No 10. We both scratched our heads.
>
> I noted we needed a way forward that allowed the MPA consultation to continue and ensured that the issue did not become a political burden to the Government here. I passed across the draft letter I had shared with you yesterday and explained that, if we sent such a letter, a conciliatory reply from the Mauritians would go a long way to resolving things. Boolell suggested a number of changes to the letter.[183]

143. On 20 January 2010, the British High Commissioner met with Prime Minister Ramgoolam on the subject of the MPA consultations. The United Kingdom's record of this conversation is, in relevant part, as follows:

> PM Ramgoolam reiterated his record of the bilateral with Gordon Brown: Brown had been 'very thankful' for all Ramgoolam had done sorting out the CHOGM Summit impasse with Sri Lanka—enabling Sri Lanka to climb down without being humiliated. When Ramgoolam had begun setting out his case on BIOT, Brown had 'interrupted' him

[182] Note Verbale dated 30 December 2009 from the Ministry of Foreign Affairs, Regional Integration and International Trade, Mauritius to the UK Foreign and Commonwealth Office, No. 1197/28/4 (Annex MM-158).

[183] E-mail from John Murton, British High Commissioner in Port Louis, Mauritius to Joanne Yeadon, BIOT Administrator, 14 January 2010 (UK Arbitrator's Folder, Tab 77).

to say 'Navin, what do you want?'. Ramgoolam says he had asked for the MPA consultation to be stopped, and Brown had agreed: "It's done." Hence Mauritius' upset when David Miliband's letter of 15 December indicated the consultation was ongoing.

I went through our version of events and explained the readout we had received from the meeting. I noted that, although I obviously hadn't been present, I knew and trusted the PM's [Private Secretary]. In light of the readout we'd received, David Miliband's letter was written in good faith as a constructive gesture. We'd been stung by the reaction it had met, particularly by the mis-reporting of Boolell's comments in the press and the claim we'd been 'dishonest'. Discussions with Koonjul and Boolell had revealed that the MFA here hadn't been fully aware of the extent of consultations we'd had with Ramgoolam himself, and this had (wrongly) coloured their advice to the PM. Mauritian non-participation at recent seminars wasn't helpful; they could easily have taken part under some form of disclaimer on sovereignty. More willingness to engage from them could have dispelled a lot of misunderstanding. He took these points.

Looking forward, I explained how my goal in meeting the PM was to enable both sides to move forward without humiliation and to avoid any further painting-into-corners. Ramgoolam jumped in: should he write to Gordon Brown to clarify the outcome of the CHOGM meeting? I sought to deflect him from this: for such a move not to backfire, the PM would have to be sure that he'd get the answer he wanted from Gordon Brown—there were political issues in the mix in the UK too. Was he sure this would work? Ramgoolam pondered aloud about what he perceived as David Miliband's strong commitment to the MPA and whether recent political events in the UK might inhibit Gordon Brown from pushing Miliband to rein in the consultation, even if he'd wanted to.

I noted that I had been working with Boolell to draft a letter that might help both sides move forward. Boolell was keen for the PM to see it. I didn't want to send the letter until I knew it would help the situation. The draft answered all of Mauritius' concerns re consultation with [the Government of Mauritius] taking place through bilateral talks, sovereignty, non-prejudice to settlement case at ECHR etc. Ramgoolam undertook to look at it with Ruhee. He was glad no other copies existed yet.

[...]

I followed up afterwards by telephone with Ruhee, principally to alert him to the [Public Consultation] facilitator's impending arrival (there hadn't been a good moment to raise this in the meeting). We'd need to factor a line on this into the letter to clear the way for her to come without it becoming a politically exploitable issue here.[184]

---

[184] E-mail from John Murton, British High Commissioner in Port Louis, Mauritius to Joanne Yeadon, BIOT Administrator, and Colin Roberts, BIOT Commissioner and Director of the Overseas Territories Directorate, 20 January 2010 (UK Arbitrator's Folder, Tab 78).

144. On 4 February 2010, Mauritius submitted written evidence to the UK House of Commons Select Committee on Foreign Affairs in respect of the MPA:

> 2. Since there is an on-going bilateral Mauritius-UK mechanism for talks and consultations on issues relating to the Chagos Archipelago, it is inappropriate and insulting for the British Government to pursue consultations globally on the proposal for the establishment of an MPA around the Chagos Archipelago outside this bilateral framework. This position was brought to the attention of the British Government by way of Note Verbale dated 23 November 2009 issued by the Ministry of Foreign Affairs, Regional Integration and International Trade of the Republic of Mauritius to the UK Foreign and Commonwealth Office. We have not received any answer yet whilst the FCO continues to defy our deep concerns on this process.
>
> 3. The manner in which the Marine Protected Area proposal is being dealt with makes us feel that it is being imposed on Mauritius with a predetermined agenda.
>
> 4. The establishment of an MPA around the Chagos Archipelago must be compatible with the sovereignty of Mauritius over the Chagos Archipelago. Any endorsement of the proposed unilateral initiative of the FCO's, particularly in some scientific quarters, would be tantamount to condoning the violation of international law and the enduring human tragedy.
>
> 5. Moreover, the issue of resettlement in the Chagos Archipelago, access to the fisheries resources, and the economic development of the islands in a manner which would not prejudice the effective exercise by Mauritius of its sovereignty over the Chagos Archipelago are matters of high priority to the Government of Mauritius.
>
> 6. The exclusion of such important issues from any MPA project and a total ban on fisheries exploitation would not be compatible with resolution of the issue of sovereignty over the Chagos Archipelago and progress in the ongoing talks between Mauritius and the United Kingdom.
>
> 7. The existing framework of talks between Mauritius and the UK on the Chagos Archipelago and the related environmental issues should not be overtaken or bypassed by the public consultation launched by the British Government on the proposed establishment of an MPA around the Chagos Archipelago.
>
> 8. The establishment of any MPA around the Chagos Archipelago should also address the benefits that Mauritius should derive from any mineral or oil that may be discovered in or near Chagos Archipelago (as per the undertaking given in 1965).[185]

[185] Written Evidence of the Mauritius High Commissioner, London, on the UK Proposal for the Establishment of a Marine Protected Area around the Chagos Archipelago, to the House of Commons Select Committee on Foreign Affairs (Annex MM-160).

145. On 8 February 2010, the British High Commissioner met again with Foreign Minister Boolell on the subject of the MPA. The United Kingdom's record of this conversation is, in relevant part, as follows:

> Much of the time was spent covering old ground, including [Government of Mauritius] unhappiness with the way the consultation was launched and the divergent readouts from the PM-PM meeting at CHOGM. We noted that repeated media briefing from the Mauritian side was unhelpful (e.g. Saturday's Mauricien).
>
> Boolell raised the issue of Chagossian resettlement and the meaning of our 'without prejudice' phrase in the MPA consultation document. We noted it meant respect for the [European Court of Human Rights] judgement. We then sought to unpick the issue of resettlement from the MPA, underlining once more the risks that resettlement potentially posed to our commitment to cede the islands when no longer needed for defence purposes. There was considerable discussion of the role of the Chagossian community in this process.
>
> [...]
>
> In discussing the way forward from here, Boolell suggested that we meet with Cabinet Secretary Seebaluck [*sic*] to request bilateral talks. We might do so using a 'short' letter: our earlier draft had been too 'long' and 'open to misinterpretation'. Once the 12th February [the originally scheduled end of the Public Consultation] was past, the atmosphere would be 'conducive' and 'welcoming' to a new round of talks. We alluded to the fact that we might not find it easy to draw a line under the consultation without some form of engagement with the Chagossians, noting that some argued there was a requirement to engage fully even with those not able to respond to a written consultation process.
>
> It was clear that the Mauritians would not welcome the visit of the facilitator. Boolell noted that a visit would be a 'slight' on the people and Government of Mauritius. They wanted to retain their 'sovereign rights'. We asked if a [video teleconference]-based consultation be easier [*sic*] for the Mauritians to swallow? Boolell could only agree to take note of this and consider the matter, but didn't commit.
>
> We said that, if talks could be restarted (and we'd been waiting for the Mauritians to discuss dates since 22 January), they'd be productive only if Mauritius came with a clear sense of what it realistically wanted rather than either (*a*) demanding sovereignty as they had done in London or (*b*) dwelling only on those things that were unacceptable to Mauritius. It would be best to focus on areas of common ground and potential cooperation. The idea of an MPA provided areas for joint work—the Mauritian Finance Minister had set aside money for MPAs in his recent budget. We thought there was enough common ground for this to be a constructive area.
>
> Boolell took the point and raised a couple of issues that could be profitably discussed:
>
> - demarcation of the continental shelf;

- the terminology 'MPA'. Marine Protected Area gave the idea of 'ownership' and the UK 'protecting' its sovereignty claim. Conservation/Preservation were better words, or at least 'the protection of the marine environment'. Mauritius was increasingly recognising it was an 'Oceanic state' and cooperation around this sphere could be helpful;
- future PM–PM engagement;
- trilateral discussions with the US [we countered this wasn't within our gift];
- a rest from nuclear ships visiting DG (just to give some political space at home in Mauritius).[186]

146. On 15 February 2010, the United Kingdom wrote to Mauritius, referencing the latter's Note Verbale of 30 December 2009 and enquiring only as to "an indication as to when the Government of Mauritius would be willing to reschedule such a meeting: either in London or Port Louis."[187] The Secretary to the Cabinet of Mauritius, Mr. Seeballuck, responded on 19 February 2010, referencing the CHOGM discussion and stating:

> 3. I wish to reiterate the position of the Government of Mauritius to the effect that the consultation process on the proposed MPA should be stopped and the current Consultation Paper, which is unilateral and prejudicial to the interests of Mauritius withdrawn. Indeed, the Consultation Paper is a unilateral UK initiative which ignores the agreed principles and spirit of the ongoing Mauritius-UK bilateral talks and constitutes a serious setback to progress in these talks.
>
> 4. I further wish to inform you that the Government of Mauritius insists that any proposal for the protection of the marine environment in the Chagos Archipelago area needs to be compatible with and meaningfully take on board the position of Mauritius on the sovereignty over the Chagos Archipelago and address the issues of resettlement and access by Mauritians to fisheries resources in that area.
>
> 5. I also wish to state that the Government of Mauritius is keen to resume the bilateral talks on the premises outlined above.[188]

147. On 19 March 2010, the British High Commission responded to Mauritius' Note of 15 February 2010, reiterating the United Kingdom's views on sovereignty over the Archipelago and on resettlement, and stating with respect to the MPA Public Consultation as follows:

> The United Kingdom should like to reiterate that no decision on the creation of an MPA has yet been taken. However, as stated previously in dis-

[186] E-mail from John Murton, British High Commissioner in Port Louis, Mauritius to Joanne Yeadon, BIOT Administrator, 8 February 2010 (UK Arbitrator's Folder, Tab 79).

[187] Note Verbale No. 6/2010 from British High Commission to Mauritius Ministry of Foreign Affairs, 15 February 2010 (Annex UKR-64).

[188] Letter dated 19 February 2010 from the Secretary to Cabinet and Head of the Civil Service, Mauritius to the British High Commissioner, Port Louis (Annex MM-162).

> cussions between Ministers and Officials and set out clearly in the MPA consultation document, the establishment of any marine protected area will have no impact on the United Kingdom's commitment to cede the Territory to Mauritius when it is no longer needed for defence purposes. Additionally, the United Kingdom is keen to continue dialogue about environmental protection within bilateral framework or separately. The public consultation does not preclude, overtake or bypass these talks. [189]

The High Commissioner further stated that "[l]ike Mauritius, the UK is keen to continue these bilateral talks as there are many other things we can discuss with regards to BIOT."[190]

3. The Declaration of the MPA

148. The Public Consultation ran until 5 March 2010. Thereafter, the Foreign Secretary received a detailed report from the consultation facilitator summarizing the consultation process and the comments received. The summary of the facilitator's report presented the consultation as follows:

> [...]
>
> 6. The response was wide ranging, with a global reach. It included inputs from private individuals, academic and scientific institutions, environmental organisations and networks, fishing and yachting interests, members of the Chagossian community, British MPs and peers and representatives of other governments.
>
> 7. The great majority of respondents—well over 90%—made clear that they supported greater marine protection of some sort in the Chagos Archipelago in principle. However, views on this proposal were more mixed, covering a wide spectrum of views. Responses did not confine themselves to the options listed in the Consultation Document.
>
> 8. The main difference between the responses was their view on potential resettlement of members of the Chagossian community, and whether this question should be tackled before designation of any MPA, or whether changes could be made later if circumstances changed, in an MPA agreed, as the Consultation Document suggests, in the context of the Government's policy on the Territory, without prejudice to ongoing legal proceedings.
>
> 9. Of those who supported one of the three listed options the great majority supported Option 1, *a full no-take marine reserve for the whole of the territorial waters and Environmental Preservation and Protection Zone (EPPZ)/Fisheries Conservation and Management Zone (FCMZ).* The

[189] Letter dated 19 March 2010 from the British High Commissioner, Port Louis, to the Secretary to Cabinet and Head of the Civil Service, Mauritius (Annex MM-163). The same details were transmitted by Note Verbale on 26 March 2010. Note Verbale dated 26 March 2010 from British High Commission, Port Louis, to the Ministry of Foreign Affairs, Regional Integration and International Trade, Mauritius, No. 14/2010 (Annex MM-164).

[190] *Ibid.*

reasons given were generally very much in line with the conservation, climate change and scientific benefits set out in the Consultation Document. A number also highlighted a legacy element, as well as the opportunity to show leadership and provide an example for others, while contributing to meeting a number of global environmental commitments.

10. In terms of numbers, support for options 2 and 3 was limited. However, they were universally the choice of the Indian Ocean commercial tuna fishing community, as well as a number of regional interests. While agreeing that there was a strong case for protecting the fragile reef environment, this group considered that the scientific case for the extra benefits of option 1 was not strongly demonstrated and the group did not want to see a negative economic impact on the tuna industry. In addition, a limited number of private individuals thought that controlled, licensed fishing at around the current level was sufficient protection and was not causing significant decline or degradation.

11. A significant body of response did not support proceeding with any of the three listed options at the current time. Of this group, some, including most but not all of the Chagossian community, argued simply for abandoning or postponing the current proposal until further consultation and agreement could take place, while others proposed one or another different option (a 'fourth option'), which sought to take account of Chagossian (and in some cases other regional) requirements.

12. As well as their headline comments on preferred options, respondents raised a number of issues of interest or concern to them. These included: the consultation process itself; the rights and interests of the Chagossian community; regional interests and concerns; enforcement of an MPA; costs associated with an MPA; yachting interests; piracy; Diego Garcia and the US base; bycatch from commercial fishing, including sharks and fragile species; fish stocks; reputational issues; and other proposed environmental measures. These are described in more detail in a final section which summarises the issues covered in responses received to each of the Consultation questions.[191]

149. The United Kingdom's further decision-making with respect to the MPA was then marked by significant differences between the political and diplomatic/civil service level. On 30 March 2010, the BIOT Administrator made a submission to the Parliamentary Under Secretary and Foreign Secretary entitled "British Indian Ocean Territory (BIOT): Proposed Marine Protected Area (MPA): Next Steps". Summarizing relevant considerations, including *vis-à-vis* Mauritius, the submission recommended as follows:

Preferred options

That the Foreign Secretary announces the publication of the report on the responses to the FCO public consultation into whether to create an MPA in the Territory; commenting on the level of interest in the

[191] R. Stevenson, Consultation Facilitator, '*Whether to establish a marine protected area in the British Indian Ocean Territory: Consultation Report*', Executive Summary (Annex UKCM-121).

consultation and general support for environmental protection and for a no-take fishing zone; noting that the consultation has thrown up a range of views which need to be explored further; stating that he believes that the establishment of an MPA is the way ahead for the protection of the environment of the Territory and that he will ask officials to work towards this. But he should stop short of announcing that he is going to ask the BIOT Commissioner to declare an MPA in the Territory at this stage. I attach a draft statement which could be used as both as a press statement and as a Written Ministerial Statement.[192]

150. After receiving an indication that the Foreign Secretary was contemplating moving ahead directly with the declaration of the MPA, the BIOT Commissioner and BIOT Administrator exchanged correspondence with the British High Commissioner in Mauritius regarding the likely Mauritian reaction to such action. In the course of internal correspondence, the British High Commissioner stated his view that "to declare the MPA today could have very significant negative consequences for the bilateral relationship. It would be seen by the Government here in general, and by PM Ramgoolam in particular, as exceedingly damaging timing."[193] Reacting to this concern, on 31 March 2010, the BIOT Administrator provided a further minute to the Foreign Secretary as follows:

> 1. The FS has said that, in an ideal world, he would like to declare an MPA in BIOT and spend 3 months reaching some sort of agreement with the Mauritian government on the governance of the area but making it clear that we will have 3 months to consult them but if they won't come to an agreement, we will go ahead without them. You have asked for options, whether this is feasible and possible implications. We have discussed this with our High Commissioner in Port Louis.
>
> 2. The "3 months", or any defined period, to hammer out details of some sort of management structure will not fly in Mauritius. Ramgoolam would not be able to commit to negotiating in this framework if an MPA had already been declared. Any such offer would be seen as forcing them into a position and would only antagonize them further.
>
> 3. What might work in Mauritius is the announcement as suggested in my submission of 30 March. Our High Commissioner thinks that there might be a market for a proposal to work with Mauritius as a privileged partner on management issues but this would need to be done prior to a final decision and such talks would have to precede any formal announcement of an MPA. If Mauritius were not prepared to engage

[192] Submission dated 30 March 2010 from Joanne Yeadon, Head of BIOT & Pitcairn Section, to Colin Roberts, Director, Overseas Territories Directorate, the Private Secretary to Parliamentary Under Secretary Chris Bryant and the Private Secretary to the Foreign Secretary, "British Indian Ocean Territory (BIOT): Proposed Marine Protected Area (MPA): Next Steps" (Annex MR-152).

[193] E-mail dated 31 March 2010 from John Murton, British High Commissioner to Mauritius, to Colin Roberts, Director, Overseas Territories Directorate and Joanne Yeadon, Head of BIOT & Pitcairn Section, UK Foreign and Commonwealth Office (Annex MR-156).

> in any sensible way, we would want to press on without them, but we would want to give them time to reflect and ourselves time to manage the negative consequences.
>
> 4. The High Commissioner has asked that the Foreign Secretary be made aware that the timing could not be worse locally than to declare a full no-take MPA today. The Parliamentary Labour Party of Mauritius is currently in a closed door meeting and it is expected that they will announce their own elections during the course of today. All Ministers are uncontactable and so the High Commission have no capacity to manage political reactions. He also wanted to point out that declaring an MPA today could have very significant negative consequences for the bilateral relationship. It would be seen, especially by Ramgoolam, as exceedingly damaging timing and pressure would be on for him to commit to taking legal action to challenge the establishment of an MPA. The Foreign Secretary will recall the atmospherics of his telephone conversation with Ramgoolam on the day the consultation was launched.[194]

151. On 31 March 2010, the Private Secretary to the Foreign Secretary wrote to the BIOT Administrator, conveying the following decision:

> The Foreign Secretary was grateful for your submission and the copy of the report on the consultations. He has carefully considered the arguments in the submission and the views expressed during the consultation. He was grateful for your further note today. He has considered the submission in light of the High Commissioner's views and has given serious thought to the different possible options for announcing an MPA.
>
> The Foreign Secretary has decided to instruct Colin Roberts [the BIOT Commissioner] to declare the full MPA (option one) on 1 April. There will then need to be an announcement to this effect.
>
> I would be grateful if you could take forward both.[195]

152. On 1 April 2010, the BIOT Commissioner issued Proclamation No. 1 of 2010, formally establishing the MPA.[196] Before the Proclamation was made public, the UK Foreign Secretary placed a call to the Prime Minister of Mauritius. According to the United Kingdom FCO's minute of the call:

> 1. The Foreign Secretary said that he wanted to inform the Mauritius Prime Minister that he would today instruct the BIOT Commissioner to establish a Marine Protected Area (MPA) in the British Indian Ocean Territory. We were telling the Prime Minister this in advance as we did not want there to be any surprises.

---

[194] Minute dated 31 March 2010 from Joanne Yeadon, Head of BIOT & Pitcairn Section, UK Foreign and Commonwealth Office to Colin Roberts, Director, Overseas Territories Directorate and the Private Secretary to the Foreign Secretary, "British Indian Ocean Territory: MPA: Next Steps: Mauritius" (Annex MR-158).

[195] E-mail exchange between Catherine Brooker, Private Secretary to the Foreign Secretary and Joanne Yeadon, Head of BIOT & Pitcairn Section, UK Foreign and Commonwealth Office, 30–31 March 2010 (Annex MR-155).

[196] British Indian Ocean Territory Proclamation No. 1 of 2010 (Annex MM-166).

2. The Foreign Secretary said that both the UK and Mauritius were commited [*sic*] to the environmental agenda and the establishment of the MPA had no impact on the UK commitment to cede BIOT to Mauritius when the territory was no longer needed for defence purposes. Nor would it prejudice the legal position of Mauritius or the Chagos Islanders. The UK valued the relationship with Mauritius and the Foreign Secretary hoped that we could cooperate together to ensure that the MPA was a success.

3. The Foreign Secretary said there had been a very large response to the consultation exercise with about a quarter of a million responses. This was a remarkable number. The majority of the responses were straightforward but there had also been responses from the environmental, political, governmental and scientific communities and some from the business community. The consultation showed that those arguing for commercial exploitation of the area were clearly in the minority. There had been some debate around the no-take approach and there was overwhelming support for that.

4. Ramgoolam said that he was disappointed that there had not been bilateral discussions. He asked if it might be possible to delay the announcement until after the Mauritius elections. It was a controversial issue in Mauritius. The Foreign Secretary said that the consultation had been thorough and there had already been an extension to the consultation period. It would not be possible to delay the announcement. The UK would stress that the decision was without prejudice to the legal position of the Chagos Islanders or to the discussions with Mauritius on the Territory.

5. The Foreign Secretary said he would say very clearly that we would work with all interested parties, in Britain and internationally, on the implementation of the no-take approach. He would also make clear that our commitment to the government and people of Mauritius in respect of ceding sovereignty at the appropriate time was strong and clear. While recognising the disagreement with the Mauritius Government on the process leading up to the establishment of the MPA, he hoped that this could bring the two governments together to work in the best interests of the environment.

6. Ramgoolam said that he had to take the line that Mauritius disagreed with the decision on the MPA but he would like to say that he and the Foreign Secretary had talked about sovereignty. The Foreign Secretary stressed that the sovereignty issue had not changed and Ramgoolam should not seek to suggest that was the purpose of the phone call. If it would help, Ramgoolam could say that if both governments were re-elected then there could be early bilateral talks on the implementation of the MPA.

7. Ramgoolam said that when the Mauritians tried to talk to the United States about BIOT the Americans took the line that Mauritius needed to settle the sovereignty issue with the UK first. The Foreign Secretary

> said that our position was clear. We would cede the Territory to Mauritius when we no longer required the base.[197]

153. On 2 April 2010, Mauritius protested against the declaration of the MPA in the following terms:

> The Government of the Republic of Mauritius strongly objects to the decision of the British Government to create a marine protected area (MPA) around the Chagos Archipelago, as announced by UK Secretary of State for Foreign and Commonwealth Affairs David Miliband yesterday.
>
> The Government of the Republic of Mauritius wishes to recall that on several occasions following the announcement by the British authorities for an international consultation on their proposal for the creation of an MPA in the waters of the Chagos Archipelago, the Government of Mauritius conveyed its strong opposition to such a project being undertaken without consultation with and the consent of the Government of the Republic of Mauritius. In this regard, the Ministry refers to its Notes Verbales No. 1197/28/10 dated 23 November 2009 and No. 1197/28/4 dated 30 December 2009 in particular. The position of the Government of Mauritius was also conveyed directly by the Prime Minister of Mauritius to British Prime Minister Gordon Brown during the Commonwealth Heads of Government Meeting (CHOGM) in Port of Spain last November and earlier to British Foreign Secretary David Miliband over the phone. The Minister of Foreign Affairs, Regional Integration and International Trade of Mauritius, Dr. the Hon. Arvin Boolell, also communicated the position of Mauritius to Foreign Secretary Miliband during CHOGM in Port of Spain and to the British High Commissioner at several meetings.
>
> It was explained in very clear terms during the above-mentioned meetings that Mauritius does not recognize the so-called British Indian Ocean Territory and that the Chagos Archipelago, including Diego Garcia, forms an integral part of the sovereign territory of Mauritius both under our national law and international law. It was also mentioned that the Chagos Archipelago, including Diego Garcia, was illegally excised from Mauritius by the British Government prior to grant of independence in violation of United Nations General Assembly resolutions 1514 (XV) of 14 December 1960 and 2066 (XX) of 16 December 1965.
>
> The Government of the Republic of Mauritius further believes that the creation of an MPA at this stage is inconsistent with the right of settlement in the Chagos Archipelago of Mauritians, including the right of return of Mauritians of Chagossian origin which presently is under consideration by the European Court of Human Rights following a representation made by Mauritians of Chagossian origin.
>
> The Government of the Republic of Mauritius will not recognize the existence of the marine protected area in case it is established and will

---

[197] Notes of telephone call from Foreign Secretary to Mauritius' Prime Minister of 1 April 2010 in e-mail of 1 April 2010 from Global Response Centre (Annex UKR-67).

look into legal and other options that are now open to it. The more so, the Anglo-US Lease Agreement in respect of the Chagos Archipelago, concluded in breach of the sovereignty rights of Mauritius over the Chagos Archipelago, is about to expire in 2016 and the Chagos Archipelago, including Diego Garcia, should be effectively returned to Mauritius at the expiry of the Agreement.[198]

154. On 6 April 2010, the United Kingdom declared a general election. In response to a question posed during the hearing regarding the speed with which the decision to declare the MPA was taken, the United Kingdom noted as follows:

> there was an election due at the beginning of May, which was a little over four weeks later. In the British system of government, when an election is called, essentially government stops. No new policies can be introduced. So, either Mr. Miliband took his decision on 1 April—which is the last possible date he could do so before the election—or he could leave the decision for the incoming government four weeks later. He took the decision, he did lose office, a new government came in, and they confirmed his decision.[199]

4. Consultations between the United Kingdom and Mauritius following the Declaration of the MPA

155. On 3 June 2010, Prime Minister Ramgoolam raised the issue of the MPA declaration during a meeting with the new UK Foreign Secretary, William Hague.[200]

156. On 1 September 2010, the BIOT Administrator made a submission to the Foreign Secretary regarding the implementation and financing of the MPA. This submission recounted the United Kingdom's analysis of the Mauritian attitude to the MPA in the following terms:

> 9. At his meeting with Prime Minister Ramgoolam on 3 June, the Foreign Secretary advised that he would familiarise himself with the issues surrounding the MPA but would not raise Ramgoolam's hopes. He stressed that he could not give Ramgoolam any reason to hope for a change in policy but that he and Mr. Bellingham did want to work closely with Ramgoolam and his government. Mr. Bellingham repeated

[198] Note Verbale dated 2 April 2010 from Ministry of Foreign Affairs, Regional Integration and International Trade, Mauritius to the British High Commission, Port Louis, No. 11/2010 (1197/28/10) (Annex MM-167).

[199] Final Transcript, 888:22 to 889:4.

[200] While a new government had since assumed office in the United Kingdom, the Mauritius general election conducted on 5 May 2010 returned the government to power. There is no joint record of this meeting. For Mauritius' record, see Extract of Information Paper CAB (2010) 295—Official Mission to France and the United Kingdom, 9 June 2010 (Annex MR-161). For the United Kingdom's record of the same meeting, see United Kingdom record of meeting of 3 June 2010 (Annex UKCM-116).

these messages when he met Foreign Minister Boolell at the AU Summit on 22 July 2010. The Acting High Commissioner in Port Louis has also recently informed Foreign Minister Boolell of the Minister for Africa's letters to Lord Luce and Olivier Bancoult. However, the Mauritians are likely still to be disappointed: they had high hopes for the new Government. This issue is likely to continue to cause tension in our otherwise good bilateral relations with Mauritius, and could impact on our wider bilateral objectives, including working with Mauritius on counter piracy in the Indian Ocean.

10. The decision to continue with the MPA of itself is unlikely to push Mauritius to seek an Advisory Opinion at the International Court of Justice. But Boolell warned the Acting High Commissioner in Port Louis on 23 August that they would be prepared to do so if there were no progress on sovereignty. They would also seek compensation for income accrued over the period of time which the "UK had denied them their rights over the Territory". While we are confident in the strength of our legal case, a decision by Mauritius to challenge our position on sovereignty would be awkward. We will need to develop an active approach to Mauritius, therefore, being clear about our red lines, but being positive about bilateral talks and options for an advisory role in the implementation of the MPA. This might include options, such as offering Mauritius a "privileged partnership" where Mauritius could play an advisory role in the management of the MPA, which does not impact on the sovereignty position. While we are not obliged to offer Mauritius this, it might help to bring them along with us on the issue. We expect the new High Commissioner to have opportunities to take stock of Mauritian thinking in his introductory meetings.

11. There is a slim chance that Mauritius may raise the issue of their historical fishing rights in the Territory. During negotiations over the excision of the Chagos Archipelago between Mauritius and the UK in 1965, the UK gave an undertaking that HMG would use their good offices with the US government to ensure that certain facilities including fishing rights in Chagos would remain available "as far as was practicable". Over the years, these rights have come to mean free fishing licences to Mauritian-flagged vessels upon application. In our exchanges on the MPA to date the Mauritians have never raised the question of fishing rights. This may be because they see it as inconsistent with their sovereignty claim. Mauritius has shown interest only in trying to secure a percentage of the fishing licence money generated by the Territory's fisheries. They do not accept our figures which show that the fishery operates at a substantial loss. Very few Mauritian-flagged vessels have fished in the Territory's Fishing (Conservation and Management) Zone. Only a couple of Mauritian-flagged vessels are run by Chagossians and

their "rights" are being taken up in the Judicial Review into the MPA case being brought by Clifford Chance against the Secretary of State.[201]

157. On 9 September 2010, the new British High Commissioner in Mauritius, Mr. Nicholas Leake, met with the then President of Mauritius, the Rt. Hon. Sir Anerood Jugnauth KCMG QC GCSK PC,[202] Prime Minister Ramgoolam, and Foreign Minister Boolell while presenting his credentials. The High Commissioner's account of that conversation is as follows:

> [...] The talks were wide-ranging, and other bilateral points will be reported separately to Africa Directorate. However, they all took the opportunity to raise Chagos/BIOT, which remains an irritant following the decision to establish a Marine Protection Area (MPA) in BIOT.
>
> 2. [President] Jugnauth said that he understood that the UK position was that sovereignty would be ceded to Mauritius once Diego Garcia was no longer needed for military purposes. But Mauritius had always understood that this meant the Cold War. The Cold War was now over, so was Diego Garcia still needed for military purposes? And if so, would there not always be a reason why the island was still needed? Jugnauth later added that the UK should just hand back the Territory; Mauritius had no problem with the US continuing to use the base, but they should pay rent to Mauritius.
>
> 3. Prime Minister Ramgoolam said that he appreciated you seeing him at Carlton Gardens on his recent visit to London. He rehearsed his disappointment following his CHOGM meeting with Gordon Brown, where he felt he had been promised that the MPA would be put on hold. But he was in "more sorrow than anger" mode. I said that we did not want to raise any hopes of a change of policy. The UK recognised the Mauritian position on sovereignty, and we trusted that the Mauritians understood ours. But, aside from sovereignty, there were a number of issues which could be discussed, and we hoped for a resumption of bilateral talks. The excellent and important relationship between the two countries should allow constructive discussions. You would be writing to set out the position. Ramgoolam said he would wait for the letter before considering his next move, but if there was no progress he would "have to do something".
>
> 4. Foreign Minister Boolell was grateful that Mr. Bellingham had met him in Kampala at the recent [AU] summit. On BIOT, he said that the MPA consultation had marred the relationship, but if there was a will we could make progress. Mauritius was keen to restart bilateral talks, but 2014 was just around the corner and this was an important date

[201] Submission dated 1 September 2010 from Joanne Yeadon, Head of BIOT & Pitcairn Section, to Colin Roberts, Director, Overseas Territories Directorate, UK Foreign and Commonwealth Office, the Private Secretary to Henry Bellingham and the Private Secretary to the Foreign Secretary, "British Indian Ocean Territory (BIOT): Marine Protected Area (MPA): Implementation and Financing" (Annex MR-164).

[202] President of Mauritius, October 2003 to March 2012. Prime Minister of Mauritius, June 1982 to September 1995, September 2000 to October 2003, and December 2014 to the present.

under the UK/US agreement. They would like more clarity on this—the Government was under increasing pressure "from African Union friends" to take action ahead of that date. Boolell also mentioned Mauritius' responsibilities under the Pelindaba Treaty (which says that there should be no nuclear weapons on the territory of AU members).

5. Boolell recognised that the US base was here to stay, but Mauritius wanted to exercise its "legitimate rights" over the territory. They wanted to be part of any discussions, and were unhappy that the US refused to engage with them and kept telling them to discuss all BIOT issues with us. Boolell drew attention to the Chagossian case in the ECHR, and said that this was a rare case where the Mauritian government and opposition were united. He also hinted at "mobilising world opinion", an ICJ case, and seeking "compensation for lost revenue" since independence.[203]

* * *

Chapter IV. Relief Requested

158. Mauritius' final submissions are as follows:

On the basis of the facts and legal arguments presented in its Memorial, Reply, and during the oral hearings, Mauritius respectfully requests the Arbitral Tribunal to adjudge and declare, in accordance with the provisions of the 1982 United Nations Convention on the Law of the Sea ("the Convention"), in respect of the Chagos Archipelago, that:

(1) the United Kingdom is not entitled to declare an "MPA" or other maritime zones because it is not the "coastal State" within the meaning of *inter alia* Articles 2, 55, 56 and 76 of the Convention; and/or

(2) having regard to the commitments that it has made to Mauritius in relation to the Chagos Archipelago, the United Kingdom is not entitled unilaterally to declare an "MPA" or other maritime zones because Mauritius has rights as a "coastal State" within the meaning of *inter alia* Articles 56(1)(*b*)(iii) and 76(8) of the Convention; and/or

(3) the United Kingdom shall take no steps that may prevent the Commission on the Limits of the Continental Shelf from making recommendations to Mauritius in respect of any full submission that Mauritius may make to the Commission regarding the Chagos Archipelago under Article 76 of the Convention;

(4) The United Kingdom's purported "MPA" is incompatible with the substantive and procedural obligations of the United Kingdom under the Convention, including *inter alia* Articles 2, 55, 56, 63, 64, 194 and 300, as well as Article 7 of the Agreement for the Implementation of

[203] United Kingdom record of meeting between British High Commission in Port Louis and President, Prime Minister and Foreign Minister of Mauritius on 9 September 2010 (Annex UKCM-119).

the Provisions of the United Nations Convention on the Law of the Sea of 10 December 1982 Relating to the Conservation and Management of Straddling Fish Stocks and Highly Migratory Fish Stocks of 4 August 1995.

159. The United Kingdom's final submissions are as follows:

For the reasons set out in the Counter-Memorial, the Rejoinder and these oral pleadings, the United Kingdom of Great Britain and Northern Ireland respectfully requests the Tribunal:

(i) to find that it is without jurisdiction over each of the claims of Mauritius;

(ii) in the alternative, to dismiss the claims of Mauritius.

In addition, the United Kingdom of Great Britain and Northern Ireland requests the Tribunal to determine that the costs incurred by the United Kingdom in presenting its case shall be borne by Mauritius, and that Mauritius shall reimburse the United Kingdom for its share of the expenses of the Tribunal.

* * *

CHAPTER V. THE TRIBUNAL'S JURISDICTION

160. The United Kingdom objects to the Tribunal's jurisdiction to consider the claims arising in respect of each of Mauritius' four final submissions. The United Kingdom also contends that Mauritius has failed, in respect of each of its submissions, to meet the procedural requirement in Article 283 to exchange views regarding the settlement of the Parties' dispute. Mauritius, in turn, contends that the Tribunal has jurisdiction to consider each of its claims and that the procedural conditions to exercising this jurisdiction have been met.

161. Set out in brief, the Parties' differing views on the Tribunal's jurisdiction reflect their differing interpretations of the dispute settlement provisions of Part XV of the Convention. Mauritius considers that the United Kingdom bears the burden of establishing that an express exception to the Tribunal's jurisdiction, such as those set out in Articles 297 and 298, is applicable. The United Kingdom, in contrast, considers these proceedings to be an attempt to "stretch the jurisdiction of courts and tribunals under Part XV" beyond permissible boundaries.[204] The United Kingdom believes that the Tribunal must instead focus on the "carefully negotiated preconditions, limitations and exceptions" contained in the Convention[205] and that so doing will lead the Tribunal to uphold the United Kingdom's objections.

162. In approaching the question of its jurisdiction, the Tribunal will first consider its jurisdiction with respect to Mauritius' First and Second Sub-

[204] Final Transcript, 647:3–6.

[205] Final Transcript, 651:20–22.

missions. Although addressed by the United Kingdom collectively, the Tribunal considers it appropriate to address Mauritius' First and Second Submissions separately and in turn. The Tribunal will then go on to consider its jurisdiction with respect to Mauritius' Fourth Submission and the question of the compatibility of the MPA with the Convention. Thereafter, the Tribunal will address its jurisdiction with respect to Mauritius' Third Submission concerning submission to the CLCS. Finally, the Tribunal will proceed to examine whether Mauritius has met the requirements of Article 283 with respect to those submissions over which the Tribunal would otherwise have jurisdiction.

A. The Tribunal's Jurisdiction over Mauritius' First Submission

163. In its First Submission, Mauritius requests the Tribunal to adjudge and declare that –

> (1) the United Kingdom is not entitled to declare an "MPA" or other maritime zones because it is not the "coastal State" within the meaning of *inter alia* Articles 2, 55, 56 and 76 of the Convention; and/or
>
> [...]

164. The United Kingdom maintains that the Tribunal lacks jurisdiction over Mauritius' First Submission, which it characterizes as Mauritius' "sovereignty claim". According to the United Kingdom, sovereignty over the Chagos Archipelago constitutes "the real issue in the case"[206] and is a matter that falls outside the dispute settlement provisions of the Convention. Mauritius, in contrast, submits that "there are no grounds for determining that any aspect of the dispute is beyond the Tribunal's jurisdiction, based on an ordinary interpretation of the Convention."[207]

1. The Parties' Arguments

165. The Parties' arguments in respect of this objection divide broadly into those concerning the scope of jurisdiction under Articles 286 and 288 of the Convention, the relevance of Article 293 concerning the applicable law, the background understanding of the drafters of the Convention with respect to jurisdiction over land sovereignty issues, and the implications of accepting or rejecting jurisdiction in the present proceedings. Each issue is addressed in turn in the sections that follow.

---

[206] The United Kingdom's Counter-Memorial, paras. 4.3–4.9.

[207] Mauritius' Reply, para. 7.6.

(a) The Tribunal's Jurisdiction over Mauritius' First Submission

i. Articles 286 and 288 and the Scope of Compulsory Jurisdiction under the Convention

166. Articles 286 and 288 of the Convention condition recourse to, and the jurisdiction of, a court or tribunal pursuant to the compulsory procedures entailing binding decisions set out in section 2 of Part XV of the Convention.

167. Article 288 provides for the Tribunal's jurisdiction in the following terms:

Article 288 Jurisdiction

> 1. A court or tribunal referred to in article 287 shall have jurisdiction over any dispute concerning the interpretation or application of this Convention which is submitted to it in accordance with this Part.
>
> 2. A court or tribunal referred to in article 287 shall also have jurisdiction over any dispute concerning the interpretation or application of an international agreement related to the purposes of this Convention, which is submitted to it in accordance with the agreement.
>
> [...]

168. Article 286 links the Tribunal's compulsory jurisdiction with the non-binding mechanisms for the settlement of disputes, set out in section 1 of Part XV, as follows:

Article 286

Application of procedures under this section

> Subject to section 3, any dispute concerning the interpretation or application of this Convention shall, where no settlement has been reached by recourse to section 1, be submitted at the request of any party to the dispute to the court or tribunal having jurisdiction under this section.

The United Kingdom's Position

169. Within Part XV, the United Kingdom notes, Articles 286 and 288 of the Convention permit recourse to compulsory settlement, but are subject to "carefully negotiated preconditions, limitations and exceptions."[208] Article 286 applies only where "no settlement has been reached by recourse to section 1" and only subject to the limitations and exceptions specified in section 3. The United Kingdom emphasizes that "the obligation to accept compulsory procedures entailing binding decisions applies only to disputes 'concerning the interpretation or application of this Convention'."[209] That this provision was

[208] Final Transcript, 651:20–22.

[209] Final Transcript, 654:3–5.

intended to restrain the Tribunal's jurisdiction is, in the United Kingdom's view, implicit from Article 288(2). That provision extends jurisdiction over related agreements that expressly refer disputes to Part XV of the Convention, but only to the extent that such an agreement is "related to the purposes of this Convention".[210] Because the possibility of jurisdiction over expressly related agreements is constrained, jurisdiction over disputes which fall to be decided under agreements unrelated to the Convention or under customary international law must also be constrained. According to the United Kingdom, the same conclusion follows from the context of the carefully constructed exclusions to jurisdiction set out in Article 297.[211] As a result of the ordinary meaning of Article 288, the United Kingdom submits that "[d]isputes concerning matters that are wholly exterior to the Convention do not fall within Article 288(1), and that result cannot be avoided by presenting matters as a dispute over who is the coastal State."[212]

170. The United Kingdom objects to the Tribunal's jurisdiction on the grounds that questions of sovereignty lie "at the heart of the current claim"[213] and that it is "self-evident ... that a dispute concerning sovereignty over land territory is not a dispute concerning the interpretation or application of the law of the sea convention".[214]

171. "Part XV of the Convention," the United Kingdom recalls, "is not a General Act for the Pacific Settlement of International Disputes."[215] While some courts and tribunals applying the Convention may have exercised a broader jurisdiction, they have done so only in cases where their jurisdiction arose (as in *Peru* v. *Chile* before the International Court of Justice (the "ICJ") (*Maritime Dispute (Peru* v. *Chile), Judgment of* 27 *January 2014*)) from other instruments such as the Pact of Bogotá that provide for the settlement of disputes in terms that are notably broader than those of the Convention itself.[216] Where jurisdiction arises under Part XV, the United Kingdom emphasizes, it –

> is confined to disputes concerning the interpretation or application of UNCLOS. It concerns UNCLOS and UNCLOS alone. It does not, unless expressly extended, concern other treaties, even other treaties on the law of the sea. Nor does it cover customary international law, even the customary international law of the sea such as is applicable between parties and non-parties or between non-parties.[217]

172. With respect to the characterization of the Parties' dispute, the United Kingdom recalls that the issue of sovereignty over the Chagos Archi-

---

[210] Final Transcript, 676:20–23.

[211] Final Transcript, 677:7–15.

[212] Final Transcript, 666:14–16.

[213] Final Transcript, 666:17–19.

[214] Final Transcript, 654:16–17.

[215] Final Transcript, 659:2–3.

[216] Final Transcript, 674:21 to 675:11.

[217] Final Transcript, 659:6–10.

pelago is a longstanding point of contention. The formulation of the dispute as a matter arising under the Convention, however, is of recent origin and, according to the United Kingdom, arose only with the commencement of these proceedings.[218] It is telling, the United Kingdom argues, that the relief sought by Mauritius "has been formulated not in terms of a declaration of breach of UNCLOS, which is what one would expect to see if this were truly an UNCLOS claim."[219] Despite presenting its claim as one over the interpretation of the term "coastal State", the United Kingdom observes, Mauritius' written pleadings do not contain "a single sentence on the correct interpretation of the term".[220] Indeed, "the principal declaration sought by Mauritius is that the UK is not the coastal State."[221] Along the way to granting such relief, the United Kingdom notes, Mauritius invites the Tribunal to apply the law of self-determination to events in 1965 and to declare that Mauritius has retained sovereignty over the Chagos Archipelago. In the United Kingdom's view, Mauritius is requesting the Tribunal to permit "an artificial re-characterization of the long-standing sovereignty dispute as a 'who is the coastal State' dispute."[222]

173. While other courts and tribunals exercising jurisdiction under the Convention have addressed some issues beyond the strict confines of the Convention itself, in the United Kingdom's view none have done so to the extent now suggested by Mauritius. The United Kingdom distinguishes both *Guyana* v. *Suriname* (*Award of* 17 *September 2007, PCA Award Series*, p. 1, RIAA, Vol. XXX, p. 1) and *MV Saiga (No. 2)* (*(Saint Vincent and the Grenadines* v. *Guinea), Judgment, ITLOS Reports 1999*, p. 10) on the grounds that in each case "some incidental issue arose in relation to what was plainly a dispute as to the interpretation or application of UNCLOS."[223] Here, in contrast, sovereignty is the principal issue and if the Tribunal were to decide that issue in Mauritius' favour, "[t]here would be no UNCLOS case left ... to decide".[224] In short, the United Kingdom concludes, "the characterization of this long-established sovereignty claim as an UNCLOS claim, or as ancillary or incidental to a claim that could correctly be brought under UNCLOS, is untenable."[225]

174. According to the United Kingdom, this result is unaffected by the debate surrounding jurisdiction over mixed disputes involving the determination of maritime boundaries in areas where sovereignty over land features is also disputed. The present case does not arise in the context of a maritime boundary delimitation, the United Kingdom notes, and the arguments advanced in favour of jurisdiction over mixed disputes (discussed in greater

[218] Final Transcript, 662:18–20.

[219] Final Transcript, 664:18–21.

[220] Final Transcript, 1171:9–14.

[221] Final Transcript, 664:21–22.

[222] Final Transcript, 660:19–20.

[223] Final Transcript, 668:9–13.

[224] Final Transcript, 667:2–5.

[225] Final Transcript, 660:13–16.

detail in the context of Article 298(1)(*a*)(i) below) are specific to that context and can be left for other tribunals. The United Kingdom summarizes its objection as follows:

> We do not, of course, contend for the existence of any implicit exclusion of all land sovereignty matters from article 288(1), [...]. We say that Mauritius' 'we are the coastal State' claim is predicated on the determination of a long-standing dispute over a sovereignty that it wishes to be decided by reference to sources exterior to the Convention and, as such, on the ordinary meaning of article 288(1), the dispute is not one concerning the interpretation or application of the Convention.[226]

Mauritius' Position

175. Mauritius submits that "all aspects of this dispute ... are firmly within the jurisdiction of the Tribunal."[227]

176. Mauritius is not, it emphasizes, attempting to force a sovereignty dispute into the confines of the Convention. Instead, it is "inviting the Tribunal to determine whether or not the UK is a 'coastal State' within the meaning of the Convention, so that it is entitled to create the 'MPA' it has purported to establish."[228] According to Mauritius, it "is not asking the Tribunal to widen or to extend its jurisdiction by looking at matters other than those 'concerning the interpretation and application of the Convention' under Article 288(1)."[229] As Mauritius understands the issue:

> Whether a state qualifies as "the coastal state" under the Convention (or "a coastal state," and we note the Convention uses both formulations) in respect of a particular state of affairs is a question arising under the Convention, and it can only be resolved by reference to the Convention itself and by general international law applicable in accordance with the Convention.[230]

177. In Mauritius' view, "[t]he starting point is not the *a priori* question of whether Mauritius does or does not have sovereignty .... The correct starting point is whether or not this part of Mauritius' claim concerns the interpretation or application of the Convention."[231] Mauritius considers that it obviously does. Having then raised a question relating to the interpretation and application of the Convention, Mauritius submits that the relevant question is "what other questions of public international law may be sufficiently closely connected to that dispute that they are questions the Tribunal can *and must*

[226] Final Transcript, 1168:18–24.

[227] Final Transcript, 429:15–16.

[228] Final Transcript, 430:1–3.

[229] Final Transcript, 434:4–6.

[230] Final Transcript, 435:8–12.

[231] Final Transcript, 1002:1–3.

consider."[232] Where such issues do arise, Article 293 then permits the Tribunal to apply the other sources of international law necessary to resolve them.[233]

178. According to Mauritius, "[c]ompulsory procedures entailing binding decisions are available in every dispute concerning the interpretation or application of the Convention, unless an exception applies."[234] Since neither the automatic exceptions to jurisdiction in Article 297 of the Convention, nor the optional ones in Article 298, are applicable, Mauritius submits that the United Kingdom is asking the Tribunal to find "that any dispute which may be construed as necessarily involving a question of sovereignty is inherently beyond the jurisdiction of a Part XV Tribunal despite the fact that there is nothing in the Convention that says that."[235]

179. Reviewing the drafting history of the Convention and the implications of Article 298(1)(*a*) (discussed in detail below), Mauritius submits that there is no basis for such an exception –

> the idea of sovereignty was within the contemplation of the negotiators; they thought about it, they talked about it. Despite this, no consensus was reached on an explicit exclusion. If they truly did not wish a Tribunal such as this to deal with the words that are before you, such an express exclusion [...] could have been drafted and would have been included.[236]

Nor does Mauritius consider jurisdiction over land sovereignty issues to be relevant only in the context of maritime boundary delimitations.

ii. The Relevance of Article 293 to the Jurisdiction of the Tribunal

180. Article 293 of the Convention provides as follows:

> **Article 293**
>
> *Applicable law*
>
> 1. A court or tribunal having jurisdiction under this section shall apply this Convention and other rules of international law not incompatible with this Convention.
>
> 2. Paragraph 1 does not prejudice the power of the court or tribunal having jurisdiction under this section to decide a case *ex aequo et bono*, if the parties so agree.

181. While the Parties are largely in agreement that Article 293 does not, of itself, constitute a basis of jurisdiction, they differ regarding the implications of this provision.

[232] Final Transcript, 438:13–15.

[233] Final Transcript, 438:8–12.

[234] Final Transcript, 441:17–19.

[235] Final Transcript, 442:15–18.

[236] Final Transcript, 1017:23 to 1018:3.

Mauritius' Position

182. Mauritius submits that Article 293 of the Convention establishes that "issues 'closely linked or ancillary' to questions arising directly under the Convention are also questions 'concern[ing] the interpretation or application of the Convention.'"[237] Mauritius "is not," it emphasizes, "asking this Tribunal to extend its jurisdiction by reference to rules of international law other than the Convention."[238] Instead, Mauritius argues, "in compulsory jurisdiction cases, the Tribunal may have to decide matters of general international law that are not part of the law of the sea, and Article 293(1) allows for this."[239] Mauritius summarizes the logical sequence as follows:

> All the Convention asks us to consider first is whether there's a dispute falling within the interpretation and application of the Convention (Article 288) and it then directs, if [the Tribunal is] satisfied that that is the case, [the Tribunal] "*shall* apply this Convention and other rules of international law not incompatible with this Convention" (Article 293).[240]

183. According to Mauritius, "ITLOS and Annex VII Tribunals have, on numerous occasions, indicated where other rules of international law are to be applied."[241] In this respect, Mauritius points to the application of the UN Charter provisions on the use of force in *Guyana* v. *Suriname* (*Award of* 17 *September 2007, PCA Award Series*, pp. 166–171, RIAA, Vol. XXX, p. 1 at p. 119, para. 425 *et seq.*) and of the determination of the permissibility of force as a matter of general international law in *M/V "Saiga" (No. 2) ((Saint Vincent and the Grenadines* v. *Guinea), Judgment, ITLOS Reports 1999*, p. 10 at p. 63, para. 159). [242] Mauritius also points to the considerations of human rights law at issue in *Arctic Sunrise ((Kingdom of the Netherlands* v. *Russian Federation), Provisional Measures, Order of* 22 *November 2013, ITLOS Reports 2013*, p. 230 at para. 33).[243]

The United Kingdom's Position

184. According to the United Kingdom, Article 293 "cannot be invoked to support an expanded vision of the jurisdiction of a court or tribunal acting under section 2 of Part XV."[244]

185. In the United Kingdom's view:

> The purpose of the reference to "other rules of international law not incompatible with this Convention" is to dispel any doubt that, in inter-

[237] Final Transcript, 446:2–4.

[238] Final Transcript, 434:1–2.

[239] Final Transcript, 435:13–15, *quoting* A.E. Boyle, "Dispute Settlement and the Law of the Sea Convention: Problems of Fragmentation and Jurisdiction" (1997) 46 *International and Comparative Law Quarterly* at p. 49 (Annex MR-103).

[240] Final Transcript, 438:8–12.

[241] Final Transcript, 438:15–17.

[242] Final Transcript, 439:3–8.

[243] Final Transcript, 439:11–21.

[244] Final Transcript, 659:14–15.

> preting and applying the provisions of the Convention, a Part XV court [or] tribunal may have recourse to such secondary rules as the law of treaties, State responsibility, diplomatic protection et cetera, and may apply other rules of international law when directed to do so expressly by a provision of the Convention.[245]

It is "most certainly not to empower a Part XV court or tribunal to decide disputes which have arisen in fields of international law that lie outside the provisions of the Convention."[246]

186. This distinction, the United Kingdom submits, was clearly established by the Order of 24 June 2003 in the *MOX Plant Case* (*(Ireland* v. *United Kingdom), Order of 24 June 2003, PCA Award Series*, p. 47 at p. 52, para. 19),[247] and is supported by the approach of the ICJ in the *Application of the Convention on the Prevention and Punishment of the Crime of Genocide* (*(Bosnia and Herzegovina* v. *Serbia and Montenegro), Judgment, I.C.J. Reports 2007*, p. 43 at p. 104, para. 147) with respect to the comparable articles 36 and 38 of the ICJ Statute.[248] It was also the approach of the *Eurotunnel* Tribunal with respect to the applicable law provisions of the contract at issue in those proceedings (*Eurotunnel (Channel Tunnel Group and France-Manche* v. *UK and France), Partial Award of* 30 *January 2007, PCA Award Series p. 61*, 132 ILR p. 1 at p. 54, para. 152).[249]

iii. The Relevance of Article 298(1)(*a*)(i)

187. The Parties disagree as to whether the effect of a declaration under Article 298(1)(*a*)(i) in excluding a dispute concerning sovereignty over land territory from compulsory conciliation implies *a contrario* that such a dispute would be subject to compulsory dispute resolution in the absence of such a declaration.

188. Article 298 of the Convention provides in relevant part:

> 1. When signing, ratifying or acceding to this Convention or at any time thereafter, a State may, without prejudice to the obligations arising under section 1, declare in writing that it does not accept any one or more of the procedures provided for in section 2 with respect to one or more of the following categories of disputes:
>
> (*a*) (i) disputes concerning the interpretation or application of articles 15, 74 and 83 relating to sea boundary delimitations, or those involving historic bays or titles, provided that a State having made such a declaration shall, when such a dispute arises subsequent to the entry into force of this Convention and where no agreement within a reasonable period of time is reached in negotiations between the parties, at the request

---

245 Final Transcript, 656:8–12.

246 Final Transcript, 656:16–18.

247 The United Kingdom's Counter-Memorial, para. 4.22.

248 The United Kingdom's Counter-Memorial, paras. 4.25–4.28.

249 The United Kingdom's Counter-Memorial, paras. 4.23–4.24.

> of any party to the dispute, accept submission of the matter to conciliation under Annex V, section 2; and provided further that any dispute that necessarily involves the concurrent consideration of any unsettled dispute concerning sovereignty or other rights over continental or insular land territory shall be excluded from such submission;

Mauritius' Position

189. According to Mauritius, "there is no *exclusion* in the Convention of jurisdiction over mixed disputes either in the narrow sense of those arising in maritime delimitation cases or the broader sense of questions of public international law over which a Part XV Tribunal may properly exercise incidental or ancillary jurisdiction."[250]

190. Mauritius submits that the United Kingdom seeks to impose an artificial distinction and limit jurisdiction to the context of maritime boundaries. "The United Kingdom is wrong," Mauritius suggests, "to argue that the inference from the academic writings and from Article 298(1)(*a*)(i) itself is that sovereignty questions could only arise under Part XV where they are 'mixed' with a *delimitation* dispute."[251] While "[d]elimitation is simply the most obvious case in which [a mixed dispute] could arise",[252] Mauritius considers that the reasoning supporting such jurisdiction applies equally to other issues that "cannot be determined in isolation without reference to territory."[253] Nevertheless, Mauritius recalls the dispute between the Parties concerning Mauritius' submissions to the CLCS in respect of the Chagos Archipelago and argues that "we do now have a situation of maritime boundaries in this case because the delineation issue, we say, is a maritime boundary issue."[254] In Mauritius' view, there is simply no reason for delimitation and delineation to be treated differently with respect to jurisdiction.[255]

191. According to Mauritius, this interpretation follows from the inclusion in the Convention of Article 298(1)(*a*)(i): "If, indeed, mixed disputes were not otherwise covered by the Convention's jurisdiction, there would have been no need for the specific exclusion in the last clause of Article 298(1)(*a*)(i)."[256] It also follows from the negotiating records of the Convention, insofar as, according to Mauritius, "an express exclusion [of jurisdiction over land sovereignty] was proposed and it was rejected" during the Third United Nations Conference on the Law of the Sea (the "Conference").[257] The Report of the President

---

[250] Final Transcript, 450:9–12.

[251] Final Transcript, 449:23–25.

[252] Final Transcript, 450:2–3.

[253] Final Transcript, 445:6–7.

[254] Final Transcript, 445:20–21.

[255] Final Transcript, 449:25 to 450:3.

[256] Final Transcript, 450:23–24.

[257] Final Transcript, 452:10–11.

of the Conference of 23 August 1980, Mauritius notes, records that a proposal was made to make "the exclusion of past or existing delimitation disputes as well as disputes relating to sovereignty over land or insular territories from the compulsory dispute settlement procedures and from compulsory submission to conciliation procedures"[258] part of the automatic exclusions from jurisdiction (now set out in Article 297), but that this was rejected.[259] Taken as a whole, Mauritius argues:

> The *travaux* plainly point to one conclusion. The issue of sovereignty over land was addressed, and a majority wanted a compulsory dispute settlement system capable of touching on such questions. A minority did not. All the minority got was the opt-out in Article 298(1)(*a*)(i), and that became part of the package deal.[260]

192. Mauritius discounts the academic commentaries assembled by the United Kingdom to suggest that land sovereignty must be outside the Tribunal's jurisdiction. According to Mauritius, of the authorities offered by the United Kingdom:

> Many, [...] merely assert that Part XV cannot cover issues of territorial sovereignty: they offer no footnote and no explanation and no reasoning, beyond—at most—a bald reference to the words of Article 298(1)(*a*)(i), unaccompanied by any further textual analysis. [...] Another three attempt some explanation of their views but offer no reasoning at all beyond a sentence or two (that is Churchill, Oxman and Thomas). Closely read, at least two of the authors cited do not actually seem to rule out the possibility of jurisdiction in at least some sovereignty disputes (Torres Bernárdez and Smith). In fact quite a few of the authors cited use language along the lines of the Convention *seeming*, or *appearing* to, or *probably*, excluding such disputes, but they don't actually offer a firm conclusion. One author (Adede) makes the historical point that the President of the Conference in 1977 said, *in his view*, territorial disputes would not fall within Part XV and another, Yee, simply repeats that observation.[261]

193. Mauritius summarises its position as follows:

> The result of a proper *a contrario* understanding of Article 298(1)(*a*)(i) is not that all sovereignty disputes are automatically included under the Convention, it is that such disputes *are not automatically excluded*. Not every question relating to land will fall within the Convention, only those which must necessarily be dealt with in order to resolve a dispute that is within the Convention. The question is, as Professor Treves has

[258] Third United Nations Conference on the Law of the Sea, Official Records Vol. XIV, Report of the President on the work of the informal plenary meeting of the Conference on the settlement of disputes, 23 August 1980, A/CONF.62/L.59, at para. 6 (Annex MR-81).

[259] Final Transcript, 452:10 to 453:2.

[260] Final Transcript, 1020:18–21.

[261] Final Transcript, 456:6–19.

put it, "whether the dispute, [...] as a whole, can be seen as being about the interpretation or application of the Convention."[262]

The United Kingdom's Position

194. The United Kingdom acknowledges that there is an extensive debate in the academic literature as to whether issues of land sovereignty may be decided through compulsory dispute settlement under the Convention when they arise incidentally to a maritime boundary delimitation. As the present proceedings do not involve the delimitation of a maritime boundary, the United Kingdom is of the view that the Tribunal "need not and should not enter into the debate on mixed disputes to decide this case."[263] To the extent the question is relevant, however, the United Kingdom endorses the view that land sovereignty disputes were excluded from jurisdiction under the Convention and cites numerous authorities in support of this view.[264]

195. In the United Kingdom's view, "the proviso to Article 298(1)(*a*)(i) merely clarifies that the general exclusion of unsettled territorial sovereignty disputes from compulsory dispute settlement also applies in the context where such a dispute would fall for consideration ... in the context of mandatory conciliation".[265] But whatever one makes of the *a contrario* argument, the United Kingdom submits, it does not assist Mauritius in the present case.

[262] Final Transcript, 450:14–20, *quoting* T. Treves, "What have the United Nations Convention and the International Tribunal for the Law of the Sea to offer as regards maritime delimitation disputes?" in R. Lagoni and D. Vignes (eds.), *Maritime Delimitation* (2006), p. 77.

[263] The United Kingdom's Rejoinder, para. 4.42.

[264] The United Kingdom's Rejoinder, para. 4.42, *citing* A.O. Adede, *The System for Settlement of Disputes under the United Nations Convention on the Law of the Sea*, pp. 132, 159, para. 7.4; Churchill, "The Role of the International Court of Justice in Maritime Boundary Delimitation", in Elferink and Rothwell, *Oceans Management in the 21st Century: Institutional Frameworks and Responses* (2004) p. 136; Elferink, "The Islands in the South China Sea: How Does Their Presence Limit the Extent of the High Seas and the Area and the Maritime Zones of the Mainland Coasts?" (2001) 32 *Ocean Development & International Law* 169, 172; Guillaume, *La Cour internationale de Justice à l'aube du XXIème siècle. Le Regard d'un juge* (2003), pp. 300–301; L.B. Sohn and K. Gustafson, *The Law of the Sea in a Nutshell* (1984) 24; P.C. Irwin, "Settlement of Maritime Boundary Disputes: An Analysis of the Law of the Sea Negotiations" (1980) 8 ODIL 105, 114–15, 138–39; K. Kittichaisaree, *The Law of the Sea and Maritime Boundary Delimitation in South-East Asia* (OUP 1987) 140; B.H. Oxman, "The Third United Nations Conference on the Law of the Sea: The Ninth Session" (1981) 75 AJIL 211, 233 fn. 109; M.C. Pinto, "Maritime Boundary Issues and Their Resolution", in N. Ando et al (eds), *Liber Amicorum Judge Shigeru Oda*, p. 1115 at p. 1130; R.W. Smith, "The Effect of Extended Maritime Jurisdictions", in Koers and Oxman, *The 1982 Convention on the Law of the Sea: Proceedings, Law of the Sea Institute* (1984), at 343; L.B. Sohn, "Peaceful Settlement of Disputes in Ocean Conflicts: Does UNCLOS III Point the Way?" (1983) 46 LCP 195; S. Talmon. "The South China Sea Arbitration: Is there a case to answer?", Bonn Research Papers in International Law, No. 2/2014, 9 February 2014; R.W. Smith and B.L. Thomas, Maritime Briefing, vol. 2(4), "Island Disputes and the Law of the Sea: An Examination of Sovereignty and Delimitation Disputes" (1998); S. Torres Bernárdez, "Provisional measures and Interventions in Maritime Delimitation Disputes", in Lagoni and Vignes, *Maritime Delimitation* (2006); Weckel, report on the Juno Trader case, 2005 R.G.D.I.P. 230; S. Yee, "Conciliation and the 1982 UN Convention on the Law of the Sea", ODIL, 44, 315 at 324.

[265] Final Transcript, 693:15–20.

Article 298(1)(*a*)(i) "is concerned only with disputes over maritime delimitation and historic bays or titles."[266] For the United Kingdom, it therefore follows that any *a contrario* reading of the provision is similarly limited to maritime boundary delimitation. Rather than infer, as Mauritius asks the Tribunal to do, that "because jurisdiction can be excluded pursuant to a declaration in context 'A', it must therefore be included in context 'B'," the United Kingdom submits that "[t]he more obvious conclusion is that [jurisdiction] was not included in context 'B' in the first place."[267] Moreover, the United Kingdom argues, Mauritius' interpretation is illogical:

> It posits certain States being utterly unwilling to agree to determine territorial disputes where these arose in the context of maritime delimitation claims, and insisting on the terms of the Article 298 opt-out (which excludes sovereignty disputes even from conciliation), but at the same time those very same States being willing to agree to the compulsory determination of such disputes in the far broader context of claims made wherever the Convention refers to a coastal state.[268]

Were this the case, the United Kingdom submits, "there would be an opt-out for 'who is the coastal State' disputes".[269]

196. Turning to the negotiating record of Article 298(1)(*a*)(i), the United Kingdom emphasizes that all of the statements identified by Mauritius as allegedly supporting jurisdiction over land sovereignty disputes were made in the context of Negotiating Group 7 and "in each case, the delegate relied on had been making a statement on land sovereignty issues in the specific context of maritime delimitation disputes."[270] Simply put, the United Kingdom argues –

> The debates do not reflect any consideration of any kind of the possibility that a justiciable dispute as to land sovereignty could be raised in the context of [...] who was the, or indeed a, coastal State. The supposed majority does not exist, because no one was considering what Mauritius is now proposing.[271]

Instead, "the negotiating history does no more than confirm that there is no foundation whatsoever for the radical and unwarranted jurisdiction that Mauritius contends for in this case."[272]

---

[266] Final Transcript, 681:17–19.

[267] Final Transcript, 682:10–13.

[268] Final Transcript, 682:14–19.

[269] Final Transcript, 682:21–23.

[270] Final Transcript, 1186:20 to 1187:1.

[271] Final Transcript, 1191:21–24 (emphasis in original).

[272] The United Kingdom's Rejoinder, para. 4.43.

(b) The Implications of Finding Jurisdiction over Mauritius' First Submission

The United Kingdom's Position

197. The United Kingdom advances a cautionary argument against finding jurisdiction over Mauritius' First Submission. In the United Kingdom's view, the risks involved in disregarding limits to jurisdiction were recalled by Judge Koroma in the context of comparable provisions in *Georgia* v. *Russia* –

> a link must exist between the substantive provisions of the treaty invoked and the dispute. This limitation is vital. Without it, States could use the compromissory clause as a vehicle for forcing an unrelated dispute with another State before the Court.
>
> (*Application of the International Convention on the Elimination of all Forms of Racial Discrimination (Georgia* v. *Russian Federation), Preliminary Objections, Judgment, Separate Opinion of Judge Koroma, I.C.J. Reports 2011*, p. 183 at p. 185, para. 7.)

198. Here, the United Kingdom submits that the open-ended approach to jurisdiction advocated by Mauritius risks opening the door to a wide range of latent sovereignty disputes among States worldwide, brought on the pretext that one State or another is not the "coastal State" with respect to the territory in question. For the United Kingdom, there is a "grave danger in abuse of Part XV represented by Mauritius' arguments in the present case," and "[t]he arguments of Mauritius' lawyers risk undermining the system of Part XV" as States would be dissuaded from acceding to the Convention or accepting the jurisdiction of other courts and tribunals.[273]

199. While Mauritius contends that its case is *sui generis* and limited by the colonial history of the Chagos Archipelago, the United Kingdom submits that –

> [t]here is no wording in Articles 288(1) or 298(1) to suggest that they somehow apply differently in different circumstances. No references to the impacts of undertakings or jurisdiction with respect to former colonies. So if Mauritius is correct in its interpretation of Article 288(1), then, as long as the claimant State can plausibly assert that the respondent State is exercising the rights or duties of a coastal State, that claimant State will be able to bring a claim challenging the territorial sovereignty of the respondent State.[274]

Mauritius' Position

200. Mauritius rejects the United Kingdom's concerns about the consequences of finding jurisdiction in this case. Mauritius describes an evolutionary process in the application of compulsory dispute settlement under the Convention –

---

[273] Final Transcript, 648:10–13.

[274] Final Transcript, 673:1–6.

> with the passage of time, as dispute settlement under the 1982 Convention and Part XV has become increasingly established and settled, as the International Tribunal for the Law of the Sea and Annex VII Tribunals have been confronted with a range of issues and questions that may not have been at the forefront of the minds of the drafters of the Convention, or indeed in their minds at all, sensible solutions have been found, and the law has evolved. Those solutions have been practical and they have been effective. It is true that they may have taken the interpretation of the Convention to a place where some of the early writings that the United Kingdom likes to rely upon may not have foreseen and may not like. But it cannot be said that disaster has followed.[275]

201. The result of that process, according to Mauritius, is not a threat to the system, but the effective application of the Convention to resolve disputes –

> the reality is the very opposite of what the United Kingdom argues: far from undermining the whole Convention, if [the Tribunal] take[s] jurisdiction over this case, [it] will strengthen the dispute settlement structure of the Convention; to decline jurisdiction will be to exacerbate the dispute, to prolong it unnecessarily, and to signal that Part XV serves to perpetuate a colonial era dispute such as this one.[276]

202. In any event, however, Mauritius contends that the circumstances of the Chagos Archipelago are unique:

> The United Kingdom has consistently described Mauritius as having rights in reversion of the islands. It has described itself as a mere "temporary freeholder." This fact alone places this dispute in a category of one. No other case like it anywhere, and the United Kingdom has not been able to find one for us.[277]

According to Mauritius, this "is the key to this case. It allows you to open the door that leads to the particular facts of this unique dispute."[278] However, "to admit one dispute touching upon such matters is not to admit them all," and "not all such disputes will necessarily come within the jurisdiction of a Part XV court or tribunal."[279] In Mauritius' view, the Tribunal should concern itself "with the facts of this case and this dispute and this case and this dispute only and no other."[280]

2. The Tribunal's Decision

203. Mauritius' First Submission asks the Tribunal to interpret and apply the term "coastal State" as it is used in the Convention. This term is not

[275] Final Transcript, 428:6–14.

[276] Final Transcript, 430:14–19.

[277] Final Transcript, 431:11–14.

[278] Final Transcript, 462:16–17.

[279] Final Transcript, 461:21 to 462:1.

[280] Final Transcript, 462:1–2.

defined in the Convention, although its usage in the text makes evident that it was intended to denote a State having a sea coast, as distinct from a land-locked State. Nowhere, however, does the Convention provide guidance on the identification of the "coastal State" in cases where sovereignty over the land territory fronting a coast is disputed. Nor is provision made for circumstances of war or secession in which a coast might effectively be occupied by authorities exercising *de facto* governmental powers, or other complex permutations of territorial sovereignty, such as condominium governments. In each of these cases, the identity of the coastal State for the purposes of the Convention would be a matter to be determined through the application of rules of international law lying outside the international law of the sea. Whether the Tribunal, or other courts and tribunals convened pursuant to Part XV of the Convention, may apply such exterior sources of law and address such matters raises a question of the scope of jurisdiction under the Convention. On this point, the United Kingdom objects to Mauritius' First Submission.

204. The Tribunal's subject matter jurisdiction is set out in Article 288(1) of the Convention, which provides as follows:

> 1. A court or tribunal referred to in article 287 shall have jurisdiction over any dispute concerning the interpretation or application of this Convention which is submitted to it in accordance with this Part.

205. Although expressed in general terms, Article 288(1) is then limited by the provisions of section 3 of Part XV, which restrict the compulsory settlement of disputes with respect to certain subject matters. Within section 3, Article 297 sets out a series of limitations and exceptions to compulsory settlement that apply automatically and which will be discussed in the Tribunal's consideration of Mauritius' Fourth Submission (see paragraphs 283–323 below). Article 298 permits States, by declaration, to exclude certain additional matters from compulsory settlement.

206. Neither Party has suggested that any of the automatic exceptions set out in Article 297 bears upon the Tribunal's jurisdiction with respect to Mauritius' First Submission. Nor has either Party made any relevant declaration pursuant to Article 298. The question of the Tribunal's jurisdiction therefore hinges entirely on whether the issues raised in Mauritius' First Submission represent a dispute "concerning the interpretation or application" of the Convention. In the Tribunal's view, this question consists of two parts: first, what is the nature of the dispute encompassed in Mauritius' First Submission? Second, to the extent that the Tribunal finds the Parties' dispute to be, at its core, a matter of territorial sovereignty, to what extent does Article 288(1) permit a tribunal to determine issues of disputed land sovereignty as a necessary precondition to a determination of rights and duties in the adjacent sea?

(a) The Nature of the Dispute in Mauritius' First Submission

207. As set out above (see paragraph 172), the United Kingdom considers Mauritius' First Submission to be "an artificial re-characterisation of the long-standing sovereignty dispute as a 'who is the coastal State' dispute."[281] Mauritius, in turn, (see paragraphs 176–177 above) considers that it is merely asking the Tribunal to interpret the term "coastal State" as it is used repeatedly in the text of the Convention itself.

208. Ultimately, it is for the Tribunal itself "while giving particular attention to the formulation of the dispute chosen by the Applicant, to determine on an objective basis the dispute dividing the parties, by examining the position of both parties" (*Fisheries Jurisdiction (Spain* v. *Canada), Jurisdiction of the Court, Judgment, I.C.J. Reports 1998*, p. 432 at p. 448, para. 30) and in the process "to isolate the real issue in the case and to identify the object of the claim" (*Nuclear Tests (New Zealand* v. *France), Judgment, I.C.J. Reports 1974*, p. 457 at p. 466, para. 30).

209. In the Tribunal's view, the record (see paragraphs 101–107 above) clearly indicates that a dispute between the Parties exists with respect to sovereignty over the Chagos Archipelago. Since at least 1980, Mauritius has asserted its sovereignty over the Chagos Archipelago in a variety of fora, including in bilateral communications with the United Kingdom and in statements to the United Nations. Mauritius has also challenged the circumstances by which the Archipelago was detached; questioned the validity of the Mauritius Council of Ministers' approval of that decision; enshrined a claim to sovereignty over the Archipelago in its Constitution and legislation; and declared its own exclusive economic zone in the surrounding waters. Finally, the pleadings in these proceedings are replete with assertions of Mauritian sovereignty over the Chagos Archipelago.

210. In the Tribunal's view, however, a dispute also exists between the Parties with respect to the manner in which the MPA was declared and the implications of the MPA for the Lancaster House Undertakings, made by the United Kingdom in connection with the detachment of the Archipelago. This dispute is distinct from the matter of sovereignty and will be the subject of further consideration in connection with Mauritius' Fourth Submission.

211. Finally, the Parties clearly differ regarding the identity of the "coastal State". For the purpose of characterizing the Parties' dispute, however, the Tribunal must evaluate where the relative weight of the dispute lies. Is the Parties' dispute primarily a matter of the interpretation and application of the term "coastal State", with the issue of sovereignty forming one aspect of a larger question? Or does the Parties' dispute primarily concern sovereignty, with the United Kingdom's actions as a "coastal State" merely representing a manifestation of that dispute? In the Tribunal's view, this question all but

[281] Final Transcript, 660:19–20.

answers itself. There is an extensive record, extending across a range of fora and instruments, documenting the Parties' dispute over sovereignty. In contrast, prior to the initiation of these proceedings, there is scant evidence that Mauritius was specifically concerned with the United Kingdom's implementation of the Convention on behalf of the BIOT. Moreover, as Mauritius itself has argued its case, the consequences of a finding that the United Kingdom is not the coastal State extend well beyond the question of the validity of the MPA. In the words of Mauritius' counsel, the Tribunal is "entitled" to –

> rule that the United Kingdom is [...] not "the coastal State" of the Chagos Archipelago. The skies will not fall if [the Tribunal] so rule[s], although this "Marine Protected Area" will. The Tribunal will do no more than state that Mauritius is the "coastal State" in relation to the Chagos Archipelago and that the Chagos Archipelago forms an integral part of the Republic of Mauritius. The American base will not be affected, as we have shown. The British will leave. The former residents of the Chagos Archipelago who wish to return finally will be free to do so and their exile will come to an end. Contrary to the United Kingdom's submissions, [...] those are the consequences that flow from applying the law, from exercising jurisdiction and interpreting and applying the words that sit in the Convention.[282]

These are not the sort of consequences that follow from a narrow dispute regarding the interpretation of the words "coastal State" for the purposes of certain articles of the Convention.

212. Accordingly, the Tribunal concludes that the Parties' dispute with respect to Mauritius' First Submission is properly characterized as relating to land sovereignty over the Chagos Archipelago. The Parties' differing views on the "coastal State" for the purposes of the Convention are simply one aspect of this larger dispute.

(b) The Tribunal's Jurisdiction to Decide Issues of Disputed Land Sovereignty in Connection with Determining Rights and Duties in the Adjacent Sea

213. The Tribunal's conclusion that the Parties' dispute in respect of Mauritius' First Submission is, at its core, a dispute over sovereignty does not definitively answer the question of jurisdiction. There remains the question of the extent to which Article 288(1) accords the Tribunal jurisdiction in respect of a dispute over land sovereignty when, as here, that dispute touches in some ancillary manner on matters regulated by the Convention.

214. In the course of these proceedings, the Parties devoted a great deal of argument to whether jurisdiction over issues of land sovereignty was, or was not, contemplated by the drafters of the Convention. The Parties also debat-

[282] Final Transcript, 1030:13–21.

ed whether an *a contrario* reading of Article 298(1)(*a*)(i) supports the view that land sovereignty is generally within the jurisdiction of a Part XV court or tribunal. Article 298(1)(*a*)(i) permits States to exclude disputes regarding maritime boundaries and historic bays or titles from compulsory settlement, requires submission instead to compulsory conciliation, and provides that "any dispute that necessarily involves the concurrent consideration of any unsettled dispute concerning sovereignty or other rights over continental or insular land territory shall be excluded from such submission [to conciliation]."

215. In the Tribunal's view, much of this argumentation misses the point. The negotiating records of the Convention provide no explicit answer regarding jurisdiction over territorial sovereignty. The Tribunal considers that the simple explanation for the lack of attention to this question is that none of the Conference participants expected that a long-standing dispute over territorial sovereignty would ever be considered to be a dispute "concerning the interpretation or application of the Convention."

216. The negotiation of the Convention involved extensive debate regarding the extent to which disputes concerning its provisions would be subject to compulsory settlement. The distrust with which some participants at the Conference viewed compulsory settlement is evidenced by the inclusion in the final texts of substantial carve outs, in Article 297, for disputes relating to the exercise of sovereign rights and jurisdiction in the exclusive economic zone. It is also apparent in the option, in Article 298(*a*)(i), for States to exclude the delimitation of maritime boundaries from dispute settlement, subject only to the requirement of compulsory conciliation. Given the inherent sensitivity of States to questions of territorial sovereignty, the question must be asked: if the drafters of the Convention were sufficiently concerned with the sensitivities involved in delimiting maritime boundaries that they included the option to exclude such disputes from compulsory settlement, is it reasonable to expect that the same States accepted that more fundamental issues of territorial sovereignty could be raised as separate claims under Article 288(1)?

217. In the Tribunal's view, had the drafters intended that such claims could be presented as disputes "concerning the interpretation or application of the Convention", the Convention would have included an opt-out facility for States not wishing their sovereignty claims to be adjudicated, just as one sees in Article 298(1)(*a*)(i) in relation to maritime delimitation disputes.

218. Mauritius suggests that the opposite conclusion can be reached by reading Article 298(1)(*a*)(i) *a contrario*: if it was necessary for that Article to expressly state that disputes concerning sovereignty over continental or insular land territory are excluded from compulsory conciliation when a declaration pursuant to the Article is made, then *a fortiori* it must be the case that such disputes fall within the ambit of compulsory settlement when no such declaration is made. The Tribunal is not convinced by this argument. Article 298(1)(*a*)(i) relates only to the application of the Convention to disputes involving maritime boundaries and historic titles. At most, an *a contrario* reading of the

provision supports the proposition that an issue of land sovereignty might be within the jurisdiction of a Part XV court or tribunal if it were genuinely ancillary to a dispute over a maritime boundary or a claim of historic title.

219. This case, however, is not such a dispute. In the Tribunal's view, to read Article 298(1)(*a*)(i) as a warrant to assume jurisdiction over matters of land sovereignty on the pretext that the Convention makes use of the term "coastal State" would do violence to the intent of the drafters of the Convention to craft a balanced text and to respect the manifest sensitivity of States to the compulsory settlement of disputes relating to sovereign rights and maritime territory. Such sensitivities arise to an even greater degree in relation to land territory.

220. As a general matter, the Tribunal concludes that, where a dispute concerns the interpretation or application of the Convention, the jurisdiction of a court or tribunal pursuant to Article 288(1) extends to making such findings of fact or ancillary determinations of law as are necessary to resolve the dispute presented to it (*see Certain German Interests in Polish Upper Silesia, Preliminary Objections, Judgment of* 25 *August 1925, P.C.I.J. Series A, No. 6*, p. 4 at p. 18). Where the "real issue in the case" and the "object of the claim" (*Nuclear Tests (New Zealand* v. *France), Judgment, I.C.J. Reports 1974*, p. 457 at p. 466, para. 30) do not relate to the interpretation or application of the Convention, however, an incidental connection between the dispute and some matter regulated by the Convention is insufficient to bring the dispute, as a whole, within the ambit of Article 288(1).

221. The Tribunal does not categorically exclude that in some instances a minor issue of territorial sovereignty could indeed be ancillary to a dispute concerning the interpretation or application of the Convention. That, however, is not this case, and the Tribunal therefore has no need to rule upon the issue. The Parties' dispute regarding sovereignty over the Chagos Archipelago does not concern the interpretation or application of the Convention. Accordingly, the Tribunal finds itself without jurisdiction to address Mauritius' First Submission.

B. The Tribunal's Jurisdiction with regard to Mauritius' Second Submission

222. In its Second Submission, Mauritius requests the Tribunal to adjudge and declare that –

> [...]
>
> (2) having regard to the commitments that it has made to Mauritius in relation to the Chagos Archipelago, the United Kingdom is not entitled unilaterally to declare an "MPA" or other maritime zones because Mauritius has rights as a "coastal State" within the meaning of *inter alia* Articles 56(1)(*b*)(iii) and 76(8) of the Convention; and/or
>
> [...]

1. The Parties' Arguments

The United Kingdom's Position

223. The United Kingdom objects to the Tribunal's jurisdiction to address Mauritius' claim that it has rights as "a" coastal State for the same reasons for which it objects to Mauritius' First Submission that the United Kingdom is not the coastal State.

224. According to the United Kingdom, Mauritius "again is asking the Tribunal to engage in issues of sovereignty, although it is some sort of reversionary rather than actual sovereignty, and it follows from that that the jurisdictional issues are the same."[283] "The only basis", in the United Kingdom's view, "for saying that Mauritius is 'a' coastal State is understood to be that it has what are said to be certain attributes of a coastal State, i.e., some reversionary interest in sovereignty."[284] Accordingly, "the only difference … is that [the Tribunal is] not being asked to interpret and apply the laws on self-determination, but instead other sources of alleged international law exterior to the Convention, which sources are said to establish the form of reversionary sovereignty".[285] In the United Kingdom's view, this amounts to a legal construct: "Mauritius wishes [the Tribunal] to interpret and apply the 1965 understandings, in one way or another, and it looks for some hook in the 1982 Convention."[286]

225. In any event, the United Kingdom notes, "there is no suggestion anywhere in UNCLOS that there could be more than one coastal State in the way that Mauritius contends for."[287]

Mauritius' Position

226. Mauritius distinguishes the question of the Tribunal's jurisdiction to find that Mauritius "has the attributes of a coastal State" from the question of jurisdiction to declare that the United Kingdom is not the coastal State.

227. According to Mauritius, in addressing Mauritius' Second Submission, the Tribunal does –

> not have to consider whether Part XV excludes all, or any, disputes related to land sovereignty. These aspects of our claim do not require [the Tribunal] to consider which State is currently exercising sovereignty over the Chagos Archipelago. We are proceeding here on the basis that the Archipelago will be returned to the sovereignty of Mauritius when it is no longer needed for defence purposes and because of the exclusive rights in regard to the living and non-living resources with which Mauritius has

[283] Final Transcript, 694:11–13.

[284] Final Transcript, 1196:21–24.

[285] Final Transcript, 1197:1–5.

[286] Final Transcript, 1197:20–21.

[287] Final Transcript, 694:20–22.

> already been vested. Our claims of entitlement to be regarded as a coastal State for purposes of Articles 56(1)(*b*)(iii) and 76(8), because of the attributes of a coastal State which Mauritius acquired as a result of the UK's undertakings, are indisputably matters calling for [the Tribunal's] interpretation and application of those two provisions of the Convention, and the meaning of the words "coastal State" under them and, as such, they plainly fall within [the Tribunal's] jurisdiction under Article 288(1).[288]

Mauritius considers that "[t]here can be no reason … why the dispute about how the Convention can be applied in the light of [Mauritius'] rights and [the United Kingdom's] undertakings should be excluded from [the Tribunal's] jurisdiction."[289]

2. The Tribunal's Decision

228. The Parties disagree both as to whether Mauritius' Second Submission presents a distinct issue from the First Submission, which the Tribunal has already considered, and as to whether the Tribunal's jurisdiction extends to Mauritius' Second Submission. In the United Kingdom's view, the issues raised by the two submissions are the same, except that in its Second Submission, Mauritius claims only a form of reversionary sovereignty. According to Mauritius, its Second Submission is distinct and does not require a determination of sovereignty. Instead, Mauritius claims that the Lancaster House Undertakings endowed Mauritius with the attributes of a coastal State for the purposes of the Convention.

229. The Tribunal agrees with Mauritius that the issues presented by its First and Second Submissions are distinct, but is nevertheless of the view that Mauritius' Second Submission must be viewed against the backdrop of the Parties' dispute regarding sovereignty over the Chagos Archipelago. Although in its Second Submission Mauritius asks only for the Tribunal to determine that it has rights as "a coastal State", the Tribunal considers that such a determination would effectively constitute a finding that the United Kingdom is less than fully sovereign over the Chagos Archipelago. As with Mauritius' First Submission, the Tribunal evaluates where the weight of the Parties' dispute lies. In carrying out this task, the Tribunal does not consider that its role is limited to parsing the precise wording chosen by Mauritius in formulating its submission. On the contrary, the Tribunal is entitled, and indeed obliged, to consider the context of the submission and the manner in which it has been presented in order to establish the dispute actually separating the Parties. Again, the Tribunal finds that the Parties' underlying dispute regarding sovereignty over the Archipelago is predominant. The question of the "coastal State"—now presented in terms of the "attributes of a coastal State"—remains merely an aspect of this larger dispute.

---

[288] Final Transcript, 1089:23 to 1090:10.

[289] Final Transcript, 435:23 to 436:2.

230. The Tribunal accepts that a dispute exists between the Parties concerning the manner in which the MPA was declared. Nevertheless, the Tribunal is of the view that the true "object of the claim" (*Nuclear Tests (New Zealand* v. *France), Judgment, I.C.J. Reports 1974*, p. 457 at p. 466, para. 30) in Mauritius' Second Submission is to bolster Mauritius' claim to sovereignty over the Chagos Archipelago. The Tribunal also notes that the relief sought by Mauritius in its First and Second Submissions is the same: a declaration that the United Kingdom was not entitled to declare the MPA. Accordingly, and notwithstanding the difference in presentation, the Tribunal concludes that Mauritius' Second Submission is properly characterized as relating to the same dispute in respect of land sovereignty over the Chagos Archipelago as Mauritius' First Submission. The Tribunal therefore finds itself without jurisdiction to address Mauritius' Second Submission.

C. The Tribunal's Jurisdiction with regard to Mauritius' Fourth Submission

231. The United Kingdom objects to the Tribunal's jurisdiction over Mauritius' Fourth Submission and its claims concerning the compatibility of the MPA with the Convention (what the United Kingdom describes as the "non-sovereignty claims"). Mauritius maintains its position that the Tribunal has jurisdiction over these claims.

1. The Parties' Arguments

232. Both Parties approach this question with reference to the mandatory exceptions to compulsory jurisdiction set out in Article 297 of the Convention. Broadly speaking, Mauritius contends that the MPA is an environmental measure and that the jurisdiction of this Tribunal is therefore established by Article 297(1)(*c*) concerning the protection of the environment. The United Kingdom, in contrast, considers the MPA to be a measure relating to "sovereign rights with respect to living resources" in the exclusive economic zone and argues that jurisdiction is precluded by Article 297(3)(*a*) concerning fisheries. The United Kingdom also objects, separately, to jurisdiction over Mauritius' claims regarding straddling and highly migratory fish stocks, fisheries access in both the territorial sea and exclusive economic zone, the harvesting of the sedentary species of the continental shelf, marine pollution, and the abuse of rights. The Parties' positions on each of these issues will be set out in turn in the sections that follow.

(a) *The Application of Article 297(1)(c) of the Convention*

233. Article 297(1) of the Convention provides as follows:

Article 297

Limitations on applicability of section 2

1. Disputes concerning the interpretation or application of this Convention with regard to the exercise by a coastal State of its sovereign rights or jurisdiction provided for in this Convention shall be subject to the procedures provided for in section 2 in the following cases:

(*a*) when it is alleged that a coastal State has acted in contravention of the provisions of this Convention in regard to the freedoms and rights of navigation, overflight or the laying of submarine cables and pipelines, or in regard to other internationally lawful uses of the sea specified in article 58;

(*b*) when it is alleged that a State in exercising the aforementioned freedoms, rights or uses has acted in contravention of this Convention or of laws or regulations adopted by the coastal State in conformity with this Convention and other rules of international law not incompatible with this Convention; or

(*c*) when it is alleged that a coastal State has acted in contravention of specified international rules and standards for the protection and preservation of the marine environment which are applicable to the coastal State and which have been established by this Convention or through a competent international organization or diplomatic conference in accordance with this Convention.

The United Kingdom's Position

234. The United Kingdom submits that "Article 297(1)(*c*) provides no basis for jurisdiction over the declaration of an MPA or the ban on commercial fishing."[290] According to the United Kingdom –

> the purpose of this provision, like paragraph (1) as a whole, is to protect freedom of navigation, or the other freedoms referred to in Article 58, against misuse by the coastal States of their power to regulate marine pollution. It does not cover environmental disputes in general, and specifically it does not cover this dispute.[291]

235. The United Kingdom looks to the structure of Article 297(1), and notes that it is generally concerned with navigation, overflight, cables, and pipelines. Fishing and the management of living resources are distinct, the United Kingdom argues, and "obviously fall[] outside the context of Article 297(1) read as a whole."[292] Thus, the United Kingdom concludes "even if we do characterise the MPA and the ban on commercial fishing as having an

[290] Final Transcript, 790:15–16.

[291] Final Transcript, 796:14–18.

[292] Final Transcript, 797:13–14.

environmental purpose, this will not be sufficient to bring the present case within Article 297(1)(*c*)."[293]

236. The United Kingdom emphasizes the requirement in Article 297(1) *c*) that a dispute concern "specified international rules and standards for the protection and preservation of the marine environment which are applicable to the coastal State."[294] Where the phrase "international rules and standards" appears in the Convention, the United Kingdom notes, it is consistently to "empower or require coastal States, flag States, or port States to regulate and enforce regulations for the prevention of marine pollution from ships, aircraft, and seabed activities,"[295] and "none of these articles covers anything resembling a marine protected area whose purpose is to manage and conserve living resources in the EEZ".[296]

237. With respect to fisheries, the United Kingdom argues, the Convention's approach is different: "far from endorsing any commitment to international regulation, in Part V it is the laws of the coastal State that prevail."[297] The United Kingdom continues:

> There are no internationally agreed rules and standards on those subjects, none on the conservation and management of marine living resources which could fit within the terminology used in Article 297(1)(*c*) and the other articles of the Convention to which Mauritius refers do not do so. There is no fisheries equivalent of MARPOL or SOLAS or the London Dumping Convention.[298]

238. Turning to the various articles of the Convention itself invoked by Mauritius, the United Kingdom submits that "the very general wording of articles 55, 56, 63, 64, and 194 also contradicts any suggestion that they could constitute 'specified international rules and standards.'"[299] In the United Kingdom's view:

> (*a*) Article 55 "simply defines the exclusive economic zone";[300]
>
> (*b*) Article 56 "provides the legal basis for the United Kingdom's right as a coastal State to regulate the exclusive economic zone of BIOT and, in particular to regulate conservation and management of living resources, but it specifies no particular international rules and standards for doing so";[301]

---

[293] Final Transcript, 797:21–23.

[294] Final Transcript, 798:4–6.

[295] Final Transcript, 798:20–22.

[296] Final Transcript, 798:25 to 799:2.

[297] Final Transcript, 799:22–23.

[298] Final Transcript, 803:5–9.

[299] Final Transcript, 800:8–10.

[300] Final Transcript, 801:9–11.

[301] Final Transcript, 801:18–21.

(*c*) Articles 63 and 64 require international cooperation, but neither "identifies specific international rules and standards: at best they encourage States to negotiate such rules and standards";[302] and

(*d*) "Article 194 sets out the obligation of States parties to take measures necessary to prevent reduce and control pollution,"[303] but "does not itself constitute or incorporate specified international rules and standards; indeed it makes no reference to them".[304]

239. In sum, the United Kingdom concludes –

> the point of Article 297(1)(*c*)—and this is entirely consistent with articles 297(1)(*a*) and (*b*)—is to protect freedom of navigation, or the other freedoms referred to in Article 58, against misuse by coastal States of their power to regulate marine pollution. And that interpretation is consistent with the two previous sub-paragraphs and it reflects their focus on navigation and pipelines and it reflects the wording of the article itself. But bringing articles 55, 56, 63, 64 and 194 into the ambit of Article 297(1)(*c*) achieves neither coherence nor contextual consistency with the rest of Article 297(1).[305]

Mauritius' Position

240. Mauritius contends that the Tribunal has jurisdiction to address the compatibility of the MPA with the Convention because Mauritius' claims "concern the contravention of specified international rules or standards for the protection and preservation of the marine environment, matters over which [the Tribunal has] jurisdiction under Article 297(1)."[306]

241. Mauritius rejects the objection that Article 297(1) is limited to the context of navigational rights, overflight, cables and pipelines. Mauritius notes that that "limitation appears only in (1)(*a*) and (1)(*b*). It does not appear in (1) *c*)."[307] For Mauritius, this is significant, and reflects the intention for Article 297(1)(*c*) to be of broader application than the preceding provisions. For similar reasons, Mauritius also rejects the United Kingdom's attempt to limit Article 297(1)(*c*) to the context of marine pollution. In Mauritius' view, "marine pollution may fall within the general category of environmental protection and preservation, but there is no textual basis on which to conclude that 297(1) *c*) is confined solely and exclusively to marine pollution."[308]

242. With respect to whether the identified provisions of the Convention are rules or standards within the meaning of Article 297(1)(*c*), Mauritius submits simply that "each of the articles alleged to have been contravened by the UK—Article 194 stands out in particular—establish a binding obligation

[302] Final Transcript, 802:6–8.

[303] Final Transcript, 802:8–10.

[304] Final Transcript, 802:13–15.

[305] Final Transcript, 802:21 to 803:2.

[306] Final Transcript, 468:3–5.

[307] Final Transcript, 1116:21–22.

[308] Final Transcript, 1117:8–11.

and each relates to the protection or preservation of the marine environment. Nothing more is required."[309]

243. Finally, Mauritius submits that the Tribunal need not be concerned that the MPA deals with both the marine environment and fisheries. According to Mauritius, the interplay between Article 297(1)(*c*) and Article 297(3) operates as follows:

> 297(1)(*c*) and 297(3) are both affirmative grants of jurisdiction, though in the case of 297(3) the grant is limited by an exception. The fact that 297(1)(*c*) and 297(3) are *independent* grants of jurisdiction means that an Applicant need only satisfy one of them. It also means that a dispute that falls within a Tribunal's jurisdiction because it concerns an alleged contravention of an international rule or standard for the protection or preservation of the marine environment, *cannot* be excluded from jurisdiction if it may also be said to involve a coastal State's sovereign rights over the living resources of the EEZ or their exercise. If a dispute falls within 297(1)(*c*), jurisdiction is established. The exception contained in 297(3) is irrelevant.[310]

(b) The Application of Article 297(3)(a) of the Convention

244. Article 297(3)(*a*) provides as follows:

> **Article 297**
>
> *Limitations on applicability of section 2*
>
> [...]
>
> 3. (*a*) Disputes concerning the interpretation or application of the provisions of this Convention with regard to fisheries shall be settled in accordance with section 2, except that the coastal State shall not be obliged to accept the submission to such settlement of any dispute relating to its sovereign rights with respect to the living resources in the exclusive economic zone or their exercise, including its discretionary powers for determining the allowable catch, its harvesting capacity, the allocation of surpluses to other States and the terms and conditions established in its conservation and management laws and regulations.

The United Kingdom's Position

245. The United Kingdom submits that the MPA is properly characterized as a fisheries measure, noting that "whatever their purpose, the only implementation measures actually adopted so far are the ban on commercial

[309] Final Transcript, 1118:17–19.

[310] Final Transcript, 469:11–18.

fishing and the new regulations on illegal fishing."[311] As such, it is properly subject to the limitation on jurisdiction expressed in Article 297(3)(*a*). According to the United Kingdom –

> a dispute relating to conservation and management of fish stocks and other living resources in the exclusive economic zone is excluded from compulsory jurisdiction by Article 297(3)(*a*) unless the coastal State agrees. This provision [...] is fatal for Mauritius' challenge to the ban on commercial fishing within the BIOT MPA. And it is fatal even if the MPA's purpose is characterised as environmental, since the wording of Article 297(3)(*a*) takes no account of the purpose for which the discretionary powers of the coastal State have been exercised.[312]

246. "Article 297(3)(*a*)", the United Kingdom argues, "is unambiguous and there is no basis for looking beyond its clear terms."[313] In the United Kingdom's view, Article 297(3)(*a*) grants jurisdiction over fisheries disputes generally and then excludes jurisdiction over fisheries disputes in the exclusive economic zone. As a result, "high seas fisheries disputes are within compulsory jurisdiction, EEZ living resources, quite deliberately, are not."[314] According to the United Kingdom, this result is "entirely consistent with the UNCLOS negotiating record."[315] Recalling that record, the United Kingdom submits that "the object of this whole provision, particularly 297(3), is to keep coastal State fisheries disputes out of court as far as possible. That's what coastal States wanted, particularly Developing States, when they asked for creation of the exclusive economic zone."[316] As such, the United Kingdom submits, "[i]n advocating an evolutionary and environmental interpretation of Article 297 Mauritius invites you to overturn a clear policy preference of the negotiating States at [the Conference]."[317]

247. For the United Kingdom, Mauritius' attempt to parse the language of Article 297(3)(*a*) and to distinguish between fishing in the exclusive economic zone and the exercise of sovereign rights in the exclusive economic zone (and to argue that the former is permitted) fails. According to the United Kingdom, "Article 297(3) makes no jurisdictional distinction between an exercise of sovereign rights that affects other states and one that does not affect other states",[318] and "[i]t seems self-evident that the grant or denial of a licence to fish in the EEZ involves the exercise of sovereign rights over conservation

[311] Final Transcript, 1274:22–23.

[312] Final Transcript, 804:2–8.

[313] Final Transcript, 806:15–16.

[314] Final Transcript, 804:24–25.

[315] Final Transcript, 810:23 to 811:1.

[316] Final Transcript, 815:22–24.

[317] Final Transcript, 812:1–3.

[318] Final Transcript, 1278:14–16.

and management of living resources, ... and that it will do so even if the rights of other states are thereby terminated."[319]

248. Nor, for the United Kingdom, does it matter if the MPA is characterized as environmental in nature, as "almost any modern fisheries conservation and management measure will serve ... multiple objectives".[320] "We can characterise the ban on fishing in the MPA as 'environmental,'" the United Kingdom submits, "but it does not follow that it therefore ceases to be about conservation and management of living resources, or that the environmental purpose prevails over the conservation and management purpose for jurisdictional purposes, or that it falls outside the very broad terms of Article 297(3) (*a*)."[321]

Mauritius' Position

249. "[T]aken as a whole," Mauritius submits, Article "297(3) provides that fisheries disputes are within a tribunal's jurisdiction unless they fall within the categories of disputes that are excluded."[322] Even if the Tribunal does not accept that the MPA is an environmental measure, for which Article 297(1)(*c*) would apply, this Tribunal has jurisdiction because the exclusions in Article 297(3) "do not apply here."[323]

250. In applying Article 297(3), Mauritius distinguishes between the effect of the provision on the sovereign rights of the coastal State and the rights of third States in the exclusive economic zone. According to Mauritius:

> The dispute is *not* based on the purported sovereign rights of the UK as a coastal State in relation to the living resources in the EEZ. That is not how the dispute should be characterized. As Mauritius has shown in its written pleadings, and emphasized in these oral pleadings, the dispute concerns the *rights of Mauritius*, this includes *its* right to fish in the EEZ of the Chagos Archipelago; *its* right to be consulted about matters that can affect *its* interests; *its* right to have fulfilled the undertaking given by Prime Minister Brown to Prime Minister Ramgoolam. It is *these* rights—the rights of *Mauritius*—that are at issue. For that reason, even if the dispute were to be characterized as a fishing dispute, it would not fall within the exception to jurisdiction located in 297(3). That exception, as the text makes unmistakably clear, pertains only to disputes relating to the rights of a *coastal* State; it does *not* concern disputes relating to the rights of *other* States in the EEZ arising under rules of international law.[324]

251. In Mauritius' view, this division mirrors the distinction in Article 56 between the rights of the coastal State and the rights of other States,

[319] Final Transcript, 1278:9–12.

[320] Final Transcript, 809:17–18.

[321] Final Transcript, 809:12–16.

[322] Final Transcript, 477:16–17.

[323] Final Transcript, 477:18.

[324] Final Transcript, 477:19 to 478:4.

and there is, accordingly, "a correlation between Article 56 and 297."[325] Within Article 56, Mauritius submits:

> Subparagraph (1)(*a*) concerns a coastal State's "sovereign rights," including sovereign rights for the purpose of conserving and managing living resources. Jurisdiction in the EEZ, on the other hand, is addressed in subparagraph (1)(*b*), including specifically "jurisdiction" concerning "the protection and preservation of the marine environment," as set out in subparagraph (1)(*b*)(iii).
>
> Article 297(3)'s exclusion mentions only sovereign rights. It does not mention jurisdiction. This must have been deliberate. When the drafters of 297 intended a jurisdictional clause to cover both "jurisdiction" and "sovereign rights," they did so expressly. [...] This, we submit, is a clear indication that the drafters intended only disputes over "sovereign rights" under Article 56(1)(*a*) to be covered by the exclusion. Disputes relating to "jurisdiction" under 56(*b*)(iii) were not. The latter category of disputes thus falls within the general grant of jurisdiction over fisheries disputes, not the exclusion.[326]

252. Moreover, according to Mauritius, the exclusion in Article 297(3) does not apply to procedural obligations such as those that Mauritius has alleged in respect of the obligation to consult in Articles 63 and 64 of the Convention and Article 7 of the 1995 Fish Stocks Agreement. In support of this position, Mauritius relies on the award of the tribunal in *Barbados/Trinidad and Tobago* (*Award of* 11 *April 2006, PCA Award Series*, p. 1, RIAA, Vol. XXVII, p. 147) and the separate opinion in *Southern Bluefin Tuna* (*(New Zealand* v. *Japan, Australia* v. *Japan), Award of* 4 *August 2000, Separate Opinion Of Justice Sir Kenneth Keith*, RIAA, Vol. XXIII, p. 49), both of which, according to Mauritius, proceeded to consider Articles 63 and 64 on the grounds that there was no bar to jurisdiction.[327]

(c) Jurisdiction with respect to Straddling and Highly Migratory Fish Stocks

253. In its final submissions, Mauritius claims that the MPA is incompatible with Articles 63 and 64 of the Convention, as well as Article 7 of the 1995 Fish Stocks Agreement.

254. Article 63 provides as follows:

---

[325] Final Transcript, 1119:8.

[326] Final Transcript, 1121:14 to 1122:7.

[327] Final Transcript, 478:5–13.

Article 63

Stocks occurring within the exclusive economic zones of two or more coastal States or both within the exclusive economic zone and in an area beyond and adjacent to it

1. Where the same stock or stocks of associated species occur within the exclusive economic zones of two or more coastal States, these States shall seek, either directly or through appropriate subregional or regional organizations, to agree upon the measures necessary to coordinate and ensure the conservation and development of such stocks without prejudice to the other provisions of this Part.

2. Where the same stock or stocks of associated species occur both within the exclusive economic zone and in an area beyond and adjacent to the zone, the coastal State and the States fishing for such stocks in the adjacent area shall seek, either directly or through appropriate subregional or regional organizations, to agree upon the measures necessary for the conservation of these stocks in the adjacent area.

255. Article 64 provides as follows:

Article 64

Highly migratory species

1. The coastal State and other States whose nationals fish in the region for the highly migratory species listed in Annex I shall cooperate directly or through appropriate international organizations with a view to ensuring conservation and promoting the objective of optimum utilization of such species throughout the region, both within and beyond the exclusive economic zone. In regions for which no appropriate international organization exists, the coastal State and other States whose nationals harvest these species in the region shall cooperate to establish such an organization and participate in its work.

2. The provisions of paragraph 1 apply in addition to the other provisions of this Part.

256. Article 7 of the 1995 Fish Stocks Agreement provides as follows:

Compatibility of conservation and management measures

1. Without prejudice to the sovereign rights of coastal States for the purpose of exploring and exploiting, conserving and managing the living marine resources within areas under national jurisdiction as provided for in the Convention, and the right of all States for their nationals to engage in fishing on the high seas in accordance with the Convention:

   (*a*) with respect to straddling fish stocks, the relevant coastal States and the States whose nationals fish for such stocks in the adjacent high seas area shall seek, either directly or through the appropriate mechanisms for cooperation provided for in Part III, to agree upon the measures necessary for the conservation of these stocks in the adjacent high seas area;

(*b*) with respect to highly migratory fish stocks, the relevant coastal States and other States whose nationals fish for such stocks in the region shall cooperate, either directly or through the appropriate mechanisms for cooperation provided for in Part III, with a view to ensuring conservation and promoting the objective of optimum utilization of such stocks throughout the region, both within and beyond the areas under national jurisdiction.

2. Conservation and management measures established for the high seas and those adopted for areas under national jurisdiction shall be compatible in order to ensure conservation and management of the straddling fish stocks and highly migratory fish stocks in their entirety. To this end, coastal States and States fishing on the high seas have a duty to cooperate for the purpose of achieving compatible measures in respect of such stocks. In determining compatible conservation and management measures, States shall:

(*a*) take into account the conservation and management measures adopted and applied in accordance with article 61 of the Convention in respect of the same stocks by coastal States within areas under national jurisdiction and ensure that measures established in respect of such stocks for the high seas do not undermine the effectiveness of such measures;

(*b*) take into account previously agreed measures established and applied for the high seas in accordance with the Convention in respect of the same stocks by relevant coastal States and States fishing on the high seas;

(*c*) take into account previously agreed measures established and applied in accordance with the Convention in respect of the same stocks by a subregional or regional fisheries management organization or arrangement;

(*d*) take into account the biological unity and other biological characteristics of the stocks and the relationships between the distribution of the stocks, the fisheries and the geographical particularities of the region concerned, including the extent to which the stocks occur and are fished in areas under national jurisdiction;

(*e*) take into account the respective dependence of the coastal States and the States fishing on the high seas on the stocks concerned; and

(*f*) ensure that such measures do not result in harmful impact on the living marine resources as a whole.

> 3. In giving effect to their duty to cooperate, States shall make every effort to agree on compatible conservation and management measures within a reasonable period of time.
>
> 4. If no agreement can be reached within a reasonable period of time, any of the States concerned may invoke the procedures for the settlement of disputes provided for in Part VIII.
>
> 5. Pending agreement on compatible conservation and management measures, the States concerned, in a spirit of understanding and cooperation, shall make every effort to enter into provisional arrangements of a practical nature. In the event that they are unable to agree on such arrangements, any of the States concerned may, for the purpose of obtaining provisional measures, submit the dispute to a court or tribunal in accordance with the procedures for the settlement of disputes provided for in Part VIII.
>
> 6. Provisional arrangements or measures entered into or prescribed pursuant to paragraph 5 shall take into account the provisions of this Part, shall have due regard to the rights and obligations of all States concerned, shall not jeopardize or hamper the reaching of final agreement on compatible conservation and management measures and shall be without prejudice to the final outcome of any dispute settlement procedure.
>
> 7. Coastal States shall regularly inform States fishing on the high seas in the subregion or region, either directly or through appropriate subregional or regional fisheries management organizations or arrangements, or through other appropriate means, of the measures they have adopted for straddling fish stocks and highly migratory fish stocks within areas under their national jurisdiction.
>
> 8. States fishing on the high seas shall regularly inform other interested States, either directly or through appropriate subregional or regional fisheries management organizations or arrangements, or through other appropriate means, of the measures they have adopted for regulating the activities of vessels flying their flag which fish for such stocks on the high seas.

The United Kingdom's Position

257. The United Kingdom objects to the Tribunal's jurisdiction over Mauritius' claims in relation to straddling and highly migratory fish stocks on four grounds:

- First, the United Kingdom argues that none of the relevant provisions specify "international rules or standards", such that "Article 297(1)(*c*) … cannot provide a jurisdictional foundation for them."[328]
- Second, according to the United Kingdom, Article 297(3)(*a*) bars jurisdiction over measures relating to straddling and highly migratory stocks in the exclusive economic zone. On this basis, the United Kingdom notes, the tribunal in *Barbados/Trinidad and Tobago*

[328] Final Transcript, 816:20–23.

"found that disputes about straddling fish stocks in adjacent EEZs were outside their jurisdiction."[329]

- Third, "Mauritius has the burden of proving ... that Mauritian vessels fish in high seas areas adjacent to the BIOT MPA or in the same region," absent which "it has no standing to invoke a dispute".[330] According to the United Kingdom, Mauritius has offered evidence only of fishing within BIOT waters.[331]
- Finally, insofar as Mauritius' claim relates to a failure to cooperate with the Indian Ocean Tuna Commission (the "IOTC"), the United Kingdom notes that the Agreement for the Establishment of the Indian Ocean Tuna Commission[332] (the "IOTC Agreement") includes its own procedure for the settlement of disputes involving a conciliation commission, followed by recourse to the Convention or to the ICJ. According to the United Kingdom, Mauritius' failure to initiate a conciliation commission precludes jurisdiction as Article 282 of the Convention gives priority to jurisdiction under other agreements providing for the binding resolution of disputes. Alternatively, the United Kingdom submits that jurisdiction would also be precluded by Article 281 (applicable where an agreement between the Parties excludes any further procedure) following the reasoning of the Tribunal in the *Southern Bluefin Tuna* arbitration.[333]

Mauritius' Position

258. Mauritius submits that it does have standing to assert claims in relation to straddling and highly migratory fish stocks:

> The UK does not deny that the relevant stocks occur within the EEZ of both the Chagos Archipelago (assuming *quod non* the UK is the coastal State) and Mauritius, for purposes of 63(1). Mauritius is also a "State fishing for stocks" in an area adjacent to the Chagos Archipelago's EEZ in the sense of 63(2).[334]

Mauritius relies, in this respect, on the records of the IOTC Scientific Committee regarding the issuance of Mauritian tuna licenses, and submits that there is no authority for the United Kingdom's suggestion that such fishing is located too far away from the Chagos Archipelago.[335]

---

[329] Final Transcript, 817:7–9.

[330] Final Transcript, 818:14–17.

[331] Final Transcript, 818:17–18.

[332] Agreement for the Establishment of the Indian Ocean Tuna Commission, 25 November 1993, 1927 UNTS 330.

[333] Final Transcript, 818:19 to 819:24.

[334] Final Transcript, 335:17–20.

[335] Final Transcript, 335:20 to 336:10.

259. At the same time, Mauritius rejects the proposition that the dispute resolution provisions of the IOTC Agreement pose any bar to this Tribunal's jurisdiction. First, Mauritius notes, it "has not made any claims under the IOTC Agreement; all of its claims are based upon breaches of UNCLOS or the 1995 Fish Stocks Agreement."[336] Equally important, however, Mauritius emphasizes, the IOTC Agreement does not provide for the mandatory submission of disputes to a binding procedure: "Disputes are initially referred to conciliation, which Article XXIII takes pains to say is 'not binding in character.' If conciliation does not settle the dispute, the Parties 'may'—but are not required to—refer the dispute to the ICJ."[337] On its face, Mauritius argues, the criteria for exclusion in Article 282 are not met. As for Article 281, Mauritius endorses the separate opinion of Judge Keith in *Southern Bluefin Tuna*, to the effect that "[t]he requirement is that the Parties have agreed to exclude any further procedure for the settlement of the dispute concerning UNCLOS… . They require opting out. They do not require that the Parties positively agree to the binding procedure by opting in."[338]

260. With respect to the application of Article 297(3)(*a*) to straddling stocks and highly migratory species,[339] Mauritius raises three arguments:

(*a*) First, "297(1)(*c*) and 297(3) are independent grounds for exercising jurisdiction" and the dispute is properly characterized as "the UK's contravention of specified international rules or standards for the protection and preservation of the marine environment".[340]

(*b*) Second, "[t]he dispute is *not* based on the purported sovereign rights of the UK as a coastal State in relation to the living resources in the EEZ"; instead "the dispute concerns the *rights of Mauritius*."[341]

(*c*) Third, relying on Judge Keith's separate opinion in *Southern Bluefin Tuna*, "[p]rocedural obligations of consultation and cooperation under [Article 63, Article 64, or Article 7 of the 1995 Agreement] fall outside the 297(3) exclusion."[342]

(d) Jurisdiction over Mauritius' Claims relating to Access to Fish Stocks in the Territorial Sea and Mauritian Rights in the Exclusive Economic Zone

261. In its final submissions, Mauritius claims that the MPA is incompatible with Articles 2(3) and 56(2) of the Convention, insofar as the Lancaster

[336] Final Transcript, 475:13–15.

[337] Final Transcript, 475:20–22.

[338] Final Transcript, 476:5–8.

[339] *See also* Mauritius' arguments concerning Article 297(3)(*a*) at paragraphs 249–252 above.

[340] Final Transcript, 476:13–17.

[341] Final Transcript, 477:19–25.

[342] Final Transcript, 478:7–8.

House Undertakings give Mauritius rights in the territorial sea and exclusive economic zone of the Chagos Archipelago.

262. Article 2(3) provides as follows:

Article 2

Legal status of the territorial sea, of the air space over the territorial sea and of its bed and subsoil

[...]

3. The sovereignty over the territorial sea is exercised subject to this Convention and to other rules of international law.

263. Article 56(2) provides as follows:

Article 56

Rights, jurisdiction and duties of the coastal State in the exclusive economic zone

[...]

2. In exercising its rights and performing its duties under this Convention in the exclusive economic zone, the coastal State shall have due regard to the rights and duties of other States and shall act in a manner compatible with the provisions of this Convention.

[...]

The United Kingdom's Position

264. The United Kingdom objects to the jurisdiction of the Tribunal in respect of Mauritius' claimed rights to fish in the territorial sea of the Chagos Archipelago on the grounds that "a dispute concerning the status and interpretation of a fisheries access agreement is not a dispute concerning interpretation and application of UNCLOS unless there is a provision for dispute settlement meeting the terms of Article 288(2) of UNCLOS."[343] No such provision exists. In the United Kingdom's view, this bar cannot be evaded by incorporating the undertaking giving Mauritius fishing rights into Article 2(3) itself. For the United Kingdom, "whether the alleged agreement is viewed separately from Article 2(3) or as part of Article 2(3), there must still be provision for dispute settlement in accordance with Article 288(2) in order for that dispute about a fisheries access agreement to fall within Part XV jurisdiction."[344]

265. Similarly, the United Kingdom argues with respect to Article 56(2) that "an agreement on access to EEZ stocks is ... subject to compulsory juris-

[343] Final Transcript, 820:13–16.

[344] Final Transcript, 822:3–6.

diction only if it so provides in accordance with Article 288(2)."[345] Any other interpretation would be contrary to State practice in the area of fisheries access agreements.[346]

266. In sum, the United Kingdom concludes:

> Mauritius and the United Kingdom never agreed to any mechanism to settle disputes with respect to Mauritian fishing in the territorial sea or in the waters out to 200 nm, and UNCLOS Part XV cannot now be invoked to solve that omission or the legal consequences that flow from it.[347]

Mauritius' Position

267. Mauritius submits that a dispute over Mauritian fishing rights in the territorial sea exists by virtue of the subjection in Article 2(3) of sovereignty over the territorial sea to other rules of international law. Mauritius contends that by extinguishing the Lancaster House Undertakings, the United Kingdom acted in contravention of such other rules of international law. According to Mauritius, the Tribunal's jurisdiction is then "plainly established" by the simple fact that "none of the exceptions to jurisdiction that the drafters of the Convention adopted in Articles 297 and 298 are applicable such as to exclude the Tribunal's jurisdiction in relation to a dispute under Article 2(3)."[348]

268. Mauritius rejects the suggestion that, in respect of the territorial sea, it has not raised a dispute concerning the interpretation or application of the Convention, but only of the Lancaster House Undertakings. Among the disputes directly relating the Convention, Mauritius identifies the following:

> Does Article 2(3) impose upon the UK an obligation to respect 'other rules of international law' in exercising its purported sovereignty over the Territorial Sea around the Chagos Archipelago? Do those 'rules of international law' encompass the obligation to respect, for example, recognized fishing rights, or the obligation to respect legally binding undertakings? Has the UK breached Article 2(3) by failing to respect those rules of international law?[349]

Mauritius considers the link to the interpretation and application of the Convention to be self-evident and notes that the Parties are in agreement on the permissibility of applying other rules of international law where—as in Article 2(3)—the Convention provides an express *renvoi*.[350]

269. Mauritius similarly rejects the idea that Article 288(2) limits the Tribunal's jurisdiction. According to Mauritius:

[345] Final Transcript, 820:24 to 821:2.

[346] Final Transcript, 821:6–8.

[347] Final Transcript, 823:6–9.

[348] Final Transcript, 291:19–21.

[349] Final Transcript, 481:4–9.

[350] Final Transcript, 482:5–21.

> Article 288(2) applies only to cases submitted pursuant to the provisions of a dispute settlement clause of an international agreement other than the Convention itself. Mauritius' claims were not submitted in accordance with the dispute settlement provisions of any other agreement. They were submitted by Mauritius in accordance with the dispute settlement provisions of Part XV of the Convention itself, invoking the Tribunal's jurisdiction expressly under Article 288(1), because they arise directly under various substantive articles of the Convention, including Article 2(3), whose interpretation or application is clearly called for.[351]

(e) Jurisdiction regarding Mauritius' Claims relating to the Continental Shelf and Sedentary Species

270. Mauritius raised claims that the MPA breached Article 78 of the Convention in its pleadings but did not include such a claim in its final submissions.

271. Article 78 provides as follows:

> **Article 78**
>
> *Legal status of the superjacent waters and air space and the rights and freedoms of other States*
>
> 1. The rights of the coastal State over the continental shelf do not affect the legal status of the superjacent waters or of the air space above those waters.
>
> 2. The exercise of the rights of the coastal State over the continental shelf must not infringe or result in any unjustifiable interference with navigation and other rights and freedoms of other States as provided for in this Convention.

The United Kingdom's Position

272. The United Kingdom objects to the Tribunal's jurisdiction over any claim regarding an alleged right to seabed minerals and sedentary species on the grounds that this "requires interpretation of the understanding reached in 1965, an issue that falls outside the scope of [the Tribunal's] jurisdiction under Article 288 of the Convention".[352] Additionally, the United Kingdom submits that there is no evidence that Mauritian nationals have ever harvested sedentary species.

Mauritius' Position

273. According to Mauritius, "[t]here can be no doubt about the jurisdiction of this Tribunal."[353] "Nothing in Article 297," Mauritius submits,

---

[351] Final Transcript, 484:6–13.

[352] Final Transcript, 824:1–3.

[353] Final Transcript, 478:15–16.

"excludes from your jurisdiction the dispute over the right to harvest sedentary species on the Continental Shelf. The 297(3) exclusion applies only to the EEZ, it does not apply to the Continental Shelf."[354]

274. Additionally, Mauritius argues, "it was immaterial that Mauritius did not exploit sedentary species in 1965, since the undertaking was intended to 'safeguard' Mauritius' *future* uses of the sea. It was *not* the intention that Mauritius would be forever constrained by its 1965 fishing practices."[355]

(f) Jurisdiction regarding Mauritius' Claims relating to the Protection of the Marine Environment

275. In its final submissions, Mauritius claims that the MPA is incompatible with Article 194 of the Convention, which provides in relevant part as follows:

> **Article 194**
>
> *Measures to prevent, reduce and control pollution of the marine environment*
>
> 1. States shall take, individually or jointly as appropriate, all measures consistent with this Convention that are necessary to prevent, reduce and control pollution of the marine environment from any source, using for this purpose the best practicable means at their disposal and in accordance with their capabilities, and they shall endeavour to harmonize their policies in this connection.
>
> [...]
>
> 4. In taking measures to prevent, reduce or control pollution of the marine environment, States shall refrain from unjustifiable interference with activities carried out by other States in the exercise of their rights and in pursuance of their duties in conformity with this Convention.
>
> [...]

The United Kingdom's Position

276. The United Kingdom objects to any claim regarding Article 194 on the grounds that "[a]t present the MPA involves no new laws or policies on marine pollution."[356] In any event, the United Kingdom argues, "although Article 194 is undoubtedly concerned with protection and preservation of the marine environment, it does not constitute the 'specified international rules and standards' whose contravention comes within [the Tribunal's] jurisdiction under Article 297(1)(*c*)".[357]

---

[354] Final Transcript, 478:16–18.

[355] Final Transcript, 341:20–22.

[356] Final Transcript, 824:23.

[357] Final Transcript, 825:5–7.

Mauritius' Position

277. According to Mauritius, the United Kingdom "concedes that Article 194 is a provision relevant to the protection and preservation of the marine environment," that would fall under Article 297(1)(*c*).[358] The only objection to jurisdiction left to it is to claim that no dispute exists.[359]

278. Mauritius contends that this is wrong on the facts as the Parties disagree as to whether the MPA is an environmental or a fisheries measure, and that therefore "there is plainly a dispute over the interpretation or application of Article 194 over which [the Tribunal] may exercise jurisdiction."[360] Mauritius summarizes its position as follows:

> The United Kingdom does not argue it is excluded by 297. Its only argument is that the UK has not yet enacted new laws or regulations on marine pollution. The UK seems to be saying there will be jurisdiction, but *not yet*. [...] Article 194(1) obligates States to "endeavour to harmonize their policies" in connection with marine pollution. This is an obligation that, self-evidently, attaches *prior* to the enactment of such rules since it is concerned with the development of regulatory policies. The UK avers that the BIOT administration is drafting these laws, so the dispute is ripe.[361]

(g) Jurisdiction regarding Mauritius' Claims relating to the Abuse of Rights

279. In its final submissions, Mauritius claims that the MPA is incompatible with Article 300 of the Convention, which provides as follows:

> **Article 300**
>
> *Good faith and abuse of rights*
>
> States Parties shall fulfil in good faith the obligations assumed under this Convention and shall exercise the rights, jurisdiction and freedoms recognized in this Convention in a manner which would not constitute an abuse of right.

The United Kingdom's Position

280. According to the United Kingdom, the Parties agree that –

> this Tribunal would have jurisdiction over its abuse of rights claim only to the extent that it already has jurisdiction over a dispute concerning other provisions of the Convention. So, if Article 297(1)(*c*) does not give

---

[358] Final Transcript, 471:6–7.

[359] Final Transcript, 471:14–20.

[360] Final Transcript, 474:4–5.

[361] Final Transcript, 1125:3–11.

> you jurisdiction over the MPA declaration or the fishing ban, or if Article 297(3)(*a*) excludes jurisdiction, then there is likewise no jurisdiction over the related article 300 claim.[362]

281. The United Kingdom submits, however, that "[t]he core of Mauritius' case on abuse of rights is the denial of fishing rights, and the Convention has its own special regime for abuse of rights claims in that context—that's Article 297(3)(*b*) … [which] mandates compulsory conciliation as the remedy for abuse of coastal State rights over fishing."[363] Mauritius has not requested conciliation and the United Kingdom considers its Article 300 claim to have been foreclosed by this separate regime.

Mauritius' Position

282. According to Mauritius:

> Article 300 establishes an independent obligation under the Convention and, to that extent, it is an independent basis of the claim. What the Convention requires, as construed by the tribunal in the *Virginia* case, is that the abuse be linked with the exercise of one of the substantive rights provided in the Convention.[364]

2. The Tribunal's Decision

283. The Tribunal considers that the question of its jurisdiction over Mauritius' Fourth Submission—concerning the compatibility of the MPA with the Convention—hinges on the characterization of the Parties' dispute and on the interpretation and application of Article 297.

284. As set out above, Mauritius contends that the MPA is a measure "for the protection and preservation over the marine environment" and bases the Tribunal's jurisdiction on Article 297(1)(*c*) of the Convention. The United Kingdom, in turn, contends that the MPA is an exercise of "its sovereign rights with respect to the living resources of the exclusive economic zone" and argues that the Tribunal's jurisdiction is precluded by Article 297(3)(*a*). The Parties thus differ sharply in their interpretation of the factual record and their characterization of the MPA.

285. As set out above (see paragraph 208), it is for the Tribunal to characterize the dispute dividing the Parties. In so doing, the Tribunal considers that it is essential to evaluate both the scope of the MPA, as the measure complained of, and the scope of the rights that Mauritius alleges have been violated.

---

[362] Final Transcript, 825:12–16.

[363] Final Transcript, 825:19–23.

[364] Final Transcript, 1126:2–5.

(a) *The Scope and Character of the MPA*

286. Turning first to the characterization of the MPA, the Tribunal does not accept that the MPA is solely a measure relating to fisheries. While in these proceedings the United Kingdom has sought, at times, to characterize the MPA as relating only to fisheries, noting its suspension of commercial fishing licences, the United Kingdom has justified the measure in far broader terms. In the Public Consultation preceding the decision to create the MPA, the United Kingdom FCO answered the question of "what would be the added value of creating a marine protected area?" as follows:

> There is sufficient scientific information to make a convincing case for designating most of the Territory as a marine protected area (MPA), to include not only protection for fish-stocks but also to strengthen conservation of the reefs and land areas.
>
> [...]
>
> There is high value to scientific/environmental experts in having a minimally perturbed scientific reference site, both for Earth system science studies and for regional conservation management.
>
> [...]
>
> MPA designation for BIOT would safeguard around half the high quality coral reefs in the Indian Ocean whilst substantially increasing the total global coverage of MPAs. If all the BIOT area were a no-take MPA, it would be the world's largest site with that status, more than doubling global coverage with full protection.
>
> [...][365]

287. In the BIOT Proclamation No. 1, establishing the MPA, the United Kingdom described it as follows:

> 1. There is established for the British Indian Ocean Territory a marine reserve to be known as the Marine Protected Area, within the Environment (Protection and Preservation) Zone which was proclaimed on 17 September 2003.
>
> 2. Within the said Marine Protected Area, Her Majesty will exercise sovereign rights and jurisdiction enjoyed under international law, including the United Nations Convention on the Law of the Sea, with regard to the protection and preservation of the environment of the Marine Protected Area. The detailed legislation and regulations governing the said Marine Protected Area and the Territory will be addressed in future legislation of the Territory.
>
> [...][366]

---

[365] UK Foreign and Commonwealth Office, Consultation on Whether to Establish a Marine Protected Area in the British Indian Ocean Territory, November 2009 (Annex MM-152).

[366] British Indian Ocean Territory Proclamation No. 1 of 2010 (Annex MM-166).

288. The FCO Press Release of 1 April 2010, announcing the creation of the MPA, described it in similarly expansive terms:

> The MPA will cover some quarter of a million square miles and its establishment will double the global coverage of the world's oceans under protection. Its creation is a major step forward for protecting the oceans, not just around BIOT itself, but also throughout the world.
>
> This measure is a further demonstration of how the UK takes its international environmental responsibilities seriously.
>
> The territory offers great scope for research in all fields of oceanography, biodiversity and many aspects of climate change, which are core research issues for UK science.[367]

289. In these proceedings the United Kingdom has sought to justify the MPA by submitting scientific writings describing its purpose as follows:

> the Chagos/BIOT MPA was not primarily initiated as a fisheries management tool, rather to conserve the unique and rich biodiversity of this region, both in the coastal and pelagic realm. The relatively pristine nature of the coral reefs of Chagos/BIOT is particularly important considering the 2008 Status of the World's coral reefs report reporting 19% of the original global coral reef area has already been lost through direct human impacts, with a further 15% seriously threatened within 10–20 years, and another 20% under threat in 20–40 years. These predictions do not take into account the accelerating problem of climate change on the oceans. There remains a critically urgent need for more effective management that conserves remaining coral reefs, particularly those in areas of low anthropogenic pressure and thus likely to be most resilient to climate change impacts.[368]

290. Finally, before this Tribunal, the Attorney-General of the United Kingdom defended the MPA on the basis of its broad environmental benefits:

> We are committed to furthering biodiversity of the oceans, and we believe that one significant way of doing this is through the establishment of marine protected areas.
>
> [...]
>
> The BIOT MPA is a regionally and internationally critical step in beginning to address the risk of irreversible damage to the oceans. It has substantially increased the global coverage of MPAs. [That] [t]he scientific case for the BIOT MPA is robust actually hasn't been challenged in this case at all. The waters around British Indian Ocean Territory are some of the most pristine in the Indian Ocean, indeed on the planet, and have

[367] UK Foreign and Commonwealth Office Press Release, 1 April 2010, "New Protection for marine life" (Annex MM-165).

[368] H. Koldewey, D. Curnick, S. Harding, L. Harrison, M. Gollock, 'Potential benefits to fisheries and biodiversity of the Chagos Archipelago/British Indian Ocean Territory as a no-take marine reserve', 60 *Marine Pollution Bulletin* 1906 (2010) (Annex UKR-63) (references omitted).

a genuinely world-wide importance: scientists agree it is an exceptional place and merits protection.[369]

291. Having argued for the necessity and importance of the MPA by reference to environmental concerns that extend well beyond the management of fisheries, it is not now open to the United Kingdom to limit the jurisdiction of this Tribunal with the argument that the MPA is merely a fisheries measure. The Tribunal is entitled to hold the United Kingdom to the manner in which it has characterized the MPA in these proceedings and in numerous public pronouncements. The Tribunal also notes that the initiation of this arbitration, only nine months after the declaration of the MPA, may well have delayed the introduction of further implementing measures. In any event, the UK's declared object and purpose of the MPA are certainly relevant to Mauritius, a country with a reversionary interest in the area.

292. The Tribunal now turns to the rights that Mauritius' alleges to have been violated.

(b) The Scope and Character of Mauritius' Rights

293. Mauritius contends that the MPA is incompatible with the United Kingdom's obligations under Articles 2, 55, 56, 63, 64, 194, and 300 of the Convention, as well as Article 7 of the 1995 Fish Stocks Agreement.[370] Among these provisions, Articles 2(3) and 56(2), regarding the exercise of sovereignty or sovereign rights over the territorial sea and exclusive economic zone, respectively, make reference to "other rules of international law" or an obligation to "have due regard to the rights and duties of other States". These provisions require the Tribunal to consider Mauritius' legal rights as they otherwise arise as a matter of international law, as well as Mauritius' rights arising under the Convention. Articles 63, 64, and 194, in contrast, create obligations on the United Kingdom, arising entirely within the Convention itself, to consult with other States regarding certain fisheries measures and regarding the harmonization of measures in respect of marine pollution. Article 55 describes the exclusive economic zone. Article 300 requires that the United Kingdom not exercise its rights in a manner that would constitute an abuse of rights.

294. For the purposes of Articles 2(3) and 56(2), the Tribunal considers the rights at issue to be those originating in the Lancaster House Undertakings made by the United Kingdom to Mauritius on 23 September 1965, in connection with the detachment of the Chagos Archipelago. As set out in detail above (see paragraphs 74–79), following that meeting Sir Seewoosagur Ramgoolam

[369] Final Transcript, 45:4–6, 48:14–19.

[370] As set out above (see paragraphs 270–274), Mauritius raised arguments relating to Article 78 of the Convention and sedentary species, but did not claim a violation of this provision in its final submissions. The Tribunal will consider its jurisdiction only with respect to those provisions of the Convention that Mauritius has alleged to have been breached by the declaration of the MPA.

wrote to the Colonial Office, supplementing the undertakings set out in the draft record. Following the inclusion of these additions, the final minutes of the meeting record the undertakings as follows:

(i) negotiations for a defence agreement between Britain and Mauritius;

(ii) in the event of independence an understanding between the two governments that they would consult together in the event of a difficult internal security situation arising in Mauritius;

(iii) compensation totalling up to £3m. should be paid to the Mauritius Government over and above direct compensation to landowners and the cost of resettling others affected in the Chagos Islands;

(iv) the British Government would use their good offices with the United States Government in support of Mauritius' request for concessions over sugar imports and the supply of wheat and other commodities;

(v) that the British Government would do their best to persuade the American Government to use labour and materials from Mauritius for construction work in the islands;

(vi) the British Government would use their good offices with the U.S. Government to ensure that the following facilities in the Chagos Archipelago would remain available to the Mauritius Government as far as practicable:

(*a*) Navigational and Meteorological facilities;

(*b*) Fishing Rights;

(*c*) Use of Air Strip for emergency landing and for refuelling civil planes without disembarkation of passengers.

(vii) that if the need for the facilities on the islands disappeared the islands should be returned to Mauritius;

(viii) that the benefit of any minerals or oil discovered in or near the Chagos Archipelago should revert to the Mauritius Government.[371]

295. These undertakings were then conveyed to the Mauritius Council of Ministers, who were asked to indicate their agreement to the detachment of the Chagos Archipelago and did so on 5 November 1965, subject to the understanding that –

(1) statement in paragraph 6 of your despatch "H.M.G. have taken careful note of points (vii) and (viii)" means H.M.G. have in fact agreed to them.

(2) As regards (vii) undertaking to Legislative Assembly excludes

[371] Record of a Meeting held in Lancaster House at 2.30 p.m. on Thursday 23rd September [1965], Mauritius Defence Matters, CO 1036/1253 at paras. 22–23 (Annex MM-19).

(*a*) sale or transfer by H.M.G. to third party or

(*b*) any payment or financial obligation by Mauritius as condition of return.

(3) In (viii) "on or near" means within area within which Mauritius would be able to derive benefit but for change of sovereignty. I should be grateful if you would confirm this understanding is agreed.[372]

296. Mauritius contends that these undertakings were binding as from their acceptance by the Council of Ministers and became so as a matter of international law upon the independence of Mauritius. Mauritius further contends that in declaring the MPA, the United Kingdom failed to exercise its jurisdiction subject to these undertakings (Article 2) and failed to give due regard to them (Article 56). For the purposes of determining its jurisdiction, however, the Tribunal's concern is with the scope and character of the rights that Mauritius alleges to have been violated. The existence and binding nature of these alleged rights are matters for the merits that the Tribunal will address subsequently (see paragraphs 417–456 below). For present purposes, the Tribunal needs only to satisfy itself that the rights asserted by Mauritius are such as to justify the provisional conclusion that they may have been binding as a matter of international law and relevant to the application of Articles 2 and 56 (*Interhandel Case, Judgment of March 21st 1959: I.C.J. Reports 1959*, p. 6 at p. 24; *see also Ambatielos case (merits: obligation to arbitrate), Judgment of May 19th, 1953: I.C.J. Reports 1953*, p. 10 at p. 18). Having reviewed the role of the undertakings in the Mauritian Ministers' agreement to the detachment of the Archipelago, the Tribunal finds that this test is satisfied.

297. Among the undertakings made by the United Kingdom, the Tribunal notes that (vi)(*b*), relating to fishing rights; (vii), relating to the return of the Archipelago when no longer needed for defence purposes; and (viii), relating to the benefit of oil and mineral resources, are potentially implicated by the declaration of the MPA. The United Kingdom's undertaking with respect to fishing rights is clearly related to living resources and—insofar as it applies to the exclusive economic zone—falls under the exclusion from jurisdiction set out in Article 297(3)(*a*). In this respect, the Tribunal does not accept Mauritius' argument that a distinction can be made between disputes regarding the sovereign rights of the coastal State with respect to living resources, and disputes regarding the rights of other States in the exclusive economic zone (with only the former excluded from compulsory settlement). In nearly any imaginable situation, a dispute will exist precisely because the coastal State's conception of its sovereign rights conflicts with the other party's understanding of its own rights. In short, the two are intertwined, and a dispute regarding Mauritius' claimed fishing rights in the exclusive economic zone cannot be separated

[372] Mauritius Telegram No. 247 to the Colonial Office, 5 November 1965, FO 371/184529 (Annex MM-25).

from the exercise of the United Kingdom's sovereign rights with respect to living resources.

298. The United Kingdom's remaining undertakings, however, are evidently broader. In the Tribunal's view, the United Kingdom's undertaking to return the Chagos Archipelago to Mauritius gives Mauritius an interest in significant decisions that bear upon the possible future uses of the Archipelago. Mauritius' interest is not simply in the eventual return of the Chagos Archipelago, but also in the condition in which the Archipelago will be returned. In this respect, the question of whether the Archipelago will or will not be covered by an MPA in the potentially extended period prior to its return significantly affects the nature of what Mauritius will eventually receive and the uses Mauritius will be able to make of it. The Tribunal does not accept the United Kingdom's argument that the MPA is irrelevant to the return of the Archipelago merely because the applicable regulations could potentially be undone. As the record of diplomatic correspondence in these proceedings amply demonstrates, the creation of the MPA was a significant political decision. If it were to remain and be developed over the course of many years, it could well become impractical or impolitic for Mauritius to adopt a radically different course. In short, the MPA's very existence bears upon the choices that Mauritius will have open to it when the Archipelago is eventually returned. In a like manner, the Tribunal considers that the benefit of the minerals and oil in the surrounding waters, which Mauritius will receive when the Archipelago is returned, may be significantly affected by the MPA, in particular in light of the expansive objective of environmental protection declared by the United Kingdom.

299. Turning now to Mauritius' rights to consultation and coordination pursuant to Articles 63, 64, and 194 of the Convention and Article 7 of the 1995 Fish Stocks Agreement, the Tribunal notes that the rights Mauritius claims to have been violated are not dependent on undertakings by the United Kingdom, but arise directly from the Convention itself. Articles 63 and 64 of the Convention, and Article 7 of the 1995 Fish Stocks Agreement, apply wherever the nationals of another State fish for straddling or highly-migratory fish stocks. Meanwhile, Article 194(1) imposes an obligation to "endeavour to harmonize" policies on pollution of the marine environment whenever joint action is "appropriate".

300. The Tribunal accepts that Articles 63 and 64 (as well as the 1995 Fish Stocks Agreement) are, on their face, measures in respect of fisheries and in their application in the exclusive economic zone are subject to the exclusion in Article 297(3)(*a*) (*see Arbitration between Barbados and the Republic of Trinidad and Tobago, Award of* 11 *April 2006, PCA Award Series*, p. 121, RIAA, Vol. XXVII, p. 147 at p. 226, para. 283). As set out above, the Tribunal does not accept that a distinction can be made between disputes in the exclusive economic zone over sovereign rights and those over the rights of another State (see paragraph 297). The Tribunal also finds no basis, in either *Barbados/Trinidad*

and Tobago or *Southern Bluefin Tuna* (including the Separate Opinion) for the proposition that the exclusion in Article 297(3) does not apply to procedural obligations. In *Barbados/Trinidad and Tobago*, that tribunal expressly held that it had it no jurisdiction to establish a right of access for Barbadian fisherman in Trinidadian waters precisely because Article 297(3) applied. That tribunal went on to address the straddling flying fish stocks and Article 63 of the Convention only to the extent of "draw[ing] attention to certain matters that are necessarily entailed by the boundary line that [the Tribunal] has drawn" and of recording certain commitments made by Trinidad and Tobago during the hearing (*Award of* 11 *April 2006, PCA Award Series*, pp. 122–124, RIAA, Vol. XXVII, p. 147 at pp. 226–228, paras. 284–293). *Southern Bluefin Tuna*, in turn, involved a dispute over catch allowances for highly migratory species applicable "principally in the high seas" (*(New Zealand* v. *Japan, Australia* v. *Japan), Award of* 4 *August 2000*, RIAA, Vol. XXIII, p. 1 at p. 8, para. 21). Neither the Award nor the Separate Opinion make any suggestion that the jurisdictional exclusion in the exclusive economic zone pursuant to Article 297(3) was potentially applicable, nor is Japan recorded as having raised any objection on this basis.

301. Finally, the Tribunal is aware of the view, advanced in certain academic settings, that Article 297(3) should be construed narrowly in its application to Article 63 and Article 64 and to the 1995 Fish Stocks Agreement on the grounds that the entire purpose of the special regime for these species is to enable populations to be managed as a unified whole, and that this object and purpose is potentially frustrated by providing distinct dispute resolution regimes for such species in the exclusive economic zone and in the high seas. However desirable this purpose may be as a matter of policy, the Tribunal can see no textual basis for such a construction in either the Convention or the 1995 Fish Stocks Agreement. The latter agreement afforded ample opportunity to remedy any ambiguity of drafting in the earlier Convention, but nevertheless expressly provides that "Article 297, paragraph 3, of the Convention applies also to this Agreement" (Agreement for the Implementation of the Provisions of the United Nations Convention on the Law of the Sea of 10 December 1982 relating to the Conservation and Management of Straddling Fish Stocks and Highly Migratory Fish Stocks (with annexes), Art. 31, 4 August 1995, 2167 UNTS p. 3).

302. Article 194, however, is not so limited. The Tribunal notes that the United Kingdom's objection with respect to this final provision is merely that no dispute exists as the obligation would apply only in the event the MPA were to include new regulations on marine pollution. This, however, is a defence on the merits, and not a bar to the Tribunal's jurisdiction.

303. Finally, Mauritius has invoked Articles 55 and 300. Article 55 is principally concerned with the definition of the exclusive economic zone and, in the Tribunal's view, adds nothing to the scope of the rights that Mauritius has already asserted pursuant to Article 56 and the Lancaster House Undertakings. With respect to Article 300 and the abuse of rights, the Tribunal agrees

with the Parties that a claim pursuant to Article 300 is necessarily linked to the alleged violation of another provision of the Convention. As such, the nature of Mauritius' rights pursuant to this provision coincides with the nature of the other provisions allegedly violated.

* * *

304. The Tribunal therefore concludes that neither the MPA nor the rights asserted by Mauritius are limited to the living resources of the exclusive economic zone. The Tribunal finds that the dispute between the Parties in relation to the compatibility of the MPA with the Convention relates more broadly to the preservation of the marine environment and to the legal regime applicable to the Archipelago and its surrounding waters when it is eventually returned to Mauritius. The Tribunal's consideration of Mauritius' Fourth Submission cannot therefore be excluded entirely by the exception from jurisdiction set out Article 297(3)(*a*). This is particularly the case in light of the extensive focus by the United Kingdom on the protection of coral, a sedentary species expressly excluded from the regime for the exclusive economic zone by Article 68 of the Convention and therefore beyond any possible application of Article 297(3)(*a*). The Tribunal also emphasizes that all of the rights of a coastal State, inherent in the United Kingdom's undertaking to return the Archipelago to Mauritius, are potentially implicated and entitled to due regard pursuant to Article 56(2). In the Tribunal's view, the Parties' dispute cannot, as a whole, be dismissed as a fisheries matter.

305. Having thus addressed the objection to jurisdiction made by the United Kingdom on the basis of Article 297(3)(*a*), the Tribunal now turns to the relationship between its jurisdiction and Article 297(1)(*c*).

(c) Article 297(1)(c) and the Tribunal's Jurisdiction

306. In the sections that follow, the Tribunal will first examine the relationship between Article 288(1) and Article 297(1) and will determine which provision founds the Tribunal's jurisdiction in the present case. The Tribunal will then go on to consider the applicability of Article 297(1)(*c*) to the MPA.

i. The relationship between Article 288(1) and Article 297(1)(*c*)

307. Within the structure of the Part XV dispute settlement provisions of the Convention, Article 288(1) (contained in section 2 of Part XV) grants the Tribunal jurisdiction generally with respect to "any dispute concerning the interpretation or application of this Convention which is submitted to it in accordance with this Part." Article 297, although captioned "Limitations on applicability of section 2", then goes on to grant the Tribunal jurisdiction specifically over certain categories of disputes relating to sovereign rights, marine scientific research, and fisheries, providing that disputes relating to these matters "shall be subject to the procedures provided for in section 2" or "shall be

settled in accordance with section 2". Articles 297(2) and 297(3) also impose express limitations on the jurisdiction the Tribunal may exercise with respect to marine scientific research or to fisheries. Article 297(1), however, is phrased entirely in affirmative terms and includes no exceptions to the jurisdiction the Tribunal may exercise.

308. Article 297(1) does not state that disputes concerning the exercise of sovereign rights and jurisdiction are *only* subject to compulsory settlement in the enumerated cases. And, as a matter of textual construction, the Tribunal does not consider that such a limitation can be implied. If Article 297(1) were understood to mean that a Tribunal would have jurisdiction over the exercise of sovereign rights and jurisdiction only in the specified cases, there would have been no need for Article 297(3) to expressly exclude disputes over the living resources of the exclusive economic zone: such disputes would be excluded already, by virtue of their non-inclusion in the list of cases set out in Article 297(1). Similarly, if Article 297(1) were understood to include an implied "only" and to present an exclusive list of the cases over which the Tribunal could exercise jurisdiction, it would then conflict with the jurisdiction over marine scientific research recognized in Article 297(2), which in some cases will involve sovereign rights in the exclusive economic zone. Textually, therefore, Article 297(1) reaffirms, but does not limit, the Tribunal's jurisdiction pursuant to Article 288(1). In light, however, of the apparent ambiguity of including a jurisdiction-affirming provision in an article otherwise devoted to limitations on the exercise of compulsory dispute settlement, the Tribunal considers it useful to delve deeper into the history of this provision.

309. The Tribunal recalls that the negotiations over the provision that ultimately became Article 297 of the Convention were marked by differences over the scope of compulsory dispute settlement in the exclusive economic zone. Many coastal States sought to limit or exclude compulsory settlement in order to protect their newly won jurisdiction from the expense and burden of potentially frequent challenge. Others considered comprehensive provisions for compulsory dispute settlement to be essential to the preservation of the rights of other States in the expansive areas being incorporated into the exclusive economic zone.[373] In attempting to balance these competing interests, the text of what became Article 297 underwent a series of substantial revisions that dramatically changed its structure and content.

310. In the 1976 draft of the Convention, the Tribunal notes, what became Article 297 *did* provide that compulsory dispute resolution would only apply to the three cases now set out in Article 297(1).[374] Following textual revisions in the course of that year, the provision read as follows:

---

[373] See the summary of the debate on this provision in S. Rosenne & L. Sohn, eds., *United Nations Convention on the Law of the Sea 1982: A Commentary*, Vol. V at pp. 92–94 (M. Norquist, gen. ed., 1989).

[374] *Official Records of the Third United Nations Conference on the Law of the Sea, Volume V (Summary Records, Plenary, General Committee, First, Second and Third Committees, as well as*

> 1. Disputes relating to the exercise by a coastal State of sovereign rights, exclusive rights or exclusive jurisdiction recognized by the present Convention shall be subject to the procedures specified in section 2 only in the following cases:
>
> (*a*) When it is claimed that a coastal State has acted in contravention of the provisions of the present Convention in regard to the freedom of navigation or overflight or of the laying of submarine cables and pipelines and other internationally lawful uses of the sea related to navigation or communication; or
>
> (*b*) When it is claimed that any State, in exercising the aforementioned freedoms, has acted in contravention of the provisions of the present Convention or of laws or regulations enacted by the coastal State in conformity with the present Convention and other rules of international law not incompatible with the present Convention; or
>
> (*c*) When it is claimed that a coastal State has acted in contravention of specified international standards or criteria for the preservation of the marine environment or for the conduct of marine scientific research, which are applicable to the coastal State and which have been established by the present Convention or by a competent international authority acting in accordance with the present Convention; or
>
> (*d*) When it is claimed that a coastal State has manifestly failed to comply with specified conditions established by the present Convention relating to the exercise of its rights or performance of its duties in respect of living resources, provided that in no case shall the sovereign rights of the coastal State be called in question.
>
> 2. Any dispute excluded by paragraph 1 may be submitted to the procedure specified in section 2 only with the express consent of the coastal State concerned.
>
> 3. Any disagreement between the parties to a dispute as to the applicability of this article shall be decided in accordance with paragraph 3 of article 10 [now 288].[375]

At that time, no express exception was included with respect to either marine scientific research or fisheries.

311. In the 1977 draft of the Convention, this provision was substantially modified. Reflecting the concern with the abuse of legal process and the pos-

---

Documents of the Conference, Fourth Session), Informal Single Negotiating Text, Part IV, Art. 18, UN Doc. A/CONF.62/WP.9/Rev.1 (6 May 1976).

[375] *Official Records of the Third United Nations Conference on the Law of the Sea, Volume VI (Summary Records, Plenary, General Committee, First, Second and Third Committees, as well as Documents of the Conference, Fifth Session)*, Revised Single Negotiating Text, Part IV, Art. 17, UN Doc. A/CONF.62/WP.9/Rev.2 (23 November 1976).

sibility of frequent, frivolous challenges to the jurisdiction of the coastal State, the 1977 draft provided that any dispute involving the exercise of sovereign rights or jurisdiction would be subject to certain mandatory procedural safeguards. Compulsory dispute settlement was no longer expressly restricted to the three cases now set out in Article 297(1); instead, jurisdiction in the three cases was made conditional on the fulfilment of the procedural safeguards. New exclusions were also introduced with respect to marine scientific research and fisheries. Finally, the draft Article provided in paragraph (5) that any dispute excluded from the other paragraphs could be submitted to compulsory settlement "only by agreement of the parties to such dispute". As restructured, the draft Article read as follows:

> 1. Without prejudice to the obligations arising under section 1, disputes relating to the exercise by a coastal State of sovereign rights or jurisdiction provided for in the present Convention shall only be subject to the procedures specified in the present Convention when the following conditions have been complied with:
>
> (*a*) that in any dispute to which the provisions of this article apply, the court or tribunal shall not call upon the other party or parties to respond until the party which has submitted the dispute has established *prima facie* that the claim is well founded;
>
> (*b*) that such court or tribunal shall not entertain any application which in its opinion constitutes an abuse of legal process or is frivolous or vexatious; and
>
> (*c*) that such court or tribunal shall immediately notify the other party to the dispute that the dispute has been submitted and such party shall be entitled, if it so desires, to present objections to the entertainment of the application.
>
> 2. Subject to the fulfillment of the conditions specified in paragraph 1, such court or tribunal shall have jurisdiction to deal with the following cases:
>
> (*a*) When it is alleged that a coastal State has acted in contravention of the provisions of the present Convention in regard to the freedoms and rights of navigation or overflight or of the laying of submarine cables and pipelines and other internationally lawful uses of the sea specified in article 58; or
>
> (*b*) When it is alleged that any State in exercising the aforementioned freedoms, rights or uses has acted in contravention of the provisions of the present Convention or of laws or regulations established by the coastal State in conformity with the present Convention and other rules of international law not incompatible with the present Convention; or
>
> (*c*) When it is alleged that a coastal State has acted in contravention of specified international rules and standards for the protection and preservation of the marine environment which are applicable to the coastal State and which have been established

by the present Convention or by a competent international organization or diplomatic conference acting in accordance with the present Convention.

3. No dispute relating to the interpretation or application of the provisions of the present Convention with regard to marine scientific research shall be brought before such court or tribunal unless the conditions specified in paragraph 1 have been fulfilled; provided that:

(*a*) when it is alleged that there has been a failure to comply with the provision of articles 247 [now 246] and 254 [now 253], in no case shall the exercise of a right or discretion in accordance with article 247, or a decision taken in accordance with article 254, be called in question; and

(*b*) the court or tribunal shall not substitute its discretion for that of the coastal State.

4. No dispute relating to the interpretation or application of the provisions of the present Convention with regard to the living resources of the sea shall be brought before such court or tribunal unless the conditions specified in paragraph 1 have been fulfilled; provided that:

(*a*) when it is alleged that there has been a failure to discharge obligations arising under articles 61, 62, 69 and 70, in no case shall the exercise of a discretion in accordance with articles 61 and 62 be called in question; and

(*b*) the court or tribunal shall not substitute its discretion for that of the coastal State; and

(*c*) in no case shall the sovereign rights of a coastal State be called in question.

5. Any dispute excluded by the previous paragraphs may be submitted to the procedures specified in section 2 only by agreement of the parties to such dispute.[376]

312. In the 1979 draft, this provision was restructured yet again, and the procedural safeguards that had been a condition to the exercise of jurisdiction over the cases now set out in Article 297(1) were broken off as separate articles, eventually to become Article 294 (Preliminary Proceedings) and Article 300 (Abuse of Rights) of the final Convention. The revised draft Article on limitations to compulsory dispute settlement still provided in its final paragraph, however, that "any dispute excluded by the previous paragraphs may be submitted to the procedures specified in section 2 only by agreement of the parties to such dispute." In its 1979 form, the provision that became Article 297 thus read as follows:

[376] *Official Records of the Third United Nations Conference on the Law of the Sea, Volume VIII (Informal Composite Negotiating Text, Sixth Session)*, Informal Composite Negotiating Text, Art. 296, UN Doc. A/CONF.62/WP.10 (15 July 1977).

1. Notwithstanding the provisions of article 286, disputes relating to the interpretation or application of this Convention with regard to the exercise by a coastal State if [*sic*] its sovereign rights or jurisdiction provided for in this Convention, shall be subject to the procedures specified in this section in the following cases.

(*a*) When it is alleged that a coastal State has acted in contravention of the provisions of this Convention in regard to the freedoms and rights of navigation or overflight or of the laying of submarine cables and pipelines and other internationally lawful uses of the sea specified in article 58; or

(*b*) When it is alleged that any State in exercising the aforementioned freedoms, rights or uses has acted in contravention of the provisions of this Convention or of laws or regulations established by the coastal State in conformity with this Convention and other rules of international law not incompatible with this Convention; or

(*c*) When it is alleged that a coastal State has acted in contravention of specified international rules and standards for the protection and preservation of the marine environment which are applicable to the coastal State and which have been established by this Convention or by a competent international organization or diplomatic conference acting in accordance with this Convention.

2. No dispute relating to the interpretation or application of the provisions of this Convention with regard to marine scientific research shall be brought before such court or tribunal unless the conditions specified in article __ have been fulfilled; provided that:

(*a*) when it is alleged that there has been a failure to comply with the provision of articles 246 and 253, in no case shall the exercise of a right or discretion in accordance with article 246, or a decision taken in accordance with article 253, be called in question; and

(*b*) the court or tribunal shall not substitute its discretion for that of the coastal State.

3. (*a*) Unless otherwise agreed or decided by the parties concerned, disputes relating to the interpretation or application of the provisions of this Convention with regard to fisheries shall be settled in accordance with this section, except that the coastal State shall not be obliged to accept the submission to such settlement of any dispute relating to its sovereign rights with respect to the living resources in the exclusive economic zone or their exercise, including its discretionary powers for determining the allowable catch, its harvesting capacity, the allocation of surpluses to other States and the terms and conditions established in its conservation and management regulations.

(*b*) Where no settlement has been reached by recourse to the provisions of section 1, a dispute shall, notwithstanding article 284, paragraph 3, be submitted to the conciliation procedure provided for in Annex IV, at the request of any party to the dispute, when it is alleged that:

(i) a coastal State has manifestly failed to comply with its obligations to ensure through proper conservation and management measures that the maintenance of the living resources in the exclusive economic zone is not seriously endangered;

(ii) a coastal State has arbitrarily refused to determine, upon the request of another State, the allowable catch and its capacity to harvest the living resources with respect to stocks which that other State is interested in fishing;

(iii) a coastal State has arbitrarily refused to allocate to any State, under the provisions of articles 68, 69 and 70 and under the terms and conditions established by the coastal State consistent with this Convention, the whole or part of the surplus it has declared to exist.

(*c*) In any case the conciliation commission shall not substitute its discretion for that of the coastal State.

(*d*) The report of the conciliation commission shall be communicated to the appropriate global, regional or sub-regional intergovernmental organizations.

(*e*) In negotiating agreements pursuant to articles 69 and 70 the parties, unless they otherwise agree, shall include a clause on measures which the parties shall take in order to minimize the possibility of a disagreement concerning the interpretation or application of the agreement, and on how the parties should proceed if a disagreement nevertheless arises.

4. Without prejudice to the provisions of paragraph 3, any dispute excluded by the previous paragraphs may be submitted to the procedures specified in section 2 only by agreement of the parties to such dispute.[377]

313. In the 1980 revisions of the draft negotiating text, the provision underwent a final, major revision when the text in respect of marine scientific research was substantially re-written and the procedure for the compulsory conciliation of disputes relating to marine scientific research and fisheries was introduced.[378] The provision was moved to the newly created section 3 and renumbered as draft Article 297. At the same time, the ultimate paragraph restricting

[377] *Official Records of the Third United Nations Conference on the Law of the Sea, Volume VIII (Informal Composite Negotiating Text, Sixth Session)*, Informal Composite Negotiating Text Revision 1, Art. 296, UN Doc. A/CONF.62/WP.10/Rev.1 (28 April 1979).

[378] *Official Records of the Third United Nations Conference on the Law of the Sea, Volume VIII (Informal Composite Negotiating Text, Sixth Session)*, Informal Composite Negotiating Text Revision 2, Art. 296, UN Doc. A/CONF.62/WP.10/Rev.2 (11 April 1980).

jurisdiction over any dispute "excluded by the previous paragraphs" was deleted.[379] As redrafted, the nearly final 1980 text of Article 297 read as follows:

> 1. Disputes relating to the interpretation or application of this Convention with regard to the exercise by a coastal State of its sovereign rights or jurisdiction provided for in this Convention, shall be subject to the procedures specified in section 2 in the following cases:
>
> (*a*) When it is alleged that a coastal State has acted in contravention of the provisions of this Convention in regard to the freedoms and rights of navigation or overflight or of the laying of submarine cables and pipelines and other internationally lawful uses of the sea specified in article 58; or
>
> (*b*) When it is alleged that any State in exercising the aforementioned freedoms, rights or uses has acted in contravention of the provisions of this Convention or of laws or regulations established by the coastal State in conformity with this Convention and other rules of international law not incompatible with this Convention; or
>
> (*c*) When it is alleged that a coastal State has acted in contravention of specified international rules and standards for the protection and preservation of the marine environment which are applicable to the coastal State and which have been established by this Convention or by a competent international organization or diplomatic conference acting in accordance with this Convention.
>
> 2. (a) Disputes relating to the interpretation or application of the provisions of this Convention with regard to marine scientific research shall be settled in accordance with section 2, except that the coastal State shall not be obliged to accept the submission to such settlement any dispute arising out of:
>
> (i) the exercise by the coastal State of a right or discretion in accordance with article 246; or
>
> (ii) a decision by the coastal State to order suspension or cessation of a research project in accordance with article 253.
>
> (*b*) Disputes arising from an allegation by the researching State that with respect to a specific project the coastal State is not exercising its rights under articles 246 and 253 in a manner compatible with the provisions of this Convention shall be submitted, at the request of either party, to the conciliation procedure specified in section 2 of Annex V, provided that the conciliation commission shall not call in question the exercise by the coastal State of its discretion to designate specific areas as referred to in para-

[379] *Official Records of the Third United Nations Conference on the Law of the Sea, Volume VIII (Informal Composite Negotiating Text, Sixth Session)*, Informal Composite Negotiating Text Revision 3, Art. 297, UN Doc. A/CONF.62/WP.10/Rev.3 (22 September 1980).

graph 6 of article 246 or of its discretion to withhold consent in accordance with paragraph 5 of article 246.

3. (*a*) Disputes relating to the interpretation or application of the provisions of this Convention with regard to fisheries shall be settled in accordance with section 2, except that the coastal State shall not be obliged to accept the submission to such settlement of any dispute relating to its sovereign rights with respect to the living resources in the exclusive economic zone or their exercise, including its discretionary powers for determining the allowable catch, its harvesting capacity, the allocation of surpluses to other States and the terms and conditions established in its conservation and management regulations;

(*b*) Where no settlement has been reached by recourse to the provisions of section 1, a dispute shall be submitted to the conciliation procedure specified in section 2 of Annex V, at the request of any party to the dispute, when it is alleged that:

(i) a coastal State has manifestly failed to comply with its obligations to ensure through proper conservation and management measures that the maintenance of the living resources in the exclusive economic zone is not seriously endangered;

(ii) a coastal State has arbitrarily refused to determine, upon the request of another State, the allowable catch and its capacity to harvest the living resources with respect to stocks which that other State is interested in fishing;

(iii) a coastal State has arbitrarily refused to allocate to any State, under the provisions of articles 62, 69 and 70 and under the terms and conditions established by the coastal State consistent with this Convention, the whole or part of the surplus it has declared to exist.

(*c*) In any case the conciliation commission shall not substitute its discretion for that of the coastal State;

(*d*) The report of the conciliation commission shall be communicated to the appropriate international organizations;

(*e*) In negotiating agreements pursuant to articles 69 and 70 the parties, unless they otherwise agree, shall include a clause on measures which the parties shall take in order to minimize the possibility of a disagreement concerning the interpretation or application of the agreement, and on how the parties should proceed if a disagreement nevertheless arises.[380]

314. The Tribunal considers this extended recitation of the history of Article 297 to be warranted for the light it sheds on the intent of a provision

[380] *Official Records of the Third United Nations Conference on the Law of the Sea, Volume VIII (Informal Composite Negotiating Text, Sixth Session)*, Informal Composite Negotiating Text Revision 3, Art. 297, UN Doc. A/CONF.62/WP.10/Rev.3 (22 September 1980).

that, as drafted, remains far from clear. In the Tribunal's view, two propositions follow from the long evolution of Article 297. First, a limitation on the submission to compulsory settlement of disputes involving the exercise by a coastal State of its sovereign rights or jurisdiction in cases other than those set out in Article 297(1) was contemplated—originally in the exclusive formulation of that provision in 1976, and then in the catch-all final paragraph of the 1977 and 1979 draft Articles—but was omitted from the final text. The evolution and eventual disappearance of this restriction is noted in the Commentary, which observes that "the restrictive word 'only,' which appeared in earlier drafts of article 297, paragraph 1, and was moved to the abuse of legal process paragraph in 1977, was omitted in the final text of article 297, paragraph 1."[381] The Commentary further posits the change was linked to the addition of express limitations for fisheries and marine scientific research.[382]

315. Second, the placement of the jurisdiction affirming Article 297(1) within an Article devoted to limitations on the compulsory settlement of disputes is explained by the procedural safeguards that were briefly introduced into the Article and which ultimately became Article 294. Article 297(1) thus imposes a "limitation" on the compulsory settlement of disputes in the enumerated cases insofar as Article 294 permits a party to seek a preliminary determination, in advance of other procedures, that the application constitutes an abuse of legal process or is *prima facie* unfounded. Article 297(1) is thus not without effect within the jurisdictional structure of the Convention.

316. The Tribunal also notes that, in certain respects, Article 297(1) expands the jurisdiction of a Tribunal over the enumerated cases beyond that which would follow from the application of Article 288(1) alone. In addition to describing disputes relating to the interpretation and application of the Convention itself, each of the three specified cases in Article 297(1) includes a *renvoi* to sources of law beyond the Convention itself:

> (*a*) Article 297(1)(*a*) establishes jurisdiction "in regard to other internationally lawful uses of the sea specified in article 58" and Article 58, in turn, provides that "other pertinent rules of international law" apply to the conduct of third States in the exclusive economic zone.
>
> (*b*) Article 297(1)(*b*) establishes jurisdiction over the exercise of freedoms, rights, and uses of the sea "in contravention of ... the laws and regulations adopted by the coastal State in conformity with this Convention and other rules of international law not incompatible with this Convention".
>
> (*c*) Article 297(1)(*c*) establishes jurisdiction over acts "in contravention of specified international rules and standards for the protection and preservation of the marine environment", including

[381] S. Rosenne & L. Sohn, eds., *United Nations Convention on the Law of the Sea 1982: A Commentary*, Vol. V at p. 104 (M. Norquist, gen. ed., 1989).

[382] *Ibid.*

> those established "through a competent international organization or diplomatic conference".

Article 297(1) thus expressly expands the Tribunal's jurisdiction to certain disputes involving the contravention of legal instruments beyond the four corners of the Convention itself and ensures that such disputes will not be dismissed as being insufficiently related to the interpretation and application of the Convention.

317. The Tribunal considers that the drafting history confirms the conclusion it reached from the textual construction of Article 297. Article 297(1) reaffirms a tribunal's jurisdiction over the enumerated cases and (through Article 294) imposes additional safeguards; it does not restrict a tribunal from considering disputes concerning the exercise of sovereign rights and jurisdiction in other cases. Where a dispute concerns "the interpretation or application" of the Convention, and provided that none of the express exceptions to jurisdiction set out in Article 297(2) and 297(3) are applicable, jurisdiction for the compulsory settlement of the dispute flows from Article 288(1). It is not necessary that the Parties' dispute also fall within one of the cases specified in Article 297(1).

318. In the present case, Mauritius has directly alleged that the MPA violates certain articles of the Convention. Accordingly, having determined that the exclusion of disputes relating to the living resources of the exclusive economic zone in Article 297(3)(*a*) does not prevent the Tribunal from considering Mauritius' Fourth Submission, and considering that a dispute over the MPA's alleged violation of specific articles of the Convention is a dispute concerning the interpretation or application of the Convention, the Tribunal determines that its jurisdiction is established by Article 288(1).

ii. Article 297(1)(*c*) and the MPA

319. As set out the preceding section, the Tribunal considers that its jurisdiction is established by Article 288(1), except with respect to those portions of the Fourth Submission that the Tribunal considered subject to Article 297(3). For the sake of completeness, however, the Tribunal notes that it is also of the view that the dispute concerning Mauritius' Fourth Submission falls within the class of disputes identified in Article 297(1)(*c*). Properly characterized, the Tribunal considers that the Parties' dispute in respect of the MPA relates to the preservation of the marine environment and that Mauritius has alleged a violation of international rules and standards in this area. Article 297(1)(*c*) expressly reaffirms the application of compulsory settlement to such disputes.

320. In reaching this conclusion, the Tribunal rejects the suggestion that either Article 297(1)(*c*) or Part XII of the Convention (relating to the protection and preservation of the marine environment) are limited to measures aimed at controlling marine pollution. While the control of pollution is certainly an

important aspect of environmental protection, it is by no means the only one. Far from equating the preservation of the marine environment with pollution control, the Tribunal notes that Article 194(5) expressly provides that –

> The measures taken in accordance with this Part shall include those necessary to protect and preserve rare or fragile ecosystems as well as the habitat of depleted, threatened or endangered species and other forms of marine life.

Notably, in the Tribunal's view, this provision offers a far better fit with the MPA as presented by the United Kingdom than its characterization as a fisheries measure.

321. Neither can the Tribunal accept the proposition that Article 297(1) *c)* was intended to refer only to external conventions such as MARPOL, SOLAS, or the London Convention. Although the Tribunal considers that Article 297(1) sets out a further grant of jurisdiction over disputes relating the contravention of the standards elaborated in such conventions (see paragraph 316 above), it remains the case that Article 297(1)(*c*) also expressly refers to "rules and standards ... established by this Convention."

322. Finally, the Tribunal is unconvinced that the reference to "international rules and standards" in Article 297(1)(*c*) was intended to refer only to substantive rules and standards, and cannot therefore include the obligation to consult with or give due regard to the rights of other States. As a general matter, the Tribunal has little difficulty with the concept of procedural constraints on State action, and notes that such procedural rules exist elsewhere in international environmental law, for instance in the general international law requirement to carry out an environmental impact assessment in advance of large scale construction projects (see *Indus Waters Kishenganga Arbitration (Pakistan* v. *India), Partial Award of* 18 *February 2013, PCA Award Series*, p. 81 at pp. 291–292, para. 450; *Pulp Mills on the River Uruguay (Argentina* v. *Uruguay), Judgment, I.C.J. Reports 2010*, p. 14 at p. 83, para. 205). Such procedural rules may, indeed, be of equal or even greater importance than the substantive standards existing in international law. In the Tribunal's view, the obligation to consult with and have regard for the rights of other States, set out in multiple provisions of the Convention, is precisely such a procedural rule and its alleged contravention is squarely within the terms of Article 297(1)(*c*).

* * *

323. For the foregoing reasons, the Tribunal concludes that it has jurisdiction pursuant to Article 288(1), and Article 297(1)(*c*), to consider Mauritius' Fourth Submission and the compatibility of the MPA with the following provisions of the Convention:

(*a*) Article 2(3) insofar as it relates to Mauritius' fishing rights in the territorial sea or to the United Kingdom's undertakings to return the Archipelago to Mauritius when no longer needed for defence purposes and to return the benefit of any minerals or oil discovered in or near the Chagos Archipelago to Mauritius;

(*b*) Article 56(2), insofar as it relates to the United Kingdom's undertakings to return the Archipelago to Mauritius when no longer needed for defence purposes and to return the benefit of any minerals or oil discovered in or near the Chagos Archipelago to Mauritius;

(*c*) Article 194; and

(*d*) Article 300, insofar as it relates to the abuse of rights in connection with a violation of one of the foregoing articles.

D. The Tribunal's Jurisdiction over Mauritius' Third Submission

324. In its final submissions, Mauritius requests the Tribunal to declare that –

> the United Kingdom shall take no steps that may prevent the Commission on the Limits of the Continental Shelf from making recommendations to Mauritius in respect of any full submission that Mauritius may make to the Commission regarding the Chagos Archipelago under Article 76 of the Convention;

325. Article 76 of the Convention defines the continental shelf and provides in relevant part as follows:

> **Article 76**
>
> *Definition of the continental shelf*
>
> [...]
>
> 8. Information on the limits of the continental shelf beyond 200 nautical miles from the baselines from which the breadth of the territorial sea is measured shall be submitted by the coastal State to the Commission on the Limits of the Continental Shelf set up under Annex II on the basis of equitable geographical representation. The Commission shall make recommendations to coastal States on matters related to the establishment of the outer limits of their continental shelf. The limits of the shelf established by a coastal State on the basis of these recommendations shall be final and binding.
>
> [...]

1. The Parties' Arguments

Mauritius' Position

326. Mauritius submits that a dispute concerning the interpretation or application of Article 76(8) of the Convention "is a dispute which is plainly within the jurisdiction of this tribunal."[383]

327. According to Mauritius, there is "a dispute between the Parties as to whether or not Mauritius has standing under that article to submit information to the CLCS in respect of the Chagos Archipelago area. The resolution of that dispute requires that the Tribunal interpret or apply Article 76(8)."[384] Alternatively, Mauritius submits that –

> Another way to look at it is that there is a dispute as to whether the filing by Mauritius was effective, whether or not the clock has stopped, and whether or not Mauritius can make a full submission. There is thus a dispute as to whether the conditions exist for the CLCS to give effect to its role under Article 76(8) and Annex 2 in relation to Mauritius and the Chagos Archipelago. This is not an exhaustive list. But it is more than sufficient, [...] to establish [...] jurisdiction in regard to the issues raised under Article 76(8).[385]

328. Mauritius concludes that "[d]isputes concerning rights in the Continental Shelf, including the Extended Continental Shelf, are not subject to any of the exclusions of section 3 of Part XV. *A fortiori* the Tribunal has jurisdiction to resolve the aspects of this dispute that concern Article 76(8)."[386]

The United Kingdom's Position

329. The United Kingdom objects to the Tribunal's jurisdiction on the grounds that –

> there can be no basis whatsoever for Mauritius' new final submission (3), [...]. Even if this new claim were within the scope of the Notification and Statement of Claim, which [...] it is not, there is no way that Mauritius can show that it has complied with the requirements of section 1 of Part XV, in particular, article 283.[387]

330. The United Kingdom argues further as follows:

> The dispute that Mauritius brought up [...] over delineation is just a reiteration of the same underlying sovereignty dispute [...]. Mauritius is just saying that there is a dispute as to Article 76(8) because it is the coastal State entitled to submit information under that article. That just adds another provision to the current dispute. It makes no difference

---

383 Final Transcript, 35:5.

384 Final Transcript, 485:15–18.

385 Final Transcript, 485:19–24.

386 Final Transcript, 486:1–3.

387 Final Transcript, 1258:10–14.

whatsoever to the jurisdictional hurdles that Mauritius faces, and likewise does not impact on the fact that Mauritius' form of mixed dispute has nothing whatsoever to do with maritime delimitation.[388]

2. The Tribunal's Decision

331. The Tribunal notes that Mauritius' Third Submission did not feature in the *Notification and Statement of Claim*. At the hearings, Mauritius explained[389] that it had added this submission in response to the following statement in the United Kingdom's *Rejoinder*:

> In accordance with the terms of article 76(7), only the coastal State may delineate the outer limits of the continental shelf. In accordance with article 76(8), only the coastal State may submit information to the CLCS on the limits of the shelf beyond 200 nautical miles. Mauritius is not the coastal State in respect of BIOT and as such it has no standing before the CLCS with respect to BIOT.[390]

332. In assessing its jurisdiction, the Tribunal considers that it must first determine whether there is a dispute between the Parties regarding the issue addressed by Mauritius' Third Submission. In order to do that, it is necessary to examine the history of the position taken by each Party regarding that issue, both before and after the commencement of arbitration proceedings on 20 December 2010.

333. The question of a submission to the CLCS was discussed at the Mauritius–United Kingdom Joint Meeting on 14 January 2009. There were no official minutes of that meeting but each side kept its own record and there was a Joint Communiqué issued at the end of the meeting, all of which have been put before the Tribunal. The Mauritius record deals with the prospective CLCS submission in the following terms.[391] The matter was raised by Mr. Doug Wilson, an FCO legal adviser who was a member of the United Kingdom team. Mauritius records him as having said the following:

> Art. 76 UNCLOS provides that a state make an application to the UN for Continental Shelf beyond 200 miles zone. UK has no interest to applying to the UN for extension. There is very little prospect for oil and gas. So reference to paragraph 22 of the 1965 letter would not be an issue.
>
> We wanted to open a possibility to produce a joint submission to claim an extended Continental Shelf. That would require extensive scientific

[388] Final Transcript, 672:4–11.

[389] Final Transcript, 926:20–25; 1088:19 to 1089:16.

[390] The United Kingdom's Rejoinder, para. 8.39.

[391] Ministry of Foreign Affairs, Regional Integration and International Trade, Mauritius, "Meeting of Officials on the Chagos Archipelago/British Indian Ocean Territory held at the Foreign and Commonwealth Office, London, Wednesday 14 January 2009, 10 a.m.", 23 January 2009 at pp. 23–26 (Annex MR-129).

> research and employment of qualified scientists. We can look forward for joint submissions.

334. Mr. Suresh C. Seeballuck, the head of the Mauritian delegation, replied as follows:

> With regard to Continental Shelf, we have a deadline of 13 May 2009 to make our submission. The deadline is there. We welcome your suggestion for a joint submission and possibly we have to work in earnest to achieve it. We have, on the basis of research, some basic data. We are prepared to exchange same with the UK side for the joint submission.

335. Mr. Wilson clarified that all that was needed by 13 May 2009 was "an outline submission". In this respect, the Tribunal recalls that Article 4 of Annex II to the Convention established the procedure that –

> Where a coastal State intends to establish, in accordance with article 76, the outer limits of its continental shelf beyond 200 nautical miles, it shall submit particulars of such limits to the Commission along with supporting scientific and technical data as soon as possible but in any case within 10 years of the entry into force of this Convention for that State.

In practice, it emerged that developing States would, in many instances, have difficulty in assembling the scientific and technical data required to meet the ten year deadline. On 29 May 2001, the Meeting of States Parties to the Convention took the decision that –

> (*a*) In the case of a State Party for which the Convention entered into force before 13 May 1999, it is understood that the ten-year time period referred to in article 4 of Annex II to the Convention shall be taken to have commenced on 13 May 1999;
>
> (*b*) The general issue of the ability of States, particularly developing States, to fulfil the requirements of article 4 of Annex II to the Convention be kept under review.[392]

On 20 June 2008, with the revised deadline approaching, the Meeting of States Parties took the following further decision that preliminary outline submissions would suffice to toll the ten year deadline:

> (*a*) It is understood that the time period referred to in article 4 of Annex II to the Convention and the decision contained in SPLOS/72, paragraph (*a*), may be satisfied by submitting to the Secretary-General preliminary information indicative of the outer limits of the continental shelf beyond 200 nautical miles and a description of the status of preparation and intended date of making a submission in accordance with the requirements of article 76 of the Convention and with the Rules of Procedure and the Scientific and Technical Guidelines of the Commission on the Limits of the Continental Shelf;

---

[392] United Nations Convention on the Law of the Sea, Meeting of States Parties, *Decision regarding the date of commencement of the ten-year period for making submissions to the Commission on the Limits of the Continental Shelf set out in article 4 of Annex II to the United Nations Convention on the Law of the Sea*, UN Doc. SPLOS/72 (29 May 2001).

> (*b*) Pending the receipt of the submission in accordance with the requirements of article 76 of the Convention and with the Rules of Procedure and the Scientific and Technical Guidelines of the Commission, preliminary information submitted in accordance with subparagraph (*a*) above shall not be considered by the Commission;
>
> (*c*) Preliminary information submitted by a coastal State in accordance with subparagraph (*a*) is without prejudice to the submission in accordance with the requirements of article 76 of the Convention and with the Rules of Procedure and the Scientific and Technical Guidelines of the Commission, and the consideration of the submission by the Commission;
>
> (*d*) The Secretary-General shall inform the Commission and notify member States of the receipt of preliminary information in accordance with subparagraph (*a*), and make such information publicly available, including on the website of the Commission;
>
> [...][393]

336. In the course of the Joint Meeting, Mr. Roberts, the BIOT Administrator, then added:

> We have no expectation of deriving any benefit from what we will get. It will flow to Mauritius when the territory will be ceded to you. It is one of the reasons why we have not invested resources to collect data. We recognize the underlying structure of this discussion. You may wish to take action and we will provide political support.

337. After a brief discussion, Mr. Seeballuck reiterated "our willingness to join the UK on the joint submission notwithstanding our sovereignty position".

338. The United Kingdom record of the talks is very similar. The United Kingdom record summed up the discussion of the possible CLCS submission in the following terms:

> The UK opened up the possibility of co-operating with the Mauritians, under a sovereignty umbrella, on an extended continental shelf agreement (i.e., a joint submission to the Commission on the Limits of the Continental Shelf). We had no interest ourselves in seabed mineral extraction. That would be for Mauritius when we have ceded BIOT. There would be no exploration or exploitation until then. It would require much expensive scientific and research work to collect and analyse data but it could be done if both sides agreed that a joint submission was appropriate.
>
> The Mauritian delegation welcomed the UK statement about a joint submission but was concerned that the deadline was 30 May 2009 so much

[393] United Nations Convention on the Law of the Sea, Meeting of States Parties, *Decision regarding the workload of the Commission on the Limits of the Continental Shelf and the ability of States, particularly developing States, to fulfil the requirements of article 4 of Annex II to the United Nations Convention on the Law of the Sea, as well as the decision contained in SPLOS/72, paragraph (a)*, UN Doc. SPLOS/183 (20 June 2008).

> work would need to be done. They already had some basic data that could help. Mauritian agreement to a joint submission would, however, be conditional upon an equitable exploitation of resources whenever they may occur.
>
> The UK delegation clarified that all that was needed by May was an outline submission. The UK delegation reiterated that the UK had no expectation of deriving commercial or economic benefit from anything discovered on the continental shelf. Our understanding was that this would flow to Mauritius once the territory had been ceded. This was one of the reasons why the UK had not invested resources in collecting data. What we were talking about was legal and political co-operation to secure the continental shelf on the premise that it is scientifically possible to do this.
>
> The Mauritians questioned why the UK was insisting on its position on sovereignty but prepared to accept a joint submission to the Continental Shelf? We explained that the Mauritians should not see our position as a sign of weakness or obligation. We wanted to be helpful where we could within the limits set out on sovereignty and treaty obligations. Our offers were on specific subjects we thought would be useful.[394]

339. The Joint Communiqué issued at the end of the talks made only a brief reference to the discussions having included the topic of the continental shelf. The Communiqué did, however, make clear that the talks had been held under a "sovereignty umbrella":

> Both Governments agreed that:
>
> nothing in the conduct or content of the present meeting shall be interpreted as:
>
> (*a*) A change in the position of the United Kingdom with regard to sovereignty over the British Indian Ocean Territory/Chagos Archipelago;
>
> (*b*) A change in the position of Mauritius with regard to sovereignty over the British Indian Ocean Territory/Chagos Archipelago;
>
> (*c*) Recognition of or support for the position of the United Kingdom or Mauritius with regard to sovereignty over the British Indian Ocean Territory/Chagos Archipelago;
>
> (*d*) No act or activity carried out by the United Kingdom, Mauritius or third parties as a consequence and in implementation of anything agreed to in the present meeting or in any similar subsequent meetings shall constitute a basis for affirming, supporting, or denying the position of the United Kingdom or Mauritius regarding sovereignty of the British Indian Ocean Territory/Chagos Archipelago.[395]

---

[394] Record of the meeting of 14 January 2009 prepared by the Overseas Territories Directorate dated 15 January 2009 at s. 6(2) (Annex UKCM-94)(Annex MR-128).

[395] Joint communiqué of meeting of 14 January 2009 (Annex UKCM-93)(Annex MM-137).

340. In May 2009, Mauritius filed preliminary information with the CLCS.[396] Paragraph 6 of that document was entitled "unresolved land and maritime disputes" and stated that –

> The Republic of Mauritius states that the Chagos Archipelago is and has always formed part of its territory. The Republic of Mauritius wishes to inform the Commission, however, that a dispute exists between the Republic of Mauritius and the United Kingdom over the Chagos Archipelago. Discussions are ongoing between the two governments on this matter. The last bilateral talks were held in London, United Kingdom, in January 2009.

341. The second round of Mauritius–United Kingdom talks took place in Port Louis on 21 July 2009. The Mauritius record of those talks (contained in a briefing document provided for the Mauritian Cabinet) described the discussion of the extended continental shelf in the following terms:

> The British side proposed that Mauritius and the UK should make a joint submission to the United Nations Commission on the Limits of the Continental Shelf (CLCS) for an extended continental shelf around the Chagos Archipelago. The Mauritian side remarked that at the first round of talks, the UK did not show much interest in submitting a claim for an extension of the continental shelf. In the circumstances, Mauritius decided to make a unilateral submission to be within the deadline of 13 May 2009.
>
> After discussions, it was agreed that although we have already made our submission within the deadline of 13 May 2009, there is scope for Mauritius and UK to work together towards a coordinated submission and that a technical committee would be set up with officials from both sides to look into the modalities of this coordinated approach.[397]

342. The United Kingdom record contained the following passage:

> The UK delegation suggested that Mauritius and the UK could work together within the UN process to secure a claim perhaps by a coordinated submission. This could be of benefit to Mauritius because otherwise the submission would effectively be put on ice because of the sovereignty dispute. All benefits of an [extended Continental Shelf] would ultimately fall to Mauritius when BIOT was no longer required for defence purposes. Mauritius welcomed the suggestion that the UK and Mauritian teams could work together on this. The Mauritian delegation explained the reasons behind their preliminary note which flagged up their intention to lodge a submission over this area by 2012 was to ensure that they were not prejudiced by failing to meet the May 2009 deadline. The UK delegation commented that this time-frame for preparation of the sub-

[396] Preliminary Information Submitted by the Republic of Mauritius Concerning the Extended Continental Shelf in the Chagos Archipelago Region Pursuant to the Decision Contained in SPLOS/183 (Annex MM-144).

[397] Information Paper by the Prime Minister of Mauritius, Second Meeting at Senior Officials' Level between Mauritius and UK on the Chagos Archipelago, CAB(2009) 624, 12 August 2009 (Annex MR-144).

> mission seemed realistic. The UK delegation also explained that we were not proposing UK funding extensive analysis and surveys but could facilitate access to the technical sources and help with the legal process. It was agreed that the best way forward would be a coordinated submission under a sovereignty umbrella and that technical experts from both sides should get together. Comment: there was a need, as in the January talks, to reiterate the fact that the UK had no intention of benefiting from an [extended Continental Shelf]. Any exploitation would be for the benefit of Mauritius. Our proposal was to get an [extended Continental Shelf] established. We would then talk about the basis on which exploitation could begin. We could not define a date when BIOT will no longer be needed for defence purposes but this was one way of ensuring that the [extended Continental Shelf] could be established in principle pending the area being eventually ceded to Mauritius.[398]

343. The Joint Communiqué issued after the talks stated:

> Both delegations were of the view that it would be desirable to have a coordinated submission for an extended continental shelf in the Chagos Archipelago/British Indian Ocean Territory region to the UN Commission on the Limits of the Continental Shelf, in order not to prejudice the interest of Mauritius in that area and to facilitate its consideration by the Commission. It was agreed that a joint technical team would be set up with officials from both sides to look into possibilities and modalities of such a coordinated approach, with a view to informing the next round of talks.[399]

344. As recorded above (see paragraphs 146–147), the further rounds of talks envisaged at the second round in July 2009 never took place. Nor has the joint technical team been set up.

345. Mauritius' *Notification and Statement of Claim* referred to the issue of submissions to the CLCS only to the extent of stating that "[i]n 2009, Mauritius submitted to the United Nations Commission on the Limits of the Continental Shelf a preliminary claim to an extended continental shelf in areas beyond 200 miles from the archipelagic baselines of the Chagos Islands."[400] In its *Memorial*, Mauritius referred to the preliminary information which it had submitted to the CLCS and the absence of protest by the United Kingdom and argued that "the absence of protest on the part of the UK appears to be a clear recognition that Mauritius has sovereign rights in relation to the continental shelf".[401] The United Kingdom responded, in its *Counter-Memorial*, by contending that this argument was unfounded insofar as everything had been done under the sovereignty umbrella agreed upon at the first round of talks and that the CLCS Rules of Procedure expressly dealt with submissions

---

[398] Overseas Territories Directorate record of discussion in Port Louis on 21 July 2009 dated 24 July 2009 (Annex UKCM-101)(Annex MR-143).

[399] Joint Communiqué, Second round of bilateral talks between Mauritius and the UK on the Chagos Archipelago, 21 July 2009, Port Louis, Mauritius (Annex MM-148)(Annex MR-142).

[400] Mauritius' Notice of Arbitration, para. 3.

[401] Mauritius' Memorial, para. 6.32.

in respect of an extended continental shelf where there was a land or maritime dispute. The United Kingdom also highlighted the fact that Mauritius had stated in its submission of preliminary information that a dispute with the United Kingdom existed in respect of the Chagos Archipelago.[402]

346. In its *Reply*, Mauritius maintained that the fact that there had been no United Kingdom submission to the CLCS, together with the absence of protest by the United Kingdom regarding Mauritius' preliminary information, suggested an acknowledgment that Mauritius possessed rights in respect of the continental shelf around the Chagos Archipelago.[403] Mauritius contrasted the absence of protest by the United Kingdom in this case with its protest regarding the submission made by Argentina in respect of the Falkland Islands/Islas Malvinas.[404] The United Kingdom countered, in its *Rejoinder*, that Mauritius "cannot alter the status of the BIOT continental shelf by making its own submission to the CLCS with respect to BIOT".[405] It was in this context that the United Kingdom made the comment quoted in paragraph 331 above, which Mauritius claimed at the hearings gave rise to an additional dispute between the Parties.[406] Mauritius expressed its grave concern that what it considered to be a new position taken by the United Kingdom risked permanently precluding Mauritius from enjoying the benefits of an extended continental shelf.[407]

347. In response, the United Kingdom denied that there was any such dispute. It maintained that it had raised the argument set out in its *Rejoinder* (and the earlier argument in its *Counter-Memorial*) merely in order to respond to the attempt by Mauritius to invoke the filing of preliminary information and the absence of a protest by the United Kingdom as support for its claim with regard to the issues raised in Mauritius' first two submissions.[408] The United Kingdom contended that it had offered at the two rounds of bilateral talks to make a joint submission under a sovereignty umbrella, in order to avoid any risk that Mauritius would be deprived of the chance to secure an extended continental shelf and that the United Kingdom itself had no intention of securing any benefit from the establishment of an extended continental shelf. Counsel for the United Kingdom told the Tribunal:

> Mauritius mischaracterises the statement in paragraph 8.39, ignoring both context and content. First, it is a single sentence forming part of a legal argument made by one party to another in the course of arbitral proceedings. As Mauritius rightly points out, the United Kingdom has not protested to the United Nations. Second, it was a statement that Mauritius itself had provoked, by its arguments in these arbitral pro-

[402] The United Kingdom's Counter-Memorial, paras. 7.51–7.58.

[403] Mauritius' Reply, para. 6.90.

[404] Mauritius' Reply, para. 6.90 n. 684.

[405] The United Kingdom's Rejoinder, para. 8.39.

[406] Final Transcript, 33:18 to 40:7; 275:1 to 282:2.

[407] Final Transcript, 921:15 to 922:16; 1075:15 to 1085:1 to 1090:10.

[408] Final Transcript 502:19 to 503:11.

> ceedings. The UK was reacting, in the context of these legal proceedings, to Mauritius' argument that "[t]he absence of protest on the part of the UK appears to be a clear recognition that Mauritius has sovereign rights in relation to the continental shelf."
>
> On content, Mauritius places an absolute interpretation on the statement in the Rejoinder. It means, they say, that the submission of the *Preliminary Information* is a nullity; that the clock has not been stopped and cannot now be stopped. That is not the position. In any event, as the Agent said yesterday, we now hear that Mauritius may be in the position to make a full submission later this year. If so, we look forward to discussing with Mauritius how this might be taken forward. If a State puts in an objection to another State's submission to the CLCS, that is not the end of the matter. Objections can always be lifted. In fact, the practice in the CLCS suggests that an objection can be the start of a dialogue, part of an ongoing diplomatic process between the States concerned. Moreover, the CLCS's backlog is so great that many years are likely to elapse before the Commission would be ready to proceed to consider a new submission and the situation then might be very different. During that period it would be incumbent on the United Kingdom and Mauritius to discuss how to take the matter forward, as the Agent indicated yesterday.[409]

348. The Tribunal has reviewed this record in detail, because it considers that it was a necessary step in determining whether a separate dispute between the Parties has come into existence regarding the subject-matter of Mauritius' Third Submission. It is not suggested that there was a dispute between Mauritius and the United Kingdom regarding the question of submissions to the CLCS prior to the filing of the *Notification and Statement of Claim*. On the contrary, the record of the two rounds of bilateral talks confirms that no such dispute existed at that time. Rather, Mauritius maintains that such a dispute was created by the language used by the United Kingdom in its *Rejoinder* (in the passage quoted above). The Tribunal considers that that passage has to be seen in the light of the exchange of legal arguments between the Parties. The United Kingdom was responding to an argument by Mauritius regarding whether Mauritius was the (or, at least, a) coastal State in respect of the Chagos Archipelago. That argument was advanced in the context of a dispute over which the Tribunal has already held that it lacks jurisdiction. The United Kingdom was not raising an objection before the CLCS. In the course of the hearings, the United Kingdom made clear that the offer of co-operation, under a sovereignty umbrella, regarding the full submission to the CLCS, which the United Kingdom had already extended at the July 2009 bilateral talks after Mauritius had filed preliminary information with the CLCS, was still open. The Tribunal considers, therefore, that there is no risk of Mauritius losing the possibility of seeking an extended continental shelf by reason of the expiry of the 13 May 2009 deadline.

---

[409] Final Transcript 734:20–735:17.

349. In view of the willingness of the United Kingdom that the submission to the CLCS proceed under a sovereignty umbrella—a willingness which the United Kingdom expressed in both rounds of the bilateral talks and repeated in the course of the oral proceedings in the present case—and of Mauritius' acceptance of such an approach in the bilateral talks, the Tribunal considers that there is no dispute between the Parties regarding this issue.

350. Accordingly, the Tribunal considers that it is not required to rule on whether it has jurisdiction over Mauritius' third submission, nor upon the merits of that submission.

E. Whether the Parties "Exchanged Views" Pursuant to Article 283

351. The United Kingdom further objects to the jurisdiction of the Tribunal on the grounds that, prior to initiating this arbitration, Mauritius failed to engage in the exchange of views required by Article 283(1). In the United Kingdom's view, such an exchange is a precondition to jurisdiction under the Convention that was not met with respect to any of Mauritius' claims.[410]

352. Article 283 of the Convention provides as follows:

Article 283

Obligation to exchange views

> 1. When a dispute arises between States Parties concerning the interpretation or application of this Convention, the parties to the dispute shall proceed expeditiously to an exchange of views regarding its settlement by negotiation or other peaceful means.
>
> 2. The parties shall also proceed expeditiously to an exchange of views where a procedure for the settlement of such a dispute has been terminated without a settlement or where a settlement has been reached and the circumstances require consultation regarding the manner of implementing the settlement.

353. Mauritius submits that the requirements of Article 283(1) are plainly met as it "repeatedly raised" the subject matter of all claims in these proceedings[411] "over several decades, in bilateral and multilateral contexts".[412] In any event, Mauritius emphasizes, the requirements of Article 283 are "not onerous", and a Party is not required to continue negotiations indefinitely.

---

[410] Final Transcript, 737:3–6.

[411] Mauritius' Reply, para. 4.3.

[412] Final Transcript, 398:5–8.

354. As the Tribunal has already decided that it has jurisdiction only with respect to Mauritius' Fourth Submission, it will examine the application of Article 283 only with respect to that portion of the Parties' dispute.

1. The Parties' Arguments

(a) The Interpretation of Article 283

The United Kingdom's Position

355. According to the United Kingdom –

> Article 283, in practical terms, requires as a first step communication by one party, received by the other party which results in a shared understanding as to what the dispute or disputes are and likewise that they are under the 1982 Convention. This is implicit from the requirement that the parties exchange views over its peaceful settlement or negotiation: they must have a shared understanding about what they are talking about in order to exchange views on it.[413]

356. This requirement, the United Kingdom submits, is not part of customary international law,[414] but arose instead from the particular context of the negotiations at the Third UN Conference on the Law of the Sea. It was intended both to ensure that States would not be taken by surprise by the introduction of binding dispute settlement procedures, and "to allow a State to rectify any possible wrongdoing or violation of the [Convention] prior to the initiation of an interstate dispute."[415] While this requirement may be unusual, the United Kingdom considers it to have been an essential part of the overall bargain in the Convention, as "[t]he requirement for prior attempts to settle disputes without recourse to compulsory procedures was seen as a central element in the negotiations that led to the acceptance of Part XV by the Conference."[416] Compulsory jurisdiction under Article 286, the United Kingdom submits, is thus contingent upon compliance with the provisions for settlement through non-binding means, including Article 283.

357. Although the United Kingdom considers Article 283 to be distinct from compromissory clauses requiring prior attempts at negotiation,[417] it submits that international jurisprudence reinforces the importance of such conditions to jurisdiction. The United Kingdom notes, in particular, the ICJ's observation in *Georgia* v. *Russia* that such provisions are important to give notice to the Respondent, to encourage the parties to settle their dispute, and to limit the scope of States' consent to dispute settlement (*Application of the*

[413] The United Kingdom's Rejoinder, para. 6.10.

[414] Final Transcript, 744:3–6.

[415] Final Transcript, 745:19–20.

[416] Final Transcript, 742:13–16.

[417] Final Transcript, 739:14–19.

International Convention on the Elimination of All Forms of Racial Discrimination (Georgia v. Russian Federation), Preliminary Objections, Judgment, I.C.J. Reports 2011, p. 70 at p. 124, para. 131). The United Kingdom also recalls the ICJ's emphasis that "[w]hen that consent is expressed in a compromissory clause in an international agreement, any conditions to which such consent is subject must be regarded as constituting the limits thereon" (*Armed Activities on the Territory of the Congo (New Application: 2002) (Democratic Republic of the Congo v. Rwanda), Jurisdiction and Admissibility, Judgment, I.C.J. Reports 2006*, p. 6 at p. 39, para. 88).

358. With respect to the specific steps required by Article 283, the United Kingdom submits that –

- There must be a "dispute" between the States Parties to the Convention;
- The dispute must concern "the interpretation or application of the Convention";
- And the parties to the dispute must have "proceeded expeditiously to an exchange of views regarding its settlement by negotiation or other peaceful means".[418]

359. While the United Kingdom does not consider that such exchanges must be lengthy, it does submit that the exchange must be sufficiently clear as to put the respondent on notice and to give it "the opportunity to redress the issues and to even modify its behaviour."[419] Moreover, "[s]ince the exchange of views must concern the modalities of settlement of disputes," the United Kingdom considers that the requirement cannot be met "without identifying the specific treaty and provisions concerned, since the range of settlement means available will depend upon the provisions at issue."[420]

Mauritius' Position

360. Mauritius submits that –

> the requirements of Article 283 are not particularly onerous. They form a threshold jurisdictional requirement to ensure that parties are not taken by surprise by the initiation of proceedings, but they do not require lengthy exchanges, they do not require reference to specific treaties or provisions, and the State's judgment as to when to terminate exchanges will be accorded considerable respect. This is an area where the law is concerned with substance, not with form.[421]

361. According to Mauritius, each of these propositions is supported in prior international jurisprudence. First, *Mavrommatis Palestine Concessions* provides that "[n]egotiations do not of necessity always presuppose a more

---

418 Final Transcript, 748:17–20.

419 Final Transcript, 1266:16.

420 Final Transcript, 739:15–19.

421 Final Transcript, 402:1–6.

or less lengthy series of notes and dispatches; it may suffice that a discussion should have commenced, and this discussion may have been very short" (*Mavrommatis Palestine Concessions, Jurisdiction, Judgment of* 30 *August 1924, PCIJ Series A, No. 2*, p. 6 at p. 13). Second, *Guyana* v. *Suriname* (*Award of* 17 *September 2007, PCA Award Series*, 158–159, RIAA, Vol. XXX, p. 1 at p. 113–114, paras. 407–410) and *Land Reclamation by Singapore in and around the Straits of Johor ((Malaysia* v. *Singapore), Provisional Measures, Order of* 8 *October 2003, ITLOS Reports 2003*, p. 10) (in the context of Article 283), and *Georgia* v. *Russia* (generally) stand for the proposition that "it is not necessary that a State must expressly refer to a specific treaty in its exchanges with the other State"[422] (*Application of the International Convention on the Elimination of All Forms of Racial Discrimination (Georgia* v. *Russian Federation), Preliminary Objections, Judgment, I.C.J. Reports 2011*, p. 70 at p. 84, para. 30). Finally, *Land Reclamation* and *Mavrommatis* both support the view that a State is "not obliged to continue with an exchange of views when it concludes that the possibilities of reaching agreement have been exhausted" (*Land Reclamation by Singapore in and around the Straits of Johor (Malaysia* v. *Singapore), Provisional Measures, Order of 8 October 2003, ITLOS Reports 2003*, p. 10 at para. 47) and further that "States *themselves* are 'in the best position to judge as to political reasons which may prevent the settlement of a given dispute' [*Mavrommatis Palestine Concessions, Jurisdiction, Judgment of* 30 *August 1924, PCIJ Series A, No. 2*, p. 6 at p. 15]".[423]

362. According to Mauritius, the United Kingdom seeks to read into Article 283 requirements that are nowhere to be found in the accumulated case law. When it insists that an exchange of views must make specific reference to the Convention, Mauritius argues, the United Kingdom "ignore[s] the clear words of the International Court in *Georgia* v. *Russia*".[424] And in limiting what it considers to be relevant exchanges to a narrow window of time, Mauritius considers the United Kingdom to have adopted an overly formalistic approach and neglected to examine the record as a whole.[425]

363. In sum, Mauritius concludes, the jurisprudence on the application of Article 283 indicates that it imposes a hurdle of only "very modest height" that can be "stepped over lightly," "[s]o long as the applicant can produce some evidence of relevant exchanges."[426]

---

[422] Final Transcript, 400:16–18.

[423] Final Transcript, 401:15–20.

[424] Final Transcript, 949:22–23.

[425] Final Transcript, 950:8 to 951:2.

[426] Final Transcript, 949:9–18.

(b) The Application of Article 283 to Mauritius' Fourth Submission

The United Kingdom's Position

364. The United Kingdom submits that Mauritius has not met the requirements of Article 283 in respect of its Fourth Submission, relating to the compatibility of the MPA with the Convention and the alleged breach of undertakings made by the United Kingdom. According to the United Kingdom, "there is nowhere any Statement from Mauritius that challenges the legality of MPA on the basis of UNCLOS provisions x, y, and z, and then concludes with an invitation to discuss some form of exchange of views. And there is nothing in this record that could be treated as somehow of equivalent effect."[427]

365. Turning to the correspondence advanced by Mauritius, the United Kingdom considers that "all the documents that Mauritius relies on to establish the existence of a dispute and an exchange of views for the purposes of its breach of UNCLOS strand [of argument] concern fishing rights, which is also the principal element in [relation to the claimed breach of undertakings]."[428] With respect to correspondence prior to 2009, the United Kingdom argues that insofar as "these communications pre-date the MPA proposal, and even the ideas of Pew and the Chagos Conservation Trust for large-scale marine park in the BIOT, a dispute about the MPA proposal or the MPA could not have been raised."[429]

366. Moreover, according to the United Kingdom, whenever "Mauritius responded to the various restrictions on its ability to fish over the years, it did not object on the grounds that the UK was acting in breach of UNCLOS but cast its case in terms of its sovereignty claim, which … was not with reference to UNCLOS."[430] Reviewing Mauritius' correspondence piece by piece, the United Kingdom concludes that it "all com[es] down to the sovereignty issue"[431] and submits that "Mauritius is unable to point to any exchange of views in relation to a claim of alleged breaches of UNCLOS."[432]

Mauritius' Position

367. Mauritius divides the relevant correspondence between that pre-dating and that post-dating Mauritius learning of the MPA proposal in February 2009. Before February 2009, Mauritius argues, correspondence is relevant because it shows "Mauritius continuously asserting its rights over the Archipelago, including the fishing rights which would be brought to an end by

[427] Final Transcript, 771:20–23.

[428] Final Transcript, 772:6–8.

[429] The United Kingdom's Rejoinder, para. 6.35.

[430] Final Transcript, 772:16–19.

[431] Final Transcript, 779:23.

[432] Final Transcript, 784:11–12.

the decision to impose a no-take MPA."[433] Mauritius recalls what it describes as a "huge number of occasions on which Mauritius asserted its specific rights in the Archipelago,"[434] including fishing rights, and concludes that "UK officials ... were well aware of the fact that Mauritius had raised these specific rights".[435]

368. After February 2009, Mauritius points to a series of exchanges that it considers make clear its diplomatic protest against the infringement of its rights in the Chagos Archipelago. In particular, Mauritius recalls:

(*a*) The Joint Communiqué[436] of the July 2009 talks between the two governments, which according to Mauritius indicates that "the Mauritian delegation made it quite clear that the proposed MPA would have to accommodate its rights in the Chagos Archipelago";[437]

(*b*) Mauritius' Note Verbale of 23 November 2009, which provided as follows:

> The Government of Mauritius considers that an MPA project in the Chagos Archipelago should not be incompatible with the sovereignty of the Republic of Mauritius over the Chagos Archipelago and should address the issues of resettlement, access to the fisheries resources, and the economic development of the islands in a manner which would not prejudice an eventual enjoyment of sovereignty. A total ban on fisheries exploitation and omission of those issues from any MPA project would not be compatible with the long-term resolution of, or progress in the talks, on the sovereignty issue.[438]

(*c*) A letter dated 30 December 2009 from the Mauritius Minister of Foreign Affairs, which provided as follows:

> Moreover, the issues of resettlement in the Chagos Archipelago, access to the fisheries resources and the economic development of the islands in a manner that would not prejudice the effective exercise by Mauritius of its sovereignty over the Chagos Archipelago are matters of high priority to the Government of Mauritius. The exclusion of such important issues in any discussion relating to the proposed establishment of a Marine Protected Area would not be compatible with resolution of the issue of sovereignty over the Chagos Archipelago

[433] Final Transcript, 406:7–9.

[434] Final Transcript, 406:18–19.

[435] Final Transcript, 408:1–2.

[436] Joint Communiqué of Meeting on 21 July 2009 (Annex UKCM-100).

[437] Final Transcript, 409:8–9.

[438] Note Verbale dated 23 November 2009 from the Ministry of Foreign Affairs, Regional Integration and International Trade, Mauritius to the UK Foreign and Commonwealth Office, No. 1197/28/10 (Annex MM-155).

and progress in the ongoing talks between Mauritius and the United Kingdom.[439]

(*d*) A letter dated 19 February 2010 from the Secretary to Cabinet and Head of the Civil Service, which provided as follows:

> I further wish to inform you that the Government of Mauritius insists that any proposal for the protection of the marine environment in the Chagos Archipelago area needs to be compatible with and meaningfully take on board the position of Mauritius on the sovereignty over the Chagos Archipelago and address the issues of resettlement and access by Mauritians to fisheries resources in that area.[440]

369. In sum, Mauritius concludes, it "made it clear that, in its view, [the MPA] would violate its substantive and procedural rights—rights which Mauritius had asserted for many years, of which the UK was fully aware, and which in many cases were self-evidently incompatible with a no-take MPA."[441]

(c) *The Utility of Further Exchanges*

370. In addition to disagreeing as to whether the requirements of Article 283 were met, the Parties differ as to whether it would have been futile to continue negotiations.

The United Kingdom's Position

371. The United Kingdom dismisses Mauritius' arguments about the supposed futility of further talks as "pure assertion."[442] On the contrary, the United Kingdom submits, "Mauritius, according to its own pleadings, had not even sought to communicate with the United Kingdom about the MPA for over eight months between 2 April 2010 and 20 December 2010 when it submitted its Notification and Statement of Claim."[443]

372. To the extent that Mauritius alleges that further exchanges were futile on the basis of the United Kingdom's failure to honour a purported undertaking by then British Prime Minister Gordon Brown to suspend the Public Consultation, the United Kingdom denies that any undertaking was made. In any event, however, the United Kingdom denies that "a failure to withdraw the public consultation could possibly make it 'clear' that any further

---

[439] Letter dated 30 December 2009 from the Minister of Foreign Affairs, Regional Integration and International Trade, Mauritius to the UK Secretary of State for Foreign and Commonwealth Affairs (Annex MM-157).

[440] Letter dated 19 February 2010 from the Secretary to Cabinet and Head of the Civil Service, Mauritius to the British High Commissioner, Port Louis (Annex MM-162).

[441] Final Transcript, 415:14–17.

[442] The United Kingdom's Counter-Memorial, para. 5.46.

[443] The United Kingdom's Counter-Memorial, para. 5.46.

exchanges in relation to the dispute notified in Mauritius' application would be 'futile and without purpose'."[444]

373. According to the United Kingdom, it –

> does not dispute the well-established principle that a party is not obliged to continue with an exchange of views when the possibilities of settlement have been exhausted. Its contention is that Mauritius cannot even establish that it raised the UNCLOS claims which it now raises, let alone that an exchange of views had taken place and that the possibilities of a settlement had been exhausted.[445]

Mauritius' Position

374. Mauritius maintains that the British Prime Minister Gordon Brown made a commitment, in November 2009, to put the MPA on hold that was "expressed in the clearest possible terms."[446] Notwithstanding this commitment the United Kingdom declared the MPA on 1 April 2010.

375. Mauritius identifies communications between April and November 2010[447] by which it conveyed "strong opposition" to the MPA[448] and raised the inadequacy of the United Kingdom's consultation process[449] and the failure of the United Kingdom to honour the assurance by former Prime Minister Gordon Brown.[450]

376. In Mauritius' view, the "violation of the commitment given at the highest level" made it plain that "no diplomatic solution was possible" and accordingly, continuing exchanges on the issue would have been futile.[451] Moreover, Mauritius submits that it was entirely reasonable to consider that further exchanges after initiation of these proceedings would have been futile in view of the circumstances.[452]

2. The Tribunal's Decision

377. As set out above, the Parties disagree both as to the interpretation of Article 283 and as to its application to Mauritius' Fourth Submission. Mauritius' account of its compliance with Article 283 ranges widely through the history of the Parties' diplomatic exchanges regarding the proposed MPA. The United Kingdom, in contrast, points to the absence of a specific communica-

---

444 The United Kingdom's Counter-Memorial, para. 5.48.

445 The United Kingdom's Counter-Memorial, para. 5.50.

446 Mauritius' Reply, paras. 4.46–4.47.

447 Mauritius' Reply, paras. 4.57–4.61.

448 Mauritius' Reply, para. 4.57.

449 Mauritius' Reply, para. 4.59.

450 Mauritius' Reply, para. 4.61.

451 Mauritius' Reply, para. 4.63.

452 Final Transcript, 951:21 to 952:3.

tion setting out a particular dispute by reference to the Convention and either proposing an approach for its resolution, or inviting an exchange of views.

378. In the Tribunal's view, much of the argument on this issue has tended to confuse two related, but distinct concepts. Article 283 requires the Parties to "proceed expeditiously to an exchange of views regarding [the] settlement [of the dispute] by negotiation or other peaceful means." Article 283 thus requires the Parties to exchange views regarding the means for resolving their dispute; it does not require the Parties to in fact engage in negotiations or other forms of peaceful dispute resolution. As a matter of textual construction, the Tribunal considers that Article 283 cannot be understood as an obligation to negotiate the substance of the dispute. Read in that manner, Article 283(1) would, redundantly, require that parties "negotiate regarding the settlement of the dispute by negotiation". The Tribunal also notes that Article 283(2) requires a further exchange of views upon the failure of a dispute settlement procedure. If an exchange of views were taken to involve substantive negotiations, this would literally require that, upon the failure of negotiations, the parties must engage in negotiations: such a construction cannot be correct. Finally, the drafters of this provision saw fit to include an exhortation that the parties proceed "expeditiously" to an exchange of views. Given the clear and understandable preference among the participants at the Third UN Conference on the Law of the Sea that disputes be resolved by negotiation whenever possible, the Tribunal cannot accept that the final text could have included a provision that would have the effect of rushing, or potentially imposing a time limit on, substantive negotiations. Article 283 is thus a provision particular to the Convention and distinct from a requirement that parties engage in negotiations prior to resorting to arbitration.

379. The Convention includes no express requirement that parties engage in negotiations on the substance of a dispute before resorting to compulsory settlement. To the extent that such a requirement could be considered to be implied from the structure of sections 1 and 2 of Part XV, the Tribunal has no hesitation in concluding that Mauritius has met such a requirement. The Parties discussed the proposed MPA during the bilateral talks in July 2009, in diplomatic correspondence, at CHOGM, and in a number of conversations between Prime Minister Ramgoolam and Foreign Minister Boolell and the British High Commissioner in Mauritius, Mr. John Murton. With respect to any obligation to carry out substantive negotiations, the Tribunal considers it to be settled international law that "it is not necessary that a State must expressly refer to a specific treaty in its exchanges with the other State to enable it later to invoke that instrument," but that "the exchanges must refer to the subject-matter of the treaty with sufficient clarity to enable the State against which a claim is made to identify that there is, or may be, a dispute with regard to that subject-matter" (*Application of the International Convention on the Elimination of All Forms of Racial Discrimination (Georgia* v. *Russian Federation) Preliminary Objections, Judgment, I.C.J. Reports 2011*, p. 70

at p. 85, para. 30; *see also Military and Paramilitary Activities in and against Nicaragua (Nicaragua* v. *United States of America), Jurisdiction and Admissibility, Judgment, I.C.J. Reports 1984*, p. 392 at pp. 428–429, para. 83). Moreover, States themselves are in the best position to determine where substantive negotiations can productively be continued, and "if finally a point is reached at which one of the Parties definitely declares himself unable, or refuses, to give way, and there can therefore be no doubt that *the dispute cannot be settled by diplomatic negotiation*" (*Mavrommatis Palestine Concessions, Jurisdiction, Judgment of* 30 *August 1924, PCIJ Series A, No. 2*, p. 6 at p. 13, 15). As set out in the factual record, Mauritius engaged in negotiations with the United Kingdom regarding the steps that would be taken before an MPA might be declared (see paragraphs 128–147 above). Mauritius' decision that substantive negotiations could not continue in parallel with the United Kingdom's Public Consultation, or that negotiations did not warrant pursuing after the MPA was declared on 1 April 2010, did not violate any duty to negotiate in respect of the Parties' dispute.

380. Article 283, however, concerns an exchange of views on the means to settle the dispute, whether by negotiation or other peaceful means. In the Tribunal's view, the most unequivocal example of compliance with this provision is that offered by Australia and New Zealand in the *Southern Bluefin Tuna* arbitration. In identical Notes Verbales dated 15 September 1999, Australia and New Zealand each set out a history of diplomatic communications recording the termination of negotiations, the possible submission of the dispute to mediation, Japan's preference for arbitration under the 1993 Convention for the Conservation of Southern Bluefin Tuna, and Australia and New Zealand's rejection of this option and intent to submit that dispute to arbitration under the Convention (*Southern Bluefin Tuna (New Zealand* v. *Japan)*, Request for the Prescription of Provisional Measures Submitted by New Zealand at Annex 1, New Zealand's Diplomatic Note 701/14/7/10/3 to Japan dated 15 July 1999, *reproduced in* International Tribunal for the Law of the Sea, *Pleadings, Minutes of Public Sittings and Documents, Vol. 4 (1999)* at p. 14; *Southern Bluefin Tuna (Australia* v. *Japan)*, Request for the Prescription of Provisional Measures Submitted by Australia at Annex 1, Australia's Diplomatic Note No. LGB 99/258 to Japan dated 15 July 1999, *reproduced in* International Tribunal for the Law of the Sea, *Pleadings, Minutes of Public Sittings and Documents, Vol. 4 (1999)* at p. 82). The United Kingdom points to the absence of a similar record of views exchanged in these proceedings and would have the Tribunal deny jurisdiction on those grounds.

381. The Tribunal, however, is sensitive to the concern expressed by the tribunal in *Barbados/Trinidad and Tobago* that an overly formalistic application of Article 283 does not accord with how diplomatic negotiations are actually carried out (*Award of* 11 *April 2006, PCA Award Series*, pp. 94–96, RIAA, Vol. XXVII, p. 147 at pp. 206–207, paras. 201–205). In practice, substantive negotiations concerning the parties' dispute are not neatly separated from

exchanges of views on the preferred means of settling a dispute, and the idealized form exhibited in *Southern Bluefin Tuna* will rarely occur. Accordingly, it is unsurprising that in the jurisprudence on Article 283 it is frequently not clear as to whether the communications that were considered sufficient for the purposes of Article 283 were substantive or procedural in nature.

382. Nevertheless, Article 283 forms part of the Convention and was intended to ensure that a State would not be taken entirely by surprise by the initiation of compulsory proceedings. It should be applied as such, but without an undue formalism as to the manner and precision with which views were exchanged and understood. In the Tribunal's view, Article 283 requires that a dispute have arisen with sufficient clarity that the Parties were aware of the issues in respect of which they disagreed. In the present case, the Tribunal considers that a dispute regarding the manner in which the United Kingdom was proceeding with the proposed MPA had arisen at least as of Mauritius' Note Verbale of 23 November 2009. In that communication, Mauritius set out its concern regarding the impact of the MPA on issues of sovereignty, resettlement, and fisheries. Mauritius also stated its view that these issues should be addressed in the bilateral framework between the two governments and that this should be done before the United Kingdom undertook to consult with the public:

> [...]
>
> Furthermore, the Ministry of Foreign Affairs, Regional Integration and International Trade would like to state that since there is an on-going bilateral Mauritius-UK mechanism for talks and consultations on issues relating to the Chagos Archipelago and a third round of talks is envisaged early next year, the Government of the Republic of Mauritius believes that it is inappropriate for the consultation on the proposed marine protected area, as far as Mauritius is concerned, to take place outside this bilateral framework.
>
> The Government of Mauritius considers that an MPA project in the Chagos Archipelago should not be incompatible with the sovereignty of the Republic of Mauritius over the Chagos Archipelago and should address the issues of resettlement, access to the fisheries resources, and the economic development of the islands in a manner which would not prejudice an eventual enjoyment of sovereignty. A total ban on fisheries exploitation and omission of those issues from any MPA project would not be compatible with the long-term resolution of, or progress in the talks, on the sovereignty issue.
>
> The stand of the Government of Mauritius is that the existing framework for talks on the Chagos Archipelago and the related environmental issues should not be overtaken or bypassed by the consultation launched by the British Government on the proposed MPA.[453]

[453] Note Verbale dated 23 November 2009 from the Ministry of Foreign Affairs, Regional Integration and International Trade, Mauritius to the UK Foreign and Commonwealth Office,

383. Once a dispute has arisen, Article 283 then requires that the Parties engage in some exchange of views regarding the means to settle the dispute. As is apparent from Foreign Secretary David Miliband's letter of 15 December 2009, the United Kingdom considered it appropriate to continue with a third round of bilateral talks in parallel with the Public Consultation:

> [...]
>
> At our meeting, you mentioned your concerns that the UK should have consulted Mauritius further before launching the consultation exercise. I regret any difficulty this has caused you or your Prime Minister in Port Louis. I hope you will recognize that we have been open about the plans and that the offer of further talks has been on the table since July.
>
> I would like to reassure you again that the public consultation does not in any way prejudice or cut across our bilateral intergovernmental dialogue with Mauritius on the proposed Marine Protected Area. The purpose of the public consultation is to seek the views of the wider interested community, including scientists, NGOs, those with commercial interests and other stakeholders such as the Chagossians. The consultations and our plans for an MPA do not in any way impact on our commitment to cede the territory when it is no longer needed for defence purposes.
>
> Our ongoing bilateral talks are an excellent forum for your Government to express its views on the MPA. We welcome the prospect of further discussion in the context of these talks, the next round of which now look likely to happen in January.
>
> As well as the MPA there are, of course, many other issues for bilateral discussion. My officials remain ready to continue the talks and I hope that Mauritius will take up the opportunity to pursue this bilateral dialogue.
>
> [...][454]

384. Mauritius, in contrast, considered that the dispute should be resolved through bilateral talks, but that pending such talks the United Kingdom's Public Consultation should be put on hold. This is apparent from Mauritius' account of the conversation at CHOGM (see paragraphs 135–138 above) and, in any event, from Foreign Minister Arvin Boolell's letter of 30 December 2009:

> During our recent meeting in the margins of the Commonwealth Heads of Government Meeting, I had expressed the concerns of the Government of Mauritius about the Marine Protected Area project. I had stated that it was inappropriate for the British authorities to embark on consultations on the matter outside the bilateral Mauritius-United Kingdom mechanism for talks on issues relating to the Chagos Archipelago.
>
> [...]

No. 1197/28/10 (Annex MM-155).

[454] Letter dated 15 December 2009 from the UK Secretary of State for Foreign and Commonwealth Affairs to the Minister of Foreign Affairs, Regional Integration and International Trade, Mauritius (Annex MM-156).

> In these circumstances, as I have mentioned, Mauritius is not in a position to hold separate consultations with the team of experts of the UK on the proposal to establish a Marine Protected Area.
>
> You will no doubt be aware that, in the margins of the last CHOGM, our respective Prime Ministers agreed that the Marine Protected Area project be put on hold and that this issue be addressed during the next round of Mauritius-United Kingdom bilateral talks.[455]

385. Although this correspondence also dealt with substantive matters (as would be expected), the Parties' views on the settlement of the dispute by negotiation were clearly exchanged in December 2009. This is all that Article 283 requires. It is not necessary for the Parties to comprehensively canvas the means for the peaceful settlement of disputes set out in either the UN Charter or the Convention, nor was Mauritius "obliged to continue with an exchange of views when it concludes that the possibilities of reaching agreement have been exhausted" (*Land Reclamation in and around the Straits of Johor (Malaysia* v. *Singapore), Provisional Measures, Order of* 8 *October 2003, ITLOS Reports 2003*, p. 10 at para. 47). Nor, importantly, does Article 283 require that the exchange of views include the possibility of compulsory settlement or that—before resorting to compulsory settlement—one party caution the other regarding the possibility of litigation or set out the specific claims that it might choose to advance. In the present case, both Parties preferred to address their dispute through negotiations, albeit subject to incompatible conditions that ultimately prevented further talks from taking place. The exchange of views took place on this basis. Thereafter, Mauritius determined that the possibility of reaching agreement on the conditions for further negotiations had been exhausted and elected to proceed with compulsory settlement through arbitration. Nothing further was called for.

386. Accordingly, the Tribunal concludes that Mauritius has met the requirement of Article 283 to exchange views regarding the settlement, by negotiation or other peaceful means, of the dispute underpinning Mauritius' Fourth Submission.

* * *

Chapter VI. Merits

387. As set out in the preceding Chapter, the Tribunal has found that it has jurisdiction with respect to Mauritius' Fourth Submission, requesting the Tribunal to adjudge and declare that –

> (4) The United Kingdom's purported "MPA" is incompatible with the substantive and procedural obligations of the United Kingdom under

[455] Letter dated 30 December 2009 from the Minister of Foreign Affairs, Regional Integration and International Trade, Mauritius to the UK Secretary of State for Foreign and Commonwealth Affairs (Annex MM-157).

the Convention, including *inter alia* Articles 2, 55, 56, 63, 64, 194 and 300, as well as Article 7 of the Agreement for the Implementation of the Provisions of the United Nations Convention on the Law of the Sea of 10 December 1982 Relating to the Conservation and Management of Straddling Fish Stocks and Highly Migratory Fish Stocks of 4 August 1995.

388. Among the provisions of the Convention invoked by Mauritius in this submission, the Tribunal has held (see paragraph 323 above) that it has jurisdiction with respect to:

(*a*) Article 2(3) insofar as it relates to Mauritius' fishing rights in the territorial sea or to the United Kingdom's undertakings to return the Archipelago to Mauritius when no longer needed for defence purposes and to return the benefit of any minerals or oil discovered in or near the Chagos Archipelago to Mauritius;

(*b*) Article 56(2), insofar as it relates to the United Kingdom's undertakings to return the Archipelago to Mauritius when no longer needed for defence purposes and to return the benefit of any minerals or oil discovered in or near the Chagos Archipelago to Mauritius;

(*c*) Article 194; and

(*d*) Article 300, insofar as it relates to the abuse of rights in connection with a violation of one of the foregoing articles.

389. The Tribunal will now proceed to consider the merits of the claims Mauritius has advanced pursuant to these provisions. The Tribunal will first address the content of Mauritius' rights, both pursuant to the Convention and otherwise, in the territorial sea, exclusive economic zone, and continental shelf areas affected by the MPA. The Tribunal will then address whether the United Kingdom's declaration of the MPA was in breach of its obligations under the aforementioned provisions of the Convention.

A. Mauritius' Rights in the Territorial Sea, Exclusive Economic Zone, and Continental Shelf

1. The Parties' Arguments

390. The Tribunal has set out the Lancaster House Undertakings made by the United Kingdom to Mauritius on 23 September 1965 (see paragraphs 74–79 above).

391. Mauritius contends that these undertakings were binding legal commitments and give Mauritius rights as a matter of international law, including fishing rights in the waters of the Chagos Archipelago, mineral and oil rights in the seabed and subsoil, and a right to the return of the Chagos Archipelago to Mauritius when it is no longer needed for defence purposes. The United Kingdom, in contrast, categorically denies that the undertakings

could have been legally binding as a matter of British constitutional law and argues that the scope of any such rights would, in any event, be limited.

392. Separately, Mauritius also claims traditional fishing rights in the waters of the Chagos Archipelago. The United Kingdom does not accept that Mauritius has made out a case for the existence of such rights.

(a) The Nature of the United Kingdom's Undertakings and the Existence of a Binding Agreement

Mauritius' Position

393. Mauritius' primary position in these proceedings is that no valid agreement was reached in 1965 at Lancaster House or in the subsequent approval of the detachment of the Chagos Archipelago by the Mauritius Council of Ministers. According to Mauritius, the United Kingdom was in violation of its obligations with respect to self-determination, the linkage between detachment and independence imposed by the United Kingdom put the Mauritius Council of Ministers under duress, and any purported consent "was not given in accordance with the applicable standards for the treatment of a colonizer towards an independence movement."[456]

394. Nevertheless, Mauritius argues, even though there was no valid agreement, "the U.K.'s undertakings to Mauritius, all of which were repeated and expressly renewed by successive British governments over the next four and a half decades after Mauritius became an independent State, still constitute binding legal obligations."[457] According to Mauritius, the binding nature of the undertakings stems not from Mauritius' agreement to detachment, but from the fact that the United Kingdom retained the Archipelago after making them:

> The United Kingdom, on independence, not after independence—on independence—retained the Archipelago. It therefore affirmed the conditions on which it had come to receive the Archipelago, even if the consent given was vitiated.
>
> [...]
>
> [The 1965 agreement] was not a treaty, nor was it intended as a binding arrangement under British law [...]. It was an arrangement made in the context of negotiations for independence which take some time between persons who knew what they were doing in virtue of independence.
>
> [...]
>
> At the very second of independence, when the excision was affirmed by the continued presence of the United Kingdom in the Archipelago, the United Kingdom disabled itself from denying the conditions attached to its presence. [...] [T]his is a situation in which the colonial authority

[456] Final Transcript, 977:17–19; *see generally*, Final Transcript, 231:22 to 255:5; 953:13 to 985:5.

[457] Final Transcript, 260:7–9.

> exercising its power assumed a responsibility which it affirms not after independence, but on independence, the very second of independence, because otherwise it would have to hand the territory back. […] [I]n the circumstances, the United Kingdom is bound by the obligations it assumed while it holds on to the territory […].[458]

395. In the alternative, Mauritius submits that if "there was a lawful agreement on detachment of the Archipelago, then the consideration for Mauritius' consent must include the undertakings that the United Kingdom expressly gave in exchange for it. They would then be legally binding terms of a lawful agreement under international law."[459]

396. Under either view, Mauritius argues that the applicable test is whether the United Kingdom intended to be bound by the undertakings.[460] In this respect, Mauritius maintains that the contemporaneous documentary evidence –

> shows that, at all times, the United Kingdom intended and considered the undertakings to be legally binding, establishing legal obligations for the U.K. and legal rights for Mauritius. This is reflected in the language and circumstances of the exchanges made at Lancaster House in September 1965 and subsequently, and in the consistent pattern of statements and actions by responsible U.K. representatives and officials, including its Legal Advisers.[461]

Moreover, the specific undertakings were part of the *quid pro quo* or "package of inducements" given in exchange for what the United Kingdom regarded as Mauritius' consent to the detachment of the Chagos Archipelago.[462] In assessing the United Kingdom's understanding of the undertakings, Mauritius argues that the consistent internal opinions held by the United Kingdom's own Legal Advisers "carry special weight" in assessing the United Kingdom's intent.[463] According to Mauritius, there is no evidence that the United Kingdom's Legal Advisers ever held a contrary view prior to April 2010.[464]

---

[458] Final Transcript, 981:12–14; 982:10 to 983:4.

[459] Final Transcript, 259:24 to 260:2.

[460] Final Transcript, 260:9–11.

[461] Final Transcript, 258:9–13.

[462] Final Transcript, 258:16 to 259:2; 977:14–17.

[463] Final Transcript, 260:15–17 to 262:6, *citing* Minute dated 26 February 1971 from A.I. Aust to Mr. D. Scott, "BIOT Resettlement: Negotiations with the Mauritius Government" (Annex MR-73); Minute dated 1 July 1977 from [name redacted], Legal Advisers to Mr. [name redacted], East African Department, UK Foreign and Commonwealth Office, "BIOT: Fishing Rights" (Annex MR-79); Minute dated 13 October 1981 from A.D. Watts to [name redacted], "Extension of the Territorial Sea: BIOT" (Annex MR-83); Note dated 2 July 2004 by Henry Steel, "Fishing by Mauritian Vessels in BIOT Waters" (Annex MR-109); E-mail dated 9 July 2009 from Development Director of MRAG to Joanne Yeadon, Head of BIOT & Pitcairn Section, UK Foreign and Commonwealth Office, and "MRAG Comments on the proposal to designate the BIOT FCMZ as a marine reserve" (Annex MR-137).

[464] Final Transcript, 262:7–10.

397. In any case, Mauritius submits that the subsequent practice of the United Kingdom, in repeatedly renewing and reconfirming all of the undertakings after Mauritius' independence and until the declaration of the MPA, confirmed the United Kingdom's understanding of the undertakings and is itself an independent source of obligation binding on the United Kingdom.[465] According to Mauritius, the United Kingdom, "having on many occasions stated that the undertaking is binding, is now estopped from claiming otherwise in these proceedings."[466] Mauritius goes on to recall the *Argentina-Chile Frontier Case ((Argentina* v. *Chile), Award of* 9 *December 1966*, R.I.A.A. Vol. XVI, p. 109, at p. 164 (1969)) and submits that –

> "there is in international law a principle, which is moreover a principle of substantive law and not just a technical rule of evidence, according to which, 'a State party to an international litigation is bound by its previous acts or attitude when they are in contradiction with its claims in the litigation.'" Accordingly, "inconsistency between claims or allegations put forward by a State, and its previous conduct in connection therewith, is not admissible (*allegans contraria non audiendus est*)."[467]

In the alternative, Mauritius considers that the reaffirmation of the undertakings would "represent the repetition of undertakings under international law which are binding [on the United Kingdom] on the *Nuclear Tests* principle", pursuant to which unilateral declarations may be endowed with binding effect.[468]

398. Finally, Mauritius argues, the legally binding character of the United Kingdom's undertaking with respect to fishing rights is undiminished by the inclusion in the undertaking of words to the effect that the United Kingdom would "use its good offices" to secure fishing rights.[469] According to Mauritius, what the undertaking with respect to fishing rights entailed was –

> a commitment to obtain for Mauritius the broadest possible fishing rights first by making best efforts to get the U.S. to consent to them and then, if successful, to establish and preserve them in the exercise of the U.K.'s own power, and that is exactly how the U.K. interpreted and understood its obligation as the contemporaneous documents show.[470]

In practice, which was "consistent and uninterrupted … over 45 years", Mauritius argues that this undertaking "came to be understood by both parties as the right to fish in all the BIOT waters, out to 200 miles … subject to licences issued freely by the BIOT administration to Mauritian-flagged vessels without charge."[471]

---

[465] Final Transcript, 260:5–9.

[466] Mauritius' Reply, para. 6.53.

[467] Final Transcript, 262:13–18.

[468] Final Transcript, 254:3–6.

[469] Final Transcript, 266:22 to 271:19.

[470] Final Transcript, 269:5–9.

[471] Final Transcript, 1051:10–15.

The United Kingdom's Position

399. In the course of these proceedings, the Agent for the United Kingdom set out his government's view of what it refers to as the "1965 understandings" in the following terms:

> We consider all of the understandings reached in 1965 to be important political commitments on both sides, typical of the friendship our two countries shared at the time they were given.
>
> As to the question whether the UK could cede BIOT to a third State, our long-standing position is that the United Kingdom does not recognise the claim by Mauritius to sovereignty over the British Indian Ocean Territory. But, the United Kingdom has previously recognised Mauritius as the only State which has a right to assert a claim of sovereignty when the United Kingdom relinquishes its own sovereignty, and successive Governments have given political undertakings to the Government of Mauritius that the territory will be ceded when it is no longer required for defence purposes.[472]

400. The United Kingdom submits that "in assessing the status of the 1965 understandings, one needs to look not to international law, but to British law, including British constitutional law. And it is clear that under British law the understandings were not legally binding or otherwise intended to have legal effect."[473] In this respect, the United Kingdom submits[474] that –

> It is not possible for overseas territories to conclude an agreement binding under international law with another overseas territory or for one or more overseas territories to conclude such an agreement with the United Kingdom. This is because internationally the Territories are not legal entities separate from each other or from the United Kingdom.[475]

Accordingly, the United Kingdom argues, "arrangements of this sort between, to put it at its most formal, the Crown in right of the United Kingdom and the Crown in right of the Colony of Mauritius, could not be legally binding. They were at most political understandings, not enforceable in the courts."[476]

401. In the United Kingdom's view, in the absence of a legally binding agreement at the time the Archipelago was detached, Mauritius' case depends upon establishing that the United Kingdom undertook a binding unilateral commitment. The United Kingdom considers the relevant standard to have been set out in the *Nuclear Tests* proceedings (*(Australia* v. *France), Judgment, I.C.J. Reports 1974,* p. 253; *(New Zealand* v. *France), Judgment, I.C.J. Reports 1974,* p. 457) and contends that Mauritius must "mak[e] out a case under *Nuclear Tests,* and ... as part of requiring that there be an intention to be bound,

[472] Final Transcript, 1163:4–13.

[473] Final Transcript, 847:7–10.

[474] Final Transcript, 846:18–24.

[475] *Ibid., citing* I. Hendry & S. Dickson, *British Overseas Territories Law* at 261 (2011).

[476] Final Transcript, 847:12–15.

it has to show clarity as to what the undertaking, the alleged undertaking, actually provides for."[477]

402. With respect to binding intent, the United Kingdom submits that "there never was any intention on the part of the United Kingdom to be bound by reference to what was and always has been a non-binding understanding on fishing rights."[478] According to the United Kingdom, the official record of the meeting of 23 September 1965 "contains a series of understandings, not legally binding obligations".[479] With respect to the matter of "fishing rights", the United Kingdom notes that this reference is preceded by the commitment to "use 'good offices'" with an object "to ensure that the ... facilities would remain available";[480] and the qualifier "as far as practicable".[481]

403. Essentially, the United Kingdom argues, Mauritius "sought preference with respect to fishing rights to the extent such were granted, and that grant would be pursuant to domestic, not international, law".[482] Moreover, the qualifying words meant there was "no absolute obligation" but what was practicable; [483] and "fishing rights", properly construed, is not an unqualified or unambiguous term.[484]

404. With regard to the position after independence, the United Kingdom maintains that –

> any renewal of the 1965 statements post-independence would bring one back to the agreed record, as to which the criteria established in the ICJ jurisprudence and reflected in the 2006 ILC Guiding Principles would not be met, not least because there was never any intention to be bound.[485]

405. The United Kingdom does not accept that any transposition of the understandings to the international plane changes their status as "nonbinding understandings, commitments ... but political commitments by each side,"[486] and further argues that its own internal comments on the status of these commitments have limited legal significance,[487] on which the Tribunal should be "very wary of placing weight."[488]

406. In the alternative, even accepting the existence of a binding unilateral undertaking on fishing rights, the United Kingdom contends that it

[477] Final Transcript, 834:14–16.

[478] Final Transcript, 828:15–17.

[479] Final Transcript, 828:21–22.

[480] Final Transcript, 842:8–9.

[481] Final Transcript, 843:3–15.

[482] Final Transcript, 842:22–24.

[483] Final Transcript, 843:4–7.

[484] Final Transcript, 843:16–20.

[485] Final Transcript, 852:23 to 853:1.

[486] Final Transcript, 1253:3–16.

[487] Final Transcript, 858:4–6.

[488] Final Transcript, 860:4–7.

is entitled to revoke this undertaking. The United Kingdom relies upon the International Law Commission (the "ILC")'s *Guiding Principles Applicable to Unilateral Declarations of States Capable of Creating Legal Obligations*[489] (the "ILC Guiding Principles") for the proposition that international law prohibits only the arbitrary revocation of a unilateral undertaking.[490] In the present circumstances, the United Kingdom submits that revocation would not have been an arbitrary step.[491]

(b) The Scope of Mauritius' Fishing Rights

407. The Parties do not differ with respect to the content of any Mauritian rights to the return of the Chagos Archipelago when it is no longer needed for defence purposes[492] or to the benefit of minerals and oil in its surrounding waters.[493] With respect to fishing rights, however, the Parties part company. The Parties agree that the insertion of the reference to "fishing rights" into the official record at the behest of Sir Seewoosagur Ramgoolam was not a correction of a deficient minute, but a renegotiation of the package.[494] The Parties also agree that the content of this undertaking was not specifically elaborated in the official record of the Lancaster House Meeting.[495] Where they disagree is on the meaning the Tribunal should accord to the reference to "fishing rights" in the United Kingdom's undertaking.

Mauritius' Position

408. Mauritius maintains that the undertaking given with respect to fishing rights was broad and –

> translated into Mauritius' right to have its vessels fish anywhere in the Chagos waters except in the immediate vicinity of Diego Garcia Island, and for any species, subject only to the requirement that they obtain fishing licences, which were issued freely and without charge.[496]

This right stems from the Lancaster House Undertakings, but its content is informed by the Parties' subsequent practice in applying the fishing rights undertaking. Ultimately, Mauritius argues, this right to fish extended to 200

---

489 Report of the International Law Commission, Fifty-eighth session, (1 May-9 June and 3 July-11 August 2006), G.A.O.R. Sixty-first session, Supplement No. 10, UN Doc. A/61/10 at p. 366.

490 Final Transcript, 860:11–15.

491 Final Transcript, 860:16–24.

492 Final Transcript, 1047:11–15.

493 Even though Mauritius accepts that "[a]t one time, until 1973, there were two different interpretations of this undertaking," it appears to have subsequently accepted the United Kingdom's position that the benefits from any prospecting activities reverted to Mauritius even though the United Kingdom retained a broad discretion with respect to such prospecting activities: Final Transcript, 1047:16 to 1049:21.

494 Final Transcript, 840:4–9; 1037:9–23; 1286:18–1287:2.

495 Final Transcript, 1051:7–10.

496 Final Transcript, 167:11–13.

nautical miles, and is "reflected in the contemporaneous documentation, *via* consistent and uninterrupted subsequent practice over 45 years".[497]

409. According to Mauritius, there is no basis to limit its fishing rights to "preferential treatment" or to link them to the rights of other States.[498] The only reference to "preferential treatment" with respect to fishing rights occurred early in the documentary record at a time when the Mauritian Ministers were still insisting on a long-term lease. As the Lancaster House Undertakings were ultimately developed, however, the discussion shifted to one of fishing "rights".[499] Nor, in Mauritius' view, is the content of the undertaking significantly limited by the reference to the use of "good offices" with the United States. Mauritius explains this issue as follows:

> The entire purpose of detaching the Archipelago was to secure it for the establishment of the U.S. military base. The U.S. might have been concerned that expansive fishing rights for Mauritius or anyone else, for that matter, especially in close proximity to the islands, might compromise the security of the base. The U.K. [...] could not ensure Mauritius' fishing rights without first obtaining the consent of the United States. Hence, the undertaking was to use "good offices" with the Americans to ensure fishing rights for Mauritius "as far as practicable." [...] The U.K.'s good offices were successful. The Americans agreed to the very broad array of fishing rights to Mauritius that the U.K. proposed [...]. After obtaining American consent, the U.K. then took steps directly to ensure all of these fishing rights for Mauritius exercising its powers as administrator of the "BIOT."[500]

Nevertheless, Mauritius argues, the inclusion of this condition does not give the United Kingdom the power to itself constrain Mauritian fishing rights. According to Mauritius,

> It would make absolutely no sense, [...] to interpret the 1965 undertaking so as to obligate the U.K. to endeavor to obtain U.S. consent to Mauritian fishing rights as far as practicable but then after this consent was obtained, to allow the U.K. to unilaterally choose not to give effect to those rights or to give effect to them briefly and then immediately abolish them. That surely would have been bad faith, and that surely was not what the U.K. intended when it gave Mauritius its undertaking in regard to ensuring fishing rights as far as practicable.[501]

410. Finally, Mauritius submits that its fishing rights were consistently exercised by Mauritian flagged vessels until the declaration of the MPA and

---

[497] Final Transcript, 1051:10–12.

[498] Final Transcript, 1056:12–15.

[499] Final Transcript, 168:11–24.

[500] Final Transcript, 267:21 to 268:21.

[501] Final Transcript, 268:23 to 269:4.

were a matter of great importance.[502] Mauritius also notes that the United Kingdom continued to grant fishing licences to Mauritius even when no other State was permitted to fish.[503]

The United Kingdom's Position

411. According to the United Kingdom, it is clear that the meaning of "fishing rights" in the official record of the Lancaster House Meeting was "preferential fishing rights if granted".[504] In the United Kingdom's view, the phrase is to be understood in the context of the limited fishing practices of the inhabitants of the Chagos Archipelago in 1965.[505]

412. The undertaking was not, the United Kingdom submits, "a perpetual and absolute right to all such fishing rights as could be granted as a matter of international law as it developed".[506] Instead, the United Kingdom argues, "the 1965 statement on fishing rights is hedged about with soft language and qualifications, with fishing rights being described as a form of 'facility.'"[507] Moreover, any subsequent attempt by Mauritius to advance an expansive interpretation of the commitment was consistently rejected by the United Kingdom.[508]

413. The United Kingdom also regards Mauritius' lack of objection when measures impacting fishing in BIOT waters were introduced and duly notified by the United Kingdom as inconsistent with the extensive rights Mauritius now claims.[509] As a matter of fact, the United Kingdom argues that Mauritians have demonstrated "minimal interest" in the exploitation of Mauritius' fishing rights.[510]

(c) Mauritius' Traditional Fishing Rights in the Territorial Sea surrounding the Chagos Archipelago

Mauritius' Position

414. Mauritius submits that it possesses traditional fishing rights in the territorial sea[511] and the exclusive economic zone[512] surrounding the Chagos

[502] Final Transcript, 169:5 to 170:5, *citing* Letter dated 13 December 2007 from the Prime Minister of Mauritius to the Prime Minister of the United Kingdom (Annex MM-135) and Letter dated 1 December 2005 from the Prime Minister of Mauritius to the Prime Minister of the United Kingdom (Annex MM-132).

[503] Final Transcript, 168:4–10.

[504] Final Transcript, 595:18–20; 853:15–17.

[505] Final Transcript, 834:4–12.

[506] Final Transcript, 853:12–14.

[507] Final Transcript, 853:8–9.

[508] Final Transcript, 604:17 to 606:4.

[509] Final Transcript, 606:23 to 605:4.

[510] Final Transcript, 613:1 to 614:9.

[511] Mauritius' Memorial, paras. 7.19–7.20; Mauritius' Reply, paras. 6.39, 6.59.

[512] Mauritius' Memorial, paras. 7.31–7.32.

Archipelago. According to Mauritius, "even if the Chagos Archipelago was lawfully detached from Mauritius ... , the detachment cannot render void any existing rights of access or use, or other rights related to the exploitation of natural resources."[513]

415. The standard for such rights, Mauritius argues, is merely that they have been exercised "for many years ... in the waters in question."[514] Moreover, in Mauritius' view, "decades of the UK's own practice" unambiguously confirm Mauritius' long standing rights in the territorial sea[515] and the exclusive economic zone.[516]

The United Kingdom's Position

416. The United Kingdom submits that "Mauritius has no traditional fishing rights"[517] and recalls the extremely limited scope of fishing in 1965 for the domestic purposes of the Chagossians.[518] In any case, the United Kingdom argues that this limited fishing does not come close to any form of historic dependence as commonly understood by traditional fishing.[519]

2. The Tribunal's Decision

(a) The Nature of Mauritius' Rights Pursuant to the 1965 Undertakings

417. Mauritius' claim that the United Kingdom has violated Article 2(3) and 56(2) of the Convention, as those provisions relate to the Lancaster House Undertakings made in connection with the detachment of the Chagos Archipelago, requires the Tribunal to determine the nature of Mauritius' rights pursuant to the undertakings.

418. The Tribunal approaches this task conscious of the findings it has made with respect to the scope of its own jurisdiction. It is common ground between the Parties that there was agreement between the United Kingdom and the Mauritius Council of Ministers in 1965 to the detachment of the Archipelago (the "1965 Agreement"). The Parties disagree, however, regarding whether Mauritian consent was freely given, whether any agreement is valid or binding, and even regarding what was agreed. In the course of these proceedings, the validity or otherwise of the 1965 Agreement was a central element of the Parties' submissions on Mauritius' First and Second Submissions,

513 Mauritius' Memorial, para. 7.10.

514 Mauritius' Reply, paras. 6.60–6.61.

515 Mauritius' Reply, paras. 6.56–6.59.

516 Mauritius' Reply, para. 6.80.

517 Final Transcript, 873:23 to 874:1.

518 Final Transcript, 861:4–5.

519 The United Kingdom's Counter-Memorial, para. 8.32; Final Transcript, 861:6–8.

sovereignty, and the identity of the coastal State. The Tribunal has found that it lacks jurisdiction to consider these submissions.

419. At the same time, the legal effect of the 1965 Agreement is also a central element of the Parties' submissions on Mauritius' Fourth Submission, insofar as it involves the Lancaster House Undertakings. The Tribunal finds that its jurisdiction with respect to Mauritius' Fourth Submission (see paragraph 323 above) permits it to interpret the 1965 Agreement to the extent necessary to establish the nature and scope of the United Kingdom's undertakings.

420. The Tribunal will approach the Lancaster House Undertakings by considering how the Parties understood the 1965 Agreement at the time it was concluded. The Tribunal will then go on to consider the legal status of the 1965 Agreement and the extent to which the Tribunal is called upon to engage with Mauritius' arguments regarding its validity. Finally, the Tribunal will address the legal significance of the United Kingdom's repetition of its undertakings in the years following the independence of Mauritius, as well as the ultimate scope of the undertaking made with respect to fishing rights.

i. The Parties' Intent in 1965

421. Having examined the extensive documentary record provided by the Parties (see paragraphs 69-87 above), the Tribunal considers that the undertakings provided by the United Kingdom at Lancaster House formed part of the *quid pro quo* through which Mauritian agreement to the detachment of the Chagos Archipelago from Mauritius was procured. The Tribunal notes in particular the following facts:

(*a*) The initial position of the Mauritian Ministers, when the proposal for detachment was first conveyed to them in July 1965 was to object and to propose instead a 99-year lease, on the condition that "provision should be made for safeguarding mineral rights to Mauritius and ensuring preference for Mauritius if fishing or agricultural rights were ever granted".[520]

(*b*) During the first meeting in London on 13 September 1965, the Mauritian participants pressed the United Kingdom regarding the amount of compensation being proposed and the possibility of securing sugar quotas from the United States in exchange for detachment.[521]

(*c*) During the second meeting in London on 20 September 1965, the Mauritian participants reiterated their preference for a lease, dismissed the £1 million in compensation then being offered as inadequate, and continued to press the United Kingdom regarding the possibility of additional compensation from the United States.

[520] Mauritius Telegram No. 175 to the Colonial Office, 30 July 1965, FO 371/184526 (Annex MM-13).

[521] Mauritius—Defence Matters: record of a meeting in the Secretary of State's room in the Colonial Office at 10.30 a.m. on Monday 13 September 1965 (Annex UKR-6).

Sir Seewoosagur Ramgoolam also proposed for the first time the condition that the Archipelago revert to Mauritius when no longer needed for defence purposes:

> Sir Seewoosagur Ramgoolam said that [...] it should in any case be provided if the islands ceased to be needed for defence purposes they would revert to Mauritius
>
> Sir H. Poynton [Permanent Under-Secretary of State for the Colonies] mentioned the precedent of certain U.S. bases in the West Indies, leased in 1940 and no longer needed, which had reverted to the jurisdiction of the Government concerned.[522]

(*d*) During the Lancaster House Meeting on 23 September 1965, the United Kingdom initially indicated that it could go no further than a defence agreement, consultations in the event of an internal security situation, good offices with the United States with respect to the supply of commodities, and £3 million in compensation.[523] The United Kingdom also noted that "it would be possible for the British Government to detach [the Chagos Archipelago] from Mauritius by Order in Council."[524] The Mauritian delegation then raised the return of the Archipelago when no longer needed for defence purposes and the possibility of approaching the United States regarding the use of Mauritian supplies and manpower in support of the planned defence facility.[525] The United Kingdom's representatives indicated that both conditions should be possible. The list of commitments tentatively agreed to during the Lancaster House Meeting was ultimately set out in the draft record of that meeting.[526]

(*e*) Following the meeting, Sir Seewoosagur Ramgoolam continued to press the United Kingdom regarding further concessions and secured the inclusion of the additional commitments set out in his handwritten note in respect of –

> (vii) Navigational & Meteorological facilities
>
> (viii) Fishing rights
>
> (ix) Use of Air Strip for Emergency Landing and if required for development of the other islands
>
> (x) Any mineral or oil discovered on or near islands to revert to the Mauritius Government.[527]

---

522 Record of a Meeting in the Colonial Office at 9.00 a.m. on Monday, 20th September, 1965, Mauritius—Defence Issues, FO 371/184528 (Annex MM-16).

523 Records relating to meetings on 23 September 1965 at p. 1 (Annex UKR-8).

524 *Ibid.* at p. 1.

525 *Ibid.* at p. 1–2; Record of a Meeting held in Lancaster House at 2.30 p.m. on Thursday 23rd September [1965], Mauritius Defence Matters, CO 1036/1253 at paras. 3–4 (Annex MM-19);

526 Records relating to meetings on 23 September 1965 at pp. 3–4 (Annex UKR-8).

527 Manuscript letter of 1 October 1965 (Annex UKCM-9).

These further conditions were incorporated into paragraph 22 of the final record of the Lancaster House Meeting,[528] and the Parties are in agreement that Sir Seewoosagur Ramgoolam's further conditions were in addition to those agreed in the course of the meeting itself.[529]

> (*f*) Finally, when the Mauritius Council of Ministers was formally asked to approve detachment, subject to the Lancaster House Undertakings, it did so while imposing a further understanding, set out in the telegram from Governor Rennie to the Secretary of State for the Colonies:
>
>> Council of Ministers today confirmed agreement to the detachment of Chagos Archipelago on conditions enumerated, on the understanding that
>>
>> (1) statement in paragraph 6 of your despatch "H.M.G. have taken careful note of points (vii) and (viii)" means H.M.G. have in fact agreed to them.
>>
>> (2) As regards (vii) undertaking to Legislative Assembly excludes
>>
>>> (*a*) sale or transfer by H.M.G. to third party or
>>>
>>> (*b*) any payment or financial obligation by Mauritius as condition of return.
>>
>> (3) In (viii) "on or near" means within area within which Mauritius would be able to derive benefit but for change of sovereignty. I should be grateful if you would confirm this understanding is agreed.[530]

422. Taken as a whole, this record clearly indicates the importance of the undertakings to the Mauritian Ministers. The commitments made by the United Kingdom increased substantially between the proposal of detachment and the Mauritius Government's ultimate acceptance on 5 November 1965. Even at the last minute, the Mauritian Ministers continued to press for further details and concessions. Given all of this, the Tribunal considers the Lancaster House Undertakings to have been an essential condition to securing such Mauritian consent to the detachment of the Archipelago as was given. Without yet passing on the legal nature of these commitments or the validity of Mauritian consent, the Tribunal is confident that, without the United Kingdom's undertakings, neither Sir Seewoosagur Ramgoolam nor the Mauritius Council of Ministers would have agreed to detachment.

423. At the same time, the Tribunal can see no hint, in the record of the United Kingdom's approach to the negotiations, that the United Kingdom

---

528 Record of a Meeting held in Lancaster House at 2.30 p.m. on Thursday 23rd September [1965], Mauritius Defence Matters, CO 1036/1253 at para. 22 (Annex MM-19); Note on Mauritius and Diego Garcia dated 12 November 1965 (Annex UKR-13).

529 Final Transcript, 1037:4–23; 1287:1–2.

530 Mauritius Telegram No. 247 to the Colonial Office, 5 November 1965, FO 371/184529 (Annex MM-25).

intended anything less than a firm commitment that would shape its relations with Mauritius following independence. By the time the conditions were formally presented to the Mauritius Council of Ministers for their agreement to detachment, the United Kingdom had already adopted, at the close of the 1965 Constitutional Conference, the "view that it was right that Mauritius should be independent and take her place among the sovereign nations of the world."[531] Independence in the near future was expected, and the commitments made by United Kingdom were not aimed at the narrow window of time between detachment and independence, but at future relations between the United Kingdom and an independent Mauritius. Moreover, the United Kingdom itself described its commitment in the language of obligation. In requesting that the conditions be presented to the Mauritian side, the Governor of Mauritius was asked on 6 October 1965, to secure Mauritian agreement to detachment "on the conditions" set out in the Lancaster House Meeting.[532] To the Tribunal, these are not the words of a voluntary intent to assist Mauritius to the extent politically feasible, but of an offer made on the basis of an intent to be bound.

ii. The Place of the Undertakings in International Law

424. Regarding the legal status of the 1965 Agreement, the Tribunal accepts the United Kingdom's submission that, as a matter of British constitutional law, an agreement between the British Government and a non-self-governing territory would not be governed by international law. For the purposes of British constitutional law, the Tribunal notes –

> It is not possible for overseas territories to conclude an agreement binding under international law with another overseas territory or for one or more overseas territories to conclude such an agreement with the United Kingdom. This is because internationally the Territories are not legal entities separate from each other or from the United Kingdom. [...] [R]egardless of the form they take, probably the most that these instruments could be is a contract binding upon the Parties under domestic law.[533]

Accordingly, although the Tribunal finds that both Parties were committed to honouring the 1965 Agreement in their post-independence relations, they were legally disabled from expressing that commitment as a matter of international law for such time as Mauritius remained a colony.

425. Had Mauritius remained part of the British Empire, the status of the 1965 Agreement would have remained a matter of British constitutional law. The independence of Mauritius in 1968, however, had the effect of elevat-

---

[531] Mauritius Constitutional Conference 1965, presented to Parliament by the Secretary of State for the Colonies by Command of Her Majesty, Command Paper 2797 (October 1965) (Annex UKCM-11).

[532] Colonial Office Despatch No. 423 to the Governor of Mauritius, 6 October 1965, FO 371/184529 (Annex MM-21).

[533] I. Hendry & S. Dickson, *British Overseas Territories Law* (2011), p. 261 (Authority UKR-30).

ing the package deal reached with the Mauritian Ministers to the international plane and of transforming the commitments made in 1965 into an international agreement. In return for the detachment of the Chagos Archipelago, the United Kingdom made a series of commitments regarding its future relations with Mauritius. When Mauritius became independent and the United Kingdom retained the Chagos Archipelago, the Parties fulfilled the conditions necessary to give effect to the 1965 Agreement and, by their conduct, reaffirmed its application between them.

426. While the Tribunal readily accepts that States are free in their international relations to enter into even very detailed agreements that are intended to have only political effect, the intention for an agreement to be either binding or non-binding as a matter of law must be clearly expressed or is otherwise a matter for objective determination. As recalled by the ICJ in *Aegean Sea Continental Shelf*, "in determining what was indeed the nature of the act or transaction embodied in the [agreement], the [Tribunal] must have regard above all to its actual terms and to the particular circumstances in which it was drawn up" ((*Greece* v. *Turkey*), *Judgment, I.C.J. Reports 1978*, p. 3 at p. 39, para. 96).

427. The Parties did not themselves characterize the status of the 1965 Agreement either at its conclusion or at the moment of Mauritian independence. The Tribunal, in turn, does not consider the circumstances in which the Agreement was initially framed—as a matter between the United Kingdom and its colony—to be determinative of the Parties' intent with respect to its eventual status. Objectively, the Tribunal considers the subject matter of the 1965 Agreement—an agreement to the reconstitution of a portion of a soon-to-be-independent colony as a separate entity in exchange for compensation and a series of detailed undertakings—to be more in the nature of a legal agreement than otherwise. And, as set out above, the Tribunal sees no hint in the course of negotiations or in the language used in 1965 that anything less than a firm commitment was intended.

428. Accordingly, the Tribunal concludes that, upon Mauritian independence, the 1965 Agreement became a matter of international law between the Parties. Moreover, since independence the United Kingdom has repeated and reaffirmed the Lancaster House Undertakings on multiple occasions. This repetition continued after Mauritius began proactively to assert its sovereignty claim in the 1980s, and even after such a claim was enshrined in the Constitution of Mauritius in 1991. As the Tribunal will set out in the sections that follow, the United Kingdom's repetition of the undertakings, and Mauritius' reliance thereon, suffices to resolve any concern that defects in Mauritian consent in 1965 would have prevented the Lancaster House Undertakings from binding the United Kingdom.

iii. The Repetition of the Lancaster House Undertakings since 1965

429. The undertakings were renewed collectively in 1973 in a letter from the United Kingdom to Prime Minister Sir Seewoosagur Ramgoolam, which contained "an assurance that there is no change in the undertakings, given on behalf of the British Government and set out in the record, as then agreed, of the meeting at Lancaster House on 23 September 1965."[534] The undertakings were also reaffirmed individually. The Tribunal will review each undertaking in turn and then consider the legal significance of this repeated reaffirmation.

430. The United Kingdom has renewed its commitment eventually to return the Chagos Archipelago to Mauritius, when no longer required for defence purposes, on numerous occasions and in unambiguous language:

(*a*) On 23 March 1976, the Parliamentary Under Secretary of State, Mr. Ted Rowlands, wrote to the Mauritius High Commissioner in London, Sir Leckraz Teelock, as follows:

> I also take this opportunity to repeat my assurances that Her Majesty's Government will stand by the understandings reached with the Mauritian Government concerning the former Mauritian islands now forming part of the British Indian Ocean Territory; and in particular that they will be returned to Mauritius when they are no longer needed for defence purposes in the same way as the three ex-Seychelles islands are now being returned to Seychelles.[535]

(*b*) On 11 July 1980, the Prime Minister of the United Kingdom, the Rt. Hon. Margaret Thatcher, stated publicly in the House of Commons as follows:

> When the Mauritius Council of Ministers agreed in 1965 to the detachment of the Chagos Islands to form part of British Indian Ocean territory, it was announced that these would be available for the construction of defence facilities and that, in the event of the islands no longer being required for defence purposes, they should revert to Mauritius. This remains the policy of Her Majesty's Government.[536]

(*c*) On 1 July 1992, the British High Commissioner in Port Louis, Mr. Michael Howell, wrote to the Prime Minister of Mauritius, Sir Anerood Jugnauth, as follows:

> The British Government has always acknowledged however that Mauritius has a legitimate interest in the future of these islands and recognises the Government of the Republic of Mauritius as the only State which has a right to assert a claim to sovereignty when the United Kingdom relinquishes its own sovereignty.

[534] Letter from United Kingdom to Mauritius, 3 May 1973 (Annex UKCM-24).

[535] Letter dated 15 March 1976 from Parliamentary Under Secretary of State, UK Foreign and Commonwealth Office, to the Mauritius High Commissioner, London (Annex MM-78).

[536] Hansard, House of Commons Debates, 11 July 1980, vol. 988 c314W (Annex MM-94).

> The British Government has therefore given an undertaking to the Government of the Republic of Mauritius that, when the islands are no longer needed for the defence purposes of the United Kingdom and the United States, they will be ceded to Mauritius. There will be no sale or transfer by the British Government to a third party or any payment or financial obligation by Mauritius as a condition of such transfer.[537]

(*d*) On 10 November 1997, the Foreign Secretary of the United Kingdom, Mr. Robin Cook, wrote to the Prime Minister of Mauritius, Dr. Navinchandra Ramgoolam, as follows:

> I am pleased to reaffirm, as was publicly stated in 1992 under the previous Administration, the Territory will be ceded to Mauritius when no longer required for defence purposes.[538]

(*e*) On 12 December 2003, the Parliamentary under Secretary of State at the United Kingdom's Foreign & Commonwealth Office, Mr. Bill Rammell, wrote to the Mauritian Minister of Foreign Affairs and Regional Cooperation, the Honourable AK Gayan MLA as follows:

> [s]uccessive British Governments have given undertakings to the Government of Mauritius that the Territory will be ceded when no longer required for defence purposes subject to the requirements of international law. This remains the case.[539]

431. The United Kingdom has similarly renewed its commitment concerning the benefit of any minerals or oil discovered in or near the Chagos Archipelago:

(*a*) In response to a Note Verbale from the Mauritian Prime Minister's Office dated 19 November 1969,[540] the British High Commission clarified that the scope of the undertaking concerning minerals or oil meant "that the benefit of any minerals or oil discovered in or near the Chagos Archipelago should revert to the Government of Mauritius".[541] The United Kingdom further explained:

> It is not considered that the wording of the understanding can be construed as indicating any intention that ownership of minerals or oil in the areas in question should be vested in the

---

[537] Letter dated 1 July 1992 from the British High Commissioner, Port Louis, to the Prime Minister of Mauritius (Annex MM-103).

[538] Letter dated 10 November 1997 from the UK Secretary of State for Foreign and Commonwealth Affairs to the Prime Minister of Mauritius (Annex MM-105).

[539] Letter dated 12 December 2003 from the Minister responsible for Overseas Territories, UK Foreign and Commonwealth Office to the Minister of Foreign Affairs and Regional Cooperation, Mauritius (Annex MM-124).

[540] Note Verbale dated 19 November 1969 from the Prime Minister's Office (External Affairs Division), Mauritius to the British High Commission, Port Louis, No. 51/69 (17781/16/8) (Annex MM-54).

[541] Note Verbale dated 18 December 1969 from the British High Commission, Port Louis, to the Prime Minister's Office (External Affairs Division), Mauritius (Annex MM-55).

> Government of Mauritius or that the Authorities of Mauritius should have any right to legislate with respect to or otherwise regulate matters relating to the ownership, exploration or exploitation of such minerals or oil ...[542]

(*b*) Notwithstanding this initial disagreement over the interpretation of the undertaking, Mauritius subsequently accepted the British position on the content of the oil and minerals undertaking in 1973.[543]

(*c*) The undertaking was renewed on 1 July 1992 by the British High Commissioner in Port Louis, Mr. Michael Howell, to Prime Minister Sir Anerood Jugnauth:

> The British Government also reaffirms its undertaking that there is no intention of permitting prospecting for minerals and oils while the islands remain British. There are no plans to establish an exclusive economic zone around the Chagos islands.[544]

(*d*) On 10 November 1997 the undertaking was again renewed by the Foreign Secretary of the United Kingdom, Mr. Robin Cook, to the Prime Minister of Mauritius, Dr. Navinchandra Ramgoolam:

> I also reaffirm that this Government has no intention of permitting the prospecting for oil and minerals while the Territory remains British, and acknowledge that any oil and mineral rights will revert to Mauritius when the Territory is ceded.[545]

432. With respect to fishing rights, the Tribunal notes that—notwithstanding the Parties' disagreement over the scope of those rights—the United Kingdom has recognized the existence of fishing rights and reaffirmed its obligations in this regard. Of particular significance is the manner in which the United Kingdom has acted consistently with its undertaking in connection with its regulation of fishing in Chagos waters over several decades and the treatment of Mauritian vessels, being given fishing licences at no cost in the waters of the Archipelago for many years until the no-take MPA was proclaimed.

433. When the fishing ordinance was adopted by the BIOT in 1971 (and subsequently amended in 1984), fishing within the 12 nautical mile zone around the Chagos Archipelago was prohibited with the exception of Mauritius, which was specifically designated in 1984 as a country whose vessels

[542] *Ibid.*; Pacific and Indian Ocean Department (Foreign and Commonwealth Office), Visit of Sir Seewoosagur Ramgoolam, Prime Minister of Mauritius, 4 February 1970, Speaking Note, 2 February 1970 (Annex MM-56). Mauritius notes that Annex MM-56 is a "composite exhibit, and attached at the end of this exhibit ... is a note dated 15 December 1969 from the British High Commissioner to the Prime Minister of Mauritius". *See* Final Transcript, 272:23–25.

[543] *See* Final Transcript, 1047:16–1049:21, *referring to* Final Transcript, 851:22–852:1.

[544] Letter dated 1 July 1992 from the British High Commissioner, Port Louis, to the Prime Minister of Mauritius (Annex MM-103).

[545] Letter dated 10 November 1997 from the UK Secretary of State for Foreign and Commonwealth Affairs to the Prime Minister of Mauritius (Annex MM-105).

could be issued licenses to fish and at no charge (see paragraph 118 above). In 1991, when the United Kingdom extended the fishery limits to 200 nautical miles, access to BIOT waters in the new 200-nautical mile limit was granted to Mauritian fishermen on the same terms as within the previous limits.[546] On 1 July 1992, a letter from the British High Commissioner, Mr. Michael Howell, to Prime Minister Sir Anerood Jugnauth acknowledged this long-standing commitment and the United Kingdom's intention to continue to honour this commitment in the following terms:

> The British Government has honoured the commitments entered into in 1965 to use its good offices with the United States Government to ensure that fishing rights would remain available to Mauritius as far as practicable. It has issued free licences for Mauritius fishing vessels to enter both the original 12 mile fishing zone of the territory and now the wider waters of the exclusive fishing zone. It will continue to do so, provided that the Mauritian vessels respect the licence conditions laid down to ensure proper conservation of local fishing resources.[547]

This system remained in place until the introduction of the MPA.

iv. Estoppel, Representation, and Reliance

434. All told, the Tribunal is faced with undertakings given as part of an agreement concluded in 1965 between the United Kingdom and one of its colonies, that became a matter of international law upon the independence of Mauritius, and that were reaffirmed in correspondence between the Parties in the decades since independence.

435. Estoppel is a general principle of law that serves to ensure, in the words of Lord McNair, "that international jurisprudence has a place for some recognition of the principle that a State cannot blow hot and cold—*allegans contraria non audiendus est*."[548] The principle stems from the general requirement that States act in their mutual relations in good faith and is designed to protect the legitimate expectations of a State that acts in reliance upon the representations of another. The principle as it exists in international law was well summarized by Judge Spender in the *Temple of Preah Vihear*:

> the principle [of estoppel] operates to prevent a State contesting before the Court a situation contrary to a clear and unequivocal representation previously made by it to another State, either expressly or impliedly, on which representation the other State was, in the circumstances, entitled to rely and in fact did rely, and as a result the other State has been prejudiced or the State making it has secured some benefit or advantage for itself.

[546] Telegram from R.G. Wells (East African Department) to M.E. Howell (Port Louis), 3 April 1992 (Annex UKR-40).

[547] Letter dated 1 July 1992 from the British High Commissioner, Port Louis, to the Prime Minister of Mauritius (Annex MM-103).

[548] A.D. McNair, "The Legality of the Occupation of the Ruhr", 5 *British Year Book of International Law* 17, 35 (1924).

((Cambodia v. *Thailand), Judgment of* 15 *June 1962, Dissenting Opinion of Judge Spender, I.C.J. Reports 1962*, p. 101 at pp. 143–44).

436. Estoppel in international law differs from "complicated classifications, modalities, species, sub-species and procedural features" of its municipal law counterpart (*Temple of Preah Vihear (Cambodia* v. *Thailand), Judgment of* 15 *June 1962, Separate Opinion of Vice President Alfaro, I.C.J. Reports 1962*, p. 39; *see also ibid., Separate Opinion of Sir Gerald Fitzmaurice, I.C.J. Reports 1962*, p. 52 at p. 62), but its frequent invocation in international proceedings has added definition to the scope of the principle. The Permanent Court of International Justice declined to apply the principle in *Serbian Loans*, noting the absence of a "clear and unequivocal representation by the bondholders upon which the debtor State was entitled to rely and has relied" (*Payment of Various Serbian Loans Issued in France, Judgment of* 12 *July 1929, P.C.I.J. Series A, Nos. 20/21*, p. 5 at p. 39). In *Barcelona Traction, Light and Power Company, Limited*, the Court dismissed a Spanish claim of estoppel in the absence of evidence that "any true prejudice was suffered by the Respondent" (*(Belgium* v. *Spain) Preliminary Objections, Judgment, I.C.J. Reports 1964*, p. 3 at p. 25) and a requirement of detrimental reliance has featured repeatedly in the Court's subsequent judgments.[549] In *Gulf of Maine*, the Court held that representations must be made by an official authorized to commit his or her government (*Delimitation of the Maritime Boundary in the Gulf of Maine Area (Canada v United States of America), Judgment of* 12 *October 1984, I.C.J. Reports 1984*, p. 246 at pp. 307–308). And in *North Sea Continental Shelf*, the Court declined to find estoppel in the absence of what it described as "past conduct, declarations, etc., which not only clearly and consistently evinced [the representation alleged as the basis for estoppel], but also had caused [the opposing parties], in reliance on such conduct, detrimentally to change position or suffer some prejudice" (*(Federal Republic of Germany/Denmark; Federal Republic of Germany/Netherlands), Judgment, I.C.J. Reports 1969*, p. 3 at p. 26, para. 30).

437. Additionally—and in contrast to at least some forms of estoppel in municipal law—the principle in international law does not distinguish between representations as to existing facts and those regarding promises of future action or declarations of law. The question of estoppel in *North Sea Continental Shelf* concerned whether the Federal Republic of Germany had clearly and consistently demonstrated an acceptance of the legal regime set out in the 1958 Convention on the Continental Shelf to which it had not acceded. The ICJ declined to reach such a finding, not on the grounds that the subject matter was incapable of leading to estoppel, but rather insofar as neither the alleged

[549] *See Military and Paramilitary Activities in and against Nicaragua (Nicaragua v United States of America) (Jurisdiction) I.C.J. Reports 1984*, p. 392 at p. 414; *Land, Island and Maritime Frontier Dispute (El Salvador v Honduras) (Application by Nicaragua to Intervene) I.C.J. Reports 1990*, p. 92 at p. 118; *Land and Maritime Boundary between Cameroon and Nigeria (Cameroon v Nigeria) (Merits) I.C.J. Reports 1998*, p. 275 at p. 304; *see also* D.W. Bowett, "Estoppel before International Tribunals and Its Relation to Acquiescence," *British Yearbook of International Law*, Vol. 33, p. 176 (1957).

representation, nor the purported reliance, were unequivocally apparent on the facts presented (*North Sea Continental Shelf (Federal Republic of Germany/Denmark; Federal Republic of Germany/Netherlands), Judgment, I.C.J. Reports 1969*, p. 3 at p. 26, paras. 31–32). The Tribunal is of the view that the forms of representation capable of giving rise to estoppel are not strictly defined in international law and notes in particular the observation of Judge Fitzmaurice regarding the interplay between estoppel and undertakings given by a State:

> The real field of operation, therefore, of the rule of preclusion or estoppel, *stricto sensu*, in the present context, is where it is possible that the party concerned did not give the undertaking or accept the obligation in question (or there is room for doubt whether it did), but where that party's subsequent conduct has been such, and has had such consequences, that it cannot be allowed to deny the existence of an undertaking, or that it is bound.
>
> *Temple of Preah Vihear (Cambodia* v. *Thailand), Judgment of* 15 *June 1962, Separate Opinion of Sir Gerald Fitzmaurice, I.C.J. Reports 1962*, p. 52 at p. 63).

438. Further to this jurisprudence, estoppel may be invoked where (*a*) a State has made clear and consistent representations, by word, conduct, or silence; (*b*) such representations were made through an agent authorized to speak for the State with respect to the matter in question; (*c*) the State invoking estoppel was induced by such representations to act to its detriment, to suffer a prejudice, or to convey a benefit upon the representing State; and (*d*) such reliance was legitimate, as the representation was one on which that State was entitled to rely.

439. In the present case, the Tribunal considers the first two elements of estoppel to have been readily fulfilled. As set out in the preceding section, the United Kingdom made repeated representations in respect of all three undertakings over the course of over 40 years. These representations took the form both of confirmation that the United Kingdom had given an undertaking in the past (i.e., "[t]he British Government has therefore given an undertaking to the Government of the Republic of Mauritius that, when the islands are no longer needed for the defence purposes of the United Kingdom and the United States, they will be ceded to Mauritius"[550]) and of independent promises (i.e., "the Territory will be ceded to Mauritius when no longer required for defence purposes"[551]), and were made in statements by the Prime Minister and Foreign Secretary of the United Kingdom, who were unequivocally authorized to speak for it on this matter. The Tribunal also considers that the United Kingdom's consistent, unvaried practice of permitting Mauritian fishing in the waters of the Archipelago constituted a representation by conduct that such fishing

---

[550] Letter dated 1 July 1992 from the British High Commissioner, Port Louis, to the Prime Minister of Mauritius (Annex MM-103).

[551] Letter dated 10 November 1997 from the UK Secretary of State for Foreign and Commonwealth Affairs to the Prime Minister of Mauritius (Annex MM-105).

rights would be continued, not necessarily unconditionally, but at least in the absence of an exceptional change of circumstances. The remaining questions are therefore whether Mauritius did in fact rely upon these representations to its detriment and, if so, whether such reliance was legitimate.

(a) Whether Mauritius relied to its detriment on the United Kingdom's representations

440. The Tribunal considers that evidence of opportunities foregone in reliance upon a representation constitutes one of the clearest forms of detrimental reliance, although a benefit conveyed on the representing State will also suffice. With respect to the undertakings eventually to return the Chagos Archipelago when no longer required for defence purposes and to preserve the benefit of mineral and petroleum resources for Mauritius, pending return, the Tribunal notes that Mauritius, during the January 2009 bilateral talks, declined an express offer to begin the process of formalizing the United Kingdom's undertakings in the form of a treaty. Mauritius considered instead that the existing undertakings were sufficient. The United Kingdom's record of the meeting provides that –

> The UK delegation reiterated its sovereignty position, suggested formalising this in a Treaty while pointing out that this would not be easy for us to achieve.
>
> [...]
>
> In response to the proposed Treaty, the Mauritian delegation said that this was not necessary. They had our government's undertakings already. In any case, an open-ended Treaty would not serve any purpose. The Treaty would need to include a definite time when the Chagos Archipelago would be ceded.[552]

Mauritius' record of the same conversation provides as follows:

> *Mr. Colin Roberts*
>
> We have undertaken to cede the territory to Mauritius when no longer required. We have also suggested a sort of formalising it into a treaty.
>
> [...]
>
> *Mr. Seeballuck*
>
> Chair, on item (5) we humbly believe that a treaty which would [sic] restrict merely to cede a territory when no longer required would not reflect any step forward on the issue. We have several letters from the UK Government, replies given to questions in the House of Commons where the UK Government has stated that the Chagos Archipelago will revert to Mauritius when no longer required for military purposes. And we have no reason to put in doubt the contents of these documents.

---

552 UK Foreign and Commonwealth Office, Overseas Territories Directorate, "British Indian Ocean Territory: UK/Mauritius Talks", 14 January 2009 (Annex MR-128).

> A treaty that would simply say that it will cede a territory when no longer required—we consider that unless the treaty includes a definite time—an open ended treaty will not be for any benefit.
>
> [...][553]

441. There is no evidence that the United Kingdom corrected Mauritius' view on the equivalence of the undertakings with a treaty commitment.

442. Stepping back from this specific example, however, the Tribunal is also of the view that Mauritius' entire course of conduct with respect to the Chagos Archipelago was undertaken in reliance on the full package of undertakings given at Lancaster House. From independence until at least 1980, Mauritius was silent as to the legitimacy of detachment. Since 1980, while the dispute over sovereignty has assumed an increasingly prominent position in the two States' bilateral relations, Mauritius and the United Kingdom have nevertheless maintained a productive and friendly relationship on other matters, often pursuant to a sovereignty umbrella. The Tribunal considers this initial silence, and Mauritius' comparatively restrained assertion of its sovereignty claim thereafter, to have been a result of the undertakings given by the United Kingdom. In so relying, Mauritius forewent the opportunity of asserting its sovereignty claim more aggressively, in particular in the early years following independence, when sentiments in favour of decolonization were still running high, before the existence of the BIOT as an independent entity had been firmly established, and at the time when portions of the BIOT were even being returned to the Seychelles. Had the package of undertakings not been given, the Tribunal considers it beyond question that Mauritius would have asserted its claim to the Archipelago earlier and more directly, and would have withheld its cooperation in other areas of the Parties' bilateral relations, as indeed occurred in 2009 and 2010 when the United Kingdom appeared (at least to Mauritius) to have set aside its concern for Mauritian rights in favour of the pursuit of the MPA.

443. Accordingly, the Tribunal concludes that Mauritius relied, both specifically and generally, on the package of undertakings given and reaffirmed by the United Kingdom. In so doing, Mauritius forewent the opportunity of pressing its sovereignty claim in the initial years following independence, forewent the United Kingdom's offer to conclude a treaty formalizing the commitment to eventually return the archipelago, and conveyed a benefit on the United Kingdom through the cooperation on other matters that the Tribunal believes would otherwise have been withheld.

444. Like the United Kingdom's repetition of the undertakings, Mauritius' reliance continued after it began actively to assert a claim to sovereignty over the Archipelago and therefore stands apart from the legal status of the

[553] Ministry of Foreign Affairs, Regional Integration and International Trade, Mauritius, "Meeting of Officials on the Chagos Archipelago/British Indian Ocean Territory held at the Foreign and Commonwealth Office, London, Wednesday 14 January 2009, 10 a.m.", 23 January 2009 (Annex MR-129).

undertakings at the time they were first given. In this respect, the Tribunal notes with approval Judge Fitzmaurice's observation (see paragraph 437 above) that estoppel is most at home in situations in which the existence of a formal agreement may be in doubt, but the course of the Parties' subsequent conduct has consistently been as though such an agreement existed (*Temple of Preah Vihear (Cambodia* v. *Thailand), Judgment of* 15 *June 1962, Separate Opinion of Sir Gerald Fitzmaurice, I.C.J. Reports 1962*, p. 52 at p. 63).

(b) Whether Mauritius was entitled to rely upon the United Kingdom's representations

445. Having concluded that Mauritius did in fact rely upon all three of the undertakings at issue in these proceedings, the Tribunal turns to the question of whether Mauritius was entitled to so rely, or—phrased differently—whether such reliance was legitimate. Not all reliance, even to the clear detriment of a State, suffices to create grounds for estoppel. A State that elects to rely to its detriment upon an expressly non-binding agreement does not, by so doing, achieve a binding commitment by way of estoppel. Such reliance is not legitimate. Nor does a State that relies upon an expressly revocable commitment render that commitment irrevocable.

446. At the same time, the Tribunal does not consider that a representation must take the form of a binding unilateral declaration before a State may legitimately rely on it. To consider otherwise would be to erase any distinction between estoppel and the doctrine on binding unilateral acts. While the ILC excluded estoppel from the scope of its study on unilateral acts, the course of its debates clearly recognized the distinct legal origins of the two related concepts:

> the distinction between the two [i.e., between a unilaterally binding promise and estoppel] consists in the way the obligation is created: whereas a promise is a legal act, the obligation arising from the manifestation of the author's will, estoppel acquires its effect, not from that will as such, but from the representation of the author's will made in good faith by the third party.[554]

In the course of these proceedings, the Parties argued for and against the existence of one or more binding unilateral acts by reference to the *Nuclear Tests* cases (*(Australia* v. *France), Judgment of* 20 *December 1974, I.C.J. Reports 1974*, p. 253; *(New Zealand* v. *France), Judgment of* 20 *December 1974, I.C.J. Reports 1974*, p. 457). The sphere of estoppel, however, is not that of unequivocally binding commitments (for which a finding of estoppel would in any event be unnecessary (see *Temple of Preah Vihear (Cambodia* v. *Thailand), Judgment of* 15 *June 1962, Separate Opinion of Sir Gerald Fitzmaurice, I.C.J. Reports 1962*, p. 52 at p. 63)), but is instead concerned with the grey area of representations and commitments whose original legal intent may be

[554] V.R. Cedeño, "Seventh Report on Unilateral Acts of States," UN Doc. A/CN.4/542 at para. 17 (22 April 2004).

ambiguous or obscure, but which, in light of the reliance placed upon them, warrant recognition in international law.

447. On the facts before it, the Tribunal considers that Mauritius was entitled to rely upon the representations made by the United Kingdom which were consistently reiterated after independence in terms which were capable of suggesting a legally binding commitment and which were clearly understood in such a way. The Tribunal also sees no evidence that Mauritius should have considered the United Kingdom's undertakings revocable. The ILC considered the question of revocability generally in the course of its examination of unilateral acts. In the absence of an express indication, the ILC concluded that a unilateral promise may not be revoked arbitrarily and that a significant factor in whether revocation would be considered arbitrary is "[t]he extent to which those to whom the obligations are owed have relied on such obligations."[555] The Tribunal considers this to be self-evident and a background assumption that would have guided Mauritius' reaction to the United Kingdom's representations. Where, as here, the United Kingdom has repeatedly committed to a future course of action with knowledge that another State is acting in reliance upon that commitment, both Mauritius and the Tribunal are entitled to presume that the United Kingdom did not consider such commitments freely revocable. To assume otherwise would be contrary to the "well established principle of law according to which bad faith is not presumed" (*Affaire du lac Lanoux (Spain/France), Award of 16 November 1957*, RIAA, Vol. XII, p. 281 at p. 305).[556]

* * *

448. On the basis of the foregoing, the Tribunal concludes that, after its independence in 1968, Mauritius was entitled to and did rely upon the Lancaster House Undertakings to (*a*) return the Chagos Archipelago to Mauritius when no longer needed for defence purposes; (*b*) preserve the benefit of any minerals or oil discovered in or near the Chagos Archipelago for the Mauritius Government; and (*c*) ensure that fishing rights in the Chagos Archipelago would remain available to the Mauritius Government as far as practicable. The Tribunal, therefore, holds that the United Kingdom is estopped from denying the binding effect of these commitments, which the Tribunal will treat as binding on the United Kingdom in view of their repeated reaffirmation after 1968.

(b) The Scope of the Lancaster House Undertaking with Respect to Fishing Rights

449. The Tribunal has found that the United Kingdom's undertaking regarding fishing rights was legally binding on the United Kingdom, yet the

---

[555] International Law Commission, *Guiding Principles Applicable to Unilateral Declarations of States Capable of Creating Legal Obligations*, at principle 10(b).

[556] In the original French text of this decision: "il est un principe général de droit bien établi selon lequel la mauvaise foi ne se présume pas."

Parties remain in disagreement as to what this undertaking entailed. Moreover, the Parties agree that at the time fishing rights were included in the record of the Lancaster House Meeting, the content of the undertaking was unclear to the participants themselves. Since then, the Parties have adopted diametrically opposed views. Mauritius advocates "the maximum possible benefit" within the constraints imposed by the qualifying terms "use of good offices" and "as far as practicable". The United Kingdom, in contrast, argues for a narrow interpretation by reference to the very limited fishing practice in 1965 and the express wording of the undertaking. Ultimately, the Tribunal recalls the Parties' agreement that "[i]t is for the Tribunal to interpret [the Lancaster House Undertakings] and to determine whether they establish legal obligations on the United Kingdom and, if so, what those obligations are."[557]

450. As an initial matter, the Tribunal is not convinced that the scope of the undertaking can, as the United Kingdom suggests, be determined by reference to the type and scale of fishing actually practised in the Archipelago at the time of the undertaking. The Tribunal notes in particular:

(*a*) The existence of clear, forward-looking statements, expressed by Sir Seewoosagur Ramgoolam and other Mauritian Ministers during negotiations, regarding an intent to secure future benefits in the form of sugar quotas and trade arrangements;

(*b*) The fact that other undertakings given at Lancaster House related to facilities not yet constructed (such as the air strip) and concerned future events, including some in the potentially distant future, such as the eventual return of the Archipelago to Mauritius;

(*c*) The clear intent of the Secretary of State for the Colonies to "secure the maximum benefit for Mauritius", and the subsequent conduct of the British Government in carrying this out so as to assure the maximum possible fishing rights for Mauritius over the maximum possible area, as far as practicable, limited only by specific defence needs at particular islands;[558]

(*d*) The acknowledgement by the Commonwealth Office that –

> we are very much concerned to keep in mind the importance of the fishing grounds to Mauritius, for instance the possible importance of fishing in Chagos as a source of food, in view of the rapidly increasing population;[559]

(*e*) The recognition by the United Kingdom that its reference to contemporaneous fishing practices was "about appreciating the

[557] Final Transcript, 256:10–12; The United Kingdom's Rejoinder, para. 8.10.

[558] Minute by Mr. Fairclough of the Colonial Office, 15 March 1966 (Annex UKCM-16); Letter dated 12 July 1967 from the UK Commonwealth Office to the Governor of Mauritius, FCO 16/226 (Annex MM-50/MR-60).

[559] Letter dated 12 July 1967 from the UK Commonwealth Office to the Governor of Mauritius, FCO 16/226 (Annex MM-50/MR-60).

context of discussions in 1965 and understanding why the issue of fishing rights received only *very* limited attention".[560]

451. Addressing the Parties' positions in turn, the Tribunal does not consider that Mauritius' rights pursuant to the undertaking amount to a "perpetual and absolute right" to fish. If nothing else, such a conclusion is precluded by the express qualifying terms in the undertaking itself. At the same time, the Tribunal does not accept that the United Kingdom undertook merely to give "preference with respect to fishing rights to the extent such were granted."[561] The Tribunal considers the unique position of Mauritius in comparison to third States to be significant. Mauritius was granted rights in the territorial sea and contiguous zone even when other States were not and continued to receive licenses when other States did not. As the fishing regime surrounding the Archipelago developed and expanded, Mauritius continued to enjoy priority in the extended zones. Rather than representing the United Kingdom's understanding of its "moral obligation",[562] the Tribunal considers the best explanation for the United Kingdom's actions to be the recognition of an obligation to respect Mauritius' rights.

452. In the Tribunal's view, the extent of Mauritius' rights and the United Kingdom's obligations should, as far as possible, be interpreted by reference to the express words of the undertaking. The Tribunal is also guided by what the United Kingdom itself considered to have been the extent of its obligation. In this context, the Tribunal considers the undertaking with respect to fishing rights to be a positive obligation subject to some limitations. The positive aspect of the obligation is found in the words "ensure" and "would remain available" whereas the limitations are found in the words "use their good offices with the U.S. Government" and "as far as practicable". The connection to the United States Government is inescapable, considering the totality of the arrangement to detach the Archipelago for the promotion of defence purposes as requested by the United States. Thus, the qualifying words "use their good offices with the U.S. Government" are to be understood by reference to the defence needs of the United States. Nevertheless, the Tribunal considers that the United Kingdom retained the ultimate discretion to determine how any conflict between U.S. defence needs and Mauritian fishing rights would be resolved.[563]

453. Subject to these limitations, the United Kingdom is under a positive obligation to "ensure" that fishing rights "would remain available" to Mauritius. The United Kingdom has acted consistently over a number of dec-

[560] Final Transcript, 1295:17–1296:3, *referring to* Debate in Mauritius' Legislative Assembly of 21 December 1965 (Annex UKCM-15).

[561] Final Transcript, 842:23.

[562] Final Transcript: 1296:17.

[563] The Tribunal considers this interpretation to be entirely consistent with the existence of qualifying words and conditions in the terms of the other undertakings. The obligation to return the Archipelago is conditioned upon the disappearance of defence needs. In turn, the obligation to return the benefit of any minerals or oil to the Mauritius Government is conditioned upon the eventual return of the Archipelago itself.

ades to comply with this obligation, most significantly reflected in permitting Mauritius to fish in the 3 nautical mile territorial sea and in the maritime zones beyond as they moved progressively out to 200 nautical miles. On each occasion, the United Kingdom has "ensured" that fishing rights "would remain available" on the same terms, even as other States' rights were being curtailed.

454. The Tribunal considers the introduction of the licensing system pursuant to the Fishing Ordinances of 1971 and 1984, to be highly relevant to the United Kingdom's compliance with its obligation. Having "used its good offices with the United States" to "ensure" that fishing in the prohibited zones "would remain available" to Mauritius, the United Kingdom exercised its discretion permitted by the qualifying terms "as far as practicable" to determine the *manner* in which fishing rights were granted to Mauritius (i.e., subject to licenses granted free of charge).

455. In all the circumstances, the Tribunal is of the view that Mauritius enjoyed rights to fish in the waters of the Chagos Archipelago—in particular in the territorial sea with which the Tribunal is solely concerned—subject to licences issued freely by the BIOT administration to Mauritian-flagged vessels, but dependent on the overarching defence needs of the United States and the United Kingdom's discretion in the routine management of the fishery. Such discretion was nevertheless to be exercised consistently with the obligation to "ensure" that fishing rights "would remain available".

(c) Mauritius' Claim to Traditional Fishing Rights in the Territorial Sea

456. In light of the Tribunal's conclusion that Mauritius is entitled to fishing rights in the Territorial Sea pursuant to the United Kingdom's undertaking at Lancaster House, the Tribunal considers it unnecessary to address the question of whether Mauritius possessed traditional fishing rights independently of any commitment by the United Kingdom.

B. The Interpretation and Application of Articles 2(3), 56(2), 194 and 300 of the Convention

457. The Parties are at odds over the interpretation and application of the various Articles of the Convention. Mauritius claims that the United Kingdom has violated Articles 2(3), 56(2), 194 and 300 in connection with its declaration of the MPA on 1 April 2010. In particular, Mauritius considers that the extinction of its rights in the territorial sea "with immediate effect, without notice, without consultation" to have been a violation of Article 2(3).[564] Mauritius further considers the manner in which the United Kingdom conducted itself prior to the declaration of the MPA to have violated the United King-

[564] Final Transcript, 290:14 to 291:2.

dom's obligation to accord due regard, pursuant to Article 56(2), to Mauritius' rights and to endeavour to harmonize its policies on marine pollution pursuant Article 194. The crux of Mauritius' complaint is that –

> The UK did not inform Mauritius of its plans; it provided Mauritius with inaccurate information; and it ignored Mauritius' repeated calls for bilateral consultations, insisting on proceeding instead with a fundamentally flawed Public Consultation all despite a commitment by the UK Prime Minister to his Mauritian counterpart that the MPA would be put on hold.[565]

Finally, Mauritius submits that the MPA was not actually declared in pursuit of the environmental objectives that were used to justify it and that its declaration constitutes an abuse of rights within the context of Article 300.

458. The United Kingdom neither accepts Mauritius' interpretation of the Convention nor concedes that it has violated any obligation thereunder. According to the United Kingdom, Article 2(3) does not impose an obligation of compliance, and the meaning of "due regard" in Article 56(2) does not mean to "give effect to" the rights of other States.[566] The United Kingdom similarly disputes that Article 194 imposes a duty with respect to marine pollution and argues that Article 300 applies only in conjunction with the violation of another provision of the Convention. In any event, the United Kingdom considers the fulsome bilateral exchanges and public consultations regarding the establishment of the MPA to have satisfied any potentially applicable obligation.

1. Parties' Arguments

(a) The Interpretation and Application of Article 2(3)

459. Article 2(3) of the Convention provides as follows:

> **Article 2**
>
> *Legal status of the territorial sea, of the air space over the territorial sea and of its bed and subsoil*
>
> [...]
>
> 3. The sovereignty over the territorial sea is exercised subject to this Convention and to other rules of international law.

Mauritius' Position

460. According to Mauritius, Article 2(3) of the Convention imposes an obligation of compliance that requires the United Kingdom to exercise

[565] Final Transcript, 336:18 to 337:2.

[566] Final Transcript, 1104:22 to 1105:8.

its sovereignty "limited by" [567] obligations arising out of the Convention and "other rules of international law." This interpretation is based on the ordinary meaning of the provision,[568] Mauritius submits, and is consistent with the intention of the drafters of the 1958 Convention on the Territorial Sea and the Contiguous Zone and the 1982 Convention. [569] Mauritius notes that "there is no material difference [in the language] between the two" treaties.[570]

461. Mauritius relies on the ILC's commentary on the 1958 Convention on the Territorial Sea to emphasise that the intended purpose of Article 2(3) is to operate as a reservation.[571] Mauritius does not accept that the provision is "merely descriptive",[572] and submits that an obligation of compliance is apparent from the French[573] and Russian[574] texts of the Convention. Mauritius also notes that a review of comparable provisions establishes that the Convention's use of "is" and "shall" is not consistent and that an obligation of compliance is not limited to the latter terminology.[575]

462. Turning to the interpretation of the phrase "other rules of international law," Mauritius argues that these are "broad and open-ended words," which are neither intended to be limitative,[576] nor expressly qualified.[577] The four categories of those "other rules of international law", Mauritius submits, are –

(i) the rules of international law that require a coastal State to respect traditional fishing rights, as affirmed in the UK's undertakings;

(ii) the rule of international law that requires a State to respect its undertakings more generally, including those that protect fishing and mineral rights;

(iii) the rule of international law that requires a State to comply with a commitment it has given, through its head of government, to the head of government of another State; and

(iv) the rule of international law that requires a coastal State to consult in regard to matters that can affect the rights of another State.[578]

463. All of these, according to Mauritius, were breached by the United Kingdom when:

---

567 Final Transcript, 291:23 to 292:2.

568 Final Transcript, 294:2–14.

569 Mauritius' Reply, paras. 6.8–6.9; Final Transcript, 294:15–22.

570 Final Transcript, 291:10–16.

571 Final Transcript, 295:1–20.

572 Final Transcript, 868:21 to 869:2.

573 Mauritius' Reply, paras. 6.10, 6.12; Final Transcript, 296:7–16.

574 Mauritius' Reply, para. 6.11; Final Transcript, 297:2–5.

575 Mauritius' Reply, paras. 6.13–6.14; Final Transcript, 297:20–22.

576 Final Transcript, 299:1–9.

577 Final Transcript, 299:9–12.

578 Final Transcript, 292:4–11.

> In April 2010 it purported to extinguish the entirety of Mauritius' fishing rights, whether traditional or other, whether inshore, or within three miles of the coast, or within 12 miles of the coast, or within 200 miles of the coast. In April 2010 by that decision, the UK failed to respect the undertakings that it had, on its own account, given to Mauritius. In April 2010 it also failed to honour the commitment that was given by Prime Minister Gordon Brown to Prime Minister Ramgoolam in November 2009 that the "MPA" would be put "on hold". In the period leading up to the announcement of the decision taken in April 2010, as we have seen, the United Kingdom manifestly failed to consult with Mauritius, instead Mauritius was presented with a *fait accompli*, it was communicated in a telephone call unexpectedly on the morning of 1 April 2010 by Mr. David Miliband to Prime Minister Ramgoolam. By establishing and applying the "MPA" in this manner which purports to deny the exercise by Mauritius of its rights, the UK, we say, is in manifest violation of Article 2(3) of the Convention.[579]

The United Kingdom's Position

464. The United Kingdom's primary position is that the Lancaster House Undertakings in relation to fishing rights are not binding and are therefore irrelevant to any application of Article 2(3).[580] The Tribunal has already comprehensively addressed this issue.

465. Nevertheless, the United Kingdom submits that "there are two points of disagreement [concerning the interpretation of Article 2(3)]—over the meaning of 'is exercised' and, then, over the intended scope of 'other rules of international law.'"[581]

466. According to the United Kingdom, Article 2(3) of the Convention is "descriptive rather than executory".[582] The United Kingdom argues that the ILC Commentary on the 1958 Convention on the Territorial Sea—which Mauritius has invited the Tribunal to consider—"is more suggestive of the wording being descriptive as opposed to establishing any obligation of compliance."[583] Moreover, the United Kingdom considers that the other treaty provisions relied on by Mauritius as a point of linguistic comparison must be examined individually and the specific wording considered in context.[584] The United Kingdom also disputes that any point regarding binding intent can be derived from the French text of the Convention.[585]

579 Final Transcript, 293:6–18.

580 Final Transcript, 828:14–17.

581 Final Transcript, 869:3–4.

582 Final Transcript, 869:10–13.

583 Final Transcript, 870:1–4.

584 Final Transcript, 872:6–19.

585 Final Transcript, 872:23 to 873:15.

467. The United Kingdom maintains that the phrase "other rules of international law" is "correctly interpreted as a reference to general rules of international law",[586] noting the explanation in the ILC's 1956 Report to the General Assembly that –

> Incidents in the territorial sea raising legal questions are also governed by the general rules of international law, and these cannot be specially codified in the present draft for the purposes of their application to the territorial sea. That is why 'other rules of international law' are mentioned in addition to the provisions contained in the present articles.[587]

Moreover, there is nothing to suggest that the drafters intended to establish "an entirely open-ended obligation of compliance with the entirety of international law in the territorial sea".[588] Such a separate "free-standing and unlimited" obligation, the United Kingdom contends, would have been exceptional, and the drafters would have "at least ... used the language of obligation ... as used in other provisions of the Convention."[589]

468. The United Kingdom rejects the existence of a customary law obligation to consult with other States that would apply by way of Article 2(3).[590] Unlike established precedents requiring consultation, the United Kingdom notes, the present case does not concern shared natural resources or common property resources, or relate to transboundary harm.[591] Even in the event that the Tribunal were to accept an obligation to consult in the present circumstances, the United Kingdom considers that the scope of such an obligation would be limited. According to the United Kingdom, the nearest analogy would be the rule on consultation in cases of transboundary harm codified by Principle 19 of the Rio Declaration on Environment and Development, which requires no more than the provision of prior and timely notification and relevant information, and consultation in good faith at an early stage.[592] Based on these criteria, the United Kingdom submits that it "did in fact consult Mauritius fully, at an early stage, with adequate information, and well before declaring the MPA... . [I]f there is any legal obligation to consult before exercising sovereign rights, ... then there has been no breach."[593]

469. Moreover, the United Kingdom rejects any notion that consultations must "continue indefinitely, ... [or] continue until the other party is

[586] The United Kingdom's Counter-Memorial, para. 8.6; Final Transcript, 870:9–15.

[587] The United Kingdom's Counter-Memorial, para. 8.6, *citing* Report of the International Law Commission covering the work of its eighth session, 23 April-4 July 1956, doc. A/3159, *YILC*, Vol. II, 253 at 265.

[588] Final Transcript, 871:9–11; *see also* The United Kingdom's Counter-Memorial, para. 8.5, The United Kingdom's Rejoinder, para. 8.2.

[589] The United Kingdom's Counter-Memorial, para. 8.5(*c*)–(*d*).

[590] Final Transcript, 890:4–7.

[591] Final Transcript, 876:21 to 877:6.

[592] Final Transcript, 878:3–7.

[593] Final Transcript, 878:14–17.

happy, any more than consultations under article 283 have to carry on indefinitely".[594] According to the United Kingdom, the necessary consultations took place in July 2009 and events subsequent thereto are "not material to Mauritius' case".[595] In all the circumstances, the United Kingdom considers that it –

> clearly did all it could to try to bring these consultations to an amicable and reasonable conclusion, but at the end of the day, it was Mauritius which unquestionably pulled out of the consultations as it said because it did not wish to see the Public Consultation proceed and that's why it terminated the bilateral consultations with the United Kingdom.[596]

(b) The Interpretation and Application of Article 56(2)

470. Article 56(2) of the Convention provides as follows:

> **Article 56**
>
> *Rights, jurisdiction and duties of the coastal State in the exclusive economic zone*
>
> [...]
>
> 2. In exercising its rights and performing its duties under this Convention in the exclusive economic zone, the coastal State shall have due regard to the rights and duties of other States and shall act in a manner compatible with the provisions of this Convention.
>
> [...]

Mauritius' Position

471. According to Mauritius, Article 56(2) of the Convention requires, as a mandatory and unambiguous obligation,[597] the United Kingdom to have "due regard" for the rights of other States in the exclusive economic zone. Mauritius argues that this formulation obliges the United Kingdom "to respect the rights of Mauritius".[598] Relying on the *Virginia Commentary* to the Convention, Mauritius considers that such due regard and respect requires the United Kingdom "to refrain from acts that interfere with [Mauritius' rights]".[599] Mauritius also relies on the ILC's commentary on the comparable provisions of the 1958 Convention on the High Seas, which "interpreted the obligation to have 'reasonable regard' for the interests of other States as meaning that, '[s]tates are bound to refrain from any acts that might adversely affect the

---

594 Final Transcript, 880:24–881:2.

595 Final Transcript, 881:14–16.

596 Final Transcript, 888:4–8.

597 Final Transcript, 322:7–17.

598 Final Transcript, 322:19–21.

599 Final Transcript, 323:1–5.

use of the high seas by nationals of other States.'"[600] Accordingly, Mauritius submits, "[b]y prohibiting Mauritius from exercising [its rights], the UK has breached Article 56(2). To put it in the terms of that provision, the UK has failed to have due regard for the rights of Mauritius."[601]

472. Mauritius rejects the United Kingdom's argument that the obligation to "have due regard" under Article 56(2) "stops well short of an obligation to give effect to such rights"[602] and extends only to "taking account" of or "giving consideration" to Mauritian rights.[603] In Mauritius' view, this interpretation is unsupported, and runs "contrary to its ordinary meaning as elucidated by the *Virginia Commentary* and the ILC, both of which require States to *refrain* from acting in ways that interfere with the rights of other states *regardless* of the strength of the reasons for doing so."[604]

473. In any event, Mauritius argues, Article 56(2) "necessarily implies an obligation to consult with other States when their rights or duties can be affected"[605] and the United Kingdom "has *also* violated that provision by failing to consult with Mauritius."[606] Mauritius relies on the *Fisheries Jurisdiction* cases (*(United Kingdom & Germany* v. *Iceland), I.C.J. Reports 1974*, p. 3 at p. 32, paras. 74–75; *(Federal Republic of Germany* v. *Iceland), I.C.J. Reports 1974*, p. 175 at p. 201, paras. 66–67), which held that the "obligation to negotiate flows from the very nature of the respective rights".[607] Although those cases concerned the exercise of preferential rights in the high seas, Mauritius argues that the underlying principle is that "where two States seek to exercise rights in a manner that may be incompatible, consultation is required."[608] The "proper balance in any particular set of circumstances", Mauritius asserts, "is achieved through consultation".[609]

474. Finally, Mauritius submits that "even under the standard posited by the United Kingdom, the obligation plainly has been breached."[610] In Mauritius' view, "[t]he United Kingdom did *not* … have 'good reasons for overriding the rights' of Mauritius to fish in the EEZ. It had no reasons at all, and … there is no indication that Mauritius' entitlement to fish, or its exercise of fishing rights, had any adverse environmental impacts."[611]

---

[600] Final Transcript, 323:7–10.

[601] Final Transcript, 332:12–14.

[602] The United Kingdom's Counter-Memorial, para. 8.36.

[603] Final Transcript, 1104:22 to 1105:8.

[604] Final Transcript, 1105:13–16.

[605] Final Transcript, 332:21–22.

[606] Final Transcript, 332:15–16.

[607] Final Transcript, 333:10–11.

[608] Final Transcript, 333:17–18

[609] Final Transcript, 333:20–21.

[610] Final Transcript, 1105:16–17.

[611] Final Transcript, 1105:17–21.

The United Kingdom's Position

475. With respect to Article 56, the United Kingdom submits that the "straightforward point" is that "the formulation 'shall have due regard to' does not somehow mean 'shall give effect to'".[612]

476. According to the United Kingdom, "'due regard' means what it says: It means take account of, give consideration to, do not ignore."[613] The United Kingdom also adopts the observation of the *Virginia Commentary* that "[t]he significance of [Article 56(2)] is that it balances the rights, jurisdiction and duties of the coastal State with the rights and duties of other States in the exclusive economic zone."[614] At the same time, the United Kingdom argues, "[i]f there are good reasons for overriding the rights of other States in the EEZ, then article 56(2) allows that."[615]

477. The United Kingdom does not accept that Article 56(2) imports an obligation to consult with other States. In the United Kingdom's view, if "having 'due regard' for the rights of other states means consulting them, we would suggest the text would have said so. Other articles of the Convention do expressly require consultation when the rights of other states may be affected."[616] "[I]t is quite possible," the United Kingdom argues, "to have regard for the rights of other states without consulting them: states do so on a daily basis."[617]

478. Against this standard, the United Kingdom submits that "there is no breach of article 56(2)."[618] Examining the record of discussions prior to the declaration of the MPA, the United Kingdom notes as follows:

- That there were meaningful and initially constructive consultations between the parties with regard to the declaration of the MPA.
- Secondly, that those consultations were undertaken well before the MPA declaration was adopted and in circumstances designed to give Mauritius every opportunity to influence the design and implementation of the project.
- The consultations ensured that the Mauritian government at all levels was fully informed of what was proposed and given the opportunity to respond.
- Mauritius' response was focused largely on joint management of resources and activities which could advance its sovereignty claim.

---

612 Final Transcript, 874:8–10.

613 Final Transcript, 822:12–13.

614 Final Transcript, 822:13–15, *quoting* M. Norquist, ed. *United Nations Convention on the Law of the Sea 1982: A Commentary*, Vol. II at p. 543 (1989).

615 Final Transcript, 822:17–18.

616 Final Transcript, 890:9–12.

617 Final Transcript, 890:13–14.

618 Final Transcript, 890:21.

- After October 2009 Mauritius chose not to engage in the Public Consultation or in further bilateral talks on the MPA proposal.
- It was only once that was clear and the Public Consultation was complete, did the United Kingdom proceed with the declaration of the MPA on 1 April 2010.[619]

479. The United Kingdom considers that –

> the evidence shows that the United Kingdom acted in good faith throughout these consultations in an attempt to engage Mauritius on the substance of the proposal, and that it did so before taking any decision to implement the MPA. It sought and it wished to continue discussions with Mauritius. The decision to end those consultations was taken not by the United Kingdom but by Mauritius.[620]

480. In short, the United Kingdom concludes, "both the internal United Kingdom documentary record on which Mauritius relies, and the bilateral negotiations to which the United Kingdom has referred, amply demonstrate that due regard has indeed been paid to the claimed rights of Mauritius."[621]

(c) *The Interpretation and Application of Article 194*

481. Article 194 of the Convention provides as follows:

> **Article 194**
>
> *Measures to prevent, reduce and control pollution of the marine environment*
>
> 1. States shall take, individually or jointly as appropriate, all measures consistent with this Convention that are necessary to prevent, reduce and control pollution of the marine environment from any source, using for this purpose the best practicable means at their disposal and in accordance with their capabilities, and they shall endeavour to harmonize their policies in this connection.
>
> 2. States shall take all measures necessary to ensure that activities under their jurisdiction or control are so conducted as not to cause damage by pollution to other States and their environment, and that pollution arising from incidents or activities under their jurisdiction or control does not spread beyond the areas where they exercise sovereign rights in accordance with this Convention.
>
> 3. The measures taken pursuant to this Part shall deal with all sources of pollution of the marine environment. These measures shall include, *inter alia*, those designed to minimize to the fullest possible extent:

---

[619] Final Transcript, 889:8–20.

[620] Final Transcript, 889:21–25.

[621] Final Transcript, 890:18–21.

(*a*) the release of toxic, harmful or noxious substances, especially those which are persistent, from land-based sources, from or through the atmosphere or by dumping;

(*b*) pollution from vessels, in particular measures for preventing accidents and dealing with emergencies, ensuring the safety of operations at sea, preventing intentional and unintentional discharges, and regulating the design, construction, equipment, operation and manning of vessels;

(*c*) pollution from installations and devices used in exploration or exploitation of the natural resources of the seabed and subsoil, in particular measures for preventing accidents and dealing with emergencies, ensuring the safety of operations at sea, and regulating the design, construction, equipment, operation and manning of such installations or devices;

(*d*) pollution from other installations and devices operating in the marine environment, in particular measures for preventing accidents and dealing with emergencies, ensuring the safety of operations at sea, and regulating the design, construction, equipment, operation and manning of such installations or devices.

4. In taking measures to prevent, reduce or control pollution of the marine environment, States shall refrain from unjustifiable interference with activities carried out by other States in the exercise of their rights and in pursuance of their duties in conformity with this Convention.

5. The measures taken in accordance with this Part shall include those necessary to protect and preserve rare or fragile ecosystems as well as the habitat of depleted, threatened or endangered species and other forms of marine life.

Mauritius' Position

482. Mauritius argues that the MPA is "a measure … intended to protect the environment" and therefore "falls to be considered by reference to the requirements of Part XII" of the Convention.[622] In Mauritius' view, any attempt to characterize the MPA as "merely introduc[ing] a ban on commercial fishing"[623] is disingenuous and inconsistent with the terms on which the United Kingdom carried out its Public Consultation[624] and with the terms of the MPA itself.[625]

483. With respect to the interpretation of Article 194(1), Mauritius submits that this provision imposes an obligation to "endeavor to act in harmony" which "requires that States must try hard to do or achieve harmonization of

622 Final Transcript, 304:9–14.

623 Final Transcript, 313:4.

624 Final Transcript, 313:20 to 314:19.

625 Final Transcript, 306:23 to 307:4.

policies regarding pollution prevention."[626] At a minimum, this translates to "undertaking such efforts to make pollution-related policies for the Chagos Archipelago consistent or compatible with those of other States in the region. It requires the sharing of information, the exchange of ideas, and some degree of consultation."[627]

484. According to Mauritius, the United Kingdom violated Article 194(1) as "it went out of its way to avoid finding a way to work with Mauritius."[628] In Mauritius' view –

> One would have thought that it would bend over backwards to achieve protections of these waters, and atolls, and reefs and for the biodiversity, but No. [...] The U.K. proceeded unilaterally and without proper notice. [...] [T]he U.K. simply refused to engage with Mauritius. When establishing the "MPA", there was no meaningful attempt to find out what Mauritius wanted to know, and no attempt to harmonize marine pollution policies.[629]

485. Turning to Article 194(4), Mauritius argues that this provision is plainly applicable because "[t]he 'MPA' and the implementing regulations which may one day come are measures to prevent, reduce or control pollution of the marine environment".[630] Accordingly, this provision requires the United Kingdom to "refrain from unjustifiably interfering with activities carried out by Mauritius in the exercise of its rights in conformity with the Convention."[631] Essentially, this obligation requires an assessment of whether the interference to Mauritius' rights is "justifiable". Mauritius alleges that the United Kingdom has not introduced any evidence to show that Mauritius' fishing activity was a source of pollution or harm and –

> mounts no real effort, no effort at all to persuade this Tribunal that a total ban on Mauritian fishing in these waters was justifiable. The burden is on the United Kingdom to show that it was a justifiable decision. In the absence of any evidence, we simply do not see how they can do that. There is no evidence, there is no argument.[632]

486. In all the circumstances, Mauritius argues that there is a "manifest and clear"[633] violation of Article 194(4) as the MPA is "a total ban on all activity. It's an anti-pollution measure. It very obviously interferes with the fishing rights of Mauritius. It is unjustifiable."[634]

---

[626] Final Transcript, 311:3–5.

[627] Final Transcript, 311:6–9.

[628] Final Transcript, 311:9–10.

[629] Final Transcript, 312:11–18.

[630] Final Transcript, 318:20–22.

[631] Final Transcript, 318:16–17.

[632] Final Transcript, 319:22to 320:1.

[633] Final Transcript, 321:1–6.

[634] Final Transcript, 320:21–22.

The United Kingdom's Position

487. The United Kingdom does not accept that it has a duty to coordinate its policy on marine pollution with Mauritius pursuant to Article 194(1) or that it must not legislate on marine pollution in a manner that interferes with Mauritius' right to fish in the MPA under Article 194(4).[635]

488. With respect to Article 194(1), the United Kingdom asserts that this is "simply the chapeau to the more specific treatment of different sources of marine pollution set out in paragraph (3)", which refers to Articles 207 and 212.[636] Accordingly, the United Kingdom does not accept that the obligation to harmonize policies under this provision can be isolated from the differing standards laid down by those Articles.[637]

489. With respect to Article 194(4), the United Kingdom notes that pollution has been strictly regulated in the MPA under existing laws for many years, and there has been no suggestion that these laws have interfered with Mauritius' fishing activities in BIOT waters.[638]

(d) The Interpretation and Application of Article 300

490. Article 300 of the Convention provides as follows:

> **Article 300**
>
> *Good faith and abuse of rights*
>
> States Parties shall fulfil in good faith the obligations assumed under this Convention and shall exercise the rights, jurisdiction and freedoms recognized in this Convention in a manner which would not constitute an abuse of right.

Mauritius' Position

491. Mauritius submits that the United Kingdom has breached Article 300 of the Convention by exercising its right under Article 56(1)(*b*)(iii) "to take measures for 'the protection and preservation of the marine environment' in the waters around the Archipelago"[639] in ways that constitute an abuse of right.[640]

492. According to Mauritius, Article 300 imposes two requirements:

> First, the right must not be exercised for a purpose that is entirely different from the purpose for which the right was created—especially if this

[635] Final Transcript, 897:18 to 898:3.

[636] Final Transcript, 897:22–898:1.

[637] Final Transcript, 898:1–3.

[638] Final Transcript, 899:3–5.

[639] Final Transcript, 377:12–13.

[640] Mauritius' Memorial, para. 7.81.

> comes at the expense of the rights or legally-protected interests of others, of other States, or indeed, of other uses of the oceans. Second, where a State takes measures in the exercise of a jurisdictional right, those measures must at least be capable of fulfilling the purpose for which the right was exercised. If they are not, the manner in which the right is being exercised is objectionable, even if that is capable of repair. If it's not repaired, then there is a breach of Article 300.[641]

493. The establishment of the MPA, Mauritius submits, violates the requirements of Article 300 of the Convention because "the record ... casts serious doubt on the purposes behind the proclamation of the 'MPA', and the manner in which it has been designed and implemented is certainly not conducive of the objectives officially declared."[642]

494. Mauritius relies upon a document that is purported to be the reproduced text of a cable from the U.S. Embassy, reporting on a meeting on 12 May 2009 with the then BIOT Commissioner, Mr. Colin Roberts, and then BIOT Administrator, Ms. Joanne Yeadon.[643] In particular, Mauritius relies upon the portion of that report that records Mr. Roberts as having said that "the BIOT's former inhabitants would find it difficult, if not impossible, to pursue their claim for resettlement on the islands if the entire Chagos Archipelago were a marine reserve", that "according to the HGM,s [*sic.*] current thinking on a reserve, there would be 'no human footprints' or 'Man Fridays' on the BIOT's uninhabited islands", and that "establishing a marine park would ... put paid to resettlement claims of the archipelago's former residents." Mauritius submits that these remarks "put[] into question the purposes behind the proclamation of the 'MPA,'"[644] which serves to fulfil the United Kingdom's political aims.[645]

495. Moreover, even if the United Kingdom's motives "were in principle purely environmental," Mauritius contends, there is still a breach of Article 300 because "there has been no serious attempt to follow up on those objectives."[646] Mauritius asks –

> whether it can be said that, whatever the actual purposes of individuals might have been, the "MPA" is still capable of succeeding in fulfilling its official purpose—the protection of the living resources and the environment of the waters around the Archipelago? Can it be said that the design

[641] Final Transcript, 377:19 to 378:3.

[642] Final Transcript, 378:11–13.

[643] Cable from US Embassy, London, on UK Government's Proposals for a Marine Reserve Covering the Chagos Archipelago, May 2009 (Annex MM-146).

[644] Final Transcript, 379:13–14.

[645] Final Transcript, 377:19–378:3.

[646] Final Transcript, 381:14 to 382:13, *citing Whaling in the Antarctic (Australia* v. *Japan: New Zealand Intervening), Judgment of* 31 *March 2014*, para. 97.

> and implementation of the "MPA" is reasonable in relation to achieving its stated objective? The answer to these questions is 'no', categorically.[647]

In support, Mauritius notes five ways in which the MPA fails to meet its environmental objectives: the insufficiency of scientific justification by the United Kingdom; the lack of regulations; the lack of financing; the severe inadequacy of enforcement; and the "exclusion zone covering Diego Garcia and its territorial waters."[648]

The United Kingdom's Position

496. The United Kingdom advances four propositions with respect to the abuse of rights:

> First, abuse of rights is not an independent basis of claim, and Mauritius appears to have conceded this point …
>
> Second, the burden of proving abuse of rights is on the party alleging it. In this respect the normal rules of international litigation apply, and Mauritius does not argue otherwise. However […] Mauritius has failed even to adduce *prima facie* evidence of improper purposes or bad faith.
>
> Third, clear and convincing proof of injury is required […] [and] without serious injury there would perhaps be no reason for a court to adjudicate on such a claim of abuse. […] If proof of serious injury is required for an abuse of rights claim to succeed, then […] Mauritius fails at the first hurdle.
>
> [And] fourth […], the rights in question must have been used in an abusive manner.[649]

497. In response to the issues advanced by Mauritius, the United Kingdom rejects the evidence relied on by Mauritius to establish improper purposes, arguing that "none of [the evidence] … adds up or comes near to the necessary evidential burden which Mauritius must discharge to prove this claim".[650] The United Kingdom responds to the alleged U.S. account of a 12 May 2009 meeting in the following terms:

> Mr. Roberts denied on oath in the domestic proceedings that he had repeated the words in question. Ms. Yeadon corroborated this, and confirmed that she would have reported to her superiors if Mr. Roberts had used the words. And the High Court accepted that the words were not said. […] [T]he UK Government strongly objects to the entirely unwarranted slurs which have been cast upon its officials, and the implication that the Court was not competent to decide the veracity of their statements.[651]

[647] Final Transcript, 382:14–18.

[648] Final Transcript, 382:21 to 387:13.

[649] Final Transcript, 900:1 to 901:5.

[650] Final Transcript, 901:24 to 902:2.

[651] Final Transcript, 1165:13–19.

498. In contrast, "there is ample evidence," the United Kingdom submits, "to demonstrate the real purpose for creating the MPA and for concluding that it was reasonable to proceed as proposed."[652] In response to Mauritius' argument that "there is no sufficient evidential basis for a no-take policy," the United Kingdom contends that –

> First, it's not an abuse of rights claim [...] what we are actually faced with here is a need to balance the competing rights of coastal states and of others fishing in their EEZ, and the relevant rules are articles 56, 58, 61 and 62. So the question [...] is whether in closing the MPA to foreign fishing to Mauritian fishing the United Kingdom has acted consistently with those articles, and that is not an appropriate question for an abuse of rights discussion.
>
> Secondly, [...] Mauritius has not shown that the decision to ban all commercial fishing in the MPA lacks scientific justification. All it can point to are the differing opinions of scientists about whether to ban fishing or continue with the previous policy. [...] But [...] justifying measures of the kind taken by the United Kingdom, in order to conserve fish stocks, biodiversity and the marine ecosystems on which they depend does not require strong and cogent evidence.
>
> [...]
>
> So it follows [...] that if Mauritius wishes to cast doubt on the scientific justification for the no-take MPA [...], it will have to provide much stronger and far more cogent evidence that clearly and convincingly contradicts the existing scientific and environmental basis for the no-take policy on fishing. Notwithstanding anything said by Mauritius last week, it comes at the moment nowhere near doing so.[653]

2. The Tribunal's Decision

(a) The Interpretation of Article 2(3)

499. Turning first to Article 2(3), the Tribunal is confronted with the stark difference between the Parties as to whether the provision gives rise to any obligation at all. Mauritius contends that the Article creates an obligation under the Convention to comply with other requirements of international law in the exercise of sovereignty in the Territorial Sea. The United Kingdom considers the text to be purely descriptive.

500. For its part, the Tribunal considers the English-language formulation of Article 2(3)—providing that "sovereignty over the territorial sea is exercised subject to this Convention and to other rules of international law"—to be ambiguous. The Tribunal agrees with Mauritius, however, that a sense of obligation is more readily apparent in the non-English versions of this pro-

[652] Final Transcript, 903:1–2.

[653] Final Transcript, 903:22 to 905:17.

vision. Furthermore, the Tribunal observes that differences between "is" and "shall" in the English text of the Convention are not consistently reflected by comparable distinctions in the non-English texts[654] and is therefore cautious of ascribing any significant consequence to such usage.

501. Pursuant to Article 320 of the Convention, "the Arabic, Chinese, English, French, Russian and Spanish texts are equally authentic". Article 33 of the Vienna Convention on the Law of Treaties governs the interpretation of a treaty authenticated in multiple languages and provides that, unless otherwise indicated, "the text is equally authoritative in each language".[655] The Convention includes no provision for the resolution of differences between its authentic texts. Therefore it is possible to have recourse to the Vienna Convention. Article 33 of the Vienna Convention further provides that "when a comparison of the authentic texts discloses a difference of meaning which the application of articles 31 and 32 does not remove, the meaning which best reconciles the texts, having regard to the object and purpose of the treaty, shall be adopted."[656]

502. Approaching first the text of Article 2(3), the Tribunal is of the view that the balance of the authentic versions favours reading that provision to impose an obligation.

503. The Tribunal also considers this interpretation to be consistent with the placement of Article 2(3) within the structural context of the Convention. The formulation of Article 2(3) is identical to that of Article 87(1), concerning the high seas, and any interpretation the Tribunal may reach regarding the

---

[654] As but one example, the English text of Article 87, concerning the freedom of the high seas, includes a distinction, within a single article, between the formulations "is exercised" and "shall be exercised":

> 1. The high seas are open to all States, whether coastal or land-locked. Freedom of the high seas is exercised under the conditions laid down by this Convention and by other rules of international law. It comprises, *inter alia*, both for coastal and land-locked States:
>
> [...]
>
> 2. These freedoms shall be exercised by all States with due regard for the interests of other States in their exercise of the freedom of the high seas, and also with due regard for the rights under this Convention with respect to activities in the Area.

In the French text, however, the same provisions are set out without distinction, using the formulation "exerce" in the present tense and differing only in the reflexive orientation of the former sentence:

> 1. La haute mer est ouverte à tous les Etats, qu'ils soient côtiers ou sans littoral. La liberté de la haute mer s'exerce dans les conditions prévue par le dispositions de la Convention et les autres règles du droit international. Elle comporte notamment pour les Etats, qu'ils soient côtiers ou sans littoral:
>
> [...]
>
> 2. Chaque Etat exerce ces libertés en tenant dûment compte de l'intérêt que présente l'exercice de la liberté de la haute mer pour les autres Etats, ainsi que des droits reconnus par la Convention concernant les activités menées dans la Zone.

[655] Vienna Convention on the Law of Treaties, art. 33, 22 May 1969, 1155 UNTS 331.

[656] *Ibid.*

scope of obligation embodied in the former provision would apply equally to the latter. Looking across the various maritime zones created by the Convention, the Tribunal notes that each of the territorial sea (Article 2(3)), international straits (Article 34(2)), the exclusive economic zone (Article 56(2)), the continental shelf (Article 78(2)) and the high seas (Article 87(2)) includes a provision to the effect that States will exercise their rights under the Convention subject to, or with regard to, the rights and duties of other States or rules of international law beyond the Convention itself. While the language of these provisions is not harmonized, a *renvoi* to material beyond the Convention must be interpreted in a manner that is coherent with respect to all of the foregoing maritime zones.

504. Recalling the object and purpose of the Convention, the Tribunal notes the express references in its preamble to the need to consider the "closely interrelated" problems of ocean space "as a whole," and the "desirability of establishing through this Convention, … a legal order for the seas and oceans." In the Tribunal's view, these objectives—as well as the need for coherence in interpreting Article 2(3) within the context of the provisions for other maritime zones—are more readily achieved by viewing Article 2(3) as a source of obligation. As discussed in the paragraphs that follow, this view is confirmed by an examination of the origin of Article 2(3).

505. As noted by both Parties, the text of what is now Article 2(3) was derived from Article 1 of the 1958 Geneva Convention on the Territorial Sea and the Contiguous Zone which provided as follows:

Article 1

> 1. The sovereignty of a State extends, beyond its land territory and its internal waters, to a belt of sea adjacent to its coast, described as the territorial sea.
>
> 2. This sovereignty is exercised subject to the provisions of these articles and to other rules of international law.

The Tribunal considers the text in this form to be identical to the 1982 Convention for present purposes, and notes that the five authentic language versions of the 1958 text do nothing to reconcile the ambiguity in the later treaty.

506. Article 1 of the 1958 Convention had its origins, in turn, in the Draft Articles on the Law of the Sea prepared by the International Law Commission in 1956, where it was proposed by the Commission's Special Rapporteur, Mr. J.P.A. François. As set out in the ILC's Draft Articles, Article 1 provided as follows:

Article 1

> 1. The sovereignty of a State extends to a belt of sea adjacent to its coast, described as the territorial sea.

2. This sovereignty is exercised subject to the conditions prescribed in these articles and by other rules of international law.

507. While the intent of Article 2(3) does not appear to have been significantly discussed during the negotiations leading to the adoption of the Convention,[657] the provision was the subject of significant debate during the preparation of the ILC Draft Articles.[658] For the Tribunal, a review of the record of these debates makes the following points apparent.

508. First, the Special Rapporteur adopted the provision from the draft Regulations prepared by the League of Nations Codification Conference in The Hague in 1930, where it was included in light of perceived differences between the exercise of sovereignty over the territorial sea and sovereignty over land. The Committee Report from the 1930 Conference, recalled as guidance by the ILC's Rapporteur, described the purpose of the provision in the following terms:

> Obviously sovereignty over the territorial sea, like sovereignty over the domain on land, can only be exercised subject to the conditions laid down by international law. As the limitations which international law imposes on the power of the State in respect of the latter's sovereignty over the territorial sea are greater than those it imposes in respect of the domain on land, it has not been thought superfluous to make special mention of these limitations in the text of the article itself.[659]

509. Second, a number of members of the Commission sought to delete the provision as superfluous, either because "[t]he sovereignty of the State, wherever exercised, was always limited by the rules of international law"[660] or because they considered that there were no limitations on sovereignty in the territorial sea beyond the right of innocent passage.[661]

510. Conversely, a number of members believed that "the Commission's function was to promote the codification of existing international law. Accord-

[657] Debate on the territorial sea during the Third UN Conference on the Law of the Sea appears to have been consumed almost entirely with the question of whether the concept of a unified territorial sea should be disposed of in favor of recognizing a plurality of legal regimes with overlapping, but not congruent, geographical scope. *See* M. Norquist, ed., *United Nations Convention on the Law of the Sea 1982: A Commentary*, Vol. II at pp. 64–74 (1989).

[658] *See* International Law Commission, Summary Record of the 165th Meeting, UN Doc. A/CN.4/SR.165 (16 July 1952); International Law Commission, Summary Record of the 253rd Meeting, UN Doc. A/CN.4/SR.253 (23 July 1954); International Law Commission, Summary Record of the 295th Meeting, UN Doc. A/CN.4/SR.295 (20 May 1955); International Law Commission, Summary Record of the 324th Meeting, UN Doc. A/CN.4/SR.324 (1 July 1955); International Law Commission, Summary Record of the 361st Meeting, UN Doc. A/CN.4/SR.361 (6 June 1956).

[659] International Law Commission, Summary Record of the 165th Meeting, UN Doc. A/CN.4/SR.165 at para. 25 (16 July 1952).

[660] International Law Commission, Summary Record of the 253rd Meeting, UN Doc. A/CN.4/SR.253 at paras. 2, 12 (23 July 1954).

[661] International Law Commission, Summary Record of the 165th Meeting, UN Doc. A/CN.4/SR.165 at paras. 26, 38 (16 July 1952).

ingly, it should formulate all the provisions of the international law in force", rather than include a general reference.[662]

511. Ultimately, these views were opposed by the strong views of other members of the Commission that "[i]t was vital that specific reference should be made to the limitations imposed by international law on sovereignty over the territorial sea, particularly in view of the recent tendency to increase the breadth of that sea"[663] and that –

> it was not permissible for the Commission to assume that the draft articles covered the entire topic so that the residuary reference to "other rules of international law" was unnecessary. In the first place, allowance had to be made for the possibility of an involuntary omission; secondly, there were certain general rules of international law which were applicable in the matter, as indeed to other topics of international law, such as the principle prohibiting the abuse of rights and, generally, the law of state responsibility.[664]

This latter view prevailed in the Draft Articles as finally adopted.

512. The ILC's Draft Articles were not prepared with dispute resolution in mind and, indeed, at the time of the foregoing remarks, it remained unclear whether the final product of the Commission's work would be a draft convention or some less formal instrument without binding effect. From the record of the discussions, the Tribunal understands the Commission's view of its task to have been to codify in the Draft Articles the obligations then existing with respect to the territorial sea, with specific language where possible and general references where necessary. The Tribunal also views the consideration given to whether it would be possible to fully specify the limitations on sovereignty in the territorial sea to be incompatible with the interpretation of draft article 1(2) as merely an introductory description.

513. During the First UN Conference on the Law of the Sea that led to the adoption of the 1958 Convention on the Territorial Sea and the Contiguous Zone, Article 1(2) received little attention, none of which appears to bear on the question before the Tribunal. Discussion was instead focussed on resolving deeply held differences as to the breadth of the territorial sea. Nevertheless, the Tribunal notes that the 1958 Conference did engage in discussion on the addition to Article 2 of the Convention on the High Seas of the comparable provision that "[f]reedom of the high seas is exercised under the conditions laid down by these articles and by the other rules of international law." Such text was not included in the ILC Draft Articles and its addition was derived from the ILC's commentary and Article 1(2) of the Draft Articles, concerning the terri-

---

[662] International Law Commission, Summary Record of the 253rd Meeting, UN Doc. A/CN.4/SR.253 at paras. 9, 17 (23 July 1954).

[663] International Law Commission, Summary Record of the 165th Meeting, UN Doc. A/CN.4/SR.165 at para. 34 (16 July 1952).

[664] International Law Commission, Summary Record of the 253rd Meeting, UN Doc. A/CN.4/SR.253 at para. 10 (23 July 1954).

torial sea.[665] The addition was supported on the grounds that "any freedom that was to be exercised in the interests of all entitled to enjoy it must be regulated"[666] and that "freedom of the high seas should be made subject to the articles of the convention and the other rules of international law".[667] In the Tribunal's view, the comments made in relation to this amendment were uniformly of the view that its addition constituted a restriction on the freedom of the seas.

514. Accordingly, the Tribunal concludes that the multi-lingual "terms of the treaty in their context and in the light of its object and purpose",[668] together with the negotiating history of the Convention, lead to the interpretation that Article 2(3) contains an obligation on States to exercise their sovereignty subject to "other rules of international law". Having reached this conclusion, however, the Tribunal notes that the Parties remain in dispute with respect to the intended scope of "other rules of international law", to which the Tribunal will now turn.

515. Both Parties have referred the Tribunal to the ILC's commentary on Article 1(2) of its Draft Articles, which provided in relevant part as follows:

> (3) Clearly, sovereignty over the territorial sea cannot be exercised otherwise than in conformity with the provisions of international law.
>
> (4) Some of the limitations imposed by international law on the exercise of sovereignty in the territorial sea are set forth in the present articles which cannot, however, be regarded as exhaustive. Incidents in the territorial sea raising legal questions are also governed by the general rules of international law, and these cannot be specially codified in the present draft for the purposes of their application to the territorial sea. That is why "other rules of international law" are mentioned in addition to the provisions contained in the present articles.
>
> (5) It may happen that, by reason of some special relationship, geographical or other, between two States, rights in the territorial sea of one of them are granted to the other in excess of the rights recognized in the present draft. It is not the Commission's intention to limit in any way any more extensive right of passage or other right enjoyed by States by custom or treaty.[669]

516. While the Parties draw different conclusions regarding the implications of these comments, the Tribunal understands them to indicate that the Commission understood Article 1(2) of the Draft Articles to require States

---

[665] First UN Conference on the Law of the Sea, Official Records, Vol. IV (Second Committee, High Seas: General Regime), Summary Records of Meetings and Annexes, UN Doc. A/CONF.13/40 at p. 37.

[666] *Ibid.* at p. 39.

[667] *Ibid.* at pp. 42, 43.

[668] Vienna Convention on the Law of Treaties, art. 31(1), 22 May 1969, 1155 UNTS 331.

[669] International Law Commission, Articles concerning the Law of the Sea with Commentaries, *Report of the International Law Commission on the Work of its Eighth Session, 23 April to 4 July 1956*, Official Records of the General Assembly, Eleventh Session, Supplement No. 9, UN Doc. A/3159 at p. 265.

to exercise their sovereignty in the territorial sea subject to the general rules of international law. The Commission also recognized that States may possess particular rights in the territorial sea by virtue of bilateral agreements or local custom, but noted merely that the Articles were not intended to interfere with such rights. In the Tribunal's view, this accords with the discussions of the provision in the Commission, in which the only references to other rules of international law were to such matters as the abuse of rights and the law of State responsibility. There is no indication that through this provision the Commission intended to create an obligation of compliance with any bilateral commitment a State might undertake in the territorial sea, nor is there any basis to assume that the intent of the provision changed between the Commission's formulation of the Draft Articles and the adoption of the Convention in 1982. The Tribunal therefore concludes that the obligation in Article 2(3) is limited to exercising sovereignty subject to the general rules of international law.

517. Turning to the implications of this provision in the present case, the Tribunal does not consider that the Lancaster House Undertakings represent part of the general rules of international law for which the Convention creates an obligation of compliance. The Tribunal does, however, consider that general international law requires the United Kingdom to act in good faith in its relations with Mauritius, including with respect to undertakings. Whether this requirement has been met in the creation of the MPA will be evaluated below.

(b) The Interpretation of Article 56(2)

518. In contrast to Article 2(3), the English text of Article 56(2) leaves no doubt that the provision imposes an obligation on the coastal State:

> In exercising its rights and performing its duties under this Convention in the exclusive economic zone, the coastal State shall have due regard to the rights and duties of other States and shall act in a manner compatible with the provisions of this Convention.

The difference between the Parties, therefore, concerns what is meant by "due regard" and the extent to which this implies an obligation to consult, or even of non-impairment.

519. In the Tribunal's view, the ordinary meaning of "due regard" calls for the United Kingdom to have such regard for the rights of Mauritius as is called for by the circumstances and by the nature of those rights. The Tribunal declines to find in this formulation any universal rule of conduct. The Convention does not impose a uniform obligation to avoid any impairment of Mauritius' rights; nor does it uniformly permit the United Kingdom to proceed as it wishes, merely noting such rights. Rather, the extent of the regard required by the Convention will depend upon the nature of the rights held by Mauritius, their importance, the extent of the anticipated impairment, the nature and importance of the activities contemplated by the United Kingdom, and the availability of alternative approaches. In the majority of cases,

this assessment will necessarily involve at least some consultation with the rights-holding State.

(c) *The Application of Articles 2(3) and 56(2)*

520. Mauritius' rights in the territorial sea and exclusive economic zone pursuant to the Lancaster House Undertakings have been identified above (see paragraphs 417–456). Article 2(3) requires the United Kingdom to exercise good faith with respect to Mauritius' rights in the territorial sea. Article 56(2) requires the United Kingdom to have due regard for Mauritius' rights in the exclusive economic zone. The Tribunal considers these requirements to be, for all intents and purposes, equivalent.

521. There is no question that Mauritius' rights have been affected by the declaration of the MPA. In the territorial sea, Mauritius' fishing rights have effectively been extinguished. And as set out above (see paragraph 298), the Tribunal considers that the United Kingdom's undertaking for the eventual return of the Archipelago gives Mauritius an interest in significant decisions that bear upon its possible future uses. The declaration of the MPA was such a decision and will invariably affect the state of the Archipelago when it is eventually returned to Mauritius. The Tribunal considers Mauritius' rights to be significant and entitled, as a matter of good faith and the Convention, to a corresponding degree of regard.

522. The Tribunal has put on record the events from February 2009 to April 2010 concerning the initial steps taken to establish the MPA and the bilateral consultations between the United Kingdom and Mauritius. The Tribunal takes issue with several aspects of these events.

523. First, the MPA was originally notified to Mauritius not by the United Kingdom, but by a London newspaper article of 9 February 2009,[670] despite the following facts:

> (*a*) In advance of the Mauritius–United Kingdom Joint Meeting on 14 January 2009, internal United Kingdom communications dated 31 December 2008 proposed the inclusion of the following agenda item:
>
> > iv) Fishing rights/protection of the environment; [Means of discussing current/possible Mauritian rights in BIOT waters and introducing discussion of Pew ideas, if not name].[671]
>
> (*b*) This was included in the proposed agenda for the meeting, sent by Note Verbale dated 6 January 2009, which included the reference to –

[670] S. Gray, "Giant marine park plan for Chagos", The Independent, 9 February 2009 (Annex MM-138).

[671] E-mail dated 31 December 2008 from Andrew Allen, Overseas Territories Directorate, to Joanne Yeadon, Head of BIOT & Pitcairn Section, UK Foreign and Commonwealth Office (Annex MR-125).

iv) Fishing rights/protection of the environment".[672]

(*c*) Nevertheless, the possibility of something like the MPA appears to have been raised in only the vaguest possible terms during the meeting. The United Kingdom's record records only an indication that "the UK was also looking at more ambitious approaches to managing the marine resource", without further specification.[673]

(*d*) Mauritius' record of comments during the January 2009 meeting by Mr. Colin Roberts, the BIOT Commissioner, confirms this impression:

> The second is the environment issue. The coral structure has become the most important coral structure. The value lies more in the capacity of the coral structure for re-growth of all coral structures of the Indian Ocean. As government we have not formed a policy on this. The fishing industry is not very vibrant. We should look to it in the broader perspective to the benefits to the international community.[674]

524. Even accepting the United Kingdom's explanation that "officials simply would not have engaged in formal discussions on the proposal with third States until the policy to move forward with it had been adopted by Ministers", which occurred on 7 May 2009,[675] there is no evidence that bilateral consultations with Mauritius, either formal or informal, commenced until July 2009. This was notwithstanding:

(*a*) a clear reference to the need for talks with Mauritius in Mr. Roberts' paper on the marine reserve concept dated 5 May 2009, which provided that –

> If Ministers wish to proceed next steps would include:
>
> [...]
>
> – opening talks with Mauritius
>
> – opening talks with the US[676]

(*b*) an exchange between Mr. Roberts and Mr. Gould on 7 May 2009 in which Mr. Roberts proposed –

1) to continue our private "bilateral" engagement of stakeholders

---

[672] Note Verbale dated 6 January 2009 from UK Foreign and Commonwealth Office to Mauritius High Commission, London, No. OTD 01/01/09 (Annex MR-127).

[673] UK Foreign and Commonwealth Office, Overseas Territories Directorate, "British Indian Ocean Territory: UK/Mauritius Talks", 14 January 2009 (Annex MR-128).

[674] Ministry of Foreign Affairs, Regional Integration and International Trade, Mauritius, "Meeting of Officials on the Chagos Archipelago/British Indian Ocean Territory held at the Foreign and Commonwealth Office, London, Wednesday 14 January 2009, 10 a.m.", 23 January 2009 (Annex MR-129).

[675] Final Transcript, 554:3–5.

[676] Paper submitted on 5 May 2009 by Colin Roberts, Director, Overseas Territories Directorate, to the Private Secretary to the Foreign Secretary, "Making British Indian Ocean Territory the World's Largest Marine Reserve" (Annex MR-132).

> [...]
>
> 3) to devise a public consultation process which takes account of the key legal and political risks identified, but is not dependent on resolution of all issues. I would aim to launch a consultation process in the second half of this year[677]

(*c*) a meeting between Mr. Roberts and representatives from the U.S. Embassy on 12 May 2009 to discuss the proposal and the two concerns expressed by the United States, to the effect:

> (1) that any marine park would not interfere with US military vessels/submarines operating in the area [...]
>
> (2) that there would not be a decision five years down the line that a military base would be seen as incompatible with the MPA";[678]

(*d*) and an e-mail dated 4 June 2009 stating "we have not yet engaged with Mauritius on the proposal but we will be doing so soon".[679]

525. In fact, the meeting of 21 July 2009 comprised the entirety of bilateral consultation, which, the United Kingdom argues, were "the necessary consultations [that] took place".[680] Despite this, the Tribunal notes the following:

(*a*) According to the United Kingdom's record of the meeting, the United Kingdom's delegation explained that –

> not many details were available as the UK wanted to talk to Mauritius before proposals were developed. If helpful the UK could, for the purposes of discussion, produce a proposal with variations on paper for the Mauritians to look at.[681]

The United Kingdom further indicated that it was considering a "standard public consultation", but noted that "the UK had wanted to speak to Mauritius about the ideas beforehand". The United Kingdom's record also included the comment that "[m]uch remains to talk about as far as a marine protected area is concerned".[682]

(*b*) The United Kingdom also presented evidence from Mr. Roberts recalling that he –

> raised the possibility that a formal public consultation might be conducted and invited Mauritius to join with us in the consultation, e.g. by launching an international consultation by a

---

[677] E-mail exchange between Colin Roberts, Director, Overseas Territories Directorate, and Matthew Gould, Principal Private Secretary to the Foreign Secretary, UK Foreign and Commonwealth Office, 7 May 2009 (Annex MR-134).

[678] E-mail exchange between Joanne Yeadon, Head of BIOT & Pitcairn Section, UK Foreign and Commonwealth Office and Ian [surname redacted], 4 June 2009 (Annex MR-135).

[679] *Ibid.*

[680] Final Transcript, 881:14–16.

[681] UK Foreign and Commonwealth Office, Overseas Territories Directorate, "UK/Mauritius Talks on the British Indian Ocean Territory", 24 July 2009 (Annex MR-143).

[682] *Ibid.*

joint press statement by the two Governments or by referencing Mauritius in the consultation document.[683]

(*c*) Mauritius' record of the meeting confirms that it was intended to be the start of discussions, noting that "the UK Government wished to start dialogue on a proposal made … to establish a marine protected area in the region of the Chagos Archipelago".[684]

(*d*) The Parties contemplated further cooperation in the form of joint action by a team of marine scientists, which never took place. What is more, the Joint Communiqué records that the Mauritian side "agreed that a team of officials and marine scientists from both sides meet to examine the implications of the concept with a view to informing the next round of talks".[685]

(*e*) The Parties continued to contemplate further joint action with respect to fishing licenses, as the Joint Communiqué goes on to record:

> The Mauritian side reiterated the proposal it made in the first round of the talks for the setting up of a mechanism to look into the joint issuing of fishing licences in the region of the Chagos Archipelago/British Indian Ocean Territory. The UK delegation agreed to examine this proposal and stated that such examination would also include consideration of the implications of the proposed marine protected area.[686]

526. There is a stark contrast between the United Kingdom's consultations with the United States and those that took place with Mauritius, in particular:

(*a*) Mr. Roberts met with the representatives from the U.S. Embassy on 12 May 2009, only days after the Ministerial-level decision to move forward with the MPA proposal.[687]

(*b*) Internal United Kingdom correspondence dated 3 and 14 July 2009 demonstrates extensive concern with the U.S. reaction to the MPA proposal. British representatives laying the ground for the MPA noted the need –

> i) to establish clearly that the creation of an MPA (excluding DG itself and its 3 mile zone) is consistent with the existing [exchanges of notes]. One question here is whether any of our agreements with the US have any application beyond the 12 mile territorial limit.

---

683 Colin Roberts' 3rd Witness Statement, para. 20 (Annex UKR-74).

684 Information Paper by the Prime Minister of Mauritius, Second Meeting at Senior Officials' Level between Mauritius and UK on the Chagos Archipelago, CAB(2009) 624, 12 August 2009 (Annex MR-144).

685 Joint Communiqué, Second round of bilateral talks between Mauritius and the UK on the Chagos Archipelago, 21 July 2009, Port Louis, Mauritius (Annex MM-148/MR-142).

686 *Ibid.*

687 E-mail exchange between Joanne Yeadon, Head of BIOT & Pitcairn Section, UK Foreign and Commonwealth Office and Ian [surname redacted], 4 June 2009 (Annex MR-135).

ii) refine a set of commitments to reassure the US, but which do not undermine the fundamental value of the MPA. My suggestions are:

- Nothing we are proposing will require any change to the [exchanges of notes] governing the territory.
- MPA designation a matter fully within the UK's sovereign powers. But will of course want to consult US.
- Diego Garcia and its 3mile limit will be excluded from the MPA (so no relevance to the anchor/buoy question [in] the lagoon).
- There will be no change to the rights and freedoms currently enjoyed by the US government in the territory under the [exchanges of notes] (However any recreational fishing will be banned in the MPA and separately we are proposing to ban recreational fishing in DG's 3-mile limit and the lagoon). The US must recognise that we do not exclude the possibility of future strengthening of environmental controls. But as in the past these would come through negotiation with the US. We do not propose any stricter controls on the US by virtue of creating an MPA.
- We are not aware of any US activity in the proposed MPA which would be inconsistent with the MPA. However, if the US think they do or will want to do anything inconsistent with an MPA, now is the time to tell us. They may find it useful to consider the extent to which the US Marine National Monuments have constrained any military activities. The BIOT MPA will be *sui generis*. If necessary we can consider a specific "military exclusion" in the MPA legislation.
- there will be no change to the fundamental purpose of BIOT: to serve the defence interests of the UK and US.[688]

(*c*) On 7 September 2009, the BIOT Administration made a formal submission concerning the "Implications for US Activities in Diego Garcia and BIOT", setting out the "two or three models for providing a framework for this [MPA]" and the assurances given to the United States as contemplated by the e-mail dated 3 July 2009.[689]

527. In the same internal correspondence, British representatives appear to have been aware of Mauritius' rights in the Archipelago (whatever their view as to their precise legal status), noting the need for "a full analysis of the history of fishing and environmental protection in BIOT" and "an authoritative state-

[688] E-mail exchange between Colin Roberts, Director, Overseas Territories Directorate, and Joanne Yeadon, Head of BIOT & Pitcairn Section, UK Foreign and Commonwealth Office, 13 & 14 July 2009 (Annex MR-138).

[689] Submission dated 7 September 2009 from BIOT Administration, "BIOT Marine Reserve Proposal: Implications for US Activities in Diego Garcia and British Indian Ocean Territory" (Annex MR-145).

ment of what we think are Mauritius' rights today to fish in BIOT waters".[690] Nevertheless, further discussion was largely limited to the possibility of policy "sweeteners" to secure Mauritian agreement and concluded that while "we might explore these issues in talks, I don't think we can commit at this stage".[691]

528. In the Tribunal's view, the United Kingdom's approach to consultations with the United States provides a practical example of due regard and a yardstick against which the communications with Mauritius can be measured. The record shows that the United States was consulted in a timely manner and provided with information, and that the United Kingdom was internally concerned with balancing the MPA with U.S. rights and interests.

529. In contrast, the 21 July 2009 meeting with Mauritius reminds the Tribunal of ships passing in the night, in which neither side fully engaged with the other regarding fishing rights or the proposal for the MPA. Indeed, the United Kingdom's record suggests the differing agendas and understandings at play in its comment that –

> There was a short discussion about access to fishing rights. The Mauritians wanted to manage jointly the resources. This was simply put on the table for the UK to consider. Comment: this all seemed a bit surreal when we'd spent the last half hour discussion [*sic*] the possible ban on any fishing in the territory but the Mauritians had warned us that this would remain an agenda item.[692]

530. The Tribunal's overall impression of the meeting was that there remained a number of issues unanswered, information that the United Kingdom promised to provide to Mauritius, and further work and consultations that would be jointly undertaken. It is difficult for the Tribunal to conclude, based on the foregoing, that this one meeting could satisfy the obligation to have "due regard" or to consult.

531. The Tribunal notes the United Kingdom's position that a further round of talks with Mauritius was contemplated, but did not take place in light of Mauritius' refusal to discuss the issue in parallel with the United Kingdom's Public Consultation. The Tribunal notes the United Kingdom's point that it was Mauritius which declined to agree upon a date for talks[693] and accepts the argument that consultation need not continue indefinitely or "until the other party is happy".[694] That being said, the United Kingdom created an expectation that further bilateral consultation "about the ideas [would take place] beforehand" and that Mauritius would be offered a further opportunity for

---

690 E-mail exchange between Colin Roberts, Director, Overseas Territories Directorate, and Joanne Yeadon, Head of BIOT & Pitcairn Section, UK Foreign and Commonwealth Office, 13–14 July 2009 (Annex MR-138).

691 *Ibid.*

692 UK Foreign and Commonwealth Office, Overseas Territories Directorate, "UK/Mauritius Talks on the British Indian Ocean Territory", 24 July 2009 (Annex MR-143).

693 Final Transcript, 561:16 to 564:12.

694 Final Transcript, 880:24 to 881:7.

discussion before a final decision was taken. As late as March 2010, the United Kingdom assured Mauritius that "no decision on the creation of an MPA has yet been taken" and that "the United Kingdom is keen to continue dialogue about environmental protection within bilateral framework or separately. The public consultation does not preclude, overtake or bypass these talks."[695] Only days later, the United Kingdom nevertheless decided to announce the creation of the MPA. The Tribunal finds it difficult to reconcile this course of events with the spirit of negotiation and consultation or with the need to balance the interests at stake in the waters of the Archipelago.

532. The Tribunal also observes that the meeting between then Prime Minister Brown and Prime Minister Ramgoolam added to the confusion and atmosphere of cross purposes between the Parties. Whatever was actually said at CHOGM, it had the effect of creating additional expectations that were not met by the United Kingdom. While the United Kingdom has shown the Tribunal the steps it took to mend such fences, it did not pursue renewed consultations with Mauritius in early 2010 and elected instead to press ahead with the final approval of the MPA.

533. Turning to the final events in March to April 2010, the Tribunal notes that the United Kingdom has not been able to provide any convincing explanation for the urgency with which it proclaimed the MPA on 1 April 2010.[696] The Public Consultation closed only on 5 March 2010. The facilitator's report on the Public Consultation was only received "sometime in March".[697] And the BIOT Administration's submission to the UK Ministers was made on 30 March 2010, only two days before the declaration of the MPA. The Tribunal finds it difficult to account for the haste with which the United Kingdom acted and would have expected significant further engagement with Mauritius following the Public Consultation. To the extent that the timing of the declaration of the MPA was in fact dictated by the electoral timetable in the United Kingdom or an anticipated change of government, the Tribunal does not accept that such considerations can justify the disregard of the United Kingdom's obligations to Mauritius. The absence of any justifiable rationale for the United Kingdom's haste—which, the Tribunal notes, stands in sharp contrast to the absence of implementing measures following the MPA's declaration—exacerbates the inadequacy of the prior consultation with Mauritius.

534. The Tribunal considers that the United Kingdom's obligation to act in good faith and to have "due regard" to Mauritius' rights and interests arising out of the Lancaster House Undertakings, as reaffirmed after 1968, entails, at least, both consultation and a balancing exercise with its own rights

---

[695] Letter dated 19 March 2010 from the British High Commissioner, Port Louis, to the Secretary to Cabinet and Head of the Civil Service, Mauritius (Annex MM-163); Note Verbale dated 26 March 2010 from British High Commission, Port Louis, to the Ministry of Foreign Affairs, Regional Integration and International Trade, Mauritius, No. 14/2010 (Annex MM-164).

[696] Final Transcript, 592:24 to 593:2; 593:16–19; 888:22 to 889:4.

[697] Final Transcript, 591:3–5.

and interests. With respect to consultations, the Tribunal does not accept that the United Kingdom has fulfilled the basic purpose of consulting, given the lack of information actually provided to Mauritius and the absence of a reasoned exchange between the Parties, exemplified by the misunderstanding that characterized the 21 July 2009 meeting. Furthermore, the United Kingdom's statements and conduct created reasonable expectations on the part of Mauritius that there would be further opportunities to respond and exchange views. This expectation was frustrated when the United Kingdom declared the MPA on 1 April 2010.

535. The Tribunal also concludes that the United Kingdom failed properly to balance its own rights and interests with Mauritius' rights arising from the Lancaster House Undertakings. Not only did the United Kingdom proceed on the flawed basis that Mauritius had no fishing rights in the territorial sea of the Chagos Archipelago, it presumed to conclude—without ever confirming with Mauritius—that the MPA was in Mauritius' interest. This approach is to be contrasted with the one adopted with respect to the United States, as another State with rights and interests in the Archipelago. There, the record demonstrates a conscious balancing of rights and interests, suggestions of compromise and willingness to offer assurances by the United Kingdom, and an understanding of the United States' concerns in connection with the proposed activities. All these elements were noticeably absent in the United Kingdom's approach to Mauritius.

536. Accordingly, the Tribunal concludes that the United Kingdom has breached Articles 2(3) and 56(2) and therefore finds that the proclamation of the MPA was incompatible with the Convention.

(d) The Interpretation and Application of Article 194

537. Article 194 sets out two provisions that potentially bear on the declaration of the MPA. Article 194(1) requires that –

> States shall take, individually or jointly as appropriate, all measures consistent with this Convention that are necessary to prevent, reduce and control pollution of the marine environment from any source, using for this purpose the best practicable means at their disposal and in accordance with their capabilities, and they shall endeavour to harmonize their policies in this connection.

Article 194(4) then requires that –

> In taking measures to prevent, reduce or control pollution of the marine environment, States shall refrain from unjustifiable interference with activities carried out by other States in the exercise of their rights and in pursuance of their duties in conformity with this Convention.

The Parties differ as to whether the former provision gives rise to an obligation and whether the latter has any bearing on the MPA.

538. In the Tribunal's view, the Parties' disagreement regarding the scope of Article 194 is answered by the fifth provision of that Article, which expressly provides that –

> The measures taken in accordance with this Part shall include those necessary to protect and preserve rare or fragile ecosystems as well as the habitat of depleted, threatened or endangered species and other forms of marine life.

Article 194 is accordingly not limited to measures aimed strictly at controlling pollution and extends to measures focussed primarily on conservation and the preservation of ecosystems. As repeatedly justified by the United Kingdom, the MPA is such a measure.

539. The Tribunal concludes that in establishing the MPA, the United Kingdom was under an obligation to "endeavour to harmonize" its policies with Mauritius. Article 194(1), however, is prospective and requires only the United Kingdom's best efforts. It does not require that such attempts precede any action with respect to the marine environment, nor does it impose any particular deadline. The Tribunal does not therefore see in the limited life of the MPA to date that the United Kingdom has violated an obligation pursuant to Article 194(1).

540. Article 194(4) imposes a different type of obligation. The Tribunal considers the requirement that the United Kingdom "refrain from unjustifiable interference" to be functionally equivalent to the obligation to give "due regard", set out in Article 56(2), or the obligation of good faith that follows from Article 2(3). Like these provisions, Article 194(4) requires a balancing act between competing rights, based upon an evaluation of the extent of the interference, the availability of alternatives, and the importance of the rights and policies at issue. Article 194(4) differs, however, in that it facially applies only to the "activities carried out by other States" pursuant to their rights, rather than to the rights themselves. Mauritius' rights to the eventual return of the Archipelago and to the benefit of oil and minerals are prospective in nature: there are no activities presently carried out pursuant to these undertakings. Accordingly, the Tribunal considers that Article 194(4) is applicable only to Mauritian fishing rights, which in turn the Tribunal is considering only in respect of the territorial sea.

541. The Tribunal does not exclude the possibility that environmental considerations could potentially justify, for the purposes of Article 194(4), the infringement of Mauritian fishing rights in the territorial sea. Such justification, however, would require significant engagement with Mauritius to explain the need for the measure and to explore less restrictive alternatives. This engagement is nowhere evident in the record. Accordingly, and for the reasons already largely set out in the application of Articles 2(3) and 56(2), the Tribunal concludes that the declaration of the MPA was not compatible with Article 194(4) and Mauritian fishing activities in the territorial sea.

(e) *The Role for Article 300*

542. Mauritius' submissions pursuant to Article 300 are based primarily, although not exclusively, on the alleged U.S. record of a meeting with BIOT officials on 12 May 2009. The Tribunal has reviewed the record of the English court proceedings that considered the matter and sees no basis to question the conclusion reached following the examination of the relevant individuals, that the content of that meeting was not as recorded in the leaked cable. Nor does the Tribunal consider it appropriate to place weight on a record of such provenance.

543. The Tribunal has before it a substantial amount of internal United Kingdom correspondence concerning the MPA, none of which suggests an ulterior motive or improper purpose. Having already concluded that the declaration of the MPA was not in keeping with Articles 2(3), 56(2), and 194(4) of the Convention, the Tribunal sees no need to comment further on Article 300 or the abuse of rights.

C. Final Observations

544. In concluding that the declaration of the MPA was not in accordance with the provisions of the Convention, the Tribunal has taken no view on the substantive quality or nature of the MPA or on the importance of environmental protection. The Tribunal's concern has been with the manner in which the MPA was established, rather than its substance. It is now open to the Parties to enter into the negotiations that the Tribunal would have expected prior to the proclamation of the MPA, with a view to achieving a mutually satisfactory arrangement for protecting the marine environment, to the extent necessary under a "sovereignty umbrella".

* * *

Chapter VII. Costs

545. In its Final Submissions, the United Kingdom requested that the Tribunal "determine that the costs incurred by the United Kingdom in presenting its case shall be borne by Mauritius, and that Mauritius shall reimburse the United Kingdom for its share of the expenses of the Tribunal." Additionally, in its decision on the challenge to Judge Greenwood, the Tribunal decided (further to the request of the United Kingdom) "[t]o defer any decision regarding the costs of the Challenge."

546. This arbitration has presented a number of difficult issues in the interpretation of the Convention with respect to which the Parties were genuinely in dispute. Although Mauritius has not prevailed on the entirety of its submissions, it has succeeded in significant part. The Tribunal also considers

that the Parties' legal arguments were carefully considered, whether or not they prevailed, and that the Parties acted with skill, dispatch, and economy in presenting their respective cases. The United Kingdom's application for costs is accordingly dismissed. Each Party shall bear its own costs. The costs of the Tribunal shall be shared equally.

* * *

CHAPTER VIII. DISPOSITIF

547. For the reasons set out in this Award, the Tribunal decides as follows:

A. In relation to its jurisdiction, the Tribunal,

(1) FINDS, by three votes to two, that it lacks jurisdiction with respect to Mauritius' First and Second Submissions;

(2) FINDS, unanimously, that there is not a dispute between the Parties such as would call for the Tribunal to exercise jurisdiction with respect to Mauritius' Third Submission;

(3) FINDS, unanimously, that it has jurisdiction pursuant to Article 288(1), and Article 297(1)(*c*), to consider Mauritius' Fourth Submission and the compatibility of the MPA with the following provisions of the Convention:

a. Article 2(3) insofar as it relates to Mauritius' fishing rights in the territorial sea or to the United Kingdom's undertakings to return the Archipelago to Mauritius when no longer needed for defence purposes and to return the benefit of any minerals or oil discovered in or near the Chagos Archipelago to Mauritius;

b. Article 56(2), insofar as it relates to the United Kingdom's undertakings to return the Archipelago to Mauritius when no longer needed for defence purposes and to return the benefit of any minerals or oil discovered in or near the Chagos Archipelago to Mauritius;

c. Article 194; and

d. Article 300, insofar as it relates to the abuse of rights in connection with a violation of one of the foregoing articles;

(4) AND DISMISSES, unanimously, the United Kingdom's objection to the jurisdiction of the Tribunal over Mauritius' Fourth Submission with respect to the aforementioned provisions of the Convention.

B. In relation to the merits of the Parties' dispute, the Tribunal, having found, *inter alia*,

(1) that the United Kingdom's undertaking to ensure that fishing rights in the Chagos Archipelago would remain available to Mauritius as far as practicable is legally binding insofar as it relates to the territorial sea;

(2) that the United Kingdom's undertaking to return the Chagos Archipelago to Mauritius when no longer needed for defence purposes is legally binding; and

(3) that the United Kingdom's undertaking to preserve the benefit of any minerals or oil discovered in or near the Chagos Archipelago for Mauritius is legally binding;

DECLARES, unanimously, that in establishing the MPA surrounding the Chagos Archipelago the United Kingdom breached its obligations under Articles 2(3), 56(2), and 194(4) of the Convention.

C. In relation to the costs of these proceedings, the Tribunal DECIDES that each Party shall bear its own costs and that the costs of the Tribunal shall be shared equally by the Parties.

Done at The Hague, this 18th day of March 2015,

[*Signed*]
JUDGE RÜDIGER WOLFRUM
[concurring in part and dissenting in part]

[*Signed*]
JUDGE SIR CHRISTOPHER GREENWOOD CMG

[*Signed*]
JUDGE JAMES KATEKA
[concurring in part and dissenting in part]

[*Signed*]
JUDGE ALBERT HOFFMANN

[*Signed*]
PROFESSOR IVAN SHEARER AM, PRESIDENT

[*Signed*]
MR. BROOKS W. DALY, REGISTRAR

Chagos Marine Protected Area Arbitration

(Mauritius v. United Kingdom)

Dissenting and Concurring Opinion

Judge James Kateka and Judge Rüdiger Wolfrum

1. To our regret we are not able to agree with the reasoning and the findings of the Tribunal on Mauritius' Submissions Nos. 1 and 2; we, however, concur with the findings on Submissions Nos. 3 and 4, although not with all the relevant reasoning.

2. This Opinion will concentrate on the areas of disagreement, namely the characterization of the legal dispute between the Parties and the jurisdiction of the Tribunal concerning Submissions Nos. 1 and 2 of Mauritius. It will also deal with some issues concerning the merits of the case.

A. Characterization of the Dispute

1. Final Submission No. 1 of Mauritius[1]

3. The Parties differ on the characterization of the dispute. Mauritius states that its case is that the MPA is unlawful under the Convention. The United Kingdom, for its part, argues that the dispute is one about sovereignty over the Chagos Archipelago. In its Final Submission No. 1, Mauritius requested the Tribunal to adjudge and declare that the United Kingdom is not entitled to declare an "MPA" or other maritime zones because it is not the "coastal State within the meaning of *inter alia* Articles 2, 55, 56 and 76 of the Convention." During the oral hearing, Mauritius put it this way: "[t]he central question before this Tribunal is not whether the United Kingdom has sovereignty, it is whether the United Kingdom for the purposes of the Convention is 'the coastal State' and was, as such, entitled to act as it does".[2] This statement was made without prejudice to the fact that there exists a longstanding dispute between the parties about sovereignty over the Chagos Archipelago.

4. We agree with the Award that it is for the Tribunal to characterize the dispute (*see* Award, para. 208). However, we differ from the approach taken in the Award in characterizing the dispute. Two different issues have to be decided in this context: namely, (*a*) whether the dispute between Mauritius and the

---

[1] Final Submission No. 1 reads: "the United Kingdom is not entitled to declare an 'MPA' or other maritime zones because it is not the 'coastal State' within the meaning of *inter alia* Articles 2, 55, 56 and 76 of the Convention".

[2] Final Transcript, 999:16–18.

United Kingdom is a dispute about the interpretation and the application of the Convention or a dispute on the sovereignty over the Chagos Archipelago, and (*b*) whether the Tribunal has jurisdiction over the dispute however defined. Logically one has to turn to the characterization of the dispute first and to other issues concerning jurisdiction second. We note that the Award, without consequently separating these two issues (*see* Award, para. 209), touches upon both of them while concentrating on the United Kingdom's argument as to whether the First Submission is to be considered an artificial re-characterization of the long-standing sovereignty dispute (*see* Award, para. 207).

5. We disagree with the approach taken by the Tribunal, which does not fully reflect the established jurisprudence of the ICJ in its *Fisheries Jurisdiction* case (*(Spain* v. *Canada), Judgment of* 4 *December 1998, I.C.J. Reports 1998*, p. 432 at p. 447, paras. 29 *et seq.*), to which the Award briefly refers in its paragraph 208. This judgment refers to several other cases, in particular to *Nuclear Tests ((Australia* v. *France), Judgment, I.C.J. Reports 1974*, p. 253 at p. 260, para. 24). This jurisprudence may be summarized as follows.

> (*a*) that it is for the Court itself to determine the dispute dividing the parties, (*Fisheries Jurisdiction (Spain* v. *Canada), Judgment of* 4 *December 1998, I.C.J. Reports 1998*, p. 432 at p. 449, paras. 30–31);
>
> (*b*) to do so on an objective basis while giving particular attention to the formulation of the dispute chosen by the Applicant by examining the position of both parties, (*ibid.*); and
>
> (*c*) to distinguish between the dispute itself and the arguments advanced by the parties, (*ibid.* at para. 32).

6. The above jurisprudence of the ICJ[3] has to be seen in its context. It focuses on the interpretation of a declaration made by Canada. Nevertheless, some of the principles expressed in this judgment are of relevance for the issue to be decided here, in particular since they are based upon previous rulings of the ICJ. These principles are, first, that the decision on the characterization of the legal dispute has to be made by the Tribunal on objective grounds "giving particular attention to the formulation of the dispute chosen by the Applicant" (*ibid.* at para. 30), and, second, that it is necessary to distinguish between the dispute itself and the arguments advanced by the parties.

7. Considering the jurisprudence of the ICJ,[4] the question raised in paragraph 209 of the Award is not formulated appropriately.

8. Mauritius centres its case in Submission No. 1 on the meaning of the term "coastal State" and accordingly qualifies it as a case on the interpretation and application of the Convention within the jurisdiction of the Tribunal (Article 288 of the Convention). It argues that the meaning of the words "coastal State" and the issues of sovereignty are interwoven in the present case.

---

[3] See the cases set out in paragraph 5 above.

[4] *Ibid.*

We are sympathetic with this reasoning, but at the same time we emphasize that the case is not only a sovereignty claim as the United Kingdom qualifies it.

9. The following are the factual and legal grounds why we believe that the dispute cannot be qualified as a dispute about the sovereignty of the Chagos Archipelago:

10. First, it has to be noted that in its Submission No. 1, Mauritius only questioned the competence of the United Kingdom to be the coastal State in respect of establishing the MPA. This was emphasized and re-emphasized in the written, as well as in the oral, proceedings. From the very wording of Submission No. 1, it is clear that the claim advanced by Mauritius is not on the territorial sovereignty of the United Kingdom over the Chagos Archipelago but only covers an aspect thereof: namely, the establishment of the MPA ("The United Kingdom is not entitled to declare an "MPA" or any other maritime zone"). It is evident that territorial sovereignty encompasses more than the establishment of an MPA.

11. Second, it is undisputed that the issue concerning the sovereignty of the Chagos Archipelago was raised in general at some stage before the arbitral proceedings were initiated, but there was no indication that third party dispute settlement was sought. The United Kingdom criticized this within the context of Article 283 of the Convention. It is worth noting in this regard that, although Mauritius maintained its claim concerning its sovereignty over the Chagos Archipelago, it was satisfied with the assurance by the United Kingdom that the Archipelago would be returned at a future date. Mauritius did not even seek an agreement with the United Kingdom to that extent. The United Kingdom offered to conclude an agreement, but Mauritius declined. This indicates that, while Mauritius maintained its claim to sovereignty over the Chagos Archipelago, this was not its primary concern in the context of the claim now before the Tribunal.

12. Third, Mauritius initiated these proceedings against the United Kingdom only after the establishment of the MPA. It was clear right from the beginning that without this development Mauritius would not have initiated a dispute settlement procedure.

13. Fourth, Mauritius does not advance in its Submission No. 1 any argument concerning the exercise of territorial sovereignty over the islands. Its Submission No. 1 is clearly limited.

14. Fifth, account has to be taken of the limited scope of Submission No. 1 of Mauritius and that this has an impact upon the jurisdiction of the Tribunal. Under this submission, the Tribunal could not decide on the sovereignty of the United Kingdom over the Chagos Archipelago as such—even if it had the competence to do so—since the submission limits the jurisdiction of the Tribunal in this respect. It would be illogical if the Tribunal declared that this dispute was on the sovereignty over the Chagos Archipelago while

being aware that, due to the limited scope of Submission No. 1, it was unable to decide on a dispute with such a broad scope.

15. We have noted that in some instances statements by counsel for Mauritius referred to the territorial sovereignty of Mauritius over the Chagos Archipelago. These are arguments, in the words of the ICJ (*Fisheries Jurisdiction (Spain* v. *Canada), Judgment of 4 December 1998, I.C.J. Reports 1998*, p. 432 at p. 449, para. 35), to be clearly separated from the case. Apart from that, in our view an overstatement by counsel for Mauritius of the Applicant's case should not dilute the thrust of the argument about the unlawfulness of the establishment of the MPA.

16. The United Kingdom emphasized that questions of sovereignty lie "at the heart of the current claim"[5] and that the issue of sovereignty over the Chagos Archipelago is a longstanding point of contention. It considers the claim an "artificial re-characterization of a long-standing sovereignty dispute."[6]

17. The Tribunal comes to the same conclusion as the United Kingdom by emphasizing the references to the sovereignty dispute "across a range of fora and instruments" (Award, para. 211), without, however, considering in detail the wording of Mauritius' Submission No. 1. This is to be regretted. The wording of paragraph 212 of the Award is quite telling. It states "... that the Parties' dispute with respect to Mauritius' First Submission is properly characterized as relating to land sovereignty over the Chagos Archipelago. The Parties' differing views on the "coastal State" for the purposes of the Convention are simply one aspect of this larger dispute". On the basis of Mauritius' Submission No. 1, it is exactly the other way around. The differing views on the coastal State are the dispute before the Tribunal and the issue of sovereignty over the Chagos Archipelago is merely an element in the reasoning of Mauritius and not to be decided by the Tribunal.

2. Final Submission No. 2 of Mauritius[7]

18. As far as Submission No. 2 is concerned, we disagree with the Tribunal's qualification in paragraph 229 of the Award that the Second Submission "... must be viewed against the backdrop of the Parties' dispute regarding sovereignty over the Chagos Archipelago." Here again, no distinction is being made between the submission and the reasoning. The submission states: "having regard to the commitments that it has made to Mauritius in relation to the Chagos Archipelago, the United Kingdom is not entitled unilaterally to declare

[5] Final Transcript, 666:18–19.

[6] Final Transcript, 660:19–20.

[7] Final Submission No. 2 reads: "having regard to the commitments that it has made to Mauritius in relation to the Chagos Archipelago, the United Kingdom is not entitled unilaterally to declare an 'MPA' or other maritime zones because Mauritius has rights as a 'coastal State' within the meaning of *inter alia* Articles 56(1)(*b*)(iii) and 76(8) of the Convention".

an 'MPA' or other maritime zone because …". We consider that the remaining part is reasoning.

19. We disagree that this is a dispute on the sovereignty over the Chagos Archipelago. In our view, this is a dispute as to whether the United Kingdom has ceded one or more rights as a coastal State in the commitments made in the Lancaster House Undertakings. Submission No. 2 is the opposite of a claim questioning the sovereignty of the United Kingdom over the Chagos Archipelago since it proceeds from the assumption that the United Kingdom had territorial sovereignty and had ceded certain rights as the sovereign.

B. Jurisdiction

20. The relevant provisions on jurisdiction are Articles 286, 287(5) and 288(1) of the Convention.

21. Mauritius ratified the Convention on 4 November 1994 and has made no declaration. The United Kingdom acceded to the Convention on 25 July 1997 and in a declaration of the same date extended the Convention to, amongst others, the BIOT. Another declaration of the United Kingdom excludes disputes under Article 298(1)(*b*) and (*c*) of the Convention from compulsory dispute settlement. These declarations are not of direct relevance for this case.

1. Final Submission No. 1

22. In considering this submission, it may be noted that for jurisdictional purposes, the Tribunal does not have to determine that the United Kingdom has violated the provisions relied upon by Mauritius. The Tribunal merely has to establish whether the provisions relied on apply to the Applicant's claims. In determining whether it has jurisdiction, the Tribunal must establish a link between the facts advanced by the Applicant and a particular provision to show that this provision can sustain the claim (*M/V "Louisa" (Saint Vincent and the Grenadines* v. *Kingdom of Spain), Judgment, ITLOS Reports 2013*, p. 4 at para. 99; *Oil Platforms (Islamic Republic of Iran* v. *United States of America), Preliminary Objection, Judgment, I.C.J. Reports 1996*, p. 803 at p. 810, para. 16). The Award refers to this principle in paragraph 296.

23. Article 288(1) of the Convention sets out when international courts or tribunals under Part XV of the Convention have jurisdiction. They have jurisdiction over "any dispute concerning the interpretation or application of the Convention". Although this provision is broadly phrased, it contains a limitation: namely, the dispute must be on the interpretation or application of the Convention. It is crucial to establish whether Mauritius advances such a claim.

24. Mauritius invokes in its Submission No. 1 Articles 2, 55, 56 and 76 of the Convention. These provisions refer to the status and competences of coastal States. Mauritius argues that Article 288(1) of the Convention does not say

that disputes concerning the interpretation or application of the words "coastal State" are excluded from the jurisdiction of a court or tribunal referred to in Article 287 of the Convention. Mauritius also disagrees with the United Kingdom's argument that the words "coastal State" are to be determined as a matter of fact[8] and do not require the interpretation or application of the Convention. For Mauritius, it is a legal question. Linked with its consideration of Article 288(1) is Mauritius' consideration of the limitations and exceptions in section 3 of Part XV, namely Articles 297 and 298. It argues that jurisdiction is not excluded by section 3. Mauritius argues that Article 297 has nothing to say about the entitlement of a State to be able to claim that it is the "coastal State".

25. We raise these details of Mauritius' arguments on jurisdiction because we feel that the Tribunal has neglected some of Mauritius' arguments due to its focusing its attention on the question "... of the extent to which Article 288(1) accords the Tribunal jurisdiction in respect of a dispute over land sovereignty when, as here, that dispute touches in some ancillary manner on matters regulated by the Convention" (Award, para. 213). This approach narrows the issue of jurisdiction and prevents the Tribunal from considering the issue from a broader perspective, as required by Article 288(1) of the Convention.

26. But apart from that, we consider the subsequent reasoning of the Tribunal (*see* Award, paras. 214–221) not convincing; in particular, it does not sufficiently deal with the arguments advanced by both Parties concerning the "*a contrario* argument". The Tribunal merely states that "much of this argumentation misses the point" (Award, para. 215). Instead the Tribunal emphasizes that the negotiation records of the Convention provide no firm answer regarding jurisdiction over territorial sovereignty. With this we would agree. But as will be demonstrated below, we draw a different conclusion therefrom.

27. Furthermore, the reasoning of the Tribunal is not fully coherent. How is it possible to state in paragraph 215 of the Award that the negotiating records of the Convention provide no firm answer regarding jurisdiction over territorial sovereignty and to assume in paragraphs 216 and 217, on the basis of Articles 297 and 298(1) of the Convention, that if the drafters had anticipated the possibility of territorial disputes they would have provided an opt-out facility? That the drafters did not foresee the possibility does not in itself justify reading a limitation into the jurisdiction of the international courts and tribunals acting under Part XV of the Convention.

28. There is no reasoning by the Tribunal concerning the argument put forward by Mauritius. According to Mauritius, sovereignty disputes are not necessarily excluded by Article 298(1)(*a*) of the Convention; they may be resolved under Part XV when they form a necessary part or have a "genuine link" to a dispute concerning the interpretation and application of any pro-

[8] Counsel for the United Kingdom dismissively said that the term "coastal State" should detain the Tribunal no more than ten seconds as it means the State with the coast adjacent to the maritime zone with which the given provision of the Convention is concerned. *See* Final Transcript, 665:14–16.

vision of the Convention. This, according to Mauritius, does not mean every dispute touching on sovereignty automatically falls within the Convention. The Tribunal does not take into account this argument since it considered the sovereignty issue the "real issue in the case" and the "object of the claim" (Award, para. 220), a statement we already have dealt with and do not consider sustainable. In the following paragraphs we will set out our position on the jurisdiction of this Tribunal on the basis of a comprehensive analysis of Articles 297, 298 and 288 of the Convention.

2. Limitations to jurisdiction

29. As stated above, Article 288(1) establishes that an international court or tribunal has jurisdiction over any dispute "concerning the interpretation or application of this Convention". It is evident that the jurisdiction of international courts and tribunals is thus limited. Exceptions to the jurisdiction of international courts and tribunals under Part XV of the Convention are contained in Articles 297 and 298 of the Convention.

30. We shall first establish whether the dispute between Mauritius and the United Kingdom is excluded by the exceptions as contained in Articles 297 and 298 of the Convention. Thereafter, we shall return to Article 288(1) of the Convention, dealing with the question as to whether that provision excludes the jurisdiction over disputes which necessarily involves the concurrent consideration of any unsettled dispute concerning sovereignty or other rights over continental or insular land territory.

31. Apart from the wording of Articles 297 and 298 of the Convention, their relationship to each other has to be taken into account, as well as the system of exceptions in the Convention seen as a whole and their legislative history. It is also relevant in this context that the Geneva Conventions on the Law of the Sea only provided for an Optional Protocol on dispute settlement, whereas under the Convention a mandatory dispute settlement system exists in spite of the exceptions provided under Articles 297 and 298 of the Convention.

32. On the basis of a purely textual analysis of Article 297 of the Convention, it is evident that its exclusion of the jurisdiction of international courts and tribunals under Part XV of the Convention does not embrace the exclusion of disputes for the reason that the decision on them would involve the consideration of any unsettled dispute concerning continental or insular land territory.

33. Article 298(1)(*a*) of the Convention provides that any State Party when signing, ratifying or acceding to the Convention may declare that it does not accept the third party dispute settlement procedures provided for in section 2 of Part XV of the Convention with respect to one or more of the three categories of disputes referred to in Article 298(1)(*a*)(i) to (iii) of the Convention. The first category deals with sea boundary delimitation. The relevant paragraph (1)(*a*)(i) contains the following clause:

> ... at the request of any party to the dispute, accept submission of the matter to conciliation under Annex V, section 2; and provided further that any dispute that necessarily involves the concurrent consideration of any unsettled dispute concerning sovereignty or other rights over continental or insular land territory shall be excluded from such submission;

34. Since the United Kingdom has not submitted such a declaration and since the present dispute is not a dispute on sea boundaries, this exception clause cannot be applied to the case before the Tribunal.

35. It has been argued by the United Kingdom, though, that this clause should be read into Article 297 of the Convention on exceptions to the jurisdiction of international courts and tribunals under Part XV of the Convention. This view is not supported by the legislative history of Articles 297 and 298 of the Convention as will be set out below.

36. The clause "... that any dispute that necessarily involves the concurrent consideration of any unsettled dispute concerning sovereignty or other rights over continental or insular land territory shall be excluded from such submission" was introduced in part into Article 297 of the ICNT[9] (today Article 298 of the Convention) to avoid the possibility of using the dispute settlement system of the Convention on the Law of the Sea for deciding territorial claims. Attempts were made to have this clause transferred to Article 297 of the Convention containing the automatic exceptions but no majority was found to that extent.[10] This is explained by the President of the Third UN Conference on the Law of the Sea in his Report on the work of the informal plenary meeting of the Conference on the settlement of disputes of 23 August 1980.[11] He stated:

> 6. The course of the negotiations conducted in the informal plenary meetings may be summarized as follows. Informal suggestions were made by some of the participants in the course of their interventions. These included suggestions regarding both drafting and substance. In particular, two suggestions were made which touched upon questions of delimitation, which were firstly, that a cross-reference to article 298*bis* of

[9] *Official Records of the Third United Nations Conference on the Law of the Sea, Volume VIII (Informal Composite Negotiating Text, Sixth Session)*, Informal Composite Negotiating Text, Art. 296, UN Doc. A/CONF.62/WP.10 (15 July 1977); *see also* S. Rosenne & L. Sohn, eds., *United Nations Convention on the Law of the Sea 1982: A Commentary*, Vol. V at p. 112 (M. Norquist, gen. ed., 1989). The idea of conciliation was introduced in *Official Records of the Third United Nations Conference on the Law of the Sea, Volume VIII (Informal Composite Negotiating Text, Sixth Session)*, Informal Composite Negotiating Text Revision 1, Art. 296, UN Doc. A/CONF.62/WP.10/Rev.1 (28 April 1979).

[10] *See* P.C. Irwin, "Settlement of Marine Boundary Disputes: An Analysis of the Law of the Sea Negotiations," *Ocean Development & International Law*, Vol. 8(2) at p. 105 (1980).

[11] *Official Records of the Third United Nations Conference on the Law of the Sea, Volume XIV (Summary Records, Plenary, General Committee, First and Third Committees, as well as Documents of the Conference, Resumed Ninth Session (28 July to 29 August 1980))*, Report of the President on the work of the informal plenary meeting of the Conference on the settlement of disputes, UN Doc. A/CONF.62/L.59 (23 August 1980).

> document SD/3 be made in article 298.1(*a*) (ii); secondly, the exclusion of past or existing delimitation disputes as well as disputes relating to sovereignty over land or insular territories from the compulsory dispute settlement procedures and from compulsory submission to conciliation procedures as provided in article 298, paragraph 1(*a*). These should be included in article 296 with the other exceptions in that article. The exclusion of future delimitation disputes by declaration would remain in article 298. Where no settlement had been reached, such disputes would be submitted to conciliation at the request of any party and the other party would be obliged to accept this procedure.
>
> 7. The President had stressed, both in document SD/3 and at the commencements of these negotiations, that changes of substance should be avoided, in particular, any changes to the text of article 296, paragraph 2 and 3. Since delicate compromises that had been very carefully negotiated are contained in that article, any attempt to raise these questions should be avoided. He pointed out that article 298, paragraph 1 (*a*) was closely linked to the delimitation issue. The president further stressed that attention should be concentrated on the structural changes alone to the exclusion of substantive changes. So far as paragraph 1 (*a*) was concerned even structural changes should be avoided.

37. The negotiating history of Articles 297 and 298 of the Convention shows clearly several issues. First, that the "exclusion of past or existing delimitation disputes as well as disputes relating to sovereignty over land or insular territories from compulsory dispute settlement procedures …" was touched upon. Second, that this issue was taken up in Article 298(1)(*a*) of the Convention, which provides for the possibility of making optional exemptions in the context of delimitation disputes. Third, that the initiative to make such (or a similar) exception a general one under Article 297 of the Convention did not prevail. In particular, this means that one cannot read an additional exception into Article 297 of the Convention.

38. On the basis of what we have stated in paragraph 37 above, contrary to what the United Kingdom asserts, a dispute which necessarily involves the concurrent consideration of an unsettled dispute concerning sovereignty or other rights over continental or insular land territory is not excluded from the jurisdiction of international courts or tribunals under Part XV by Article 298 of the Convention. Therefore it is necessary to return to Article 288(1) of the Convention. It has to be considered whether the reference in Article 288(1) of the Convention to disputes concerning the interpretation or application of the Convention excludes disputes which require sovereignty over continental or insular land territory.

39. In our view, there are several reasons why a clause such as is contained in Article 298(1)(*a*) of the Convention cannot be read into Article 288(1) of the Convention.

40. If such an inherent restriction for the jurisdiction of international courts and tribunals under Part XV of the Convention existed, it would not have been necessary to include it in Article 298(1)(*a*) of the Convention.

41. It is equally not sustainable to argue, as the United Kingdom does, that the clause in Article 298(1)(*a*) of the Convention is of a declaratory nature only.[12] The legislative history of this provision proves that there existed some concern in that respect and for that reason this clause was introduced into Article 298(1) of the Convention. When the initiative was launched to transfer such clause to Article 297 of the Convention, the President of the Conference argued against changes, pointing out that the delimitation issue was negotiated intensively and should not be touched. This does not point in the direction of this clause being of a declaratory nature. On the contrary, such change was considered to be substantial.

42. In our view, there are many situations referred to in the Convention in which, when it comes to a legal dispute, it is necessary to establish whether the State taking action is competent to do so. In many instances these disputes require a decision on the existence of competences or their scope and thus on the sovereignty of the State concerned. So far, the issue has come up only in connection with delimitation and flag State issues. The particularity of the present case is that the issue of sovereignty comes up not in the delimitation context but in the context of the application of Article 56 of the Convention. It is to be noted that the issue of sovereignty will be a crucial factor in the reasoning.

43. As to the argument by the United Kingdom that allowing decisions under Part XV of the Convention touching on sovereignty issues would provide for a too broad jurisdictional power of the dispute settlement institutions referred to in Part XV,[13] one has to bear in mind that such a limitation does not apply to the ICJ, which has a broader mandate unless it decides under Part XV of the Convention. This means such a possibility already exists, albeit under a different dispute settlement regime.

44. In our view, the limitations on the exercise of jurisdiction under Part XV rest in Article 288(1) of the Convention (disputes "concerning the interpretation or application of the Convention") and the exceptions provided for in Articles 297 and 298 of the Convention. This ensures that a required nexus between the claim and the law of the sea exists, but there is in our view no justification to create another jurisdictional limitation beyond the ones of the Convention. It has been stated that Part XV constitutes a well-negotiated text. But exactly that puts into question the introduction of limitations to the jurisdiction of international courts and tribunals acting under Part XV beyond those explicitly provided for.

45. To conclude, according to Article 288(1) of the Convention, a nexus between the case in question and the Convention has to exist. Such a nexus

[12] Final Transcript, 693:15–20.

[13] Final Transcript, 648:10–13.

exists in this case through Article 56 of the Convention. In that respect we disagree with the Tribunal's finding in paragraph 220 of the Award which states: "Where the 'real issue in the case' and the 'object of the claim' do not relate to the interpretation or application of the Convention, however, an incidental connection between the dispute and some matter regulated by the Convention is insufficient to bring the dispute, as a whole, within the ambit of Article 288(1)" on two grounds. We differ in respect of the qualification of the dispute, which is for us a dispute about the interpretation of Article 56 of the Convention, and we consider it permissible to decide incidentally about sovereignty issues. That it will be necessary to consider the sovereignty issue by having recourse to general international law or specific international agreements is anticipated in the Convention. To introduce a new limitation to the jurisdiction of international courts and tribunals acting under Part XV of the Convention would change the balance achieved at the Third UN Conference on the Law of the Sea in respect of the dispute settlement system. The Tribunal lacks the competence do so.

3. Final Submission No. 2

46. As far as the jurisdiction of the Tribunal is concerned, this claim requires the Tribunal to analyse the commitments made by the United Kingdom. The United Kingdom argued that the Tribunal lacks the competence to do so.

47. The Tribunal does not deal with the arguments advanced by both Parties, due to its qualification of the dispute as sovereignty related. The Tribunal should have considered further whether the dispute under Submission No. 2 was one on the competences of the coastal State and whether the undertakings in the Lancaster House Understanding were to be considered as rights under Article 56(2) of the Convention. We regret the fact that the Tribunal did not do so.

4. Final Submission No. 3[14]

48. As far as Mauritius' Submission No. 3 (alleged violation of Article 76(8) of the Convention) is concerned, we agree with the Tribunal that this submission is different from the above two submissions. The United Kingdom did not object to Mauritius' submission of preliminary information to the CLCS. In fact the United Kingdom encouraged Mauritius to file the preliminary information at the January 2009 meeting. It was only at the stage of its *Rejoinder* that the United Kingdom seemed to have had a second thought. During the oral hearing the United Kingdom suggested a possible joint full

[14] Final Submission No. 3 reads: "the United Kingdom shall take no steps that may prevent the Commission on the Limits of the Continental Shelf from making recommendations to Mauritius in respect of any full submission that Mauritius may make to the Commission regarding the Chagos Archipelago under Article 76 of the Convention".

submission with Mauritius. In any case, the United Kingdom says it has no interest in the development of mineral resources in the outer continental shelf.

49. We agree with the extensive review of the record with the view to determining whether a separate dispute between the Parties has come into existence regarding the subject-matter of Mauritius's Submission No.3. We agree that there was no such dispute at the time when the *Application*, *Memorial* and *Counter-Memorial* were filed. Considering the exchange of views between the Parties at the hearing, we agree that there is no dispute between the Parties regarding this issue. We also agree that accordingly the Tribunal is not required to rule on whether it has jurisdiction over Mauritius' Submission No. 3 (*see* Award, paras. 348–350).

5. Final Submission No. 4[15]

50. As far as the fourth submission is concerned, it deals with the violation of Articles 2(3), 55, 56, 63, 64, 194 and 300 of the Convention. We agree with the Tribunal that jurisdiction over Mauritius's Submission No. 4 depends upon the characterization of the Parties' dispute and on the interpretation and application of Article 297 of the Convention (*see* Award, para. 283).

51. Mauritius argues that the MPA deals with the protection of the marine environment and accordingly any dispute would come under Article 297(1)(*c*) of the Convention in connection with Article 194. The United Kingdom advances several counter-arguments, including that the MPA does not—at least not yet—regulate marine pollution, but deals with fishing. It points out that Article 297(1)(*c*) covers—by pointing to Part XII to the Convention—pollution only. Therefore the Tribunal's jurisdiction would not cover the establishment of the MPA. In response thereto Mauritius argues that the declarations made by the United Kingdom at the occasion of the establishment of the MPA indicated that the MPA was devoted to protect the marine environment at large, as well as the territorial environment (except Diego Garcia). The implementation regulations announced are meant to replace the BIOT legislation protecting the environment, flora and fauna of the islands and their waters. Only later did the United Kingdom state that implementing legislation was not necessary since the relevant rules were in place. The Award sets out quite in detail that the MPA was designed by the United Kingdom as a means for the protection of the marine environment (*see* Award, paras. 286–291); we agree with this assessment of the background for the establishment of the MPA.

[15] Final Submission No. 4 reads: "The United Kingdom's purported 'MPA' is incompatible with the substantive and procedural obligations of the United Kingdom under the Convention, including *inter alia* Articles 2, 55, 56, 63, 64, 194 and 300, as well as Article 7 of the Agreement for the Implementation of the Provisions of the United Nations Convention on the Law of the Sea of 10 December 1982 Relating to the Conservation and Management of Straddling Fish Stocks and Highly Migratory Fish Stocks of 4 August 1995."

52. As far as the jurisdiction of the Tribunal is concerned, the starting point has to be the wording of Article 297(1)(*c*) of the Convention which refers to the protection of the marine environment ("... acted in contravention of specified international rules and standards for the protection and preservation of the marine environment ..."). Article 297(1)(*c*) of the Convention has to be read together with Article 56(1)(*b*)(iii) and Part XII of the Convention, which specifies the competences of the coastal Sates under that article (*see M/V "Virginia G" (Panama/Guinea-Bissau), Judgment of* 14 *April 2014, ITLOS Reports 2014*; *ibid., Joint Declaration of Judges Kelly and Attard*). The coastal State must have violated those rules (or standards), which may have been established by the Convention or through a competent international organization or diplomatic conference.

53. The Award provides a detailed description and assessment of the relationship between Articles 288 and 297 of the Convention based upon the legislative history of these provisions (see Award, paras. 307–317) which we share. The plain reading seems to indicate that the language of Article 297(1)(*c*) of the Convention covers a rather narrow scope of disputes; it would not cover every activity undertaken by the coastal State under Article 56(1)(*b*)(iii) of the Convention. We are not convinced by that argument of the United Kingdom.[16] One has to look closely at Part XII since Article 297(1)(*c*) of the Convention does not only refer to rules and standards established through an international organization, but also to rules established by the Convention.

54. As far as the competences of the coastal States in respect of the EEZ are concerned, Article 211(5) of the Convention (also dealing with pollution) is of relevance. Part XII of the Convention does not provide a general competence for coastal States to issue rules on the protection of the marine environment. This is of relevance. Taking this into consideration, T. Mensah says: "For example, disputes could arise where it is alleged that a coastal state has exceeded the powers given to it by the Convention to take measures for environmental protection against a foreign vessel ...".[17] This means cases where the coastal State has exceeded its regulatory powers concerning the protection of the marine environment come under the clause of Article 297(1)(*c*) of the Convention. As Mensah points out, the jurisdiction of any court or tribunal is not subject to any of the limitations on jurisdiction specified in Article 297 or the optional exceptions to jurisdiction under Article 298 of the Convention.

55. What Mauritius in fact alleges is that the United Kingdom had no competence under the Convention to establish an MPA and thus is in breach of the Convention. Therefore, we agree with the Award that the Tribunal has

[16] Final Transcript, 802:21 to 803:2.

[17] T. Mensah, "Protection and Preservation of the Marine Environment and the Dispute Settlement Regime in the United Nations Convention on the Law of the Sea," *in* A. Kirchner, ed., *International Marine Environmental Law: Institutions, Implementation and Innovations*, p. 9 at p. 11 (2003).

jurisdiction to decide on alleged breaches of the rules of the Convention on the protection of the marine environment.

56. The United Kingdom further argues that the MPA was established in the exercise of its sovereign rights under Article 56(1)(*a*) of the Convention and refers to the exception clause of Article 297(3)(*a*) of the Convention.[18] As far as Article 297(3)(*a*) of the Convention is concerned, the United Kingdom accords that provision a rather broad scope which would include the protection of biodiversity under "... its sovereign rights with respect to living resources in the exclusive economic zone ...". In our view this goes clearly beyond the meaning of Article 56(1) of the Convention. The protection of the biodiversity does not come under the sovereign rights concerning the protection and management of living resources. It is a matter of the protection of the environment.

57. Considering that this is a decision on an MPA, rather than a decision on fishing, Article 297(3)(*a*) of the Convention does not apply.

58. But if that provision is considered to be applicable, it has to be taken into account that Article 297(3)(*a*) of the Convention contains two parts. The first part says that disputes concerning fisheries shall be settled in accordance with section 2 of Part XV. That is a confirmation of jurisdiction and not a limitation. The limitation starts with the word "except". If the first part of this clause—the confirmation of jurisdiction—is to retain some meaning, not all disputes on fisheries can be interpreted as "... any dispute relating to its sovereign rights with respect to living resources ...". The second part of the clause must be narrower in scope than the scope of the first part. This is not taken into account by the United Kingdom. On the basis of its approach, all disputes on fisheries would be excluded from the jurisdiction of the Tribunal, which means this interpretation would deprive Article 297(3)(*a*) of the Convention (first part) of its meaning. Apart from that, the United Kingdom expands upon the scope of the exception by including the protection of biodiversity. This is not sustained by Articles 61 and 62 of the Convention which should be correlated to Article 297(3)(*a*) of the Convention.

59. In this context, it is essential to note that the United Kingdom only later in the proceedings emphasized the fisheries aspect, whereas at the time of declaring the MPA it stressed the environmental aspect. Further, up to the conclusion of the oral proceedings, the United Kingdom was vague as to whether implementing rules were necessary and would follow. The fact that so far only the prohibition of fishing has been proclaimed does not turn this zone into a measure concerning fishing. Otherwise this would give the United Kingdom the right, by not issuing the necessary implementation legislation, or by doing so only selectively, to determine the scope of the dispute.

60. Finally, in our view it is doubtful whether a total ban on fishing is covered by the exception clause under Article 297(3)(*a*) of the Convention. The second part of Article 297(3)(*a*) of the Convention focuses on utilizing living

[18] The United Kingdom's Preliminary Objections, paras. 5.15–5.30.

resources, including their proper management and conservation, rather than banning fishing completely without a conservation objective. That fishing and management of living resources is to be seen from the perspective of their utilization is confirmed by the object and purpose of the Convention. One of the goals of the Convention, as stated in its preamble, is to establish "… a legal order for the seas and the oceans which … will promote … the equitable and efficient utilization of their resources, the conservation of their living resources … and preservation of the marine environment." As provided in article 31(1) of the Vienna Convention on the Law of Treaties, treaties should be interpreted in the light of their object and purpose.

61. To sum up, we share the conclusion of the Tribunal that it has jurisdiction pursuant to Article 288(1) and Article 297(1)(*c*) of the Convention to consider Mauritius's Submission No. 4 (*see* Award, para. 323).

6. Article 283 of the Convention

62. The "implicit legal disagreement between the Parties [concerning Article 283 of the Convention] relates to the need to refer to a specific treaty or its provisions" as counsel for Mauritius put it.[19]

63. The United Kingdom argues[20] that Mauritius should have indicated in its consultations with the United Kingdom which provisions in the Convention it considered had been violated.

64. This interpretation of Article 283 of the Convention is sustained neither by the wording of this provision, nor by the relevant jurisprudence in this respect. One should rely on the jurisprudence of the ICJ on compromissory clauses (*see, e.g., Application of the International Convention on the Elimination of all Forms of Racial Discrimination (Georgia* v. *Russian Federation), Preliminary Objections, Judgment, I.C.J. Reports 2011*, p. 70) with caution. Article 283 of the Convention is particular. Further, the jurisprudence of ITLOS is not fully coherent and mostly the result of deciding provisional measures (*see, e.g., Land Reclamation by Singapore in and around the Straits of Johor (Malaysia* v. *Singapore), Order of* 8 *October 2003, ITLOS Reports 2003*, p. 10).

65. In the present case, the dispute—or rather the dissatisfaction—with respect to the sovereignty over the Chagos Archipelago was expressed by Mauritius over a long time. The situation took a new turn with the establishment of the MPA. The opposition of Mauritius thereto was evident and clearly expressed. Apart from that, account has to be taken of the fact that Mauritius was informed rather late about the establishment of the MPA. When the public consultation process ended—a process against which Mauritius had protested—the United Kingdom acted (for domestic reasons) very quickly in

[19] Final Transcript, 949:19–20.

[20] Final Transcript, 739:14–19.

the establishment of the MPA. Thereafter there was, from the point of view of Mauritius, no point in engaging in further consultations.

66. We agree with the statement in paragraph 378 of the Award that "... Article 283 cannot be understood as an obligation to negotiate the substance of the dispute" and that Mauritius has met the requirement of Article 283 concerning its Submission No. 4 (*see* Award, para. 386).

C. Merits

67. By declining jurisdiction in respect of Submissions Nos. 1 and 2, the Tribunal missed the opportunity to deal with the separation of the Chagos Islands from Mauritius and the circumstances surrounding this separation. These issues are at the basis of what the Tribunal qualifies as the "real dispute" between Mauritius and the United Kingdom.

68. The United Kingdom emphasized that the Chagos Archipelago was a dependency of Mauritius, only attached to the latter for administrative purposes.[21] The intensive discussion of this point—the fine points of colonial constitutional law[22]—shows that the notion of dependency was used to describe situations which differed significantly. In this case it seems to be of relevance that the extension of the European Convention of Human Rights was interpreted to cover the Chagos Archipelago although the notification only referred to Mauritius. Also the Mauritius (Constitution) Order of 1964 by definition included the dependencies of Mauritius (section 90). This indicates that the Chagos Archipelago was more closely linked to Mauritius than is conceded by the United Kingdom.

69. For that reason, it is not appropriate to consider the Archipelago as an entity, somewhat on its own, which the United Kingdom could decide on without taking into account the views and interests of Mauritius. The way the detachment was executed in reality proves this view to be correct. In particular, the instructions given to the Governor of Mauritius on 6 October 1965 are a clear indication that the United Kingdom considered consent by the cabinet of Mauritius to be essential.[23]

70. This brings us to a central question: namely, as to whether the excision of the Chagos Archipelago was contrary to the legal principles of decolonization as referred to in UN General Assembly resolution 1514 and/or contrary to the principle of self-determination.[24]

71. The United Kingdom argues that the principle of self-determination developed only in 1970 (*Declaration on Principles of International Law con-*

---

[21] The United Kingdom's Counter-Memorial, para. A2.5; Mauritius' Reply, paras. 2.1–2.135.

[22] *See* Final Transcript, 640:23–25.

[23] Mauritius' Memorial, para. 3.36.

[24] *See generally* Final Transcript, 231:22 to 242:12. On the violation of the principle by detaching the Chagos Archipelago, see Final Transcript 245:11 to 247:9.

cerning Friendly Relations and Co-operation among States in accordance with the Charter of the United Nations, General Assembly resolution 2625 (24 October 1970)). In our view, the principle of self-determination developed earlier. Counsel for the United Kingdom to some extent provided information which may be taken to prove this point. Counsel rightly pointed out that between 1945 and 1965 already more than 50 States gained independence in the process of decolonization.

72. It is clearly stated in General Assembly Resolution 1514 that the detachment of a part of a colony (which in this case includes the dependency of the Chagos Archipelago) is contrary to international law. However, it is worth noting (without going into detail) that in many cases referred to by counsel for the United Kingdom, all parts of the former colonies became independent, whereas here a new colony was established.[25] The list provided by the United Kingdom does not sufficiently distinguish between cases where the detached parts of a colony became independent and cases where a new colony was established.

73. There is no bar to having recourse to international law in this respect. According to Article 293 of the Convention, the Tribunal may have recourse to international law which is not incompatible with the Convention. There is no indication that the Convention would not allow a court or tribunal acting under Part XV of the Convention to consider the international law rules concerning decolonization. We consider it appropriate to refer in this respect to Article 305 of the Convention and Resolution III of the Third UN Conference on the Law of the Sea, which clearly indicate the awareness of the Conference of the decolonization process.

74. This brings us to the consent given by the Mauritian Ministers. Two arguments are advanced in this respect by Mauritius: namely, that the consent given was contrary to the rules on self-determination since the ministers did not represent the population and that the consent was given under pressure.[26]

75. As far as "pressure" is concerned, the United Kingdom argues that negotiations can be tough. This is countered by counsel for Mauritius that, in relations between a colonial entity and the metropolitan State, the latter has some responsibility towards the former. This point was not elaborated upon, but meant that the United Kingdom, being the colonial power as well as the guardian of the colony, was under an obligation not to use pressure that could be acceptable in the relationship between two sovereign States, but not between a metropolitan State and a colony.

---

[25] On self-determination, see Mauritius' Memorial, paras. 6.10–6.22. On *uti possidetis*, see *ibid.*, paras. 6.23–6.24.

[26] Final Transcript, 248:24 to 251:21; 972:16–24.

76. It was further pointed out—correctly—that Mauritius had no choice.[27] The detachment of the Chagos Archipelago was already decided whether Mauritius gave its consent or not.

77. A look at the discussion between Prime Minister Harold Wilson and Premier Sir Seewoosagur Ramgoolam suggests that the Wilson's threat that Ramgoolam could return home without independence amounts to duress. The Private Secretary of Wilson used the language of "frighten[ing]" the Premier "with hope".[28] The Colonial Secretary equally resorted to the language of intimidation. Furthermore, Mauritius was a colony of the United Kingdom when the 1965 agreement was reached. The Council of Ministers of Mauritius was presided over by the British Governor who could nominate some of the members of the Council. Thus there was a clear situation of inequality between the two sides. As Mauritius states, if the Mauritian people, through their Government, had made a free choice without coercion, they could have given valid consent in the pre-independence period to the excision of the Chagos Archipelago. This was not the case.

78. If it is accepted that the consent given is invalid on either of the two grounds mentioned above, the question is to be raised why it took Mauritius so long to make this point. Reference was made in this context to the fact that Mauritius was economically dependent upon the United Kingdom.[29] It was argued that this has to be taken into consideration by referring to a statement made by the ICJ in *Certain Phosphate Lands in Nauru ((Nauru* v. *Australia) Preliminary Objections, Judgment, I.C.J. Reports 1992*, p. 240).[30]

79. Even if the view is taken that the consent was valid and/or that Mauritius acquiesced in the detachment (with which we would disagree) one may argue that the "agreement" reached in the Lancaster House Conference has been terminated by the United Kingdom *ex nunc* by establishing the MPA unilaterally and thus depriving Mauritius of some of the actual benefits it was meant to receive from that agreement.

80. This leads us to the conclusion that Submission No. 1 of Mauritius is well founded in fact and law on the merits.

81. According to its Submission No. 2, Mauritius claims that "… having regard to the commitments that it has made to Mauritius in relation to the Chagos Archipelago, the United Kingdom is not entitled unilaterally to declare an 'MPA' or other maritime zones because Mauritius has rights as a 'coastal State' within the meaning of *inter alia* Articles 56(1)(*b*)(iii) and 76(8) of the Convention".

---

[27] Final Transcript, 145:22 to 146:2.

[28] Colonial Office, Note for the Prime Minister's Meeting with Sir Seewoosagur Ramgoolam, Premier of Mauritius, 22 September 1965, PREM 13/3320 (Annex MM-17).

[29] Trade with the United Kingdom accounted for more than 70 percent of export earnings. *See* Final Transcript, 123:11–16.

[30] Final Transcript, 250:22 to 251:2; 976:11–15.

82. This submission requires dealing on the merits with two issues: whether legally binding commitments existed and whether they existed on the level of international law. The Parties seem to agree that the undertakings of the Lancaster House meeting in 1965 did not constitute a treaty under international law. This was explained by counsel for the United Kingdom and confirmed by counsel for Mauritius.[31] According to the United Kingdom, this undertaking was not an agreement between equals. Whether or not it was meant to be binding remains somewhat unclear.[32]

83. In our view the facts are in favour of the position that the commitments exchanged were meant to be binding. According to counsel for Mauritius: "It was an arrangement made in the context of negotiations for independence .... At the very second of independence, when the excision was affirmed by the continued presence of the United Kingdom in the Archipelago, the United Kingdom disabled itself from denying the conditions attached to its presence."[33]

84. The style of the negotiations, the report on the negotiations and the subsequent practice confirm this. This resulted in a package binding under national law which upon the independence of Mauritius devolved upon the international law level. Being part of international law, it may be read into the Convention to the extent the latter refers to international law.[34]

85. What do the commitments entail? Good offices concerning navigational and meteorological facilities; in respect of fishing rights; landing rights on an airstrip still to be built; benefits from mineral resource activities and right to have the islands returned.[35]

86. This leads to the conclusion that the United Kingdom, by establishing the MPA, violated its prior commitments *vis-à-vis* Mauritius and thus violated Article 56(2) of the Convention. As a consequence thereof the MPA is legally invalid.

87. Concerning Submission No. 4, we agree with the findings of the Tribunal that the establishment of the MPA violated Mauritius' rights under Articles 2(3), 56(2) and 194(4) of the Convention (*see* Award, paras. 536, 541).

88. We would, however, have preferred that the Tribunal had considered the promise of Prime Minister Gordon Brown to Prime Minister Navichandra Ramgoolam at the CHOGM at Port of Spain in 2009. This issue of the promise goes to the heart of the matter of Mauritius' reliance on this United Kingdom

---

[31] *See* Final Transcript, 983:10–22.

[32] *See* Final Transcript, 982:10 to 984:12.

[33] Final Transcript, 982:11–22.

[34] *See* Mauritius' Memorial, paras. 3.95–3.98; *see also* Despatch dated 2 July 1971 from M. Elliott, UK Foreign and Commonwealth Office to R. G. Giddens, British High Commission, Port Louis, FCO 31/2763 (Annex MM–63).

[35] Record of a Meeting held in Lancaster House at 2.30 p.m. on Thursday 23rd September [1965], Mauritius Defence Matters, CO 1036/1253 (Annex MM–19); Minutes of a Meeting held at 10 Downing Street, S.W.1, on Thursday, 23rd September, 1965, at 4 p.m. (Mauritius Arbitrator's Folder, Round 2, Tab 5.1); Manuscript letter of 1 October 1965 (Annex UKCM–9).

undertaking to put the MPA on hold. The United Kingdom's unilateral assurance may not be an Ihlen declaration, but it is a commitment which Mauritius relied upon to its detriment. When Prime Minister Ramgoolam went back to Port Louis after CHOGM, he called a press conference and addressed Parliament to state that the United Kingdom had promised at the highest level of Government to put the MPA on hold. In his witness statement, which was not challenged by the United Kingdom, the Prime Minister repeated the Brown assurance.

89. In this regard, we note that the Tribunal has concluded that it sees no need to comment further on Article 300 or the abuse of rights (*see* Award, para 543). We disagree with this conclusion. We feel that the Tribunal, having found that the 1965 commitments are legally valid and that the United Kingdom in establishing an MPA breached its obligations under several articles of UNCLOS including Article 56(2), should have examined the issue of good faith on the part of the United Kingdom. For we are of the view that the manner in which the United Kingdom proclaimed the MPA did not take into account the rights and interests of Mauritius, in particular under Article 56 of the Convention. Furthermore, having held that "the United Kingdom is estopped from denying the binding effect of [the 1965] commitments", (Award, para. 448) it is surprising that the Tribunal did not examine the matter further, especially when it is recalled that estoppel rests on the principle of good faith.

90. The Tribunal states that the internal United Kingdom documents in the record do not suggest any ulterior motive. While we do not completely share this observation, we are of the view that the way in which the MPA was established and the negotiations leading up to the MPA leave a lot to be desired on the part of the United Kingdom. As the ICJ stated in the *Nuclear Tests* case, "[t]rust and confidence are inherent in international co-operation" (*Nuclear Tests ((Australia* v. *France), Judgment, I.C.J. Reports 1974,* p. 253 at p. 269, para 46). In the case of the MPA, Mauritius learnt of the MPA proposal from the London newspaper, *The Independent*, on 9 February 2009 (*see* Award, para. 126). The United Kingdom went ahead with a public consultation on the MPA in spite of Mauritius' opposition and its demand that the matter should be discussed in the bilateral framework. Indeed in its written evidence to the UK House of Commons Select Committee on Foreign Affairs in respect of the MPA, Mauritius complains that "[t]he manner in which the MPA is being dealt with makes us feel that it is being imposed on Mauritius with a predetermined agenda" (*see* Award, para. 144). Even British senior officials, including the British High Commissioner (*see* Award, para. 150) warned that "to declare the MPA today could have very significant negative consequences for the bilateral relationship". However, the British Government hastily went ahead and declared the MPA on 1 April 2010.

91. We complete this argument on good faith by noting disturbing similarities between the establishment of the BIOT in 1965 and the proclamation of the MPA in 2010. Although these two events are 45 years apart, they show

a certain common pattern. This is the disregard of the rights and interests of Mauritius. The 1965 excision of the Chagos Archipelago from Mauritius shows a complete disregard for the territorial integrity of Mauritius by the United Kingdom which was the colonial power. British and American defence interests were put above Mauritius' rights. Fast forward to 2010 and one finds a similar disregard of Mauritius' rights, such as the total ban on fishing in the MPA. These are not accidental happenings. We further note the observation of the arbitral tribunal in *ConocoPhillips Petrozuata B.V., ConocoPhillips Hamaca B.V., ConocoPhillips Gulf of Paria B.V., and ConocoPhillips Company* v. *The Bolivarian Republic of Venezuela* (ICSID Case No. ARB/07/30, Decision on Jurisdiction and the Merits, para. 275 (3 September 2010)) on "… how rarely courts and tribunals have held that a good faith or other related standards is breached. The standard is a high one." We take the view that, for the reasons as set out above, the United Kingdom did violate the standard of good faith.

92. We disagree with some of the reasoning of the Tribunal on Article 2(3) of the Convention (*see* Award, paras. 514–516). We read the legislative history of that provision differently.

93. In interpreting Article 2(3) of the Convention and thus determining the limits imposed upon the exercise of the costal States' sovereignty over the territorial sea it is necessary to distinguish between the reference to the Convention and "to other rules of international law". The starting point of the ILC deliberations on the law of the sea was as to whether the limits to the exercise of sovereignty by coastal States in its territorial sea set out in article 1(2) of the 1956 ILC Draft Articles are exhaustive. The ILC commentaries on that provision confirm that "the limitations imposed by international law on the exercise of sovereignty in the territorial sea" which "are set forth in the present articles" cannot "be regarded as exhaustive."[36] For this reason, "'other rules of international law' are mentioned in addition to the provisions contained in the present articles."[37] Moreover, as the ILC emphasised, draft Article 1(2) encompasses both obligations founded in general international law and specific arrangements entered into by the States: The ILC commentary stated:

> (5) It may happen that, by reason of some special relationship, geographical or other, between two States, rights in the territorial sea of one of them are granted to the other in excess of the rights recognised in the present draft. It is not the Commission's intention to limit in any way any more extensive right of passage or other right enjoyed by States by custom or treaty.[38]

---

[36] Report of the International Law Commission covering the work of its eighth session, 23 April–4 July 1956, Doc. A/3159, *YILC*, Vol. II, 253 at 265 (para. 4).

[37] *Ibid.*

[38] International Law Commission, Articles concerning the Law of the Sea with Commentaries, *Report of the International Law Commission on the Work of its Eighth Session, 23 April to 4 July 1956*, Official Records of the General Assembly, Eleventh Session, Supplement No. 9, UN Doc. A/3159 at p. 265.

94. The first sentence in paragraph 5 of the commentary to article 1(2) of the ILC Draft makes it quite plain that the draft encompasses obligations that may arise from a "special relationship, geographical or other," where one State recognises or grants the other State rights in the territorial sea.[39] This has the consequence that the reference to 'other rules of international law' not only refers to general international law but has a broader scope. This interpretation is confirmed by *Birnie, Boyle and Redgwell,* who observe that "UNCLOS establishes a twelve-mile limit for the territorial sea, over which the coastal state has sovereignty, subject to any requirements of the Convention and other rules of international law, including any conservatory conventions to which that state is party and which by their terms apply within that area."[40] Taking the ILC Commentary into account means, in our view, that the reference to "other rules of international law" encompasses obligations arising from commitments by the coastal State bilaterally or even unilaterally, as well as commitments based upon customary international law or the binding decisions of an international organization. For these reasons the undertakings of the United Kingdom in the Lancaster House Understanding have to be read directly into Article 2(3) of the Convention.

* * *

Dated: 18 March 2015

[*Signed*]
Judge Rüdiger Wolfrum

[*Signed*]
Judge James Kateka

[39] See also the Annex VII tribunal decision in *Guyana v Suriname,* interpreting terms in Article 293 "other rules of international law" as encompassing both general international law and international treaties, at para. 406.

[40] P. Birnie, A. Boyle & C. Redgwell, *International Law & the Environment*, p. 716 (3rd ed., 2009).

ISBN 978-92-1-033108-1

9 789210 331081

United Nations publication